PUBLICATIONS OF THE
UCLA CENTER FOR MEDIEVAL AND RENAISSANCE STUDIES

A Handbook of the Troubadours

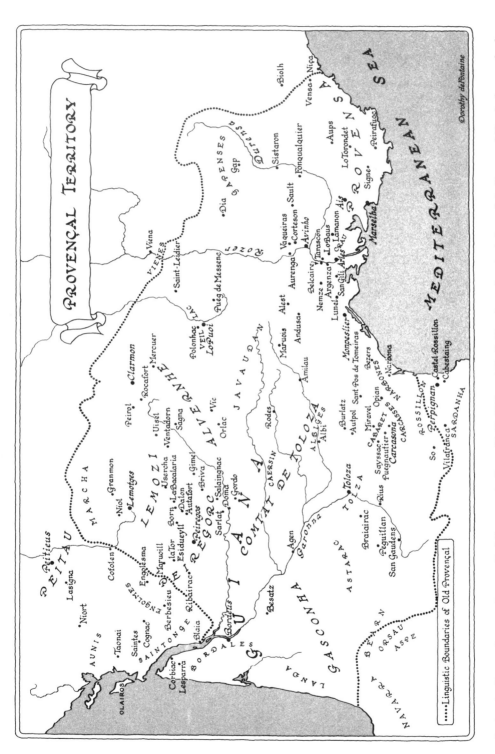

Occitania (formerly sometimes called Provence). From R. T. Hill and T. G. Bergin, eds., *Anthology of the Provençal Troubadours*, 2d ed. (New Haven: Yale University Press, 1973). Reprinted by permission of Yale University Press.

A Handbook
of the Troubadours

EDITED BY

F. R. P. Akehurst

AND

Judith M. Davis

UNIVERSITY OF CALIFORNIA PRESS

Berkeley   Los Angeles   London

University of California Press
Berkeley and Los Angeles, California

University of California Press, Ltd.
London, England

© 1995 by
The Regents of the University of California

Library of Congress Cataloging-in-Publication Data

A handbook of the Troubadours / edited by F. R. P. Akehurst and Judith M. Davis.
    p.   cm.—(Publications of the UCLA Center for Medieval and Renaissance
Studies ; 26)
    Includes bibliographical references and index.
    ISBN 0-520-07975-2 (alk. paper).—ISBN 0-520-07976-0 (pbk. : alk. paper)
    1. Provençal poetry—History and criticism—Handbooks, manuals, etc.   2. Provençal
poetry—Criticism, Textual—Handbooks, manuals, etc.   3. Troubadours—Handbooks,
manuals, etc.   I. Akehurst, F. R. P.   II. Davis, Judith M.   III. Series: Publications of
the Center for Medieval and Renaissance Studies ; 26.
PC3304.H36 1995
849′.1209—dc20   94-36018
                                                                      CIP

Printed in the United States of America
9 8 7 6 5 4 3 2 1

CONTENTS

Origins and Diffusion

General and Technical Considerations

ACKNOWLEDGMENTS

We wish to thank the following publishers and individuals for granting permission to quote portions of the works indicated: Nizet, Paris, for Jean Boutière and Alexandre H. Schutz, eds., *Biographies des troubadours: Textes provençaux des XIIIe et XIVe siècles* (Paris: Nizet, 1964); Francesco Branciforti for his edition of *Le rime de Bonifacio Calvo* (Catania: Università di Catania, 1955); Mouton de Gruyter, a division of Walter de Gruyter & Co., Berlin, for Joseph Linskill, ed., *The Poems of the Troubadour Raimbaut de Vaqueiras* (The Hague: Mouton, 1964); the University of Minnesota for Walter T. Pattison, ed., *The Life and Works of the Troubadour Raimbaut d'Orange* (Minneapolis: University of Minnesota Press, 1952, 1980); Aimo Sakari for his edition of *Poésies du troubadour Guilhem de Saint-Didier* (Helsinki: Société Néophilologique, 1956); and Cambridge University Press for Ruth Sharman, ed., *The Cansos and Sirventes of the Troubadour Giraut de Borneil: A Critical Edition* (Cambridge: Cambridge University Press, 1989).

We also wish to thank Abigail Bok, Rose Vekony, and Anne Canright for their patient assistance. On the behalf of the contributors, we dedicate this volume, gratefully and affectionately, to all our teachers and all our students, past, present, and future.

Introduction

F. R. P. Akehurst

The troubadours have been called "the inventors of modern verse,"[1] and they stand at or near the beginning of the literary history of most modern European traditions. The student of medieval literature in French, Spanish, Portuguese, German, Italian, and English cannot ignore the phenomenon often called Courtly Love, which finds its first broad expression in Old Occitan (sometimes, especially formerly, called Old Provençal) in the twelfth century. Courses on the troubadours are offered in but few universities, however, and not every year even where they are available. Consequently, many students need to be able to learn something of the troubadours on their own. This book, then, has been produced not only to serve as a text for formal courses, but also to provide the necessary secondary material for independent study. The primary material, the texts of the troubadour poems themselves, is to be found in innumerable published editions, anthologies, and translations.

This book is intended to be a reference book and a digest of the material known to every troubadour specialist. While some of the chapters present scholarship that is on the cutting edge of troubadour studies, many of the contributions contain a précis of decades or even centuries of scholarly work. Frequent reference is made to longer studies, some written by the contributors to the present volume. Each contributor is an expert in his or her own area and gives in this handbook condensed information that will be sufficient for many scholars' needs. Readers who wish to pursue in more detail some aspect of troubadour studies will find ample bibliographical references to additional secondary material.

1. James J. Wilhelm, *Seven Troubadours: The Inventors of Modern Verse* (University Park and London: Pennsylvania State University Press, 1970).

I

What the authors have done is to summarize the current consensus on their topic. This kind of "conventional wisdom" (in a positive sense) grows from a process of thesis and antithesis, leading to synthesis. Most of the present work is therefore synthesis—which may nevertheless be the starting point for a new antithesis. The contributors show the current status of troubadour studies, the basis of shared knowledge and opinion that one must take into account if one is going to make progress.

Lawyers are familiar with such digests. For those areas of the law that are governed by precedent rather than by statute, such as torts and contracts, books are published for the guidance of lawyers that state the general position of the law in boldface type (or black letters) and then give pertinent commentary and references to case law. This conventional wisdom, known as black-letter law, represents the mass of legal opinion established not by legislation but by a developmental process lasting sometimes for centuries. To contest black-letter law successfully is usually very difficult; but great advances can sometimes be made by means of such contestation.

Even in literary studies, a new and revolutionary view of the material can sometimes change a discipline. Such a view was presented in Robert Guiette's short article "D'une poésie formelle en France au moyen âge," *Revue des Sciences Humaines* 54 (1949): 61–68. The influence of this essay is everywhere felt in troubadour studies today, and it came as a challenge to the conventional wisdom of its day. For many years before Guiette's article, troubadour studies had been dominated by a few very influential scholars, especially Alfred Jeanroy. Guiette's article challenged Jeanroy's views, showing that what the earlier scholar had seen as a weakness in troubadour poetry was actually a strength. This new approach proved an inspiration to many younger researchers.

Some of the chapters of the present volume indeed contain material that is not, or not yet, part of the conventional wisdom. In areas that are seeing growth and change, the contributions are more conjectural and often more specific than the received knowledge. Such chapters include those on the trobairitz, or women troubadours (Bruckner), and on the origins of the tradition (Bond). Other essays present material that is hardly susceptible to a new interpretation, such as versification (Chambers) and language (Jensen). Yet other chapters deal with matters that are still evolving, such as bibliography (Taylor) and "courtly love" (Lazar).

Like the law, troubadour studies appear as a seamless web. Each way of approaching the material presupposes and complements all the others. The chapters of this book, which treat discrete topics, may therefore be read in any order. Nevertheless, their arrangement follows a certain pattern. Zumthor's "Why the Troubadours?" gives an overview of the place of the troubadours in European literature and their importance in literary studies. While this essay touches on a great number of different topics, and briefly alludes to the content of various of the other contributions in this volume, it also synthesizes much of Zumthor's thinking about what was to become, in his terms, the *grand chant courtois*. One of the foremost medievalists of our time, Zumthor has adorned his text with lapidary sentences that will be mined for decades by setters of examinations, used in the form of a quotation followed by the word *Discuss*.

The first section of the book, "The Essentials," deals with the primary materials of study, the lyric poems of the troubadours (Van Vleck), followed by some general considerations of those materials. One of the principal subjects of troubadour lyric poetry, *fin'amor* (Lazar), is presented, followed by the formal aspects of the poems: versification (Chambers) and the melodies that accompany the words (van der Werf). The second section, "Accessory Texts," comprises two chapters: one on the non-lyric texts (Fleischman), and one on the medieval biographies of the troubadours themselves, the *vidas* and *razos* (Poe). In the following section, "A Subgroup: The Women Troubadours," appears a single chapter, on the trobairitz (Bruckner). Next, in "Origins and Diffusion," a group of six essays deals with the origins (Bond) and the influence of the troubadours' poetry, the latter topic presented according to the country or language where the influence was felt (Nelson on northern France, Van D'Elden on the minnesingers, Snow on the Iberian Peninsula, and Martinez and Keller on Italy). Finally, in "General and Technical Considerations," the handbook is rounded out by a series of essays on more advanced aspects of troubadour studies: manuscripts (Paden), translation (Rosenstein), the Old Occitan language (Jensen), rhetoric (Smith), topoi (Schulze-Busacker), and vocabulary (Ghil). Much of the material in this last series of essays will be found to be relevant to a wider group of poets than just the troubadours. The very last chapter deals with the all-important topic of bibliography (Taylor). In the Appendix may be found a list of troubadours who left eight or more poems, and of the editions in which these may be found.

Some of the contributors (Van Vleck, Schulze-Busacker, and Bruckner) have chosen to analyze one or more troubadour poems in some depth, while others have quoted appropriate passages from a number of troubadours. The reader can form some opinion of the prestige of various poets by counting the references to their work. It will quickly become apparent that the most prolific poets are not necessarily quoted the most often; conversely, certain poets who left a very small corpus of work may be frequently cited.

Because the chapters will likely be read piecemeal, and in no particular order, each contains its own notes and/or bibliography. Nevertheless, no chapter should be completely neglected by the scholar trying to become familiar with the troubadour phenomenon. In attempting to understand or explicate a particular poem, the reader will need to draw on the different approaches of almost all of the chapters. The art of the troubadours is a complex one, and many factors contribute to each poem. Jaufre Rudel already understood this when he said,

> No sap chantar qui so non di,
> Ni vers trobar qui motz no fa,
> Ni conois de rima co's va
> Si razo non enten en si.
>   (Wolf and Rosenstein 4:1–4)[2]

> He cannot sing who makes no tune, / And he cannot write songs who makes no words, / And does not know how a rhyme works / If he does not understand the matter. (trans. Wolf and Rosenstein)

If the poet needed to be a master of all these factors, so must the reader. The poets were not naïve; nor can the reader afford to be. Attentive study of seemingly mechanical or unrelated aspects of a poem may lead to a sudden revelation of its nature. The poets themselves were not unaware of the theoretical underpinnings of their poetry, and to read the poems as mere effusions is to miss much of what they have to offer.

Strikingly absent from the volume is any consideration of the troubadours as people or as individuals. Poetic individuality has not until very recently been a preoccupation of troubadour scholarship,[3] though many troubadours present individual characteristics that make their poems more or less identifiable. A poem by Bernard de Ventadorn, for example, is easily distinguished from one by Arnaut Daniel. These differences exist, however, within a corpus of poems that are otherwise remarkably homogeneous. It is in the main the similarities, not the differences, that have been addressed by the contributors to this volume. Regardless of the poet being studied, this book's chapters on courtly love, music, versification, language, rhetoric, tropes, and vocabulary will contain much material that will aid in understanding and interpreting the body of troubadour poetry as a whole.

PRACTICAL SUGGESTIONS

For those readers wishing to learn Old Occitan so as to be able to read the troubadours in their original language, a beginning text, William D. Paden's *Introduction to Old Occitan*, is to be published by the MLA in its series Introductions to Older Languages in about 1995. This book will do for Old Occitan what William W. Kibler's *Introduction to Old French* has done for that language. Until Paden's book appears, readers may consult Nathaniel B. Smith and Thomas G. Bergin, *An Old Provençal Primer* (New York: Garland,

---

2. For an explanation of the system of citation, see "Forms of Citation," p. 6 below.

3. Sarah Kay, *Subjectivity in Troubadour Poetry*, Cambridge Studies in French (Cambridge: Cambridge University Press, 1990).

1984); and an anthology such as *Anthology of the Provençal Troubadours*, ed. R. T. Hill and T. G. Bergin (with the collaboration of Susan Olson, William D. Paden, and Nathaniel Smith), 2d ed., 2 vols. (New Haven: Yale University Press, 1973); or *Introduction à l'étude de l'ancien provençal*, ed. Frank R. Hamlin, Peter T. Ricketts, and John Hathaway, 2d ed. (Bern: Francke, 1986). Neither of these anthologies contains translations of the poems. Several bilingual anthologies have been published, including Alan R. Press, *Anthology of Troubadour Lyric Poetry*, Edinburgh Bilingual Library 3 (Austin: University of Texas Press, 1971); and Fred Goldin, *Lyrics of the Troubadours and Trouvères: An Anthology and a History* (Garden City, N.Y.: Anchor, 1973). In addition, there are several anthologies of troubadour poems prepared for a French audience, such as Pierre Bec's *Anthologie des troubadours*, 10/18 (Paris: Union Générale d'Editions, 1979). Many prose texts, which may offer an easier introduction to the language than the difficult lyric poetry, have been edited by Pierre Bec in his *Anthologie de la prose occitane du moyen âge (Xe–XVe siècle)* (Avignon: Aubanel, 1977). There are of course some rather dated accounts of the grammar of Old Occitan (often called Old or Ancien Provençal in their titles). A succinct and modern account of the language appears in the present volume (Chapter 17, by Jensen); while this chapter is not intended to teach how to read the language, it will provide a handy reference for many points of morphology and syntax.

Some troubadours write very difficult poetry, while others compose in a relatively easy style. Among those generally considered more approachable, both in language and in content, are Bernart de Ventadorn, Peirol, and Arnaut de Marueill; somewhat more difficult are Peire d'Auvernhe, Folquet de Marseilla, and Peire Vidal; and among the most difficult are Arnaut Daniel and Raimbaut d'Aurenga. All these poets are of major importance, but the reader might do well to work from the easier to the more difficult ones.

A warning is perhaps necessary with respect to the spelling of troubadour names in the present volume. Because names are spelled in various ways both in the manuscripts and in modern editions, a choice had to be made. The editors have decided to use throughout the spellings that appear in the Hill-Bergin anthology or, for the names that do not appear in Hill-Bergin, the spellings used in the Index bibliographique to István Frank's *Répertoire*.[4] This decision has caused some of us slight discomfort. A poet whom we have thought of for twenty or thirty years as William IX must here be called Guillem de Peiteus, and the poet whose one critical edition calls him Raimbaut d'Orange must be referred to as Raimbaut d'Aurenga. But Hill-Bergin is an *auctoritas*, and the reader's indulgence is requested.

---

4. István Frank, *Répertoire métrique de la poésie des troubadours*, 2 vols. (Paris: Champion, 1953–57).

FORMS OF CITATION

Parenthetical references throughout this volume are keyed both to the individual chapter's list of Works Cited and, for editions of the troubadours, to the book's Appendix. If the Works Cited lists only one work by an author, the parenthetical reference is by name only; the date of publication is added if there are multiple entries. If the Appendix shows more than one edition of a troubadour's works, a headnote to the Works Cited will state which edition is used in that chapter. Troubadour editions are always cited by the troubadour's (not the editor's) name only.

The Appendix lists the troubadour names in the numerical order of the Bartsch/Pillet-Carstens/Frank repertory (on which see Chapter 21 and its Works Cited); the result is almost completely alphabetical. References to troubadour texts are given by the poem and line number in the edition used, or very occasionally by the Pillet-Carstens number (signaled "P-C"). Not all critical editions print the poems in order of their Pillet-Carstens numbers, and two different editions of the same poet may number the poems differently (for example, the Appel and Lazar editions of Bernart de Ventadorn). However, later editions generally include a concordance showing the corresponding poem numbers in all previous editions.

THE DISCIPLINE

The field of troubadour studies may seem very well organized. For example, every troubadour poem preserved in the manuscripts has been published, generally in all the known versions. And as we have just seen, each poem has been given a standard number, making for easy reference, whether its author is known or disputed or even anonymous. Thanks to István Frank we know that there are 2,542 troubadour lyrics.[5] Not only has every poem been published and numbered, but also more than four-fifths of the poems have been entered into the computer, which allows their texts to be manipulated electronically.[6] Thus the raw material of study—the text of the poems—is available and largely accessible without recourse to the original manuscripts.

---

5. Ibid., 1:xvi.

6. The repository of the troubadour corpus is ARTFL: A Textual Database. This is a cooperative project of the Centre Nationale de la Recherche Scientifique and the University of Chicago. ARTFL stands for American and French Research on the Treasury of the French Language. Information on how to access the troubadour database may be obtained from ARTFL, Department of Romance Languages, University of Chicago, 1050 East 59th Street, Chicago, IL 60637, USA. The work of entering the whole corpus of troubadour poetry, as undertaken by an international team including F. R. P. Akehurst, Peter T. Ricketts, and Gérard Gonfroy, is nearing completion, and a complete concordance is planned, to be published probably on CD-ROM.

The scholarly aids go well beyond the mere text, however. Every poem of the 2,542 has been scrutinized, its form analyzed, its syllables counted, the sometimes convoluted patterns of its rhymes deciphered, and all the resulting data noted in tabular form. Any poem can thus be compared, as regards its form, with any other poem. It is immediately apparent whether a poem under investigation is formally unique or shares its form with one or more other poems. (For a discussion of this secondary material, see Chapter 4, by Chambers, in this volume.) A preoccupation with form was already visible in some of the earliest writers on troubadour verse, and we still use the critical vocabulary that they invented.[7]

Another aspect of the formal study of troubadour poems is the accompanying music. Already in 1972 Hendrik van der Werf published *The Chansons of the Troubadours and Trouvères, and Their Relation to the Melodies* (Utrecht: Oosthoek), and since that time two teams of editors have each published the complete repertoire of troubadour melodies.[8] In the past twenty years or so considerable interest has been shown in the performance of medieval music, including the songs of the troubadours, and many recordings by groups and individuals, in a variety of styles, are now available.[9]

The work of bringing the texts of troubadour poems before the public was first undertaken in modern times by scholars in the nineteenth century. They produced not only works about the troubadours but also collections of previously unpublished poems transcribed from manuscripts,[10] as well as early critical editions of individual poets.[11] While some poems have been published many times over in critical editions and anthologies, others published nearly a century ago have never reappeared, and some poets have not yet been given critical editions of their own.

Many of the major poets have been the subject of satisfactory critical editions. Some poets have been edited twice or more; for example, there

7. *Las leys d'amors*, ed. Joseph Anglade, 4 vols., Bibliothèque Méridionale 17–20 (Toulouse: Académie des Jeux Floraux, 1919–20).

8. Hendrik van der Werf and Text Editor Gerald A. Bond, *The Extant Troubadour Melodies: Transcriptions and Essays for Performers and Scholars* (Rochester, N.Y.: author, 1984); and Ismael Fernandez de la Cuesta and Text Editor Robert Lafont, *Las cancons dels trobadors* (Toulouse: Institut d'Etudes Occitanes, 1979).

9. See, for example, Larry S. Crist and Roger J. Steiner, "MUSICA VERBIS CONCORDET: Medieval French Lyric Poems with their Music (A Discography)," *Medievalia* 1 (1975): 35–61; also Annie Zerby-Cros, *Discographie occitane générale*, Publications du C.I.D.O., Bibliotèca d'Occitania (Béziers: Centre International de Documentation Occitane, 1979).

10. Carl A. Mahn, *Die Werke der Troubadours in provenzalischer Sprache* (1846–53; Geneva: Slatkine, 1975); Carl Appel, *Provenzalische Inedita aus pariser Handschriften* (Leipzig: Fues/R. Reisland, 1890).

11. These include some who have never been reedited, such as Raimon Gaucelm de Beziers, Guilhem Anelier de Toulouse, Blacasset, Palais, Uc Brunenc, Peire Guilhem de Luzerna, and Blacatz.

exist critical editions of Guillem de Peiteus in French, Italian, and English, and editions of Bernart de Ventadorn in German, English, and French. In addition to critical editions of individual poets, facsimile photographic editions of certain manuscripts have appeared, as well as anthologies of poems, which seem to appear at the rate of one a year.

The task of organizing a field of research such as troubadour studies often falls to a professional organization, which may sponsor a publication. Internationally, there exists the Association Internationale d'Etudes Occitanes (AIEO), which publishes irregularly the Bulletins de l'Association Internationale d'Etudes Occitanes. In North America, the Société Guilhem IX fills this role; its journal, *Tenso,* first appeared in 1985–86.[12] Each volume contains a medieval Occitan bibliography for the preceding year. An invaluable research tool is Robert Taylor's *La Littérature occitane du moyen âge: Bibliographie sélective et critique* (Toronto: University of Toronto Press, 1977), of which a new edition is being prepared.

In recent years, students and scholars have been particularly interested in women writers of the past. An edition of the known poems of women troubadours was compiled as early as 1889;[13] in 1976 Meg Bogin republished those poems with translations in both an English and a French edition.[14] More recently, the poems of na Castelloza were published by William D. Paden.[15] Other offerings include a collection of essays on the trobairitz[16] and a new edition of poems by women troubadours, containing a number of poems not attributed to women poets by Bogin.[17]

The subject matter of the troubadour poems is also of much interest to scholars. Since over a century ago, the terms *amour courtois* and *courtly love* have been applied to the variety of male-female relationship described by the troubadours in many of their poems. Called *fin'amor* by the medieval poets, this phenomenon has been investigated in its nature, its origin, and its subsequent literary history by probably hundreds of scholars. Frequently cited among those who have written on the topic is Moshe Lazar,[18] who

12. Information on both these organizations may be obtained from Wendy Pfeffer, Editor in Chief, *Tenso,* Department of Modern Languages, University of Louisville, Louisville, KY 40292, USA.

13. Oscar Schultz-Gora, *Die provenzalischen Dichterinnen* (Leipzig: Gustav Foch, 1888).

14. Meg Bogin, *The Women Troubadours* ([1976] New York: Norton, 1980).

15. William D. Paden et al., "The Poems of the Trobairitz Na Castelloza," *Romance Philology* 35 (1981): 158–82.

16. William D. Paden, ed., *The Voice of the Trobairitz: Perspectives on the Women Troubadours* (Philadelphia: University of Pennsylvania Press, 1989).

17. Angelica Rieger, ed., *Trobairitz. Der Beitrag der Frau in der altokzitanischen höfischen Lyrik. Edition des Gesamtkorpus,* Beihefte zur Zeitschrift für romanische Philologie 233 (Tübingen: Niemeyer, 1991).

18. Moshé Lazar, *Amour courtois et fin'amors dans la littérature du XIIe siècle* (Paris: Klincksieck, 1964).

provides a summary of the subject for this volume. For the poems that do not deal with *fin'amor*, a thorough treatment is to be found in Suzanne Méjean's book *Les Poésies satiriques et morales des troubadours.*[19]

Given this abundance of material, a student may well ask if anything remains to be done. Even if it were true that nothing remained to be done, the troubadours would be worth reading for their own sake. Each new reader may find something new to enjoy in each poem; and the more one reads, the greater the understanding and the greater the *joy*. However, much indeed does remain to be done. The psychological aspects of troubadour verse remain relatively unexplored, and questions about performance have not yet found a definitive answer. Troubadour poems form a convenient-sized, well-defined corpus, to which any literary theory might be applied. They have been remarked upon by writers such as Goethe, Stendhal, and Nietzsche. We have hardly seen the last of theory; and a scholar who has mastered the corpus of the troubadours will be in a position to apply to that corpus each new theory that comes along.

19. Suzanne Thiolier-Méjean, *Les Poésies satiriques et morales des troubadours du XIIe siècle à la fin du XIIIe siècle* (Paris: Nizet, 1978).

ONE

An Overview: Why the Troubadours?

Paul Zumthor

The poetry of the troubadours is the finest flower produced in its most flourishing period by Occitan "culture": viewed from the distance lent by the passage of time, the former is, in our eyes, largely identified with the latter.

We must in fact speak of an "Occitan culture." Seen from twentieth-century America, the distinguishing characteristics of the lands lying west and south of the Massif Central and east of the Rhône, whether in turn of mind, in customs, or in speech, seem negligible. Much more noticeable in ancient Gaul and medieval France, these characteristics correspond to profound cultural differences, discernible in the settlement, political history, structures of society, religious tendencies, a certain more or less diffuse "national" consciousness, and the language of the region. It was only beginning in the thirteenth century that these differences gradually diminished, but they were still palpable in 1789; and contemporary provincialist movements are not entirely mistaken in demanding the recognition of a southern cultural autonomy. In this sense, it is not improper to suggest that France as we know it was formed between the fourteenth and the eighteenth centuries by the slow fusion of two nations.

The Occitan as opposed to the French language remained for a long time the vehicle and the sign of this difference (see Chapter 17). Much earlier than in the north, a fairly homogeneous literary koiné emerged from its various dialects, attested already in the eleventh century by several narrative poems, such as the *Boeci* from the Limoges area, whose special features were confirmed by the first troubadours. From 1100 to about 1400 this standard Occitan was one of the principal poetic languages of Europe. French drove

Translated from the French by F. R. P. Akehurst.

it back with more difficulty than the kings of France had experienced in conquering the Occitan provinces. It was not until the middle of the fifteenth century that a great southern writer, Antoine de la Sale, chose for the first time to write in French. From then on, Occitan literature went through a long decline, in spite of periodic renaissances, the best known of which took place in the nineteenth century, with Aubanel and Mistral at its center. As the language of daily use, Occitan was descending to the status of various local patois, which are still in use in several regions, and on which various groups of educated men are trying to base a new common language, modern Occitan.

On these questions in general, we refer the reader to the group synthesis published by the Institut d'Etudes Occitanes under the direction of A. Armengaud and R. Lafont, *Histoire d'Occitanie* (Paris: Hachette, 1979).

Let's return to the Middle Ages. From the year 1000 until the second half of the thirteenth century was the great Occitan period, when this culture seemed full of promise and nothing yet gave warning of its future exhaustion. Several arts of language began to flower very early on the lips of this people in love with words and singing. In the movement of musical and liturgical renewal that from the eleventh century on was centered on the abbey of Saint Martial of Limoges, there grew up a poetry in the vulgar tongue, though inspired by the church: "songs of saints" such as *Sainte Foy* (ca. 1050) or *Boeci* (ca. 1100) and liturgical plays such as the *Sponsus* (early 12th cent.). After 1150 a French influence makes itself felt, and is probably responsible for the (few) Occitan chansons de geste (*Girart de Roussillon*, 1150–80; *Daurel et Beton*, late twelfth century), whose form was borrowed by an anonymous genius from Toulouse, the author of the second part of the *Chanson de la croisade albigeoise*. It is also to this French influence, well assimilated and technically mastered, that are due the few romances and short stories of the thirteenth century, the best known of which, the masterpiece of the genre, is *Flamenca*. These romances and *novas*, which make use in narratives of various themes of troubadour lyric poetry, remain very close in form to their northern models (see Chapter 6).

Compared to the mass of literature in French from the same period, all this would not amount to very much, were it not for the troubadours, whose totally original poetry (so original that certain critics have seen in it, in the historical order, an absolute beginning) had already produced most of its "classics" before French models had left their mark on the other genres. Several critics have remarked, perhaps unjustly, that the creative genius of the Old Occitan poets seems to have been almost entirely concentrated on the lyric, to the detriment of other forms of expression.

The poets to whom we owe this art called themselves by specific terms that, in Occitan, French, Italian, and Spanish, are derived from the verbs *trobar*, *trouver, trovare, trovar,* and go back to musical composition (from the medieval Latin *tropare* 'to make tropes', a trope being "a newly composed text with music added to an established liturgical chant"),[1] while in German their self-referent, *Minnesänger,* refers to singing. A claim is thus asserted to the essentially musical nature of these poems. The Occitan word *canso* 'song' was probably forged expressly to designate the works themselves, as was *vers,* which suggests a movement of return in the melody. In spite of a widespread but erroneous opinion, it was by its musicality much more than by its themes that troubadour poetry, at the dawn of European civilization, left an indelible mark on our poetic sensibility.

During its great period, the second half of the twelfth century, this poetry is characterized by the simplicity of its formal principles and at the same time by the extreme subtlety of its nuances. The *canso* is composed of four to eight monometric stanzas, often on the same rhymes; they are followed by a *tornada* the size of a half-stanza and generally consisting in an address to the dedicatee of the song, man or woman, or to the song itself. After 1150 the number of stanzas stabilizes at five, and this rule, which became binding, survived up to the beginning of the sixteenth century in the French "chant royal," a distant descendant of the *canso.* The *sirventes* and the *planh* are *cansos* that are distinguishable by their subject matter: the first is satiric or polemic, most often with a political and feudal purpose; the second is a lament for a famous man or a beloved woman who has died. The *descort,* breathing some distraught passion, is the opposite of the *canso* in that each of its stanzas, far from being identical to all the others, is in fact quite different.

Within this framework, infinite combinations are possible, by varying the number of lines, their length, and the choice and arrangement of the rhymes (see Chapter 4). In theory, no song is like any other; when it is, a special and meaningful effect of the art is produced. The melody, normally composed at the same time as the text, is the overarching form: it gives unity to the song, guarantees its originality, and makes it into a single whole. This very fact, added to the loss over time of nine out of ten of the melodies, considerably limits our power to judge and appreciate this poetry, and we must be aware of that.

Hendrik van der Werf (Chapter 5) shows the great complexity of this problem, which has twin causes: on the one hand, the tightness of the bonds that attach, in their reciprocal structures, text and music; on the other hand, the fact that, more often than the text, the music is transmitted (and probably composed) orally, without the support of a written notation. This issue of orality, which is especially important with respect to the transmission of the melodies, extends to the whole of this poetic corpus. Between the

1. Charles M. Atkinson, "Tropes to the Ordinary of the Mass," in *Dictionary of the Middle Ages,* ed. Joseph R. Strayer (New York: Scribner, 1982–89), 12:209.

composition of a *canso* and the first manuscript in which it appears stretches a period that can reach two centuries or more. For modern editors of the troubadours, the result is some heavy constraints, which can be partially avoided by recourse to the notion of "mouvance" (see Chapter 15).

Already in the twelfth century, the regularization of this art and the different goals of its elaborators gave birth to several "styles" (among whose adherents disputes did not fail to arise): the *trobar leu*, simple and unadorned by rhetoric; the *trobar ric*, in which dazzling sonorities abound; and the *trobar clus*, based on the obscurity of its metaphors and the closure of its meaning. The latter can be considered the end-product of a poetry that consists in the simultaneous presence of a set of oppositions and a movement toward the integration of those opposites. It has sometimes been asked to what extent this play of forms is derived from the Latin rhetorical tradition. The answer is ambiguous: we know that in fact several troubadours who had attended school received some instruction in rhetorical techniques of expression; but these techniques, which were completely interiorized and spontaneously recreated, are only one of the closely intertwined elements of troubadour art (see Chapter 18). The same is true of the topics elaborated by the early troubadours, which after 1150 exhibit a remarkable stability (see Chapter 19).

At a time when the courts were the seat of political power in the framework of late feudalism, the art of the troubadours was a poetry of those courts, tightly bound to the life there, to their evolving conflicts and their prevailing ideology. Yet the social origin of these poets was very varied: a few great lords, some simple knights, bourgeois, clerks, jongleurs—all classes were represented among the troubadours. What is more, the attention of medievalists has for some years been directed to the fact, surprising as it is for the twelfth and thirteenth centuries, that a score or so of them (not a negligible proportion) were women, and of aristocratic origin: the trobairitz. Various research has been undertaken in an effort to determine the specifics of their work (see Chapter 8). In any event, the troubadour acted as a spokesman for the seigneurial clan, or a faction of the clan. Remaining outside the urban life of the bourgeois until after 1250, the troubadour undertook to defend a decaying social order. This explains the sometimes confusing nature of some of this poetry for the twentieth-century reader: one encounters, on the one hand, a set of moralizing themes, often heightened by a biting aggressivity, whether in terms of eternal commonplaces (the decadence of morals, the folly of love) or concerning local or personal quarrels; and on the other hand, a true political vein, inspired by the vicissitudes of feudal groups or the changing fortunes of some noble Maecenas (see Chapter 20).

It is, however, mostly to their love songs (more than half of what has come down to us) that the troubadours owe their survival into the twentieth century. But even here misunderstandings have been numerous. It is true that the *vidas* (biographies) and *razos* (commentaries) accompanying the songs in several manuscripts, confirmed by discoveries in the archives, have permitted a sufficiently adequate retracing of the lives of several poets to lead certain researchers to interpret the love *cansos* biographically (see Chapter 7). These texts, moreover, offer, or may offer, some reflection of contemporary manners. Nevertheless, no serious indication justifies the generalizations of those who speak of the "adulterous love" of the troubadours. Rather, a passion—real or fictitious, adulterous or not—gives rise in the case of the troubadours to a discourse that is offered as an end in itself, independent of the real-life origin. The question of "sincerity" is not worth asking; the only pertinent approach is to interrogate the elements of this discourse: vocabulary, syntax, and rhetoric.

What the troubadour speaks of is *fin'amor,* a more or less technical expression where *fin,* meaning "distilled," may be a borrowing from alchemy. Moshe Lazar's analysis (Chapter 3) shows how equivocal this term can be. *Fin'amor* is in fact silhouetted against a background of strongly sexualized (though often implicit) eroticism. *Fin'amor* strives toward a desired but unnamed good, bestowable only by a lady, herself identified only by an emblematic pseudonym: a dialogue without reply, pure song, turning into poetry the movements of a heart contemplating an object whose importance as such is minimal. All that counts is the distance separating them, a distance filled in turn by pleasure, sadness, hope, and fear. The (future or already refused) possession of the coveted good would occasion *joi,* a term that should be understood as including both the modern French words *joie* 'joy' and *jeu* 'play, game'. Illustrated in the early troubadours by fleeting narrative allusions (such as Jaufre Rudel's invocation of his Distant Princess), the discourse of *fin'amor* was gradually pared down to its basic elements, enriched by nuances of an ever-increasing subtlety, without, however, losing (in its images and choice of words) a true sensuality.

It is unlikely that a form already so elaborate in its earliest manifestations had no antecedents. On this topic various specialists have undertaken research, the results of which do not mesh well (see Chapter 9). The Romantic theories that linked this poetry to a tradition of "popular lyricism" (about which almost nothing is known from any other source) were abandoned long ago. On the contrary, everything suggests that the earliest troubadours (or the unknown poets who were their immediate predecessors) created an original form from various elements presented to them by the practices and customs of their time, which they were able to transform into a homogeneous discourse with a particular purpose. The question of "origins" comes back to an inventory of these elements, of which some are to be defined in terms of rhythms, melodies, and verse patterns, and others in terms of imagination and sensitivity, without their being entirely separable.

Certain references made by the troubadours themselves to the source of their emotion, the quality of certain images, indicate that several of them were well schooled in Latin culture, while the sensitivity of certain others was clearly nourished by the remains of Celtic myths, which had recently spread through the western world, such as the legend of Tristan. None of that could have been decisive, however. By the same token, although it has never been proved that any troubadour knew Arabic, some of them, beginning with the first, Guillem de Peiteus, were in contact with Muslim Spain and had a taste for its singers. That the themes and the metaphors used by the troubadours owe something to the mysticism of the Sufi poets or to the Platonizing treatise of Ibn Hazm *The Dove's Neck-Ring* is probably nothing but an erroneous theory . . . like the one that long ago tried to see in troubadour song an emanation of the Cathar religion. According to the German scholar Erich Köhler, demographic pressure and the subsequent impoverishment of minor noblemen, which in about 1100 forced them to live in dependence on the greatest lords, were the social conditions that allowed this poetry to be born and develop.

The only certainties concern the music and a few rhythmic forms. The former probably derived from the liturgical music developed at Saint-Martial. Among the latter, one of the most frequently occurring forms in the earliest songs of the troubadours, the *zejel* or *zadjal*, a three-line stanza with refrain, certainly comes from the Semitic world, perhaps via the numerous Jewish communities of southern France. (For the *zejel*, see also Chapter 4.)

On the scale of European history, the poetry of the troubadours lasted but a short time: a scant two centuries, from 1100 to around 1270. Until 1350 it survived while becoming ossified. It was a brief but intense flash of lightning, crossing the horizons of European cultures, marking them forever.

We know the names of more than four hundred troubadours who lived between 1100 and 1350; we have more than 2,500 of their songs. Several poets are known to us only by name, and quite a few songs are anonymous or of doubtful attribution. Finally, many assigned dates are hypothetical. A first description of troubadour poetry thus requires it to be considered as a collective and universal phenomenon.

From the first generation of troubadours, two names have come down to us: that of one of the greatest feudal lords of the time, the duke of Aquitaine, Guillem de Peiteus, who lived in Poitiers, and that of one of his vassals, the viscount Eble de Ventadour from Limousin. Eleven songs remain to give us testimony of the work of the former; nothing of the latter's work has survived. At least we know that the poetry that was then rapidly developing was doing so in the central regions of Occitania. The somewhat slight legacy of Guillem de Peiteus allows us to see the first efforts of this development, and of the progressive search for a particular model: from rather crude songs, inspired by the daily life of warrior knights, to a very subtle art, closed in on itself.

The second generation gives proof of an extension to the whole south-west of France: Cercamon and Marcabru (nicknames suggesting that they were itinerant singers) were Gascons; their contemporary Jaufre Rudel is from the Bordeaux region. With the third and fourth generations the poetry of the troubadours reaches maturity and achieves a harmony among the different elements of its form that was never again questioned. Between 1160 and 1210 came the half-century of poets like Bernart Marti, Bernart de Ventadorn, Guiraut de Bornelh, Peire Vidal, Arnaut Daniel, Raimon de Miraval, and many others; then came all those whose songs rang out during the years of the French conquest (the "Albigensian Crusade"). The Narbonne poet Guiraut Riquier, in about 1270, was nicknamed "the last of the troubadours. . . ."

The "Crusade," waged for half a century, caused a break in the tradition of troubadour poetry from which it never recovered. The effects were felt in three ways: in the impoverishment of the seigneurial courts that supported the poets, which in turn caused the gradually increasing movement of their art into urban bourgeois society (see Chapter 20); in the rising importance given to political and especially religious, even mystical, themes in the *canso;* and in the emigration of many troubadours to Spain and Italy. Before the end of the thirteenth century, poets native to these countries were composing songs in the pure troubadour style in Occitan (see Chapters 12 and 14).

In Castile, Portugal, Sicily, and Tuscany, however, the local languages were not slow in taking the place of Occitan, and in modulating the troubadour tradition to suit poetic, musical, or intellectual habits peculiar to these areas. Nevertheless, the essential element remained: the language of erotic desire, which the Occitan poets had invented. The history of these avatars is especially rich in Italy, where the triumphal path along which the torch lit by the troubadours would enter the modern world led from the "Sicilian school," to the philosopher poets of the *dolce stil nuovo,* and to Petrarch (see Chapter 13).

North of the Loire, the poetry of the troubadours had since 1160–70 been adapted to French, as it had been in German in the Rhine countries (see Chapters 10 and 11). This poetry, originally imported but then reexperienced from within, displayed a brilliance and a vigor in the thirteenth and fourteenth centuries that was to influence profoundly all literature and even all social discourse until almost our own time. Nevertheless Dante, in about 1300, when outlining in his *De vulgari eloquio* a theory of poetry, goes back (in referring to initiators and models) not to the *trouvères* or the *Minnesänger,* but to the troubadours, whom he calls in Latin *eloquentes doctores,* that is to say, masters of doctrine and language.

And there we still stand today. True, the word *troubadour* and the names of most of these poets were forgotten during the fifteenth, sixteenth, and seventeenth centuries. But the tradition they had begun and the forms of sensitivity to which they gave poetic expression remained. The mutations of the baroque era, together with the more ephemeral ones contributed by French classicism, did not change the essence: a certain way of talking about love and about what separates the sexes in their desire while at the same time bringing them together; and also a way of considering that language to be the principal source of all poetry. When the first medievalists, at the end of the eighteenth century, restored a few names to a place of honor and set about reading the old *cansos*, a new literary fashion in France was christened: the "troubadour style."

The breakthrough had been made. During the nineteenth century, scholarship and the poetic taste of European Romanticism completed the rediscovery of these venerable ancestors. After entering contemporary romance and medieval studies, this poetry, through Ezra Pound and Paul Blackburn, reentered living literature. In our own day, the translations by the French poet Jacques Roubaud of troubadour verse are authentic poems (see Chapter 16). Our century, however, especially since the Second World War, has insisted on the musical side of this poetry, and on its delicate requirement of formal harmony. Musical philological studies have been pursued, and the methodology of interpretation has been the object of much research. A growing number of bold attempts have been made to perform in their original totality the text and melody of various songs, and we now have available a fairly large number of albums. Indeed, a person beginning the study of this poetry cannot be too strongly encouraged to begin by listening to these recordings. As for the themes of the troubadour *cansos*, tirelessly inventoried and discussed by specialists, taken together they merely confirm the dictum of the French historian Charles Seignobos when he called it "Love, that invention of the twelfth century. . . ."

The Essentials

TWO

The Lyric Texts

Amelia E. Van Vleck

Poetry in Europe changed forever when the first troubadours made lyric song the foremost of verbal arts in their time. From Poitiers to Catalonia, from Gascony to Savoy and Lombardy, individual poets refined this favorite entertainment by creating a unique blend of the familiar and the strange, the conventional and the original, the silly and the serious. The phenomenon had repercussions: it invigorated vernacular poetry as an emerging competitor with Latin literature; it popularized its subject matter, the balance of power between the sexes as well as between political factions; it multiplied poetic possibilities by creating endlessly new forms of versification, and music to go with them; it inspired renewal in the medieval lyric traditions of Italy, northern France, Germany, Spain, and England.

No sooner was it composed than this poetry challenged, even defied the reader to *ben l'entendre* 'understand it properly'. The first known troubadour, Guillem de Peiteus (1071–1127),[1] set the tone of challenge to future decipherers. By mischievously remarking that one privileged recipient possessed a *contraclau* 'counterkey' for his poem, he hints that some part of its message is locked up, awaiting disclosure exclusively to the owner of the key:

Fait ai lo vers, no sai de cui;
Et trametrai lo a celui

1. For a bilingual edition of his poems, with abundant historical documentation, see Bond 1982 (listed under Guillem de Peiteus in the Appendix). Guillem's name appears in criticism as Guillem IX, referring to his status as ninth duke of Aquitaine; Guilhem VII, as the seventh count of Poitiers; the medieval anthologies and biographies designate him "Lo Coms de Peiteus" (hence his odd place in the Pillet-Carstens *Bibliographie*, among the Gr's for "Graf" (German for count), not the Gu's for "Guillem"). His given name, like those of all troubadours, is subject to various orthography (Guilhem, Guillem) as well as translation, e.g. English "William the Ninth," French "Guillaume IX," Italian "Guglielmo."

Que lo·m trametra per autrui
Enves Anjau,
Que·m tramezes del sieu estui
La contraclau.

(4:43–48)

I've done the song, about whom I don't know; and I'll send it over to the other one who will send it for me through another toward Anjou, so that [she] might send me a copy of the key to her coffer.   (trans. Bond 16–17)[2]

Not just the making of the song, but its reception as well, is part of Guillem's teasing request that the poem's receiver send him something back. As readers, we may feel distantly called upon to supply the requested item: keys from our own "coffers" to match the one that unlocks Guillem's riddles. Each generation of readers—including our own—has aspired to recapture for its own times the sense of these rather elusive lyrics.

Just as our understanding of it has undergone many transformations over time and space, so has the poetry itself taken many forms and produced variations in different places and different times. A single poem composed in one locality and performed in another might adapt a few of its details to the new audience; twenty years later the adaptation might be more drastic. Such adaptation, evident in existing manuscript copies of many lyrics, reveals poets' and performers' awareness of their audiences' capacity and need to comprehend the verses. In time, poets borrowed and varied others' innovations, added these to the inventory of workable conventions, then innovated again. In space, poets and performers not only promulgated their songs by carrying them from region to region, but they also diffused ideas for new songs: verse-forms, thematic motifs, rhetorical tropes, specialized genres, melodic forms, and ornaments. Readings of troubadour poetry, at some stages in the history of its reception, have emphasized the where and when of composition: one way to grasp a puzzling, alien, even shifting verbal artifact is first to situate it in history, in time and space, in literary and sociological contexts. Locating a song in its historical moment or at its geographic source, though, yields only an outward comprehensibility. Such

2. The last two lines are ambiguous: Guillem may be asking the addressee to send this *contraclau* 'counterkey' *from* his or her coffer. In his textual note (ed. 64), Bond explains his preference for a translation highlighting the use of the " 'counterfeit key' as an erotic symbol," but since the strophe's emphasis is on the transmission of the poem, and since the addressee's gender is not specified, the reader cannot overlook *contraclau* as the homologue of the poem: both *vers* and *contraclau* are direct objects of the verb *trametre* 'send' in a strongly parallel series. Both registers may be operating simultaneously: this is not the only case where the poet implies a parallel between imposing the text on a reader and making a sexual conquest of the reader.

location lets us situate each poem along a continuum of other poems, allows us to estimate its importance, yet leaves readers who love poetry still rattling the lock for more satisfying access.

What is constant across time and space in this poetry is the language of which it is made: from the end of the eleventh to the end of the thirteenth century and beyond, the art language that was Old Occitan remained more or less intact; its use was the sine qua non of composing troubadour poetry. In the fourteenth century, self-styled poetry experts who wanted to preserve *trobar* (in localities where the tradition was fading or imported) composed manuals for would-be troubadours that include a basic grammar of the language: how to conjugate verbs, when to add *s* to a noun to mark its case and number.[3] Some 2,500 troubadour songs are available to us as linguistic artifacts—sometimes in several copies, sometimes copied with various light "foreign accents," which reveal that Old Occitan was not the native language of all who enjoyed, received, and transmitted this poetry. Medieval speakers of Catalan, Gascon, Spanish, French, Italian, and various dialects of Occitan—all, whatever their native tongue, adopted the "art language" (*Kunstsprache*) of troubadour poetry whenever they composed it, recited it, or made copies of it. Thus these "texts," preserved in the chansonniers (medieval songbooks compiled in the thirteenth century and later), do share a consistent idiom—not just a grammar and vocabulary, but a common language for expressing a culture of aesthetic and moral values. The poetry builds, creates, reinforces this idiom with every poem—even poems that rebel against it. The modern reader enters into this culture through its language: like a traveler in a strange land for whom the surrounding voices become daily more intelligible, just so we gather slightly more familiarity, more fluency in the troubadours' idiom with each encounter. It is this language, this idiom, that eventually promises us as readers the desired access to what these poems are really made of.

THE MYSTIQUE OF PLACE

When not at home, some poets speak of their homelands with nostalgia:

Ab l'alen tir vas me l'aire
Qu'ieu sen venir de Proensa;
Tot quant es de lai m'agensa,
Si que, quan n'aug ben retraire,

3. Several such handbooks can be found in Marshall 1972. See also Chapter 6 in this volume.

Ieu m'o escout en rizen
E·n deman per un mot cen.
(Peire Vidal 20:1–6)

With my breath I draw toward me the air I feel coming from Provence;
everything from there moves me, so much that when I hear good tales of it,
I listen laughing, and for every word I ask a hundred more.

Nostalgia for troubadour territory, sometimes acquiring the compelling
force of a local "nationalism," has affected subsequent understandings of
their poetry. In the fourteenth century, the Consistori de la Subregaya
Companhia del Gai Saber was founded at Toulouse to preserve and continue a tradition of *belles lettres* in Occitan. One of the earliest literary
historians of the troubadours, Jehan de Nostredame of Aix (b. 1507), was
moved by regional loyalties to concentrate troubadour geography in Provence; he thus "relocated" some of the western poets.[4]

The mystique of troubadour territory includes speculation about the
beneficial effects on poetry of the region's "favorable conditions": a
milder climate, more dramatic landscapes set off by brighter sunlight, and
lesser Germanic interference with the Roman heritage of its *provincia* than
in the north. The obligatory southerly pilgrimage of Romantic poets
(Keats, Byron, Shelley) fueled Anglophone critics' affirmations of regional
magic. Friedrich Diez, one of the founders of Occitan philology, became
interested in troubadour studies in 1818 on the advice of the great German Romantic poet, Goethe.[5] Frédéric Mistral (1830–1914), the leading
poet in Le Félibrige, a group of poets founded in 1854 to revive Provençal
language and literature, contributed untiringly to the existence in print of
an idealized Provence full of sunlight, fields of lavender, enchanting folk
wisdom, and above all, uniquely vibrant language.[6] The American expa-
triate poet Ezra Pound, early in the twentieth century, brought troubadour
song to the attention of modernist writers and their readers with *The Spirit
of Romance*, his literary essays and letters, and his admiring adaptations and
translations.

Among the earliest "literary critics" to describe the troubadours were the
authors of the medieval *vidas* and *razos* (see Chapter 7 in this volume). As
if art were identical to life, these authors counsel us to understand the poetry
by situating its maker geographically and socially. Often they create a biography retroactively to explain the poetry: they presuppose a view that the

---

4. Jeanroy 1:8–9: "Quand il n'ose les faire naître en Provence, il les y fait du moins mourir"
(9).

5. Ibid., 22. For more on the Romantic background of Diez's scholarship, see Gumbrecht.

6. Mistral's Provençal-French dictionary, *Lou Tresor dou Felibrige*, provided a lexicon for this
movement. He was awarded the Nobel Prize in 1904. His memoirs are available in English
translation: Wickes.

poem was a direct consequence of its creator's experience, and its composition a means to obtain specified results in the poet's negotiation for love or property. Such an effort to decode the text as biography results, for example, in a thirteenth-century biographer's assertion that Bernart de Ventadorn's verses "Can vei la lauzeta mover / de joi sas alas contral rai" (When I see the lark move its wings for joy against the ray [of sunlight]; 31:1–2) were inspired one day when the poet, hidden behind a curtain in the bedroom of a lady named Alauzeta, watched her raise her arms ("wings") to embrace a lover named Rai. We may laugh at this kind of interpretation, but even the most cautious scholars still occasionally make comparable mistakes. However small the grain of true-life experience underlying a fiction, curiosity will seek it out—and will likely cause more fiction to sprout from it.

These early critics, the authors of the *vidas*, seem to care (or know) much less about the poets' position in time than in space. They subordinate chronological concerns to observations about class standing, poverty or wealth, importance or insignificance. For example, the Comtessa de Dia (d. 1212–14?) is described as the wife of Guillem de Peiteus and the lover of Raimbaut d'Aurenga—a trio of names that at best highlights the strange coincidence that the Comtessa's loved ones bore the same names as major poets, and at worst perhaps claims literary contact for three poets whose life spans did not even overlap.[7] The *vida* communicates the Comtessa's prestige—as a countess and as a poet—but is indifferent to the succession of years and decades as historical markers.

The first things the *vidas* tell us about a given troubadour are his birthplace and social rank: occasionally they are quite specific about it, as in this opening sentence: "Deude de Pradas si fo de Rosergue, d'un borc que a nom Pradas, pres de la ciutat de Rodes quatre legas, e fo canorgues de Magalona" (Daude de Pradas was from Rouergue, from a town named Pradas, only four leagues from the city of Rodez, and he was a canon of Magalona).[8] For a thirteenth-century biographer, then, identity rested on the social niche one occupied in a given locality. The exact distance from Rodez, along with Daude's ecclesiastical title, might have implied a particular stance in the religious politics of the region during his lifetime (ca.

7. See her *vida*, Boutière and Schutz 445–46; reprinted in Hill and Bergin No. 63 (1:95) with a concise explanatory note (2:31). Instead of the poet Raimbaut d'Aurenga (ca. 1144–73), the name may refer to Raimbaut IV; instead of the poet Guilhem de Peiteus (ca. 1071–1127), the biographer may mean Guilhem II de Poitiers, count of Valentinois. The dates of these namesakes are more in keeping with presumed dates of a countess of Die, who might have written poetry. Pattison's edition of Raimbaut d'Aurenga includes a detailed investigation of archival clues to this *vida* (27–30).

8. Boutière and Schutz 233.

1194–1282).[9] But the biographer could not anticipate questions about Rodez that arise seven hundred years later. Such regional and sociological identifications gives us a foothold in the referential landscape underlying the poets' language; to grasp their meaning, we can attempt (but only attempt) to put ourselves in their place.

A "map" of early troubadour activity over time would show a movement from west to east. Poitiers, the home of Guillem de Peiteus, is near the northern limit of the region that was to nurture and develop troubadour poetry. Sending one song to Anjou, another to Narbonne, he set distant boundaries at the far limits of Aquitaine for his songs' itinerary. Belligerent words against the Gascons to the south, French and Normans to the north, are in keeping with the historical count's need to stake out and hold an enormous territory; and though he imagines receiving Montpellier as a gift, his boasts of possession are centered in the Limousin. Guillem's travels as a crusader to Syria and as a diplomat to Spain doubtless broadened the worldview he had brought from his birthplace.

THE FIRST TWO GENERATIONS

From Guillem's time to that of Guiraut Riquier (fl. 1254–82), known as the "last troubadour," poets engage in a dialectic as they shape their verse-forms, their artistic and moral preoccupations, their expression of political views. It is partly because they constantly allude to contact with courts and with one another that we speak of "generations" of troubadours. Although Guillem constitutes a generation by himself, as far as extant poetry is concerned, the evidence that his poetry responds to and even parodies conventions already established makes it unlikely that Guillem was a sole inventor, creating troubadour poetry *de dreit nien* 'out of just nothing', as he says he created the riddle-song cited earlier. (See Chapter 9 in this volume.)

The second generation of troubadours offers an intense contrast between the combative Gascon poets led by Marcabru (fl. 1130–49) and the poignant *amor de lonh* 'faraway love' of Jaufre Rudel (fl. 1125–48). This second generation—Jaufre, from Blaya (modern Blaie) at the mouth of the Garonne just north of Bordeaux, and Marcabru and Cercamon (fl. 1137–49), from Gascony in the southwest—extends the use of this "art language," called "Lemosin" or later "Provençal," along the Atlantic side. Marcabru, an inventive name caller and word coiner who voices outrage at the decadence of contemporary sexual mores, hammers out the standard for po-

---

9. Daude de Pradas ed., xviii. Schutz presents the archival references to a historical Daude de Pradas but draws few conclusions.

litical and social satire (*vers,* later called *sirventes*).[10] Offering advice in verse
to princes and paupers, one surveys the symptoms of a world in decline, one
reprimands (*castiar*) specific wrongdoers either by name or with comic
nicknames, and one ridicules the victims. Strong invective requires strong
language to match:

> E ·il luxurios corna-vi,
> Coita-disnar, bufa-tizo,
>   Crup-en-cami
> Remanran inz el folpidor,
>   (Marcabru 35:46–49)

> These lustful wine-horners, dinner-rushers, coal-puffers, crouchers-in-the-
> road, they'll stay in the filth-atory.[11]

These newly minted compound words fairly spit with blistering plosive
consonants. With a fellow poet, Uc Catola, Marcabru co-authored the first
of the extant debate poems (*tensos*): the two poets argue the uses and misuses
of love, with Marcabru condemning it. Such dialogue poems are evidence
that literary contact and competition fueled the rapid development of
troubadour art. Marcabru's medieval biographer associates him with the
poet Cercamon, whose surviving works include love songs, social criticism,
and a lament (*planh*) on the pilgrimage death of Duke Guillem X of
Aquitaine (1137). Their Gascon contemporary Alegret (fl. 1145) develops
Marcabru-style invective, using some of Marcabru's techniques: personification of the virtues and vices, biblical allusion, alliterative name-calling,
"adult language" for adulterous women, and a taste for Old Testament
justice couched in proverbial style, for example: "e coven se q'ab l'enap ab
qe·ill bec / sai le cogos, beva lai le sufrens"[12] (meaning essentially, "The
cuckold's goblet is the proper cup from which the permissive man should
drink"). In the early years of troubadour lyric, oddly enough, such moral
satires outnumber songs of love.[13]

Malice is entirely absent from the six poems attributed to Jaufre Rudel:
he elaborates his *amor de lonh* 'love from afar' using simpler language and
rhetoric that evoke obsessive desire and its concomitant heightening of the

---

10. For a recent full-length study of Marcabru, see Harvey.

11. See Ricketts and Hathaway. The celebrated "Vers del lavador" (Song of the Washing-
Place) incites all good men to travel to go and fight the Moslems. The baffling word *folpidor*
can only be deciphered through etymological analysis; after much discussion, scholars tend to
agree that *folp-* has to do with uncleanliness, either of the slothful or of the lustful variety, and
that the ending *-dor* signifies the place where it occurs, as in *lavador* (lavatory, washing-place).

12. P-C 17,2; text of Riquer 1:238.

13. William D. Paden has found that of sixty songs in the period 1100–1141, there were
only thirteen *cansos* to thirty-four *sirventes* (paper delivered at the annual meeting of the
Medieval Institute, Kalamazoo, 1992).

senses. For Jaufre, it is not the perfidy of gossips that frustrates love, but desire itself:

E cre que volers m'engana
Si cobezeza la·m tol.
(4:24–25)

And I think desire cheats me, if wanting takes her from me.[14]

His poetry lacks allusion to the *lauzengiers* whom later love poets regularly accuse of misrepresenting them to their ladies.

Ebles II de Ventadorn (fl. 1096–1147), a legendary rival of Guillem de Peiteus and contemporary of Cercamon whose poetry has probably not survived, was lord of a castle farther inland, southeast of Limoges near the Dordogne River.[15] He appears to have been a leader in formulating a sophisticated, nonsatirical style of love poetry. Marcabru accuses him of sophistry, of confusing the nuances in his terminology of love and thereby of promoting "sentenssa follatina . . . encontra razo" (a crazy pronouncement . . . contrary to reason).[16] Later Bernart de Ventadorn (fl. 1147–70?) speaks respectfully of "l'escola n'Eblon" (the school of Ebles) as a standard he would like to live up to.[17] Alfred Jeanroy (1934, 2:13–36) established as traditional the view that the second generation of troubadours was divided into "the idealist school"—Jaufre Rudel, Ebles de Ventadorn, and their followers—and "the realist school," with Marcabru and friends.

With this second generation, the basic framework of troubadour poetry is in place. Even before the terms come into use, a central division between the love song (*canso*) and the invective (*sirventes*) takes shape, and poets tend to specialize in one type or the other.[18] The nature introduction ("exordium"), where springtime weather inspires and bird songs "teach" the poet to sing, has already developed variations: dark weather inspires dark thoughts; cackling or shrieking birds reflect traitors' counsel in contrast to the poets' own harmonious advice. One or more *tornadas*, half-strophes at the conclusion akin to the French *envoi*, commend the song to its addressee and wish for its auspicious delivery and reception. Middle stanzas also de-

14. In "Qan lo rius de la fontana" Wolf and Rosenstein translate "And I think my will deceives me, if lust takes her away from me" (139). The pair *volers* and *cobezeza* belong to an array of nuanced terms for "to desire," along with *talen*, *[aver] cor*, and *desirer*.

15. Riquer 1975, 142–47. Jean Mouzat has proposed a list of five poems possibly attributable to Ebles, but the evidence is inconclusive. For "the school of Ebles," see Dumitrescu.

16. 31.75–76; Marcabru accuses Ebles of missing the distinction between *amor* and *amar*.

17. 44.22–23: "Ja mais no serai chantaire / ni de l'escola N'Eblo, / que mos chantars no·m val gaire . . ." (I will never be a singer nor of Ebles's school, for my song is worthless to me).

18. The existence of a mixed genre, the *canso-sirventes*, "ties the theme of love to that of politics" and, "as Erich Köhler demonstrated, with this double thematics the genre once again presents the original unity of feminine praise and lordly service" (Jauss 92).

velop stable topoi on which poets can build original variations: for the love poem, motifs of the lover's madness, pleasurable pain, nearness to death, hallucinatory visions. The love song builds its central idea or emotion with rhetorical ornaments that, to an analytic eye, can seem coldly calculated, and all largely have the function of restatement: antithesis and opposition, restatement by the negative of the contrary, restatement with paired synonyms, restatement with sententiae, and, at the level of form, reinforcement by recurring rhyme-sounds or rhyme-words.[19] Imaginative paradox is one means by which the poets step out of this cumulative rhetoric: they communicate psychological depth by affirming two superficially antithetical conditions.[20]

A few genres with narrative components are already well represented by the time of the second generation. Guillem de Peiteus's "song of the red cat" boasts about an adventure with two women who, convinced that he cannot speak, carry him off for an eight-day orgy. Marcabru composed more than one *pastorella*, or "encounter with a shepherdess," a genre usually recounting an attempted seduction through dialogue between a knight and a shepherd girl. The relatively rare genre of the *alba* 'dawn song', though not appearing in troubadour poetry proper until Guiraut de Bornelh's "Reis glorios," may have existed in Provençal even before Guillem de Peiteus. Evidence for its existence is to be found in the "bilingual alba," a late-tenth-century Latin poem with a two-line refrain in early Romance (Occitan?) that is only partly decipherable.[21] The dawn song depicts a dramatic situation involving three people: an adulterous couple spending the night together, and the man's friend who serves as watchman to warn them when the sun rises and the jealous husband is likely to arrive. The situation is a bit marginal for troubadour poetry, since the dawn song finds the lovers not in the state of perpetual desire that characterizes the *canso*, but at a moment of contentment. For this reason, Raimbaut de Vaqueiras's *alba* was suspected of not being by a Provençal poet:

> Gait', amics, e veilh'e crid'e bray,
> Qu'eu sui ricx e so qu'eu plus voilh ai.
>   Mais enics sui de l'alba,
> E·l destrics que·l jorn nos fai
>   Mi desplai
>   Plus que l'alba.
>
> (25:8–13)

Stand sentinel, my friend, and keep watch and cry out and shout, for I am rich, and I have what I most desire. But I am dawn's enemy, and the swindle that the day works on us displeases me more than the dawn.

19. Dragonetti. See Chapters 18 and 19 in this volume.
20. On "poetic antithesis" see, for example, Bec.
21. See Zumthor 1984 on the bilingual *alba*.

Perhaps because its themes, with the lazy adulterers luxuriating in the moments before dawn and wishing to prolong the darkness, are slightly outside the typical love situation of the *canso*, troubadours who did compose *albas* often substituted a religious theme.

THE THIRD GENERATION AND SUCCESSORS

By the mid–twelfth century a third "generation" of poets, in communication and often professed disagreement with one another, is working out further refinements not only in the variety of stances toward love and the lady, but also in the qualities appropriate to the best poetic style. When the terms *vers*, *canso*, and *trobar* recurrently appear conjoined with adjectives like *leu*, *greu*, *plan*, *entier*, *clus*, and *natural*, we can only assume that the poets are commenting on stylistic trends. Humility belongs to the persona of the lover but not always of the poet/singer, so the open discussion of various styles takes on a competitive aspect. Peire d'Alvernhe (fl. 1149–70), whose extant corpus includes love songs, *sirventes*, and religious lyrics, was involved in early stylistic debates: he composed an enigmatic manifesto of *trobar clus* 'closed poetry', and he participated in debate with Bernart Marti on the question of "integrity" (*vers entiers*). One of his poems, a "portrait gallery" lampooning each of a dozen troubadours, seems to commemorate a special occasion when poets from a wide geographical range gathered under one roof.[22] Participants in the symposium included representatives of the Limousin, of Auvergne, of Roussillon and Catalonia and Spain, of the Rhône region, and of Lombardy. Though many of the poets mentioned are no longer known, the poem evokes a self-critical literary community, in which each poet marks his lyrics with a unique personal style.

Such exchange of ideas, and surely also of poems, invigorated this poetry with the tonic of competition. Peire Rogier advises the young and serious Raimbaut d'Aurenga to be more jocular, to act the fool among fools; a few years later, Peire d'Alvernhe makes this flippancy Raimbaut's trademark in his portrait gallery of poets. A poet named Peire debates with Bernart de Ventadorn his refusal to sing when not in love, and rebukes the latter for not manufacturing the required emotion. Untrammeled by the bonds of love, Bernart can contemplate turning the whole system of the love lyric upside down: why not let ladies humbly woo the men, he asks (poem 28). Yet Bernart's gift for tracing the movements of a tender heart, which nearly melts when he sees a lark in flight, made him one of the most successful poets of his time. Elsewhere he expounds the view that heartfelt feeling must precede good poetry, inciting his contemporaries to contemplate the interaction between sincerity and artifice, and either to echo or to protest his

---

22. See Pattison.

doctrine. Bernart's celebrated pronouncement, "Chantars no pot gaire valer / si d'ins dal cor no mou lo chans" (Singing can have little worth if the song does not issue from within the heart; 2:1–2), finds a mocking echo in Raimbaut d'Aurenga's *tenso* with Guiraut de Bornelh: "can d'als cossir, no m'es coral" (when I think of something else, it is not heartfelt for me; Raimbaut d'Aurenga 31, Guiraut de Bornelh 59). Raimbaut, a serious stylist but a playful theorist and love poet, operates on several levels; with him one arrives at the "heartfelt" only after passing through the jocular screen, the logical puzzle, and the formal prodigy. Poets in this "classic period" constantly refer to one another, whether they confirm or challenge views already put forward, whether they reopen questions of lovers' etiquette or of poetry itself.

The aesthetics of originality versus accessibility entered into the debate: songs that "anc mais non foron dig cantan" (were never before recited in song; Raimbaut d'Aurenga 16:6) were an object of pride for their composer, but their reception was problematic: "pos vers plus greu / fan sorz dels fatz" (since more difficult verses render fools deaf; Raimbaut d'Aurenga 18:5–6). The supposed polarity of *trobar clus* and *trobar leu* (closed poetry and light poetry) debated in the well-known *tenso* (Raimbaut d'Aurenga 31) between Guiraut de Bornelh and "Linhaure" (probably Raimbaut) reflects widespread debates on which poetic styles gave poems the highest intrinsic value, and which styles made poems most appreciated by their audiences. Guiraut de Bornelh favors the accessible style in this *tenso*, yet his extant lyrics show him fully capable of both easy and difficult verse. Whenever a particular adjective reappears as modifier for *vers* or *trobars*, it can be investigated as descriptive of a poetic style. Some such terms are transparent, others rather enigmatic: terms like *plan* 'plain?, smooth, polished', *prim* 'first-rate, early', *escur* 'dark', and so on fit into the discussion of intrinsic value versus audience accessibility, *clus* 'closed' versus *leu* 'light, easy';[23] others describe the poem's rhythm (Peire Vidal's *chanson viatz* 'rapid song'), its novelty or originality (the *chansoneta nueva* 'new song' and its descendants), its integrity (*enter* or *frach*, 'whole' or 'broken'), its authenticity (*trobar natural* 'natural poetry'),[24] or its mood.

Through rhyme-schemes a poet can refer to another's work—whether in approval or in challenge—and thus comment on it. Originality of rhyme-scheme was customary, and the drive toward novelty spread to other elements: striking, rare rimes (*rimas caras*) led to unusual word choices and hence to unusual images, logical leaps, unexpected causality. In a poem with a fixed rhyme on *giscle* 'switch' or 'twig', Raimbaut d'Aurenga compares his lady's eyes to "switches"; Arnaut Daniel's sestina, with *oncle* as a refrain

---

23. The landmark study of these terms is Mölk.
24. For discussions of this mysterious term, see Topsfield; also Van Vleck 139–46.

rhyme, refers to his mother as "the sister of my uncle." Ambitious rhyme schemes sometimes propelled the creation of new words to fit them. Competition both fueled originality and amplified intertextual echoing: poets tested the limits of formal complexity by building new rhyme-schemes on the innovations of their predecessors (see Chapter 4 in this volume). Bertran de Born (fl. 1181–98), a feisty satirist, occasionally borrowed the formal structure of a predecessor's sweet love song to build his harsh *sirventes* upon, though more often poets borrowed from *him* in this practice of structural imitation (ed. 45–65). Thus, in seeking a way to approach troubadour poetry, we realize that the troubadours made some of the first commentaries on their own poetry and on that of their contemporaries.

Successors who refined the art of the second generation held roughly the same geographical territory: concentrated in the area south of the Loire, west of the Rhône, north of the Pyrenees, troubadours nevertheless are to be found also along the Durance, in the coastal cities of Marseille and Montpellier, and in northern Spain. Many made their fame in the northern Spanish courts of Castile, Aragon, and Catalonia (see Chapter 12 in this volume). With the generation of circa 1180–95, we discover a refinement and synthesis of many of the most successful techniques created before. Elaborately inventive rhyme-schemes reach new heights in this period (notably in "L'aura amara" of Arnaut Daniel, in his sestina and that of Bertran de Born, in Peire Vidal's "Mout m'es bon e bel," and in the inventive Raimbaut de Vaqueiras). Yet other poets return to forms that are less flamboyant in the rotation of rhymes and more impressive for the sustained development of a single argument within a slightly longer stanza. A second "literary gallery" ("Pos Peire d'Alvernh'a chantat"), composed in 1195 by the Monge (Monk) de Montaudan (fl. 1193–1210), mentions sixteen poets, including himself and his cousin, poets born in Catalonia and Quercy, and several from the Dordogne (poem 18 in Routledge's edition). The most famous and prolific of these were Guilhem de Saint-Didier (fl. 1165–95; thirteen extant poems),[25] Raimon de Miraval (fl. 1191–1229; at least forty-five poems extant), Gaucelm Faidit (fl. 1172–1203; more than sixty-five poems surviving), Peirol (fl. 1188–1222; thirty extant poems), Folquet de Marseilla (fl. 1178–95, d. 1231; nineteen poems), Arnaut Daniel from Ribérac in the Dordogne (fl. 1180–95; eighteen or nineteen poems), Arnaut de Marueill (fl. ca. 1195; twenty-five lyrics plus five love epistles and an *ensenhamen*), and the celebrated Peire Vidal from Toulouse (fl. 1183–1204; forty-five poems).

---

25. St-Didier-en-Vélay, department of Haute-Loire; this poet is also known as Guilhem de Saint-Leidier.

This post-1180 generation diversified the minor poetic genres, using them more frequently and creating new ones.[26] For example, the Monge de Montaudon himself composed several *enueg* 'ennui' poems cataloging "the things that bother him." Clearly the *enueg* is a subcategory of the *sirventes*, but a slightly specialized one. Debate poems become prominent—the *tenson* and *partimen*, in which two voices discuss burning issues on fine points of love or morality.

The poet Raimbaut de Vaqueiras (fl. 1180–1205) exemplifies the cosmopolitan character and versatility of some poets in this period: he mastered old genres, synthesized a variety of new ones, and found patronage in Italian courts. He composed a *descort* (a "disaccord") in which, he says, "ieu fauc dezacordar / los motz e·ls sos e·ls lenguatges" (I make the words and music and languages disaccord; 16:7–8). Accordingly, the song has a strophe in Old Occitan, one in Italian, one in French, one in Gascon, one in Gallego-Portuguese, and one combining all five languages. Two of his most famous and beautiful songs have so much in common with the *cantigas d'amigo* that scholars have questioned their attribution to this Provençal poet: his "Altas undas que venez suz la mar" ([You] high waves who come over the sea, 24), lamenting from the woman's point of view her lover's absence, and his *alba* (25).[27] His *estampida* (dance song, "stamping song") "Kalenda maia" (15), with its rapid rhythm of insistently repeated rhymes, is a concert favorite for performers today. He composed a three-part "epic epistle" in praise of his Italian patron's military exploits during the Fourth Crusade.[28] One of his poems is a fictive "battle of the ladies" (18, also given the title *Carros*), featuring lady warriors from specified northern Italian localities pitched against the "citadel" of the far superior Lady Beatriz, his patron's daughter.

A few poets of the late period are known less for their own poetry than as "magnets" who drew together the best poets of their times. Among these is Dalfin d'Alvernha (ca. 1160–1235), a count whose poetic contacts and political entanglements were sometimes intertwined. Princely accusations of betrayal, verse interventions in his family squabbles, and hearty debates survive in the works of other poets as monuments to Dalfin's knack for inspiring eloquent dispute. Another "magnet" poet was Blacatz (fl. 1194–

26. William D. Paden, at the Medieval Institute's annual meeting at Kalamazoo in 1992, presented a study showing that songs composed prior to 1180 were almost exclusively *cansos* and *sirventes*, but between 1180 and 1220 almost one-fifth of the poems composed belonged to minor genres; by the late period, 1261–1300, more than one-third belong to minor genres.

27. Linskill (Raimbaut de Vaqueiras ed.) summarizes the controversy over these songs' attribution to Raimbaut de Vaqueiras because of their Catalan "flavor"; those expressing doubt include Fassbinder, Jeanroy, Lewent, Roncaglia, and Bergin.

28. Ed., 301–44.

1236), whose extant poems are all debates. His praises were sung by an impressive list of poets including Elias de Barjols, Guillem Figueira, Aimeric de Peguilhan, Lanfranc Cigala, Cadenet, Peirol, Bertran d'Alamanon, Folquet de Romans, and Peire Guillem; and when he died, Sordello lamented him in a *planh*. Some of the poets in his literary group were Italians who had come to Provence to learn the art of poetry. Lanfranc Cigala (fl. 1235–57), a Genoese, became an ambassador in the poetic field as well as the political. Critics of Italian literature traditionally consider Lanfranc an important precursor of the Italian *dolce stil nuovo*, or a bridge between the troubadours and the new Italian style (see Chapters 13 and 14 in this volume). Sordello (fl. 1255–69), a poor knight born near Mantua, moved from court to court: from Verona he traveled to Spain and possibly to Portugal, reappeared in Provence, then Montpellier, then Aix, and back to Italy again. Naturally, his extant poetry includes numerous debates with poets he met in his wide travels.[29]

After about 1220, with the Albigensian Crusade and pressure from the north to speak langue d'oïl, Occitan poetry tended to go elsewhere. "Heretics" driven out of France took some troubadour poetry with them. Very few chansonniers were copied in southern France: the earliest extant ones, with almost identical texts, date from the mid–thirteenth century; one was copied in Haute Auvergne and the other, by a southern French copyist, in Venetia.[30] In Italy and Spain, poets continued to compose songs in the art language associated with troubadour lyric (see Chapters 12 and 14 in this volume). Judging from the rise of "how to" books, lesser poets pursued an increasingly artificial cultivation of this art, aided by "handbooks of love" (that is, of poetry) that codified the "proper way to compose."[31]

In one such handbook, the *Rasos de trobar*, the author, Raimon Vidal, blames the rise of bad poetry on bad audiences of two kinds: those too ignorant to encourage good poetry, who only pretend to understand it; and those who do understand but are too polite to discourage bad poetry. Near the end of the flourishing of troubadour poetry, as at the beginning, it depended for its value on its "understanders." As readers, therefore, we are once again faced with the responsibility to interpret, not just to chronicle or map, the production of the troubadours. Successful critical approaches proposed in recent decades offer a variety of valid means to "understand" troubadour poetry. With caution and boldness in due measure, the reader can make a good attempt at escaping from Raimon Vidal's category of "li auzidor qe ren non indendon" (listeners who don't understand anything).

29. For a bilingual edition with English notes and translations, see Wilhelm.
30. I refer to MSS Rome, Bibl. Apost. Vat., lat. 5232; and Paris, B.N. fr. 1592, known by the standard sigla as MSS *A* and *B*.
31. See Marshall 1972 for texts of these rule books.

Many recent critical approaches have in common an exploration of the troubadours' contemporary audiences: who were those original *auzidors* 'listeners', and how did their experience fit into the meanings of particular songs or of whole genres?

SOCIAL AND ECONOMIC HIERARCHIES

Although using "climate" as a key does little to explain what troubadour poetry is about, one can explain better "what it is about" through the political climate: the social situation of its intended audience. The love song and the *sirventes* offer the plea of a powerless young man before, respectively, a powerful lady or a prince. Erich Köhler has argued that the poets' stance here reflects the widespread condition of a whole class of young men, young more for want of consolidated property than in terms of age, whose livelihood depended on comparable skill in the art of making requests. When the troubadours refer to their audience as a public of *entendedors*, initiates who "understand" the arts of love and poetry, they minimize the distance between a song's creator and its hearer to such an extent that addressees are occasionally asked to memorize and recite the songs. The poet, from this point of view, is truly a spokesman for his audience's prevailing needs, desires, and discontents. In the south of France, where instead of following a principle of primogeniture in matters of inheritance the custom was to parcel out ever smaller portions of land, often geographically separated and even divided temporally to the point of time-sharing, a lofty title did not guarantee power. Add to this an ethic of generosity, with the "best" people being those who give away all their goods and must finally call upon the bounty of others. The basic form of most poems, then, is as intermediary in a request: "Lady, give me your *merce*"; or "Sir, I could do you prodigious service *if only I had a horse.*"

When one looks closely at courtly texts, the evidence abounds for a preoccupation with economic concerns. It is not just class that counts, but wealth too. The *vida* of Dalfi d'Alvergne explains how the virtue of generosity led to poverty: "E per la larguesa soa perdet la meitat e plus de tot lo sieu comtat; e per avareza e per sen o saup tot recobrar, e gazaingnar plus que non perdet" (And through his generosity he lost more than half of his county; and through avarice and cleverness he managed to get it all back, and to gain more than he had lost; Boutière and Schutz 284). Peire Vidal's song "Drogoman senher, s'ieu agues bon destrier" (Sir Interpreter, if only I had a good war horse; song 29) boasts what a great warrior and protector the speaker would be if he had a proper steed and armor: his lord could sleep well at night, knowing he would not be robbed by "malvatz rocinier" (bad people riding on nags). He also promises to do physical combat against the enemies of love: jealous husbands and gossips. The horse was essential to a knight's functioning, yet its purchase, equipment, and maintenance were a heavy expense: the armor alone cost as much as a good farm, according to Georges Duby (1968, 55). In this "request for a horse," then, Peire presents the comic figure of a horseless vassal, poor but boastful, whose military prowess is realized only in grand dreams.

Erich Köhler, through his sociohistorical approach, traces the ideals in troubadour lyric to the imaginative needs of a knightly class caught in an almost untenable economic situation. Forever "young" (*jovens*) because in the second feudal age the system could not provide them all the landed property required for advancement to "mature" seignorial status, the knights develop (almost subconsciously) a utopian vision antagonistic to private property. As an example, Köhler explains troubadour poetry's rough treatment of the stereotyped "jealous husband" along with the possessive stance of the lover-turned-jealous, as expression of discontent with contemporary circumstances surrounding property ownership. The struggle for the lady's favors "is no different from the struggle for the social advancement of a group that designates itself by the name of 'joven' and that includes impoverished knights, warriors of servile ancestry, mercenary soldiers, and finally the spokesmen for them all, the poets."[32] We could thus ask, with historians in the school of Georges Duby, what the poet was eating, what he used for transportation, where he traded, whether it was so cold that year that he really needed a fur-lined coat. For example, when Bernart de Ventadorn compares his love-service (and consequent prospects for recompense) to the service and reward of an *escudier* 'squire', it is worthwhile to know the quotidian details of a squire's job:

> Servirs c'om no gazardona,
> Et esperansa bretona
> Fai de senhor escuder
> Per costum e per uzatge.
> (34:37–40)[33]

Service that is not compensated, and the hope of the Bretons, turns a lord into a squire by custom and usage.

According to Linda Paterson, the job entails "rubbing down and saddling the horses," riding on a smaller horse than the lord's, "taking messages, keeping watch, and serving at table." Their lords sometimes forget to pay them, and they sometimes neglect their errands; and when they carve meat they lazily cut the pieces too large, and "forget to clean their knives and wash

---

32. Köhler (1970, 553) here refers to his 1966 article on the term *jovens* 'youth'. See his important full-length study (1962).

33. Paterson 135. She translates *esperanza bretona* as "the hope of the Bretons, or Never-Never Land" (137).

their hands."[34] Poor recompense leads to poor service and to debasement equally in love as in chivalry.

Such material and economic studies examine what the poet really stood to gain, or lose, by exchanging his "aesthetic product," a song, for something else.[35] When poets offer their "homage," we remember that the feudal bond carried reciprocal obligation for practical as well as spiritual support. Epic poets of the period asked directly for food or money; might lyric poets have been doing the same in asking for *merce* 'mercy, reward'?[36] If so, it would revise the notion that poets' real motive in singing was purely to offer love, expecting little or nothing in return. Such a "literary socioeconomic" approach considers not only what the poet stood to gain or lose by offering his poem, but also what value such a product might have held for those who received it.[37] Because the poem as an offering participates in an exchange, to investigate a given poet's persuasive strategy should inquire what he *needed*, and what his audience as a class needed; identifying these needs provides a partial answer to the question of what motivated him to sing and the audience to listen.

Soon after the new discipline of modern philology in the nineteenth century took on the task of accounting for troubadour poetry, and once its concerted effort to publish the texts was under way, it set out to make sense of historical allusions by means of archival sources. Our understanding of elements of troubadour poetry that are bound by time and place have thus evolved along with evolutions in historical method. More recent historical approaches tend to place greater emphasis on an economic view: they look at the individual within a range of practical constraints that defined his life.

Historical inquiries into the lives of the troubadours can use the poems as historical documents, or they can use the history as a means to recapture the aesthetic monument.[38] In either case, careful application of historical or scientific method is advisable: otherwise, one can easily fabricate be-

---

34. Ibid., 135–38. Paterson finds only ten "mentions" of the *escudier* in her corpus of fifty-four lyric poets, but this figure may not include all poets' allusions to "carrying a lord's shield."

35. One detects a Marxist inspiration in this line of interpretation.

36. See the section on the *canso* as petition in R. H. Bloch 176–89, especially the discussion of *merce:* "From the Latin *mercēdem* the term came to mean 'prize' or 'gift' in Gallo-Romance and 'grace accorded by sparing' in Old French. A commonplace of feudal terminology, *merce* or *chauzimen*, the bestowal of favors, was the equivalent of salary. It was not until the fourteenth century that *merci* became a term of politeness" (184).

37. This approach is being developed with respect to the *razos* and associated texts by William Burgwinkle.

38. For an interesting way of stating the distinction between document and monument, see Zumthor 1987.

guiling "castles in the air."[39] With the help of archival studies, and by exercising great care in examining assumptions and formulating inferences, one can place one's edifice on a firmer foundation.[40] In amassing and synthesizing details toward a sort of holographic view of the poet in question—a sociological and anthropological portrait having as many dimensions as possible—very little of the amassed detail is wasted. A comprehensive theory does not supplant or render obsolete humbler studies that predate it. Rather, each fact tests the theory, eventually to support it or refute it. Theories, on the other hand, easily collapse under a light burden of counterevidence. Straightforward historical studies of all kinds, including those that simply identify proper names within a local military or political context, or those that, say, investigate the quality of the drinking water in Sistéron in 1200, remain vital to our continuing construction of a "literary anthropology" for the troubadours.

INTERPRETIVE STRATEGY AND ANACHRONISTIC EXPERIENCE

In reading a troubadour poem, one can draw on all that one brings to reading and to poetry. Yet the special properties of this lyric tradition require the modern reader to restrict some interpretive habits and to extend and enhance others. The imagination must go to work, but must constantly check itself for appropriateness. For example, suppose a troubadour complains about "the noise of a great city." The modern reader, adducing direct personal experience, might "hear" a gridlocked street churning with double-decker buses and revving motorcycles. We must of course suppress the motorcycles and visualize "great city" as it might have been in the year and locality of our poet; only then can we supply the appropriate noises. Other anachronistic evocations might color our reading more subtly. When, for instance, Peire d'Alvernhe begins "Bel m'es quan la roza floris" (I am pleased when the rose blooms; 15:1), we share his sentiment, for a rose is a rose. But what was a rose in 1150? Not a long-stemmed Baccarat; not a

---

39. Le Goff (19–45) warns that historiography can act as a mirror for the historian's own life and times, showing how Michelet's Middle Ages changed in mood in three successive editions of his *Histoire de France:* from "the beautiful Middle Ages of 1833–1844," to "the somber Middle Ages of 1855," and in 1862, to the Middle Ages as witch, spawning the natural sciences out of famine and disease.

40. Exemplary studies combining historical and literary research are Rita Lejeune's articles on Rigaut de Berbezilh (1957, 1962). More recently, a fine study in which history serves literature is Paden, Sankovitch, and Stäblein's edition of Bertran de Born: along with their rigorous and detailed historical inquiry, the authors emphatically make comprehension of Bertran's poetry the purpose, not the pretext, for investigating his biography. As they put it, one should not "denigrate the autonomy of fiction by assuming that the art of Bertran, or of any other troubadour, can be satisfactorily appreciated by tracing some subordination—real or imagined—to the circumstances of its composition" (72).

Peace rose that can flower all summer. Peire's line probably signals a very specific time of year when scrawny dog roses briefly spread their perfume; some detective work in medieval botany might yield the precise month and day to which Peire's poem refers. Other evocations of common experience can be trickier. When Guiraut de Bornelh tells his lady he could be "worse than [the] one from Béziers" (12:52), we have to find out what Guiraut finds amiss in Béziers, and whether he refers to a particular inhabitant or to the whole town.

Our very respect for poetry's perfection can overdetermine our reception of these poems. Most readers perforce begin with a detailed explication of the text that draws conclusions about its "development and organization." Subsequent interpretive efforts, no matter what critical method one follows, may rely heavily on minutiae of word choice and on broader movement observed in the sequence of words, of lines, of stanzas. Yet here one needs abundant tolerance of uncertainty. The texts themselves are in flux: most come down to us in many versions with an inordinately high proportion of variants. Hence, whether a modern edition approximates the "original" text or merely creates a new version is debatable. It is more likely that many versions circulated during the period of a given song's composition, and that the poet originating a given song contributed to its variability in performance. To some extent, this variability is part of the song, and the careful reader does well to take it into account when interpreting a poem.

Provided that we take care not to anachronize or distort, provided that we reconcile ourselves to the texts' mutability, we can bring to bear almost as many critical and theoretical approaches as exist in all our libraries, and in the minds of writers yet to come. The more one reads this poetry and the more one learns about the culture it springs from, the more easily one can remain within the range of the plausible and still enjoy its kaleidoscopic range of dimensions, its richness both in meaning and in form. As Jaufre Rudel says of his song (and many others echo the sentiment), "con plus l'auziretz, mais valra" (the more you hear it, the more it will be worth; 3:6).[41]

A number of critical methods fruitfully applied to troubadour poetry derive from comparison of one poem to another—as if to perpetuate the troubadours' own competitive, critical zest. A straightforward form of this comparative method is the study of "influence," seeking to identify the echoes and assimilations of one poet's work in another's. Another kind of comparative study, instead of seeking the "influence" of an older poet on a worshipful younger one, views poets' intertextual allusions to one an-

---

41. For a full view of the song in its manuscript transmission, see the edition of Pickens, 215–49 (song 6).

other's work (and their own) as commentary, dialogue, self-correction, elaboration of shared preoccupations.[42] Recognizing such references yields an "intertextual" network that clarifies the meaning of words, phrases, and allusions within the context of a competitive tradition. A drawback of the "influence study" is that one cannot always tell who influenced whom. Further, with medieval works, all poets tend to draw upon a common store of poetic material—topoi, motifs, conventional collocations, comparisons, and images.

Out of the realization that medieval poets influenced one another in ways particular to the period, there began in the 1950s a movement to study these commonplaces as part of the aesthetics of medieval poetry, abandoning the Romantic presupposition that whatever was original was the "good" poetry and whatever was clichéd was the "bad."[43] Acknowledging the poets' access to "networks" of linguistic "registers" and of conventional motifs recalled in endless combinations—more for purposes of aesthetic play than for catharsis of personal emotion—lets us come closer to the aesthetic motives of the troubadours and their audiences. Through comparison of these generalized and widespread recurrences, tracing the similarities among poems has led scholars to amass an extensive catalog of conventions—that is, the "expected elements" in all songs participating in lyric genres (e.g., Dragonetti 1960). When the poet says love keeps him awake at night, or when he says he will die if the lady does not help him, he elaborates on conventional symptoms of love so commonly voiced that they become almost required in a love song. In the trouvère poetry of northern France, reliance on such conventions so markedly tends to exclude the "striking and unusual" that there arose the idea of a "formal poetry" in which nothing "heartfelt," least of all love, troubles the pleasure of varying, ornamenting, and rearranging conventional motifs. For example, every lover is expected to say he will die if not satisfied soon. But if he goes further, and likens himself to a strong swimmer escaping from a sinking ship, and the lady's help to that swimming, he modifies drastically the conventional "dying for love" topos—as, for example, in this passage from Rigaut de Berbezilh (fl. 1141–60):

Aissi con de nau perida,
Don res non pot escapar
Mas per forsa de nadar,

42. See Kay 2–16 for discussion of the way models of "intertextuality" apply to troubadour song.

43. Landmark studies along this line of thought are Guiette, Dragonetti, and Zumthor 1972. These works are primarily on French poetry or on medieval literature in general, but they have modernized troubadour studies in a far-reaching way.

Atressi for'eu resors,
Dompna, ab un pauc de socors.
                    (1:23-27)

Just as if from a sinking ship from which nothing can escape except by strength
of swimming, just so I would be risen again, lady, with a little help.

If two poets use the sinking ship image, the reader might look for the rivalry
or apprenticeship of literary contact, or for a source available to both.

The bi-millennial reader, intrigued by the sinking ship image, might wish
to call on psychoanalytic theory for an interpretation. For a Freudian view,
for example, we might seek Oedipal tendencies in the image, with our
psychoanalysis running as follows: "Fear of suffocation in the drowning
image refers to the infant's experience of being born; the substitution of the
ship for the human body superposes patriarchal structure (shipbuilding,
navigation, commerce) upon the image of birth. In this context *resors* takes
on the meaning of rebirth. The swimmer escaping from the broken ship is
escaping from broken patriarchy; with rival papa submerged, he can now
return to the womb." By positioning himself as the shipwreck victim and the
lady as rescuer, does the poet ask the lady to be his mother as well as his love?
Does he attack and vanquish father figures when he sinks the ship—or, in
other passages, when he attacks the unworthy princes, jealous husbands, and
mean gossips who people the hostile society inhibiting his love? Or for a
Jungian view, we might adopt the symbolism of the sea and the swimmer,
who "saves" himself only through active (sexual) unification with this
watery feminine principle.

Perhaps more appropriate than these relatively late psychologies would
be to find the equivalent in medieval analyses of the psyche. The image of
a lady sitting by quietly while shipwreck victims are drowning can be found
in medieval bestiaries: she is the Siren, who calmly combs her hair and
ignores the swimmers' calls for help. A temptress, she is one of many
monsters who inhabit weak souls and whose living counterparts trouble
susceptible young men. One can work within medieval mythologies to
confirm—without necessarily finding a Victorian castration complex in
it—the finding that the singer does voice fear of an almost supernaturally
dangerous lady, and does try to gain pity for his own powerless position. As
reader, one can "try everything," invoking the mind's creative fancies as
well as its rational controls. If we are trying to "unlock the coffers" of
troubadour song, we can try makeshift keys, from hairpins to dynamite—
bearing in mind that the coffer's contents may melt a bit in the explosion.

Rather than speaking further in abstract terms about methodology, let
us turn to a typical troubadour poem and practice various strategies—some
optional, some not—that the reader might use to understand it. Its difficulties as well as its pleasures can serve to represent the reading of any

troubadour poem. In choosing a "typical" *canso* I am not choosing the most
conventional one or the least challenging one, but rather a song with a
typical measure of the striking, the original, the expected, and the obscure,
one that affords a sampling of the kinds of questions the reader must pose.

Guiraut de Bornelh (song 12, Sharman 1989; text from Sharman)

I. Qan lo freitz e·l glatz e la neus
    S'en fuich e torna la calors
    E reverdis lo gens pascors
    Et aug las voutas dels auzeus,
        M'es aitant beus   5
    Lo doutz temps a l'issir de martz,
    Que plus sui saillens que leupartz,
    E vils non es cabrols ni sers.
    Si la bella cui sui profers,
        Mi vol honrar   10
    De tant qe·m deigne sofertar
    Q'ieu sia sos fis entendens,
    Sobre totz sui rics e manens.

II. Tant es sos cors gais et isneus
    E complitz de bellas colors   15
    C'anc de rosier no nasquet flors
    Plus fresca, ni de nuills brondeus;
        Ni anc Bordeus
    Non ac seignor tant fos gaillartz
    Cum ieu, si ia m'acuoill ni·m partz   20
    Q'ieu sia sos dominis sers;
    E fos appellatz de Beders,
        Qan ia parlar
    M'auziri'hom de nuill celar
    Q'ella·m disses privadamens,   25
    Don s'azires lo sieus cors gens.

III. Bona dompna, lo vostr'aneus
     Qe·m detz, mi fai tant de socors
     Q'en lui refraigni mas dolors,
     Qan lo remir, e torn plus leus   30
         C'us estorneus.
     Puois sui per lui aissi ausartz
     Que no·us cuidetz lanssa ni dartz
     M'espaven ni aciers ni fers;
     E d'autra part sui plus despers   35
         Per sobramar
     Que naus, qan vai torban per mar,
     Destreicha d'ondas e de vens;
     Aissi·m destreing lo penssamens.

IV. Dompn', aissi cum us paucs aigneus   40
    Non a forssa contra un ors,
    Sui ieu, si la vostra valors
    No·m val, plus febles q'us rauseus;
       Et er plus breus
    Ma vida de las catre cartz   45
    S'uoimais mi prend neguns destartz,
    Que no·m fassatz dreich de l'envers.
    E tu, Fin'Amors, qi·m sofers,
       Qe deus gardar
    Los fins amans e chapdellar,   50
    Sias mi capteins e garens
    A ma dompna, pos aissi·m vens.

V. Dompn', aissi co·l frevols chasteus
    Q'es asetgatz per fortz seignors
    Qan la peiriera fraing las tors   55
    E·l calabres e·l manganeus,
       Et es tant greus
    La gerra davas totas partz
    Qe no lor ten pro geins ni artz,
    E·l dols e·l critz es grans e fers   60
    De cels dedinz, qe ant grans gcrs,
       Sembla·us ni·us par
    Quez aian merce a cridar,
    Aissi·us clam merce humilmens,
    Bona dompna pros e valens!   65

C, Q, Sg, and *a* also have the following:

[VI.] Messager mos moz noveus
    De chantar porteras en cors
    A la bella cui nais ricors
    E digaz li q'eu sui plus sieus
    Qe sos manteus.   70

G and *Q* also have:

[VII.] Lo segner cui es Aragon
    Sal Deu si·ll plai,
    Car ves (vos *G*) bona dompna s'atrai,
    E la mia tot eissamenz,
    Car es bella e covinenz.   75

I. When cold and ice and snow are put to flight and warmth returns with fair spring clad in green, [and I hear the trills of the birds,][44] such delight do I have in this gentle time at the end of March that I am livelier than a leopard

44. Translation of line 4 missing in Sharman.

and more fleet of foot than roe or hart. If the fair lady to whom I am devoted wishes so to honour me that she will accept me as her loyal suitor, then I am the richest and wealthiest of all people.

II. So full of joy and movement is her body, so perfect the beauty of her colouring, that no fresher bloom ever blossomed on rose or any bush; and Bordeaux never had a lord as merry as I if she ever gives me welcome and keeps me for her very own servant. And let them call me a man of Béziers if I were ever heard to speak—and so anger her gracious self—of any secret she confided to me alone.

III. Kind lady, your ring that you gave me so helps me that in gazing on it I assuage my sad longings and become more sprightly than a starling. Then it gives me such courage that, believe me, I am not afraid of any lance or dart, or weapon of steel or iron; but, on the other hand, I am in more dismay through loving too much than the ship tossed to and fro on the ocean, beset by winds and waves; for so I am beset by sad thoughts.

IV. Lady, just as a little lamb has no strength against a bear, so am I frailer than a reed without the help of your virtue. And my life will be shorter by four quarters if you delay now in any way to right the wrong you do me. And you, True Love, who are my support, and you who must guard and guide true lovers, be a defence and protection for me against my lady, since she conquers me so completely.

V. Lady, just as the weak castle is besieged by powerful lords, and perrier, catapult and mangonel shatter the towers, and the fighting is so fierce on every side that cunning and skill are of no avail to those within who are sore afraid and suffer and cry out in great anguish, and just as it seems to you quite clear that they must cry for mercy, so do I cry to you for mercy, kind, noble and virtuous lady![45]

[VI.] Messenger, my new words of a song you'll carry running to the fair one in whom wealth is born; and tell her I am more her own than her mantle.

[VII.] God save the lord to whom Aragon belongs, if it please him, for he moves toward a good lady; and God save my own lady likewise, for she is fair and proper.]

The reader may have found the poem in an anthology (it appears in Hamlin, Ricketts, and Hathaway 1967; in Hill and Bergin 1973; and in Riquer 1975) or may have singled it out in the recent critical edition by Ruth Sharman. Its form is readily apparent: *coblas unissonans* with six different rhyme-sounds, mostly in octosyllabic lines, but with two four-syllable lines per strophe—a8 b8 b8 a8 a4 c8 c8 d8 d8 e4 e8 f8 f8. Each strophe is rather long at thirteen lines.[46] Whether one finds the poem published in a sim-

---

45. Text and translation in Sharman 92–96. Since Sharman gives no notes or translation for the *tornadas*, the English for these is my own.

46. The average strophe length for Guiraut would be eleven or twelve lines; most of his contemporaries (except Arnaut Daniel, who rivals Guiraut) average seven to nine lines per strophe. Data from "Table A-I" in Van Vleck 237.

plified format or in glorious complexity makes a great difference in one's approach. Let us suppose we first read the poem in the Hill and Bergin *Anthology of the Old Provençal Troubadours*; we can then later turn to Sharman's critical edition to take advantage of the fuller apparatus of notes, variants, and indices, and of the opportunity to compare this poem with Guiraut's other works.

On reading the text in Hill and Bergin, the reader grasps an intelligible movement in five strophes. The nature introduction, a *reverdie* or "greening," specifies time of composition at the end of March. The poet likens his own energy to that of "jumping" woodland animals—leopard, hart, and stag—and asks the lady to permit his courtship. A second strophe praises her liveliness, gaiety, and rosy coloring, and imagines how happy and faithful he would be if she took him into her trust. A third (and central) strophe thanks her for the ring she gave him: looking at it gives him courage and vitality (though at times he feels like a sinking ship). Two final strophes plead the cause again with expanded similes of danger and salvation: the lady can save him as the victim of a besieged castle, or as a lamb menaced by a bear. He begs Fin'Amors to be his lord and surety, since it/she conquers him.

Based on the preliminary reading, we can discern the poem's position as a love plea. Spring inspires love and song (a standard observation), and it makes the leopards leap (a nonstandard observation). Though leopards are predatory beasts, the other leapers—stag and hart—are prey. Spring, then, provokes a chase. We can take this hunting in the context of the classical and medieval Latin literary tradition of love as a hunt, or follow a feminist, Marxist, or structuralist line of interpretation and emphasize the power struggle involved. We might even, cautiously, deconstruct the text as representative of its genre: is not this excessive humility in fact a bid for power, this self-effacement a vaunt, this harmless lamb's submission a predatory assault on (at least) the lady's purse strings? The second half of the strophe very cautiously asks *la bella* permission to offer himself, with turns of phrase rivaling the circumlocutions at the ends of formal French business letters. This exaggerated diplomacy allows us to guess what stage of the love affair is being represented here: the beginning. If we look at the poem as a movement of power, this first strophe gives most of that power to the lady. Yet in the scheme of predation and prey, the poet has already claimed the leopard's place—and then ceded it, for a safer humility.

An early stage of love, that of vision, appears to be confirmed in the second strophe.[47] Love comes in through the eye before it strikes the heart,

---

47. Love traditionally proceeds through five stages: seeing, speaking, touching, kissing, and consummating (*visum, allocutio, tactum, osculum,* and *actum* or *factum*). See Akehurst 1973 and 1989 for the troubadours' treatment of this *gradus amoris*.

and Guiraut's physical sight of the lady's body "gay, quick, and full of pretty colors," better than the flower of any rosebush, accords with the distance implied in his initial plea. But when he specifies two favors he hopes she will grant—accepting him as her servant and confiding her secrets to him—he compares his imagined, transformed self first to a "jolly lord of Bordeaux," second to someone from Béziers. The reader must gauge the affective valence of these place-names. The conditional clauses are tricky: the first expressing its result with a negative comparison ("Bordeaux never had such a merry lord as I would be if . . ."), the second wishing a puzzling doom on himself if ever he should betray her confidences ("And I would be called 'from Béziers' if ever anyone heard me speak of any secret that she might tell me privately, which might anger her gracious self"). To be "from Béziers," according to a long line of scholars' annotations, means to be a fool: the people of Béziers used to run outside the safe, fortified city walls when they were being attacked. Their town was one of the first taken in the Albigensian Crusade, apparently because they did this.[48] Guiraut's poem is probably too early to refer to Béziers as a stronghold of Cathars, but otherwise he might mean "if I betrayed her confidences, I could be called impious." The strophe begins and ends with the body; is this appropriate for a love at the vision stage? And how *galliartz*, exactly, were the lords of Bordeaux? One merry lord of Bordeaux, an on-and-off patron of Guiraut, was Richard Coeur de Lion. If the poem was composed for him, to use him as the measure of bliss is a compliment: his state is that to which the poet aspires. And since the Bordeaux lord and Béziers fool are opposed—one the speaker wishes to emulate, one he does not—the reader poses a third question: What were Richard's relations with Béziers?

Mention of the ring in the third strophe suggests a later stage in the romance. Observing the possible sexual symbolism, we can also look to medieval ceremonies involving rings. A bishop was given a ring when he passed election—and this pastoral ring, conveyed by a secular authority, represented not only the charge to take care of a "parish, diocese, or monastery," but also the right to the income from the property.[49] Among other things, rings signify agreements, and if the lady has given him one, she has already negotiated some unwritten contract with him. *Looking* at the ring (to confirm a love at the "vision" stage) renders him "light" like a starling and so "daring" that he fears neither lances nor arrows, steel nor iron. The lady's peaceable gift overcomes masculine warlike threats; possessing it, at least, the poet momentarily declares recuperation of his own power. Yet all this power is soon lost (for the conventional lover's moods fluctuate rapidly). In comparing himself to a wave-tossed ship, and then his

48. Guiraut de Bornelh ed., 75n.53, 96n.22.
49. See M. Bloch 2:349, 351, for "investiture by ring and crozier."

thoughts of excessive love to the waves and winds that will wreck that ship, Guiraut reverts to the position of helplessness.

By this time, the reader has likely sought out the critical edition with its notes on gaiety at Bordeaux and folly at Béziers. The "close reading" strategy becomes subject to compromise, to say the least, when one sees strophes four and five are printed in a different sequence in the two texts, that two *tornadas* not in Hill and Bergin are preserved, and that even the first line has changed: Hill and Bergin's "Can lo glatz e·l frechs e la neus" becomes, in Sharman's edition, "Qan lo freitz e·l glatz e la neus." Variants take up almost as much space as edited text, though printed in smaller type. To panic, on realizing the massive instability of the text, might be natural, but it is not necessary. If this were a poem coming from a poetic tradition that resolutely valued fixed and perfect texts, and no others, we might declare the "authentic poem" lost amid the rubble. But this state of affairs is the norm in troubadour poetry. True, words for textual "corruption and contamination" abound in the critical apparatus of troubadour editions, but such disparaging terms reflect an anxiety perhaps more relevant to our modern print-culture than to the troubadours themselves. "Qan lo freitz," offering only two different strophic sequences, actually reflects the norm. For the moment, all we need to understand is how the two requests for protection—one where the poet compares himself to a lamb attacked by a bear, and the other where he elaborates a comparison of his weakened state with that of a besieged castle, reasonably follow one another. We can still pursue the poet's meditation on the way love both disarms and empowers him.

The castle strophe elaborates the simile of the lover's soul as a fortress under fierce attack. In the same way that (*aissi co*, line 53) defeated inhabitants of the castle appeal for mercy, just so the poet appeals (*Aissi·us clam* 'Just so I beg you', line 64). The comparison attributes to the poet all the properties of the besieged, who undergo in ten lines a passage from valiant resistance to reluctant surrender. The strophe creates clamorous noise: we hear the machines of war battering the towers (lines 55–57), we hear cries of pain from the besieged (60–63). So the poet poses his request loudly. His greatness, making it worthwhile to conquer him, is like that of a large castle; hers, making her capable of conquering him, is like that of an army. Both lover and beloved are aggrandized. Calling her "bona domna pros e valens" (kind lady valiant and worthy), after making the reader listen to the violent siege, does not praise her gentleness: the heroic epithets understate her power to attack, to overwhelm, and to inflict damage. They call upon the warrior's ethic of forgiveness, obliging the victor to spare his fallen enemy.

The lamb hopelessly outclassed in size and strength by the bear provides another figure for the singer's position of weakness. He is the fragile lamb, and she the bear; she may either protect him—lending her *valor*—or devour him. The strophe foresees conditionally how her refusal of immediate alliance would end ("my life will be four-fourths shorter if . . ."). It proposes, as less guilt-ridden alternatives to the lady, the contrary of these conditions: her strength may be used in his favor (the contrary of *si la vostra valors no·m val* 'if your strength does not avail me'), and she may right the wrong with no further ado (the contrary of *si . . . mi prend negun destarz / Que no·m fassatz dreich* 'if I am caught by any delay in your doing me justice'). Two scenarios are available to the lady: she can behave like a nasty bear and attack an innocent lamb, trampling the weak reeds under her feet, causing instant death to her suppliant, or she can wield her strength ethically. The speaker deflects the indictment of ferocity away from the lady, urging her to cast herself instead in the role of protector. Next he does the same thing in an apostrophe to Amors, reminding the "goddess" of her obligation toward lovers and asking her to be his guarantor (*garens*)—*pos aissi·m vens* 'since I am thus conquered'. Two dangerous powers, the lady and love, have been converted to allies—but against what foe? The bear may represent more than the lady's potential cruelty. If lamb and bear stand for conflicting aspects of the singer, they show his internal struggle—a *psychomachia*. With an allegorical interpretation, the lamb stands for purity, the bear possibly for lust. At this stage in his love affair, then, Lust intimidates Purity; further, since purity is weaker, when he admits defeat he could be confessing to animal urges.

Both as victimized lamb and as besieged castle, the singer calls upon obligations that appear, looking more closely at the poem's language, to be legal ones. (See Chapter 20 in this volume.) The expression *far dreich* 'to do justice' (line 47) is the first of these terms to come to the notice of the unsuspecting reader. Once having observed that the legal register of language is present, one begins to identify a whole cluster of such terms, together creating a legal metaphor that supports the "claims" made in the love plea. After all, reasons the poet, deftly claiming his right to be loved, feudal power carries with it the obligation to protect and sustain one's vassal; not to fulfill these duties would be negligent. The fundamental metaphor of "the lady as feudal lord" appropriates the entire "feudal register" of language to the love song. Love's "duty" as lord to his vassal becomes a source of persuasive leverage for the speaker. With a hypothesis to pursue, we now reexamine the secondary meanings of any words suspected of having a legal sense. His life will be shortened by four quarters, he says, "S'uoimais mi prend neguns destartz, / Que no·m fassatz dreich de l'envers" (lines 46–47). *Destartz* 'delay' is a candidate for legal connotations,[50]

---

50. For *destart*, Raynouard quotes this very passage and no other, yet it has many synonyms meaning "delay." The verb it derives from, *destarzar*, is more than once cited as an antonym of *enansar* 'to advance' (Raynouard, *Lexique roman* 5:305). Levy, *Petit Dictionnaire*, s.v. *destart*, gives "retard, dommage."

and with it *neguns* 'any (whatsoever)' appears to be a legalistic intensifier. And one must ask what *de l'envers* means with *far dreich*: how does one "do right by the reverse"?[51] This is another probable part of the legal metaphor: according to Levy (*Petit Dictionnaire*, 156), *envers* as an adjective can mean "unjust," and as a substantive perhaps "default."[52] *Envers* may well be a synonym of *tortz* 'wrong' as used in another poem attributed to the earliest troubadour:

> Tem que la dolors me ponja,
> Si no·m faitz dreg dels tortz q'ie·us clam
> (Guillem de Peiteus 8:29–30)[53]

I am afraid grief will torment me, if you do not make right the wrongs of which I accuse you. (trans. Bond 45)

Returning to Guiraut's poem, we see that *sofers* (line 48), *gardar* (line 49), *chapdellar* (line 50), and *capteins e garens* (line 51) all suggest some contribution to the song's use of this legal register, especially with the allusion to duty (*de·us* 'you must', line 49). The pair *destreicha* and *destreign* (lines 38, 39) also shows promise as a potential addition to our list of legal terms.

Where do we look to verify these connotations? Sometimes the notes in critical editions supply the required knowledge, assuming the editor has asked the same questions we have. The critical edition's glossary, or Levy's *Petit Dictionnaire*, is usually too concise to take the reader far into semantic resonances of particular words. The multivolume dictionaries of Raynouard and Levy, however, often provide examples of usage that will confirm or reject a reading. One can also check the etymological dictionaries of Tobler-Lommatsch, von Wartburg, and Meyer-Lubke for derivation and usage. In the rare book room one can even find an early dictionary of French law.[54] For an adventure at the library, one can also check editions of nonlyric documents using the register of language one is interested in: for example, medieval how-to books on training birds of prey for falconry terms; bestiaries for lore on the behavior of lambs, leopards, stags, or bears; recipes for

---

51. Salverda de Grave (63) classifies this collocation with textile metaphors of "draperie et vêtement," referring to the right side and wrong side of cloth or garments. Guiraut's condition, then, might mean "if she does not turn (it for me) right side out."

52. The word *envers* also calls up Guiraut's rather mysterious allusions in other poems to the way his lady "turned the red side of her shield toward him"—that is, the wrong side: "Lingnaura, si·m gira·l vermeil / De l'escut cella cui reblan / Qu'euil voill dir 'a Deu mi coman,'" (Lignaura, the one whom I court turns the crimson side of the shield toward me, so that I say, "I give myself up for lost") (from Guiraut's tenso with Raimbaut d'Aurenga in Pattison ed., song 31, p. 174, lines 50–52; and Pattison's translation).

53. Of doubtful attribution.

54. Ragueau and de Laurière. Ragueau died in 1605; de Laurière edited his glossary of French law and first published it a century later.

cooking terms; theological works for religious terms. If one is lucky enough to be investigating a "register" of language in which both a Latin text and its Old Occitan translation are extant, one can compare the two versions' usage of the term in question.[55] Cartularies, or collections of charters, are records of contracts (mostly property transfers) in legal language; such documents can illustrate standard use of vernacular terminology in a non-poetic context intended to be perfectly unambiguous.[56] There are also customaries in Old Occitan:[57] at a given point, someone writes down a region's customary law. Most edited medieval texts, on any subject, have indexed glossaries. Specialized and pragmatic as they are, these resources show us the unpoetic idioms that poetic language draws upon and transforms.

When Guiraut asks love to be his *capteins* (or *capdels*) *e garans*,[58] simple dictionaries yield the synonymous pair "protector and protector." *Capdelhs*, however, turns out to have connotations of guidance for those who cannot manage by themselves.[59] The *garans* (also spelled *guirentz*) is a standard character in contracts involving property. This "guarantor" was like a co-signer, obligated to pay with his own goods if the creditor should fail to keep his side of the bargain, and at the very least obligated to put pressure on the creditor in case of default. If Love has arranged a contract between the lady and Guiraut, and if the lady fails to honor it, then Love must hold her to her word.

The very premise of the poem as a request for love now takes on the color of a legal petition. The singer's goal in lines 9–11 is stated in the form of an optimistic present conditional sentence:

> Si la bella cui sui profers
>   Mi vol honrar
> De tant qe·m deigne sofertar

---

55. One "dictionary supplement" is the *Donatz Proensals of Uc Faidit* (Marshall 1969), a bilingual grammar in Latin and Old Provençal; the last part of it is a rhyming dictionary, organized by word endings, and it includes an eclectic vocabulary from many registers. Another "dictionary supplement," primarily useful for the connotations within the register of love, is Cropp.

56. See Brunel.

57. See Carbasse.

58. Variants for *capteins* in line 51 include: *capdenz* in *D*, *captenh* in *EGT*, *capdels* in *BCMQQ2Sg* a, *capdel* in *R*.

59. In Brunel, *capdelar* shows up only twice, once for a woman whose husband is donating all his belongings to the Templars and whom they promise to *capdelar* and make her a nun, and again in a similar situation where it appears that in exchange for the donation of land, the Templars are promising to give a woman "guidance" should she travel on pilgrimage to Jerusalem: "Eil seinnor del Temple au la presa a Deu merce et a la lor que l'ajudo a capdellar aqui ond ad ella plazera en Jherusalem e per la via servidor" (Brunel 46). In poetry, however, *capdel* and its derivatives (*capdelar, capdelaire*) are quite frequent.

Q'ieu sia sos fis entendens,
Sobre totz sui rics e manens.
                    (lines 9–13)

If the fair one to whom I am a gift[60] is willing to honor me, to the extent of deigning to permit that I be her perfect understander, (then) I am rich and powerful.

Figuratively or not, he stands to gain "wealth" if his plea as *profers* is successful. Success will consist in her *honrar*, specifically by giving him that *honors* which is her consent (*sofertar*) to be her *fis entendens*. The term *honor* often referred to property rather than to the acknowledgment of personal worth. The supplicant hopes for a bargain that will transform him, through her willingness to *honrar* and *sofertar*, from *profers* to *rics e manens*. Her permission to bear the title of "true understander" would be an endowment, like a grant of property.

Another present conditional in lines 10–21 describes a contractual relationship with the lady which Guiraut wishes to establish: "Q'ieu sia sos dominis sers." This state of serfdom would paradoxically confer upon him the gaiety of a lord of Bordeaux—again he envisions wealth and power as results of his successful love plea:

Ni anc Bordeus
Non ac seignor tant fos gaillartz
Cum ieu, si ia m'acuoill ni·m partz
Q'ieu sia sos dominis sers
                    (lines 18–21)

And Bordeaux never had a lord as merry as I if she ever gives me welcome and keeps me for her very own servant. (trans. Sharman)[61]

By examining terms from the feudal and legal registers, we begin to see the persuasive aims of Erich Köhler's impoverished knight: by soliciting protection from those mightier than himself, he hopes to gain a position (that of *fis entendens*) that carries figurative wealth and power with it. Where

60. Salverda de Grave (64) classifies these lines as religious metaphor: he translates, "La belle envers qui j'ai profession," presumably using the variant *profes* instead of the *profers* in our text.

61. "Ni·m partz" is problematic to translate as "keeps me," for normally *partir* implies separation rather than greeting. At first glance, it appears to belong to an antithesis in "si ia m'acuoill ni·m partz" (if ever she welcomes me or severs/distances me; in other words, if ever she says hello or goodbye). Yet Levy gives a few definitions of *partir* that are consonant with greeting and welcoming—among transitive uses, "emmener." The usage *partir alcuns de* (*una clamor*, etc.), "accomoder un différend, en juger," would fit with the relative clause in line 21. Hence: "Nor did Bordeaux ever have a lord so gay as I would be, if ever she bid me welcome or propose that I be her servant."

does the *entendens,* 'one who understands', get so much power? One answer is to be found in lines 22–26:

E fos appellatz de Beders,
    Qan ia parlar
M'auziri'hom de nuill celar
Q'ella·m disses privadamens,
Don s'azires lo sieus cors gens.

If the speaker obtains the privileges he seeks, the lady is likely to tell him *privadamens* 'privately' some *celar* 'hidden thing', which would then be his to betray. He wavers between submitting to the lady and appropriating her value (a hesitation that we have been finding throughout the poem); the speaker first swears he will never reveal any (*nuill*) secret, then qualifies this oath in line 26: he will never reveal any secrets, at least none whose revelation "would anger her." This leaves him free to reveal secrets he judges innocuous. One glimpses the *lauzengier,* or "evil-speaking gossip" who lurks on the obverse of every praise-poet;[62] of course, no one professing love ever admits to taking part in the spread of rumors, but most claim that "everyone *else* does." To answer in advance her suspicion of potential betrayal is to admit that it could happen, and sometimes does. As *fis entendedor,* submissive and humble as ever he might be, he will have many opportunities to make her *depend* on his faith.

The *tornadas* at first glance appear to merit their exclusion. We are on our own to translate them. Recalling the original rhyme scheme a8 b8 b8 a8 a4 c8 c8 d8 d8 e4 e8 f8 f8, we see that the first *tornada* follows the scheme of the beginning of the strophe but has a hypometric line (line 66), while the second introduces new rhyme-sounds altogether. The first *tornada,* though, epitomizes what we have been noticing about the supplicant's bid for power, money, and intimate knowledge. He asks Messager to race the song to "the fair one at whom wealth originates." At the same time as he offers himself up to be possessed by her ("I am more hers than her mantle"), he proclaims a conquest: his (metaphorical) accession to a place of physical intimacy with the lady, as if he were already as close to her as her mantle:[63]

Messager mos moz noveus
De chantar porteras en cors
A la bella cui nais ricors
E digaz li q'eu sui plus sieus
Qe sos manteus.

---

62. Köhler 1970.
63. The image is parallel to, but not as extreme as, Arnaut Daniel's in his sestina where he claims to be closer to his lady than the fingernail is to the finger.

Lo segner cui es Aragon
Sal Deu si·ll plai,
Car ves bona dompna s'atrai,
E la mia tot eissamenz,
Car es bella e covinenz.

(lines 66–75)

Messenger, my new words of a song you'll carry running to the fair one in whom wealth is born; and tell her I am more her own than her mantle. God save the lord to whom Aragon belongs, if it please him, for he moves toward a good lady; and God save my own lady likewise, for she is fair and proper.

Mantel is a frequently used *senhal* of Raimon de Miraval, while *mo Messager* is a jongleur asked to carry a song for Bernart de Ventadorn.[64] Is Guiraut claiming to rival Raimon de Miraval with the same lady? Is he using the same jongleur as did Bernart de Ventadorn? When they are not cast into doubt by metrical irregularities, such *tornadas* often contribute to the web of fragile evidence used to assign a date and context to a particular poem.

Bearing in mind the importance of oral performance to this poetry and the relative instability of the written versions, we can rule out interpretations based on anagrams or visual puns,[65] though auditory puns should come into consideration: for example, when Guiraut says he is "plus vils que n'es cabrols ni cers," he could mean us to understand both *cerf* and *serf* (homophonous to the extent that the *c* and the *s* were pronounced similarly), since we have a series with woodland animals, yet the adjective *vils* usually refers to social condition.

After a detailed reading of such a poem, realizing the instability of the text and the numerous changes of metaphor, one can emerge from the text with a sense of its fragmentation. Guiraut has roved from leopards to roses, rings to shipwrecks, lambs and castles to coats—and we cannot tell whether lambs or castles come first. At such times, it would be inappropriate to superimpose the aesthetics of our own era and judge the poem as disjointed, and equally inappropriate to ignore the wild metaphorical swings and falsely assert that "it flows." Any approach that discerns structure *other* than linear or sequential can, at such times, help to restore the reader's sense of order. For example, a look at the linguistic structures might reveal a coherent pattern. Personal pronouns of the first, second, and third person mark out a distribution of influence: the lady and Love alternately are addressed in the second person and asked to help the speaker in his dealings with the third party. Verb tenses and moods superimpose a temporal and affective frame of reference, distinguishing among what is, what was, and what might

64. 25:63. References under "Messenger" and "Mantel" are in Chambers (184, 175).
65. The view that visual puns did play an important role in troubadour lyric is argued in Kendrick.

be. Figurative language can also be "sorted" in "structural" types. Guiraut appears to be using contrasts between the organic and the constructed, the weak and the strong, the broken and the whole, the passive and the aggressive, the tangible and the intangible, the natural and the social; we can find patterns of association and alternation among them without necessarily concluding that "they create an impression of unity." Each strophe, except the shipwreck strophe, uses concrete images ("the tangible") in its first half and abstract ("intangible") terms of honor, authority, fidelity, in its second half. Alternatively, we might label these as "natural" and "social" images, some attributed to the poet, some to the lady, and some to external forces of society, nature, or Love.

A popular form of criticism, one not entirely inappropriate here, is to point out how the poem is contradictory on its own terms, working against itself from within the set of values built into its very language, its very "socio-anthropological" foundation. The love plea, from this point of view, is essentially subversive: even as it praises the lady and her sovereignty, it blames her for mismanagement and seeks to reverse the order it ostensibly praises. The speaker's profound ambivalence toward the lady becomes apparent in his movement from hope (the initial petition) through memory (the ring) to visions of disaster (ship, castle). Instead of directly attributing aggression to her, he displaces the violence and blames figurative seas and winds that buffet his poor ship; or he leaves inexplicit the equation between the lady and the army assaulting the castle. In all cases, the vocabulary of governance locates all control outside the speaker, either with the lady or with Love. He says he does not resent his disempowerment, but because he presents the lyric shipwreck and castle siege as unmotivated and as causing suffering, he conceals but imperfectly his resentment of disempowerment. We have already seen evidence of a desire to reclaim dominion from the lady, if not by becoming *dominus*, then at least by claiming the lady herself.

The ring strophe, at the center of the poem when viewed as a five-stanza fixed text, is the turning point: that most simple symbol appears to unleash the speaker's fear and mistrust. He says that the ring makes him feel "light as a starling." This is odd, for although the ring signifies a social relationship, he responds to it by "becoming" a wild creature with no social ties. The delicate flower on the rosebush, once seen through the social symbol of the ring, soon transforms herself into an angry sea, a shambling bear, or a war machine. If the ring represents a pledge of fidelity, alliance, mutual trust, then nearly every one of Guiraut's metaphors belies that trust. He expects the lady to betray him by attacking the castle of his soul; and he knows she will be wary that he might tell her secrets. Within the poem, he betrays the lady before our eyes by asking Love to intervene on his behalf, to save the lamb from the bear and the castle from the battering ram. Her attacks likewise demonstrate little respect for whatever treaty the ring represents. According to this kind of interpretation, we might judge the *tornadas* to affirm the speaker's spiteful usurpation: he had called himself a gift offered to her (*profers*), but finally she is a gift to him (*la mia*); he is hers (*sui . . . sieus*), but in the same way that her coat is hers—indispensable, protective, and enveloping; he now encircles her (the coat wrapped around her body) as she had encircled him (her ring around his finger).

As for an "intertextual" reading, we might build our whole interpretation around the song's place in the literary dialogue of troubadours up to and during the period of composition, or even extend this and find allusions in later poets. The line "E fos appellatz de Beders," for one scholar, alludes to the poet's allegiances to a group of contemporary poets including Raimbaut d'Aurenga, Azalais de Porcairagues, and Guillem de St-Didier.[66] It means, in this context, that Guiraut's poet-friends from Béziers would denounce him if he betrayed a secret. If we also suspect "Manteus" of referring to Raimon de Miraval and "Messagers" to Bernart de Ventadorn, then we know where to look among Guiraut's contemporaries for shared patterns of speech, collocations, and topics that might have come under debate by this group.

The symbol of the ring, too, suggests an intertextual link between two contemporaries: Raimbaut d'Aurenga uses "Mon Anel" as a *senhal*, pretending (in a satirical "love lesson" where he explains how to woo women by "socking them on the nose" and using "ugly words") to "let slip" a secret he should not have told:

Mas mon Anel am, que·m ten clar,
Quar fon el det . . . ar son, trop sors!
Lengua, non mais! que trop parlars
Fai piegz que pechatz criminaus
                    (20:52–55)

But I do love My Ring, which keeps me radiant, for it was on the finger . . . now sound, you come forth too much! Tongue, no more! For speaking too much is worse than a mortal sin. (trans. Pattison 135)

To have said that "the ring was on the finger" is to have said too much, to have betrayed a secret that could compromise the lady. Guiraut, when he looks at his lady's ring, does not breach propriety to such an extent; he merely exhibits a violent mood swing that suggests the magnitude of the ring's meaning to him. In a nonsatirical love song, Raimbaut portrays the

66. Sharman's edition refers us to the long article by Aimo Sakari establishing, through a combination of methods (historical research and poetic interpretation), a network of literary ties among these poets. Sakari dates the poem in the spring of 1172 (p. 84).

fulfilled lover, bursting with joy but obliged to keep his happiness a secret, and he speaks in terms like Guiraut's of "kissing and looking at" his ring:

> Que ges lanza ni cairel
> Non tem, ni brans asseris,
> Can bai ni mir son anel;
> E si·n faz gran galardia
> Ben o dej faire jasse.
>   (29:57–61)

I never fear lance or bolt or steely brand when I kiss or look at her ring; and if I am vainglorious about it I ought indeed always to be so. (trans. Pattison 168)

It is as if, having passed the *factum* or "consummation" stage of love, symbolized here by the ring, the lover found himself obliged to recommence at the beginning, "looking, speaking, touching, and kissing," but displacing these stages of love contact from the lady to her token. If we are seeking intertextual ties, we can find them. Both of these "ring poems" of Raimbaut are addressed to Joglar, who is identified by Sakari as the *bederesca* 'wren' of Béziers, the trobairitz Azalaïs de Porcairagues.[67] Lexical similarities in the two poets' "Ring" songs suggest literary contact, not convention (e.g., the recurring word *gallardia/gaillarz*, the notion that the ring relieves fear of military attack, with a specific list of weapons that the speaker no longer fears: Guiraut's "lance nor arrow nor steel nor iron," Raimbaut's "lance or bolt or steely brand"). If this group of friends shares certain obscurities, composing for one another in a more private idiom than was Old Occitan itself, then they participate in a partially "closed system" of poetry that readers can unlock only by initiating themselves into the "code" of these poets.[68]

CONCLUSION

The reader of troubadour poetry today has access to a wealth of accumulated facts, methodologies, and tools—some old and some new, some anachronistic yet capable of saving us from anachronistic readings. The troubadours themselves did not have critical editions of their own works; they could not use computers to analyze the frequency of key words in their predecessors' lyrics; their own terminology did not include the adjectives *psychoanalytic, structural, intertextual,* or *deconstructive,* to name a few. Although no

---

67. Pattison dates the satire around 1168, the love poem around 1169 (Raimbaut d'Aurenga ed., 43, 44).

68. For a study of intertextuality and the question of hermeneutics in troubadour poetry, see Gruber.

one alive can ever again become a medieval *entendedor,* one can become part of the troubadours' initiated public through repeated readings of their poetry. Reading them for breadth, we bring back with us increasing familiarity with their linguistic and cultural idiom, and this understanding, this *entendenssa,* in turn enriches our in-depth readings. Acquiring the taste for it in more and more ways, one finds less and less occasion to be perplexed or bored. The reader becomes tolerant of the enigmatic, patient with the uncertain, open-minded about the difficult.

The improbability of a definitive reading, for any medieval text and specifically for a troubadour song, is becoming part of the discipline itself. In lieu of one definitive reading, multiple and varied readings must "do." This is not to say that there are no "wrong readings": to assert that Guiraut de Bornelh's pride in his "Ring" meant that he "had caught the brass ring while riding a carousel," that *anel* is a pun on French *âne* 'donkey', or that strophe three can be read backwards to yield an encoded message would in various ways cross the limits of the song's plausible meanings given its time, place, and medium of composition. It is important to reject readings that, like these, are demonstrably outside the realm of plausibility: they clutter and falsify an already-rich panoply of readings that do remain plausible.

A modern reader of troubadour poetry inevitably wavers between the sense of exclusion brought on by temporal distance from the poetry, and the sense of inclusion that increases with one's experience with the language itself and its poetic idiom. On the one hand, the printed texts we read are copies, collations, and emendations of manuscript copies (collations, emendations) that are themselves doubtful memoranda of songs made for performance: to read this poetry instead of hearing it as an entertainment is already to transpose it from one medium to another. Reading it with all the apparatus of a scholar distances us from the experience of the troubadours' contemporary public, who did not have to use dictionaries, grammars, magnifying glasses, microfilms, or ultraviolet lamps. On the other hand, the songs urgently include their audience; for want of living twelfth-century "native speakers," troubadour poetry calls upon us to complete, repeat, and understand it.

In some way these transmuted texts continue to "speak" to us, and we still "hear" over the anachronistic sounds of traffic, air conditioners, or recorded music. To "hear" more distinctly, we try to know what the medieval hearer knew: what certain words meant; what associations the place-name Béziers called forth in the spring of 1172, in certain circles; and what symbolic or historical resonances came to mind at the mention of rings and catapults. One steps momentarily out of an economic structure circumscribed by an equation of work and salary, with paper or electronic payments in standardized monetary units, and back into a system of economic exchange just beyond barter, where the relative values of service and protection, goods and land, may have had to be reasserted, claimed and re-claimed—particularly by a *servidor* who had done his service but had not yet received in payment his fur coat or his pony. In doing so, the reader becomes attuned to registers of language touching on the situation of feudal knights, whose daily idiom was transformed into the poetic idiom. The modern reader can use knowledge of that idiom to assist the imagination, to create anew the time and locality where these songs were sung, and so to rejoin the first audiences who heard troubadour poetry when it was fresh. Our re-creation of that time and space, and that music, will include some music of our own. We can learn, nonetheless, to screen out at least the airplane noise, and to replace it with a more authentic detail of the medieval audience's auditory experience. Each stage in the reader's re-creation of the *fis entendedor* leads to another. Our *contraclau* 'counterkey' at last springs the bolt; treasure sparkles from the dusty coffer—but underneath, no doubt, lies a false bottom with yet another lock.

WORKS CITED

The quotations in this chapter are from the critical editions cited in the List of Troubadour Editions in the Appendix, and in particular from the following editions: Bernart de Ventadorn (Lazar); Bertran de Born (Paden, Sankovitch, and Stäblein); Guillem de Peiteus (Bond); Guiraut de Bornelh (Sharman); Jaufre Rudel (Wolf and Rosenstein); Peire d'Alvernhe (Del Monte); Peire Vidal (Avalle); Rigaut de Berbezilh (Várvaro); and Sordello (Wilhelm). All translations are my own except as indicated.

Akehurst, F. R. P. "Les Etapes de l'amour chez Bernard de Ventadour." *Cahiers de Civilisation Médiévale* 16 (1973): 133–47.
———. "Words and Acts in the Troubadours." In *Poetics of Love in the Middle Ages: Texts and Contexts.* Fairfax, Va: George Mason University Press, 1989.
Bec, Pierre. "L'Antithèse poétique chez Bernard de Ventadour." In *Mélanges de philologie romane dédiés à la mémoire de Jean Boutière*, 107–37. Liège: Mardaga, 1971. Reprinted in Bec, Pierre. *Ecrits sur les troubadours et la lyrique médiévale.* Caen: Paradigme, 1992.
Bloch, Marc. *Feudal Society.* 2 vols. Translated by L. A. Manyon. Chicago: University of Chicago Press, 1961.
Bloch, R. Howard. *Medieval French Literature and Law.* Berkeley: University of California Press, 1977.
Boutière, Jean, and A.-H. Schutz. *Biographies des troubadours.* 2d ed. Paris: Nizet, 1964.
Brunel, Clovis. *Les Plus Anciennes Chartes en langue provençale: recueil des pièces originales antérieures au XIIIe siècle.* Paris: Picard, 1926.
Carbasse, Jean-Marie. "Bibliographie des coutumes méridionales (Catalogue des textes édités)." In *Recueil de mémoires et travaux, publié par la Société d'Histoire du Droit et des Institutions des Anciens Pays du Droit Ecrit*, 10:7–89. Montpellier: Faculté de Droit et des Sciences Economiques, 1979.

Chambers, F. M. *Proper Names in the Lyrics of the Troubadours.* University of North Carolina Studies in the Romance Languages and Literatures, 113. Chapel Hill: University of North Carolina Press, 1971.

Cropp, Glynnis. *Le Vocabulaire courtois des troubadours de l'époque classique.* Geneva: Droz, 1975.

Dragonetti, Roger. *La Technique poétique des trouvères dans la chanson courtoise.* Bruges: De Tempel, 1960.

Duby, Georges, and Robert Mandrou. *Histoire de la civilisation française,* vol. 1. Paris: Armand Colin, 1968.

Dumitrescu, Maria. "'L'escola N'Eblon' et ses représentants." In *Mélanges offerts à Rita Lejeune,* 107–18. Gembloux: Duculot, 1970.

Gruber, Jörn. *Die Dialektik des Trobar. Untersuchungen zur Struktur und Entwicklung des occitanischen und französischen Minnesangs des 12. Jahrhunderts.* Beihefte zur Zeitschrift für romanische Philologie, 194. Tübingen: Niemeyer, 1983.

Guiette, Robert. "D'une poésie formelle au moyen âge." *Revue des sciences humaines* 54 (1949): 61–68. Reprinted in *Romanica Gandensia* 8 (1960): 9–32.

Gumbrecht, Hans Ulrich. "'Un souffle d'Allemagne ayant passé': Friedrich Diez, Gaston Paris, and the Genesis of National Philologies." *Romance Philology* 40 (1986): 1–37.

Hamlin, Frank R., Peter T. Ricketts, and John Hathaway. *Introduction à l'étude de l'ancien provençal: textes d'étude.* Geneva: Droz, 1967.

Harvey, Ruth E. *The Troubadour Marcabru and Love.* Westfield Publications in Medieval Studies, 3. London: Westfield College, University of London, 1989.

Hill, R. T., and Thomas G. Bergin. *Anthology of the Old Provençal Troubadours.* 2d ed., rev. 2 vols. New Haven: Yale University Press, 1973.

Jauss, Hans Robert. "Genres and Medieval Literature." In *Toward an Aesthetic of Reception,* trans. Timothy Bahti. Minneapolis: University of Minnesota Press, 1982.

Jeanroy, Alfred. *La Poésie lyrique des troubadours.* 2 vols. Toulouse: Privat, 1934.

Kay, Sarah. *Subjectivity in Troubadour Poetry.* Cambridge: Cambridge University Press, 1990.

Kendrick, Laura. *The Game of Love: Troubadour Wordplay.* Berkeley: University of California Press, 1988.

Köhler, Erich. *Trobadorlyrik und höfischer Roman.* Berlin: Rutten & Loening, 1962.

———. "Sens et fonction du terme 'jeunesse' dans la poésie des troubadours." In *Mélanges offerts à René Crozet,* 569–83. Poitiers: Société d'Etudes Médiévales, 1966.

———. "Les Troubadours et la jalousie." In *Mélanges de langue et de littérature offerts à Jean Frappier,* 533–59. Geneva: Droz, 1970.

Le Goff, Jacques. *Pour un autre moyen âge. Temps, travail et culture en Occident.* Paris: NRF/Gallimard, 1977.

Lejeune, Rita. "Le Troubadour Rigaut de Barbezieux." In *Mélanges de linguistique et de littérature romanes à la mémoire d'István Frank,* 269–95. Annales Universitatis Saraviensis 6. Saarbrücken, 1957.

———. "Analyse textuelle et histoire littéraire: Rigaut de Barbezieux." *Moyen Age* 68 (1962): 331–77.

Marshall, John H., ed. *The "Donatz Proensals" of Uc Faidit.* London: Oxford University Press, 1969.

———. *The Razos de Trobar of Raimon Vidal and Associated Texts.* London: Oxford University Press, 1972.

Mistral, Frédéric. *Lou Tresor dou Felibrige.* 2 vols. Aix-en-Provence: Veuve Remondet-Aubin, 1879–87; repr. Geneva: Slatkine, 1979.

Mölk, Ulrich. *Trobar clus/Trobar leu: Studien zur Dichtungstheorie der Trobadors.* Munich: Fink, 1968.

Mouzat, Jean. "Quelques hypothèses sur les poèmes perdus d'Eble II." *Cultura Neolatina* 18 (1958): 11–120.

Paterson, Linda M. "The Occitan Squire in the Twelfth and Thirteenth Centuries." In *The Ideals and Practice of Medieval Knighthood,* ed. Christopher Harper-Bill and Ruth Harvey, 133–49. Suffolk: Boydell Press, 1986.

Pattison, Walter T. "The Background of Peire d'Alvernhe's 'Chantarai d'aquestz trobadors.'" *Modern Philology* 31 (1933): 19–34.

Pound, Ezra. *The Spirit of Romance.* London: Dent, 1910.

Ragueau, François, and Eusèbe de Laurière. *Glossaire du droit françois.* Paris: J. & M. Guignard, 1704; repr. Niort: Favre, 1882.

Ricketts, P. T., and E. J. Hathaway. "Le 'Vers del lavador' de Marcabrun: edition critique, traduction et commentaire." *Revue des langues romanes* 78 (1966): 1–11.

Riquer, Martín de. *Los trovadores: historia literaria y textos.* 3 vols. Barcelona: Planeta, 1975.

Sakari, Aimo. "Azalais de Porcairagues, le Joglar de Raimbaut d'Orange." *Neuphilologische Mitteilungen* 50 (1949): 23–43, 56–87, 174–98.

Salverda de Grave, J.-J. *Observations sur l'art lyrique de Giraut de Borneil.* Mededelingen der Koninklijke Nederlandsche Akademie van Wetenschappen, afd. Letterkunde, n.s., pt. 1, no. 1. Amsterdam: Noord-Hollandsche Uitgeversmaatschappij, 1938.

Topsfield, Leslie T. "The 'Natural Fool' in Peire d'Alvernhe, Marcabru, and Bernart de Ventadorn." In *Mélanges d'histoire littéraire, de linguistique et de philologie romanes offerts à Charles Rostaing,* 1149–58. Liège: Association des Romanistes à l'Université de Liège, 1974.

Van Vleck, Amelia E. *Memory and Re-Creation in Troubadour Lyric.* Berkeley: University of California Press, 1991.

Wickes, George, trans. *The Memoirs of Frédéric Mistral.* New York: New Directions, 1986.

Zumthor, Paul. *Essai de poétique médiévale.* Paris: Seuil, 1972.

———. "Un trompe-l'oeil linguistique? Le Refrain de l'aube bilingue de Fleury." *Romania* 105 (1984): 171–92.

———. "Pour une conception anthropologique du 'style' médiéval." *Medioevo Romanzo* 12 (1987): 229–40.

THREE

Fin'amor

Moshe Lazar

Contrary to the lyric love songs and romances of twelfth-century literature, the epic poetry of the preceding generations assigns scant importance to female characters and to the theme of love. Here, the masculine world of the feudal warrior is at the center of literary creativity. In examining the passage from the eleventh to the twelfth century one witnesses a major transformation of society and mentality, a rearrangement of ethical and aesthetic values, and a qualitative change in attitude toward life and its earthly pleasures. Whereas man's destiny had been exclusively oriented to serving God and the emperor, to the church and the battlefield, his calling now came from the god of love and an earthly lady, his daily battlefield being the ladies' quarters and his wounds those of wishful and unrequited love. Feudal service, warrior virtues, and harsh language were replaced by amorous service, courtly attributes, and lyric articulations of love's constant sorrows and rare blissful joys. "'We shall yet talk of this day in ladies' chambers,' said the count of Soissons, at the battle of Mansurah" (Joinville, chap. 49). The historian Marc Bloch, after quoting this statement, insightfully comments: "This remark, the equivalent of which it would be impossible to find in the chansons de geste, but which might have been heard on the lips of more than one hero of courtly romance as early as the twelfth century, is characteristic of a society in which sophistication has made its appearance and, with it, the influence of women" (Bloch 2:307). This transformation of feudal society resulted from the combined influence of various factors: economic, political, and cultural. By the end of the eleventh century, social life had begun to be organized outside church circles and sometimes in open opposition to their narrow view of human love and their focus on asceticism.

After having caught a first glimpse of the luxurious East through Spain and Sicily, which had already achieved a kind of first "Renaissance," the crusaders had discovered the marvels across the seas with their own eyes. A new world had revealed itself to them: a civilization that was not Christian, that accorded a positive attitude to life on earth, that gave free expression to love and sensual pleasures rather than dwelling on sin, contrition, and penitence. The frequent contacts with Muslim Spain and the development of commerce with the East were important factors in the transformation of thought and social demeanor, and encouraged the formation of an aristocratic society indifferent to the ascetic and reformist ideology of Cluny and other religious orders. Writers and poets, whether originating from or aspiring to be part of the new social class, soon aimed to satisfy the new needs and new tastes of those who started crowding the developing courts of various lords. The aristocratic courts, organized outside the church, needed a social and ethical code that would correspond to their new "art of living" and replace the "art of dying" (*ars moriendi*). Major aspects of this courtly code were to be first provided by a close collaboration between the ladies and the troubadours in the territories of langue d'oc.

The south of France, indeed, acted as a catalyst and disseminator of the new code of sentimental and social behavior among the courtly circles. The church there had always been more lax and less repressive than in the north. The clergy's grip on the landowning classes was almost nonexistent, leaving the latter quite free to develop an ideology of love, a code of secular ethics, a sinless joy of living, that first find their expression in the lyric songs of the troubadours and are later modulated in the lais, romances, and songs of the trouvères in northern France. The moralists of the time decried the changes happening under their eyes. Geoffroy of Vigeois fulminates:

> Now they have clothes fashioned of rich and precious stuffs, in colors to suit their humor. They snip out the cloth in rings and longish slashes to show the lining through, so they look like the devils that we see in paintings. . . . Youth affect long hair and shoes with pointed toes. . . . As for women, you might think them adders, if you judged by the tails they drag after them. (quoted by Kelly 165)

And Ordericus Vitalis lashes out:

> These effeminate men, these dirty libertines who deserve to burn in hell-fire, rejected their warrior customs and laugh at the exhortations of the priests. They spend their nights at banquets of debauchery and drunkenness, in futile talk, playing dice and other games of chance. . . . They take pains to please the women with all kinds of lasciviousness. . . . Instead of covering their heads with caps they wear ribbons, and their external appearance is the sad reflection of their souls. (quoted by Jeanroy 2:84)

These sermons, leaving aside their conventional hell rhetoric, present the clear image of a changed society, diametrically opposed to the Cluniac ideals that had dominated thought and behavior for over a century, articulated in the context of epic poetry. Man was regaining a certain autonomy and, above all, the possession of his body. "Towards the pleasures of the flesh," writes M. Bloch,

> the attitude of the knightly class appears to have to have been frankly realistic. It was the attitude of the age as a whole. The Church imposed ascetic standards on its members and required laymen to restrict sexual intercourse to marriage and the purpose of procreation. But it did not practise its own precepts very effectively, and this was especially true of the secular clergy, among whom even the Gregorian reform purified the lives of few but the episcopate. (2:308)

While preaching the sacred and indissoluble bond of marriage, the Church was unable to impose its authority on the aristocracy. Lords and nobles sought sexual gratification outside conjugal life, with their concubines. On the whole, marriage for them was merely an economic and political venture: its goals were the expansion of the fief, consolidation of power, and continuation of their lineage. The women, often wealthy heiresses of large fortunes, lived in idleness, unable to find consolation in their beauty or intelligence. Marriage, which had alienated them from their frequently absent husbands—away at their crusades, battles, tournaments, or less noble adventures—had not brought them love or happiness. It is not without reason, perhaps, that the "mal-mariées" (unhappily married women) came to play such an important role in the love literature of that time and that the *chanson de mal-mariée* even became a poetical genre. "We should not assume," writes J. F. Benton, "that a literature of loose morals was something which medieval women imposed on their men" (Benton 28). Nevertheless, there is reason to believe that the "mal-mariée" sought and found in the new modes of love songs a compensation for her disappointments, a landscape for repressed desires, and a kind of literary revenge.

We should always distinguish between, on the one hand, extraconjugal love documented by real facts and, on the other, adulterous love as a fashionable mode within the genre of love songs, encouraged and inspired by the twelfth-century ladies in southern France. "Any idealization of sexual love, in a society where marriage is purely utilitarian, must begin by being an idealization of adultery," writes C. S. Lewis, observing that "marriages had nothing to do with love, and no 'non-sense' about marriage was tolerated. All matches were matches of interest, and worse still, of an interest that was continually changing" (13). This idealization certainly inspired some of the constitutive elements of the "love service" of the Occitan troubadours. Many of the social and terminological aspects of this "love service" were in fact modeled on "feudal service"; and by calling his lady *midons* (my lord), the troubadour acknowledged her authority just as a vassal acknowledged that of his feudal lord. The troubadour thus became, in the realm of poetry and fiction at least, his lady's servant and lover.

COURTLINESS, COURTLY LOVE, AND *FIN'AMOR*

The various modes of love illustrated in medieval literature, from the twelfth to the fourteenth century, have often been designated by a single term: *amour courtois* 'courtly love'. The term *cortez'amor*, used only once in Occitan love songs (by Peire d'Alvernhe) and disseminated by Gaston Paris (see below), has since served most medievalists to characterize a variety of contradictory concepts and modes of love. When one scans through the impressive amount of studies and essays dedicated to the love literature of the Middle Ages, one is struck by the great confusion that reigns in the use of such ill-defined terms as *courtoisie* 'courtliness', *amour courtois* 'courtly love', and *fin'amor* 'perfect love'. They are used as though it were possible to lump together all the periods of the Middle Ages and to interchange the order of authors and works. This confusion has also led to a monolithic evaluation of the nature and meaning of love in medieval poetry and romance, as though the troubadours' ideology of love were identical, for example, to that of the trouvères or the Italian poets of the *dolce stil nuovo*. The confusion becomes even greater when one finds medievalists, and in their path other scholars, interchanging the concepts of courtliness and courtly love (courtliness is "the organized and codified form of courtly love" [Belperron 186]; "as is customary, we use interchangeably courtliness and courtly love" [Wettstein 10]; "Christian courtly love [and] courtliness [owe] their charm and their depth to the presence of the religious element" [ibid. 19]). While many phenomena are presented as courtly in the troubadours' songs (courtly season, courtly song, courtly speech, courtly land, courtly weather, etc.), love is generally qualified as *verai'amor, bon'amor,* or most frequently, *fin'amor.* None of these is interchangeable with *courtoisie* or its Occitan equivalent *cortezia.*

Some medievalists, although aware of the confusion between courtliness and courtly love, seem not to have seen a similar confusion existing between courtly love and *fin'amor,* as though the concept of courtly love could encompass the various modes of love articulated in the songs of the troubadours, in the romances of Béroul, Thomas, and Chrétien de Troyes, in the chansons of the trouvères, and other works. Frappier states:

> The meaning of the word *courtois* is complex: it is, in fact, sometimes used in
> a wide sense, for example when it concerns chivalrous morality and the finer

points of worldly etiquette, and, other times, with a more specific meaning, more refined, more *pure*, as when it designates an art of love not accessible to most mortals, that embellishment of erotic desire and that discipline of passion which together properly constitute courtly love. (1951, 88; my translation)

Denomy remarks: "The qualifier *courtois* essentially means: belonging to, emanating from, for and in a Court. This is a literature of the Court about courtliness and an incorporation of its ethical and social ideals"; but when speaking of the troubadours' love he states: "*courtois* bears a completely different meaning. It is the term used to designate the troubadours' kind of love" (1953, 46–47). Without going into a detailed discussion, and before attempting to analyze the various modes of love that are lumped together within the concept of "courtly love," we have to eliminate the confusion between courtliness and courtly love, and even to point to some differences between the *cortezia* of the troubadours and the *corteisie* of the writers in langue d'oïl.

Courtliness

One can be courtly, according to twelfth-century texts, without loving; but one cannot love without being courtly. Courtliness is the ethical and social ideal of chivalry, a code of good manners and a guide for a "gentleman," but it is in no way an *ars amandi*, that is, an art or a mode of love. The word *courtly* may be understood in a moral or social sense. Its opposite is *villainy*. One consists of a set of qualities and virtues, the other of a series of faults and vices. In the social sense, the same terms describe two opposite social classes. When the troubadours affirm that a villain may become courtly and that, inversely, a courtly man is liable to be or act as a villain, it is obviously the moral sense of these terms that is being used. They surely do not mean that a peasant has a chance of becoming a knight or that a noble may fall to the rank of peasant. In one of his *pastorelas*, Marcabru has a knight, impressed by the beauty, noble speech, and demeanor of a shepherd girl, making the following remark:

> Toza de gentil afaire,
> Cavaliers fon vostre paire
> Que·us engenret en la maire,
> Car fon corteza vilana.
>   (30:29–32)

Maiden of noble comportment, your father was a knight who engendered you in your mother, who was thus a courtly commoner [*corteza vilana*].

The girl's mother is courtly by her virtues and common by her social status. The girl herself delineates sharply their different worlds:

> Cerca fols sa follatura,
> Cortes cortez' aventura,
> E·il vilans ab la vilana;
>> (30:79–81)

Let the fool seek out his folly, the courtly, his courtly adventure, and leave the common girl to the commoner.

The social sense of the term is thus clearly defined. Similarly, in the *Tristan* of Thomas, the knight Cariado is depicted as "handsome, courtly," but also as "haughty and proud" (Wind, lines 811–12); the latter are not attributes of courtliness, and Iseut considers him a villain. Socially, he belongs to the nobility; morally, he lacks the necessary virtues of courtliness. When the troubadours speak of *cortezia* it is almost always in the light of a *moral preoccupation* or an *aesthetic emotion*. It is directly related to their conception of love. It does not originate in a class ideology, nor is it the exclusive lot of knighthood and aristocracy. Since loving, for them, is an *art of loving*, one who observes the essential principles and precepts of its code is necessarily courtly. It thus ensues, contrary to what has been generally stated, that "courtly love" is neither a central category of courtliness nor one of its fundamental components. The troubadours' *cortezia* is, on the contrary, essentially a product of *fin'amor*. In truth, one cannot be courtly if one does not love according to the code of *fin'amor*, for this love, "per cui a om pretz e valor" (by which man has worth and value; Bernart de Ventadorn 28:45), is the source of all courtly virtues:

> Greu er pros ni cortes
> Que ab amor no·s sap tener
>> (Bernart de Ventadorn 28:15–16)

Hardly gallant and courtly is he who cannot act in accordance with love.

It is also this love that holds power over man's inclinations:

> Per lei serai o fals o fis,
> O dreichurers o ples d'enjan,
> O totz villa o totz cortes,
>> (Cercamon 3:51–53)

Through her I shall be false or faithful, loyal or full of deceit, totally villain or totally courtly.

Whoever loves according to the principles of *fin'amor* lives "letz, cortes e sapiens" (happy, courtly, and wise; Marcabru 40:9). This love, as the source of all virtues (honesty, generosity, humility, honor, courage, wisdom, and also *cortezia*), is a poetic theme examples of which abound in the troubadours' songs.

It is not easy to determine with precision the exact value of the word *cortezia*. It sometimes presents itself as a notion encompassing all of the qualities and virtues of a perfect knight and, other times, as one component in a set of other principles that characterize the perfect lover. The troubadours were not theoreticians seeking to sharply distinguish between certain terms that they frequently used and that, very often, were synonyms complementing each other. The presence of the word *cortezia*, as well as that of other key terms, often depends upon the preceding rhyme and completes a string of attributes that, taken together, represent courtliness: *onor, donar, pretz, valor, joven, joy, mezura*, etc. In many other instances it appears in petrified expressions such as *solatz e cortezia, pretz e cortezia, cortezia e joven*, etc. Finally, we also find it invariably opposed to *vilania*, that set of uncourtly or anticourtly characteristics (greed, cowardice, avarice, disloyalty, violence, vulgarity): *cortes/vilas, encortizer/vilanejar, cortezia/vilanatge*, etc.

We may, more or less, definitely establish that *cortezia*, if it is to be fully realized, demands a certain attitude and mentality whose three fundamental requirements seem to be: to love in a courtly manner, to maintain *mezura* or moderation, and to be loyal to the guidelines of *joven* 'youth, generosity'. In the troubadours' songs, the order in which the virtues derived from *fin'amor* are presented may be considered as inconsequential. In the final analysis, however, the cardinal components of *cortezia* appear to be *pretz/valor, mezura*, and *joven*. Folquet de Marseilla writes: "Cortesia non es als mas mezura" (Courtliness is nothing else but measure; 12:41). For Marcabru, "Mesura es de gen parlar / E cortesia es d'amar" (Measure is to speak honorably, and courtliness is to love; 15:19–20).

As one can see, the term *mezura* is open to various meanings, and can be identified with both *cortezia* and *amor*. But the underlying common meaning for all troubadours seems to be the notion of moderation, a sense of balance between emotion and reason, between social and individual considerations, and whose opposite is *desmezura*, which is almost the equivalent of *folia* 'folly'. The shepherd girl, in Marcabru's *pastorela* mentioned above, declares:

En tal loc fai sens fraitura
On hom non garda mezura
　　　(30:82–83)

Reason fails there where one lacks measure.

And measure in the lady is almost always related to her way of responding to the lover's request:

> Ric' es de mezura
> E d'onor mondana
> Ab sol una vetz que·m bais.
> > (Bernart Marti 1:58–60)

She would be rich in measure and in worldly honor if only she kissed me once.

Any absence in moderation entails some punishment, as can be seen not only in the songs of the troubadours but also in some *lais* of Marie de France: *Yonec, Les Douz Amanz*, and *Guigemar*. Reason, patience, humility, poise, moderation in the request of sexual enjoyment are all part and parcel of the concept of *mezura*. True love, writes Marcabru, is essentially composed of "Jois, Sofrirs e Mesura" (Joy, Patience, and Moderation; 37:24). The latter creates the harmony between the first two: the lover's request and love requited. To act outside the prescribed guidelines of courtliness is considered foolish behavior, or *desmezura*.

Amor and *Joven*

Guillem de Peiteus writes:

> Companho, farai un vers tot covinen
> Ez aura·i mais de foudatz no·i a de sen
> Ez er totz mesclatz d'amor e de joi e de joven.
> > (1:1–3)

Companion, I shall compose a nice song, and it will have more nonsense than sense, and contain a blend of love, joy, and "youth."

And in another song:

> Farai un vers de dreyt nïen;
> Non er de mi ni d'autra gen,
> Non er d'amor ni de joven.
> > (4:1–3)

I shall compose a song about absolute nothing: about neither myself nor anyone else, neither about love nor about "youth."

With the exception of some rare occurrences, the term *joven* does not really mean young age, young person, or youth (see Köhler 1964). Rather, it appears to represent a set of duties and virtues. In spite of the technical aspect of the term, only scant attention was given to it by most of those who dealt with *cortezia*, or by the authors of entries in dictionaries and glossaries. A similar technical concept, with identical levels of meaning, exists in the hispano-arabic literature preceding the troubadours and has been investigated by several Arabists (Fackenheim; Hammer-Purgstall 1849, 1855; Taeschner; Denomy 1949). It should be noted here, incidentally, that the rejection by many scholars of a relationship between hispano-arabic poetry and troubadour songs (as proposed by Nykl) is no longer acceptable (see Pérès, Pollmann, Giffen, Menocal). Denomy was the first to draw attention to the parallel concepts in both literatures. He has noted the recurrence of *joven* thirty-nine times (though this writer counts forty-five times) in the songs of the early troubadours Guillem de Peiteus, Marcabru, Cercamon, Alegret, Bernart Marti, and Peire d'Alvernhe. It should be added also that the term appears twice in the opening lines of a song by the Comtessa de Dia:

Ab ioi et ab ioven m'apais
E iois e iovens m'apaia
(1:1-2)

with joy and youth I am filled and joy and youth fulfill me.

In the songs of Marcabru alone, the term appears thirty-one times, whereas in the songs of Jaufre Rudel and Bernart de Ventadorn, for example, the concept of *joven* is nonexistent. With the exception of its use by the Comtessa de Dia, it appears mainly in the context of social and moral criticism, or in laudatory references to some noble patron or a lady from whom the poets received or hoped to get some material reward. According to Marcabru,

Tant cant bos Jovens fon paire
Del segle e fin' Amors maire,
Fon Proeza mantenguda.
(5:37-39)

As long as noble *joven* was the father of the world, and *fin'amor* its mother, prowess was upheld.

Besides the meaning of "young in spirit," the term *joven* has the connotation of generosity, liberality, member of a group praising *joven* and *fin'amor*. Not noted by Denomy is a song by Bertran de Born that is entirely structured around the opposition between "young" and "old," which helps to interpret some of the aspects of *joven*. A lady, for example, is old when she has no knight at her service:

Vielha la tenc si de dos drutz s'apaya,
Et es vielha si avols hom lo·il fa.
Vielha la tenc s'ama dins son castelh,
Ez es vieilha qan lh'a ops de fachell.
Vieilha la tenc pos l'enueion juglar . . .
(24:11-15)

I consider her old if she takes two lovers, and she is old if a commoner does it to her; I consider her old if she loves within her castle, and she is old if she needs magic spells; I consider her old if minstrels bore her.

And as for the perfect lover:

Joves se te quan pro·l costa ostatge,
Et es joves quan fa estraguatz dos.
. . . .
Jove se te quan li plai domneyar
(24:27–28, 31)

I consider him young, if his hospitality is costly, and he is young when giving priceless gifts, . . . and he is young when he knows well the art of courting a lady.

In dedicating his song to Richard Lion-Heart, the poet advises him not to collect "old treasures," for only "young treasure" (i.e., *Joven*) can increase his merit and his fame.

The concept of *joven* is an important element in the string of virtues constituting *cortezia*; but it is not essential to the nature and quality of *fin'amor*. Most, if not all, of the troubadours who use the term *joven* (except for the Comtessa de Dia), and in particular Marcabru, seem to have traveled across the Pyrenees more than once and visited some wealthy Spanish courts. Marcabru and Cercamon admired Alphonso VII of Castile. Cercamon, in the same *planh* 'dirge' where he laments the death of Guillem VIII de Peiteus and the subsequent decline of *joy* and *joven* (1:3–6), extols Alphonso's court as the only remaining refuge where *youth* still finds *joy* (1:6, 34–36). It seems plausible, therefore, that the notion of *futuwwa* (an Arabic word meaning "youth," but including the various meanings of Occitan *joven*) was borrowed from hispano-arabic literature and added to the regular meaning of *juventus*. Marcabru, in whose songs the term *joven* is overwhelmingly present, appears to have been its catalyst and disseminator.

In the final analysis, *cortezia, mezura,* and *joven* are the three fundamental virtues of the courtly lover. They are representative of the social, psychological, and moral dimensions of courtly love. *Cortezia* of the troubadours is not completely identical with *corteisie* of chivalry. "*Cortezia* is an ideal and a virtue of the courtly lover; *courtliness* is the virtue and ideal of the knights," writes Denomy (1953, 63). And, finally, neither *cortezia* nor courtliness should be confused with either *fin'amor* or courtly love.

FIN'AMOR AND COURTLY LOVE

The three major secular modes of love represented in medieval literature, from the twelfth to the fourteenth century, have been for the past hundred years described by the single term *courtly love* ("amour courtois," coined by

Gaston Paris in his essay on Chrétien's *Lancelot*). It has served to characterize the love songs of the troubadours and the trouvères, as well as the art of love in *Lancelot* and Chrétien's other romances, in the versions of *Tristan et Iseult* by Béroul and by Thomas, and in a variety of later literary works in Germany, England, Spain, and Italy. In my doctoral dissertation (Sorbonne, 1957), later revised and published (1964), I studied in great detail the misuse of the term *amour courtois* in a restrictive and shallow definition that fails to encompass a variety of modes of love that, in spite of having in common the basic elements of courtliness and a set of canonized poetic formulas, cannot be reduced to a single common denominator. Since then, several scholars have expressed their uneasiness with the term. Jean Frappier has summarized my own findings and expanded on that analysis (1959). See also W. T. H. Jackson's statement: "One of the great disadvantages of a term like *courtly love* is the ease with which it can be stretched to cover many different types and genres" (Jackson 74). The term has been qualified as "an impediment to our understanding of medieval texts" (Robertson 17), as having "no useful meaning" and not being worth "saving by redefinition" (Benton 37; see also Frappier 1972). Finally, Gilson has pointedly remarked: "The discussions related to courtly love are sometimes conducted by the most objectionable methods. One would think that, from the first troubadours all the way to Dante, the authors and texts were interchangeable. They are not" (193).

MODES OF LOVE IN A SECULAR CONTEXT

Leaving aside late-twelfth-century and thirteenth-century "spiritualized" and "mystical" variations on the three secular modes of love, and considering only the love songs and romances of the twelfth century, one should draw a clear distinction between the following categories and groups of works:

1. The *adulterous fin'amor*, or the *aristocratic* mode: a secular unchristian ideal of love newly articulated by the Occitan troubadours, exclusively centered on a married lady, conceived as the only mode of *verai'amor* 'true love', a love dominated by a strong expression of sensuality and eroticism, free from any principle of sin and guilt, achristian and amoral in the context of prevalent Church standards, presented in a variety of stylized poetic and melodic songs. The aristocratic mode of *fin'amor* is also extolled in Chrétien's romance *Lancelot*.

2. The *passionate love*, or the *tragic-mythical* mode: adopts in the context of Celtic mythical tales all the characteristic elements of *fin'amor*, casting the lovers in an extramarital relationship; their tragic end is the result not of sin and divine punishment but of a consuming passion and the lack of a psychological-social balance (*desmezura*), which violate the principle of *me-*

zura so central to the troubadours' code of courtliness. The most representative works in this category are Thomas's *Tristan* and certain *lais* of Marie de France.

3. The *courtly conjugal love,* or the *"bourgeois" anti-fin'amor* mode: elaborated essentially in an anti-Tristan context, opposed to the adulterous relationship of the lovers as illustrated in the two previous groups of texts and critical of the idolatrous passion that leads them to their tragic end; all of Chrétien's romances except *Lancelot* promote a love relationship, based on the code of courtliness and the rules of reason, leading to and existing only in marriage. Béroul's *Tristan*, although different from both Thomas's version and the romances of Chrétien de Troyes, undermines the mode of *fin'amor* by the author's use of sin and guilt in characterizing the lovers' passionate bond.

TROUBADOURS AND *FIN'AMOR*

The love songs of the troubadours are certainly not to be considered as actual testimonies of real love affairs or frustrated amorous adventures, although some underlying ties with a historical reality might have existed, known only to the songwriters and hidden from our inquiry behind many layers of disguising devices and verbal games: euphemisms, puns, conventional signs, ambiguous expressions, mannerisms, etc. It is therefore within the fictional framework of the poetic texts that we have to define and understand the erotic-sexual language and imagery. Whether the married lady of the songs is historical or fictional does not alter the fact that the nature of *fin'amor*, as poetically articulated in these *cansos*, remains adulterous beyond any doubt. A good number of scholars have attempted to allegorize it and represent it as essentially religious and mystical in nature—for example, Appel: "There is no doubt what the meaning of fin'amor is here. . . . No more is it a worldly love. Fin'amor has ascended to heaven. It is a love that addresses itself to God and becomes one with him" (1923, 454); Wechssler: "courtly love of the troubadours took its crown from *Caritas*, the cardinal Christian virtue" (216); and Scheludko: "Marcabru has directly identified *fin'amor* with divine love" (234). Errante follows closely Wechssler's ideas (1948, 377); see also the theological and mystical interpretations by Casella (1938) and Zorzi (124–44), and a mariological connection posited by Wilcox: "the worship of women may have been suggested by the worship of Mary" (313). On the other hand, Hatzfeld has qualified *fin'amor* as a blasphemous parody "of rich passages of profound mystical meaning" (287), whereas more recently an attempt has been made to "unmarry" the married lady (Paden 1979). All these attempts constitute essentially a wishful denial of the adulterous tenor of *fin'amor* and an exercise in literary exorcism. These casuistic interpretations of the love songs have been strongly rejected by other scholars (see Briffault; Denomy 1945, 1953; Lazar; and Gilson). Considering *caritas* and *fin'amor*, Gilson writes:

> There will always be as many sophisms available as one wishes to justify such a thesis, but it will remain a sophism and for a very good reason: mystical love being the negation of carnal love, one cannot borrow the description of the former to describe the latter; it is not enough to say that their object is not the same, one must add that they cannot be of the same nature precisely because they do not have the same object. (201)

Allegorical and esoteric interpretations of *fin'amor* have been particularly applied to its elaboration in the *cansos* of Jaufre Rudel and his theme of *amor de lonh* 'love from afar', i.e., love for an unseen or dreamed lady. A detailed analysis of his love songs (Lazar 1964, 86–102) reveals that the "distant lady" is more a metaphoric embodiment of "unfulfilled love" than the incarnation of a "heavenly Mary." Jaufre Rudel's words on this point are far from ambiguous:

> Q'en breu veia l'amor de loing,
> Veraiamen en locs aizis,
> Si que la cambra e·l jardis
> Mi resembles totz temps palatz.
> (6:39–42)

May I see this far away love in reality, in an appropriate place, such as the bedroom or the garden which always seem a palace to me.

Or let us consider these lines:

> Luenh es lo castelhs e la tors
> Ont elha jay e sos maritz,
>
> . . . .
>
> Et en dormen sotz cobertors
> Es lai ab lieis mos esperitz;
> (1:17–18, 35–36)

Distant are the castle and tower where she lies with her husband. . . . And while I sleep under the sheets, my mind is over there near her.

Another example:

> Et es ben paisutz de manna
> Qui ren de s'amor gazaigna.
> (4:20–21)

Well rewarded with manna is whoever obtains something from her love.

Compare this to Marcabru's unequivocal statement:

> Que tals bad' en la peintura
> Qu'autre n'espera la mana.
> (30:89–90)

While one marvels open-mouthed at a picture, another expects from it manna.

See also Riquer's note on *manna*: "Among the troubadours, *manna*, considered a delicious food, qualifies the joy of a satisfied love" (1:14, lines 89–90).

The mode of *fin'amor* extolled by the troubadours is conceived in a purely secular framework. When they invoke God and the saints it is never to confess sin or remorse; instead it is generally to ask for assistance in obtaining the ladies' favors. In the *fin'amor* tradition of the twelfth century, one might say that God is always on the side of the adulterous lovers and never on that of the deceived husband. The Christian doctrine of love and marriage, chastity and abstinence, does not even cast a shadow on the celebration of love outside marriage—the only love to be called *bona* 'noble', *veraia* 'true', and *fina* 'perfect'. Bernart de Ventadorn clearly distinguishes between "noble love" and "common love" when he writes:

> C'amors no·n pot ges dechazer,
> Si non es amors comunaus.
> (2:17–18)

For love cannot decay unless it is a common love.

Bernart also says:

> Aisso non es amors; aitaus
> No·n a mas lo nom e·l parven.
> (2:19–20)

That is not love; of love it has only the name and appearance.

The husband of the married lady, an obstacle to the satisfaction of desire and anticipated "joy of love," merely earns epithets like "ugly," "jealous," "old," "dull," etc. In the view of the troubadours, true love simply cannot exist between husband and wife, conjugal relations being contractual rather than love relations. At best the pair can be considered as *amic* 'friends', not *amanz* 'lovers'. Whereas married women are acquired political and economical assets and the husbands their masters, *fin'amor* exists in a context of sensual longing, verbal love games, separations, frustrated sexual expectations, postponed physical union, temporary satisfactions and stolen looks or kisses, fear of competing lovers, etc. Cercamon expresses a common view of *fin'amor*:

> Ni res tan grieu no·s covertis
> Com fai cho q'ieu vauc desziran;

Ni tal enveia no·m fai res
Con fai cho q'ieu non puosc haver.

(1:9–12)

Nothing is so difficult to obtain as that which I now desire, and there is nothing that I desire more than that which I cannot obtain.

Constantly put to a test of patience and endurance, the lover's heart oscillates between sorrow and anger, and the rare *joy* granted the lucky lover is always temporary and threatened:

Ai Deus! car se fosson trian
D'entrels faus li fin amador,
E·lh lauzenger e·lh trichador
Portesson corns el fron denan!
   (Bernart de Ventadorn 1:33–36)

Oh God, that we might distinguish between faithful and false lovers; if only the adulators and deceitful wore horns on their foreheads!

In the particular type of relationship between the married lady and the noble lover, the former is the master and lord (*midons:* masculine title, "my lord") and the latter her subject and servant. Guillem de Peiteus, for example, puts it thus:

Qu'ans mi rent a lieys e·m liure,
Qu'en sa carta·m pot escriure
            (8:7–8)

I surrender and give myself up to her and she can inscribe me in her charter.

Or Bernart de Ventadorn:

E·lh serai om et amics e servire
            (9:23)

I will be her vassal, friend, and serf

Domna, vostre sui e serai,
Del vostre servizi garnitz.
Vostr' om sui juratz e plevitz.
            (10:29–31)

Lady, yours I am and will be, dedicated to serving you; I have pledged to be your sworn vassal.

Or Peire Vidal:

Per qu'ieu ai mes en vos ferma fiansa
E tot mon cor e tota m'esperansa,
E fatz de vos ma domn'e mo senhor
            (8:87–89)

For I have put in you my firm hope, all my heart and all my trust, and made you my lady and my lord.

In general, while expressing humble submission and praising the courtliness and divine beauty of the lady, almost all the troubadours poetically "undress" their desirable companion and sensually describe her fascinating body, longing to be physically united with her. Consider, for example, Bernart Marti:

> Tant m'es grail' e grass' e plana
> Sotz la camiza ransana,
> Quan la vei,
> Fe que·us dei,
> Ges no tenc envei' al rei
> Ni a comte tan ni quant,
> C'asatz fauc meils mon talant,
> Quan l'ai despoillada
> Sotz cortin' obrada.
>
> (3:37-45)

She seems to me so delicate, fleshy and plump, beneath her gown of fine cloth, that, by my faith, when I see her, I envy neither king nor count, nor anyone else, for I satisfy better my desire when I hold her undressed beneath the embroidered bedcover.

Or Peire de Valeira:

> E qar mei oill l'an chausida,
> A Deu prec que mi don vida
> Per servir son bel cors gen.
>
> (2:20-22)

Ever since my eyes gazed upon her, I pray God to grant me long life, to serve her noble and beautiful body.

Or Bernart de Ventadorn:

> Mas mas jonchas li venh a so plazer,
> E ja no·m volh mais d'a sos pes mover,
> Tro per merce·m meta lai o·s despolha.
>
> (7:40-42)

Hands clasped, I surrender to her will, and I will not move away from her feet until, by her grace, she takes me to where she undresses.

FIN'AMOR AND JOY

The word *joy* is a key term in the troubadours' love songs from Guillem de Peiteus to Guiraut Riquier, and is frequently found several times within the same song or a stanza. The poet who, more than any other, seems to have incorporated it into his refined erotic compositions is Bernart de Ventadorn: *joy* is the center of gravity of his amorous experience and dreams. The term assumes a variety of connotations. It is sometimes the vibrant expression of great happiness and illumination, sometimes a glorified personification of the lady, and sometimes a technical word in a set of courtly notions; more generally, however, it represents the erotic pleasure derived from the verbally imagined physical union and the expected sexual gratification from the game of love (see the articles of Akehurst, Smith, and Lazar in Lazar and Lacy 1989).

The origin of the word *joy* and its possible meanings have given rise to much discussion (see Casella, Settegast, Briffault, Denomy 1951, and especially Belperron and Camproux). Morphologically the term is variously represented: *joi, joy, jai, gaug*; the latter, somewhat rarer than the others, is frequently attested in Peire Vidal's songs. In my opinion, Camproux provides a most insightful and plausible explanation: the word is derived not from the Old French *joie*, but from the Latin *joculum* (< *jocum*, "play," "jest," "frolicking"); however, *joya* (resulting in Old French *joye, joie*) derives from the neuter plural *jocula*, which bore the meaning of *gifts, reward, prize* bestowed upon him who had played the game well and won it (Camproux 1956, 65). Thus, Occitan *joy* would be the result of the telescoping of two concepts, *jocus* 'play' and *gaudium* 'joy'.

As for what *joy* signifies, there is a wide spectrum of opinions, including: "spiritual and mystical exaltation of love" (Jeanroy 1927, xvi; Appel 1901); "identical to the *delectatio* of the Augustinian tradition" (Casella 160); "a combination of courtly service and love" (Settegast 125); "a purely sensual joy whose origin stems from Greek paganism" (Wechssler 35); "the moral climate in which the courtly lover becomes conscious of *mezura*" or "*Amor, joy*, and *joven*, which sum up the essence of courtliness [and] parallel the notions of love, joy, and perfection that, as symbols of the Trinity, express the existential fullness of the angel's life" (Wettstein 98, 99); "a new sentiment, unknown to antiquity and medieval Christianity, that beyond the sexual outcome creates the joy of loving, that sentimental exaltation which, not being foreign to desire, transcends it by spiritualizing it and lifts its recipient above the commoner" (Belperron 49). *Joy* bears no relationship to *delectatio* and *gaudium*, but represents a movement, the activity of a soul who loves, a source of spiritual regeneration: using "the language of the late scholastics, one could say that joy is to Courtly Love in the natural order what grace is to 'caritas' in the supernatural order" (Denomy 1951, 217); *gaug* expresses a "passive joy," whereas *joy* generally represents "an active joy, which very often and more precisely is really a game, an exercise. One could say, in a somewhat schematic manner, that *gaug* results from *joy*" (Camproux 1956, 66).

A short survey of the thematic contexts in which the term *joy* most frequently occurs will enable us to grasp its essential meaning and related connotations:

1. Springtime, being the season of mating in the animal world, inspires the poet with the joy of love and the joy of songwriting: compared to the joy of the birds,

> Eu, c'ai mais de joi en mo cor,
> Dei be chantar, pois tuih li mei jornal
> Son joi e chan, qu'eu no pes de ren al.
> > (Bernart de Ventadorn 24:6–8)

I, who have more joy in my heart, I truly must sing, for all my days are joy and song, thinking of nothing else.

> Quan lo rossinhols el follos
> Dona d'amor e·n quier e·n pren,
> E mou son chant jauzent joyos
> E remira sa par soven,
> . . . .
> Mi ven al cor grans joys jazer.
> > (Jaufre Rudel 5:1–4, 7)

When the nightingale in the foliage gives, asks for, and receives love and begins his joyous song, rejoicing and often gazing at his mate . . . a great joy settles down in my heart.

Contemplating birds, frogs, and owls in the mating season, Marcabru confesses his own frustration:

> Sesta creatura vana
> D'amor s'aparilha,
> Lur joys sec la via plana
> E·l nostre bruzilha,
> Quar nos, qui plus pot enguana.
> > (21:13–17)

These small creatures couple together out of love, their joy follows a straight path while ours strays from it, for, among us, each one cheats another.

In rare instances, some troubadours subvert the topos and relate joy with the winter season (see Bernart de Ventadorn 26:1–10), which with autumn generally introduces a song of frustrated love.

2. The lady as the supreme source of joy:

> Quar vos etz arbres e branca
> On fruitz de gaug s'asazona
> > (Peire Vidal 15:9–10)

For you are the tree and the branch upon which ripens the fruit of joy.

E vos etz lo meus jois primers,
E si seretz vos lo derrers
(Bernart de Ventadorn 10:33–34)

You are my first joy, you will also be my last.

[Fin'amor] e[s] de Joi cim' e racina
                    (Marcabru 37:33)

[*Fin'amor*] is of Joy the summit and the root.

Lady and *love* are frequently synonymous and often interchangeable, each of them being the omnipotent master of the lover's destiny, who can cure through *joy* the sickness of the longing heart.

3. Joy emanating from the lady's gaze upon the lover, or from glancing at her face:

Negus jois al meu no s'eschai,
Can ma domna·m garda ni·m ve
    (Bernart de Ventadorn 40:41–42)

No joy is comparable to mine when my lady looks and gazes at me.

Bernart also says:

C'ab sol lo bel semblan que·m fai
Can pot ni aizes lo·lh cossen,
Ai tan de joi que sol no·m scn.
                    (19:28–30)

By simply showing me her beautiful face whenever she may or the place permits, I am so filled with joy, I no longer am myself.

4. *Joy* is not only a sentimental exaltation, but a sensual and erotic pleasure experienced through the long-awaited kiss, which placates the anguish of the soul and the torments of the body. Consider the following two examples from Bernart de Ventadorn:

Per la bocha·m feretz al cor
D'un doutz baizar de fin'amor coral,
Que·m torn en joi e·m get d'ira mortal!
                    (24:30–32)

May your mouth strike me in the heart with a sweet kiss of pure love, a hearty kiss, that will deliver me to joy and save me from mortal sadness!

E baizera·lh la boca en totz sens,
Si que d'un mes i paregra lo sens
                    (20:39–40)

I would then kiss her lips over and over, so that a month later they would bear its marks.

The verb *jauzir* and its alliterative derivates frequently accentuate the sensual-erotic connotation of *joy*:

E mias sion tals amors
Don ieu sia jauzens jauzitz
　　　(Jaufre Rudel 1:11–12)

And be such loves mine in which giving joy I am enjoyed.

Quar lai ay joy meravelos
Per qu'ieu la jau joyos jauzen
　　　(Jaufre Rudel 5:17–18)

For I have there a marvelous joy by which I lie enjoyed and giving joy.

Joy don ieu suy jauzens.
　　　(Marcabru 40:2)

Joy through which I am enjoyed.

5. The *joy* of kissing is but a prelude to the supreme *joy* of the total embrace and physical union, as in Guillem de Peiteus:

A mos ops la·m vuel retenir,
Per lo cor dedins refrescar
Et per la carn renovellar,
　　　　(9:33–35)

For my needs I wish to keep it [my joy], to refresh my heart within and to rejuvenate my flesh.

And Bernart de Ventadorn:

Las! e viure que·m val,
S'eu no vei a jornal
Mo fi joi natural
En leih, sotz fenestral,
Cors blanc tot atretal
Com la neus a nadal,
Si c'amdui cominal
Mesurem s'em egal?
　　　　(17:33–40)

Alas! What is my life worth if every day I do not see my loyal and natural joy in bed, beneath the window, with her body as fair as the snow at Christmas, so that together we may measure to see if we are matching?

In another of his songs Bernart writes:

Qui ve sas belas faissos,
Ab que m'a vas se atraih,

Pot be saber atrazaih
Que sos cors es bels e bos
E blancs sotz la vestidura
—Eu non o dic mas per cuda—
Que la neus, can ilh es nuda,
Par vas lei brun' et escura.

(16:33–40)

He who has seen her radiant face, by which she drew me to her, may know with certitude that her body is noble and beautiful and fair beneath her clothing—I say so only by guessing—so fair that, when this body is naked, the snow beside it seems dark and brown.

Compare these lines of Bernart de Ventadorn with the following stanza of a goliardic poet:

Non in visu defectus,
Auditus nec abiectus;
Eius ridet aspectus,
Sed et istis iocundius:
Locus sub veste tectus;
In hoc declinat melius
Non obliquus, sed rectus.

(Hilka, Schumann, and Bischoff, No. 164, lines 22–28)

Without blemish is her face, composed is her speech, a most harmonious presence; but the most pleasant place remains hidden beneath her clothing; to decline there is better erect than oblique.

Or compare with the stanza of an anonymous Catalan monk (late 12th cent.), nicknamed by his editor Nicolau d'Olwer, "the Anonymous Lover":

Et tuarum
Papillarum
Forma satis parvula
Non tumescit,
Sed albescit
Nive magis candida.

(d'Olwer, No. 22, lines 55–60)

And your teats, small shaped, not fully grown, that shine brighter than immaculate snow.

The same monk, in another song, describes his *joc d'amor* 'game of love' and *joy d'amor* 'joy of love' as follows:

Cuius crus tenerum tenui, quod non negat ipsa,
Insuper et coxas, sponte sua tetigi.

Nec vetuit niveas post me tractare papillas,
Quas tractare mihi dulce nimis fuerat.
Venimus ad lectum, conectimur insimul ambo;
Cetera, que licuit sumere, non piguit.

(d'Olwer, No. 23, lines 17–22)

Tenderly I held her legs, without her resisting, and moreover her thighs, freely
offered by her; neither did she deny me then caressing her snowy teats whose
touch was the sweetest thing for me. We went to bed, both our bodies intertwined; and the *et cetera*, offered for my taking, was not unpleasant.

(We shall consider later the frequent use of this "et cetera," and other
similar euphemisms, among the troubadours and the goliardic songwriters.)

It is thus clear that, except in some cases where *joy* expresses a general
feeling of happiness, the term typically connotes sensual, erotic, and sexual
gratification. Nowhere does it allude to the mystical and metaphysical realms
of *delectatio, gratia,* and *caritas* that are brought to bear upon the concept by
the scholars mentioned above. A passage in Thomas's romance *Tristan*
exemplifies the troubadours' implied meaning of *joy*: Tristan, exiled from
the court, suffers from knowing that Iseut is in King Mark's bed:

Pur vostre cors su jo em paine,
Li reis sa joie en vos maine;
Sun deduit maine e sun buen,
Ço que mien fu ore est suen.

(Wind, lines 17–20)

For your body I am in pain, the king seeking his joy in you, taking his pleasure
and contentment; what was mine is now his.

The above-mentioned aspects of *joc d'amor* 'game of love' and *joy d'amor* 'joy
of love', so central to the mode of *fin'amor*, are also the essential components
of many Latin love songs composed by the much maligned and discredited
goliards, generally presented as drunkards and fornicators, living in and
writing about lechery. The *Carmina Burana*, in many of its songs, testifies to
the influence of the *fin'amor* tradition. One of the goliardic poets—who,
contrary to the *fin'amor* mode, prefers young maidens to married ladies—
presents the same love-game's strategy in five stages (see below, *gradus
amoris*) as profusely illustrated in the Occitan *cansos*. He writes:

Ut, quem decet fieri
Ludum faciamus.
Volo tantum ludere,
Id est: contemplari,
Presens loqui, tangere,
Tandem osculari;

Quintum, quod est agere
Noli suspicari.

(Hilka, Schumann, and Bischoff, No. 88, lines 41–48)

Within decency's boundaries let us play a game. I want so much to play, namely: gaze at you, then converse, caress, and kiss at last; fifth, which is "to do it," let's not mention it.

Another goliardic songwriter defines unequivocally the fifth stage:

Felicitate Iovem supero,
Si me dignetur, quam desidero,
Si sua labra semel novero,
Una cum illa si dormiero.

(Hilka, Schumann, and Bischoff, No. 116, lines 5–8)

I would be happier than Jupiter if the one I desire would let me kiss her lips and let me sleep with her.

FIN'AMOR, EROS, AND SEXUALITY

Metaphors, metonyms, euphemisms, and other hermetic expressions are used by the troubadours as disguising devices in the representation of real or imagined sexual activities. The art of sublimating metaphorically and metonymically the erotic register of *fin'amor* increases in sophistication when we compare the songs of the *trobar leu* (plain song) to those of the *trobar clus* (hermetic song) groups. William D. Paden writes, "The language of eroticism in troubadour's lyric is distinguished by a pervasive ambiguity of reference which functions on linguistic levels from vocabulary to syntax, and in the poetic conventions as well. Such ambiguity masks the poet's reference to chaste or sexual love and calls our attention instead to the language itself, to the literal material of the poetry" (1979, 73). But, at the same time, the joys of lovemaking and songmaking, even when not inspired by a real life experience but only imagined in daydreams, should not be considered as limited to a purely verbal game independent of the principle of erotic and sexual pleasure shared affectively and emotionally between the writer/ performer and the reader/listener (Lazar 1991). The inhibiting moral and social conventions around them actually serve to heighten and intensify their awareness of and pleasure in implied sexual messages. The afore-mentioned Neoplatonic and mystical interpretations of *fin'amor*, as well as the statement by Wettstein that in the amorous relationship between the lover and the lady "the body remains insensitive as the soul contemplates the lady" (107–8), are not so much in the eye of the beholder as in the inhibited minds of "idealistic" and "moralizing" scholars.

Let us have a closer look at some topical areas of the troubadours' *ars amandi* 'art of loving':

1. The *locus amoenus* of the lovers: the discreet garden and the lady's alcove.

> Morrai, pel cap sanh Gregori,
> Si no·m bayza en cambr'o sotz ram.
> (Guillem de Peiteus 8:17–18)

I shall die, by Saint Gregory, if she does not kiss me in the alcove or beneath the boughs.

After praising the rare virtues of his lady and her fair body, Cercamon prescribes the cure that could bring him back the joy of living and loving:

> Qu'eu non puesc lonjamen estar
> De sai vius ni de lai guerir,
> Si josta mi despoliada
> Non la puesc baizar e tenir
> Dinz cambra encortinada.
> (4:45–49)

For I cannot live away from her sight, nor be cured by her, unless at my side and undressed I may kiss and embrace her in a carpeted alcove.

And elsewhere:

> E si·m fezes tant de placer
> Qe·m laisses pres de si jaser,
> Ja d'aquest mal non morira.
> (5:53–55)

And if only she would grant me that pleasure, letting me lie beside her, I would not die from this illness.

Marcabru instructs his messenger bird as follows:

> Vol' e vai
> Tot dreit lai,
> E·l retrai
> Qu'ieu morrai,
> Si no sai
> Consi jai
> Nuda o vestia.
> (25:49–55)

Go and fly straight to her, and tell her that I shall die, unless I know whether she sleeps nude or clothed.

And Bernart de Ventadorn:

> Mal o fara, si no·m manda
> Venir lai on se despolha
> (29:29–30)

She will do wrong if she fails to order me to come where she undresses

and

> Si no·m aizis lai on ilh jai,
> Si qu'eu remir son bel cors gen,
> Doncs, per que m'a faih de nien
> Ai las! com mor de dezire!
> (19:46–49)

If she does not invite me where she sleeps, so that I may gaze at her noble body, why then did she raise me from nothingness? Alas! I am dying from desire!

To show that this topos is common to several generations of troubadours, one could adduce the following examples:

> Molt mi fera gran secors,
> S'una vetz per aventura[1]
> Mi mezes lai o·s despuelha.
> (Peire Rogier 1:47–49)

She would be of noble succor to me if once, on a dark night, she took me where she undresses.

And, in transferring his repressed sexual desires to the nocturnal dream, Arnaut de Marueill writes:

> Mai volria jauzens dormir
> Qe velhan deziran languir.
> (Salut d'amors I, 152–53; Bec ed., 85)

I would rather have my joy while asleep than languish of desire awake.

Finally, Arnaut Daniel, quite hermetic in general, has clearly summarized in two lines the mode of *fin'amor*, its implied sexuality and the favorite site for its consummation:

> Del cors li fos, no de l'arma,
> E consentis m'a selat dinz sa chambra!
> (18:13–14)

May I be hers, in flesh, not in soul; and she, consenting to me, secretly, in her alcove.

---

1. For "per aventura," manuscript *C* has *ab nueg escura* and manuscript *R* has *de nueg escura.*

There is no attempt either to conceal the adulterous nature of *fin'amor* in the song of the trobairitz Comtessa de Dia, nor does she disguise metonymically her desire:

> Ben volria mon cavallier
> Tener un ser e mos bratz nut,
>
> . . . .
>
> Bels amics, avinens e bos,
> Cora·us tenrai en mon poder,
> E que iagues ab vos un ser
> E qe·us des un bais amoros!
> Sapchatz gran talan n'auria
> Qe·us tengues en luoc del marit.
>
> (4:9–10, 17–22)

I would very much like to hold my knight some evening, naked between my arms. . . . My lover, generous and kind, may I hold you in my power and sleep with you one night, and give you a loving kiss. Know also that I have a great desire to embrace you rather than my husband.

2. Erotic games and consummation of love:

> Enquer me lais Dieus viure tan
> C'aia mas mans soz so mantel!
>   (Guillem de Peiteus 10:23–24)

May God grant I live to see the day when I may put my hands beneath her cloak!

and

> Que tal se van d'amor gaban;
> Nos n'avem la pessa e·l coutel!
>   (Guillem de Peiteus 10:29–30)

Let others boast of love, for we have the piece and the knife!

Elsewhere, stating that he is no beginner at the *juec d'amor* 'game of love', he boasts:

> Qu'ieu sai joguar sobre coisi
> A totz tocatz;
>
> . . . . . .
>
> Qu'ieu ai nom: "maistre serta":
> Ja m'amigu'a nueg no m'aura
> Que no·m vueill'aver l'endema;
>
> . . . .
>
> Mas ela·m dis un reprovier:
> "Don, vostres datz son menudier,
> Ez ieu revit vos a doblier!"
>
> . . . .

Et quant l'aic levat lo taullier,
Espeis lo datz;
E·ill dui foron cairat, vallier,
E·l terz plombatz.
    (6:25–26, 36–38, 50–52, 57–60)

For I know how to play on a cushion, all kinds of games; . . . For I have the fame of a consummate master; my lover will never have me for a night without wanting to have me the next day. . . . Yet she says to me in a reproach: "Sire, your dice are small, and I invite you to cast them again!" . . . And when I had lifted up the apron, I cast the dice and two of them went rolling while the third was loaded.[2]

Marcabru, whom some have considered to be a defender of conjugal love against *fals'amor* (see Appel 1923, Jeanroy), sends his messenger bird to the lady with a demand to settle their quarrel (she had left him waiting outside her castle an entire night):

Del deslei
Que me fai
Li fauc drei,
E·il autrei,
Mas sotz mei
A plat sei
Qu'ela·m lass'e·m lia.
    (25:78–84)

For the suffering she caused me I forgive her and grant her pardon if beneath me she would lie and hug and embrace me.

The bird brings back the lady's answer (dreamed up most probably by Marcabru himself):

Son joc revit, si·l m'envida

. . . .
La cambr'er de cel guarnida,
D'un ric jauzir per jauzida,
C'ab doutz baizar s'es sentida
Desotz se plat de plazensa.
Vai e·l di
Qu'el mati
Si·aissi,
Que sotz pi

2. On the frequent use of the dice game in an erotic context, see Marcabru 25:27–29, 6:29–32; and Bédier, *Tristan*, lines 1655–59 and related note.

Farem fi,
Sotz lui mi,
D'esta malvolensa.

(26:47, 56–66)

I accept his game, if he so invites me. . . . The alcove shall have as its roof the sky, a rich pleasure and enjoyment to her who by a sweet kiss already felt herself with pleasure lying flat beneath him. Go and tell him that come the morning he should be here so that, beneath the pine tree, we might appease, me beneath him, this misfortune.

In a dramatic manner, Bertran de Born (accused by some jealous gossipers of having betrayed his lady) puts a curse upon himself to prove that he had not desired any other woman:

Autr' escondich vos farai plus sobrier,
E no·m puosc orar plus adorer d'encombrier:
S'ieu anc failli vas vos, neis del pensar,
Qan serem sol dinz cambr'o en vergier
Failla·m poders davas mon compaignier
De tal guisa que no·m posc'aiudar.

(6:13–18)

I cannot wish a greater misfortune: if ever I betrayed you, even in thought, when we are alone in the alcove or garden, may I lose my vigor before my beloved so that not even she could help me!

3. The *surplus*, the *promised thing*, the *rest*, the *et cetera*, the *sweet secret*—these and other related euphemistic expressions, in both the Provençal strategy of lovemaking as well as that found in the *Carmina Burana*, belong to the fifth stage of the game of love or *gradus amoris* 'scale of love' so frequently outlined in the literature of the time (see the articles of Carlson, Smith, Akehurst, and Lazar in Lazar and Lacy 1989): (a) gazing at the lady's body; (b) courtly conversation; (c) caressing her body; (d) exchanging kisses; (e) *far lo* 'do it', obtaining from the lady the ultimate *joy*, invariably called *lo al* 'the other thing', *lo plus* 'the surplus, the rest of it', or the *et cetera*. For example, in Bernart de Ventadorn:

E car vos plac que·m fesetz tan d'onor
O jorn que·m detz en baizan vostr'amor,
Del plus, si·us platz, prendetz esgardamen!

(13:16–18)

And since it pleased you to grant me such honor that day you sealed your love with a kiss, do take care, if you please, of the rest.

In a song by Gautier de Châtillon, "Declinante frigore," following the conventional descriptions of spring, the beauty of the lady's body, the desire to be with her, and so on, we read:

> Ad hec illa frangitur
> Humi sedet igitur,
> Et sub fronde tenera,
> Dum vix moram patitur,
> Subici compellitur.
> Sed quis nescit cetera?
> P[r]edicatus vincitur.
>> (Strecker 17:43–49)

Now she lost her resistance, sat down on the ground and beneath the tender foliage let herself be conquered without delay. But who could ignore the "et cetera"? It surpassed every expectation.

The Catalan monk mentioned above concludes one of his songs:

> Genas deosculans, papillas palpito,
> Post illud dulcius secretum compleo.
>> (d'Olwer, No. 26, lines 33–34)

Kissing her cheeks, caressing her teats, then concluding with the sweet secret.

4. God, the lovers, and the husband: *fin'amor* must triumph over social and religious conventions because it alone is "true love." And even God is called upon to be on the side of the lovers, not on the side of the "old" and "jealous" husband. Raimbaut d'Aurenga, alluding to Iseut's trial by ordeal in Béroul's *Tristan*, where she was declared "not guilty" thanks to her linguistic trickery and punning,[3] advises his lady to follow her example:

> Vejatz, dompna, cum Dieus acor
> Dompna que d'amar s'agrada.
> Q'Iseutz estet en gran paor,
> Puois fo·n breumens conseillada,
> Qu'il fetz a son marit crezen
> C'anc hom que nasques de maire,
> Non toques en lieis. Mantenen,
> Atrestal podetz vos faire!
>> (27:41–48)

See, lady, how God assists a lady who gives herself to love. When Iseut was stricken with fear she found advice at the right time, for she could make her husband believe that no man, born of a mother, had ever touched her; now, you too can do the same.

---

3. See Muret, *Tristan*, lines 4205–8, for the passage referred to by Raimbaut.

Cercamon, having just left the "most perfidious woman God ever created," summons Christ to assist him in obtaining a rendezvous with another lady, "the most noble" in the world:

> Saint Salvador, fai m'albergan
> Lai el regne on mi donz estai,
> Ab la genzor si q'en baizan
> Sien nostre coven verai,
> E qe·m do zo qe m'a promes;
> Pueis al jorn m'en ira[i] conqes,
> Si be l'es mal al gelos brau.
>
> (7:43–49)

Holy Savior, find me lodging in the land where my lady dwells, near this most noble, so that in kissing we may truly realize our agreement, so she may grant me what she promised; then, in the morning, she would depart conquered even if this displeases the jealous villain.

And just as Aucassin would gladly give up Paradise to retain his beloved Nicolette (Matarasso 28–29), the troubadour Raimon Jordan would do the same if only he could spend one night with his lady:

> Que tan la desir e volh
> Que, s'er' en coita de mort,
> Non queri' a Deu tan fort
> Que lai el seu paradis
>   M'aculhis
>   Com que·m des lezer
> D'una noit ab leis jazer.
>
> (13:48–54)

For I want and desire her so much that, were I in the pangs of death, I should not more fervently pray God to welcome me into his Paradise than to give me time to spend the night beside her.

TRANSFORMATIONS OF *FIN'AMOR*

The love songs of the trouvères in the north of France, during the last decades of the twelfth century, select a number of elements from *cortezia*, leaving out *mezura* and *joven* (except for one mention of "joie et jovent" [joy and youthful gaiety; Grace Brulé 21:4, trans. Rosenberg and Danon]), and adapt a greater number of components from the *fin'amor* tradition developed by the Occitan troubadours. Conon de Béthune, Guiot de Provins, Châtelain de Coucy, Gace Brulé, and even Chrétien de Troyes in his romances (while excluding the adulterous and sexual nature of *fin'amor* in all of them but *Lancelot*) borrow their major themes, motifs, metaphors, topoi, and vocabulary from the *cansos*. The resemblances in language and style often seem straight translations from langue d'oc into langue d'oïl. For example, in two songs of Châtelain de Coucy we find:

Ainz ai mis en li servir
Cuer et cors, force et pooir;
(10:21–22)[4]

In serving her I have invested body and heart, strength and power.

Quar g'i met tout, cuer et cors et desir,
Force et pooir, . . .
(3:21–22)[5]

For I invest everything, heart and body and desire, strength and power.

Compare with their corresponding source in Bernart de Ventadorn:

Cor e cors e saber e sen
E fors' e poder i ai mes
(1:5–6)

I have invested heart and body, and wisdom and knowledge, and strength and power.

Or take the opening lines of a poem by Gace Brulé:

Qu'onques ne fis chançon jor de ma vie,
Se fine amor nel m'enseigna avant
(13:2–3)[6]

For I never made a song in my whole life, unless Fine Amor taught it to me first

and set them alongside these by Bernart de Ventadorn:

Chantars no pot gaire valer
Si d'ins dal cor no mou lo chans,
Ni chans no pot dal cor mover
Si no·i es fin'amors coraus.
(2:1–4)

A song has no real value if the song does not surge from within the heart, and a song cannot not surge from the heart if it has no heartfelt *fin'amor* in it.

---

4. Quotations from the Châtelain de Coucy are taken from Alain Lerond, ed., *Chansons attribuées au Chastelain de Couci (fin du XIIe–début du XIIIe siècle)*, Publications de la Faculté des Lettres et Sciences Humaines de Rennes 7 (Paris: Presses Universitaires de France, 1964).

5. In some mss. line 22 reads *Sens et savoir* 'knowledge and wisdom', but this only strengthens my case.

6. Quotations from Gace Brulé are taken from Samuel N. Rosenberg and Samuel Danon, eds. and trans., *The Lyrics and Melodies of Gace Brulé* (New York: Garland, 1985).

But beyond the similarity in certain areas of the register of courtly vocabulary, *fine amour* and *joie* (or *delit*) have lost the erotic and sexual density we uncovered in *fin'amor* and *joi*. Expressions such as "secret meeting in the garden or alcove," "see the lady when and where she undresses," "lie beside her under the embroidered bedcover," "caress her fair body," "obtain from her, after the kiss, the supreme joy of the 'other thing,'" are most often replaced by innocent demands such as to see the lady's "sweet face," her "sweet look," her "gentle body." One exception occurs in Châtelain de Coucy (once more imitating Bernart de Ventadorn):

> Or me lait Diex en tele honor monter
> Que chele u j'ai mon cuer et mon penser,
> Tieigne une foiz entre mes braz nuete
> Ainçoiz qu'aille outremer.
>
> (5:5–8)

May God grant me such an honor that the one in whom I put my heart and thought, I could once hold nude in my arms before I depart beyond the sea.

In general, the *fine amour* of the trouvères is closest to the mode of "courtly love" articulated in the romances of northern France.

With the growing influence of Bernard de Clairvaux's allegorical interpretation of the biblical *Song of Songs* toward the end of the twelfth century, and particularly after the crusade against the Albigensians (the heretic Cathars), which prompted the demise of the secular culture of the south, there begins a process of psychological inhibition and repression in the domain of love songs, a trend toward spiritualization and allegorization that would eventually lead to the *Roman de la Rose*, to the *dolce stil nuovo* of a Guido Guinizelli or Cavalcanti, and to the *Vita nuova* of Dante. During this process, some aspects of the courtly vocabulary will also be transferred to the love hymns addressed to Mary, "*our* Lady" replacing now "*my* lady" and "*midons*" of the troubadours. During the thirteenth century, in a changing cultural context, poets now invest their talent in "divine love" songs. *True love* and *good love*, fair body and sweet face, kisses and embraces, desire and joy, garden of delights and dying from passionate love, are so many expressions recuperated from the troubadours' vocabulary by the devotional hymns to Mary, including *fine amour* and *fin amant*, but totally emptied of their profane erotic and sexual connotations. Whatever latent eroticism remains in these hymns is common to all mystical love literature in which human love is sublimated, spiritualized, and allegorized.

In the late-twelfth-century Old French metrical paraphrase of Psalm 44, *Eructavit* (dedicated to Marie de Champagne), troubadour vocabulary and imagery, often adapted from Bernart de Ventadorn's *cansos*, permeate an allegorical and mystical epithalamium:

> D'une douçor ai plain li cuer,
> Ne puis soffrir n'en isse fuer.
> > (Jenkins, lines 205–6)

My heart is full of sweetness, I cannot keep it from coming forth.

> Qui est cist sire qui tant l'aimme
> Que sa douce amie la claimme,
> Qui por li aidier au secors
> Vost morir par fines amors?
> > (Jenkins, lines 1263–66)

Who is this lord who so loves her that he calls her his sweetheart, who wished to die through perfect love to help her in her need?

> Se l'ame qui a Dé s'est jointe
> Por sa folie ailors s'acointe.[7]
> > (Jenkins, lines 1605–6)

If the soul, that was wedded to God, through its folly [sin] loves somewhere else.

The Virgin is so beautiful "qu'au deviser n'ot que redire" (that no reproach was possible in describing her; line 1669); cf. Bernart de Ventadorn: "e l'autre cors, que res non es a dire" (and the rest of her body, perfect beyond any reproach; 21:21).

> Ele s'oblie antre lor braz
> De la grant joie et del solaz;
> Une douçor au cuer li vient
> Si que de li ne li sovient.
> > (Jenkins, lines 1779–82)

She loses herself in his arms, for great are the joy and solace; a sweetness so swells her heart that she does not remember herself.

Compare these lines with their source in Bernart de Ventadorn:

> Can vei la lauzeta mover
> De joi sas alas contra·l rai
> Que s'oblid'e·s laissa chazer
> Per la doussor c'al cor li vai.
> > (31:1–4)

---

7. *Ailors*: somewhere else, outside the bond of divine love.

When I see the lark move with joy its wings against the rays, losing consciousness, slowly falling because of sweetness swelling its heart.

These lines are echoed later again in Dante (*Paradiso* XX, 73–75).

By contrast, in two anonymous poetic and allegorized adaptations of the
Song of Songs (Paris, B.N., MS. 14966 [13th cent., unpublished], and Le
Mans, MS. 173 [12th cent., ed. Pickford]) we witness a similar use of *fin'amor*
vocabulary, frequently accompanied by some remarkable gloss that alerts
the reader/listener to the fact that *fine amour*, as used in the devotional
context, is neither sinful nor a source of torment like the *fin'amor* of secular
love literature. In the first text (fol. 1v), we read that *fine amour* is " . . . plus
honeste que n'est celle / dou romant c'on dist [de] la Rose" (more virtuous
than the one in the so-called *Romance of the Rose*); it is not "un amour qui
sanble estre fole" (a love that appears to be sinful).[8] *Fin amant*, in this text,
designates the divine lovers. In the second text, the warning gloss contrasts
two modes of love, *good love* (holy, peaceful) and *sinful love* (secular, painful):

L'amor dont il ici parole
N'est pas del siecle, n'est pas fole,
Enz est amors e bone e sainte
Dunt il ne vient mals ne complainte.
(Pickford, lines 11–14)

The love spoken about here is not the worldly and sinful one; it is, on the
contrary, good and holy, never causing evil nor complaint.

Whereas the courtly lady of the *fin'amor* tradition chooses her lover
outside marriage, in the Hebrew Scriptures (Isaiah, Jeremiah, etc.), as well
as in the esoteric love literature derived from the allegoric interpretation
of the *Song of Songs*, the soul—that is, the bride, wedded to God, her
bridegroom—commits a sin of fornication if she seeks love outside the
sacred bond (see above, in *Eructavit*: "se l'ame qui a Dé s'est jointe / por
sa folie ailors s'acointe"). One can clearly detect here the subversion of the
Provençal aristocratic mode of *fin'amor*, and its constitutive elements, in the
context of a moralizing and bourgeois mentality in the north of France,
which finally produced a reconversion and recuperation of the secular
vocabulary and metaphors within the allegorized mode of divine love; the
concepts of *fin'amor*, *bon'amor*, *verai'amor*, *joy*, although verbally preserved,
have now lost the original contextual meaning they had in troubadour
songs. During the course of the thirteenth century, following the crusade
against the Albigensians and some threatening warnings addressed to the
late troubadours, the number of antifeminist treatises and invectives against

8. For *folia* in the troubadours, see Akehurst 1978.

secular love poetry increased dramatically. In the thirteenth century, Matfre Ermengaud composed his *Lo Breviari d'Amor* (a poetic apology of spiritual love, some 34,000 lines long!). In the latter part of this work he anthologizes a great number of stanzas from many troubadours, showing off his knowledge of them in order to better reject the "courtly love" games. He even offers the suffering courtly lovers a remedy: imagine your lady as rich in imperfections, as ugly and repulsive, without makeup and fashionable clothing, and you will be cured. He then concludes:

E volon tot jorn biordar,
Tornejar, ab donas dansar;
E sabchas senes dubtansa
Que·l diables mena lur dansa,
Et escompren tan lur folor
E tant abraza lur ardor
Le Satans que per sobr'amar
Lur fai lurs donas azorar;
Quar aichi cum lo Creator
Devon amar de bon'amor,
De tot lur cor, de tot lur sen
E de tot lur entendemen
Amon lurs donas e peccat
Don d'ellas fan lur deitat.
E sabchatz que las azoran,
Azoro per cert lo Satan
E fan lur dieu del deslial
Diable, Satan, Belial;
          (Ricketts 27451–68)

And those who want to be in tournaments, dance with ladies, should know without any doubt that the devil leads the dance; as they increase their folly, Satan, in his pride, incites their passion and has them worship women; whereas men should love their Creator with pure love, with all their heart and soul, and all their intelligence, these men sinfully love women and transform them into goddesses. And know that those who worship them truthfully worship Satan and take as God the treacherous devil, Satan, Belial.

To illustrate the recycling of concepts and topoi of the *fin'amor* tradition in thirteenth-century devotional songs, let us examine a number of interesting examples. Bernart d'Auriac writes:

Be volria de la mellor
De totas far chanso plazen,
Quar d'autra chantar non enten
Mas de la Verge de doussor
. . . .
Nuls hom no val ni a valor

Si non lauza la plus valen,
La maire de Dieu, doussamen.
   (Oroz, No. 5, lines 1–4, 25–27)

I would like to compose a pleasant song about the best of all ladies, for I don't intend to sing but about the sweet Virgin. . . . No man has worth or value if he does not sweetly praise the most precious, the mother of God.

Daude de Pradas opens a song in the following manner:

Qui finamen sap cossirar
Lo dous dezir, lo dous pensar
Que fis cors a per fin'amor,
Finamen ab fina sabor
En fin'amor si deu fizar.
amors vens tot'autra doussor;
Quals amors? Silh que tot perpren,
Ses fin e ses comensamen:
Dieus es fin'amors e vertatz,
E qui Dieu ama finamen
Finamen es de Dieu amatz.
   (13:1–11)

Whoever considers with perfection the sweet desire, the sweet thought, that a perfect heart gets from *fin'amor*, perfectly, with perfect taste, should confide in perfect love. Love surpasses any other sweetness. Which love? The one which contains all, without beginning nor end: God is *fin'amor* and truth, and whoever loves perfectly perfectly is he loved by God.

Folquet de Lunel opens his song with the traditional spring stanza, praises the beauty and the virtues of his "midons," who rewards her "fis amans," and after five strophes reveals in the *tornada* that the "lady" is "Our Lady" (Oroz, No. 12). Finally, in Lanfranc Cigala we read:

Gloriosa sainta Maria,
Eu·s prec e·us clam merce, que·us plaia
Lo chanz que mos cors vos presenta;
E s'an iorn chantei de follia
Ni fis coblas d'amor savaia,
Ar vueill virar tota m'ententa
E chantar de vostr'amor fina;
Que autr'amors no vueill que·m vensa,
Qu'anc no·y trobei ioi, mas pezansa.
   (Oroz, No. 38, lines 1–9)

Glorious holy Mary, I mercifully beg you to accept the song my heart presents to you; and if, a time ago, I sang sinfully and composed evil love songs, I now desire to transform my intent and sing the praise of your *fin'amor*; I do not want another love to conquer me, for I did not find in it joy but sorrow.

In what might be qualified as a "mariological century," following the demise of the sensual and erotic *fin'amor* tradition, the "heavenly Lady," "Our Lady," gradually displaced in society and literature the "earthly lady," "my lady"; and so, in an ultimate refinement, the *donna* became the *Madonna*.

WORKS CITED

The quotations in this chapter are from the critical editions cited in the List of Troubadour Editions in the Appendix, and in particular from the following editions: Arnaut Daniel (Toja); Arnaut de Mareuil (*Saluts d'amour*, Bec); Bernart de Ventadorn (Lazar); Bernart Marti (Hoepffner); Bertran de Born (Paden, Sankovitch, and Stäblein); Cercamon (Wolf and Rosenstein); Guillem de Peiteus (Bond); Jaufre Rudel (Wolf and Rosenstein); Lanfranc Cigala (Branciforti); and Peire Vidal (Avalle). All translations are my own.

Akehurst, F. R. P. "La Folie chez les troubadours." In *Mélanges de philologie romane offerts à Charles Camproux*, 19–28. Montpellier: Centre d'Etudes Occitanes, 1978.
———. "Words and Acts in the Troubadours." In *The Poetics of Love in the Middle Ages: Texts and Contexts*, ed. Moshe Lazar and Norris Lacy. Fairfax, Va.: George Mason University Press, 1989.
Appel, Carl. "Wiederum zu Jaufré Rudel." *Archiv* 107 (1901): 338–49.
———. "Zu Marcabru." *Zeitschrift für romanische Philologie* 43 (1923): 403–69.
Bec, Pierre. *Burlesque et obscénité chez les troubadours: le contre-texte au moyen âge*. Paris: Stock, 1984.
Bédier, Jean, ed. *Le Roman de Tristan par Thomas: poème du XIIe siècle*. 2 vols. Société des Anciens Tests Français 46. Paris: Didot, 1902–5.
Belperron, P. *La Joie d'amour: contribution à l'étude des troubadours et de l'amour courtois*. Paris: Plon, 1948.
Benton, J. F. "Clio and Venus: An Historical View of Medieval Love." In *The Meaning of Courtly Love*, ed. F. X. Newman, 19–42. Albany: State University of New York Press, 1968.
Bloch, Marc. *Feudal Society*. Trans. L. A. Manyon. 2 vols. Chicago: University of Chicago Press, 1961.
Breul, Karl. *The Cambridge Songs: A Goliard's Song Book of the Eleventh Century*. Cambridge: Cambridge University Press, 1915.
Briffault, Robert S. *Les Troubadours et le sentiment romanesque*. Paris: Editions du Chêne, 1945. Rev. and trans. by author as *The Troubadours*. Bloomington: Indiana University Press, 1965.
Camproux, Charles. "La Joie civilisatrice chez les troubadours." *La Table Ronde* 97 (1956): 64–69.
———. *Le "Joy d'amor" des troubadours: jeu et joie d'amour*. Montpellier: Causse & Castelnau, 1965.
Carlson, David. "Religion and Romance: The Languages of Love in the Treatises of Gerard de Liège and the Case of Andreas Capellanus." In *The Poetics of Love in the Middle Ages: Texts and Contexts*, ed. Moshe Lazar and Norris Lacy, 81–92. Fairfax, Va.: George Mason University Press, 1989.

Casella, Mario. "Poesia e storia, I: Guillaume IX; II: Jaufré Rudel." *Archivo storico italiano* 96 (1938): 3–63, 153–99.

Denomy, A. J. "Fin'Amors: The Pure Love of the Troubadours, Its Amorality and Possible Source." *Medieval Studies* 7 (1945): 139–207.

———. "Jovens: The Notion of Youth Among the Troubadours, Its Meaning and Source." *Medieval Studies* 11 (1949): 1–22.

———. "*Jois* Among the Early Troubadours, Its Meaning and Possible Source." *Medieval Studies* 13 (1951): 177–217.

———. "Courtly Love and Courtliness." *Speculum* 28 (1953):44–63.

d'Olwer, Lluis Nicolau. "L'escola poetica de Ripoll en els segles X–XIII." *Institut d'Estudis Catalans*, Seccio Historico-Arqeologica, 6 (1915–20): 3–84.

Errante, Guido. *Sulla lirica romanza delle origini.* New York: Vanni, 1943.

———. *Marcabru e le fonti sacre dell'antica lirica romanza.* Florence: Sansoni, 1948.

Fackenheim, Emil. "Risalah fi'l-'Ishq." *Medieval Studies* 7 (1945): 208–28.

Fath, F. *Die Lieder des Castellans von Coucy* (diss., University of Heidelberg). Heidelberg: Horning, 1883.

Frappier, Jean. *Le Roman breton: des origines à Chrétien de Troyes.* Paris: Centre de Documentation Universitaire, 1951.

———. "Vues sur les conceptions courtoises dans les littératures d'oc et d'oïl au XIIe siècle." *Cahiers de Civilisation Médiévale* 2 (1959): 135–56.

———. "Sur un procès fait à l'amour courtois." *Romania* 93 (1972): 145–93.

Friedman, Lionel. "Gradus Amoris." *Romance Philology* 19 (1965): 167–77.

Giffen, Lois Anita. *Theory of Profane Love Among the Arabs: The Development of the Genre.* New York: New York University Press, 1971.

Gilson, Etienne. *La Théologie mystique de Saint Bernard.* Paris: J. Vrin, 1934.

Hammer-Purgstall, J. "Sur la chevalerie des Arabes antérieure à celle d'Europe, sur l'influence de la première sur la seconde." *Journal Asiatique* 4 (1849): 1ff.

———. "Sur les passages relatifs à la chevalerie chez les historiens arabes." *Journal Asiatique* 5 (1855): 282ff.

Hatzfeld, H. "Critical Review of Denomy's 'The Heresy of Courtly Love.'" *Symposium* 2 (1948): 285–88.

Hilka, A., O. Schumann, and B. Bischoff, eds. *Carmina Burana.* 3 vols. Heidelberg: Carl Winter, 1930–70.

Huet, G. *Les Chansons de Gace Brulé.* Paris: Didot, 1902.

Imbs, Paul. "De la *fin'amor.*" *Cahiers de Civilisation Médiévale* 12 (1969): 265–85.

Jackson, W. T. H. "Faith Unfaithful: The German Reaction to Courtly Love." In *The Meaning of Courtly Love*, ed. F. X. Newman, 55–76. Albany: State University of New York Press, 1968.

Jeanroy, Alfred. *La Poésie lyrique des troubadours.* 2 vols. Paris: H. Didier, 1934.

Jenkins, T. Atkinson, ed. "*Eructavit*": *An Old French Metrical Paraphrase of Psalm XLIV.* Gesellschaft für romanische Literatur 20. Dresden: Niemeyer, 1909.

Kelly, Amy. *Eleanor of Aquitaine and the Four Kings.* Cambridge, Mass.: Harvard University Press, 1963.

Köhler, Erich. *Trobadorlyrik und höfischer Roman.* Berlin: Rutten & Loening, 1962.

———. "Observations historiques et sociologiques sur la poésie des troubadours." *Cahiers de Civilisation Médiévale* 7 (1964): 27–51.

Lazar, Moshe. *Amour courtois et fin'amors dans la littérature du XIIe siècle.* Paris: Klincksieck, 1964.

————, ed. *Bernard de Ventadour: chansons d'amour.* Paris: Klincksieck, 1966.

————. "Lancelot et la *mulier mediatrix*." *L'Esprit Créateur* 11 (1969): 243–56.

————. "Carmina Erotica, Carmina Iocosa: The Body and the Bawdy in Medieval Love Songs." In *The Poetics of Love in the Middle Ages: Texts and Contexts*, ed. Moshe Lazar and Norris Lacy, 249–76. Fairfax, Va.: George Mason University Press, 1989.

Lazar, Moshe, and Norris Lacy, eds. *The Poetics of Love in the Middle Ages: Texts and Contexts.* Fairfax, Va.: George Mason University Press, 1989.

Lewis, C. S. *The Allegory of Love.* New York: Oxford University Press, 1960.

Margoni, Ivos. *Fin'Amors, mezura, e cortezia: saggio sulla lirica provenzale del XII secolo.* Milan, 1965.

Matarasso, Pauline, trans. *"Aucassin and Nicolette" and Other Tales.* Baltimore, Md.: Penguin Books, 1971.

Menéndez Peláez, Jesús. *Nueva visión del amor cortés.* Oviedo: Universidad de Oviedo, 1980.

Menocal, María Rosa. *The Arabic Role in Medieval Literary History.* Philadelphia: University of Pennsylvania Press, 1987.

Mölk, Ulrich. *Trobar clus, trobar leu. Studien zur Dichtungstheorie der Trobadors.* Munich: Fink, 1968.

Muret, Ernest, and L. M. Defourques [Lucien Foulet and Mario Roques]. *Béroul: Le Roman de Tristan.* Paris: Champion, 1947.

Newman, F. X., ed. *The Meaning of Courtly Love.* Albany: State University of New York Press, 1968.

Nykl, Alois Richard. *Hispano-Arabic Poetry and Its Relations with the Old Provençal Troubadours.* Baltimore: J. H. Furst, 1946.

Oroz Arizcuren, Francisco J. *La lírica religiosa en la literatura provenzal antigua.* Pamplona: Institución Príncipe de Viana, 1972.

Paden, William D. "The Troubadour's Lady: Her Marital Status and Social Rank." *Studies in Philology* 72 (1975): 28–50.

————. "*Utrum Copularentur:* Of *Cors*." *L'Esprit Créateur* 19 (1979): 70–83.

Paris, Gaston. "Etudes sur les romans de la Table Ronde: Lancelot du Lac." *Romania* 12 (1883): 459–534.

Pérès, Henri. *La Poésie andalouse en arabe classique au XIe siècle: ses aspects généraux, ses principaux thèmes et sa valeur documentaire.* Paris: Maisonneuve, 1953.

Pickford, Cedric E., ed. *The Song of Songs: A Twelfth-Century French Version* [Ms. 173, Bibl. Mun. Le Mans]. London: Oxford University Press for the University of Hull, 1974.

Pollmann, Leo. *"Trobar Clus." Bibelexegese und hispano-arabische Literatur.* Forschungen zur romanischen Philologie, 16. Münster: Aschendorff, 1965.

Ricketts, Peter T., ed. *Le Breviari d'Amor de Matfre Ermengaud.* Vol. 5. Leiden: E. J. Brill, 1976. [Only vols. 2 and 5 have been published.]

Riquer, Martín de. *Los trovadores. Historia literaria y textos.* 3 vols. Barcelona: Editorial Planeta, 1975.

Robertson, D. W. "The Concept of Courtly Love as an Impediment to the Understanding of Medieval Texts." In *The Meaning of Courtly Love*, ed. F. X. Newman, 1–18. Albany: State University of New York Press, 1968.

Rosenberg, Samuel N., and Samuel Danon, eds. and trans. *The Lyrics and Melodies of Gace Brulé.* New York: Garland, 1985.

Saville, Jonathan. *The Medieval Erotic Alba: Structure as Meaning.* New York: Columbia University Press, 1972.

Scheludko, Dimitri. "Über die Theorien der Liebe bei den Trobadors." *Zeitschrift für romanische Philologie* 60 (1940): 191–234.

Settegast, F. "*Joi* in der Sprache der Trobadors." *Berichte der Kaiserlichen Sächsischen Gesellschaft der Wissenschaften* 41 (1899): 99–154.

Smith, Nathaniel B. "Games Troubadours Play." In *The Poetics of Love in the Middle Ages: Texts and Contexts,* ed. Moshe Lazar and Norris Lacy, 3–15. Fairfax, Va.: George Mason University Press, 1989.

Strecker, Karl, ed. *Die Gedichte Walters von Chatillon.* Berlin: Weidmannsche Buchhandlung, 1925.

Taeschner, F. "Die islamischen Futuwwabünde." *Zeitschrift der Deutschen Morgenländishcen Gesellschaft* 87, neue Folge 12 (1934): 6–49.

Topsfield, Leslie T. *Troubadours and Love.* Cambridge: Cambridge University Press, 1975.

Wechssler, Eduard. *Das Kulturproblem des Minnesangs,* vol. 1: *Minnesang und Christentum.* Halle: Niemeyer, 1909 [only volume published].

Wettstein, J. *"Mezura," l'idéal des troubadours, son essence et ses aspects* (diss., University of Zurich, 1945). Zurich: Leemann, 1945; repr. Geneva: Slatkine, 1974.

Wilcox, J. "Defining Courtly Love." *Papers of the Michigan Academy of Science, Arts, and Literature* 12 (1930): 313–25.

Wind, Bartina H., ed. *Les Fragments du roman de Tristan.* Leiden: Brill, 1950.

Zorzi, Diego. *Valori religiosi nella letteratura provenzale.* Publ. Univ. Catolica del S. Cuore, n.s., 44. Milan: Vita & Pensiero, 1954.

FOUR

Versification

Frank M. Chambers

The centuries following the decline and fall of the Roman Empire witnessed another decline and fall—that of classical Latin quantitative metrics, inherited from the Greeks and based on the length or duration of syllables, some inherently long, others inherently short. All verse was made up of various combinations of the two types, or "feet." For example, the standard epic line was nominally composed of six dactyls (long short short), but with important possibilities of modification: the sixth foot always had only two syllables, a long as in a dactyl, followed by either a short or a long; and in all other feet except the fifth the dactyl could be replaced by a spondee, consisting of two long syllables. Consequently, a dactylic hexameter might have as few as thirteen syllables or as many as seventeen. This quantitative system took no account of word accent, except insofar as the poet wove it into the longs and shorts of his verse for stylistic effects, just as he used alliteration and other rhetorical devices for similar purposes. The interplay of this accentual element with the rhythm of quantitative meters contributed greatly to the musical quality of the poem, but it had nothing to do with the technique of versification.

In time, the feeling for differences in quantity between one syllable and another was lost; but the cases in which word accent fell on a long syllable, as it often did, and unstressed syllables coincided with those that were metrically short, probably paved the way for a transition from the quantitative system to one based on word accent. At any rate, the meter of many late Latin poems is purely of this second kind:

Aestuans intrinsecus / ira vehementi
In amaritudine / loquar meae menti;

Factus de materia / levis elementi
Folio sum similis / de quo ludunt venti.[1]

Burning inwardly with vehement wrath, I speak in the bitterness of my mind. Transformed into the semblance of a light element, I am like a leaf, the plaything of the winds.

The structure of these lines is so regular that they resemble doggerel: each verse has precisely the same number of syllables (thirteen), each is divided into two parts by a caesura falling at precisely the same spot (after the seventh syllable), the meter consists of a succession of stressed and unstressed syllables (corresponding to the classical trochee), except that after the seventh syllable, which has a secondary accent because it is always final in a proparoxytone (e.g. *intrínsecùs*), the expected unstressed syllable is replaced by a pause (the caesura). In addition to metrical considerations, notice that this poem introduces another totally new element: the use of rhyme, which was never present in classical Latin verse, but which divides this little composition into monorhyme stanzas of four lines each. Throughout, all the rhymes are feminine, to use a later word: *ménti*, *móri*, *dátur*, and the like.

Poets who composed in the Romance vernaculars followed these late Latin models. In addition, however, a number of scholars believe that another influence was operative in the development of Romance, and particularly Occitan, verse: namely, that of the brilliant Hispano-Arabic culture to the south. It is undeniable that many contacts took place between Christians in the south of France and Muslims in Spain long before the time of the earliest troubadour whose work has been preserved, so that there was plenty of opportunity for poets of the Midi to become familiar with Arabic music, meters, and rhyme-schemes. Ramón Menéndez Pidal, in his *Poesía árabe y poesía europea*, makes a good case for their borrowing from at least one Arabic source, the *zejel* (also transcribed *zajal* or *zagal*). Poems of this type, written in a colloquial Arabic far removed from the older classical language, consist of four-line stanzas rhyming *aaab*, in which the *a*-rhymes change from stanza to stanza, whereas *b* remains constant throughout. There are sixteen Occitan poems composed in this pattern (e.g. No. 44 in Frank's *Répertoire métrique*); six of these are late religious pieces not usually considered part of the troubadour lyric legacy, although one, a *sermo* in seventy-eight stanzas, is the work of a recognized troubadour, Peire Cardenal. Of the remaining ten, only three belong to the early

1. The Archpoet, "His Confession, to the Arch-chancellor, Rainald of Dassel," *The Oxford Book of Medieval Latin Verse*, ed. F. J. E. Raby (Oxford: Clarendon Press, 1959), p. 263, lines 1–4.

period of Occitan verse: Guilhem VII's "Pos de chantar m'es pres talenz," Marcabru's "Emperaire, per vostre pretz," and a *tenso* or poetic debate between Marcabru and Uc Catola, "Amics Marchabrun, car digas." Now, the vast majority of *zejels* have one further element, two or more introductory verses, whose rhyme is picked up by the *b*-rhyme of the stanzas. This feature is not present in any of the poems mentioned thus far, but it does appear in five of the other compositions (all *dansas*) listed by Frank: one each by Cerveri de Girona and Guiraut d'Espanha, and three anonymous, which follow the *zejel* pattern exactly (aside from some apparent scribal blunders) and would seem to be imitations of it. To justify the earlier songs without the opening verses matching the *b*-rhyme, Menéndez Pidal points out that a few of the Hispano-Arabic *zejels* also lack these preliminary lines. Taking all these considerations into account, I think we should admit the strong possibility that the *zejel* served as a model for some troubadour songs, perhaps acting through the medium of popular verse.

The number of syllables in a line, once it had been decided upon, was fixed, with no permissible substitution of two unstressed for one stressed syllable, as might have been suggested by Latin versification. There was some tendency to alternate stress and the lack of it, so that one fairly often receives the impression of a trochaic or iambic meter; but this alternation was seldom considered obligatory, and eventually gave way in most areas to a simple counting of syllables, in which word accent merely played the role of a very effective rhetorical device, as it had done in classical days. Rhyme, however (sometimes weakened to assonance), was a sine qua non. One reason for this insistence on rhyme was doubtless the lessened importance of word stress as a determining factor in versification. Another reason was its usefulness as a mnemonic prompter for purveyors of songs in a largely illiterate society. Eight or ten syllables with relatively weak word accent (as compared, for example, with English or German), and with no obvious break into individual verses, would lack a strong, memorable quality and could easily be taken for prose. These, then, were the two main criteria for the identification of verse: a rigorous count of syllables in each line, and an identity of final sounds that served as a connecting link between two or more adjacent lines.

The troubadours, following these criteria, wove the raw material of medieval Occitan into a multiplicity of structural patterns ranging from the simple and unpretentious to the most elaborate, with many very beautiful songs in all parts of the spectrum. The first criterion, as we have seen, was an undeviatingly exact count of syllables in every line. The basic number, however, must be understood as applying to lines with oxytonic endings, abundant in Occitan, which were called masculine (*mascle*) by the poets themselves; paroxytonic (feminine, *femeni, femel*) rhymes added an extra syllable:

> Lo vers dech far en tal rima,
> Mascl'e femel que ben rim.
>> (Gavaudan 9:1–2).

> One must end a verse with a suitable rhyme sound, masculine or feminine, to match the rhyme scheme.

These designations were obviously inspired by adjectives, which had predominantly oxytonic endings in the masculine, paroxytonic in the feminine: *bel, bela.*

The number of syllables in troubadour verses varied from one to fourteen, the most frequently used being ten, eight, seven, and six, either alone or in a dazzling array of combinations, and the shortest occurring almost exclusively with other verses. The longer lines (ten syllables or more) invariably have a caesura: decasyllables after the fourth syllable, or occasionally after the sixth; alexandrines after the sixth. The syllable immediately preceding the caesura is ordinarily stressed, and final in its word (normal or oxytonic caesura):

> Ni richas cortz / ni beill don aut e gran.
>> (Gaucelm Faidit 50:30)

> Nor rich courts, nor fine gifts great and tall.

Sometimes, however, it is followed in the same word by an unstressed syllable, which is treated in two different ways. It may simply be counted as one of the syllables needed to fill out the rest of the line ("Italian" caesura), as in the second of these verses of eleven syllables, regularly broken after the seventh:

> Compaigno, non puesc mudár / qu'eo no m'effrei
> De novellas qu'ai auzi- / -das et que vei.
>> (Guillem de Peiteus 2:1–2)

> Comrades, I cannot help being upset by reports which I have heard and seen. (trans. Bond 7)

Or it may, on the other hand, be supernumerary, totally outside the normal count, thus giving an extra syllable to the line. This is called an "epic" caesura, from its frequent use in chansons de geste and other narrative poems:

> Ladoncs auziratz pla- / -nher / tans baros cavalers.
>> (*Croisade albigeoise*, ed. Martin-Chabot, vol. 3, line 208)

> Then you will hear many noble knights lament.

In relatively rare cases, the caesura falls after an unstressed syllable that occupies the place regularly reserved for the precaesural strong syllable ("lyric" caesura), as in the second verse here:

Ni que farán / li liurat a maltraire,
Cill que s'éran / en vostre servir mes . . .
(Gaucelm Faidit 50:32–33)

And what will *they* do, those who entered your service, and who will be abandoned to mistreatment?

This is not to be confused with Italian or epic caesura, in both of which the expected break comes in the middle of a word.

In addition to such disturbances as epic caesuras and feminine rhymes, certain other apparent anomalies complicate the counting of syllables. One is the optional elision of practically any unstressed final vowel before a word beginning with a vowel, in which case the two words are written as one in the manuscripts, although modern editors supply an apostrophe:

Don per lair vente giscle plou [l'air vent' e giscl' e plou]
(Raimbaut d'Aurenga 10:2)

[Now I see somber, dark, and stormy skies] because of which, in the atmosphere, the wind blows and whistles, and it rains. (trans. Pattison 100)

Similar to elision is the practice of suppressing a vowel or a consonant of a weak word and linking the remainder to a stronger word as an enclitic; the manuscripts treat the combination as one word, but the custom nowadays is to insert a raised period or a hyphen for the reader's benefit:

Amors, a vos meteussam [meteusa·m or meteussa-m] clam de vos
(Aimeric de Peguilhan 7:1)

Love, I make my complaint about you to you.

S'es quil [qui·l] tenha ni gen l'aplanh
(Peire Vidal 34:12)

If there is someone who will hold it [a hawk] or caress it.

Rassa, aissous [aisso·us] prec que vos plassa
(Bertran de Born 13:45)

Rassa [Geoffrey of Brittany], I pray that this may please you.

The full forms of the enclitics here are, of course, *me, lo* and *vos.*

The reduction of two syllables to one, as in elision and enclisis, is also achieved by blending the final and initial vowels of adjacent words together in pronunciation (synalœpha); this is not indicated at all in the text, as in the second of these heptasyllables:

> Ieu sui Arnautz qu'amas l'aura
> E chatz la lebr*e a*b lo bou.
> > (Arnaut Daniel 10:43–44)

I am Arnaut, who pile up the breeze and use the ox to hunt the hare.

Very frequently, however, contiguous vowels retain their full value (hiatus); this is also not indicated in the manuscripts or modern printed texts:

> Long*a ira a*t avol vid'auran
> Et totz temps dol, q'enaissi lor es pres.
> > (Gaucelm Faidit 50:37–38)

They [the friends of Richard Lion-Heart] shall have great sorrow and a sad life, for this is their fate.

> Es sa colors teun' e flaca,
> E fuelh e flors chai jos dels rams
> Si *que en* plais ni en blaca . . .
> > (Raimbaut d'Aurenga 10:8–10)[2]

Its [the sun's] light is now weak and feeble, and leaves and flowers fall from the branches, so that neither in hedges nor in groves [do I hear songs]. (trans. Pattison 100)

The reader must therefore decide, in this case as well, whether to treat adjacent vowels as one syllable or two; only the meter provides the correct answer.

The lyric poems (more accurately, songs) of the troubadours are with very few exceptions composed of stanzas designed to be sung to the same tune throughout any given piece, and necessarily uniform in metrical structure. Deviations are almost always the result of faulty transmission. But if the pattern of any particular poem remains constant from stanza to stanza, the sum total of all troubadour patterns is enormous. To begin with, the number of lines in a stanza may be anything from three to forty-two, although these extremes are rare: more usual line counts fall between five and twelve. The lines themselves differ greatly in length, and a stanza may have exclusively lines of the same dimension (isometric) or a combination of varying lengths (heterometric). Thus the possibilities for original patterns were superabundant, and a large number of them were turned to good use.

Rhyme-schemes gave additional opportunities for variation: coupled with those afforded by meter, they brought the stock of available patterns to an almost astronomical figure. I would estimate that, of the over 2,500 trou-

---

2. This poem is of disputed attribution. Its number in Pillet-Carstens is 392.5.

badour lyrics now extant, at least some 1,500 are unique in their precise combinations of meters and rhyme-schemes, not to mention the further distinctions of masculine and feminine rhymes and the order in which these
are placed. István Frank, in his *Répertoire*, lists 884 different rhyme-schemes,
and of these, 541 are represented by only one poem apiece. The others include from 2 to 306; the longest (that of the popular rhyme-scheme *abbaccdd*)
distinguishes 54 separate metrical patterns, taking into account the gender
of the rhymes, the isometric or heterometric nature of the stanzas, the length
of the verses, and the arrangement of these disparate elements.

Volume 2 of Frank's *Répertoire* contains a numbered list of all known
troubadour songs, arranged in alphabetical order, first by author and then
by incipits under each poet—a system originated by Karl Bartsch and greatly
amplified by Pillet and Carstens in their *Bibliographie der Troubadours*. From
these entries, reference is made to the appropriate rhyme-schemes of
volume 1, also arranged alphabetically and numbered, from *aaa* (1) to
abcdefghijklmn (884). To cite an example, the *canso* by Pons de Chapteuil
beginning "Tan mi destrenh" bears in volume 2 the composite number
375,24, with a reference to rhyme-scheme number 377:1. Turning to number 377 in volume 1, we find that it describes two poems under the scheme
ababccdc, as follows:

377
a b a b c c d c
10 10′ 10 10′ 10 10 10′ 10   1. Po Chapt. 375,24.   a: e‿en. b: ire‿aja.
                                   ch. 4 a 8, 1-4   c: en‿e. d: aja‿ire.
                                                          Capcaud.

8 8 8 8 7′ 7′ 8 7′   2. Rb Or. 389,36.   eis, ic, enga, ec.
                                   ch. 7 u 8, 2-4   Vers 5: «lenga».

In the first column, under the rhyme-scheme, we see that Pons's stanzas are
isometric, since all the lines are decasyllabic; the prime signs indicate
feminine rhymes. In the second column, there is an abbreviated identification of the poem in question, followed by the information that it is a *canso*
(*ch.* for *chanson*) consisting of four stanzas of eight lines each and that the
rhymes alternate from one stanza to the next (*a* for *coblas alternadas*). The
1-4 means that it has one *tornada* or *envoi* of four lines. In the third column,
we learn what the rhyme-sounds are, and how they alternate: *e* and *en*
changing places between *a* and *c*, *ire* and *aja* between *b* and *d*. "Capcaud"
means that these stanzas are *coblas capcaudadas:* the last rhyme-sound of one
stanza becomes the first of the next.

The second poem (with rhyme-scheme number 377:2) has a different
metrical structure, a combination of masculine octosyllables and feminine
heptasyllables. The author is Raimbaut d'Aurenga, whose identifying number is 389, and this poem is alphabetically the thirty-sixth of his composi-

tions. It too is a *canso* (*ch.*); it has seven stanzas of eight lines each, all of which have the same rhyme-sounds throughout the poem (*u* is for *coblas unissonans*), and it has two *tornadas* of four lines each. The third column gives us the rhyme-sounds, and tells us that the fifth line of each stanza ends with the word-refrain *lenga*.

In addition to the *coblas alternadas* and *unissonans* that we have just mentioned, other arrangements of rhymes by stanzas are *coblas singulars* (each stanza has a new set of rhymes) and *coblas doblas* (the stanzas rhyme together two by two). *Coblas retrogradadas*, a more elaborate version of *capcaudadas*, present the same rhyme sounds in all the stanzas, but the order is reversed from one stanza to the next:

> I. Mandat m'es que no·m recreia
> De cantar ni de solatz;
> E quar plus soven no fatz
> Chansos, m'o tenon a mal
> Sill a cui chans e deportz abelis;
> Et a grat de sos amis
> Deu hom far, com que l'en prenda.

> II. Tota corteza fazenda,
> Solatz, chant e joc e ris,
> Mou ben d'Amor, so m'es vis.
> Qu'en tot pretz ajud' e val
> Amors trop mais d'autra re, so sapchatz;
> Et ades n'es hom coitatz
> De far so que ben esteia.
>   (Pons de la Guardia 6:1–14)

I. People ask me not to give up song and merriment; those who like songs and amusement are annoyed with me because I don't compose anymore. One has to respond to the wishes of one's friends, no matter what happens.

II. Every courteous act, merriment, songs, and games and joy come from Love, in my opinion. In every detail of honor, Love helps you much more than anything else, you should know that. It is for the effect that one always wishes to do what is proper.

In the present poem, this system amounts to changing the rhyme-scheme from *abbcdde* to *eddcbba; c* remains constant, while *a* and *e* (both feminine) change places, as do *b* and *d* (both masculine).

Coblas capfinidas involve the repetition of the final rhyme-word of one stanza (or some form of it) in the first line of the next, not as a rhyme, but elsewhere in the line. Sometimes this repetition is carried through a number of verses; the first stanza of Raimbaut d'Aurenga's "Ab nou cor et ab nou talen" ends with the word *renovellar*, which leads to this second stanza:

> Qu'ieu *renovel* mon ardimen
> (Qu'ai *novel* ab veil pessamen)

Franc de *novel* ab ferm parven,
E chantem al *novel* temps clar
Que·l *novels* fruitz naison desen
E·l *novels* critz on Jois s'empren
E·ill auzeill intron en amar.

(35:8–14)

I renew my passion (for I have a new thought with the old) again sincere with a firm intention, and let us sing to the bright new season for there are brought forth swiftly the new fruit and the new cries in which joy is kindled, and the birds begin to love. (trans. Pattison 184)

In a number of poems, genuine rhymes are replaced or supplemented by *rims derivatius* (derivative or grammatical rhymes), of which this is a sample:

I. Bel m'es oimais qu'eu retraja
   Ab leugieira razon plana
   Tal chanson que cil l'entenda
   A cui totz mos cors s'aclina,
   Q'en la soa desmesura
   Mi part de si e·m desloigna:
   Tant m'es de merce estraigna
   Que no·l platz que jois m'en venga.

II. Non sai si·m muor o viu o veing
    O vau, c'a mal seignor estraing
    Serv que no·m met neus terme loing
    Que ja jorn vas me s'amesur.
    Et on ieu plus l'estau capcli,
    Negun de mos precs non enten,
    Anz sai qe m'aucirant de pla
    Li ben c'om de lieis mi retrai.

(Guilhem de Saint-Didier 4:1–16)

I. It pleases me to repeat in the future a certain song, simple and easy, so that she to whom my whole heart bows may hear it, she who in her injustice separates me from her and banishes me; she is so devoid of mercy toward me that it does not please her that joy should come to me.

II. I do not know whether I am living or dying or coming or going, for I serve a cruel, wicked suzerain who does not grant me even a remote appointed time, for now a day measures itself for me; and when I'm most humble toward her, she will hear none of my prayers; rather, I know that the good things people tell me about her will kill me.

Strictly speaking, all these verses are *rims estramps*, rhyming with no others in their own stanza but theoretically with corresponding verses in other stanzas. Such lines occur in many troubadour poems. Here, however, the "rhymes" in the next stanza are other forms of the same words (*veigna, veing;*

estraigna, estraing; etc.), and these occur in reverse order (*retrogradadas*). Another exceptional feature of these lines is that the first stanza has exclusively feminine rhymes, the second stanza exclusively masculine. This violates the normal troubadour insistence on an exact correspondence between stanzas in such matters, and would seem to create problems with the use of the same melody for all stanzas. In this case, the discrepancy is solved by making the feminine lines heptasyllabic and the masculines octosyllabic, with the result that all the verses have exactly eight syllables, although the rhythm differs notably between the two stanzas.

Tornadas, which we have mentioned in passing, consist of a few closing verses that almost invariably follow the structure and the rhymes of those immediately preceding in the last full stanza. They often indicate the person to whom the poem is to be sent, either by his or her own name or by a *senhal* or pseudonym. A song may have more than one *tornada*—commonly two, but sometimes as many as four. Here are the last stanza and the two tornadas of Raimon de Miraval's "S'a dreg fos chantars grazitz":

> VI. Domna, vos m'es del tot guitz,
> Qu'ieu non ai foldat ni sen
> Mas al vostre mandamen.
> Tan m'es lo dezirs corals
> Q'us ans me sembla jornals;
> Si·m fai loncs atens paors
> E si·m par mos chans folhors,
> Qu'en domney ses totz enguans
> Es greus termes de tres ans.
>
> VII. *Mais d'amic,* d'autras ricors,
> Que·us semblarian majors,
> Vos val Miravalh dos tans,
> Quar l'avetz ses totz engans.
>
> VIII. *N'Audiartz,* totas valors
> Daura domneys et amors,
> E no·us segra mais balans,
> Pus a vos platz que s'enans.
>
> (10:46–62)

VI. Lady, you are my guide in all things, for I have neither folly nor sense except by your orders. The desire I have at heart is so burning that a year seems like a day to me; however, a long wait frightens me, and my song seems senseless to me, because in a love free from all deceit, a delay of three years is hard.

VII. Better-than-Friend, Miraval is worth for you twice as much as any other wealth that might seem more valuable, for you own it without having to fear any fraud.

VIII. Sir Audiart, gallantry and love gild any value, and you will no longer be a prey to indecision, since it pleases you to exalt them.

"Mais d'amic" and "N'Audiartz" have been identified as *senhals* designating Loba de Puegnautier and Raimon VI of Toulouse, respectively.

Many troubadour lyrics contain refrains, which are treated rather differently in different genres. In *cansos* and frequently elsewhere, the complete refrain of two or more verses is repeated at the end of each stanza, as in this *sirventes* by Guilhem de Berguedan:

> Cansoneta leu e plana,
> Leugereta, ses ufana,
> Farai, e de Mon Marques,
> Del traichor de Mataplana,
> Q'es d'engan farsitz e ples,
> *A, Marques, Marques, Marques,*
> *D'engan etz farsitz e ples.*
> (10:1–14)

I shall make a light, plain little song, unpretentious, about my Marquis, the traitor of Mataplana, who is stuffed and filled with deceit. *Ah, Marquis, Marquis, Marquis, you are stuffed and filled with deceit!*

In *albas*, or dawn songs, the refrain usually consists of a single line, ending with the word *alba*, and likewise repeated at the end of every stanza:

> I. Reis glorios, verais lums e clartatz,
>   Deus poderos, Senher, si a vos platz,
>   Al meu companh siatz fizels aiuda;
>   Qu'eu no lo vi, pos la nochs fo venguda,
>   *et ades sera l'alba!*
>
> II. Bel companho, si dormetz o velhatz,
>   No dormatz plus, suau vos ressidatz,
>   Qu'en orien vei l'estela creguda
>   C'amena·l jorn, qu'eu l'ai be conoguda,
>   *Et ades sera l'alba!*
>   (Guiraut de Bornelh 54:1–10)

I. King of Glory, true light and brightness, lord God almighty, I beseech You to take my friend into Your loyal care; for I have not seen him since night fell, and the dawn will soon be here!

II. Fair friend, are you awake or sleeping still? Sleep no longer, gently rouse yourself; for I see the star that brings the day, rising in the East—for I recognized it well, and the dawn will soon be here! (trans. Sharman 167)

In *baladas*, the refrain (called a *respos*) usually consists of two verses, which serve as an overture to the poem. The first verse is repeated after the first line of every stanza (and after the second as well in longer stanzas), and the entire refrain is repeated at the end of each stanza:

> *Coindeta sui, si cum n'ai greu cossire*
> *Per mon marit, qar ne·l voil ne·l desire.*

Q'eu be·us dirai per qe son aisi drusa:
Coindeta sui, si cum n'ai greu cossire,
Qar pauca son, iuveneta e tosa,
Coindeta sui, si cum n'ai greu cossire
E degr'aver marit dunt fos ioiosa,
Ab cui totz temps pogues iogar e rire,
Coindeta sui, si cum n'ai greu cossire
*Per mon marit, qar ne*l voil ne·l desire.
(Anonymous, P-C 461,69:1–9)

I am pretty, and yet I am miserable because of my husband, for I neither want
him nor desire him, and I will tell you what I would like. I am pretty and yet
I have great misery; for I am small and young and tender, and I should have
a husband who would make me happy, with whom I could play and laugh. I
am pretty, and yet I am miserable because of my husband, for I neither want
him nor desire him.

At least, this is how modern editors treat the *respos* in *baladas;* the manuscripts give it in full at the beginning, but only use a word or two to signal
the repetitions.

In a *dansa*, the *respos* is longer than the refrain of a *balada*. It comes at the
beginning of the poem, as in the other genre, but it is not a true refrain and
is not repeated in any of the stanzas. Instead, the final verses of each stanza
simply echo the rhymes and the structure of the *respos.*

Similar to the full-fledged refrain of one or more verses is the repetition,
in the rhyming position, of the same word in every stanza of a song. The most
famous, and probably the most effective, use of such word-refrains is Jaufre
Rudel's insistence upon the very appropriate word *loing* in his song about
distant love:

  I. Lan qand li jorn son lonc e mai
     M'es bels douz chans d'auzels de *loing,*
     E qand me sui partitz de lai
     Remembra·m d'un' amor de *loing;*
     Vauc, de talan enbroncs e clis,
     Si que chans ni flors d'albespis
     No·m platz plus que l'inverns gelatz.

  II. Ja mais d'amor no·m gauzirai
      Si no·m gau d'est amor de *loing,*
      Qe gensor ni meillor non sai
      Vas nuilla part ni pres ni *loing.*
      Tant es sos pretz verais e fis
      Qe lai el renc dels Sarrazis
      Fos eu per lieis, chaitius clamatz.
                    (5:1–7, 8–14)[3]

---

3. In Pickens's edition, p. 164, version 1, the lines are 1–14; lines 8–14 of Pickens correspond to lines 29–35 of Jeanroy.

I. When the days are long in May I like a sweet song of birds from afar, and when I have gone away from there I am reminded of a love from afar; I go bent and bowed with desire, so that song nor hawthorn flower pleases me more than frozen winter.

II. Never shall I enjoy love if I do not enjoy this love from afar; for fairer nor better do I know anywhere near or far. So much is her worth true and fine that there in the kingdom of the Saracens would I be called, for her sake, captive. (trans. Pickens 165)

Notice that *loing* occurs not once but twice in every stanza, in the second and fourth verses.

Marcabru employs the word-refrain *vilana* in a *pastorela* to stress the difference in rank between the speaker (doubtless a knight) and the shepherdess he is trying to seduce:

I. L'autrier jost'una sebissa
Trobei pastora mestissa,
De joi e de sen massissa,
Si cum filha de *vilana:*
Cap' e gonel' e pelissa
Vest e camiza treslissa,
Sotlars e caussas de lana.

II. Ves lieis vinc per la planissa:
—Toza, fi·m ieu, res faitissa,
Dol ai car lo freitz vos fissa.
—Seigner, so·m dis la *vilana,*
Merce Dieu e ma noirissa,
Pauc m'o pretz si·l vens m'erissa,
Qu'alegreta sui e sana.

(30:1–14)

I. The other day, near a hedge, I found a humble shepherdess, full of joy and discretion. Like the daughter of a peasant woman, she wore a cape, a gown, a pelisse, and a knitted shirt, with coarse shoes and stockings of wool.

II. I went to her through the fields. "Girlie," I said, "pretty thing, I'm sorry the wind is chilling you." "Sire," said the peasant girl, "thanks to God and the one who gave me milk, I'm not worried about the wind that rumples my hair, because I'm happy and healthy."

The troubadours aimed at making each poem (or at least each *canso* or love song) a unique combination of meter, rhyme, and melody; and their structural originality was most impressive, as we have seen from István Frank's figures. They did, however, admit some important exceptions to the rule of a new form for every song. Certain "lesser" genres such as *sirventes* (polemic compositions), *coblas esparsas* (poems consisting of a single stanza), *tensos* and *partimens* (poetic discussions or debates involving two or more authors), and a few others were commonly excepted from the expectation of formal novelty; it became not only permissible, but very common practice, to set these poems to tunes already familiar, but with other words. Such an imitation is called a *contrafactum*. Since the number of troubadour poems accompanied in the manuscripts by musical notation is relatively small, it seldom happens that imitation can be proved by the identity of written music for two songs; evidence must therefore be sought elsewhere, and it assumes several forms. First of all, indebtedness may be taken for granted in a poem replying to another with the same metrical form and rhyme-scheme. An example of this is the series of *planhs* or funeral laments begun by the Italian troubadour Sordel in five monorhyme stanzas of eight alexandrines with a new rhyme sound for each stanza; here is the first:

> Planher vuelh en Blacatz en aquest leugier so,
> Ab cor trist e marrit; et ai en be razo,
> Qu'en luy ai mescabat senhor et amic bo,
> E quar tug l'ayp valent en sa mort perdut so;
> Tant es mortals lo dans qu'ieu non ai sospeisso
> Que jamais si revenha, s'en aital guiza no;
> Qu'om li traga lo cor e que·n manio·l baro
> Que vivon descorat, pueys auran de cor pro.
>
> (26:1–8)

I want to lament Sir Blacatz in this simple tune, with a sad, afflicted heart, and I have reason to do so, for in him I lost a master and a good friend, and because all worthy qualities have been lost in his death. So fatal is the damage that I have no hope that it will ever recover unless it be in this manner: let his heart be taken out, and let the barons who live without hearts eat of it. Then they will have heart in abundance.

Bertran d'Alamanon replied in a poem of the same format, but with different rhyme-sounds. The first stanza begins and ends with the following lines:

> Mout m'es greu d'En Sordel, car l'es faillitz sos senz . . .
> Mas ia no·i er perduz entrels flacs recrezenz;
>
> (15:1)

I am deeply grieved for Sir Sordel, since he has lost his mind . . . this heart shall not be wasted on heartless cowards.

Not to be outdone by these two, Peire Bremon Ricas Novas added a third *planh*, beginning thus:

> Pus partit an lo cor En Sordels e·N Bertrans . . .
>
> (20:1)

Since Sir Sordel and Sir Bertran have divided the heart [of Blacatz] . . .

All three poems follow the same pattern, including the optional use of epic caesuras, as in Sordel's sixth line, with an extra syllable after the sixth: *revenha*. There can be no doubt that all three were sung to the *leugier so* 'easy tune' mentioned by Sordel in his first verse, and presumably invented by him.

In a few cases, the author of a *contrafactum* admits his borrowing more or less explicitly. Guilhem de Berguedan, for example, begins one of his poems with these lines:

> Cavalier, un chantar cortes
> Aujatz *en qest son q'ai apres;*
> Et aujatz d'en Guillem pajes
>   Per qal raizon
> Mi clam de lui ni el de mi depois naison.
>
>   (17:1–5)

Cavaliers, hear a courtly song in this tune that I have learned, and hear for what reason I have been complaining of Sir Guillem the Catalonian, or he of me since we were born.

The words "to this tune that I have learned" refer quite clearly to a song by Guillem de Peiteus, the only other troubadour poem with precisely the same combination of meter and rhyme-scheme:

> Farai un vers, pos mi sonelh,
> E·m vauc e m'estauc al solelh;
> Domnas i a de mal conselh
>   E sai dir cals:
> Cellas c'amor de chevaler tornon a mals.
>
>   (5:1–5)

I shall do a song, since I am dozing and riding and staying in the sun. There are ladies who are ill-advised, and I can say which: those who turn a knight's love into pain. (trans. Bond 19)

Martín de Riquer, in his edition of Berguedan, names as the model Guillem's poem "Un vers farai de dreit nien," similar in form, but differing from the two we have considered in having an extra rhyme that divides the final alexandrine into two lines—one of eight syllables and one of four:

> Un vers farai de dreit nien:
> Non er de mi ni d'autra gen,
> Non er d'amor ni de joven,
>   Ni de ren au,
> Qu'enans fo trobatz en durmen
>   Sus un chivau.
>
>   (4:1–6)

I'll do a song about nothing at all: it won't be about me nor about anything else, for it was composed earlier while [I was] sleeping on a horse. (trans. Bond 15)

The most famous example of acknowledgment by a troubadour that he is indebted to another for the melody he is using comes in Bertran de Born's song "D'un sirventes no·m cal far loignor ganda," the fourth stanza of which runs as follows:

Conseill vuoill dar *el son de n'Alamanda*
Lai a·n Richart, si tot no lo·m demanda:
Ja per son frair mais sos homes non blanda.
Nonca·is fai el, anz asetg' e·ls aranda,
Tol lor chastels e derroc' et abranda
　　Devas totz latz!
E·l reis tornei lai ab cels de Guarlanda
　　E l'autre, sos coignatz.

(11:25–32)

[First line: I won't put off a *sirventes* any longer.] I want to give some advice to Richard, there, to the tune of Lady Alamanda, though he hasn't asked me for it: no more should he flatter his men for fear they might turn to his brother. He never does anyway; instead he besieges them and chases them around, steals their castles, and smashes and burns in every direction! Meanwhile, I suppose, the Young King will tourney up there with the men of Guarlanda, and the other one, too, his brother-in-law. (trans. Paden, Sankovitch, and Stäblein 387)

Bertran's contemporaries could identify "el son de n'Alamanda" at once as an allusion to the *tenso* purportedly composed by Guiraut de Bornelh and a lady named Alamanda, but very possibly the work of Guiraut alone:

S'ie·us qier cosseill, bell'ami'Alamanda,
No·l me vedetz, q'om cochatz lo·us demanda;
Qe so m'a dich vostra dompna truanda
Que loing sui fors issitz de sa comanda
Que so qe·m det m'estrai er'e·m desmanda.
　　Qe·m cosseillatz?
C'a pauc lo cors dinz d'ira no m'abranda,
　　Tant fort en sui iratz.

(57:1–8)

If I seek your advice, my fair, sweet Alamanda, do not refuse me this, for a desperate man asks it of you; for your deceitful mistress has told me that I have strayed far beyond the bounds of her authority, so that what she [once] granted me she now takes back and retracts. What do you advise me to do? For this fills me with such sorrow that grief almost sets the depths of my heart on fire. (trans. Sharman 387)

Bertran's frank admission that the source of his *sirventes* was Guiraut's *tenso*, though interesting, was not necessary; his imitation would have been obvious without it. His *contrafactum* has not only the same metrical format and rhyme-scheme as his model, but also the same rhyme-sounds as those of Guiraut's first stanza; and this brings us to the clearest and most reliable evidence of formal borrowing among the troubadours. Beginning with Bertran de Born, or at any rate contemporaneously with him, it became quite customary to include rhyme-sounds among the features that were appropriated from the work of earlier poets. This was evidently not frowned upon in the lesser genres, but was perhaps even considered a compliment to the original composer. The word *composer* is used advisedly. We must not forget that troubadour lyrics were not simply poems, but songs. Two important words in the declarations of indebtedness we have read stress this fact: *el son* 'to (literally "in") the tune' of such and such a poem. To the troubadours, the tune was an integral part of the song, composed by them along with the words, and if a song was imitated, it was primarily because of the tune.

No description of troubadour versification would be complete without some consideration of non-lyric verse, although this is far less important from our point of view than the songs we have been considering. The fundamental difference in form between the two types of verse is that the lyric is strophic, divided into uniform stanzas, while the non-lyric is not. Even a love letter or *salut (d'amor)*, though closely related to the courtly lyrics in theme, is not made up of stanzas, but follows the same pattern as one group of narrative poems: octosyllables (or occasionally hexasyllables), rhyming in pairs (*rimes plates*). But the *salut*, which ordinarily begins with the word *Domna*, may have the same word as an unrhymed ending, or *bioc*, as in these lines:

> Dona, no·us aus de pus prejar,
> Mas Dieu vos sal e Dieu vos *gar,*
> Sie·us play, rendetz me [ma] salut,
> Pus Amors m'a per vos vencut,
> Vensa·us per mi tot eyssamens
> Amors, qe totas cauzas vens!
> [Domna].

(Arnaut de Marueill, Salut d'amour 1:203–9)

Lady, I do not dare to pray for you anything more than God save you and God guard you. If it please you, return to me my greetings; since Love has conquered me through you, may it conquer you likewise, through me, Love which conquers all things, Lady!

Verse novels, such as *Flamenca* and *Jaufre*, are also written in rhyming couplets of octosyllables. Here is a short passage from *Flamenca:*

> Mais anc no·i ac domna neisuna
> Non volgues Flamenca semblar;
> Qu'aissi con es soleils ses par
> Per beutat e per resplandor,
> Tals es Flamenca entre lur,

Quar tant es fresca sa colors,
Siei esgart douz e plen d'amors,
Siei dig plazent e saboros,
Que la bellazers e·l plus pros
E que plus sol esser jugosa
Estet quais muda et antosa.
            (Gschwind ed., lines 536–46)

Among the ladies, there was not one who would not have wished to resemble Flamenca, for just as the sun has no equal for beauty and brilliance, such is Flamenca among women. So fresh is her color, so sweet and full of love her words, that the most beautiful and the worthiest, and the one who was wont to be the most playful, remained as if mute and ashamed.

The other main type of non-lyric verse is that used in epics and similar poems. The basic lines have either ten or twelve syllables—the same throughout the poem—and they are grouped in *laisses* of indeterminate length, like those of the French chansons de geste; but the Occitan epics differ from the French in the use of full rhyme instead of assonance to set each *laisse* apart from the others. The following verses are from the most famous Occitan epic, *Girart de Rossilhon*:

Ben pro de li se trais: non si fain muz:
"Donne, per amor Deu, qui fait vertuz,
E per amor des sains qu'avez quesuz,
E per amor Girart qui fun tes druz,
Donne, te cri marcet qu'ere m'ajuz."
La reïne li dis: "Bons om barbuz,
Que sabez de Girart? Qu'es devenguz?"
            (Hackett ed., vol. 2, lines 7818–23)

He moved close to her; he did not pretend to be mute. "Lady, for the love of God, who works miracles, and for the love of the saints whom you have implored, and for the love of Girart, who was your lover, lady, I beg your mercy, that you help me now." The queen said to him: "Good bearded man, what do you know about Girart? What has become of him?"

Notice that the caesura in these verses falls after the sixth syllable, rather than the fourth, which is more usual in the decasyllable.

The *Chanson de la croisade albigeoise* is written in alexandrines, with a verse of six syllables at the end of each *laisse*, which is attached to the following *laisse* in one of two ways. In the first section of the poem, by Guilhem de Tudela, it rhymes with the following *laisse*, while in the anonymous second section it is repeated more or less exactly as the first half of the next line. This passage is taken from the anonymous part of the epic:

Mas de laïns perdero tal que i era mestiers,
N'Aimeriguet lo jove, cortes e plazentiers;

Don fo grans lo dampnatges e·l mals e·l desturbiers
    A totz cels de la vila.
A totz cels de la vila, car en Symos moric,
Venc aitals aventura que l'escurs esclarzic,
Car la clartatz alumpna, que granec e fluric
E restaurec Paratge e Orgolh sebelic.
            (Martin-Chabot ed., 3:208–12)

[In the fall of the city] those within lost one who was needed, Sir Aimeriguet the young, courteous and agreeable, whose loss was a great injury and harm and confusion to all those of the city.

    But to all those of the city, Sir Simon's death brought such good fortune that the darkness lighted up, the clarity grew brighter and budded and flowered and restored nobility and buried arrogance.

After the death of their leader, Simon de Montfort, the crusaders withdrew from Toulouse, which they had besieged, leaving much of their gear behind them; and those in the city, though they too had suffered the loss of a noble soldier, rejoiced greatly at the end of the siege. Notice, incidentally, that each of the alexandrines quoted here has an epic caesura; this is characteristic of the second part of the *Chanson de la croisade albigeoise.*

The troubadours are credited with having invented (or popularized) the concept of "courtly love," which influenced the course of European poetry for centuries, and which has been discussed elsewhere in this book. But perhaps as important as the content of their verse is the form in which this content is presented. On numerous occasions, troubadours express concern with the art and craftsmanship that go into the making of a poem. They often use the vocabulary of woodworking to describe their efforts, as in these lines of Aimeric de Peguilhan, which echo similar verses by Raimbaut d'Aurenga, Arnaut Daniel, and others:

Ses mon apleich   non vau ni ses ma lima
Ab que fabreich motz   et aplan e lim,
Car ieu non veich   d'obra sotil e prima
De nuilla leich   plus sotil ni plus prim,
Ni plus adreich   obrier en cara rima
Ni plus pesseich   sos digz ni meills los rim.
            (47:1–6)

I do not go about without my plane and my file, with which I fabricate words and plane and file them, for I see no subtle and delicate work of any sort subtler or more delicate (than mine), nor a more skillful worker in precious rimes, nor one who breaks up his words more, nor who rimes better (than I). (trans. Shepard-Chambers ed., 224)

In other words, a poem demands hard work and great care on the part of its author. This belief in poetry as a true art form, which is evident both in their precepts and in their practice, is a second great contribution of the troubadours to subsequent generations of poets.

WORKS CITED

The quotations in this chapter are from the critical editions cited in the List of Troubadour Editions in the Appendix, and in particular from the following editions: Guiraut de Bornelh (Sharman); Jaufre Rudel (Pickens). All translations are my own except as indicated.

Chambers, Frank M. *An Introduction to Old Provençal Versification.* Memoirs of the American Philosophical Society, 167. Philadelphia: American Philosophical Society, 1985.

Frank, István. *Répertoire métrique de la poésie des troubadours.* Bibliothèque de l'Ecole des Hautes Etudes, 302, 308. 2 vols. Paris: Champion, 1953–57.

Jeanroy, Alfred. *La Poésie lyrique des troubadours.* 2 vols. Paris: Privat, 1934.

Menéndez Pidal, Ramón. *Poesía árabe y poesía europea.* 2d ed. Buenos Aires: Espasa-Calpe Argentina, 1943.

Nykl, Allardyce R. *Hispano-Arabic Poetry and Its Relations with the Provençal Troubadours.* Baltimore: Johns Hopkins University Press, 1946.

Pillet, Alfred and Henry Carstens. *Bibliographie der Troubadours.* Schriften der Königsberger Gelehrten Gesellschaft, Sonderrreihe, 3. Halle: Niemeyer, 1933; repr. New York: Burt Franklin, 1968.

FIVE

Music

Hendrik van der Werf

THE MUSIC AND ITS RELATION TO THE POETRY

Over the centuries, and almost without interruption, the poems of the troubadours have received considerable attention from literary critics. This tradition started with treatises written during the late thirteenth century and reached one of its culminations in Dante's fascinating evaluations of poets and poems. Johannes de Grocheio, writing late in the thirteenth century, was the only music theorist of the time to mention secular monophonic song. He seems to have been quite familiar with trouvère songs, but he gave no evidence of having known any troubadour. Furthermore, the little he wrote about French songs is far from explicit, and, in this century, it has caused considerable confusion and some heated debate. It was not until very late in the nineteenth century that the melodies preserved with medieval poems started to attract serious attention from scholars. Musicians, in general, are not overly interested in music for a single voice without instrumental accompaniment; this may account for the fact that the first studies and editions of troubadour and trouvère songs were written not by conservatory-trained musicians but by scholars who had received their higher education in departments of Romance literature.

Making the melodies available in modern notation was one of the primary concerns of these early experts, so that issues of rhythm and meter stood in the foreground of study and debate. At that time, it was virtually taken for granted that all music was precisely measured. Although in the second half of the thirteenth century so-called "mensural" notation enabled music scribes to indicate duration of individual pitches with great precision, the vast majority of the troubadour and trouvère melodies are extant in a nonmensural notation. Consequently, establishing the original meter of a given melody was the first task faced by editors of these songs.

What seemed to be a great break in this search came with the discovery of what came to be called "modal rhythm." Several thirteenth-century authors described in minute detail the various "modes" in which motets and related genres could be measured. A motet is a composition for two, three, or four voices in which each voice sings its own text. Each rhythmic mode involves a consistent alternation of short and long syllables in a ratio of either 1:2 or 1:2:3. The precise sequence of events is unclear, but Johann Baptist Beck and Pierre Aubry more or less simultaneously published the theory that all troubadour and trouvère songs were in the same rhythmic modes as the motets. Although the evidence for the theory was very thin, it led to a bizarre and tragic episode when Beck and Aubry became embroiled in a dispute about who had been the first to discover modal rhythm in chansons. Shortly after a jury of lawyers decided in favor of Beck, Aubry was fatally wounded while training for a duel; Beck immigrated to the U.S.A.

Even after this sad incident, modal rhythm in troubadour and trouvère songs remained a subject of great controversy and, sometimes, unscholarly debate. At its center was the theory that textual accentuation was assumed to indicate which of the rhythmic modes described in treatises about polyphonic music was valid for a given monophonic song. Friedrich Gennrich, whose university training had been primarily in literature, became a prolific and adamant advocate of the modal theory. Most other literary experts remained on the side lines; some expressed doubt, but only one took a strong position. Seemingly exasperated with the dismal state of affairs, Carl Appel in 1934 took it upon himself to publish the melodies of Bernart de Ventadorn. In the introduction to this work, *Die Singweisen Bernarts von Ventadorn*, he conclusively showed that accentuation in the text did quite the opposite of proving any alternation of long and short syllables in a musical performance. In his transcriptions, as some had done before him and as many more did after him, Appel resorted to a nonmensural form of modern notation. His efforts did not have much effect. Perhaps in part because Appel made a few errors in his transcriptions, the few trained musicologists who paid attention to nonliturgical monophonic song were divided, and, until very recently, almost all authors of textbooks on the history of music unquestioningly accepted the modal theory.

Apparently, my first writings about accentuation and duration in troubadour and trouvère songs, beginning with a chapter in my Columbia dissertation of 1964, were not as clear as they should have been; they may even have caused some confusion. Especially my using the term *declamatory rhythm* may have led some readers to think that, in a medieval performance, all syllables were of approximately equal duration. Instead, my research made me conclude that the notes in the manuscripts represent pitches of more or less equal duration and that, therefore, the songs were performed in a somewhat freely flowing rhythm that allowed composers and performers to do as much justice to pitches, syllables, and words as tradition prescribed. Despite its shortcomings, my reasoning on this topic prompted many scholars, especially experts on medieval literature, to discard or at least to question the validity of the modal theory. It has been especially pleasing that my reasoning encouraged professional performers of early music to abandon modal rhythm altogether, but I fear that my inadequate presentation of the positive aspects of my conclusions may have contributed to the fairly widespread practice of performing medieval songs in a somewhat isosyllabic manner. Considering the strong hold the modal theory once had upon certain groups of scholars, especially experts on medieval music, it is not surprising that some continue to defend it. In the mid-1970s, the musicologist Hans Tischler suddenly became the most prolific and eager proponent of modal rhythm. It should be pointed out, however, that much of his argumentation is essentially a reiteration of statements made by such early experts as Aubry, Beck, and Gennrich.

In part because I have already had several opportunities to discuss the weakness of the modal theory, it will receive little attention in this essay. Instead, accentuation and duration will be treated in a largely positive fashion based on my analysis of the melodies, especially those that have come to us in multiple versions. Above all, I want to discuss how and when the melodies were preserved, how the troubadours as composers may have functioned in a musical culture that may not have used notation, and to what extent there was an intimate relationship between a poem and its melody.

THE EXTANT MELODIES

No more than four of the many manuscripts that preserve troubadour poems also contain music, and none of these has the melody for every poem it contains. The largest of the four (manuscript *R*) is the only one from the region where Occitan was the primary language, while the second largest (*G*) was compiled in northern Italy (see Chapter 15 for more on troubadour manuscript sigla). The other two (*W* and *X*) stem from France and are primarily trouvère manuscripts that contain sections with troubadour poems, most of them with music. In the latter two sources, the texts are "Frenchified," as illustrated in the *W* versions of Examples 1, 2, and 3 (examples appear in the appendix to this chapter, p. 149). (In the trouvère bibliographies these two sources carry the sigla *M* and *U*, respectively.) The two trouvère manuscripts date from the middle of the thirteenth century and thus are among the earliest sources for troubadour and trouvère songs; the two troubadour manuscripts date from ca. 1400 and thus are rather late sources. To these we may add the *Breviari d'amor* by Matfre Ermengau, three copies of which contain the music for one of Matfre's own poems

(P-C 297,4). Obviously, songs of the latest authors do not occur in manuscripts *W* and *X*, but all four contain compositions by early troubadours, most notably Bernart de Ventadorn and Jaufre Rudel. However, they preserve not one single melody by either Guillem de Peiteus or Cercamon. Together, these collections preserve some 250 troubadour melodies, in other words, there is music for only approximately 10 percent of the extant Occitan poems. These melodies stem from some forty-five different composers, slightly more than 10 percent of the troubadours known by name. In comparison to the enormous wealth of Gregorian chant, and even in comparison to the approximately 1,400 extant trouvère melodies, this is a meager legacy. It is even smaller than the melodic treasure preserved on the Iberian Peninsula with the *Cantigas de Santa Maria*. But in comparison to medieval melodies with German, Italian, or English texts, it is a rich harvest.

The musical repertory of the troubadours has been published three times, namely by Friedrich Gennrich (1958–65); by Ismael Fernandez de la Cuesta, with Robert Lafont as text editor; and by Hendrik van der Werf, with Gerald A. Bond as text editor (1984). These editions differ from one another on some important points. With very few exceptions, the melodies of the troubadours have been preserved in a notation that does not indicate duration. Accordingly, Fernandez de la Cuesta and van der Werf transcribe the melodies in a modernized version of the medieval notation and they give all extant versions in their entirety. For all songs, the former gives the shape of the medieval notes above his transcriptions,[1] the latter does so only in the few cases in which a scribe seems to have differentiated between long and short notes. In his volume with transcriptions (1958), Gennrich gives all melodies in modal rhythm, and, with little or no discussion thereof, he makes numerous corrections and emendations. In the volume with commentary (1960), he gives the melodies from manuscript *R* in diplomatic transcription but without text. In the transcriptions, multiple versions are conflated into one melody; at the end of the volume with commentary, they are given in juxtaposition but without text. In order to keep down the size of their publications and avoid unnecessary duplication, none of the editors gives texts beyond the first strophes. Both Gennrich and Lafont give texts conflated from all sources; Bond gives each text as it occurs in the manuscript(s) with music. Although the above editions serve well to supply the melodies for poems already available in modern edition, it is hoped that future editions will contain both texts and melodies, as was done in the recent editions of the songs by Bertran de Born (Paden) and Raimon de Miraval (Switten).

---

1. In this edition, all liquescent notes, or plicas, are erroneously printed as square notes with a stem.

The songs that have music in manuscripts *G, R, W,* and *X,* and that are attributed in these or other sources to a known troubadour, form a remarkably uniform group. All but two of them are strophic songs (i.e., all strophes are sung to the same music), and the texts of most of them deal with *fin'amor.* Where form is concerned, a lai by Aimeric de Peguilhan (P-C 10,45) is the most direct departure from this norm, while an estampida by Raimbaut de Vaqueiras ("Kalenda maya," P-C 392,9) is both an estampida and a strophic song, in that each strophe is an estampida. (Cf. van der Werf 1980, and Chapter 2 in this volume.) Other and more substantial departures are to be noted in a relatively small number of anonymous songs, most of which occur exclusively in sources other than the four mentioned above or were added to manuscript *W* by various scribes late in the thirteenth or early in the fourteenth century. The main link between these songs and the troubadour repertory is their language, and even that link often is tenuous because in many of the anonymous songs the Occitan is contaminated in a way that makes Occitan origin doubtful. The difference between the central and peripheral sources is interestingly illustrated by editorial decisions made for the three existing editions of all troubadour melodies. Gennrich and Fernandez de la Cuesta take the language, even when it is contaminated, as sole or primary criterion. Gennrich includes every song, and Fernandez de la Cuesta almost every song, that has, at least in part, an Old Occitan text. Van der Werf and Bond draw upon outside sources only for contrafacts of troubadour melodies that also occur in manuscripts *G, R, W,* and *X,* and thus exclude songs whose music and melodic rhythm are better studied in a different context.[2] By not publishing them again, they hope to encourage others to describe and edit them in a more appropriate context, as suggested below. To a large extent, van der Werf and Bond's criteria for inclusion coincide with the distinction between "high" and "lower" styles proposed recently by Christopher Page (16).

For the sake of completeness, we may briefly survey the Occitan songs that have been preserved with music but are atypical for the troubadour repertory. In addition to the lai by Aimeric de Peguilhan, four anonymous songs of the sequence type ("descort" or "lai") have been preserved with music.[3] It is to be hoped that they will soon be included in a large-scale study of Latin, French, German, and Occitan songs belonging to the vast sequence

2. Two strophic songs are excluded from their edition, namely, "A l'entrada del tens clar" and "L'autrier m'iere levatz" (P-C 461,12 and 461,148). The former is a dancing song whose original language is likely to have been French; the latter is a contrafact of the Latin song "Homo considera." See Gennrich 1958, nos. 244, 252; Fernandez de la Cuesta 721 and 794.

3. P-C 10,45, 461,37 (preserved exclusively as a late addition to manuscript *W*), 461,122, and 461,124 (both occur only in manuscript *W* and trouvère manuscript *T*). See Gennrich 1958, nos. 182, 280–82; Fernandez de la Cuesta 402, 732, 749, and 765.

family. Several songs of the virelai type were added by later scribes to manuscript *W*.[4] They should be included in a much-needed study of the monophonic songs of that genre dating from the thirteenth and fourteenth centuries. A late-eleventh- or early-twelfth-century Aquitanian manuscript containing Latin religious songs for one or two voices has three songs with Occitan or mixed Latin-Occitan texts.[5] They belong in a study of the monophonic *versus* of the eleventh and twelfth centuries. Furthermore, their melodies are notated without staffs or clefs, so that transcription must be rather conjectural. Four motets exist that have "Frenchified" Old Occitan texts (or, more likely, "Occitanized" French texts).[6] They are compositions for two or three voices, each voice with its own text. They have been preserved exclusively in French manuscripts with polyphonic music, and as such they have been published repeatedly in modern editions of motets. Two paper sheets, now lost, stemming from Catalonia and dating from the later thirteenth century contained four songs with Occitan (or "Occitanized") texts.[7] In contents, their texts are only minimally related to a typical troubadour song; their form suggests that they would be of great interest in a study of the fourteenth-century virelai and its predecessors. Finally, a fourteenth-century dramatization of the life of St. Agnes contains several songs, including two contrafacts of known troubadour songs (Jeanroy).[8] Most of their melodies are very poorly notated. The contrafacts can be transcribed only with the help of their models, and the other songs cannot be transcribed with sufficient accuracy to allow meaningful study of the music. (The contrafacts are included in van der Werf 1984.)

For about one-fourth of the troubadour melodies we have multiple versions, either because the song involved occurs with music in more than one source or because its melody was also used for another song, a so-called

---

4. P-C 461,20a, 461,51a, 461,92, 461,196, 461,230 (all five are preserved exclusively as late additions to manuscript *W*), and 461,192a (preserved only in trouvère manuscript *V*). See Gennrich 1958, nos. 257–62; Fernandez de la Cuesta 726, 738, 741, 805, and 810.

5. Paris, B.N., f. lat. 1139; Gennrich 1958, nos. 1–3. These songs are not included by Fernandez de la Cuesta. Gennrich includes three more religious texts with music, including two troped epistles, or "epîtres farcies," that fall outside of the troubadour repertory (Gennrich 1958, nos. 4–6).

6. Gennrich 1958, nos. 283–86. By omitting the tenor, Fernandez de la Cuesta (746, 788, 796, 801, and 812) edits the motets as monophonic songs. See also Tischler 1982, nos. 34, 71, 212; and Tischler 1978, no. 170.

7. Gennrich 1958, nos. 246, 255, 258; Fernandez de la Cuesta 728, 730, 804, and 809. These songs were published with complete texts, extensive discussion, and photocopies of the manuscript in Bond.

8. Gennrich 1958, nos. 265–79; Fernandez de la Cuesta 740, 745, 786, 791, 814. One of the songs is a contrafact of the alba by Guiraut de Bornelh (P-C 242,64; van der Werf and Bond 1984, 163*). A fragmentary melody is said to stem from Guillem de Peiteus (P-C 183,10; van der Werf 1984, 151*).

contrafact. Most of the contrafacts with music come from outside the troubadour repertory and are found in sources other than the four mentioned above. Not surprisingly, most of them are trouvère songs, and almost all of the others have a Latin text. In addition, a contrafact of a song by Cadenet (P-C 106,14) occurs among the *Cantigas de Santa Maria,* and a song by Walther von der Vogelweide has been preserved with a melody found also with a song by Jaufre Rudel (Example 1). Multiple versions of a given melody never are identical to one another. The differences among them range from relatively minor (Example 2) to very significant (Example 1); in some cases one may even wonder whether the tunes preserved with a given text are related to one another. It seems that, for a long time, the differences among multiple versions caused editors considerable problems. In recent research, however, the similarities and differences among multiple versions have become a rich source of information about the composition, the transmission, and even the performance of the songs. This different way of seeing the manuscript tradition is reflected in the manner in which multiple versions are treated. Whereas earlier editors conflated multiple versions into one melody, it now is general practice to include all of them in their entirety.

ORAL AND WRITTEN TRANSMISSION

It would have been helpful for our evaluation of the differences and similarities among multiple versions if we had had detailed and reliable information about those who participated in relaying the songs from poet-composer to extant manuscript. Now we must judge these intermediaries' ability, interest, and attitude by the differences and the similarities among multiple versions. For some scholars, this approach comes dangerously close to circular reasoning; for example, we may conclude from the nature of the variants that they were made by connoisseurs, defending our conclusion by arguing that songs of such an esoteric character could have been transmitted only by connoisseurs. For others, including myself, the following reconstruction of the transmission is a "package deal" in which each component either stands or falls with all the other components. Study of multiple versions shows clearly that the melodies were not transmitted exclusively in written form, as was generally accepted until early in this century. Instead, the songs were initially disseminated by word of mouth (or rather by word and pitch of mouth) and written down at some later date. In other words, the differences among multiple versions were not caused exclusively, and not even primarily, by incompetence and inaccuracy on the part of medieval copyists. Instead, most differences represent variants that occurred during oral transmission. As far as the music is concerned, this conclusion may be drawn from the sheer number of variants. If the differences are due to scribal errors, the extant manuscripts contain more wrong than correct notes. The connoisseurs involved in collecting the songs would not have been so ignorant as to accept—and pay for—faulty collections. More important, scribal errors should have resulted in incoherent or awkward melodies, whereas the extant melodies, in general, are far from awkward, and, as will be discussed shortly, many melodies are quite cohesive. The strongest and most objective evidence for oral transmission comes from songs in which the first and second pair of verses are sung to the same music (their form may be represented as AB AB X).[9] As in Examples 1 and 5, multiple versions of such songs differ much less from one another in the AB than in the X section. If the differences had been due to scribal inaccuracy, one would have to assume that, for almost every song in this form, the scribes were alert when copying the first four verses, that they suddenly turned sleepy and sloppy exactly at the beginning of the fifth verse, and again became alert when starting on the next melody. When learning a song upon hearing it, however, one would learn the A and B melodies better than those of the X section because the former occur twice as often as the latter.

Since oral transmission of the melodies must have taken place in audible form, we may refer to all participants as "singers" or "performers," leaving out of consideration whether they were professional entertainers and whether they should be called "jongleurs," "minstrels," or yet something else. Although the assumption that differences among multiple versions represent variants made by medieval connoisseurs and experts is not new, we are still engaged in studying its far-reaching and numerous implications. Unlike their twentieth-century successors, medieval singers were not required to perform a song always in exactly the same way. If those involved in the oral tradition were, indeed, experts and connoisseurs, they may well have improved upon the quality of a song. Hence, we are unable to determine the original text and melody of a troubadour song. Components that were considered essential either for a given song or for the repertory in general are likely to have been less subject to variation than incidental elements. The rhyme-sounds and the syllable count of a poem rarely vary from one version to another, and we may conclude that they were among the most essential elements of a troubadour text. On the opposite extreme, the many variants in the number and order of strophes for a given song suggest that singing all strophes and singing them in a specific order were not absolute requirements. In the music, we find that maintaining a song's melodic contour and underlying structure (to be discussed shortly) was essential, whereas retaining the precise number of pitches and, to some

---

9. In discussions of notational peculiarities, most notably chromatic alterations, one often must distinguish between what is entered on one line of the manuscript and what constitutes one line in a printed edition of a poem. For that reason, I habitually use the word "verse" for the latter and restrict usage of the word "line" to the former.

extent, even the precise level of the pitches for a given syllable must have been of much less importance. Despite the inherent danger of assessing the relative value of textual and musical variants, we can safely say that, in general, the variants in the music are not only more numerous but also more significant than the variants in the text. Thus we may conclude that the transmitters of the songs paid close attention to form and content of the poems while treating most melodic aspects more freely.

Tracing the dissemination from its starting point, we must not lose sight of the simple fact that the poet-composer was also the first performer of a song. Thus, it was the troubadour himself, or the trobairitz herself, who set the way a given text and melody would be performed. For the next stage, we must keep in mind that a troubadour song was not the normal fare for lower-class performers who eked out a living by entertaining bystanders at the medieval version of a county fair. Conversely, performing for pecuniary or other tangible remuneration does not seem to have been a very lucrative occupation. Thus, a count of Poitiers, a comtessa de Dia, a prince de Blaya, and anyone who had a choice would have turned to more secure sources of income than were available to jongleurs and minstrels. This, however, does not mean that a financially secure person would never sing for his or her equals; on the contrary, most troubadours and trobairitz are likely to have been active participants in the transmission of songs, and they probably did not restrict that activity to their own creations. The poet-composer of a song may have performed his or her creation on several occasions and for different audiences. He or she thus may have been the first to vary text and melody. Finally, those who, during the second half of the thirteenth century, commissioned a written collection of troubadour songs are likely to have been connoisseurs who would not entrust this costly task to scribes who knew nothing about the art of "finding" and performing cansos and verses (see also van der Werf 1993).

The individual stages of writing down and copying songs may need some elaboration. Various characteristics of the manuscripts, including the neatness with which they are executed and the order in which the songs are entered, tell us that the songs were not written down onto the extant parchment immediately upon hearing them or directly from memory.[10] Instead, the scribes must have copied from written models, or "exemplars." For a song by Guiraut Riquier (P-C 248,57), the end of which is lacking, for example, the copyist of manuscript *R* makes a direct reference to his model when he writes that the song is deficient because it was deficient in the exemplar (*deficit quia deficiebat in exemplari*). Accordingly, it is wise to dis-

---

10. The above-mentioned play of St. Agnes seems to present us with a telling exception to this practice. Its scribe may well have written down the melodies from memory without first making an exemplar.

tinguish between several stages in the transmission from author to extant manuscript. The earliest, for many songs even the major, part of the transmission consisted exclusively in an oral tradition of texts and melodies. Many if not most of the differences among multiple versions must have come about at this stage. At some time near the middle of the thirteenth century, a fashion arose to collect troubadour (and trouvère) songs in writing. At that time, a given song may have been collected on several occasions and as it was performed by different singers. The persons who were the first to write down a given melody (we may call them "notators") either knew the songs and wrote them down from memory, or notated what someone else sang to them. In the next stage, someone acting like a modern editor, or redactor, may have consciously made some changes before the copyists of the extant manuscripts did their part of the work.

Finally, various features strongly suggest that the copyists did not work like automatons. It appears that a music copyist sang to himself part of the melody and then wrote down not what he had seen but what he had heard; he thus put himself, as it were, into the shoes of a performer and notated his own rendition of the melody. In this process the copyist may have made some variants of the same type that performers were likely to make. Obviously, we do not know to what extent notator, redactor, and copyist were one person. Nor do we know, in the event that they were different persons, how a song traveled from one to the other. For that reason, it seems wise to take the expression "the scribe of [a given] manuscript" as some kind of umbrella term that refers to all who, in one way or another, contributed a given song to a given source. In some cases, however, we may have to distinguish between text and music scribes.

Turning to some specific issues, it is well known that, for many texts, manuscript G is related to manuscript Q; that is, in these sources, large groups of poems were entered in the same order and with very few variants. This leads to the conclusion that, for the texts involved, the scribes copied, directly or indirectly, from the same exemplars. However, manuscript Q has no music, and we do not know whether the exemplars contained music. Essentially the same situation pertains to manuscripts R and C, the cansos and verses by Guiraut Riquier being an interesting case in point. The scribe of manuscript C claims to have copied Guiraut's poems from a book written by the poet himself. However, manuscript C does not have any of the melodies, whereas manuscript R does so for most of the songs involved. It is clear that the two scribes copied the poems, directly or indirectly, from one batch of exemplars. These exemplars almost certainly came directly or indirectly from Guiraut, but it is far from certain that they came in the form of a book, nor is it certain that they contained music (van der Werf 1984, 24–28). In opposition to all of this, three copies of the treatise *Breviari d'amor* by Matfre Ermengau preserve almost identical versions for one of Matfre's songs (P-C 297,4), and this may well be the only case in which two or more copyists shared an exemplar for a troubadour melody.

Since the musical legacy of the trouvères is quite large, its extant sources provide more insight into the process of collecting and copying melodies than can be gleaned from the troubadour repertory alone.[11] Clearly, the copyists of trouvère manuscripts *K, N, P,* and *X* shared exemplars for most of the songs (text and music) they preserved (van der Werf 1972, 30–31, 108–15.) The similarities among the versions of these songs lead to the reassuring conclusion that medieval scribes could copy very accurately. The differences among those same songs—and there are relatively few—show that these scribes were human beings and made some errors; but much more important, we learn that someone, perhaps the music copyists themselves, also made some deliberate changes in the melodies, though we lack the means to determine what was actually in the exemplar and what was the scribal variant.

Trouvère manuscripts *M* and *T* (the former is troubadour manuscript *W*) reveal yet another aspect of transmission. Although their text copyists likely shared exemplars for certain groups of songs, it can be proven that the music copyists did not copy from the same models (van der Werf 1972, 31–32). Nevertheless, the similarity among the *M* and *T* melodies of these songs is greater than is normal in the trouvère repertory. This duality suggests a conclusion that is both disturbing and fascinating: either the music scribes of manuscripts *M* and *T* did not copy the melodies from the exemplars used by the text copyists, or only one of the music scribes had access to them. Thus, we must admit the possibility that the extant text and the extant music for a given song did not necessarily come from one singer. By the same token, the close similarity between the versions of some songs poses two equally interesting possibilities: either the notators worked with the same informant(s) but on different occasions, or certain melodies in these two sources came from connoisseurs who had been in close contact, perhaps as teacher and pupil or as fellow pupils of one teacher.

COMPOSING IN A NOTATIONLESS CULTURE

Thirteenth-century poets and scribes would probably be dazzled if they could see the ease and speed with which we read and write. But exactly this mastery may well be our greatest impediment to full appreciation of medieval literature. Similarly, the rapid and effortless ways in which today's musicians read notes probably impede our efforts to understand medieval music life. It will not solve all problems, but it is illuminating to stand still for a moment and ponder the meaning of terms we habitually use in

---

11. For multiple versions of many trouvère melodies, see van der Werf 1977–79.

reference to the creation of literary and musical works of art. During the last several centuries, most plays, poems, and symphonies were written down virtually at the moment of being created, and it is common to say that such works were "written" even though, by itself, the verb "to write" does not even come close to covering all aspects of creation. We do not know who among the troubadours could read and write, but even those who had mastered those arts wrote and read more slowly and with greater difficulty than we do (Chaytor 5–21). It may be advisable, therefore, to consider all implications of the term when we refer to troubadours as "authors" who "wrote" certain types of poems; for many, perhaps even for most of them, writing down a poem while creating it may well have been more a hindrance than a help.

We may safely assume that very few troubadours, if any, were familiar with the art of notating a melody. In reference to music, the verbs "to compose" and "to write" are so nearly synonymous that even the former may have undesirable associations in the present context. To avoid that problem, I often use the verb "to improvise" for the act of creating a melody without the help of notation. For some readers, unfortunately, that term evokes a picture of someone making up an exuberant, unorganized, or rhapsodic melody at the very moment of performing it for an audience. That association could not have arisen in the mind of anyone familiar with melodies such as the one for Bernart's "Quan vei la lauzeta mover" (Example 2), which is a true masterpiece of simplicity and balance. Furthermore, the music world has long known the practice of organists *improvising* a fugue on a theme that they have *not seen before.* By its very nature, a fugue is far from unorganized or rhapsodic, and no organist would be able to *improvise* a fugue for four voices without having studied and played hundreds of fugues *written* by composers of the past few centuries.

We have no documentary information as to how and when troubadours made up their melodies. It is helpful, therefore, that the present field of popular music knows many composers who cannot read music, and whom we often call "musically illiterate." It is known that they normally compose while singing, playing, or singing-and-playing and that it usually takes many run-throughs before a piece is considered ready for presentation in public. At the actual world premiere, therefore, the music is in essence a *remembered improvisation.* For a typical troubadour, making up a melody probably was a deliberate act that strongly relied upon familiarity with existing melodies. The more time and attention given to the act of composing and, especially, the greater the understanding of existing tunes, the better the result was bound to be. (How we would love to know whether, or to what extent, a troubadour simultaneously improvised text and melody!) The melodies preserved with the poems attributed to Jaufre Rudel probably are among the oldest extant melodies for nonliturgical texts in a language other than

Latin. Yet they are stylistically quite different from plainchant, they are far from primitive or incoherent, and they strongly contradict the old notion that the earliest troubadours were the first composers of nonliturgical music.

Without paying much attention to its literal meaning, I have habitually used the term *oral tradition* in reference to the unwritten dissemination of medieval songs. But when reading exams of young music students, I never could find fault with those who wrote of "aural" tradition because the ear of the listener is as much involved as the mouth of the performer. Even though the mouth is not the determinant factor in the creation of a text, experts on medieval literature often write and speak of "oral" composition; some even discuss in great detail the "orality" of certain medieval genres. In reference to music, such terms probably are even less appropriate because the repertory of medieval musicians, in general, must have comprised large quantities of instrumental music, and it would be rather awkward to talk of the "oral" composition of music for shawm, sackbut, and lute. Personally, moreover, I find it neither mellifluous nor elegant to associate refined music and poetry with "mouthliness." Contrarily, in its acquired meaning of "to invent" or "to find," the verb *trobar* seems wondrously appropriate for the art of creating a song without the intervention of script and notation.

So as to minimize undesirable associations, I have often spoken of the "notationless" musical culture of the Middle Ages (van der Werf 1965). The suffix of that term, however, may make the absence of notation seem to be a deficiency. Of course it all depends on rather subjective evaluations, but a culture that is notation*less* also is notation *free*. In certain respects, the troubadours may have been at a disadvantage in that they were unable to work out certain complex passages with the help of writing gear, but they also had the freedom to incorporate in their melodies details that cannot be captured in notation. Most important, today's musicians must perform every sonata and concerto exactly "as written." The medieval performers did not know written texts and tunes, and this may well explain why they had far greater artistic freedom than their successors of today.

It is difficult to determine to what extent it is a consequence of the medieval way of composing, but conjunct motion is one of the most striking characteristics of troubadour music, that is, their melodies move primarily in small steps, the second being the most frequently occurring interval by far.[12] The interval of the third is the next favorite move, followed closely by

12. The nomenclature for intervals does not measure the interval itself, but rather indicates the number of pitches that are encompassed by the interval. Thus, a step from one pitch on the scale to the next (e.g., from *C* to *D*) is called a "second"; an interval comprising two seconds (e.g., going from *C* to *E* without touching the pitch *D*) is called a "third"; an interval comprising seven seconds (e.g., from low *C* directly to high *c*) is an "octave."

reiteration of a pitch over a few consecutive syllables. Most troubadour melodies span approximately an octave, but the melody for one verse often encompasses only part of that total range; a part of the total range (often the higher part) may occur in only one or two verses. If the music of the troubadours had been the only or the largest extant medieval repertory, it would have been unwise to extend melodic analysis much beyond a description of intervals, repetition, contour, and the like. If, moreover, musicologists had restricted their attention to Western music, we might not have had any criteria by which to analyze a troubadour melody. Over the past century, however, examination of non-Western music has led to the recognition of organizing principles other than major or minor scales.[13] Application of these findings to plainchant and trouvère songs, two repertories rich in multiple versions, has taught that, in many medieval melodies, certain pitches are more prominent than others and thus provide an overall tonal structure.

A pitch can stand out or attract attention by being reiterated over consecutive syllables. Next, since the second is the most frequently occurring interval, the pitches of wider intervals are likely to be perceived as prominent. Similarly, in songs in which many or most syllables receive only one pitch each, groups of pitches over one syllable are likely to stand out, and, within such a group, the first pitch appears to be more prominent than subsequent ones. A pitch that occurs noticeably more frequently than others also is likely to be perceived as prominent. Finally, it seems fairly well accepted that most pitches in a troubadour melody were of more or less equal duration;[14] thus, the pitches that we know to have been longer than average are likely to have been more prominent than the ones of average duration. (The music scribes indicated lengthening of a pitch by writing it as a double note.) Pitches that, within a given melody, frequently stand out by position, reiteration, longer duration, or frequency of occurrence form what may be called the "underlying structure" of the melody; they seem to serve as the frame of reference over which the composer draped the melody,

13. The most extensive description of such principles in non-Western music is still Sachs 1961; see also Sachs 1943. For an application of these principles to medieval music, see van der Werf 1983, pt. 1, 43–100. In discussions of medieval music, it is customary to identify pitches in the following manner:

A B C D E F G a b c d e f g

14. Kippenberg presents a discussion and evaluation of the many studies that since the beginning of this century have been devoted to duration in medieval nonliturgical song. For detailed commentary on the so-called "modal theory," see van der Werf 1982; 1972, 35–46.

or, in somewhat less poetic terms, they provided the composer with the pegs on which to hang the melody.

Obviously, not all troubadour melodies have equally clear underlying structures. Moreover, the total troubadour repertory is comparatively small, and it is poor in multiple versions, so that outside help is more than welcome. Both from Gregorian chant and from the trouvère repertory, we know that melodies ending on *D* are likely to have the pitches *D, F, a,* and *c* as structural pitches. Using this knowledge, we can easily recognize that Bernart de Ventadorn's most famous melody (Example 2), as well as the only extant melody attributed to the Comtessa de Dia (Example 3), has the chain *D-F-a-(c)* as underlying structure. The structural pitches manifest themselves by serving often in intervals wider than a second, and as initial pitch of a group of pitches over one syllable. In Bernart's tune, the first verse immediately displays the underlying structure by beginning with the skip from *D* to *F* and by reiterating the *a* over two or three consecutive syllables. In the melody by the Comtessa de Dia, the *a* is reiterated in the beginning of the first, the third, and the fifth verse, and the total melody consists of three parts (AB AB CDB) all three of which end on *D*. Verses 1, 3, and 6 end on the nonstructural tone *E*, and thus seem unfinished or in need of a follow-up sentence. In Bernart's tune, most verses end on a structural pitch, and the total melody consists of two parts of equal length, the first of which ends on *D* in most versions, the second of which ends that way in all versions.

Bernart's tune for "Quan vei la lauzeta mover" has come down to us in twelve versions, nine of which have been preserved with contrafacts (three in French, one in Latin, and a fourteenth-century Occitan one). When evaluating the similarities and differences among these versions, we must keep in mind that the melody lived in an oral tradition for almost a century before its oldest extant version was copied. From this point of view, the great similarity among the twelve versions fills us with awe for the medieval connoisseurs who so well retained the melody's essential features without the help of written notes. Examination of many medieval melodies in multiple versions helps us understand how singers of the time retained them. In order to remember a melody, or in order to reconstruct a melody from memory, the performers needed to retain the underlying structure; they also needed to know which segments thereof were used for a given part of the song. The clear underlying structure of Bernart's melody must have made it easy for several generations of connoisseurs to preserve it rather precisely. The close similarity among so many versions suggests that this structure may well have been with this melody from its inception. Because the song by the Comtessa de Dia has been preserved only in the version presented here, we do not know how well her melody fared in the oral tradition by which the song traveled from composer to notator. We do not even know how closely the preserved tune resembles the one with which she sent her poem into the world.

Although Guiraut Riquier's melody for "Jhesu Crist filh de Dieu vieu" (Example 6) moves almost exclusively in seconds, it contains just enough hints of the structural chain *D-F-a-c*. Almost all intervals wider than a second skip from one structural pitch to another. In addition, almost all of the many syllables that are sung to a group of pitches have *D*, *F*, or *a* as initial pitch. The manner in which Guiraut's songs have been preserved suggests that he could write, but the character of the melodies does not indicate that he also could notate music (van der Werf 1984, 24–28; Mölk). Most notably, it is by no means evident that he designed the form of his tune with greater care than other composers did. The overall form of the melody (AB AB CDE) is very common, and, as is almost usual, the two statements of the AB section are not identical to one another. The song is unusual in having many instances in which a syllable is sung to a group of from six to twelve pitches, but there seems to be no system as to where such groups come; for instance, the string of seven pitches over the fourth syllable of verses 1 and 3 recurs over the first syllable of verses 2 and 4 and again over the fourth syllable of verse 7. Most of the groups of pitches over one syllable share at least some melodic material, but we do not know how much of this repetition was due to conscious design on the part of the composer and how much came about by a confluence of necessity and chance because Guiraut made the melody go up and down in small steps within the *D-F-a-c* mold.

It is difficult to determine the underlying structure of Aimeric de Peguilhan's song given as Example 5. In the first four verses, the chain *G-b-d* seems as strong (or as weak) as the chain *(D)-F-a-c*, but the latter is decidedly stronger from the fifth verse on. Even though twentieth-century experts on medieval music may have difficulty finding a clear structure in this song, the medieval singers must have sensed some tonal organization. Although the versions differ considerably from one another where pitches for a given syllable are concerned, they are very similar in melodic contour; they are even identical in regard to closing pitches for every verse. Example 4, by Folquet de Marseilla, has an even less clearly structured melody. In this case, the many and significant differences among its versions suggest that even medieval singers did not find much coherence in it. For us, therefore, it is difficult to understand how the singers retained as much similarity in melodic contour as they actually did; we must return to that problem when examining the relation between a given group of syllables and their segment of the melody.

In Gregorian chant, we find many melodies in which a tertial chain (e.g., *D-F-a-c*) occurs side by side with a quartal one (e.g., *D-G-c* or *C-F-b♭*). In some versions of such a melody, the tertial chain may be the stronger one, while the quartal one prevails in other versions. Detailed study of many such melodies in multiple versions led me to the hypothesis that plainchant started out as a quartally structured repertory, that a conversion of these structures into tertial ones was started before any melodies were written down, and that this conversion was halted before it was completed (van der Werf 1983, pt. 1, 109–20). Consequently, those who knew Gregorian chant were accustomed to hearing (and singing) melodies with a dualistic tertial-quartal structure.

Perhaps this knowledge can help us understand the variants among the multiple versions for Jaufre Rudel's melody for "Lanquan li jorn son lonc en mai" (Example 1). By a stroke of great fortune, we have five versions of its melody, only three of which appear with Jaufre's text. As Heinrich Husmann discovered a few decades ago, a poem by Walther von der Vogelweide has been preserved with a melody that resembles Jaufre's melody. The resemblance is too close to have come about by chance, so we must accept that Walther modeled his song directly or indirectly on Jaufre's. It is also possible that Jaufre and Walther, independently of one another, modeled their respective tunes upon an older, now lost song. Subsequently, Ursula Aarburg found a religious Latin poem that had been preserved with yet another relative of Jaufre's melody, which may or may not be older than Jaufre's tune.

In Walther's version, the total melody is clearly based on the tertial chain *D-F-a-c.* In Jaufre's version, the *F* and the *c* are similarly strong structural pitches, but for the rest the structure is considerably more complex. At the basis of the melody, the *D* shares its structural function with its lower neighbor, *C.* Except for the function of the *c*, the structure for the higher region is somewhat elusive, so that we must leave analysis of that segment to someone who is willing to make a large-scale study of underlying structures in medieval music in general. It may be noted, however, that similarly elusive structures are found frequently in Gregorian chant, specifically in melodies assigned to the second and the eighth mode.

The AB AB X form in Examples 1 and 3 draws attention to a specific difference between Walther's and Jaufre's versions of the melody. The melody by the Comtessa de Dia illustrates a characteristic found in many songs in that form: the A and the B melodies relate to each other as antecedent and consequent—that is, neither can stand on its own, and only the B melody has a final pitch that we perceive as a good ending tone. Since the late thirteenth or early fourteenth century, such endings have been referred to as "open" and "closed." In all three versions of Jaufre's tune, the A melody ends on *D*, while the B melody ends on *C.* In Walther's melody, however, the *C* serves as the open ending tone for the antecedent, while the *D* is the final of the consequent. It is unwise to speculate about the nature of the melody in Jaufre's time (a century or so before the earliest extant version was copied), but it appears that, at the time of preservation, the configuration *C/D-F* was part of its underlying structure.

The chain *D-f-a-c* is not the only structure found in troubadour melodies. In the absence of precise statistics, I may present my impression that tertial structures occur much more often than quartal ones, and that the ones with a minor third (e.g., *D-F*) at the bottom occur more often than the ones with a major third (e.g., *C-E* or *G-b*) in that position. As is to be expected, we find differences from one composer to another in respect to the use and the pervasiveness of a given structure. A detailed study of such differences is bound to reveal more interesting and more precise information than can be given here. We have nineteen melodies with poems attributed to Bernart de Ventadorn, fourteen for Gaucelm Faidit, and thirteen for Folquet de Marseilla; moreover, for most of these songs we have two or three versions. In quantity this is sufficient to venture some generalizations and oversimplifications concerning these composers' ability, or interest, in giving tonal structure and cohesion to their melodies. Both from individual versions and from differences among the multiple versions we may conclude that Bernart's melodies are the most cohesive ones in this group, that Folquet's are the least cohesive, and that Gaucelm's ability or interest in this area comes close to that of Bernart. It would be premature to give up on the melodies in which we now perceive no structure because future research may yet reveal some underlying principles, or at least some reason may be uncovered why seemingly unstructured melodies existed next to clearly organized ones.

Unfortunately, no medieval author, whether his primary interest was poetry or music, writes about or alludes to the underlying structures that we perceive in medieval music. Consequently, we do not know how aware the troubadours were of their choice of structure for a given melody, nor do we know to what extent they consciously understood the way in which, and the degree to which, they maintained it throughout a tune. When trying to form an opinion about this fascinating issue we run the risk of erroneously equating effect and intention. For example, the stronger and the more pervasive the underlying structure of a given melody is, the more likely it is to contain repetitions of short melodic turns. But it is open to question whether the repetition or the pervasive structure was the composers' primary goal. (Interestingly, repetitiveness does not necessarily yield a strong underlying structure.) We must also keep in mind that the preference for conjunct motion within the span of an octave almost forced the composers to return many times to a limited number of melodic ideas.[15] Furthermore, as will be discussed next, some aspects of the relation between text and

---

15. Since terms such as "motive" and "formula" are associated with precise repetition, the term melodic "idea" may be more suited to recurrence in troubadour melodies.

melody contributed to repetition of certain ideas at specific places in the song. Finally there is the difficulty of determining what is a recurrent motive. Obviously, the shorter a motive, the more frequently it is likely to recur, and if we take every two- or three-pitch sequence as a motive, all music is exclusively based upon recurring motives. Whatever the reason for the recurrence, much is to be learned from the synopsis of "literal and varied repetitions of small units" that Margaret Switten has culled from fourteen of the twenty-one songs attributed to Raimon de Miraval.

POEM AND MELODY

In respect to a song's largest component, the strophe, there is a complete correspondence between poem and melody.[16] In the music, there is nothing beyond the strophe because the melody preserved with the first strophe serves all subsequent ones. The practice of singing all strophes to the same melody requires that all of them have the same number of verses, and that a given verse has the same number of syllables in all strophes. However, there is no tradition that the high point of the text come in the same verse in all strophes or that word accents, other than those in the rhyme (and the caesura), come on the same syllables in all verses. The text of each strophe normally is a self-contained unit, so much so that, for many songs, performers and scribes could scramble the order of their strophes without altering their message or value. Interestingly, however, the first strophe almost always retains its position at the head of the poem.

A strophe's subdivision into verses does not always match the poem's syntax and content, but it is strongly marked by rhyme. In the music, that subdivision ranges from obvious to elusive. Speaking generally, only a few possibilities exist for a melodic contour. The melody for a verse, or a melody-verse, can rise or fall, it can stay more or less at one level, and it can be in the shape of an arch or an inverted arch. Preference for one shape over another varies from song to song and, perhaps, from troubadour to troubadour, but two things stand out: remarkably many melody-verses are in the shape of an arch, while the inverted arch occurs only rarely. Obviously, an archlike melody-verse does not necessarily end on the pitch on which it started; nor does a rising melody-verse always go straight up without any digression. For example, a melody-verse may rise more or less directly for about an octave and then descend a fourth or a fifth, so that it is both an overall rising and an arch-shaped melody.

Returning for a moment to the form of the strophe, we may observe that the troubadours liked to begin a song with a rising passage or with reiter-

16. Concerning the relationship between music and text see also Page; Switten; Stevens; van der Werf 1972, 1989.

ation of a selected pitch. Such reiteration often is slightly adorned, as in verse 5 of Example 3, and the ascending opening begins more often at the lowest level than in the middle of the song's total range. Only rarely did a composer start a song at the summit of its range, as Aimeric de Peguilhan did in Example 5. Toward the end, almost all melodies make a generally descending motion, often going down to a second under the closing pitch. These preferred ways to begin and end a song, together with the preference for arch-shaped melody-verses, go hand in hand with the reliance on typical opening passages, typical closing passages, and passages that would not serve well either as opening or closing. The word "typical" does not imply that such passages were fixed formulas, the pitches of which could not be altered; on the contrary, they were melodic ideas that could take on almost any sequence of pitches (van der Werf 1967a).

To a large extent, the troubadours, as composers, treated melody-verses as separate entities. Groups of pitches over a single syllable come much more often toward the end than in the course of a verse. In melodies with a strong underlying structure, melody-verses end remarkably often on structural pitches. Melody-verses with a so-called open ending often end on a nonstructural pitch, whereas those with a "closed" ending usually end on a structural pitch. (See the A and B melodies of Example 3.) Finally, although multiple versions do not always agree on the final pitch of each verse, they are more often in agreement on that pitch than on other ones (see Example 5).

The last feature leads us again to the influence of the poet-composer as the first performer of a song and the initiator of its dissemination. Even when the troubadour or trobairitz, as composer, failed to mark verse end-ings, he or she still may have done so as performer. In some way, the performer may have made the final pitch of a verse stand out so that subsequent singers maintained its precise level, even if they varied almost every preceding pitch. We have no way of knowing how much of a break medieval singers made between verses. Making a verse more ornate toward its end probably caused a slowing down in the presentation of the text. However, the final pitch of a verse is never written as a double note, and it is not certain that lengthening the last few pitches, and more or less dou-bling the very last one, was the primary way by which the first performer made the end of the verse stand out. Moreover, we may assume special attention for the rhyme syllable(s) on the part of the person who learned a song by listening to it being performed, so that the last pitch, or the last few pitches, also received his special attention.

The separation between melody-verses is unusually clear in the song by the Comtessa de Dia (Example 3), the form of which can graphically be represented as AB AB CDB. The A and the B melodies relate to each other as antecedent and consequent, and only the B melody has a final pitch that we perceive as a good ending tone. In fact, the *D* comes close to performing the function carried out by the tonic in music of more recent centuries. In this case, the relation between verses is particularly strong owing to yet more repetition of melodic material. The opening passage of the A melody returns, in a varied form, at the beginning of verse 5, while its closing passage returns at the ending of verse 6. The entire B melody is heard again with the text of verse 7. Over the last two syllables, the A and the B melodies are related to each other by having a three-note descending figure, after which the melody goes up by a second to *E* or *D*, respectively. Curiously, in verse 5 the closing figure of the A melody appears not over the rhyme-word, but over syllables 8 and 9, which leads to some questions about scribal accuracy. It is possible, but not certain, that the trobairitz wanted verse 5 (with its masculine rhyme) to end differently from the other six. It is also possible, however, that a copyist skipped a neume earlier in that verse and, unconsciously, made up for this error by writing the first pitch of verse 7 over the last syllable of verse 6. If the former hypothesis is correct, the last three verses have descending closing pitches, *F, E, D*, but if the latter is the case, the composer gave her song a remarkably clear and consistent subdivision into melody-verses. (As the text editor points out in the notes to the transcription, the seventh verse should have had a masculine ending but the manuscript has a neume over the unaccented syllable of the feminine ending. Thus we know that something is wrong with the music of the last verse.)

Content and syntax often divide a strophe into two or three distinct sections. In many songs, the poet managed to give all strophes the same subdivision. Repetition of entire melody-verses often was related to the textual form. Similarly, there was often a relation between the poet's choice of rhyme-scheme and the form of the strophe. Thus, rhyme-scheme and melodic form can be related indirectly. Typically, we do not know what came first: systematic subdivision on the basis of content and syntax, or a specific repetition of melody-verses and rhyme-sounds. All we do know is that certain subdivisions of a strophe were (or became) favorite already among the earliest known troubadours. In many songs, including our Example 1, the first and the second pair of verses share not only rhyme-sounds but also melodic sentences. As far as the music is concerned, this sequence of melody-verses can adequately be represented with the formula AB AB X, because the A and the B melodies, in their entirety, do not often recur in the X section. (In a comparatively small number of songs, the B melody recurs at the end of the song, not necessarily along with a recurrence of the *b* rhyme.) In reference to the rhyme-scheme, the formula *ab ab x* is somewhat less appropriate because the *a* and the *b* rhyme frequently recur in the *x* section.[17]

---

17. The songs included in this essay were selected to illustrate many and varying characteristics in no more than a few complete songs. The fact that four of the six have the AB AB X

For some time, probably on the basis of studies by Friedrich Gennrich, it was assumed that the troubadours (and trouvères) sought a close relation between rhyme-scheme and melodic form. However, even a superficial examination of randomly selected songs reveals that neither the troubadours nor the trouvères considered it mandatory that rhyme-scheme match melodic form. All one can conclude is that both the AB AB X melodic form and the *ab ab x* rhyme-scheme occur frequently, that they often were combined, but that one could also occur without the other (Examples 2 and 5). Beyond the combination of these favorite forms, there are no cases in the troubadour repertory (and only very few cases in the trouvère repertory) in which a song's rhyme-scheme matches its melodic form, and there is no indication that the poet-composers considered that an ideal for which to strive (van der Werf 1972, 63–68).

Quite frankly, recurrence of melody-verses is an elusive issue, as is interestingly illustrated in Bernart de Ventadorn's song of the lark (Example 2). In manuscript *R*, verses 4 and 7 are identical to each other; in manuscript *W*, they are identical except over the very last syllable; in manuscript *G*, they resemble each other closely without being identical. The differences in the degree of similarity among the extant versions (including the contrafacts) forcefully remind us that we do not know Bernart's original tune. Possibly, in Bernart's very first version, those melody-verses were identical to one another, and some of the transmitters failed to maintain that important characteristic. Yet we must reckon with the possibility that, initially, these verses resembled each other only in contour and general pitch level, that the degree of similarity was (gradually) increased during the subsequent oral transmission, and that it was a redactor who, pen in hand, made them identical. If the former was the case, Bernart must have been fully aware of what he was doing, he may even have planned it from the outset. If the latter was the case, we have no way of knowing whether Bernart planned it; we do not even know whether he was fully aware of the similarity. Our uncertainty is deepened by analysis of the text. It is of minor importance that verses 4 and 7 do not rhyme with each other, and that these two verses have no similarity in syntax or content in any of the seven strophes.[18] However, it may be crucial that these verses have different strophic functions. In rhyme (*ab ab cd cd*) and content, every strophe is divided into two sections of four verses each. If Bernart had made the fourth and the eighth melody-verses identical

---

form and that two of the them end with the B melody is coincidence and does not reflect formal preferences in the troubadour repertory, in general.

18. In Bernart's song "Cant l'erba fresqu' e·l fuelha par" (P-C 70,39), the melody of which has been preserved exclusively in manuscript *R*, verses 5 and 6 have a remarkable textual similarity ("joy ai de luy e joi ai de la flor / joi ai de mi e de midons major") and share the music. However, there is no such textual relation in subsequent strophes.

or similar to each other, we would have admired the care with which he designed the form of his melody. Now, we can only wonder about his intentions and interests.

Repetition of entire melody-verses must have been an important compositional device for the troubadours. It also must have played an important role in the manner in which performers reconstructed melodies from memory. Nevertheless, we have serious problems in reconstructing a song's original form. The extant music shows that, for songs that appear to be in the AB AB X form, note-for-note repetition was not a standard requirement. Multiple versions show that what once were identical melody-verses may have grown apart while similarly sounding phrases may have become identical. Unfamiliar as we are with the art of composing in a notationless culture, we do not know to what extent melodic repetition was planned and to what extent it merely happened in the course of finding a melody. We do not even know to what extent medieval composers were aware of using precise repetition, modified repetition, or a faint echo of an earlier-used melodic idea. A music scribe may have been more aware of precise pitch levels than were either the composer or the other participants in the oral tradition. Certainly we, trained as we are in analysis of printed music, are more conscious of such things than were the musicians in the notationless culture of the Middle Ages.

Recently, two experts on medieval song have expressed dismay at my apparent downgrading of the value of the music in the songs of the troubadours and trouvères (Stevens 40–41; Switten 22). A brief discussion of the apparent difference of opinion may further our understanding of the melodies and their relation to the poems. Probably, our differences are more a matter of degree than of principle; the passage that offended them involved repetition in the melodies *in comparison to* "the care with which the troubadours and trouvères designed the form of their poems" (van der Werf 1972, 63). Unconsciously, I directed those observations primarily to fellow musicians, and especially to fellow History of Music teachers. In our training, most of us listened to and analyzed many examples of what usually is called the "art song" of the nineteenth century before we came across medieval melodies. Our knowledge of the former had raised certain expectations about the latter. In addition, most of us had been required to study various publications by Friedrich Gennrich, who emphatically states that medieval poet-composers consciously sought a close relationship between the rhyme-scheme of the poem and the form of the melody (Gennrich 1932, 18). I need not apologize for having spent some effort counteracting certain notions we acquired as music students, but I do regret that some readers now think that, in my opinion, the music of the troubadours and trouvères lacks artistic value. All that aside, however, I happen to be more interested in the reasons for the recurrence of melodic ideas than in the fact of occurrence itself. All in all, I may not have used superlatives in my discussions of the melodies, but I hope to have made a positive contribution to the appreciation of medieval music by drawing attention to some of the means by which the composers made their melodies hang together.

The smallest component in the relation between poem and melody is the syllable with its segment of the music. In general, the troubadour songs are fairly syllabic, in that most syllables receive no more than one pitch each. Groups of pitches over one syllable are more likely to appear toward the end than at the beginning of a verse. In such "neumatic" passages, groups of from two to four pitches are the norm.[19] The most notable exception to this generalization is Guiraut Riquier's song "Jhesu Christ, filh de Dieu vieu" (Example 6), in which most syllables are sung to anywhere from six to twelve pitches, while the others receive one single pitch each. The Old French repertory contains two similarly ornate songs, namely "Belle Doette" and "En un vergier" (R 1352 and R 594; both are narrative and both are anonymous). In comparison to the troubadour and trouvère songs, in general, these three songs are very ornate, but in comparison to certain genres of Gregorian chant, such as Graduals, they hardly qualify for the epithet "melismatic."[20] These melodies, and less ornate ones as well, clearly show that there is no systematic relation between the number of pitches sung over a given syllable and its role in the word or the sentence. Nor does there seem to be a consistent relation between the nature or content of the poem and the degree of the melody's ornateness. As further research may well disclose, some composers liked ornate songs, while others tended to keep theirs more syllabic. Jaufre Rudel's song about the faraway beloved may be somewhat more ornate than most troubadour songs, but I would not dare attribute that to the composer's attempts at providing an expressive melody for his sad poem. Probably, the number of pitches over the word *lonh* is

19. A neume is a notational symbol normally written in one stroke of the pen; it may be simple and comprise only one note, or it may be compound and comprise several notes. The term "neumatic" rather vaguely refers to melodies with many instances in which one compound neume was needed to notate the pitches for a given syllable.

20. A melisma is a lengthy garland of pitches sung over one syllable; in Gregorian chant, melismas of thirty or forty pitches are common. Melismatic chants contain no more than one or a few melismas, while the rest of the chant ranges from neumatic to syllabic. The degree of ornateness of a given chant is exclusively linked to liturgical function; in the Mass, for example, Introit antiphons are neumatic, Graduals are melismatic, regardless of whether they were sung on a high feast day or on a weekday in Lent. Concerning the poems, we can only say that hymns and sequences generally are syllabic or neumatic, but they are not melismatic. This stylistic uniformity among chants with the same liturgical function is likely to have been the result of a conscious redesign of plainchant, carried out during the Carolingian era (see van der Werf 1983, pt. 1, 120–32). The word "ornate" in the above discussion does not imply that only the first pitch of a melisma or a compound neume is essential to the melody and that all subsequent pitches are mere ornaments.

related more to its position at the end of the verse than to its meaning. The group of pitches at the beginning of verse 5 in Bernart's song is well suited to the exclamation at that point in the first strophe, but on its subsequent occurrences it does not seem to serve any expressive function. Guiraut Riquier may simply have been one of those composers who liked ornate melodies. Thus, we should be cautious in attaching specific meaning to the ornate style of his song "Jhesu Christ, filh de Dieu vieu."

Perhaps the most striking aspect of the relation between a syllable and its segment of the melody is its variability. To a large extent, the nature of words and sentences determined the order of the syllables in a poem. To a limited extent, the underlying structure and the overall contour determined the order of pitches in a melody. However, as especially the opening verses of Example 5 illustrates, the relation between individual syllables and individual pitches could fluctuate considerably. Not only the number of pitches but, with certain limitations, also the precise level of the pitches over a given syllable may vary from one version to another. Both in number and in nature, the variants are such that they can have come about only in a performance in which neither the pitches nor the syllables had a fixed duration.

In a treatise dating from the late thirteenth century, Johannes de Grocheio (whom French scholars now call Jean de Grouchy) divided the music of his time into precisely measured and not-so-precisely measured ("non ita precise mensurata") genres (Rohloff 124). It is fairly clear that individual pitches in troubadour and trouvère songs, in general, were not precisely measured. In a positive formulation of this important phenomenon, we may say that the notes in the manuscripts represent pitches that were of *more or less* equal duration, with double notes representing pitches that were *more or less* twice as long as pitches of *average* duration. Multiple versions often differ as to whether a given pitch should be entered as a single or as a double note. For instance, the *W* version of Example 1 has double notes over the fifth syllable of verses 1, 2, and 3. Even though the music for verse 4 is essentially the same as that for verse 2, the fifth syllable of verse 4 has a single note. This and many similar differences between otherwise identical melody-verses suggest that the medieval scribes either had difficulty with, or were not overly concerned about consistently distinguishing between, pitches of long and pitches of average duration. Music scribes are not likely to have had difficulties in this respect, or to have been unconcerned, if pitches always were of precisely equal duration and if long pitches always were exactly twice as long as short pitches. (See also van der Werf 1967b and 1972, 35–45.)

The formulation "more or less equal" is deliberately vague because precise terms would negate the freedom composers and performers appear to have had in subtly altering duration of individual pitches, syllables, and words. This freedom provided singers with ample opportunity to be as expressive as they wished. It also explains how one single melody could do justice to several strophes of widely different meaning and with a different flow of words and accents. In conclusion, the most important relationship between poem and melody lay not in the form of either component, but in the manner in which the song (text and melody) was performed. In this respect, we must again keep in mind that the troubadour or the trobairitz also was the first performer of a song and thus could set whatever relation he or she wished between words and pitches. In all probability, the manner in which certain passages of a song were performed played an important role in their transmission, allowing even a seemingly incoherent or unstructured melody to be remembered remarkably well.

In his recent book *Words and Music,* John Stevens returns to the theory that not the notes but the syllables were of more or less equal duration. Although he rejects modal rhythm for monophonic songs, he comes close to advocating performance in the so-called "fifth rhythmic mode." He softens this stand by writing that "the equality of the syllables in an iso-syllabic rendering must . . . be approximate, sensitively judged, not metro-nomic" (501). Where syllabic and near-syllabic songs are concerned, this theory is not far from mine; perhaps one could even say that we have come to essentially the same conclusion. But for even moderately ornate songs, such as Examples 2, 3, 4, and 5, we are far apart. It is almost impossible to imagine an isosyllabic performance of Examples 1 and 6. It should be noted that in his reasoning Stevens pays no attention to variants among multiple versions, and that his conclusions are based on a rather questionable theory of numbers (van der Werf 1989) and on statements in medieval treatises in which troubadour songs are not considered.

CONCLUSION

Repetition of melodic material has come up so frequently in the last several pages that a recapitulation may clarify the issues. For a variety of reasons, it is risky to go into great detail when discussing troubadour music in general, and the relation between poem and melody in particular. Because the majority of troubadour songs are extant in only one version, we are inclined to consider that version's melody as the one with which the poet sent his text into the world. My research on a multitude of multiple ver-sions for plainchant and trouvère songs has made me very reluctant to discuss a composer's intentions. We simply do not know them! To begin with, we know next to nothing about the troubadours' methods of com-posing, although it is clear that most, perhaps even all of them, made up their melodies in their head and while singing out loud. This method of finding a melody must have been conducive to repetitiveness because, for a given song, one is likely to improvise in a certain vein and to return frequently (and perhaps unconsciously) to a few melodic ideas. A given idea may vary from one occurrence to another, but its recurrence contributes to the cohesiveness of the total melody. Also, the similarity among motives with the same function, such as opening or closing, tends to increase the homogeneity among melody-verses. At first encounter, the troubadours' manifest preference for conjunct motion in arch-shaped melodies, ranging not much wider than an octave, may seem a severe limitation; but greater familiarity with the entire repertory breeds respect for the manner in which a melody was given its own character and essence. In the songs of the troubadours, as in all music, variety plays at least as great a role as recurrence.

Both repetition of melodic material and appearance of new melodic ideas serve to set individual melody-verses apart. Many troubadour and trouvère melodies are "through-composed" (that is, no melody-verse recurs in its entirety) and they are not necessarily less melodious than other ones. A troubadour is likely to have predetermined the rhyme-scheme and syllable count of his poem, just as he is likely to have decided in advance whether he was going to make his melody in the AB AB X form. Beyond this standard repetition pattern, we are in the dark about his intentions and awareness, as was discussed in reference to verses 4 and 7 in Bernart's song and in reference to the garlands of pitches in Guiraut's tune. Similarly, it is far from certain that the Comtessa de Dia decided in advance to use one basic ending formula for each verse of her song given here as Example 3. If that similarity stems from the trobairitz herself, it may have come about in the process of her improvising one melody-verse at a time. All in all, troubadours and trobairitz are likely to have taken more care with details when selecting the form of a poem than when deciding on the mix of variety and repetition in the melody. As was said before, we do not know who among the troubadours could read and write, but the form of the poem (number of verses, number of syllables, and rhyme-scheme) could have been designed with the help of script, whereas the melodies bear all the hallmarks of music that originated in a notationless culture. This is no condemnation of the music; on the contrary!

A melody's underlying structure is deduced from the manner in which certain pitches repeatedly appear in prominent positions; in other words, repetition also is one of the contributors to structural unity in the music. As was said above, the stronger and the more pervasive the underlying structure of a given melody is, the more likely it is to contain repetitions of a limited number of short melodic turns. Some (much?) of the repetition was judiciously applied; the rest just happened to come about when the composer was improving within a certain framework. Clearly, we need to know much more about the workings of underlying structures before we can fully understand the how and why of melodic repetition.

Once more, we may turn to multiple versions for elucidation. What in one manuscript is a note-for-note repetition, is often a modified repetition, or merely a similar-sounding passage, in another source. In one version, certain melody-verses may have identical opening statements, but in another one they may hardly resemble one another in any aspect other than general contour. A certain pitch sequence may span three consecutive syllables in one version, while it covers four or five syllables in another one. Clearly, repetition was one of the aspects that could be varied by experts and connoisseurs during the transmission from composer to extant manuscript. In spirit, repetition was an integral feature of troubadour music; in detail and in reality, however, it was not a sacred component that was to be left untouched. The attitude of the poet-composers and other medieval experts toward melodic repetition seems to have differed greatly from their approach to rhyme and syllable count.

The art song of the nineteenth and twentieth centuries has caused a famous controversy. In the opinion of some, Schubert's settings often enhanced the poem involved. Others, including Goethe, have held an almost diametrically opposite point of view. Knowing where the troubadours stood in this controversy would have helped the present discussion. Alas, we cannot even guess what prompted the medieval poets to provide a melody for their poems. We do not know whether they did so in order to make the text more beautiful, or whether they did so merely because it was tradition. As some of us know from experience, it is easier to attract attention and to be heard when singing a poem than when speaking it. However, singing is not only a convenient way to raise one's voice; it also is a means by which to set a poem apart from more ordinary communication. In the song about the faraway beloved and in the one about the lark, the respective poet-composers "found" a melody that helped raise the poem immeasurably far above the level of everyday communication.

In summary, despite much uncertainty, we have a fair knowledge of general habits and accomplishments of the troubadours as composers, but we would like to have far more information on matters of detail. It is my impression that with respect to overall melodic flow (that is, movement in small steps and reliance on structural pitches), the tunes of the troubadours as a group are not very different from those of the trouvères as a group, but for many of the individual composers we can point out personal habits and preferences; in other words, we also need more studies of individual troubadours. Needless to say, no poet-composer can be studied effectively without reference to others in the same group, and no single repertory can be studied effectively without reference to other repertories.

APPENDIX: MUSIC EXAMPLES

In order to make examination of the melodies easier for those unfamiliar with medieval notation, the neumes of the medieval sources have been replaced with modern notes on five-line staffs with modern clefs. In agreement with the nonmensural character of the medieval notation, however, the notes do not have the usual stems, flags, and dots, because these indicate duration. The flat signs in the *W* reading of Example 1 are due to its having been transposed. All other flat signs were copied exactly where they appear in the manuscript; we do not precisely know how long such a sign was valid, but a given sign often seems to pertain to the rest of the staff on which it stands (van der Werf 1984, 38–61). Where desirable, the transition to a new line in the manuscript is marked with an apostrophe (').

Notes with a descending or ascending curved stem represent a liquescent neume in the manuscript; the implication of these neumes for actual performance is still unknown, but it is clear that, depending on the direction of the stem, the main note in the manuscript was followed by either its upper or its lower neighbor. In verse 6 of Example 1, however, the scribe of manuscript *X* indicated that the added pitch was a third lower than the main pitch.

Examples 1–6 follow on pages 150–62; the list of Works Cited begins on page 163.

Example 1. Jaufre Rudel de Blaja (P-C 262,2)

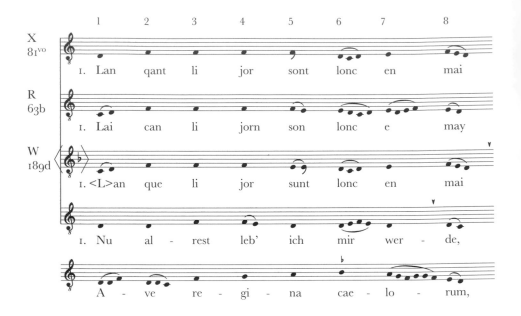

Example 1 (*continued*)

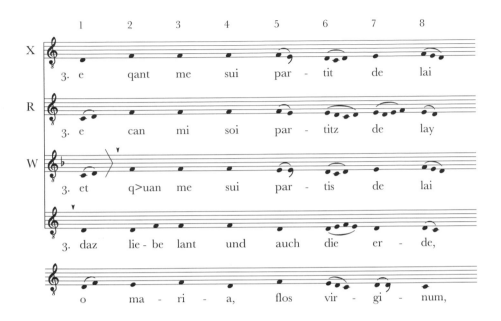

Example 1   (*continued*)

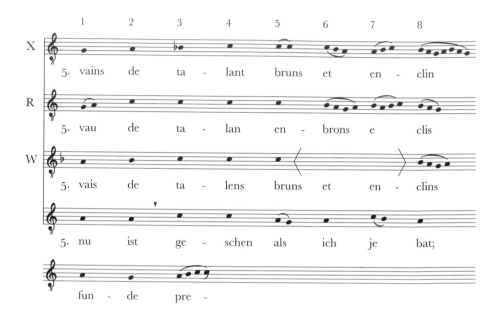

X: 5. vains de ta - lant bruns et en - clin

R: 5. vau de ta - lan en - brons e clis

W: 5. vais de ta - lens bruns et en - clins

5. nu ist ge - schen als ich je bat;

fun - de pre -

X: 6. si que chant ne flors d'au - bes - pin

R: 6. si que chans ni flors dels bels pis

W: 6. si que chanz ne flors d'au - bes - pins

6. ich byn ko - men an die stat,

ces ad fi - li - um

Example 1   (*continued*)

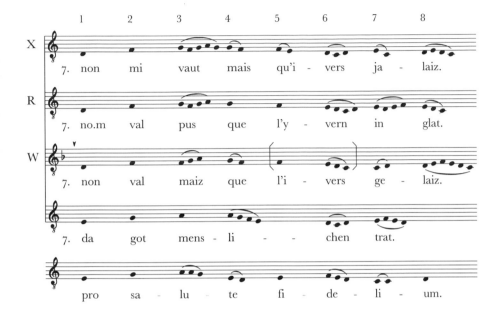

NOTES: The version in manuscript *W* is notated a fifth higher than given here; it was transposed here to facilitate comparison with the other extant versions. Due to mutilation of the manuscript, the version of *W* is incomplete; the missing passages of verses 1–4 were copied (and given between angular brackets) from appropriate places in the same manuscript within the AB AB form. The lost passage in verse 5 is more difficult to reconstruct but may well have been similar to the corresponding section in the other two versions. Finally, as discussed in van der Werf 1984, an error seems to have crept into the notation of verses 6 and 7; the notes given between square brackets are no more than a proposal for a correction.

Example 2. Bernart de Ventadorn (P-C 70,43)

Example 2   (*continued*)

Example 2   (*continued*)

NOTES: In comparison to other versions, the text scribe of manuscript *X* reversed verses 3 and 4, causing a rhyme problem as well as an apparent contextual disorder. In the same manuscript, the music of verse 5 seems to have a supernumerary neume, and the last three notes are crowded over the last two syllables. My transcription is based on the assumption that, at the transition to a new line, the music scribe split the neume for the first syllable into a single note and a group of three notes, giving the former in its appropriate position and erroneously placing the latter over the second syllable of that verse, which happened to be the first syllable of a new line. The subsequent notes for that verse seem to come one syllable too late. However, it is also possible that the individual neumes are placed over the appropriate syllable and that the contraction toward the end of the verse received two neumes rather than one.

Example 3. La Comtessa [Beatriz] de Dia (P-C 46,2)

NOTES: In verse 2, the words *cele* and *amigs* suggest that the scribe assumed the speaker to be male, even though the meter and the number of neumes demand the feminine form *amie*. At the end of verse 7, the rhyme and meter, as deduced from other versions, demand the adjective *desavinen(t)*. Accordingly, the melody for that verse should have been one neume shorter, but beyond that simple observation it is impossible to determine what exactly is wrong. For the sake of performance, almost any contraction of the melody-verse can solve the problem satisfactorily.

Example 4. Folquet de Marseilla (P-C 155,14)

Example 4 (*continued*)

Example 5. Aimeric de Peguilhan (P-C 10,25)

Example 5 (*continued*)

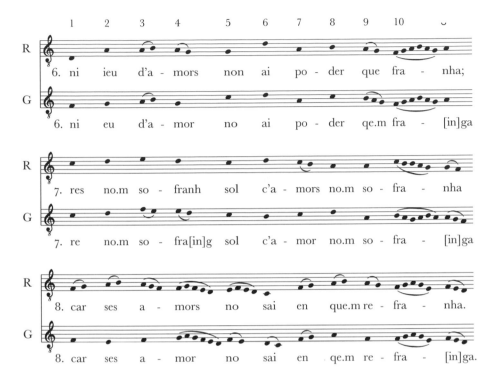

NOTES: The last word of verse 3, originally *sofranh*, was justifiably made into *franh* by expunctuation; the resulting one-syllable word has one neume, leaving both text and melody hypometric by one item. Although text and music make sense as they stand, it is possible that the first syllable and the sixth neume were erroneously omitted. For the music, we find support for this hypothesis in both versions of the first melody-verse and in the other version of the melody for verse 3. For the text, our hypothesis is supported by the other versions, all of which read "ni" at the beginning of the verse.

Example 6. Guiraut Riquier (P-C 248,46)

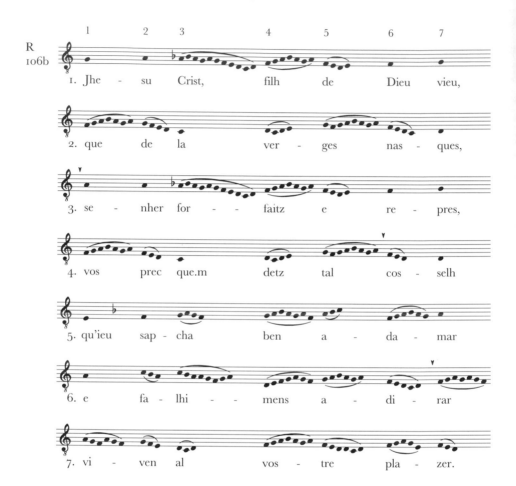

WORKS CITED

Aarburg, Ursula. "Probleme um die Melodien des Minnesangs." *Deutschunterricht* 19 (1967): 98–118.

Appel, Carl. *Die Singweisen Bernarts von Ventadorn nach den Handschriften mitgeteilt.* Halle: Niemeyer, 1934.

Bond, Gerald A. "The Last Unpublished Troubadour Songs." *Speculum* 60 (1985): 827–49.

Chaytor, Henry John. *From Script to Print: An Introduction to Medieval Vernacular Literature.* Cambridge: Cambridge University Press, 1945.

Fernandez de la Cuesta, Ismael, with Robert Lafont, text editor. *Las cancons dels trobadors.* Toulouse: Institut d'Etudes Occitanes, 1979.

Gennrich, Friedrich. *Grundriss einer Formenlehre des mittelalterlichen Liedes als Grundlage einer musikalischen Formenlehre des Liedes.* Halle: Niemeyer, 1932.

———. *Der musikalische Nachlass der Troubadours.* 3 vols. Darmstadt: author, 1958, 1960, 1965.

Husmann, Heinrich. "Das Prinzip der Silbenzählung im Lied des zentralen Mittelalters." *Die Musikforschung* 6 (1953): 8–23.

Jeanroy, Alfred. *Le Jeu de Sainte Agnès . . . avec la transcription des melodies par Th. Gérold.* Paris: Champion, 1931.

Kippenberg, Burkhard. *Der Rhythmus im Minnesang.* Munich: Beck, 1962.

Mölk, Ulrich. *Guiraut Riquier: las cansos.* Studia Romanica 2. Heidelberg: Winter, 1962.

Paden, William D., Tilde Sankovitch, and Patricia H. Stäblein, eds. *The Poems of the Troubadour Bertran de Born.* Melodies transcribed by Hendrik van der Werf. Berkeley and Los Angeles: University of California Press, 1986.

Page, Christopher. *Voices and Instruments of the Middle Ages: Instrumental Practice and Songs in France, 1100–1300.* Berkeley and Los Angeles: University of California Press, 1986.

Rohloff, Ernst. *Die Quellenhandschriften zum Musiktraktat des Johannes de Grocheio.* Leipzig: Deutscher Verlag für Musik, 1972.

Sachs, Curt. "The Road to Major." *Musical Quarterly* 29 (1943): 381–404.

———. *The Wellsprings of Music.* Ed. Jaap Kunst. The Hague: Nijhof, 1961.

Stevens, John. *Words and Music in the Middle Ages: Song, Narrative, Dance, and Drama, 1050–1350.* Cambridge: Cambridge University Press, 1986.

Switten, Margaret Louise. *The Cansos of Raimon de Miraval: A Study of Poems and Melodies.* Cambridge, Mass.: Medieval Academy of America, 1985.

Tischler, Hans. *The Montpellier Codex.* Madison, Wis.: A-R Editions, 1978.

———. *The Earliest Motets.* 3 vols. New Haven: Yale University Press, 1982.

———. *The Style and Evolution of the Earliest Motets.* 2 vols. Henryville, Ott.: Institute of Mediaeval Music, 1985.

van der Werf, Hendrik. "The Trouvère Chansons as Creations of a Notationless Musical Culture." *Current Musicology* 1 (1965): 61–68.

———. "Recitative Melodies in Trouvère Chansons." In *Festschrift für Walter Wiora,* ed. Ludwig Finscher and Christoph-Hellmut Mahling. Kassel: Bärenreiter 1967a.

————. "Deklamatorischer Rhythmus in den Chansons der Trouvères." *Die Musikforschung* 20 (1967b): 122–44.

————. *The Chansons of the Troubadours and Trouvères: A Study of the Melodies and Their Relation to the Poems.* Poems translated by F. R. P. Akehurst. Utrecht: Oosthoek, 1972.

————. *Trouvères-Melodien.* 2 vols. Monumenta Monodica Medii Aevi, 11 and 12. Ed. Bruno Stäblein. Kassel: Bärenreiter, 1977–79.

————. "Estampie." In *The New Grove Dictionary of Music and Musicians*, ed. Stanley Sadie, 6:254–58. London: Macmillan, 1980.

————. Review of *Chanter m'estuet: Songs of the Trouvères*, by Samuel N. Rosenberg and Hans Tischler. *Journal of the American Musicological Society* 35 (1982): 539–54. Subsequent discussion, 36 (1983): 341–44; 37 (1984): 206–8.

————. *The Emergence of Gregorian Chant: A Comparative Study of Ambrosian, Roman, and Gregorian Chant.* Vol. 1: *A Study of Modes and Melodies*, part 1: *Discourse*; part 2: *Transcriptions.* Rochester, N.Y.: author, 1983.

————. Review of *Words and Music in the Middle Ages: Song, Narrative, Dance, and Drama 1050–1350*, by John Stevens. *Journal of Musicological Research* 9 (1989): 378–86.

————. "The Raison d'être of Medieval Music Manuscripts." Appendix to *The Oldest Extant Part Music and the Origin of Western Polyphony*, 1:173–204. Rochester, N.Y.: author, 1993.

van der Werf, Hendrik, with Gerald A. Bond, text editor. *The Extant Troubadour Melodies: Transcriptions and Essays for Performers and Scholars.* Rochester, N.Y.: author, 1984.

Accessory Texts

SIX

The Non-lyric Texts

Suzanne Fleischman

There is no question but that our modern interest in the language and culture of medieval Provence is linked principally to the poetry of the troubadours—both as a literary-historical phenomenon in its own right and in terms of its impact on later poets and writers in various linguistic traditions. Yet there is also a body of non-lyric material that has come down to us, which in the opinion of some scholars represents but a fraction of what was once a substantial corpus of texts. Though the non-lyric texts are on the whole less well known than the lyric compositions of the troubadours, no survey of the textual production of medieval Occitania would be complete without at least a chapter devoted to them. The number of non-lyric texts that have been preserved, representing a range of literary and less literary genres, precludes any attempt at an exhaustive survey. I will therefore limit the remarks in this chapter to what I consider to be the most significant of the non-lyric genres (the *vidas* and *razos* are treated separately in Chapter 7) and, within these genres, the texts most likely to be of interest to non-specialists—both as literary "monuments" and as linguistic or literary-historical "documents" (to invoke a distinction drawn by Paul Zumthor).

Limentani characterizes the narrative genres as "exceptional" within the literary panorama of the Midi; yet their development, as he observes, was never disjunct from that of the more prominent lyric tradition. A case in point is the romance of *Flamenca*, the one universally acknowledged masterpiece of Old Occitan narrative.

THE ROMANCE TRADITION

Blending ingredients of the fabliau genre, northern French courtly romance, and the erotic casuistry of the troubadours, the anonymous verse romance *Flamenca* (composed ca. 1250) may be seen as a transposition into narrative of the social and erotic conventions of troubadour poetry, developed in a dynamic context not possible in a lyric poem with its limited temporality and even more limited point of view. The plot in brief: Archambaut de Bourbon, a prominent member of courtly society, falls prey to an all-consuming passion for Flamenca, the bride he has acquired through contracted marriage. His love deteriorates rapidly into the most vehement jealousy, which transforms the erstwhile chivalrous figure into a social recluse and courtly recreant. Obsessed by fear of betrayal, Archambaut locks his wife in a tower, limiting her exits to attendance at mass and sporadic visits to the baths, but always under guard. Enter Guilhem de Nevers, the perfect knight and potentially perfect lover, who conceives for Flamenca an *amor de lonh* à la Jaufre Rudel. Applying the strategies of his mentor the god of love, Guilhem gains access to Flamenca in church, then woos her in the privacy of his chamber, which he has contrived to link up, via subterranean tunnels, to the bathhouse where she takes her supposed cure. Ultimately, the three main characters, who have all been socially isolated during the major part of the preceding action, return to public life. Flamenca swears an oath of fidelity to her husband as specious as that which Iseut swore to Mark. Archambaut, oblivious to the deceit, is miraculously cured of his jealousy, lifts his surveillance over Flamenca, and regains his former courtly stature. Flamenca then sends her lover away to have his knightly credentials revalidated in jousts and tournaments, from which he abstained all the while he was pursuing his amorous objectives. When he returns, triumphant, to take part in Archambaut's tournament, Flamenca and Guilhem are reunited and now engage in love publicly. Amid renewed celebrations the unique manuscript breaks off.

Into the texture of this fabliau plot the *Flamenca* poet weaves a complex pattern of ideological issues relating to love and courtliness, at the crux of which is the implicit question of whether the form of love that best conforms to human passions and emotions is also most consistent with the social demands and expectations of courtly life. The narrative poet attempts what the lyric poets could not: he tests the viability of the ideals of *fin'amor* by playing them out in a purportedly real-life scenario. What emerges is, in my view, a markedly ironic and ambivalent picture of love and courtliness as embodied in the troubadour lyric (cf. Fleischman 1980).

The Occitan romance genre is represented by three other chivalric-adventure texts, two from the first half of the fourteenth century: *Blandin de Cornualha*, a relatively short (ca. 3,000 verses) anonymous romance (ed. van der Horst), and Arnaut Vidal de Castelnaudary's *Guilhem de la Barra* (ed. Meyer); the third, the anonymous *Jaufre*, was composed in the late twelfth or early thirteenth century (text available in Lavaud and Nelli, vol. 1). Of these three romances, *Jaufre* clearly has the most to offer readers, though its *literary* aspects have received relatively scant critical attention; discussion has focused instead on questions of sources, dating, authorship, and indebtedness to Chrétien de Troyes. What little attention it has received as a literary artifact has on balance been negative, in large part because Chrétien's romances have served as the yardstick for the Arthurian romance genre. The *Jaufre* poet has been faulted for repetitiveness, lack of psychological insight, overemphasis on single combat, and a loosely woven plot that strings together in seemingly random fashion similar and often gratuitous episodes. Such criticisms not only reveal a crucial misunderstanding of the role of single combat within Arthurian tradition, they also ignore the fact that sequences of disjunctive episodes constitute a distinctive structural feature of romance. Even granting that the *Jaufre* poet does draw out his tale (ca. 11,000 verses) with a series of somewhat parallel adventures, this strategy takes on an entirely different meaning if we consider that the poet sought not to imitate but to parody by exaggeration the conventions of canonical chivalric romance. If a reevaluation of this—in my view highly underrated—text is forthcoming, it will most likely emerge through an approach to the text as parody, the reading strategy that seems to yield the most compelling and coherent interpretation (see Fleischman 1981).

NOVAS

Among short narrative fiction in verse—referred to in the Occitan tradition as *novas*—mention should be made of *Castia-gilos* and the *Judici d'Amor*, both attributed to the Catalan troubadour Raimon Vidal de Besalù (late 12th or early 13th cent.), and of the *Novas del papagai* of Arnaut de Carcassès (early 13th cent.). The *Judici d'Amor* (also referred to by its first verse, "So fo el temps c'om era jais"), the longest of the three *novas* (ca. 2,000 verses), explores a question of love casuistry through the vehicle of a debate, whose participants cite *coblas* from the lyric poets in support of their respective positions.

Combining lyric and narrative elements, the brief *Novas del papagai* (just over 300 verses) treats a familiar fabliau theme that also provides the plot springboard for *Flamenca* and *Castia-gilos*: the punishment of jealousy. Limentani (61–77) looks into the manuscript tradition of this text as it relates to the question of "lyricism" vs. "narrativity." Comparing the versions given in four manuscripts, he concludes that of the two complete manuscripts, *J* comes closer to the lyric paradigm, while *R* offers a more clearly articulated narrative development. In support of his view that the narrative genres were "the exception" in Old Occitan literature, he interprets the evolution of this text, as seen through the prism of its manuscript history, as symptomatic testimony to the very partial and lukewarm reception that southern French culture accorded to the narrative mode that northern France was exporting with greater and greater impetus.

In *Castia-gilos* (see Elliott for the text with English translation), the emotion of jealousy, which the *Flamenca* poet explores in considerable psychological depth, is reduced to a stock plot device in a popular tale that might appropriately be characterized as a blend of moral fable and courtly fabliau. More interesting from a narratological point of view than the conventional bawdy-tale plot is the *skaz* structure of the 450-verse text,[1] in which the levels of fiction resemble a series of three Chinese boxes. The "tale" itself (vv. 65–411) is set into a multilevel frame that includes its supposed context of performance. Raimon Vidal—if we can equate the highest-level narrator with the poet himself—claims to have heard the tale, recounted as a historical happening, performed at the court of King Alfonso VIII of Castile (vv. 38–43). Vidal inserts this context of courtly performance twice more into the fabric of his tale—briefly at vv. 64–67, then again at the close of the tale (v. 412) as the verbal perspective returns definitively from the "now" of the events of the fiction (the innermost box, as it were) to the "now" of the performing *joglar* (the middle box). At verse 412 both the point of view and the narrative voice shift from the *joglar*-narrator at Alfonso's court back to Raimon Vidal (in the outermost box), who reports, largely via direct speech (dialogue), the exchange between the king and the *joglar* (vv. 412–43). The text concludes with a self-serving statement by Raimon testifying to the success of the tale and of the *joglar*'s performance of it. In addition to its interest from the standpoint of narrative structure, *Castia-gilos* provides us with precious documentation about story performance as carried out in the Middle Ages.

The three aforementioned *novas* all deal with courtly subject matter, specifically with love. By contrast, the *Novas del heretje* (ed. Meyer), while it bears the label of *novas*, is essentially a work of conservative propaganda directed against the Cathars. In this ca. 700-verse text from the end of the thirteenth or beginning of the fourteenth century, the poet Izarn debates with the Cathar heretic Sicart de Figueiras and ultimately convinces him of the merits of a more orthodox Christianity.

THE EPIC/HISTORIOGRAPHIC TRADITION

Texts included under these two headings are considered together here inasmuch as the overlap of the two categories makes it difficult to draw a meaningful boundary between them. As Duggan points out, for much of the Middle Ages the epic songs were *the* popular form of historiography. Only

---

1. Narrative theorists have identified a type of first-person storytelling that imitates the form of direct speech, to the extent that within the narrative itself a fictional storyteller addresses a tale to an audience whose presence is linguistically inscribed in that tale as is the voice of its teller. The Russian Formalists have labeled this style of storytelling *skaz*, a Russian word meaning "speech" (cf. Bakhtin).

verse narratives are surveyed in this section—that is, texts with some claim to a poetic function in addition to their referential function of reporting ostensibly historical information.

For this genre, as for romance, the number of Occitan texts that have survived is minimal in comparison to the number of extant Old French chansons de geste—a state of affairs all the more striking given that most of the major epic events take place in the Midi. We possess only nine epic texts composed in dialects of Oc. All have survived in unique manuscripts except *Girart de Rossilho* (mid–12th cent.), represented by three manuscripts and a fragment now lost. The other Occitan epics are *Daurel e Beto* (latter half of the 12th cent.); fragments of *Aigar e Maurin* (12th cent.); *Ronsasvals* and the comic-heroic *Rollan a Saragossa* (both early 12th cent.); a fragment of the *Canso d'Antiocha* (mid–12th cent.); the *Canso de la crozada* by Guilhem de Tudela and an anonymous continuator (composed between 1210 and 1218); *Fierabras* (ca. 1230–40); and a *Canso* chronicling the Navarrese civil war of 1276–77 by Guilhem Anelier (late 13th cent.). Also of historiographic purport, albeit considerably later (14th cent.), is the *Roman d'Arles*, an anonymous chronistic romance reworked partially in prose.

The paucity of extant Occitan epics (vis-à-vis those of Old French), together with the fact, noted above, that the major events of Gallo-Romance epic are concentrated in the south, has led a number of scholars to assume that a vigorous epic tradition once flourished in the Midi, but that for reasons unclear the majority of the texts were lost. It is difficult to accept Chaytor's suggestion that epic texts failed to survive in Occitania owing to a poorly developed sense of nationalism. Even less tenable—and no longer taken seriously by anyone—is Fauriel's proposal that the Old French chansons de geste were merely calques of an epic tradition indigenous to the Midi.

We possess incontrovertible textual evidence from lyric as well as non-lyric sources that in the twelfth century a considerable number of chansons de geste were known in Occitania (see Roques 1962; also discussion below). Yet the fact that lyric poets make reference to northern epic material cannot support the claim that this material at one time existed in Occitan texts that were later lost, through some accident of history, leaving only incomplete and ambiguous fragments. It seems more plausible to assume that southern audiences were familiar with the chansons de geste, either directly or through translations: pieces of the Roland legend, for example, survive in two Occitan fragments, *Ronsasvals* and *Rollan a Saragossa* (described below). The seven remaining epics, however, are indigenous to the Midi. While some scholars (e.g. Lejeune 1969) argue for a unified epic tradition across langue d'oc and langue d'oïl, others (e.g. Pirot 1969) insist on the existence in the south of a long epic tradition independent of that of the north.

Among the epics listed above, the most popular today is *Girart de Rossilho* (ed. Hackett), a text of some 10,000 verses. While no one would dispute that *Girart* is an epic, belonging to the cycle of "rebellious vassals," it begins like a romance (parallels with the Tristan story have been observed) and ends like a saint's life, with the hero dedicating the latter part of his life to performing good works and founding monasteries. The text recounts Girart's difficulties with his feudal lord Charles (Martel).[2] While the bulk of the narration is taken up with the stock building blocks of epic—council scenes, battles, quarrels, embassies, discussions of the duties of a vassal, etc.—there is also considerable emphasis on the psychological penetration of characters, a feature that sets this text apart from most twelfth-century epics and suggests influence from the romance tradition. *Girart* is conceivably also the only epic to develop a strong female figure, in the character of the hero's wife, Berthe. Critical discussion of this text has focused on its linguistic heterogeneity—that is, the fact that the language cannot be identified with a particular Occitan dialect. Although consensus is lacking about the dialect of the original poet-singer, there is agreement that the text we possess is written in a poetic koiné (cf. Hackett 1970, Pfister).

Also acknowledged for its literary merits is the *Canso de la crozada* (eds. Martin-Chabot; Gougaud), a historiographic epic chronicling the crusade against the Albigensians. The poem is in two parts: the shorter first part (ca. 2,800 verses) by Guilhem de Tudela takes the events up to the Battle of Muret in July 1213; the continuation (ca. 9,600 verses) by an anonymous poet, which certain critics regard as superior from a literary standpoint, follows events up to the death of Simon de Montfort in 1218.

The principal interest of *Daurel et Beto* (ed. Kimmel) is its controversial generic status—romance or "bourgeois" epic—and its use of a first-person narrator. Daurel is the sole example in Romance epic literature of a hero who narrates his own adventures (cf. Kimmel 1974; Limentani 102–10), a situation that, from a narratological perspective, provides an interesting departure from the characteristically objective epic point of view, which is connected to the usual third-person voice.

The two texts pertaining to the Roland legend, *Rollan a Saragossa* and *Ronsasvals* (both ed. Roques), are now considered to be roughly contemporaneous (early 12th cent.), at least in their original versions, and conceivably the work of a single poet. Previously *Rollan* was thought to have been composed in the fourteenth century, that is, during the period of the single extant manuscript. Lejeune's suggestion (1954) that *Ronsasvals* provided a

---

2. The character of Girart is based on a historical Count Gerardus, regent of the kingdom of Provence at the time of Charles the Bald. The historical Gerardus is known to have had difficulties with his feudal lord, who in the poem is confused with Charles Martel.

source for the *Canso d'Antiocha* (based on an allusion in the latter to the battle of Roncevaux) led her to date *Ronsasvals* before 1126–38.

HAGIOGRAPHY

The extant corpus of hagiographic narratives in Old Occitan consists of some half dozen texts, of which the best known—as a linguistic document rather than for any particular poetic value—is the *Canso de Sancta Fides* (ed. Hoepffner and Alfaric), an anonymous poem of some 600 octosyllabic verses, composed near Agen between 1060 and 1080. The poem begins by narrating the martyrdom of Saint Fides, an event situated in the context of the campaign of the Roman emperors Diocletian and Maximian against the Christians. It continues with an invective against the Roman emperors that ends in a declaration by the poet that he is too disgusted to sing of them any further. Critical discussion of this poem has focused on three issues: its geographic localization, which remains controversial (see Schwegler); the meaning of the phrase from the Prologue, "a lei francesca" (in rhyme? in the vernacular (vs. Latin)?); and stylistic parallels with the epics, in particular the use of formulas and other devices that point to composition-in-performance. In a detailed study of the social and cultural context of eleventh-century Gallo-Romance hagiography, Zahl demonstrates the extent to which hagiographic poets borrowed from the epic *jongleurs*' oral narrative techniques in order to market their didacticism more effectively (cf. note 3 and the discussion on *Boeci*, below).

Narrative *vidas* have also survived for *Sancta Doucelina* (early 14th cent.; original text in prose), *Santa Enimia* (early 13th cent.; a verse adaptation by Bertran de Marselha of an extant Latin *vita*), *Sant Frances* (first half of the 14th cent.; a learned prose adaptation, of anonymous authorship, of St. Bonaventure's *Legenda maior sancti Francisci*), and *Sant Honorat* (end of the 13th cent.; a verse adaptation by Raimon Feraut of an extant Latin text). Also considered to be a Christian saint was Buddha (known as Josaphat); the events of his youth are recounted in *Barlaam e Josafat* (ed. Keller and Linker; text and French trans. also available in Lavaud and Nelli, vol. 1), an anonymous fourteenth-century prose adaptation of a lost Latin original. (Below I discuss dramatized versions of the lives of saints.)

Today the Old Occitan saints' lives are read primarily by specialists—a statement that probably holds (with certain exceptions) for the genre as a whole, across languages. The interest of these texts is principally as cultural and historical documents rather than as literary monuments.

THE "EXCEPTIONAL" STATUS OF NARRATIVE IN OCCITANIA

As pointed out in our discussion of epic, scholars differ in how they choose to interpret the relative paucity of extant narrative texts in Old Occitan:

many believe that a once sizable narrative corpus suffered major textual losses, while others maintain that the narrative genres were cultivated primarily in the north but constituted an anomaly in the south—the *patria* of the lyric par excellence. This state of affairs bears a resemblance to that which obtained on the Iberian Peninsula, where the medieval lyric tradition flourished originally in Galician-Portuguese territory, the narrative tradition in Castile, and only later did cross-fertilization occur. As mentioned above, too, we have textual evidence—e.g. the *ensenhamen* by Guiraut de Cabreira (see below), who reproaches his *joglar* for not knowing a virtual catalog of narrative texts, also a passage from *Flamenca* (vv. 599–602, 621–706) detailing the repertoire of the *joglars* who performed at the nuptial festivities of Flamenca and Archambaut—that a significant amount of northern narrative material was in circulation in the south. What we lack are the texts themselves.

DRAMA

The dramatic literature that has survived in Old Occitan—most of it from the fourteenth century or later—is of religious inspiration (for an overview, see Jeanroy 1949; he gives particular attention to the *Esposalizi de Nostra Dona,* the *Jeu de Sancta Agnes,* and the Didot *Passion*). In Oc as in Oïl, the boundary between drama and performed narrative is often a tenuous one, the difference involving little more than the number of speakers. As mentioned above, saints' lives were commonly performed, as were the chansons de geste, and the two genres share a number of features that have been identified as characteristic of "performed stories" in general, including asides, repetitions, extensive use of direct speech (dialogue), expressive sounds and sound effects, use of motions and gestures, and tense switching.[3] The difference between presenting the events of a saint's life in the form of a *vida* or in the form of a *jeu* was often only a difference of degree (of dramatization), rather than a hard-and-fast generic distinction recognized by medieval audiences.

The corpus of extant dramatic texts in Old Occitan includes one hagiographic piece, the *Jeu de Sancta Agnes* (ed. Jeanroy), a play of about 1,200 verses (the beginning is missing) from the mid–fourteenth century, containing eighteen lyric interludes with melodic notation. There are also

---

3. The term *performed stories* was coined by Wolfson to refer to naturally occurring narrations (i.e., stories surfacing spontaneously in conversation) that share with theatrical presentations the features enumerated above. While there are undeniably important differences between the medieval texts under survey here and the unplanned anecdotes that punctuate everyday interactive discourse, the two varieties of narrative nonetheless share a number of structural and linguistic features that differentiate "performance" narratives from other verbal reports of experience (see Fleischman 1990).

several mystery plays, listed here chronologically: the *Sponsus*, also known as the *Drame de l'époux* or *Mystère des vierges sages et des vierges folles* (ed. Avalle and Monterosso), is an anonymous piece of liturgical drama (with melodic notation) from the end of the eleventh century; the 87-verse text is partly in Latin (47 verses), partly in Occitan (40 verses). The *Esposalizi de Nostra Dona* (ed. Kravtchenko-Dobelmann) dramatizes a series of episodes in the life of the Virgin Mary: her marriage to Joseph, her visit to Elizabeth, the Nativity, and the Adoration; the text of approximately 800 verses dates from the end of the thirteenth or beginning of the fourteenth century. The extant text of the anonymous fourteenth-century *Passion Occitane* (ed. Shepard) is in Occitan, though the original may have been in Catalan. The last of the dramatic texts chronologically is the *Jutgamen general* (ed. Lazar), a play from the cycle known as the *Mystères rouergats* (15th cent.); as its name suggests, the Occitan play represents the episode of the Last Judgment.

DIDACTIC LITERATURE

A variety of poetic genres come under this heading, religious as well as secular (see Segre 1968, 86–102; Monson chap. 5). An important document in this genre, until recently considered to be the oldest extant text in a dialect of Oc,[4] is the *Boeci* fragment (ed. Schwarze), composed circa 1000–1030 (dating controversial). The 258-line text, representing only a fragment of the original, offers a paraphrase in epic form (see below) of Boethius's *De consolatione philosophiae*. The poet, after some initial moralizing, proceeds to tell the life story of Boethius, whom the Middle Ages turned into a Christian martyr. He makes Boethius, like Alexis, a "count of Rome" (v. 35; presumably a confusion of CONSUL with COMES), a landed vassal owing homage to the emperor. Several studies on the narrative style of *Boeci* have linked this poem to the epic tradition, focusing in particular on its form—decasyllabic verses with a regular caesura after the fourth syllable, arranged in *laisses* of unequal length—which is the same as that of the chansons de geste save for the use of rhyme instead of assonance. Segre (1954–55) regards this text as a crucial intermediary, in the literary development of the ninth to eleventh centuries, between hagiography and the epic forms. In light of his statement and the observations made above concerning the hagiographic poets' appropriation of performance fea-

---

4. The prevailing opinion is now that the Romance refrain of the so-called bilingual *alba* (*Phoebi claro nondum orto iubare* . . .), found in a tenth-century manuscript from Fleury-sur-Loire, is in a variety of Oc and thus constitutes the earliest piece of sustained discourse in that language. The strophes of the poem, in Medieval Latin, are followed by the refrain "L'alba part umet mar atra sol / poi pasa bigil mira clar tenebras," enigmatic with respect to both dialect and meaning (cf. Hatto 77ff., 272, 280f., 353f.).

tures from their epic counterparts, it is relevant to point out the presence in *Boeci* of several distinctive marks of narrative performance: extensive use of direct speech, tense switching from past to present (cf. vv. 72–75), and words/phrases whose function in the text is a pragmatic, specifically conative one of underscoring the interactive (i.e., speaker-hearer) dimension of the storytelling situation (e.g., phrases involving direct reference to the speaker and/or addressee, such as *ecvos*, lit. 'here before you': *Ecvos Boeci cadegut en afan* 'here you have B. fallen on hard times'; or *bel sun si drap: no sai nommar lo fil* 'his clothes are elegant; I can't say exactly what the fabric is').

An important subgenre of didactic literature in Old Occitan is constituted by the nine *ensenhamens* (literally 'instructional [poems]'), of which only six bear this title in the manuscripts. Composed between the end of the twelfth and the first third of the fourteenth century, these texts represent conceivably the earliest didactic poetry in Europe of nonreligious inspiration. In an exhaustive study of the genre, Monson emphasizes that what this formally heterogeneous group of texts has in common, and what sets them apart from other doctrinal genres, is the *courtly* nature of their didacticism: in all of them a first-person speaker offers instruction on courtly doctrine by reflecting on the basic tenets of the love ethic that informed the contemporaneous courtly lyric and narrative traditions. The didacticism that is merely implicit in the *cansos* is rendered explicit in the *ensenhamens*, which seek to resolve the ambiguities and contradictions that *fin'amor* presented in the troubadour lyrics or in a romance like *Flamenca*. Several of the *ensenhamens*, such as Arnaut de Maruelh's *Razos es e mezura* (late 12th cent.; ed. Johnston) and Sordel's *Aissi co·l tesaurs es perdutz*, also known as the *ensenhamen d'onor* (mid–12th cent.; ed. Boni), elaborate on key concepts of courtliness and the moral values they imply, while others such as Amanieu de Sescars's *En aquel mes de mai* (end of the 13th cent.) are more straightforwardly pedagogical. Perhaps the best-known exemplar of the genre, Raimon Vidal's *Abril issi' e mays entrava* (ca. 1200; ed. Field), contains an *ensenhamen* addressed by the poet to a *joglar*, followed by a topical lament on the decline of poetry. The assignment of this text to the *ensenhamen* genre is not uncontroversial; certain scholars classify it, along with the other poems of Raimon Vidal, among the *novas*, while others regard it as a hybrid of the two genres.

In three other texts from the late twelfth and thirteenth centuries the poets Guiraut de Cabreira, Guiraut de Calanso, and Bertran de Paris de Rouergue similarly propose to edify their respective *joglars*, albeit in a vein more critical than constructive. Pirot (1972) coined the label *sirventes-ensenhamens* to refer to these texts, inasmuch as their form is that of a *sirventes* while their incontrovertible didacticism links them to the *ensenhamen* (Monson excludes them from the *ensenhamen* genre, labeling them simply *sirventes* addressed to jongleurs). In the earliest of these (late 12th cent.), referred to above, Guiraut de Cabreira inveighs against his *joglar* Cabra for his deficiencies as a singer, musical accompanist, and performer of other activities appropriate to the jongleuresque *métier* such as dancing and magic ("mal saps viular e pietz chanter . . . non sabs balar ni trasgitar"). However the bulk of this 216-line poem—and its principal interest for us today—is a catalog of the texts Cabra is accused of not knowing and therefore of being unable to perform. These include, in addition to a panoply of northern narrative, the work of Occitan poets both narrative (*Daurel e Beto* and the *Canso d'Antiocha*) and lyric. Among the lyric poets, Guiraut singles out Jaufre Rudel, Marcabru (the sole troubadour mentioned in *Flamenca*), Alfonso of Castile, and Eblo of Ventadorn—believed to have been the earliest of the troubadours, although none of his poetry has survived. It is in part through texts such as *Cabra joglar* and analogous intertextual citations that we have been able to reconstruct a picture of the literary culture of the Midi during the age of the troubadours and the several centuries that followed, during which time their work continued to influence poetic traditions outside Provence (see Chapter 10 in this volume).

Among secular didactic works, mention should also be made of several encyclopedic compilations in verse: the *Thezaur* of Pierre de Corbian (ed. Bertoni and Jeanroy), a text from about 1250 that has survived in two redactions of 520 and 825 verses respectively; the compendious *Breviari d'Amor* of Matfré Ermengaud, a poem of nearly 35,000 verses from the end of the thirteenth century (ed. Ricketts); and the much shorter and fragmentary *Cort d'Amor* (just over 1,700 lines; ed. Jones), composed earlier in the same century. The latter two treatises, as their titles suggest, offer comprehensive analyses of love in its diverse manifestations. Both are allegorical, though the *Breviari* aims at a christianization of the troubadours' love ethic, which was in essence secular. Allegorical too is the *Chastel d'Amors* (text in Lavaud and Nelli 1966), an anonymous satirical narrative, probably from the mid–thirteenth century. The *Breviari* is organized according to the allegorical figure of the tree of love, whose four branches Matfré examines successively: love of God and one's fellow humans, love of worldly goods, love between men and women, and love of children. It is in the second of these branches that we find the *Perilhos tractat d'amor de donas*, which explores the vicissitudes of love between the sexes in the form of a lawsuit ("en forma de plah") in which the troubadours themselves are made to speak: over two hundred strophes of their poetry are cited. In the *Cort d'Amor* judgments on *fin'amor* are likewise put forth in the form of litigation, not dissimilar in style and content from that of Raimon Vidal's *Judici d'Amor* (see above), save for the allegorical nature of certain of the protagonists. It is worth noting that several critics classify the allegorical *Chastel d'Amors* and *Cort d'Amor* as varieties of the *ensenhamen.*

TREATISES ON GRAMMAR, RHETORIC, POETICS

The vernacular *artes poeticae*, of which we possess three written in dialects of Oc, have always been of some interest for students of troubadour poetry in that they set forth the formal and compositional principles that guided the lyric enterprise, as well as providing definitions of the major poetic genres and sundry information on matters of grammar and language use. Today these texts attract the attention of a wider audience, including literary theorists interested in the history of poetics, particularly in the transmission and transformations of classical poetic theory into the medieval Latin and vernacular traditions.

Raimon Vidal's *Las razos de trobar* (ed. Marshall 1972) was composed at the beginning of the thirteenth century, making it the oldest grammatical treatise in or about a Romance language. After a rather flamboyant Prologue, which seems to promise a good deal, what follows is a lengthy and rather dry exposition of Limousin morphology. The major critical difficulty with the *Razos* concerns the relationship of the Prologue to the rest of the text, a difficulty some critics have circumvented by discounting the Prologue altogether or postulating dual authorship. A related critical debate concerns how to classify the *Razos*: as an *ars poetica* or as a grammatical manual (depending on whether one chooses to focus on the Prologue or on the body of the work). In a recent attempt to demonstrate the unity of the *Razos* and to vindicate the author of the charge of not carrying through on his promises, Poe emphasizes that Raimon Vidal was a Catalan and that he wrote this text for Catalans; he therefore stresses those aspects of *lemosi* that differ from Catalan and gives shorter shrift to those that the two languages share. This may explain what might appear to be his narrow and idiosyncratic choice of grammatical topics to treat. Moreover, he makes a point in the Prologue of defining his target audience as "prims homs"—that is, not simply hack versifiers but a select minority of skilled writers who aspire to compose poetry properly. Thus Poe maintains that Raimon never set out to teach the *saber de trobar* at all—the objective most critics have attributed to him on the basis of their reading (or misreading) of the Prologue—but merely to suggest how this *saber* might be acquired by sophisticated men of letters and to stimulate a spirit of inquiry into the process of poetic composition.

More complete and more methodical than the *Razos de trobar* as a treatise on poetics, but also drier and somewhat more mechanical, is the *Donatz proensals* (ed. Marshall), composed around 1240 by Uc Faidit and accompanied by a Latin translation. Rather than cite examples from actual troubadour texts, Uc constructs his own examples to illustrate poetic forms and techniques. His text also contains a dictionary of rhymes, of interest not only to students of poetry concerned with how the texts sounded but also to philologists in their attempt to piece together the sound system of a language no longer spoken. However, in light of the dialectally composite nature of the poetic language, determined to have been a koiné, this dictionary of rhymes is of only limited value as a window onto the phonology of Oc (or any of its dialects) as spoken in the thirteenth century.

The last of the three treatises on poetics is the *Leys d'amors*—literally "the laws of love" but understood as referring to "the rules of composing poetry," the composition of poetry having come to be equated in the troubadour tradition with skill as a lover (the topical assimilation of poetic skill to skill as a lover is given a new twist by Huchet, who proposes that the rules set forth in the *Leys* represent the displacement of desire into language, substituting love of language for an unavailable erotic and carnal love). Drawing on classical grammarians, the troubadour tradition, and contemporary ideas on linguistic usage, Guilhem Molinier compiled an initial version of the *Leys* between 1330 and 1332. This version, now lost, covered phonetics (pronunciation), grammar, rhetoric, and poetry (a summary exists in the unedited *Compendi* of Joan de Castelnou). In 1355 Guilhem produced a revised and abbreviated version. The *Leys* currently exists in three versions: A, a prose version in five books, from 1340 (two manuscripts); B, a transposition of version A into verse, in six books; and C, a prose reworking in three books of the 1355 version. The best edition available is of version C (ed. Anglade).

The *Leys* constituted the poetic code of the Consistori de la Subregaya Companhia del Gay Saber, a group founded at Toulouse in 1323 (some fifty years after the last major phase of troubadour activity) to encourage the composition of poetry in the language of the troubadours (rather than in French). This society was founded as part of a campaign to combat the decline of Occitan literature that followed the Albigensian Crusade. The *Leys* were based on the linguistic norm of Toulouse; excluding as they did both Provençal (in the narrow sense) and Gascon, they had the effect of dividing the Midi rather than unifying it, thereby undermining, paradoxically, the society's effort to revive an Occitan linguistic consciousness (cf. Lafont 1966–67). The principal value of the *Leys* for scholars and students of troubadour poetry today lies in the descriptive definitions it provides of the major poetic genres: *vers, canso, sirventes, dansa, descort, tenso, partimen, pastorela, retroncha, planh,* and *escondig* (not that these definitions are consistently borne out by the texts that bear the respective labels). The *Leys* use terms still in use today for certain poetic forms, such as the *coblas capcaudadas* (see Chapter 4 in this volume).

THE NATURAL WORLD

Under this rubric I mention briefly several texts, belonging to different genres, that share the property of dealing with elements of the natural world, in particular birds and animals. *Dels auzels cassadors* by Daude de Pradas (ed. Schutz) is a verse treatise on falconry composed in the first half of the thirteenth century. From the late thirteenth century we have an Occitan version of a bestiary that appeared in various adaptations and languages in the Middle Ages; the rubric for the Occitan version (available in Appel's *Provenzalische Chrestomathie*) is *Aiso son las naturas d'alcus auzels e d'aucunas bestias*. Finally, the *Elucidari de las proprietatz de totas res naturals* is an anonymous translation, composed in the region of Toulouse (near Foix) in the first half of the fourteenth century, of the compendious encyclopedia *De proprietatibus rerum* of Bartholomaeus Anglicus. The text of the *Elucidari* (in nineteen books) is in prose; the Prologue is in verse. Prior to publication of the recent critical edition of books 1–7 (Scinicariello), only portions of book 12 on ornithology had been edited.

It should be apparent from the foregoing discussion that the question of genres—defining them, organizing them into a coherent typology, and assigning texts to the categories of that typology—has been a major preoccupation of Occitanists over the years. This is especially true for the non-lyric genres, whose zones of overlap—with one another and with the lyric genres—significantly complicate the task of producing a genre typology that will be useful as a hermeneutic device and not merely an exercise in taxonomy for its own sake. The reviewer (who remains anonymous) of one recent genre study observes:

> On appréciera fort l'effort fait par . . . pour comparer les *ensenhamens* aux *novas*, aux allégories d'amour, aux saluts d'amour, aux épîtres, aux traités pratiques, moraux ou religieux. La mise en parallèle de ces oeuvres n'est pas inutile. Mais il faut éviter de croire que les genres littéraires du Moyen Age étaient d'une rigidité absolue. Il est vain de chercher à en donner des définitions trop strictes. On tombe vite dans l'artifice, car bien des textes sont au carrefour de plusieurs traditions. . . . (*Romance Philology* 38 [1985]: 442)

This statement is applicable a fortiori to the textual production of medieval Occitania, where the inextricable imbrication of amorous activity (real or imagined) with poetic praxis turned the formal and thematic preoccupations of the lyric tradition into the subject matter of the major non-lyric genres, which thus evolved as a metadiscourse on the troubadour's poetic project and its social implications.

WORKS CITED

The quotations in this chapter are from the critical editions cited in the List of Troubadour Editions in the Appendix, and in particular from the following editions: Arnaut de Marueil (Johnston); *La Chanson de la croisade* (Gougaud); Sordello (Boni). All translations are my own.

Anglade, Joseph. *Les "Leys d'amors," manuscrit de l'Académie des Jeux Floraux.* 4 vols. Bibliothèque Méridionale, 17–20. Toulouse: Privat, 1919–20; repr. New York: Johnson Reprint, 1971.

Avalle, D'Arco Silvio, and Raffaello Monterosso, eds. *"Sponsus," dramma delle vergini prudenti e delle vergini stolte.* Documenti di Filologia, 9. Milan: Ricciardi, 1965.

Bakhtin, Mikhail. "Discourse Typology in Prose." In *Readings in Russian Poetics: Formalist and Structuralist Views,* ed. Ladislav Matejka and Krystyna Pomorska, 176–96. Cambridge, Mass.: MIT Press, 1971.

Bertoni, Giulio, and Alfred Jeanroy. "Le *Thezaur* de Pierre de Corbian." *Annales du Midi* 23 (1911): 289–308, 451–71.

Boni, Marco, ed. *Sordello, le poesie.* Bologna: Palmaverde, 1954.

Chaytor, Henry J. *The Provençal Chanson de Geste.* London: Oxford University Press, 1946.

Duggan, Joseph J. "Appropriation of Historical Knowledge by the Vernacular Epic: Medieval Epic as Popular Historiography." In *Grundriss der romanischen Literaturen des Mittelalters,* vol. 11: *Historiographie,* ed. Hans Ulrich Gumbrecht et al., 285–311 Heidelberg: Carl Winter, 1986.

Elliott, Alison G. "Ramon Vidal de Besalù; The Punishment of the Jealous." *Allegorica* 1, no. 2 (1976): 103–30.

Fauriel, Claude. *Histoire de la poésie provençale: cours fait à la Faculté des Lettres de Paris.* Leipzig: Engelmann, 1847; repr. Geneva: Slatkine, 1969. English trans. New York: Derby, 1860; New York: Haskell House, 1966.

Field, W. H. W., ed. *Raimon Vidal: Poetry and Prose.* Vol. 2: *Abril issia.* University of North Carolina Studies in the Romance Languages and Literatures, 110. Chapel Hill: University of North Carolina Press, 1971.

Fleischman, Suzanne. "Dialectic Structures in *Flamenca.*" *Romanische Forschungen* 92, no. 3 (1980): 223–46.

———. " 'Jaufre' or Chivalry Askew: Social Overtones of Parody in Arthurian Romance." *Viator* 12 (1981): 101–29.

———. *Tense and Narrativity: From Medieval Performance to Modern Fiction.* Austin: University of Texas Press/London: Routledge, 1990.

Hackett, W. Mary, ed. *Girart de Roussillon, chanson de geste.* 3 vols. Paris: Picard, 1953–55.

———. *La Langue de Girart de Roussillon.* Publications Romanes et Françaises, 111. Geneva: Droz, 1970.

Hatto, Arthur T., ed. *Eos: An Enquiry into the Theme of Lovers' Meetings and Partings at Dawn in Poetry.* London: Mouton, 1965.

Hoepffner, Ernest, and Prosper Alfaric, eds. *La Chanson de Sainte Foy.* 2 vols. Publications de la Faculté des Lettres de l'Université de Strasbourg 32–33. Paris: Les Belles Lettres, 1926.

Huchet, Jean-Charles. "L'*Amor de lonh* du grammairien." *Médiévales* 9 (1985): 64–79.

Jeanroy, Alfred, ed. *Le "Jeu de Sainte Agnès," drame provençal du XIVe siècle, avec la transcription des mélodies par Théodore Gérold.* Classiques Français du Moyen Age, 68. Paris: Champion, 1931.

———. "Le Théâtre médiéval des origines à la fin du XIVe siècle." *Histoire littéraire de la France* 38 (1949): 431–61.

Jones, Lowanne, ed. *The "Cort d'Amor": A Thirteenth-Century Allegorical Art of Love.* University of North Carolina Studies in the Romance Languages and Literatures, 185. Chapel Hill: University of North Carolina Press, 1977.

Keller, John E., and Robert W. Linker, eds. *Barlaam et Josafat.* Madrid: Consejo Superior de Investigaciones Científicas, 1979.

Kimmel, Arthur S. *A Critical Edition of the Old Provençal Epic "Daurel et Beton."* University of North Carolina Studies in the Romance Languages and Literatures, 108. Chapel Hill: University of North Carolina Press, 1971.

———. "Le Jongleur héros épique." In *Actes du VIe Congrès International de la Société Rencesvals (Aix-en-Provence, 1973),* 461–72. Aix-en-Provence: Université de Provence, 1974.

Kravtchenko-Dobelmann, Suzanne. "'L'Esposalizi de Nostra Dona,' drame provençal du XIIIe siècle." *Romania* 68 (1944–45): 273–315.

Lafont, Robert. "Les *Leys d'amors* et la mutation de la conscience occitane." *Revue des langues romanes* 77 (1966–67): 13–59.

Lavaud, René, and René Nelli, eds. *Les Troubadours.* 2 vols. Vol. 1: *Jaufre, Flamenca, Barlaam et Josaphat.* Vol. 2: *L'Oeuvre poétique.* Bruges: Desclée de Brouwer, 1960, 1966.

Lazar, Moshe, ed. *Le Jugement dernier (Lo jutgamen general): drame provençal du XVe siècle.* Paris: Klincksieck, 1971.

Lejeune, Rita. "Une allusion méconnue à une *Chanson de Roland.*" *Romania* 75 (1954): 145–64.

———. "L'Esprit de croisade dans l'épopée provençale." *Paix de Dieu et guerre sainte en Languedoc au XIIIe siècle. Cahiers de Fanjaux* 4 (1969): 143–73.

Limentani, Alberto. *L'eccezione narrativa: la provenza medievale e l'arte del racconto.* Turin: Einaudi, 1977.

Marshall, John H. *The "Donatz Proensals" of Uc Faidit.* London: Oxford University Press, 1969.

———. *The "Razos de trobar" of Raimon Vidal and Associated Texts.* London: Oxford University Press, 1972.

Martin-Chabot, Eugène, ed. *"La Chanson de la Croisade Albigeoise," éditée et traduite du provençal.* 3 vols. Classiques Français du Moyen Age, 13, 24, 25. Paris: Champion, 1931 [rev. 1960], 1957, 1961.

Meyer, Paul. "Le Débat d'Izarn et de Sicart de Figueiras." *Annuaire-Bulletin de la Société de l'Histoire de France* 16 (1879): 233–84.

————, ed. *"Guillaume de la Barre," roman d'aventures par Arnaut Vidal de Castelnaudary*. Paris: Firmin Didot, 1895.

Monson, Don Alfred. *Les "Ensenhamens" occitans: essai de définition et de délimitation du genre*. Paris: Klincksieck, 1981.

Pfister, Max. *Lexicalische Untersuchungen zu Girart de Roussillon*. Zeitschrift für romanische Philologie, Beiheft 122. Tübingen: Niemeyer, 1970.

Pirot, François. "Olivier de Lausanne et Olivier de Verdu(n): sur les traces d'une épopée occitane." In *Mélanges offerts à Rita Lejeune*, 247–65. Gembloux: Duculot, 1969.

————. *Recherches sur les connaissances littéraires des troubadours occitans et catalans des XIIe et XIIIe siècles: les "sirventes-ensenhamens" de Guerau de Cabrera, Guiraut de Calanson et Bertrand de Paris*. Barcelona: Real Academia de Buenas Letras, 1972.

Poe, Elizabeth Wilson. "The Problem of the Prologue in Raimon Vidal's *Las Razos de Trobar*." *Res Publica Litterarum* 6 (1983): 303–17.

Ricketts, Peter T. *Le "Breviari d'Amor" de Matfré Ermengaud*. Vol. 5. Leiden: Brill, 1976.

Riquer, Martín de. *Les Chansons de geste françaises*. 2d ed. Trans. Irénée Cluzel. Paris: Nizet, 1957.

Roques, Mario. "*Ronsasvals*, poème épique provençal." *Romania* 58 (1932): 1–28, 161–89; 66 (1941): 433–50.

————. *"Roland à Saragosse," poème épique méridional du XVIe siècle*. Classiques Français du Moyen Age, 83. Paris: Champion, 1956.

————. "Poèmes épiques provençaux du XIVe siècle." *Histoire littéraire de la France* 39 (1962): 133–68.

Scinicariello, Sharon G. "A Critical Edition of Books I—VII of the *Elucidari de las Proprietatz de totas res naturals*." Ph.D. diss., University of North Carolina, Chapel Hill, 1982. [*DAI* 43:5, no. 1538A].

Schutz, Alexander H., ed. *The Romance of Daude de Pradas Called "Dels Auzels Cassadors."* Contributions in Languages and Literature, 11. Columbus: Ohio State University Press, 1945.

Schwarze, Christoph, ed. *Der altprovenzalische "Boeci."* Forschungen zur romanischen Philologie, 12. Münster, Ger.: Aschendorff, 1963.

Schwegler, Armin. "The 'Chanson de Sainte Foy': Etymology of *Cabdorn* (with Cursory Comments on the Localization of the Poem)." *Romance Philology* 39, no. 3 (1986): 285–304.

Segre, Cesare. "Il *Boeci*, i poemetti agiografici e le origini della forma epica." *Atti della Accademia delle Scienze di Torino, Classe di Scienze Morali, Storiche e Filologiche* 89 (1954–55): 242–92.

————. "Le forme e le tradizione didattiche." In *Grundriss der romanischen Literaturen des Mittelalters*, vol. 6, pt. 1: *La Littérature didactique, allégorique et satirique (partie historique)*, ed. Hans Robert Jauss and Erich Köhler, 58–145. Heidelberg: Carl Winter, 1968.

Shepard, William P., ed. *La Passion provençale du manuscrit Didot: mystère du XIVe siècle.* Paris: Champion, 1928.

van der Horst, C. H. M., ed. *Blandin de Cornouaille: introduction, édition diplomatique, glossaire.* Publications de l'Institut d'Etudes Françaises et Occitanes de l'Université d'Utrecht, 4. The Hague: Mouton, 1974.

Wolfson, Nessa. "Features of Performed Narrative: The Conversational Historical Present." *Language in Society* 7 (1978): 215–37.

Zahl, Johannes W. B. *"A lei francesca" (Sainte Foy, v. 20): étude sur les chansons de saints gallo-romanes du XIe siècle.* Leiden: Brill, 1962.

SEVEN

The *Vidas* and *Razos*

Elizabeth W. Poe

The *vidas* and *razos*, commonly referred to jointly as the biographies of the troubadours, are important for two reasons: first, they constitute the richest surviving source of information about the Old Occitan poets; and second, they represent the largest body of prose literature in this lyric-dominated tradition. If we tend to think of Jaufre Rudel dying happily in the arms of the countess of Tripoli (B-S 16–17),[1] or picture Guillem de Cabestanh, somewhat less happily, making his final appearance in the form of a cooked heart about to be served to his beloved by her jealous husband (B-S 530–55), it is less because of what these troubadours have said about themselves in their verses than because of what the biographer has recounted about them in the *vidas*. Moreover, if we know anything of the existence of the trobairitz Na Tibors (B-S 498–99), Almuc de Castelnou, and Iseut de Capio (B-S 422–23), it is only because the biographies preserve their memories and snatches of their work.

The power of the *vidas* and *razos* to determine a troubadour's reputation is nothing new. The scribes of the mid–thirteenth century who compiled the earliest organized anthologies of troubadour verse tended to put the works of Peire d'Alvernhe at the head of the collection of *cansos*, if the arrangement of poets was to be based on a combination of chronological and aesthetic criteria, and Guiraut de Bornelh's poems in the initial position if the organizing principle was to be purely aesthetic (Gröber 459–60). In awarding the place of honor to Peire or Guiraut, these scribes were relying not on their own judgment, but rather on the written authority of the *vidas*,

---

1. All references to the texts of the *vidas* and *razos* are taken from Boutière and Schutz and are indicated parenthetically here and throughout this chapter as B-S followed by a page number. All translations in this chapter are my own.

according to which Peire d'Alvernhe was the first good troubadour of widespread fame, and the best until Guiraut de Bornelh, who was the best troubadour of all time, indeed the master of them all (B-S 63–64, 39).

While the biographies have been heavily exploited in their most obvious capacity—as a source of information about the troubadours—in their other capacity, as prose compositions of intrinsic literary worth, they have been largely ignored. Scholars have overlooked the aesthetic value of the biographies partly because they have been preoccupied with other matters, such as the historical accuracy, authorship, origins, and transmission of the texts,[2] and partly because they have been deceived by the apparent naïveté of thought and childishness of syntax characteristic of these accounts.[3] This chapter, then, will not only review the standard questions raised by the *vidas* and *razos*, most of which pertain to their external worth as literary history and commentary, but also take up less obvious questions connected with their inherent value as literature in their own right.

It is common to distinguish between two different types of biography: the *vida* and the *razo*. The former is a brief account, rarely more than a few sentences long, typically explaining who the troubadour was, whence he came, what his status was, what he was like, whom he loved, what kinds of poems he wrote, and where he died. This information is often conveyed by the use of certain formulas that are the hallmark of the genre: e.g., *si fo de* 'was from', *enamoret se de* 'fell in love with', *fetz maintas bonas cansos* 'composed many good songs', *e lai el definet* 'and there he died'. The accounts may be as economical as the following:

> Richautz de Tarascon si fo uns cavalliers de Proenssa, del castel de Tarascon. Bons cavalliers fo e bons trobaire e bons servire. E fez bons sirventes e bonas cansos. (B-S 513)

> Ricau de Tarascon was a knight from Provence, from the castle of Tarascon. He was a good knight and a good troubadour and a good servant [of ladies]. He composed good *sirventes* and good *cansos*.

Or they may develop a whole story, as in the case of the *vida* about Jaufre Rudel's fateful voyage to Tripoli (B-S 16–19). *Vidas* survive for approximately a hundred troubadours, from Guillem de Peiteus to Italian poets still active in the mid–thirteenth century, like Lanfranc Cigala.

The *razo*, in contrast, is a little story in prose that attempts to explain how a particular troubadour came to compose a specific song. It tends to be somewhat longer than a *vida*, but even the longest does not exceed 2,500 words. The most common plot deals with a lovers' quarrel, but other subjects include stolen property or, on one occasion, the withholding of half a slab

---

2. See the studies by Panvini, Santangelo, Stronski, and Favati.
3. See Schutz 1951; Favati 83–84, esp. n. 136.

of bacon from a woman who wanted it to fry with her eggs (B-S 286–88). While showing somewhat more freedom than the *vidas* in their choice of expression, the *razos* also use various formulas: e.g., *si com vos ai dich* 'as I have told you', *qi fo ni don* 'who he was and from where', *si amava* 'he was in love with'. One peculiarity of the *razos* is the not infrequent intervention of the first-person narrator, usually for the purpose of reminding his audience of what he has told them in a previous account. Fewer than twenty-five troubadours have *razos* written about them, but a number of these poets inspired more than one such story. There are, for example, four *razos* pertaining to Raimon de Miraval, six to Guiraut de Bornelh, and an unparalleled nineteen to the incorrigible warmonger Bertran de Born.

Both *vidas* and *razos* function as introductions to poems, the former leading into a whole set of songs, the latter into a specific one. Many of the biographies probably originated with the jongleurs, who devised them to enliven their performance and to prepare their audience for the song or songs that were to come. From the biographer's complaint about the jongleur Guillem de la Tor's irritating habit of telling *razos* that lasted longer than his songs (B-S 236), we surmise that it was common practice for a jongleur to recite a *razo* before he began to sing. The wealth of geographical detail in the *vidas* strengthens the argument that it was traveling performers, or jongleurs, who invented the oral version of the genre (Schutz 1938, 231–32).

In their written form, the *vidas* and *razos* occur in approximately twenty manuscripts, most of which were compiled in northern Italy. Five of these manuscripts (*A, B, H, I, K*) date from the thirteenth century, virtually all the rest from the fourteenth. The manuscript tradition reflects a significant evolution in the attitude toward these biographies. In the collections of the thirteenth century, each *vida* or *razo* is placed immediately before (or in the case of the *razos* for Bertran de Born, immediately after) the poem or poems for which it was created; by the fourteenth century, however, the biographical texts stand detached from the poems, in a section unto themselves. The proportion of *vidas* to *razos* also changes dramatically between the earlier and the later chansonniers. In the thirteenth-century manuscripts the *vidas* far outnumber the *razos*. Two of these chansonniers (*I* and *K*) contain eighty-seven *vidas* each, but *razos* for only one poet; two others have approximately fifty *vidas* and no *razos* at all.[4] The fourteenth-century manuscripts, in contrast, show a more nearly equal representation of *vidas* and

4. *H* was originally misdated to the fourteenth century, and its biographies were taken to be later avatars of a well-established genre. Now that we can situate *H* among the older biography-bearing chansonniers, we can reassess the status of the biographical texts, especially the *razos*, that it contains. They may in fact be among the earlier experiments with an emerging prose genre.

razos. We gather from these trends that there was a growing appreciation of the intrinsic literary worth of the biographies, which, because of their connections with the lyric, deserved to be included in chansonniers, but which, as narratives, could also be separated from the poems for which they were first intended.

The biographies bear only two signatures: the *vida* for Peire Cardenal is signed by Miquel de la Tor (B-S 335–36), and one of the *razos* for Savaric de Mauleon gives the name of Uc de Saint-Circ, who identifies himself as having written *estas razos* 'these commentaries' (B-S 224). The *razos* to which he refers are probably all of those biographical texts in the collection in which the Savaric account is found. Indeed, Uc de Saint-Circ almost certainly wrote most of the *vidas* and *razos* that we know: there are enough common errors, cross-references, and stylistic similarities among the texts to make it clear that there was but one principal biographer (Favati 33–42, 50). That Uc was considered in the Middle Ages to be the biographer par excellence is evident from the insertion of his name next to a first-person pronoun in one version of the *vida* for Bernart de Ventadorn (Jeanroy 292n.1). Several of the *vidas* refer to events after Uc's time, hence could not have been written by him, but we can take it as a working assumption that all of the *vidas* and *razos* pertaining to events before 1257 or so were the work of Uc (Folena 534; Meneghetti 183).

To say that Uc "wrote" the biographies is not to say that he invented all of the stories. Many of the *vidas* and *razos* must have already existed in primitive form, even in writing, among the jongleurs, who performed them as part of their act. Uc, who was himself a jongleur, would have had access to these "texts." Moreover, as a cleric manqué, Uc had studied in Montpellier, where he came into contact with various materials related to the troubadours and their patrons. We know about Uc's education from his own *vida*, which is probably autobiographical (Folena 518):

> Aquest N'Ucs si ac gran ren de fraires majors de se. E volgron lo far clerc, e manderon lo a la scola a Monpeslier. E quant ill cuideront qu'el ampares letras, el amparet cansos e vers e sirventes e tensos e coblas, e·ls faich e·ls dich dels valens homes e de las valens domnas que eron al mon, ni eron estat. (B-S 239)

> This Uc had a great number of brothers older than he. And they wanted to make him a cleric, and they sent him to the school in Montpellier. And while they thought that he was learning letters, he was learning *cansos* and *vers* and *sirventes* and *tensos* and *coblas* and the deeds and words of the worthy men and of the worthy women who were or who had been alive in this world.

Uc's great contribution, then, was that he collected the stories already in circulation among his fellow jongleurs (undoubtedly adding some of his own), invested them with genealogical and historical detail gathered both from his travels and from his studies in Montpellier, and recast them in his own style: in short, he turned them into literature.

The major source for the stories told in the *vidas* and *razos* is, of course, the troubadour poems. If the *vida* of Marcabru claims that he was the son of a woman named Marcabruna (B-S 10), it is because that is what the poet has reported in one of his songs (Riquer 1:188); and if one of the *razos* for Bertran de Born recounts this poet's unfulfilling quest for a composite lady whose perfection would match that of the woman who has rejected him (B-S 75), it is because Bertran has described just such a search in the *sirventes* that the *razo* is to introduce (Paden, Sankovitch, and Stäblein 150–59). Yet not all of the "facts" in the *vidas* and *razos* can be traced back to a poet's own words. The biographer's identification of Bernart de Ventadorn's father as an oven-stoker (B-S 20) is based not on anything that Bernart ever said but, rather, on a distortion of a remark made by Peire d'Alvernhe in his satirical poem about his fellow troubadours, "Chantarai d'aquestz trobadors" (I will sing about these troubadours; Riquer 1:335). Similarly, the biographer's statement that Raimon Jordan's lady became a heretic out of grief over Raimon, whom she believed to be dead, comes directly from a second such satirical poem, "Pois Peire d'Alverne a chantat" (Since Peire d'Alvernhe sang) by lo Monge de Montaudon (Riquer 2:1040). Some of the other information recorded in the *vidas* and *razos* has no discernible poetic source, but must have come simply from Uc's general knowledge or from what he had learned in Montpellier.

Though the *vidas* and *razos* are structurally and stylistically uniform enough to be thought by some to have been created from a single mold (Jeanroy 289; B-S VIII), it seems more likely that the biographer used a variety of narrative models. For example, while it is hard to deny that the *vida* for Jaufre Rudel reads almost like a little saint's life (Bertolucci-Pizzorusso 16–19), one would be hard put to make the life of the lecher and murderer Guillem de Berguedan conform to any sort of ascetic pattern. Several of the *vidas* and *razos* are nothing more or less than prose fabliaux (Jeanroy 299). Two of these fabliau plots were such favorites that the biographer used them more than once. The tale of the lover who, disillusioned by his lady's empty promises, allows himself to be lured away by the sweet words of another woman, who proves to be just as stingy with her favors as the first, provides the plot for *razos* about three different troubadours, namely Gaucelm Faidit, Raimon de Miraval, and Uc de Saint-Circ (B-S 170–73, 393–95, 244–45). The episode of the woman who arranges to sleep with one of her two lovers in the bed of the other serves as the model for *razos* about Gaucelm Faidit and Guillem de Saint-Disdier (B-S 180–81, 274–75). Margarita Egan has speculated that most of the shorter *vidas* were patterned after the *accessus ad auctores*, or introductions to the Latin authors found in many medieval manuscripts of classical texts. The relation between the *accessus* and the *vidas* is, however, difficult to substantiate, since the resemblances between the two are not very specific. That these two genres have a common function as introductions to literary works is indisputable; but that one uses the other as a narrative model remains open to debate.

Given that the *vidas* and *razos* draw largely on lyric sources and borrow from such widely divergent narrative models as the saint's life and the fabliau, it is little wonder that they have often misled or disappointed scholars who have tried to treat them as purely historical accounts. The deceptive thing about these texts is that many of the facts that they report, sometimes even the unlikeliest, are true—that is, they are historically verifiable. Guillem de Berguedan really did assassinate Raimon Falc of Cardona (Riquer 1:519), and Bertran de Born really did enter the Order of Cîteaux at the end of his tumultuous life (Jeanroy 303–4). Virtually all of the geographical information is accurate. The summary of the Albigensian Crusade at the beginning of one of the *razos* for Raimon de Miraval is reliable in every detail:

> Quan lo coms de Toloza fo dezeretatz per la Gleiza e per los Franses, et ac perduda Argensa e Belcaire, e li Franses agron Saint-Gili et Albuges e Carcases, e Bederres fon destruitz, e·l vescoms de Bezers era mortz, e tota la bona gens d'aquelas encontradas foron morta e fugida a Toloza, Miraval era col comte de Tolosa . . . (B-S 404)

> When the Count of Toulouse was disinherited by the Church and by the French, and had lost Argence and Beaucaire, and the French had possession of Saint-Gilles and Albigeois and Carcassès, and Biterrois was destroyed, and the viscount of Béziers was dead, and all the good people of those regions had either died or fled to Toulouse, Miraval was with the count of Toulouse . . .

But when the biographer claims at the end of this same *razo* that the king of Aragon brought an army of a thousand knights to the defense of Raimon VI, count of Toulouse, as a result of a poem (a *canso* no less) written by Raimon de Miraval, we are no longer dealing with the kind of truth that can be confirmed by edicts and treaties (Jeanroy 295; Poe 1979).

The value of the biographies lies not so much in their faithful reconstruction of history, though occasionally they provide that as well, but much more in their transformation of lyric experience into prose, through a process that Jeanroy has aptly described as metaphor giving rise to anecdote (297). The *razo* for Bernart de Ventadorn's famous *canso* "Can vei la lauzeta mover" serves as a good example of this process at work. The opening verses of the song read:

> Can vei la lauzeta mover
> De joi sas alas contra·l rai,
> Que s'oblid' e·s laissa chazer . . .
>
> (Lazar ed., 180)

When I see the lark move its wings with joy against the sunray, then swoon and swoop . . .

The *razo* introducing them begins thus:

E apelava la Bernart "Alauzeta," per amor d'un cavalier que l'amava, e ella apelet lui "Rai." E un jorn venc lo cavaliers a la duguessa e entret en la cambra. La dona, que·l vi, leva adonc lo pan del mantel e mes li sobra·l col, e laissa si cazer el lieg. (B-S 29)

And Bernart called her "Lark" on account of her love for a knight who loved her, and she called him "Ray." And one day the knight came to the duchess and entered her bedroom. The lady, when she saw him, raised the hem of her cloak and put it onto his neck and let herself fall onto the bed.

The beautiful image of the lark flapping its wings against the sun is reduced in the *razo* to a banal scene of seduction. The lark becomes a lady; the sunray becomes a man; and the bird's natural swooping motion becomes a calculated enticement to erotic pleasure. The other amusing illustration of this process at work involves a metaphor taken from a *canso* by Peire Vidal, in which the poet, playing on the name of his lady Loba, claims that he has suffered such scorn at her hands that he might just as well be a wolf chased and beaten by shepherds. In this *razo*, this metaphor, which was a joke to start with, develops into a ridiculous tale in which Peire, in order to gain access to the castle where his lady resides, dons a wolfskin and sets out for his destination, only to be overtaken by some shepherds and their dogs on the way. Beaten by the former and mauled by the latter, he is brought, unconscious, to his lady, who, laughing, sends for the doctor.

It is because of *razos* like these, in which the figurative language of lyric is interpreted as though it were the literal truth, that scholars have generally accused the biographer of naïveté. One wonders, though, to what extent such accounts are supposed to be taken seriously.[5] Just because the biographer does not share the lyric idealism of Bernart de Ventadorn does not mean that he does not recognize it for what it is. Indeed, if anything, the *razo* about Lark and Ray is a deliberate mockery of Bernart's high-flown and vaguely suggestive nature imagery. Far from being naïve, *razos* of this type are sophisticated, bordering on cynical.

The biographer makes fun not only of others, but of himself as well. At least one of the *vidas*, that pertaining to Gaucelm Faidit, is a parody of its genre (Poe 1986, 21–25).

Gauselms Faiditz si fo d'un borc que a nom Userca, que es el vesquat de Lemozi, e fo filz d'un borges. E cantava peiz d'ome del mon; e fetz molt bos

5. We should note that Pierre Bec includes the *razo* about Lark and Ray among the parodistic pieces in his *Burlesque et obscénité*, 111–12.

sos e bos motz. E fetz se joglars per ocaison qu'el perdet a joc de datz tot son aver. Hom fo que ac gran larguesa; e fo molt glotz de manjar e de beure; per so venc gros oltra mesura. Molt fo longa saiso desastrucs de dos e d'onor a prendre, que plus de vint ans anet a pe per lo mon, qu'el ni sas cansos no eran grazidas ni volgudas.

E si tolc moiller una soldadera qu'el menet lonc temps ab si per cortz, et avia nom Guillelma Monja. Fort fo bella e fort enseingnada, e si venc si grossa e si grassa com era el. Et ella si fo d'un ric borc que a nom Alest, de la marqua de Proenssa, de la seingnoria d'En Bernart d'Andussa.

E missers lo marques Bonifacis de Monferrat mes lo en aver et en rauba et en tan gran pretz lui e sas cansos. (B-S 167)

Gaucelm Faidit was from a town that is named Uzerche, which is in the bishopric of Limousin, and he was the son of a burgher. And he sang worse than anyone in the world; and he made many good melodies and good words. And he became a jongleur, on account of having lost all his possessions at a game of dice. He was a man of great largesse; and he was quite gluttonous of food and drink; thus he became fat beyond measure. For a very long time he was so unlucky in his efforts to get gifts and honor that for more than twenty years he went all over the place on foot, for neither he nor his songs were well received nor desired.

And he married a prostitute, whom he took with him for a long time through the courts, and she was named Guilhelma Monja. She was quite beautiful and quite well educated, and she became as big and fat as he was. And she was from a rich town named Alest, in the march of Provence, under the lordship of Bernart of Anduza.

And the marquis Sir Boniface of Montferrat provided him with property and clothing and placed him and his songs in very great esteem.

In this text the biographer, Uc de Saint-Circ, claims that Gaucelm *cantava peiz d'ome del mon* 'sang worse than anyone in the world'. This statement is humorous for two reasons: first, because the ability to carry a tune is the very least that one can expect from someone trying to make a living as a jongleur; and second, because the specific expression used here is a perfect reversal of the standard vida formula *e cantava meilz c'ome del mon* 'and sang better than anyone in the world', applied to troubadours like Peire Vidal (B-S 351). The explanation of how Gaucelm happened to take up the jongleur's trade—namely, on account of having lost everything he had at the dice table—is more than a sarcastic commentary on Gaucelm's base inclinations. It is, in addition, a perversion of the neutral phrase *fetz se joglars* 'he became a jongleur' used in other *vidas* to indicate the same decision as though it were something respectable. Uc describes Gaucelm as a man of great *larguesa*, by which he means that he was quite fat. Now, Uc knew as well as anyone else what *larguesa* is supposed to signify, and he used it with its normal meaning of "generosity" in several *vidas*, but here he chose to take it in its most literal acceptation of "broadness," for humorous effect, just as he had done with Peire Vidal's wolf. The banter in this account continues as Uc reports of Gaucelm that *si tolc moiller una soldadera* 'he married a prostitute'.[6] The juxtaposition and equation of wife and whore is clearly a bit of misogynist wit. By characterizing this lady of the night as *bella e fort enseignada* 'beautiful and very well educated', Uc laughs at the emptiness of this phrase, which he has used in other *vidas* to describe real ladies like Na Castelloza (B-S 353). In the conclusion of this *vida* Uc manages to take a swipe at one of the great patrons of the troubadours, Boniface of Montferrat. He scoffs at him implicitly by suggesting that any patron undiscerning enough to reward this singularly untalented and unattractive jongleur has extraordinarily bad taste, and explicitly by calling his gifts *rauba*. At first glance, the words *mes lo en aver et en rauba* 'fixed him up with goods and clothes' seem innocent enough, but *rauba* is ambiguous. Although it can mean simply "clothing," more commonly it refers to stolen goods or booty. Uc has exploited this same wordplay in a *razo* about Raimbaut de Vaqueiras (B-S 462), in which the taking of a cloak allows Uc to make a double pun on *rauba* as a synonym for both "robe" and "rob."

Such wordplay is characteristic of Uc's style throughout the *vidas* and *razos*. The biographer finds puns even in the names of persons and places. He portrays Gaucelm Faidit (*faidit* 'outlaw', 'worthless one') as a failure, even though he knows that Gaucelm was a nobleman and a highly successful troubadour. Uc undoubtedly takes delight in reporting that Ademar lo Negre came from, of all places, Albi (*negre* 'black' and *alban* 'white'; B/S 432). He makes puns even when describing the most tragic of events, for example, the destruction of Rocamadour: *Rocamajor fo . . . derrocatz* 'Rocamajor was demolished' [lit. 'un-rocked'] (B-S 239). Another humorous feature of Uc's style is his use of the conjunction *and* to bring together ideas that stand in logical opposition to each other. For instance, Guillem de Peiteus is depicted as courtly and deceitful: *uns dels majors cortes del mon e dels majors trichadors de dompnas* 'one of the most courtly men in the world and one of the greatest deceivers of women' (B-S 7). And even more startlingly, Pons de Chapteuil is presented as possessing all the qualities that one would expect to find in a nobleman, including stinginess:

> Bons cavalliers fo d'armas e gen parlanz e gen domnejanz e granz e bels e ben enseingnatz e fort escars d'aver. (B-S 311)

> He was a good knight of arms and a fine speaker and a fine suitor and he was tall and handsome and well educated and very stingy.

The unexpected afterthought, one of the factors contributing to the humor of the sentence about Pons de Chapteuil, is another typical device of

---

6. A. Rieger, while admitting that the ambiguity of the term is undeniable (233–35), argues that *soudadeira* is synonymous with *joglaressa*. Lazar, however, accepts the definition "prostitute" (1989, 268–69).

Uc's style (Schutz 1951, 184–85; Favati 83n.136). He catches us off guard with this tactic at the end of the short *vida* about Peire de Valeira, for example, which he concludes with the harsh judgment: *Sei cantar non aguen gran valor* 'His songs did not have much value' . . . and just when we think that he has completed his devastating critique, he adds, *ni el* 'and neither did he' (B-S 14).

The *vidas* and *razos* have been hailed as the first attempts at literary criticism in a Romance language, and, to some extent, they are (Smith 26; Poe 1980). Uc does not hesitate to express his personal opinions of the troubadours, most of which are negative: e.g., that Peire de Valeira's poems were worthless (B-S 14), that Jaufre Rudel's words were poor (B-S 17), that Albertet's words had little value (B-S 508), that Gaucelm Faidit's singing voice was a disgrace to the profession (B-S 167). Such comments, while revealing a great deal about the tastes of Uc de Saint-Circ, tell us very little about the troubadours. A few of Uc's statements, more general and objective in nature, have greater literary-historical worth: e.g., that the difference between *vers* and *canso* is essentially chronological (B-S 12, 263); that Arnaut Daniel and Raimbaut d'Aurenga were known for their *caras rimas* 'difficult rhymes' (B-S 59, 441); that Peire Vidal was the one for whom writing poetry came most naturally (B-S 351). All of these facts probably belonged to the fund of knowledge with which Uc became familiar during his studies at Montpellier. It should be emphasized in this regard that the often farfetched stories recounted by the *razos* are not, nor were they ever intended to be, literary commentary. These accounts were designed to arouse curiosity about the upcoming song by giving a bit of background, not to kill interest in the piece about to be performed by submitting it to sterile literary analysis.

Perhaps the most significant development in our understanding of the troubadour biographies is the realization that the *razos* must have been written before the *vidas* (Favati 49). Both the manuscript evidence (i.e., the high number of *vidas* and virtual absence of *razos* in the earliest chansonniers) and the relative simplicity of the typical *vida* as compared with the greater narrative complexity of the *razos* had seemed to support the opposite view. But systematic explanation of the content of the texts shows that none of the information reported in the *razos* postdates the year 1219, while that given by the *vidas* often does (Favati 46–48). What seems to have happened is that Uc de Saint-Circ collected the material for the *razos* while he was still in southern France. In 1219 he left the Midi, taking his notes with him. By the year 1220 Uc was, according to reliable historical sources, residing in Italy. Though he may not have written the *razos* as we know them for another seven to ten years (this seven-plus–year delay has been hypothesized as an explanation for the frequent Italianisms that occur in Uc's Occitan), he did not make any effort to update his information in the meantime (Favati 68). Uc did not produce all of the *razos* as a single block. He wrote those for the *sirventes* of Bertran de Born first. These texts remained detached from the rest of the *razos* and ended up preserved in a different set of manuscripts from the others. Uc referred to them once in a *razo* about Folquet de Marseilla as *l'autre escrit* 'the other writing', thereby acknowledging that they were indeed his work, yet assigning them to an earlier period in his career (Poe 1990, 126–30).

Although this discussion began by drawing a clear-cut distinction between *vida* and *razo*, it shall end by clouding the picture somewhat, for while most of the biographies fit readily into one group or the other, a few, like the following, fall somewhere in between.

> Peire Pelisiers si fo de Martel, d'un borc del vescomte de Torrena. Borges fo valens e pros e larcs e cortes; e montet en si gran valor per proesa e per sen q·el vescoms lo fetz baile de tuta la sua terra. E·l Dalfins d'Alverne, en aqella sason, si era drutz de Na Comtor, filla del vescomte, q'era en gran prez de beutat e de valor. En Peire Pelisiers lo servia totas vetz, qant el venia, de tot so q'el volia, e·il prestava son aver. E qant Peire Pelisiers volc l'aver recobrar, lo Dalfins no·l volc pagar, e l'esqivet a rendre gierdon del servise q'el li avia fait, et abandonet la dompna de veser ni de venir en aqella encontrada on ella estava, ni mes ni letra no·il mandet; don Peire Pelisiers fetz aqesta cobla:
>
> > Al Dalfin man q'estei dins son hostal . . .
>
> Lo Dalfins respondet a Peire Pelisier vilanamen e con iniquitat:
>
> > Vilan cortes, c'avez tot mes a mal . . .   (B-S 291)
>
> Peire Pelissier was from Martel, from a burg of the viscount of Torrena. He was a valorous burgher, excellent and generous and courtly; and he rose to such a degree of valor through prowess and intelligence that the viscount made him the bailiff of his whole land. And Dauphin d'Auvergne, at that time, was courting Na Comtor, daughter of the viscount, who was greatly esteemed for her beauty and her valor. Peire Pelissier served him every time that he came, in all that he desired, and he lent him his money. And when Peire Pelissier wanted to recover his money, Dauphin refused to pay him, and would not consent to give him any compensation for the service that he had done for him, and he gave up seeing the lady and coming into that region where she lived, and he sent her neither letter nor messenger; therefore, Peire Pelissier composed this *cobla*:
>
> > I order Dauphin to stay at home . . .
>
> Dauphin answered Peire Pelissier nastily and with wickedness:
>
> > You, base courtly one, who have dissipated . . .

This text clearly begins like a *vida*, but, after the first two sentences, it proceeds like a perfect *razo*, from the standpoint both of the story that it tells and of its explicit connection with a particular exchange of *coblas*.

There are at least a dozen of these mixed texts spread throughout the chansonniers, but they are represented most prominently in the late-thirteenth-century manuscript *H*, the source of the Peire Pelissier–Dauphin d'Auvergne episode cited here. It was formerly believed that these curious biographies were transitional between the *vidas* and *razos*. Now, however, it appears that we must modify this view: they are indeed transitional, but between the *razos* and the *vidas* rather than the other way around (Favati 46–49). Regardless of the direction of generic evolution, the presence of a few specimens of the mixed variety in virtually all of the major collections of troubadour biographies, even those presumably containing only *vidas*, suggests that the medieval boundary between the two genres must have been rather fluid. At several points within the biographies, the term *razo* is applied to what we normally consider a *vida*. A good example of this imprecision of terminology occurs in the opening sentence of a *razo* for Raimon de Miraval, where the biographer reminds us that we have just heard who this troubadour was and where he came from in the *razo* that is written at the head of his *cansos*:

> Ben aves entendut d'En Raimon de Miraval qui fo ni don, en la razo que es escriuta denan las soas chansos . . .   (B-S 384)

> You have indeed heard, concerning Raimon de Miraval, who he was and from where, in the *razo* that is written before his *cansos* . . .

Both because of what this piece is supposed to have told us and because of its position at the head of a whole collection of songs, it is evident that the "*razo*" in question is really a *vida*.

Finally, it should be noted that Uc de Saint-Circ never uses any term other than *razo* as a designation of genre for those prose compositions. He calls himself the writer of *estas razos* 'these *razos*', probably referring to *vidas* as well as *razos*. On eight other occasions he employs *razo* with the meaning of 'story'; never once does he use *vida* in this sense. It is not until the fourteenth century, in the rubrics of the chansonniers, that *vida* emerges as a generic designation for the biographies of the troubadours. *Vida*, as it is used in the fourteenth century, like *razo* in the previous century, can indicate texts of either type (Poe 1988). Thus, the sharp distinction between *vida* and *razo* is more of a modern perception than a medieval reality (Schutz 1938, 225). Such a division of the texts provides a useful point of departure for discussion of the troubadour biographies, but it is deceptive, for it implies a formal rigidity that these early prose writings never had.

WORKS CITED

Bec, Pierre. *Burlesque et obscénité chez les troubadours: le contre-texte au moyen âge.* Paris: Stock, 1984.

Bertolucci-Pizzarusso, Valeria. "Il grado zero della retorica nella 'vida' di Jaufre Rudel." *Studi mediolatini e volgari* 18 (1970): 7–26.

Boutière, Jean, and Alexander H. Schutz. *Biographies des troubadours: textes proven-çaux des XIIIe et XIVe siècles.* 2d ed., with I.-M. Cluzel. Paris: Nizet, 1973.

Egan, Margarita. "'Razo' and 'Novella': A Case Study in Narrative Forms." *Medioevo Romanzo* 6 (1979): 302–14.

Favati, Guido. *Le biografie trobadoriche.* Bologna: Palmaverde, 1961.

Folena, Gianfranco. "Tradizione e cultura trobadorica nelle corti e nelle città venete." In *Storia della cultura veneta,* 1:453–562. Vicenza: N. Pozza, 1976.

Gröber, Gustav. "Die Liedersammlungen der Troubadours." *Romanische Studien* 2 (1877): 337–670.

Jeanroy, Alfred. "Les Biographies des troubadours et les *razos*: leur valeur historique." *Archivum Romanicum* 1 (1917): 289–306. Reprinted in *La Poésie lyrique des troubadours,* 1:101–32. Toulouse: Privat; Paris: Didier, 1934.

Lazar, Moshe. "*Carmina erotica, carmina iocosa*: The Body and the Bawdy in Medieval Love Songs." In *Poetics of Love in the Middle Ages: Texts and Contexts,* ed. Moshe Lazar and Norris J. Lacy, 249–76. Fairfax, Va.: George Mason University Press, 1989.

Meneghetti, Maria Luisa. *Il pubblico dei trovatori.* Repr. from 1984 edition with updated bibliography. Turin: Einaudi, 1992.

Panvini, Bruno. *Le biografie provenzali, valore e attendibilità.* Florence: Olschki, 1952.

Poe, Elizabeth Wilson. "The Meeting of Fact and Fiction in an Old Provençal *Razo*." *L'Esprit Créateur* 19 (1979): 84–94.

———. "Old Provençal *Vidas* as Literary Commentary." *Romance Philology* 33 (1980): 510–18.

———. "Toward a Balanced View of the *Vidas* and *Razos*." *Romanistische Zeitschrift für Literaturgeschichte* 1/2 (1986): 18–28.

———. "At the Boundary Between *Vida* and *Razo*: The Biography for Raimon Jordan." *Neophilologus* 72 (1988): 316–19.

———. "*L'autr' escrit* of Uc de Saint Circ: The *Razos* for Bertran de Born." *Romance Philology* 44 (1990): 123–36.

Rieger, Angelica. "Beruf: Joglaressa. Die Spielfrau im okzitanischen Mittelalter." In *Feste und Feiern im Mittelalter. Paderborner Symposium des Mediävistenverbandes,* ed. Detlef Altenburg, Jörg Jarnut, and Hans-Hugo Steinhoff. Sigmaringen: J. Thorbecke, 1991.

Riquer, Martín de. *Los trovadores: historia literaria y textos.* 3 vols. Barcelona: Planeta, 1975.

Santangelo, Salvatore. *Dante e i trovatori provenzali.* 2d ed. Catania: Facoltà di Lettere e Filosofia, 1959.

Schutz, A. H. "Where Were the Provençal *Vidas* and *Razos* Written?" *Modern Philology* 35 (1938): 225–32.

———. "Prose Style in the Provençal Biographies." *Philological Quarterly* 30 (1951): 179–85.

Smith, Nathaniel B. *Figures of Repetition in the Old Provençal Lyric.* Chapel Hill: University of North Carolina, Department of Romance Languages, 1976.

Stroński, Stanisław, ed. *Le Troubadour Folquet de Marseille, édition critique précédée d'une étude biographique et littéraire et suivie d'une traduction, d'un commentaire historique, de notes, et d'un glossaire.* Cracow, 1910; repr. Geneva: Slatkine, 1968.

———. *La Poésie et la réalité aux temps des troubadours.* Oxford: Clarendon, 1943.

A Subgroup: The Women Troubadours

EIGHT

The Trobairitz

Matilda Tomaryn Bruckner

Interest in the women troubadours, or trobairitz, as they are designated in the Provençal romance *Flamenca*, generally follows the rising and falling tides of feminism, at least if we judge by the critical tradition that accompanies and introduces us to their extant poems. It is, therefore, not without significance that this chapter is being written in a period and culture that is, at least in theory, pro-feminist. Certainly, we live in a time that is alive to the issue of gender and how it interplays with poetic production and reception. Nor is it insignificant that a woman is writing this chapter, a woman whose particular point of view will become more evident in the course of this essay, even as she tries to give a representative overview of the current status of trobairitz studies. Those studies received special impetus in the 1980s because of Meg Bogin's *The Women Troubadours* (1976; 1980 in paperback), an edition that substantially reproduces and translates the Schultz-Gora corpus of twenty-three poems. While Bogin's edition remains widely available, it must nevertheless be used with great caution.[1] Her

I would like to express my thanks to Don Monson, Laurie Shepherd, and Victoria Jordan for all their help in preparing this chapter, which was completed with the aid of a Summer Research Grant from Boston College.

1. Our deep gratitude to Bogin for bringing out her edition at so timely a moment can be outweighed only by regret that its translations are so often unreliable. Her introduction is equally marred by tendentious and naïve ideas about the trobairitz' spontaneity and directness, which ignore the highly conventional nature of troubadour art in general and the rhetorical skills of the trobairitz in particular, as they play with and against the masculine poetic system. Cf. the reviews of Anatole, Robbins (1977), and Bec (1979a). I recommend using Angelica Rieger's edition of forty-six trobairitz poems, critical editions of specific poems or poets (e.g. Kussler-Ratyé, Paden 1989), or the Garland edition and translation of thirty-six poems by trobairitz (Bruckner, Shepard, and White). In what follows, I have offered my own literal translations, unless otherwise indicated, and have furnished as many sources for the poems'

introduction and notes offer useful historical and cultural information that helps situate the trobairitz and their poems—and these surely constitute the major contribution of Bogin's volume, since the previous edition of the trobairitz as a group dates from 1946 (Véran).

In some sense, to consider the trobairitz as a group already represents an interpretation of their poetry as a kind of feminist project, inasmuch as the poems and poets themselves, as well as most of the manuscripts (chansonniers) that include their songs, do not treat them as a group to be differentiated from the male troubadours. Indeed, in their poems and in the *vidas* (biographies) and *razos* (commentaries) that introduce them in a number of manuscripts, the trobairitz are fully integrated into the network of associations that connect the producers and consumers of troubadour lyric as it functioned in the Occitanian society of the twelfth and thirteenth centuries. And yet the tendency to treat the trobairitz as a separate group already appears in the Middle Ages, in some thirteenth- and fourteenth-century manuscripts, especially Italian and Catalan ones, which group together all the poems of the trobairitz (see Bec 1979a, 262; Paden 1989, 163; and Rieger 1985, 389–91).[2] It is as if, as soon as we leave the contemporary culture of the trobairitz, their existence as a group asserts itself and proclaims the anomaly of their appearance as female poets singing in a fundamentally male-dominated world (both that of their society and that of the songs themselves). We are thus asked to read them simultaneously as part of that larger lyric system and as a coherent group of women poets, who belong to the long but continually disrupted tradition of women and poetry (cf. Woolf 1957, 79).

The poet of "No·m posc mudar" reminds us not only that woman and women are important topics of troubadour poems, but that women should feel a certain solidarity with their sisters, whom they should honor. This particular woman poet has risen to their defense against the old troubadours, like Marcabru, who "ditz mal d'aisso don nais enfansa" (speak badly of that from which a child is born; Riquer 577:30). Any woman who would follow her example in speaking honestly and honorably about the trobairitz as women and poets must pick her way carefully through the difficulties presented by their corpus, both as it relates to the troubadours' lyric production and as it stands in relation to the question of what real medieval

---

texts as I could locate among currently available editions, anthologies, etc. Jeanne Faure-Cousin's French translation of Bogin's edition corrects some but not all mistranslations.

2. Bogin follows Bartsch and lists sixteen manuscripts that include poems by trobairitz: A, B, C, D, d, F, H, I, K, M, N, N², O, Q, R, T. To these can be added G, W, Sg, V, and a (see Kussler-Ratyé's edition of the Comtessa de Dia's poems, and Kolsen's edition of Guiraut de Bornelh's *tenso* with Alamanda). Rieger (1991b, 47–49) includes twenty-eight manuscripts; Bruckner, Shepard, and White, nineteen manuscripts.

women could and did accomplish in their songs. *Ecriture féminine? Textualité féminine?* Certainly as I identify the trobairitz and their corpus, and then offer a brief literary analysis of their poems, we will discover again and again how these songs are linked to the lives of their producers (and consumers) in mysterious but seductive ways. Even when we understand, as we must, the poetic fictionalization that characterizes their representation of lovers, their emotions and experiences, the power of the poems themselves makes us react to them, at least on some level, in relation to the individual lives of women and the general society in which trobairitz and troubadours circulated their songs.

IDENTIFYING THE TROBAIRITZ

Who are the women poets we can identify as trobairitz? The question is not as simple and straightforward as it may appear. Listed by Meg Bogin in chronological order (as far as that can be determined) from about the mid–twelfth century to the mid-thirteenth, they are: Tibors, the Comtessa de Dia, Almucs de Castelnau, Iseut de Capio, Azalais de Porcairagues, Maria de Ventadorn, Alamanda, Garsenda, Isabella, Lombarda, Castelloza, Clara d'Anduza, Bieris de Romans, Guillelma de Rosers, Domna H., Alais, Iselda, and Carenza. To these we can add three more names: (1) Gaudairenca, the wife of Raimon de Miraval, is mentioned in two *razos* that describe how the troubadour used the pretext of too many poets in one home ("dui trobador en un alberc"; Boutière-Schutz 380) to divorce her in favor of another lady (who then abandoned Raimon for another man!). Though she is described there as a composer of "coblas e dansas" (380), none of her poems has survived.[3] (2) Gormonda (or Germonda) of Montpellier wrote a response to Guilhem Figueira's famous *sirventes* against Rome. And (3) Azalais d'Altier names herself as the author of a poetic letter, a kind of *salut d'amor*, in which she intercedes on behalf of a lover who has quarreled with his lady. This lady may be the trobairitz Clara d'Anduza, if we combine the suggestions of her closing lines—

> Anz li sias fina et *clara*
> Qel *noms* nil semblanz nous desmenta
> (Crescini 131:98–99; emphasis added)

rather be to him true and clear, so that neither your name nor your appearance makes you a liar

---

3. Guillelma Monja, the wife of Gaucelm Faidit, may also have been a trobairitz, if we accept Gégou's argument in favor of interpreting *soldadera* as *joglaressa* instead of "prostitute" (47–48). See Gaucelm's *vida* and *razo* F (Boutière-Schutz 167, 169n.4, 192).

—with the information offered in a *razo* on Uc de Saint-Circ concerning his amorous but troubled relationship with "una do[m]pna d'Andutz, qe avea nom ma dompna Clara" (a lady of Anduza whose name was my Lady Clara; Boutière-Schutz 244).

That brings the total to twenty-one, but that number is by no means conclusive (cf. Rieger 1991b, 29–47). We have to consider, on the one hand, an assortment of anonymous poems whose existence suggests that an undetermined number of names for other trobairitz have been lost to us. On the other hand, we cannot ignore the possibility that some of the names we have may be inventions that do not correspond to actual women poets. Meg Bogin, for example, is the first to suggest that the *tenso* between "Na Carenza" and "N'Alaisina Iselda" (Schultz-Gora 28) actually names not two, but three ladies: "N'Alais i na Iselda" (144). Patricia Anderson, however, invites us to read the names as designating types rather than real people. Their names would suggest their characters. Lady Carenza is the one "without assets" (*carenza* in Old Occitan), a nun with courtly manners and worldly graces, whose advice is sought by a young lady, Alaisina Iselda, whose two names combine elements from the highest and lowest social orders: Alice "the nut brown maid" (cf. Chaucer's Wife of Bath) and Isolde, daughter and wife of kings, the well-known lover of Tristan (57). Two or three trobairitz with names, but otherwise unknown; one anonymous trobairitz; or none at all?

Similar problems arise for other trobairitz named in *tensos* but without *vidas* to substantiate, however slightly, their earthly existence. We have a *vida* for Elias Cairel, but who is Isabella, named only by the troubadour in his *tenso* with her? Ladies who debate with well-known poets are especially vulnerable to scholars' speculations that they are simply literary fictions. Thus we have been invited to see Alamanda as the creation of Guiraut de Bornelh (Jeanroy 2:257; Tavera 141–42; but cf. Rieger 1991a) and the lady of "Amics, en gran cossirier" as the projection of Raimbaut d'Aurenga. The three manuscripts that contain the latter *tenso* name only Raimbaut, but many modern scholars and readers have followed the suggestion of the Comtessa de Dia's *vida* and name her as the female speaker: "La Comtessa de Dia si fo moiller d'En Guillem de Peitieus, bella domna e bona. Et enamoret se d'En Rambaut d'Aurenga, e fez de lui mantas bonas cansos" (The Countess of Dia was the wife of William of Poitou, a beautiful and good lady. And she fell in love with Lord Raimbaut of Orange, and made many good songs about him; Boutière-Schutz 445). Judging by the power of her poetic accomplishments, Jeanroy (2:257) even wonders if she might be the sole author of both voices. While Pattison (27–30) argues convincingly about the process whereby her biographer may have invented the *vida* based on certain situational and verbal similarities between this *tenso* and the Comtessa de Dia's poems (especially the opening line of "Estat ai en greu cossirier"), we may still reasonably wonder if Raimbaut d'Aurenga exchanged his *coblas* with a real but otherwise unknown lady (not unlike the Comtessa de Dia!). Historically and textually we can neither prove nor disprove such conjectures. Pattison links the *tenso* to Raimbaut d'Aurenga's corpus because both speakers express ideas typical of the troubadour and because he judges the lady's wit to be "more in keeping with Raimbaut's other works than those of the Countess" (157). Neither argument excludes the possibility of a female poet exchanging stanzas with Raimbaut.

That some *tensos* were feigned is well established: we can readily accept that the poets were feeding made-up words to God and their assorted horses, birds, and hearts (Shapiro 1981, 292–94). That some *tensos* between troubadours and anonymous ladies were fictional dialogues is indisputable. When, for example, Aimeric de Peguilhan's *tenso* "Domna, per vos estanc en greu turmen" alternates *Domna* and *Senher* line by line for three stanzas, we can imagine a real lady speaking, but when *Amors* and *Amics* take over the dialogue for two more stanzas the fiction stands revealed as part of Aimeric's poetic skill. When Raimbaut de Vaqueiras exchanges a *tenso* with a Genoese lady, though the rubric of the manuscript may identify it as "Rambautz de Vaqueras e de la domna" (P-C 392,7), the linguistic fireworks displayed in the contrasts of Occitan and Genoese dialects, of courtly *requête d'amour* and popular insults, which characterize male and female speakers respectively, suggest that the troubadour, who also shows his multilingual skill elsewhere in his corpus, is indeed the sole author in question (Hill-Bergin 2:51; but see Gaunt).

In the corpus of nine or ten fictional *tensos* between male and female speakers identified by Shapiro (1981, 292–93, 293n.10, 299n.10), most of the designations regarding their fictionality seem to be based not on textual or historical evidence, but rather on stylistic evaluations: the popular language and humor (e.g. Guillem Rainol d'Apt's "Quant aug chantar lo gal sus en l'erbos"),[4] the obscenity of the speakers (e.g. Montan's "Eu veing vas vos, seigner"),[5] or perhaps the frame supplied by the male poet's opening and/or closing stanza (e.g. Pistoleta's "Bona Domna, un conseill vos deman" [Niestroy 65–67] and Guillem Rainol d'Apt's "Quant aug"). But these evaluations tend to reflect subjective and culturally determined assumptions about how "ladies" speak or what kind of humor they indulge in (cf. also Chambers and Zufferey). When we consider "fictional" *tensos*, like Bertram del Pojet's "Bona Dompna, d'una re que·us deman" (de Lollis) or those mentioned earlier in which scholars have doubted the real existence of Isabella, Alamanda, or Raimbaut d'Aurenga's *domna*, it seems

---

4. See Riquer, no. 75. Cf. the exchange of insults in the *tenso* between Isabella and Elias Cairel.

5. Montan is otherwise unknown. See Nelli 1977, 199–203.

likely that we are dealing with long-enduring presuppositions that make it hard for scholars to believe that women of whatever time or place composed poetry—even when we know that at least twenty-some women of southern France actually did.

I shall discuss below further consequences of the indeterminability that makes it impossible to say exactly how many trobairitz there were and exactly which poems they wrote, but this digression on fictional *tensos* already suggests the degree to which the poetic world of the troubadours operates in and includes a series of dialogues between men and women. While the *canso* usually offers only one half of a potential dialogue—sometimes addressed to the beloved, elsewhere to the poet's public, and most often perhaps to the poet's own self as he or she meditates on the experience and language of love—the *tenso* realizes that potential in the interplay of debate and disagreement, advice-giving and -getting. The *tensos*, which constitute such an important proportion of the trobairitz corpus, remind us that troubadour poetry lives in performance, in the face-to-face of songs produced and received in the seignorial courts of the langue d'oc. What these songs show us, in some sense, is that women are expected to participate in song as a social activity that claims to translate lived experience, however intimate, into the give-and-take of conventionalized lyric outpourings.

While a trobairitz like Castelloza may speak of the difficulty of being a woman courting her lover in song (see below), the Comtessa de Dia exuberantly calls for all women who love and choose well to sing out. The relatively small number of trobairitz may reinforce our sense that Castelloza's reserve is not totally uncharacteristic of her contemporaries—at least as far as their poetic output is concerned—but the Comtessa's attitude is not out of keeping with what we see reflected in the thirteenth- and fourteenth-century *vidas* and *razos*, our first examples of literary history and interpretation performed on the lyric corpus and based in part on verifiable information regarding people and places, in part on fictional elaborations of the poems themselves. (For more on the *vidas* and *razos*, see Chapter 7 in this volume.) Only five trobairitz have *vidas*, all of them quite short: Tibors, the Comtessa de Dia, Azalais de Porcairagues, Castelloza, and Lombarda. Lombarda's *vida* quickly becomes a more elaborate *razo* that sets into a narrative explanation the *coblas* she exchanges with Bernart Arnaut. In similar fashion, *razos* "explain" the *tensos* between Almuc de Castelnau and Iseut de Capio, Maria de Ventadorn and Gui d'Ussel,[6] Guillelma de Rosers

6. Two *razos* mention their *tenso* (Boutière-Schutz 208, 212–13). Maria de Ventadorn also appears in a lengthy *razo* on Gaucelm Faidit (Boutière-Schutz 170–76) as the object of his love and songs: she enjoys the praise, but does not return Gaucelm's love. An elaborate narrative ensues to follow the ramifications of that unrequited love. See also a *razo* for Pons de Capdoill (Boutière-Schutz 314–15). Maria was a patroness for all three of these troubadours, as for the Monk of Montaudon, Savaric de Mauleon, and Guiraut de Calanson (Bogin 169).

and Lanfranc Cigala, and Alamanda and Guiraut de Bornelh. Garsenda, the countess of Provence, is mentioned as the object of love and song in the *vidas* of Elias de Barjols and Gui de Cavaillon. Clara d'Anduza appears in a *razo* to one of Uc de Saint-Circ's songs. If we include Gaudairenca from Raimon de Miraval's *razo*, this brings the total to thirteen trobairitz named in *vidas* and *razos*, out of the hundred or so included in Boutière and Schutz's *Biographies des troubadours*. A small but not negligible number, as Bec points out (1979a).

Even more important, Bec, in his brief analysis of the length and contents of these *vidas* and *razos*, points out that biographers seem to have made no fundamental distinction between male and female poets in their use of cliché, commonplaces, or style in general (238–39). Ladies (and they are all *domnas*, an important social issue to which I will return shortly), whether they be ladies loved by troubadours, loving in turn, or only protecting the poets who sing their praises, are described with the same adjectives, the same set of qualities, taken for the most part from the troubadour lyrics themselves. The trobairitz are *gentil, bella, avinens, enseignada* (noble, beautiful, charming, educated). This last adjective seems especially important, since these women know how to compose songs (*trobar*). As Tibors's biographer says, "cortesa fo et enseignada, avinens e fort maïstra; e saup trobar" (she was courteous/courtly and educated, pleasant and very learned, and she knew how to compose poems; Boutière-Schutz 498). Maria de Ventadorn is "la plus preziada dompna qe anc fos en Lemozin, et aqella qe plus fetz de be e plus se gardet de mal. Et totas vetz l'ajudet sos senz . . . " (she was the most esteemed lady ever found in Limousin, and the one who did the most good and refrained the most from doing evil. And her good sense helped her always; Boutière-Schutz 213). We can easily compare such descriptions to those of Elias de Barjols, when he addresses his poems to Garsenda, countess of Provence, an important patroness as well as one of the trobairitz:

> Pros comtessa, qui·l ver en vol retraire
> Vos etz dona de pretz e de joven
> E guitz d'amor e caps d'ensenhamen.
> (12:51–53)

Valorous Countess, for the one who wants to tell the truth, you are a lady of worth and youthfulness, and a guide of love and a summit of good manners.

Or we can compare them to the Comtessa de Dia's own description of herself, when she enumerates her qualities: *merces, cortesia, beltatz, pretz, sens, paratges, fis coratges* ("A chantar m'er").

Each biography locates the lady in a place, gives her a lover (often named) and sometimes a husband. Castelloza, for example, is a noble lady of Auvergne, Turc de Mairona's wife—but the object of her love and songs is Lord Arman de Breon (Boutière-Schutz 333). Love and desire for fame go hand in hand in this world, as we see in the rest of Tibors's *vida* where she is described as both "enamorada" and "fort amada per amor," honored by all the good men, feared and obeyed by all the worthy ladies of the region (Boutière-Schutz 498). It is Clara d'Anduza's desire for worth and praise that inspires first Uc de Saint-Circ's songs and then their mutual love, according to the *razo* (Boutière-Schutz 244). In similar fashion we are told how Azalais loved Gui Guerrejat and "fez de lui maintas bonas cansos" (made many good songs about him; Boutière-Schutz 342). The gender of the pronouns may change, but the kinds of relationships illustrated remain the same. What we see represented in the *vidas* and *razos*, as well as in the songs, is a whole network of crisscrossed ties linking men and women, loved and loving, troubadours and trobairitz, patrons and patronesses, husbands and wives, rivals, friends, and relatives. The legendary level—the stories invented around the poems—parallels and elaborates the intertextual allusions of the songs themselves, in which trobairitz poems respond to those of the troubadours (Robbins 1979).

To what extent can we believe the information so gleaned? Scholarly research suggests that a good deal of historical information lies buried in these *vidas*, but sometimes it eludes our grasp or seems to be garbled with an overlay of romance generated by the situations implied in the lyrics (and therefore repeated from one *vida* or *razo* to another). Tibors, located by her *vida* in Provence at the castle of Lord Blacatz named "Sarenom" (Boutière-Schutz 498), is also named as the judge in a *tenso* between Bertran de Saint-Felix and Uc de la Bacalaria and may also appear as "Na Tibortz de Proensa" in a *dansa* by Guiraut d'Espanha (Boutière-Schutz 499n.2; Bec 1967b, 66–67). Although this does not give us much solid information to go on, research on Raimbaut d'Aurenga has yielded enough to suggest that Tibors (a common name at that time) was either Raimbaut's mother or, more likely, his sister and the wife of Bertrand des Baux, a major patron of the troubadours (Pattison 10–27; Bogin 162–63). The Comtessa de Dia's *vida* names her as the wife of "En Guillem de Peitieus" (Boutière-Schutz 445): could this be Beatrice, wife of William II of Poitiers, count of Valentinois, who would be contemporary with Raimbaut d'Aurenga (and whose name is often given to the Comtessa de Dia in anthologies)? Or perhaps Isoarde, the daughter of the count of Die and wife of Raimont d'Agout who lived at the time of Raimbaut IV, a generation later (Bogin 163–64; Pattison 27–30)? Or does the *vida* simply invent a literary fiction that brings her into the presence of two great troubadours, the founder

Guillem de Peiteus and Raimbaut d'Aurenga, one of the masters of *trobar* (Huchet 62–63)? We cannot decide based on the extant documents.

But with other trobairitz we have considerably more luck. Take the example of "la contesa de Proensa," as she is named in manuscript *F*: identified as Garsenda in two troubadour *vidas*, we can verify that she was the daughter of Garsenda and granddaughter of Guilhem IV, last particular count of Forcalquier (Stroński 1907, 22–23). She brought Forcalquier as a dowry upon her marriage in 1193 to Alphonse II, count of Provence and brother of Pedro II of Aragon. Until the death of her husband in 1209 there are few historical mentions of Garsenda, which is typical for a woman of this period. According to Elias de Barjol's *vida*, it was only after her husband's death that she patronized his songs. Thus after 1209 her role at the court in Aix can be divided into two periods: 1209–16—while her son lives with his uncle in Aragon, she has neither title nor official authority at Aix, these having been usurped by Pedro II—and 1216–1219/20—upon the latter's death, Garsenda reclaims the guardianship of her son, Raimon-Berengar IV, and exercises full authority in Aix until his marriage to Beatrice of Savoy. While this new countess of Provence then claims all the troubadours' attention,[7] Garsenda retires to a nearby monastery, the abbey of La Celle, where she takes her vows in 1225, with the proviso that she will retire completely only after she has settled some outstanding affairs (Stroński 1907, 23–26).

As Meg Bogin points out, "Garsenda belonged to two of the most powerful and important noble families of southern France. It is for this reason that we have relatively abundant information on her life" (172).[8] Bogin further locates her marriage as part of the power struggle between the Forcalquier family and the counts of Provence and sees it as an act of reconciliation offered by the bride's family. While none of these facts can tell us exactly why and how Garsenda herself became a trobairitz, they do tell us a lot about the kind of society in which troubadour lyric flourished and about the roles women could play in it.

Whenever we begin to consider the trobairitz we are inevitably led to ask why there was a significant group of women poets in the south of France but nowhere else in Europe, despite the spread of troubadour lyric throughout the Continent.[9] Without reaching any conclusive statements to

---

7. Consider the shift in Elias de Barjol's dedications, for example: Poems 5–8 are dedicated to Garsenda, 9–13 to Beatrice (Stroński 1906, xxi–xiii).

8. For similar reasons we can learn a fair amount about Maria de Ventadorn (see Bogin 168–69) and Azalais de Porcairagues (see Sakari 1971).

9. This is not to say that women poets do not appear elsewhere in Europe; Marie de France is an important example to the contrary. But the examples tend to be more isolated or scattered

explain their absence or presence here or there, we can speculate about the various aspects of Occitanian society that seem to favor women (relatively speaking): its easygoing, tolerant nature; its economic and cultural expansion; its preference for peacetime enjoyment of wealth and acts of largesse over more warlike pursuits; the persistence of codes of law that allowed women a more privileged status, especially in relation to inheriting property; and the effect of crusades that sent men off to war and left noble women at home with great administrative responsibilities (Bogin 20–36; Herlihy 1962). Southern France was remarkable both for the extent of women's lands and for the use of matronymics (Herlihy 1962, 108), despite feudalism's theoretical exclusion of women from seigniory. Although we should remember that politically active and powerful women like Eleanor of Aquitaine or Ermengarde of Narbonne are exceptional, such exceptions, in various degrees, are especially numerous in the south. We can usefully remember, in this respect, Eileen Power's suggestion that, despite ecclesiastic and aristocratic theories on the inferiority or superiority of women, in practical life noblewomen probably enjoyed a "rough and ready equality" (410).

The poems themselves, whether in terms of content or public addressed (be it fellow or sister poets, patrons and patronesses), suggest a society in which interchanges between the sexes and their respective balance of power have become a major focus of interest for all concerned. Does the new importance accorded by the troubadour lyric to the lady—now *midons* placed in the position of lord to the poet/lover's humble vassal—reflect a real change in medieval society? The answer on the whole appears to be negative. Historical studies have pointed out that, in fact, women's roles and their exercise of power were reduced in the course of the Middle Ages, especially at the highest and lowest levels of society (Herlihy 1985). Nor does there appear to have been a dramatic change in sexual or social mores in southern France that might correspond to an application of the ideas about love sung by the troubadours (Benton). Even in the poetry itself, recent literary analyses have stressed the extent to which the troubadours, even while elevating the lady to the status of lord, use the feudal code in which they then represent the love relationship as a way of controlling the lady's response: if the lover serves well, he can expect the *domna* to reward him accordingly, just as a lord is bound by the reciprocal rights and responsibilities of the feudal contract with his vassal (Haidu, Burns). (See Chapter 3 in this volume for a discussion of *fin'amor*.)

---

than what we see in the south of France, with the possible exception of Catalan women poets of the fourteenth and fifteenth centuries. See Massò I Torrents; Earnshaw 155–59; and especially Paden's introduction to *Voice of the Trobairitz* (1989, 1–19).

Both literary and historical analysis lead us to understand troubadour lyric and the *fin'amor* it proclaims in various ways, depending on which poet or poem we are considering, as manifestations of an elaborate social game, enjoyed, practiced, and performed in song by the men and women of the Occitanian courts. We may even speculate that the rise of woman as image—symbol of courtly society's most important values or stand-in for her husband, the real possessor of power (cf. Goldin 1967, Köhler, Warning)[10]—is a function of women's real loss of power, which liberates "woman" as a sign of something else: hence the possibility to play with the notion of the *domna* in troubadour lyric (and, to a certain extent, in courtly literature in general).

But then why spend so much time finding out about Occitanian society or who the trobairitz really were? The answer is double and leads us to the problematic relationship between life and literature, an issue already implied in the observable gap between the *domna* of troubadour lyric and the historical role played by most ladies in southern French society. Again we need to remember the exceptions, as well as the generalities, to come to grips with the past.[11] There are two faces of the life-literature continuum to consider here. On the one hand, we can observe, with the hindsight of centuries, that life does indeed reflect art, though admittedly at odd and refracted angles. The *domna* of troubadour lyric does eventually lead to the "lady on the pedestal" of nineteenth-century Victorian society and its inheritors today; we still speak of "chivalry" when a man opens the door and invites the "lady" to go first. In some way, however subtle and nuanced, the ideas about women possessing power and value that we see launched in troubadour lyric pass beyond the sphere of social game and become part of the social fabric of Western society, even if they never perfectly correspond to their literary models. Without losing sight, then, of the degree to which troubadour lyric is above all a formal, literary game involving considerable virtuosity and connoisseurship, we can also remember that it is not

10. On the other hand, feminist criticism might legitimately wonder to what extent such sociological interpretations, which recover the normal social hierarchy within the reversed hierarchy of troubadour lyric, represent an effort to explain away the shock of female power. Cf. Huchet's tendency to argue away the historical existence of the trobairitz in favor of a feminine Other.

11. In "Did Women Have a Renaissance? A Reconsideration," Herlihy analyzes the role and distribution of female saints in the Middle Ages to test to what extent feminist historians are right in maintaining that only men, not women, had a renaissance. While he confirms their views in general, he does point out that some women did rise to considerable prominence in the late medieval period through personal charisma (e.g., Joan of Arc, Catherine of Siena). For women in general, he points out the importance of family help when it comes to status, wealth, office, and power (cf. my earlier remarks on the ties that link trobairitz to male troubadours as mothers, sisters, wives, etc., as well as their privileged status in powerful families).

without consequence for the society that plays such a game, whether as performers or consumers.

The second aspect of this life-literature continuum involves the special character of troubadour lyric, as it claims to equate and represent lived experience and song. Here we stumble across one of the recurrent issues of troubadour criticism, and especially that of the trobairitz: the question of sincerity. While Jeanroy dismissed the trobairitz as "slaves of tradition" (2:316), incapable of saying anything the troubadours did not already say (cf. Ferrante 1975, 14), until recently most scholars who noticed them at all exclaimed about their spontaneity and simplicity in expressing outright their most intimate feelings—whether to be shocked by such "sincerity," as were some nineteenth-century scholars (e.g. Hueffer 282–87), or to applaud it like Bogin, inspired by twentieth-century feminism (13, 65–69). The naïve enthusiasts tend generally to insist on the contrast between the troubadours as professional poets whose poetry is a craft or trade and the trobairitz who, as noblewomen, keep their amateur status and gain in emotional intensity what they lose in rhetorical skill. While it is certainly true that as noblewomen the trobairitz did not use poetry to earn their daily bread—though there may have been *joglaressas* who composed as well as performed songs, without leaving their trace in the extant documents (cf. Dronke 1983, 98)—the same can be said of a Guillem de Peiteus or a Raimbaut d'Aurenga. We do well to remember with Dronke that "the spontaneous movement of poetic answering, and the calculated movement of literary shaping, were two constant and inseparable elements in their verse" (106)—both for the trobairitz and for the troubadours in general.

With this caveat in mind, we still have to deal with the fact that the poems themselves ask us to appreciate their sincerity, to measure the power of the song by the force of lived feelings that inspire it. As Bernart de Ventadorn tells us:

> Non es meravelha s'eu chan
> Melhs de nul autres chantador
> Que plus me tra·l cors vas amor
> E melhs sui faihz a so coman.
>   (Goldin 1973, 126:1–4)

Of course it's no wonder I sing better than any other troubadour: my heart draws me more toward love, and I am better made for his command. (trans. Goldin)

If only for the space of the song itself, we are to believe—if the poet can convince us through his or her rhetorical skill—that the topos of sincerity is not just a topic shared with other poets, whose merely conventional phrases may feign real love (see Monson, Bruckner 1986). While the writers of *vidas* and *razos*—who introduce troubadour lyric to a new public, often an Italian one, some one hundred years or more after it first appears in southern France (Boutière-Schutz, intro.)—are perhaps our own models for equating literary fiction with biographical data, we have to remember that the original public of these songs was probably neither so gullible, nor so ready to confuse poetic skill with true-life confessions.

We can certainly sympathize with the biographers' literalizing approach, when we consider not only the sincerity topos itself, but also the way troubadours and trobairitz do indeed mix their real identities into their poetic outpourings. We have to verify, however, the particular ways in which poets, male and female, interlace life and literature in the troubadour lyric system. In this respect, we can usefully begin by considering the use of proper names in troubadour songs and the chansonniers that preserve them. This chapter began with a list of names: twenty-one trobairitz whose names are supplied by the poems themselves or by the manuscripts, whether in rubrics, *vidas*, or *razos*. We have a total of over four hundred names for troubadours. Conditioned as we are by modern notions of authorship, we have tended to read the "I" of troubadour lyric in light of these names as biographical indicators. Michel Zink has most usefully shown how the choice of named authorship or anonymity often reflects a generic consideration, the latter generally preferred in popular lyric traditions like the *pastourelle, chanson de toile*, rondeau, etc. (1980, 423-29). While only the *canso* contains signatures within the lyric itself (423), the proper names supplied elsewhere constitute an invitation to identify our own lived experience with that of the poet's "I," an illusion of contact based on the emotion created by the song itself (423-24) and not necessarily coincident with the direct, lived experience of the historical poet.

Zink's analysis connects the proper names of the poets to the recipients of the poems, as a kind of guarantee that these songs do indeed sing of human experience. It is surely significant that one of the most important sources of proper names in troubadour lyric is the *tornada*, those closing verses where the poet sends his or her song to fellow poets, patrons and patronesses. Paul Zumthor sees the envoi as gratuitous as far as the "grand chant courtois" is concerned (218), which may be true of the poetic system as it passes from troubadour to trouvère lyric. But these proper names are an important indication of the social role played by the poets and their poems within Occitanian society. They are the concomitant, in some sense, of the *senhal* that maintains the illusion of secrecy around the beloved.

The "I" who speaks, then, is referable to a proper name, often named by the poetic partner. "She" calls "Gui d'Ussel," "N'Elias Cairel," "Guiraut," "Amic Lanfrancs"; "he" addresses "Dompna na Maria," "bell'ami-'Alamanda," "Ma domn'Isabella," "Na Guillelma." And yet the poetic identities thus named should not be confused with or simply conflated with the historical personages designated. Even in the *sirventes*, a genre that frequently alludes to specific circumstances and historic people, the poet creates a fiction of himself that does not quite coincide with his own historical reality, as the most recent editors of Bertran de Born's poetry have so masterfully demonstrated (Paden, Sankovitch, and Stäblein). This gap between fiction and reality needs especially to be kept in mind when the poetry itself appears to invite us to identify social and poetic realities. Consider, for example, the debate of the "ric ome," in which at least two trobairitz participated (Sakari 1965). Should a lady love a man only if his social position is inferior to hers (i.e., should social reality and the reversed hierarchy of *fin'amor* poetry coincide)? Is she dishonored if the man is her social superior (and can, therefore, effectively buy her love)? Or does love itself create hierarchies that are independent of the lovers' social ranks? The response of troubadours and trobairitz may vary, but the questions themselves remind us that the issues of life and poetry overlap. Even if the poems themselves constitute a game in connoisseurship, even if they cannot be referred immediately to the historical reality of a given poet's private experience, they do set into play a series of enticing voices that keep us curious about the people, their poems, and the social arena in which they circulated.

THE TROBAIRITZ CANON

Small as the trobairitz canon may seem in comparison with the total number of troubadour songs extant (around 2,500), delineating it with some exactitude is as problematic as counting the number of identifiable trobairitz. One of the great values of Meg Bogin's edition is to make easily available a considerable proportion of their poems. The hidden danger in that gift, already apparent in some otherwise excellent pieces the edition has generated, is that poems not included will be lost to sight just when the trobairitz are receiving renewed critical attention. Bogin's edition includes twenty-three poems (counting the *tenso* between Raimbaut d'Aurenga and an anonymous lady). Tibors has only part of one stanza; all the other trobairitz are represented by a single poem, except the Comtessa de Dia (four *cansos*) and Castelloza (three *cansos*). We should compare this with the extant norm for troubadours in general, which Tavera calculates at three or four poems apiece (146). To Bogin's list we can add two poems by named trobairitz: "Greu m'es a durar" by Na Gormonda (or Germonda) of Montpellier (P-C 177,1), a *sirventes* that responds to Guillem Figueira's "D'un sirventes far" and uses the same rhymes and metric form;[12] and "Tanz salutz e tantas amors" by Azalais d'Altier (P-C 42), a kind of *salut d'amor* with 101 verses

12. Levy 74–78; Städler 130–37; Bruckner, Shepard, and White 106–19; Véran 196–201. See Thiolier-Méjean 359n.2; and Rieger 1987.

in rhyming couplets. A number of other poems spoken in a woman's voice may have been composed by anonymous trobairitz:

1. "Quan vei los praz verdesir" (P-C 461,206), a *canso* with five stanzas and a *tornada*, a springtime opening and a refrain: "Aie!" (Véran 64–66)
2. "Per joi que d'amor m'avegna" (P-C 461,191), a *canso* with five stanzas[13]
3. "No·m posc mudar no diga mon veiaire" (P-C 404,5), a *sirventes* with four stanzas[14]
4. "Ab greu cossire" (P-C 371,1), a *sirventes* with six stanzas (Rieger 1991b, 691–93; Bruckner, Shepard, and White 1995, 102–5)
5. "Ab lo cor trist environat d'esmay" (P-C 461,2), a *planh* with five stanzas plus *tornada* (Rieger 1991b, 662–63; Bruckner, Shepard, and White 1995, 120–23)
6. "Dieus sal la terra e·l pa[is]" (P-C 461,81), one stanza of a *canso* or a *chanson d'ami*[15]
7. "Cant me donet l'anel daurat" (P-C 461,203a), a *cobla dobla* (Rieger 1991b, 657)
8. "Coindeta sui, si cum n'ai greu cossire" (P-C 461,69), a *chanson de mal mariée* in the form of a *ballada* (dance song) with five stanzas; the refrain "coindeta sui" is repeated four times in the opening stanza, which contains two extra introductory lines, three times in each of the remaining four (Véran 61–63; Bec 1979b, 57–58; Bruckner, Shepard, and White 1995, 130–33)
9. "En un verger sotz fuella d'albespi" (P-C 461,113), an *alba* spoken by a female voice, five 4-line stanzas, with the refrain: "Oi deus, oi deus, de *l'alba*! tan tost ve" (Véran 68–69; Bec 1979b, 57–58; Bruckner, Shepard, and White 1995, 134–35)

Uncertainty about the gender of the poet remains irreducible, as we proceed down this list, especially in regard to the last two items from the

13. See Paden et al.'s edition of Castelloza's poems, where he argues for attributing it to her as her fourth *canso* (163–64, 179–82). Rieger's edition includes it among Castelloza's poems (1991b, 549–50); Bruckner, Shepard, and White 26–29 follows *N* and presents it as anonymous.

14. Riquer 576–77; Rieger 1991b, 704–5; Bruckner, Shepard, and White 98–101. Though *C* attributes this *sirventes* to Raimon Jordan, the poem itself argues for a trobairitz, given the closing verses: "car domna deu az autra far onransa, / e per aisso ai·n eu dit ma semblansa" (for a lady should honor other ladies, and for this reason I have said what I think about it; 39–40).

15. Kolsen 289, 303–4; Rieger 1991b, 652; Bruckner, Shepard, and White 36–37. This *cobla* appears in *H*: the miniature that accompanies the poem represents a trobairitz (Rieger 1985, 392).

popularizing genres. "Coindeta sui" and "En un verger" are certainly spoken by female voices, but since they appear anonymously in the chansonniers, we have no way of knowing whether they were composed by male or female poets. The distinction between poet and voice is an important one: we know that troubadours did compose songs in which they invented a female speaker (we do not know if the reverse ever happened within this corpus). But as the discussion about fictive *tensos* has already suggested, we cannot always be sure that "Anonymous" was a man. Hence the difficulty of delineating with exactitude the trobairitz corpus involves not only the identity of the women poets, but also the role of anonymity, especially in the popularizing genres, and the possible gender gap between poet and speaking voice (cf. inventories in Paden 1989, 227–37; and Rieger 1991b).

If we appraise the thirty or so poems identified in terms of their distribution by genre, we find the majority divided between *cansos* and *tensos*.[16] The remaining include three *sirventes*, one *planh*, one *salut d'amor*, one *alba*, one *chanson de mal mariée*, one *cobla dobla*, and one stanza of a *canso* or a *chanson d'ami*. Commentators of the trobairitz corpus have frequently remarked what is not there, as well as what is. Despite the certain existence of Gormonda's political *sirventes* within that corpus, and the probable inclusion of "No·m posc mudar" and "Ab greu cossire" (a protest against laws curbing rich dress), even as careful a scholar as Pierre Bec has commented that the trobairitz wrote neither *sirventes* nor *planh*, "parce que les motivations socio-politiques de ces deux genres ne les concernaient pas directement" (1979a, 237). While it is true that only exceptional medieval women played an active political role, we have already noted that such exceptions are particularly remarkable in Occitanian society. Three *sirventes* may seem few indeed when compared with the total troubadour output; it is therefore all the more important not to forget them—even if a defense of Rome like Gormonda's may not be a popular political choice from the modern point of view. No *planh*? Sakari has argued convincingly for seeing some of the irregularities of Azalais de Porcairagues's *canso* as an effort to transform it, at least in part, into a *planh* in memory of Raimbaut d'Aurenga (1949, 180–81; 1971). Rieger and my co-editors have included in our editions "Ab lo cor trist environat d'esmay," an anonymous *planh* spoken in a female voice. It is likewise worthwhile to notice that the springtime opening of "Quan vei los praz" doubles (along with Azalais's inverted use) the number of times the trobairitz use that topos (cf. Bec 1979a, 238 and n. 15). These are still small numbers, but each addition makes us

---

16. The number of *tensos* is particularly difficult to ascertain: Rieger includes twenty-six in her edition; the Garland edition (Bruckner, Shepard, and White) includes sixteen. See also Bruckner 1994; and Napholz.

aware of how cautiously we should proceed to generalize about what trobairitz typically do or do not do.

The large number of *tensos* has elicited some comment. While I think we can quickly pass beyond Jeanroy's disparaging comment that the trobairitz choose mostly "inferior" genres that require "mediocre effort" (2:315), we should keep in mind that every one of the *tensos* is by a different trobairitz. The total does not, therefore, represent an abnormality in terms of an individual poet's corpus, though it does differ from the troubadour corpus as a whole, where the *canso* definitely dominates by a large proportion. The balance within the trobairitz corpus—however accidental it may be, given the likelihood that any number of poems have been lost—does make an interesting comment on the question of hierarchy and the balance of power between the sexes, a major issue of troubadour lyric, as indicated above. Where the troubadour's *canso* enacts through a single voice the reversed hierarchy of *fin'amor*—though with the power still ultimately held by the speaking poet/lover—the *tenso* asks questions about that balance of power within the more equal confrontation of the debate form. Huchet has argued that it is the role of the feminine Other to put into question the fundamental givens of the troubadours' poetic system. I would see this contestation rather as already inscribed in the *tenso* as one of the major lyric genres, even when it occurs between two male poets. The *tensos* remind us repeatedly that disagreement, different points of view, different ideals, are as much a part of troubadour lyric as the shared motifs, vocabulary, and themes that make so many songs seem similar. But I agree with Huchet that the introduction of a woman's point of view makes that *mise en question* more striking—and, especially important, introduces it not only in the male/female *tensos*, but in the *canso* as well, where two speaking voices can never be heard at once (except insofar as the public itself supplies the echoes from other songs).

A number of scholars have described the *canso* as a genre at least partially defined by the exclusion of the lady as participant in a dialogue set in motion by the poet's apostrophes, but resolutely monologistic in form (cf. Blakeslee's discussion of hybrid types). Paden has pointed out how logical it is for the "speechless *domna*" to adopt the persona of the male speaker "and with it a version of his courtly love" (1979, 80). Thus we may not be as surprised as Jeanroy (2:315) that the trobairitz initiate their own *requête d'amour*, rather than simply responding to that of the troubadours (though some like Garsenda and the anonymous lady of "Si·m fos grazitz" seem to do that as well). As Paden remarks, the shift in gender changes the typical moment of the *requête* "not for poetic reasons, but for subordinate reasons of a cultural order: the male lover tends to experience unhappiness before love becomes reciprocal, and the female after, because the cultural model of love calls for the male to be active and the female passive" (81). In fact, the trobairitz play with the opposition of active and passive roles (Bruckner 1985, 1992), but it is important to stress as well how the poetic system, in some sense, overrides the (apparent) difference of gender: "The unrequited lover and the abandoned mistress correspond because the model of love is dominated by the model of poetry, in which they are both unhappy speakers" (Paden 1979, 81). Though all is not doom and gloom, among the troubadours and the trobairitz (see especially the Comtessa de Dia's "Ab ioi"), the preponderance of sorrow and pain in troubadour lyric in general no doubt reflects what Clifford Davidson observes about the function of separation in love poems of whatever type: the most moving are not those in which erotic gratification is close (458).

The important number of *tensos* in the trobairitz corpus suggests we should give some brief attention to its character. The *tenso* is formally indistinguishable from the *canso* inasmuch as it is usually modeled on a *canso*'s form and melody. It is a genre that "takes off" from the *canso*, allows its speakers more freedom from courtly constraint (Paden 1979, 81), and easily accommodates humor and wit (Pattison 157). The word *tenso* itself operates as a general term to describe poetic discussion or debate and includes a variety of subgenres like the *partimen* or *joc partit*, based on a more rigorous debate in which the two speakers take up opposite sides of the dilemma proposed, or the *cobla*, a short exchange of one or two stanzas. Camproux (63) remarks that *coblas*, *tensos*, and *partimen* are genres practiced by many personalities who had little in common with professional troubadours (and who, therefore, express quite different points of view). He emphasizes as well how the *partimen* functions as a highly appreciated courtly game, in which the participants can say something different (78; cf. Cropp 108).

These observations furnish a useful background for analyzing the trobairitz' own participation in the genre. Four *tensos* take the form of a *partimen*, each one posing a specific problem. Na Carenza and Alaisina Iselda discuss the relative merits of marriage and chastity. Maria de Ventadorn and Gui d'Uisel debate the hierarchy between lovers: Gui argues for equality, Maria for maintaining the superiority of the lady. Two other *partimen* viewed together show the unpredictability of male and female positions. Guillelma de Rosers and Lanfranc Cigala discuss the conduct of two lovers on a stormy night: one obeys his lady and hastens to meet her, despite some strangers' need for hospitality; the second disobeys his lady's call, in order to serve the gentlemen. Guillelma supports the obedient lover, Lanfranc the other. But when Domna H. calls on Rofin (or Rosin) to choose which lover acts better—the one who quickly swore to his lady that he would do no more than kiss and hold her if she let him in her bed (for him oaths meant little) or the one who dared not swear—Rofin argues for the humbleness and timidity of the second, Domna H. for the boldness of the first (see Kay 1990, 99;

Bruckner 1994). In both of these *partimen* what starts out as an impersonal debate ultimately shifts to the relationship between the two speakers—a maneuver especially related to the gender of the participants. Of the four *partimen*, three are male/female, one female/female.

Three of the *tensos* (and also Azalais d'Altier's poetic letter sent to another lady) enact a similar situation, in which a lover (or a representative speaking for him) seeks help to patch up a quarrel with his lady. Thus, Iseut intervenes on behalf of Almuc's lover; an anonymous *donzella* speaks out for the sake of her *domna*'s lover, while Guiraut seeks the help of Alamanda, who ultimately agrees to assist him with his lady (also named Alamanda in the *razo* that introduces this *tenso*). Two other *tensos* show the lovers themselves in direct confrontation: Isabella and Elias Cairel (who explains that his love songs are professional rather than personal) and Raimbaut d'Aurenga with his *domna* (who disagrees as to how much he should fear the *lauzengiers*). In this group, we have three male/female *tensos*, two female/female (plus the *salut d'amor*).

To the lovers who debate each other in song we have to add three more sets, each one using a slightly different form of *tenso*. Garsenda and her anonymous interlocutor (identified as Gui de Cavaillon by a manuscript rubric, probably as a result of Gui's *vida;* Boutière-Schutz 505) exchange *coblas*, one stanza apiece, in which she encourages him to be less timid and speak out. He wittily responds with the hope that deeds may serve just as well as words. Bernart Arnaut and Lombarda exchange what appear to be two *cansos* built on the same metric form and rhymes (his has two heterometric stanzas and a *tornada*, hers two stanzas; for an analysis, see Sankovitch). A *vida-razo* that preserves the only copy of their songs fits them into an elaborate narrative that describes Bernart's arrival in Toulouse to see the lady he has heard so much about, their love, and then his departure without taking leave of her, followed by their exchange of songs. We can recognize in this plot an interesting variation on the Jaufre Rudel *vida*. The last example concerns the *tenso* between an anonymous lady and Raimon de las Salas (Anonymous III in Bogin), which begins with three stanzas of the man's complaint, to which respond two of the lady's, reassuring him of her love and attributing her appearance of "non-chaler" (not caring) to the opposition of "gens enoiosa e fera" (troublesome and savage people; Bruckner, Shepard, and White 1995, 86, v. 33).

From this sample of twelve *tensos*, then, three are exchanged by female poets, while eight play off male and female voices against each other (cf. Rieger 1990). Of the latter, five are initiated by the trobairitz (this includes the *tenso* with Raimbaut d'Aurenga, which may be fictional). If we judge by these statistics, however limited (cf. the twenty-six *tensos* included in Rieger's maximal corpus, 1990 and 1991b), we may surmise that, unlike the cultural model of the lady afraid to speak out about love, once ladies found their voices in song they showed themselves to be more like the unashamedly outspoken lady of the Comtessa de Dia than the self-conscious persona of Castelloza.

THE TROBAIRITZ AND FEMALE POETIC VOICE

Any analysis of the trobairitz' songs needs to understand their relation to the larger question of female voice. Pierre Bec has most usefully reminded us that the lady who decides to compose in the aristocratic style of the troubadour also has at her disposal a range of female voices from the popularizing genres, the various "women's songs": the *chanson d'ami*, with its subgenres, the *chanson de départie* and *chanson de délaissée; alba; chanson de mal mariée;* and *chanson de toile.* Moreover, the troubadours themselves offer models for just such generic overlapping from the earliest generations. Marcabru's "A la fontana" (Bec 1967b, 88–89; Goldin 1973, 54–56) mixes elements of a *pastorela* (the motif of a meeting and dialogue between a knight and a maiden, found all alone), a *chanson de femme* (the lady's lamentation over her beloved's departure), and a crusading song (the lover has left to serve God with King Louis; Bec 1967b, 91). Marcabru also sets the tone for the aristocratic version of the *pastorelas* found in Occitanian verse, with "L'autrier jost'una sebissa" (Goldin 1973, 70–76), most of which is a spirited *tenso* between the would-be seducer and a shepherdess, who is more than a match for his elegant arguments (cf. Gui d'Uisel's "L'autrier cavalcava," in Bec 1967b, 53–55).

These examples have clearly been written by a male troubadour who invents both the male and female personae (cf. Earnshaw 155–59). We have seen the same process for creating a "textualité féminine" (Bec 1979a, 258) in the fictive *tensos* discussed earlier. Here as there, the distinction between poet and speaking voice is a crucial one, when we consider the problem of gender and how it is actualized in the extant corpus. I have already mentioned how difficult it is to determine the sex of the poet from the speaking voice—a difficulty that blurs considerably the delineation of the trobairitz corpus. Similar difficulties arise when we consider the *chansons de femme,* relatively rare in the Occitanian corpus, but more abundant in northern French and Gallego-Portuguese collections, for example (Bec 1974). The existence of the trobairitz themselves suggests a tradition of women's song in the south of France, even if it was not often set down in manuscript (Bec 1979a, 254). Within the Gallego-Portuguese corpus, we can identify both male and female authors, but what about the large quantity of anonymous lyrics? Once again although we cannot determine the gender of the poets, it does not seem unreasonable to suppose some of them to be women.

What are the characteristics of the female persona offered in women's songs? Bec defines the general poetic model as a lyric monologue with sorrowful overtones, spoken by a woman (1979a, 252). Clifford Davidson identifies the two basic elements of the mythos of women's songs: desire and separation (456). These same elements appear whether we consider the *Song of Songs*, the Mozarabic *kharjas*, or the Comtessa de Dia's *cansos*. In her analysis of *Women in the Medieval Spanish Epic and Lyric Traditions*, Lucy Sponsler summarizes the various types of female speaker that appear in the eleventh-, twelfth-, and thirteenth-century *kharjas*, romance lyrics inserted as refrains in Arabic and Hebrew poems. They include a young girl confiding in her mother and afraid to follow her longings, a woman who worries about the welfare of her man, a woman dreading abandonment by her lover on whom all her happiness and ecstasy depend, and a seductress revealing her charms and physical desires. Women speaking in these poems may also describe their lover's physical charms, usually his coloring and physical appeal (51). Peter Dronke gives several examples from the *kharjas* in discussing the unity of popular and courtly love lyric:

> Ven, sidi, veni
> El querer es tanto beni . . .

> Come, my lord, come! Love-longing is so great a good.

> Tan t'amaray, tant t'amaray,
> Habib, tan t'amaray,
> Enfermeron welyos, †guay Deus†,
> Ya dolen tan male!
> (Dronke 1968, 29)

> I shall love you so, love you so; beloved, love you so, my eyes languish, ah God, ah they hurt me so!

Many of these same characteristics appear in the *cantigas de amigo* of the Gallego-Portuguese tradition, where the woman's physical desire is present along with her emotional needs (Sponsler 63). Suspicion about the man's infidelity is less important in these songs, which concentrate on the importance of loyalty (64–65). Where the women of the *kharjas* demonstrate great submissiveness to their lovers and fall into despair without them, the female speakers of the *cantigas de amigo* may avoid these extremes, but they nonetheless suffer great pain (65).

In similar fashion, we find direct expressions of the woman's desire in *chansons de femme* from northern France, as well as her complaint about the lover's absence, intermingled with the description of his charms:

> La froidor ne la jalee
> Ne puet mon cors refroidir;
> Si m'ait s'amor eschaufee,
> Dont plaing et plor et sospir.

Car toute me seux donee
A li servir.
(Bec 1977, vol. 2, 9:1–6)

Neither cold nor frost can cool down my body; his love, for which I lament
and cry and sigh, has warmed me so. For I have given myself entirely to serve
him.

As Bec points out, along with Jean-Marie d'Heur, the same expressions
of desire may seem tiresomely conventional and repetitive when they appear
in the troubadour *canso*, but often strike the same critics as "sincere" and
"spontaneous" when attributed to a female speaker (1979a, 253). The
gender of the speaking voice is a powerful signal to the literary public that
cannot be discounted among the rhetorical effects of a lyric poem. What we
know—or think we know—about the gender of the poet behind the poetic
voice also influences in conscious and unconscious ways how we react to a
given poem or set of poems. Since "feminine" and "masculine" are un-
avoidably cultural constructs, at least in part, our reception of certain
poems—whether in terms of believability, acceptability, and so on—will be
different depending on who we know (or believe) to be the poet and what
kind of voice he or she chooses to invent.

This seems to be particularly important with the trobairitz, for whom, as
Robbins points out, the *fait littéraire* is so indissolubly tied to the *fait social*
(1979, 5). To take only the most obvious and extreme example for the
moment, consider the case of "Bieris de R," as the poet is identified in *T*,
the only manuscript that records the *canso* "Na Maria, pretz e fina valors."
Considerable speculation has gone into trying to decide if this is Beatrice
of Romans or perhaps Alberico de Romano (Bogin 176–77): neither identity can be proven or disproven, but the choice of male or female poet leads
to radically different readings and interpretations of the same poem—
allegory being the road most favored by those who, while accepting Beatrice
as a trobairitz, find her expression of love for Lady Maria (in all ways
identical to that of the troubadour lover for his lady) too uncomfortably
suggestive of lesbianism. A perfect expression of heterosexual or homo-
sexual love, or a nuptial union with the Virgin Mary? Or simply an expression of friendship between two women couched in the language of the
troubadours (cf. Rieger 1989)? All depends on what we know or believe to
know about gender, poet, and voice. What we see is determined, at least to
a degree, by who we are and what we expect or want.

Here again it strikes me as important not to replace the historical existence of these women poets with a construct of the feminine Other, even
if we do need to compare the speaking voice of the trobairitz with the variety
of female voices and personae circulating in women's songs (composed by
men and women), as well as in troubadour lyrics which integrate that

archaizing and popularizing tradition. It is when we see the trobairitz at the crossroads of so many literary models that we can appreciate the effects of their innovation: they do what troubadours generally do not, when they combine within a single female speaker the aristocratic and the popularizing female personae.[17]

Nanette Paradis Segouffin (35–38) and Michel Zink (1972, 74–118) have both suggested that the lady of the troubadour *canso* finds her counterpart in the shepherdess of the *pastorela:* that is, the lower class woman functions as a kind of escape valve for letting out, often in violent form, the constrained desires of the male lover. The division of woman into Mary and Eve (or their equivalents) has a long tradition and seems to take this particular form in the generally amoral world of the Occitanian lyric (at least in its early and classical period; Zink 1972, 118). Bec reminds us that the *pastorela* itself belongs to the larger tradition of the *contrasto*, not only in terms of the debate it often includes, but also in the contrast between (noble) man and (peasant) woman (1979a, 260). We have also seen this tendency to polarize male and female voices in the fictional *tensos*; but what stand out by contrast against this system of polarized types are the *cansos* in which the trobairitz themselves bring back together, in a variety of different ways, their fragmented identities as *domna* and *femna* (Bruckner 1992). They are ladies *and* women who play with and against the balance of power and hierarchy between the sexes that constitute so much of the interest in troubadour lyric and *fin'amor*.

LITERARY ANALYSIS OF THE TROBAIRITZ CORPUS

Much remains to be done in the detailed analysis of the trobairitz corpus, which has begun to attract attention from scholars and critics of troubadour lyric.[18] Some recent work suggests how promising such analyses can be, but they also show some of the difficulties—avoidable and unavoidable—that such work entails. All readers would agree that the poems of the trobairitz must be located within the poetic system of the troubadours, since they are conceived and operate with respect to that masculine system. But it does not necessarily follow that the women troubadours can say only what the male poets have already said. On the one hand, we have just explored the availability of female voices from other lyric types, which may intersect with

17. The same combination also appears later in the fourteenth and fifteenth centuries in Catalan lyric, where there is a group of women poets (see Massó I Torrents).

18. In addition to the collective volume edited by William D. Paden, *Voice of the Trobairitz*, see volume 7 (Spring 1992) of *Tenso*, a special issue dedicated to the trobairitz. I would like to thank Wendy Pfeffer for sending me advance information from that issue. Paden 1992 includes an extensive bibliography on the subject, as does Rieger's edition of the trobairitz.

and modify the aristocratic genres of the *canso* and *tenso*. On the other, we need to take into account the nature of the poetic system invented by the troubadours: within the context of shared materials and forms, each poem makes its own choices and combinations. Its individual variations are as important as the common background against and within which such difference can be perceived. Just as there is ample room for any given troubadour to maneuver in, so for the trobairitz individually and as a group there is considerable play within the poetic system, which they may both confirm and contest (cf. Gravdal).

What kinds of valid generalizations can be made about the trobairitz corpus, given its extremely limited size and the uncertainties that make it difficult, if not impossible, to define in any exact way? Antoine Tavera has identified fourteen "specifically feminine traits" (144), grouped in five categories: excessive abandonment to desire, sensibility, weakness of character or tolerance, consciousness of one's superiority, and miscellaneous (159n.11). He finds these traits only in the *cansos*—in fact, only in six of the *cansos* from Bogin's edition (146). They seem to represent for Tavera a kind of "Eternal Feminine" that he associates with women poets, ancient and modern (145). While appreciating the equal status he gives to women and men within the craft of poetry, we can yet wonder if the "privilèges qui leur [women poets] sont exclusifs" (145) are exclusively theirs, and if this sort of definition is more limiting than liberating in the pursuit of what truly characterizes a quite varied group of women poets who choose to operate within the constraints and possibilities offered by troubadour lyric.

I admit to being particularly suspicious whenever I read attempts to enumerate the "feminine traits" of the trobairitz. My first reaction is generally to think of exceptions and wonder about the hidden or not so hidden assumptions about male and female, masculine and feminine, that underlie such an enterprise. Nonetheless, useful and valid observations can be and need to be made about the troubadours and trobairitz in terms of their gender. This is immediately evident if we take, for example, the complex resonances of the term *amor* available to any troubadour, but not for the trobairitz who begins to compose a song. *Amor* is a feminine noun in Old Occitan. The troubadour can thus use *amor* and the feminine pronouns that replace it to represent and conflate his own feeling, love personified, and most important, his beloved. The mysterious charm of Jaufre Rudel's *amor de lonh* owes much of its effect to such ambiguous combinations. The masculine *amic*, by which the woman poet addresses her lover, cannot so easily be veiled by the feminine *amor*—a grammatical reality that may account in large measure for some of the statistical differences F. R. P. Akehurst has observed in the vocabulary choices made by troubadours and trobairitz. While *amor* is the noun most frequently used by twenty troubadours, it drops to fourth place on the trobairitz list.[19] The ramifications of this simple difference in gender seem obvious—and yet they have thus far passed unnoticed in trobairitz criticism.

Several studies of the trobairitz' vocabulary—though they, too, are based only on Bogin's corpus—suggest more promising and less subjective overviews of the women poets' choices. Pierre Bec (1979a, 242–43) analyzes the trobairitz' use of key terms that represent the courtly values generally endorsed by the male troubadours. He divides these into two types: sociopoetic values and psycho-poetic ones. Statistical results show the following ratios, which measure the number of occurrences against the total number of verses (almost eight hundred in Bogin's edition):

> Socio-poetic values (include all the key terms sociologically valorized, such as *valor, valer, pretz, pro, gen, largueza, connoissens, merce, cortesia, cortes, paratge, ricor, vassalatge, proeza, mesura, sen*). *Cansos* 1/9; *tensos* 1/27.
>
> Psycho-poetic values (e.g. *joi* and *joven*) and affective valorization (forty-seven lexical units express pain: *desir, cossirier, dolor*, etc; eighteen express joy: *alegransa, solatz, jauzimen*, etc.). *Cansos* 1/4; *tensos* 1/8.

Based on these statistics, Bec cautiously draws four conclusions. In terms of "lyric effusion," *cansos* are twice as marked as *tensos*, a fact that must be equally true for the troubadours. Likewise, socio-poetic values are three times more frequent in the *cansos* than in the *tensos*. Third, psycho-poetic values dominate the others within the trobairitz corpus in general. But here Bec wisely remarks that his analysis has no meaning unless it can be compared with similar analyses of the troubadours' lyric corpus. I would add a further caveat about the unequal nature of such comparisons, since only two of the trobairitz have more than one poem extant. Do we, for example, compare Bernart de Ventadorn's forty songs to Castelloza's three or the Comtessa de Dia's four? Or do we compare Bernart's corpus with that of all the *trobairitz*; or a selection of troubadours with all the trobairitz, as Akehurst has done? However we decide to carry out such comparisons, we cannot

---

19. A list of the troubadours' top twenty nouns appears in Akehurst's "The Paragram AMOR." He furnished a slightly different list during a talk at the University of Georgia, along with the following breakdown for the trobairitz: *domna* 44, *cor(s)* 39, *amic* 34, *amor* 29, *joi* 18, *pretz* 16, *mal/ven* 12, *merce* 11, *talan* 10, *cavalhers/falhimen* 9, *drut/dan* 8, *fe/semblan/amador/coratge* 7, *temps/joven/razos/valor* 6. Both troubadours and trobairitz put in third place the noun for the love object—*domna* and *amic*, respectively—whereas their self-designations vary considerably in frequency: *amic* appears sixteenth on the male list; *domna* appears first on the female list. It is also useful to notice that three other nouns that can refer to the love object appear on the trobairitz' list, but not on the troubadours': *cavalhers, drut*, and *amador*.

avoid the inconvenience of not having altogether comparable elements to work with.

Bec's fourth conclusion concerns the characterization of the Comtessa de Dia, often identified with Sappho for her passion and lyricism (in fact, Sappho's name is regularly trotted out for any number of trobairitz as a convenient term of comparison). While the Comtessa's poetry is marked affectively, it is less so, according to Bec's analysis (which he does not report in detail), than that of Castelloza or Clara d'Anduza. Furthermore, the Comtessa's poems (along with the *canso* of Bieris de Romans) are the only ones marked both affectively and sociologically: paradoxically, the Comtessa de Dia may thus appear to be the trobairitz who, in at least two of her poems (unidentified by Bec), comes closest to the masculine poetic system. At this point, however, I would suggest that we need to consider other aspects that contribute to the overall effect of these poems before we agree or disagree with such a characterization (see, e.g., Nichols, Kay 1989, and Bruckner 1992). But it is both useful and refreshing to see modern scholars attempting to furnish some sort of factual control to their descriptions of the trobairitz.

And while some of these "facts" may surprise us, others confirm our general impression of the women poets. In corroboration of Paden's observation that women are more likely to sing of love already initiated but disrupted (rather than not yet shared, as in the troubadours' complaints), both Akehurst and Robbins (1979) have pointed out how important a role the theme of trust plays in the trobairitz corpus, in terms of the vocabulary most frequently used. With the help of a computer, Akehurst has compared the twenty most frequently used nouns in the twenty-three poems of Bogin's edition with the top twenty nouns of twenty troubadours (558 poems). Of the ten nouns that appear only in the women poets' list, three in particular suggest the trobairitz' concern with fidelity and infidelity between lovers: *falhimen* (offense), *drut* (lover), and *fe* (faithfulness). My analysis of the computer printout generously supplied by Akehurst confirms that fourteen of the eighteen trobairitz included choose from this group of words at least once in their poem(s) (Bruckner 1985, 251–52n.20). The semantic field of fidelity/infidelity is richly represented among the nouns of the trobairitz corpus, including in addition to the three on the "top twenty list": *faillensa, faillida, faillir, trair, traitor, plevir, fiansa, acordamen, acord, jurar, covinen, recrezens, recrezamen, camjar,* and *camjairitz* (Robbins also adds *fegnedor* and *trichador*). *Leyal* appears only twice (in the lady's part of the *tenso* with Raimbaut d'Aurenga), and *lejalmen* once, when the anonymous *domna* of "Si·m fos grazitz" describes herself (also in "Quan vei los praz," not included in the concordance). While Akehurst relates this vocabulary group to the major complaints directed by the trobairitz against their lovers, Robbins suggests that it leads, on the one hand, to the women's desire to prove themselves worthy (while at the same time deploring the lover's unworthy betrayal) and, on the other, to the concern for reputation and the woman's particular vulnerability to the *gelos* and the *lauzengier*. All those thematic avenues suggest further useful work to be based on such vocabulary studies, especially if they are expanded to include trobairitz poems left out of Bogin's edition, as well as comparisons with similar analyses of the troubadour corpus (cf. Ferrante 1989).

A brief analysis of the major characters—self and love object—as they pass from troubadour lyric into the poems of the *trobairitz* reveals an important series of shifts and reversals, in combination with the maintenance of basic types. Marianne Shapiro has pointed out the asymmetrical polarity between courting men and courting ladies: in the troubadour's poem, the lady represents the apex of courtly values; when she leaves that place and begins to sing (i.e., takes the position of the lover), the male beloved cannot simply move into her vacated position "without exciting a polemic that would attack the core of the *humilis/sublimis* paradox as it pertains to the hierarchy of courtly love" (1978, 562). No simple reversal of the male/female relationship represented in troubadour lyric—already a reversal of the "normal" cultural ideal of man dominating woman—can be effected by the "normally" silent lady who begins to compose in the troubadour style. That seems clear enough based on the theory we might extrapolate from the masculine poetic system, but what actually happens when the trobairitz make poems? Bec's analysis of the modes of address and reciprocal designations used by troubadours and trobairitz furnishes a good starting point for the many answers that question requires (1979a, 243–44). In the *cansos*, the lady speaks to her lover, as does the female voice of the *chansons de femme*: she calls him *amic* or *bels dous amic*. When she speaks of herself or of "him" in the third person, she is *domna*, he is *cavalier* (rarely *amic* in the third person; but see Azalais de Porcairagues and "Quan vei los praz"). In the *tensos*, the trobairitz designate the troubadour either by their full names with or without a title; by first name (*Gui, Guiraut, Lanfranc*); or, more rarely, by *amics* or *amics* plus a first name (*amics Lanfrancs*). Bec sees this practice as maintaining the functional distance between highborn lady and lover of lower rank, indispensable to the ideal of *fin'amor*. The *domna* imitates the troubadour (without addressing him as such) and implies that she will never love anyone but a knight or lord. She enters the system less as a woman than as a lady, "c'est-à-dire, encore et toujours, comme protectrice et dominatrice" (244). We can already begin to see in these elements that the lady who sings does not completely vacate her position in the asymmetrical balance of power between *domna* and lover. If this is generally valid in terms of the vocabulary Bec has analyzed, we also need to explore other aspects of the trobairitz' self-representation to nuance and sometimes modify his overview for particular women poets and poems.

Much remains to be done as work on the *trobairitz* integrates new textual resources supplied by Rieger's edition, new critical tools and concepts, and new historical research made available by scholars using a variety of approaches to troubadour lyric and gender studies. As a number of promising studies have already shown, those readings of the trobairitz corpus that expect and enter into the complexity of their play within the resources and limits of the troubadours lyric system will find a variety of women's voices that continue to fascinate us with the twists and turns of their poetic (re)inventions.

WORKS CITED

Akehurst, F. R. P. "The Paragram AMOR in the Troubadours." *Romanic Review* 69 (1978): 15–21.

Anatole, Crestian. "Las trobairitz." *Gai Saber: Revista de l'Escolà Occitana* 394 (1979–80): 384–88.

Anderson, Patricia. "*Na Carenza al bel cors avinen*: A Test Case for Recovering the Fictive Element in the Poetry of the Women Troubadours." *Tenso: Bulletin of the Société Guilhem IX* 2 (Spring 1987): 55–64.

Anglade, Joseph. *Les Troubadours. Leurs vies—leurs oeuvres—leur influence.* Geneva: Paris, 1929; repr. Geneva: Slatkine, 1977.

Bec, Pierre. "Le Type lyrique des chansons de femme dans la poésie du moyen âge." In *Etudes de civilisation médiévale (IXe–XIIe siècles): mélanges offerts à Edmond-René Labande*, 13–23. Poitiers: CESCM, 1974.

———. *La Lyrique française au moyen âge (XIIe–XIIIe siècles).* 2 vols. Paris: Picard, 1977.

———. "'Trobairitz' et chansons de femme: contribution à la connaissance du lyrisme féminin au moyen âge." *Cahiers de Civilisation Médiévale* 22, no. 3 (1979a): 235–62.

———, ed. *Anthologie des troubadours.* 10/18, Série "Bibliothèque médiévale." Paris: Union Générale des Editions, 1979b.

Benton, John F. "Clio and Venus: An Historical View of Medieval Love." In *The Meaning of Courtly Love*, ed. F. X. Newman, 19–42. Albany: State University of New York Press, 1972.

Blakeslee, Merritt, R. "Apostrophe, Dialogue, and the Generic Conventions of the Troubadour *Canso*." In *The Spirit of the Court: Selected Proceedings of the Fourth Congress of the International Courtly Literature Society (Toronto 1983)*, ed. Glynn Burgess, 41–51. Dover, N.H.: Brewer, 1985.

Bogin, Meg. *The Women Troubadours.* 1976; New York: Norton, 1980.

Boutière, J., and A. H. Schutz, eds. *Biographies des troubadours: textes provençaux des XIIIe et XIVe siècles.* Paris: Nizet, 1964.

Bruckner, Matilda Tomaryn. "Na Castelloza, *Trobairitz*, and Troubadour Lyric." *Romance Notes* 25, no. 3 (1985): 239–53.

———. "Jaufré Rudel and Lyric Reception: The Problem of Abusive Generalization." *Style* 20, no. 2 (1986): 203–19.

———. "Fictions of the Female Voice: The Women Troubadours." *Speculum* 67 (1992): 865–91.

———. "Debatable Fictions: The *Tensos* of the Trobairitz." In *Literary Aspects of Courtly Culture: Selected Papers from the Seventh Triennial Congress of the International Courtly Literature Society,* ed. Donald Maddox and Sara Sturm-Maddox, 19–28. Cambridge: D. S. Brewer, 1994.

Bruckner, Matilda Tomaryn, Laurie Shepard, and Sarah White, eds. *Songs of the Women Troubadours.* New York: Garland Publishing, Inc., 1995.

Burns, E. Jane. "The Man Behind the Lady in Troubadour Lyric." *Romance Notes* 25, no. 3 (1985): 254–70.

Camproux, Charles. "On the Subject of an Argument Between Elias and His Cousin." In *The Interpretation of Medieval Lyric Poetry,* ed. W. T. H. Jackson, 61–90. New York: Columbia University Press, 1980.

Chambers, Frank. "*Las trobairitz soiseubudas.*" In *The Voice of the Trobairitz: Perspectives on the Women Troubadours,* ed. William D. Paden, 45–60. Philadelphia: University of Pennsylvania Press, 1989.

Crescini, V. "Azalais d'Altier." *Zeitschrift für romanische Philologie* 14 (1890): 128–32.

Cropp, Glynnis M. "The 'Partimen' Between Folquet de Marseille and Tostemps." In *The Interpretation of Medieval Lyric Poetry,* ed. W. T. H. Jackson, 91–112. New York: Columbia University Press, 1980.

Davidson, Clifford. "Erotic 'Women's Songs' in Anglo-Saxon England." *Neophilologus* 59 (1975): 451–62.

de Lollis, Cesare, ed. "Bertram del Pojet." In *Miscellanea di studi critici in onore di A. Graf,* 708–10. Bergamo: Instituto Italiana d'Acti Grafiche, 1903.

Dragonetti, Roger. "*Aizi* et *aizimen* chez les plus anciens troubadours." In *Mélanges de linguistique romane et de philologie médiévale offerts à M. Maurice Delbouille,* ed. J. Renson and M. Tyssens, 2:127–53. Gembloux: Duculot, 1964.

Dronke, Peter. *Medieval Latin and the Rise of European Love-Lyric.* Vol. 1: *Problems and Interpretations.* Oxford: Clarendon Press, 1968.

———. *Women Writers of the Middle Ages: Critical Texts From Perpetua (d.203) to Marguerite Porete (d.1310).* Cambridge: Cambridge University Press, 1983.

———. "The Provençal Trobairitz Castelloza." In *Medieval Women Writers,* ed. Katharina Wilson, 131–52. Athens: University of Georgia Press, 1984.

Earnshaw, Doris. *The Female Voice in Medieval Romance Lyric.* Romance Languages and Literature 68. New York: Peter Lang, 1988.

Faure-Cousin, Jeanne. *Les Femmes troubadours.* Paris: Denoël/Gonthier, 1978.

Ferrante, Joan. *Woman as Image in Medieval Literature: From the Twelfth Century to Dante.* New York: Columbia University Press, 1975.

———. "Notes Toward the Study of a Female Rhetoric in the Trobairitz." In *The Voice of the Trobairitz: Perspectives on the Women Troubadours,* ed. William D. Paden, 63–72. Philadelphia: University of Pennsylvania Press, 1989.

Finke, Laurie A. "The Rhetoric of Desire." In *Feminist Theory, Women's Writing,* 29–74. Ithaca: Cornell University Press, 1992.

Gaunt, Simon. "Sexual Difference and the Metaphor of Language in a Troubadour Poem." *Modern Language Review* 83 (1988): 297–313.

Gégou, Fabienne. "*Trobairitz* et amorces romanesques dans les 'Biographies' des troubadours." In *Studia Occitanica in Memoriam Paul Rémy*, ed. Hans-Erich Keller et al., 2:43–51. Kalamazoo, Mich.: Medieval Institute Publications, 1986.

Goldin, Frederick. *The Mirror of Narcissus in the Courtly Love Lyric.* Ithaca: Cornell University Press, 1967.

————, ed. *Lyrics of the Troubadours and Trouvères.* New York: Anchor Books, 1973.

Gravdal, Kathryn. "Metaphor, Metonymy, and the Medieval Women Trobairitz." *Romanic Review* 83 (1992): 411–26.

Haidu, Peter. "Text and History: The Semiosis of Twelfth-Century Lyric as Sociohistorical Phenomenon (Chrétien de Troyes: 'D'Amor qui m'a tolu')." *Semiotica* 33, no. 1/2 (1981): 1–62.

Herlihy, David. "Land, Family, and Women in Continental Europe, 701–1200." *Traditio* 18 (1962): 89–120.

————. "Did Women Have a Renaissance? A Reconsideration." *Mediaevalia et Humanistica: Studies in Medieval and Renaissance Culture* 13 (1985): 1–22.

Hill, Raymond T., and Thomas G. Bergin, eds. *Anthology of the Provençal Troubadours.* 2d ed., revised and enlarged by T. G. Bergin. 2 vols. New Haven: Yale University Press, 1973.

Huchet, Jean-Charles. "Les Femmes troubadours ou la voix critique." *Littérature* 51 (1983): 59–90.

Hueffer, Francis. *The Troubadours: A History of Provençal Life and Literature in the Middle Ages.* 1878; repr. New York: AMS, 1977.

Jeanroy, Alfred. *La Poésie lyrique des troubadours.* 2 vols. Paris: Privat, 1934.

Kay, Sarah. "Derivation, Derived Rhyme, and the Trobairitz." In *The Voice of the Trobairitz: Perspectives on the Women Troubadours*, ed. William D. Paden, 157–73. Philadelphia: University of Pennsylvania Press, 1989.

————. *Subjectivity in Troubadour Poetry.* Cambridge: Cambridge University Press, 1990.

Köhler, Erich. "Observations historiques et sociologiques sur la poésie des troubadours." *Cahiers de Civilisation Médiévale* 7 (1964): 27–51.

Kolsen, A. "25 bisher unedierte provenzalische Anonyma." *Zeitschrift für romanische Philologie* 38 (1917): 281–310.

Kussler-Ratyé, Gabrielle. "Les Chansons de la comtesse Béatrice de Die." *Archivum Romanicum* 1 (1917): 161–82.

Levy, Emil, ed. *Guilhem Figueira.* Berlin, 1889.

Massó I Torrents, J. "Poetesses i dames intellectuals." In *Homenatge a Antoni Rubio i Lluch*, 1:405–17. Barcelona, 1946.

Monson, Don A. "Lyrisme et sincérité: sur une chanson de Bernart de Ventadorn." In *Studia Occitanica in Memoriam Paul Remy*, ed. Hans-Erich Keller et al., 2:143–59. Kalamazoo, Mich.: Medieval Institute Publications, 1986.

Nichols, Stephen G. "Medieval Women Writers: *Aisthesis* and the Powers of Marginality." *Yale French Studies* 75 (1988): 90–91.

Napholz, Carol. "(Re)locating Lost Trobairitz: The Anonymous Female Voice in Provençal Debate Poems." *Tenso: Bulletin of the Société Guilhem IX* 7 (Spring 1992): 125–41.

Nelli, René. *L'Erotique des troubadours*. Toulouse: Privat, 1963.

————, ed. *Ecrivains anticonformistes du moyen âge occitan*. 2 vols. Paris: Phébus, 1977.

Niestroy, Erich. "Der Trobador Pistoleta." *Zeitschrift für romanische Philologie* 52 (1914): 65–70.

Paden, William D. *"Utrum Copularentur:* Of *Cors"*. *L'Esprit créateur* 19, no. 4 (1979): 70–83.

————, ed. *The Voice of the Trobairitz: Perspectives on the Women Troubadours*. Philadelphia: University of Pennsylvania Press, 1989.

————. "Some Recent Studies of Women in the Middle Ages, Especially in Southern France." *Tenso: Bulletin of the Société Guilhem IX* 7 (1992): 94–124.

Paden, William D., et al., eds. "The Poems of the *Trobairitz* Na Castelloza." *Romance Philology* 35, no. 1 (1981): 158–82.

Paden, William D., Tilde Sankovitch, and Patricia Stäblein, eds. *The Poems of the Troubadour Bertran de Born*. Berkeley and Los Angeles: University of California Press, 1985.

Pattison, Walter T. *The Life and Works of the Troubadour Raimbaut d'Orange*. Minneapolis: University of Minnesota Press, 1952.

Pillet, Alfred, and Henry Carstens. *Bibliographie der Troubadours*. Repr. New York: Burt Franklin, 1968.

Poe, Elizabeth Wilson. "Another *Salut d'amor?* Another *Trobairitz?* In Defense of *Tanz salutz et tantas amors.*" *Zeitschrift für romanische Philologie* 106 (1990): 425–42.

Pollina, Vincent. "Troubadours dans le nord: observations sur la transmission des mélodies occitanes dans les manuscrits septentrionaux." *Romantische Zeitschrift für literaturgeschichte* 3/4 (1985): 263–78.

Power, Eileen. "The Position of Women." In *The Legacy of the Middle Ages*, ed. G. G. Cramp and E. F. Jacob, 401–33. Oxford: Clarendon Press, 1926.

Rieger, Angelica. "'Ins e·l cor port, dona, vostra faisso': image et imaginaire de la femme à travers l'enluminure dans les chansonniers de troubadours." *Cahiers de Civilisation Médiévale* 28 (1985): 385–415.

————. "Un *sirventes* féminin—la *trobairitz* Gormonda de Monpeslier." In *Actes du Premier Congrès International de l'Association Internationale d'Etudes Occitanes*, ed. Peter T. Ricketts, 423–55. London: AIEO, 1987.

————. "Was Bieris de Romans Lesbian? Women's Relations with Each Other in the World of the Troubadours." In *The Voice of the Trobairitz: Perspectives on the Women Troubadours*, ed. William D. Paden, 73–94. Philadelphia: University of Pennsylvania Press, 1989.

————. "*En conselh no deu hom voler femna*: les dialogues mixtes dans la lyrique troubadouresque." *Perspectives Médiévales* 16 (1990): 47–57.

————. "Alamanda de Castelnau—Une trobairitz dans l'entourage des comtes de Toulouse?" *Zeitschrift für romanische Philologie* 107 (1991a): 47–57.

————, ed. *Trobairitz: der Beitrag der Frau in der altokzitanischen höfischen Lyrik. Edition des Gesamtkorpus*. Tübingen: Niemeyer, 1991b.

Riquer, Martín de, ed. *Los trovadores: historia literaria y textos*. 3 vols. Barcelona: Planeta, 1975.

Robbins, Kittye Delle. "Woman/Poet: Problem and Promise in Studying the *Trobairitz* and Their Friends." *Encomia* 1, no. 3 (1977): 12–14.

———. "Love's Martyrdom Revised: Conversion, Inversion, and Subversion of *Trobador* Style in *Trobairitz* Poetry." Paper presented at the Troubadour Symposium, University of California, Los Angeles, March 1979.

Sakari, Aimo. "Azalais de Procairagues, le joglar de Raimbaut d'Orange." *Neuphilogische Mitteilungen* 50 (1949): 23–43, 56–87, 174–98.

———. "Le Thème de l'amour du 'Ric Ome' au début de la poésie provençale." In *Actes et mémoires du IIIe Congrès International de langue et littérature d'oc* (Bordeaux, 3–8 Sept. 1961), 2:88–94. Bordeaux: Université de Bordeaux, Faculté des Lettres, 1965.

———. "A propos d'Azalais de Porcairagues." In *Mélanges Jean Boutière*, ed. Irénée Cluzel and François Pirot, 1:517–28. Liège: Soledi, 1971.

Sankovitch, Tilde. "Lombarda's Reluctant Mirror: Speculum of Another Poet." In *The Voice of the Trobairitz: Perspectives on the Women Troubadours*, ed. William D. Paden, 183–93. Philadelphia: University of Pennsylvania Press, 1989.

Schultz-Gora, Oskar. *Die provenzalischen Dichterinnen.* Liepzig: Gustav Foch, 1888.

Segouffin, Nanette Paradis. "Trobairitz." *Vent Terral* 8 (1982): 35–46.

Shapiro, Marianne. "The Provençal *Trobairitz* and the Limits of Courtly Love." *Signs* 3, no. 2 (1978): 560–71.

———. "'Tenson' et 'partimen': la 'tenson' fictive." In *XIV congresso internazionale di linguistica e filologia romanza: atti*, ed. Alberto Várvaro, 287–301. Naples: Macchiaroli, 1981.

Shepard, William P., and Frank Chambers, eds. *The Poems of Aimeric de Peguilhan.* Evanston, Ill.: Northwestern University Press, 1950.

Sponsler, Lucy A. *Women in the Medieval Spanish Epic and Lyric Traditions.* Lexington: University Press of Kentucky, 1975.

Städler, Katharina. "The *Sirventes* by Gormonda of Monpeslier." In *The Voice of the Trobairitz: Perspectives on the Women Troubadours*, ed. William D. Paden, 129–55. Philadelphia: University of Pennsylvania Press, 1989.

Stroński, Stanisław, ed. *Le Troubadour Elias de Barjols.* Toulouse: Privat, 1906.

———. "Notes sur quelques troubadours et protecteurs des troubadours." *Revue des langues romanes* 50 (1907): 5–44.

Tavera, Antoine. "A la recherche des troubadours maudits." *Senefiance* 5 (1978): 135–62.

Thiolier-Méjean, Suzanne. *Les Poésies satiriques et morales des troubadours du XIIe siècle à la fin du XIIIe siècle.* Paris: Nizet, 1978.

Véran, Jules. *Les Poétesses provençales du moyen âge.* Paris: Quillet, 1946.

Warning, Rainer. "Moi lyrique et société chez les troubadours." Trans. Werner Kügler. In *L'Archéologie du signe*, ed. Lucie Brind'Amour and Eugène Vance, 63–100. Papers in Medieval Studies 3. Toronto: Pontifical Institute of Medieval Studies, 1982.

Woolf, Virginia. *A Room of One's Own.* 1929; New York: Harcourt, Brace, Jovanovich, 1957.

Zink, Michel. *La Pastourelle: poésie et folklore au moyen âge.* Paris: Bordas, 1972.

———. "Remarques sur les conditions de l'anonymité dans la poésie lyrique française du moyen âge." In *Mélanges de langue et littérature françaises du moyen âge et de la Renaissance offerts à Monsieur Charles Foulon,* 421–27. Rennes: Institut de France, Université de Haute-Bretagne, 1980.

Zufferey, François. "Toward a Delimitation of the Trobairitz Corpus." In *The Voice of the Trobairitz: Perspectives on the Women Troubadours,* ed. William D. Paden, 31–43. Philadelphia: University of Pennsylvania Press, 1989.

Zumthor, Paul. *Essai de poétique médiévale.* Paris: Seuil, 1972.

Origins and Diffusion

NINE

Origins

Gerald A. Bond

The abrupt appearance of complex Occitanian lyric in the early years of the twelfth century has often puzzled literary historians: Where did it come from? This question has exerted an almost mesmerizing effect on scholars since its introduction as a serious topic into Western academic discourse during the nineteenth century. Attempts to find a primary source have repeatedly produced thorough and impressive scholarship. Nevertheless, the picture remains so confused today that skepticism reigns about even the possibility of a solution. The purpose of this chapter is to define the question and its target, to review the major theories that have been proposed, and to sketch a possible model built on my own research with the earliest known troubadour.

THE QUESTION

The methodological problems embedded in the search for the origins of troubadour lyric are fundamental. Little progress in the area of troubadour studies can be made without carefully considering these problems, because careless and inaccurate premises have frequently compromised the conclusions of much hard work. Moreover, the topic carries wider import than one might at first suspect, since theories of origins tend to determine critical attitudes, and vice versa. If we do not formulate the questions with care, we will never obtain reliable answers.

As Paul Zumthor has commented, problems arise already with the very myth of origins. Nineteenth-century scholars accepted without question, as he puts it, "the idea of an original source, the idea of the value of the past without distance, directly comparable to the world of today—or rather of the day before yesterday, because . . . the real point of reference was located

in bourgeois society of 1850 or 1880!" (1986, 42). As long as the belief in
a true and single source for the complex phenomena known today to literary
historians as "troubadour lyric" and "courtly love" continues to be em-
braced, investigations of origins will remain necessarily unsatisfactory. As
Zumthor concluded, we have to face honestly the problem of the double
historicity of the printed text before us: the shifting status of the performed
discourse it represents in its time, and the contingency of any interpretive
discourse in our own.

Taken to an extreme, this perception could lead to the conclusion that
the medieval text's fundamental otherness or "alterity" will always defeat
any modern attempt to understand its essence or its history (Jauss). I am not
so pessimistic; to my mind, phenomena *always* escape understanding, but
never *completely*. The extent of that escape can and must be limited; it begins
with careful examination of conceptual and methodological presuppositions.[1] On a general level, we can make an important start by combating the
twin effects of the object's remoteness and the mind's syncretism, constantly
reminding ourselves that troubadour lyric is not—and never was—monolithic. In fact, it varied by time, place, and troubadour to such an extent that
attempts to produce a universal theory or history must be considered
problematic from the start.

The question of origins also makes tacit assumptions about troubadour
lyric as poetry that must also be questioned, since they distort the object
whose origins are being sought. At least three considerations suggest that
a revision of these notions might be useful: the effect of literacy, the
elements of composition, and the role of "context."

Literacy and orality have been central topics in much recent thinking
(Ong, Stock, Zumthor 1987). These very different theorists share a common concern about the effect of literacy on a text's state of being and on
the work of interpretation, in the twentieth century as in the twelfth. When
we speak of the "poet," silently read a text, or even number the lines in an
edition, we take a strong position concerning its discursive status. We see the
artifact as a stable, written and verbal composition subject to the categories
of evaluation and criticism developed in antiquity (and revived across the
High Middle Ages) for "poetry." But the troubadour product can be called
properly a "poem" only when it is reduced to its verbal component, fixed
within a timeless language, and framed by the preconceptions engendered

---

1. In making such a suggestion I betray my faith that on both "sides" of troubadour song
important, common, and relatively stable semantic elements (i.e., constructs of lexical, social,
aesthetic, mythic, or other significance by and for particular communities) can be established.
Not fact in any absolute sense, such common elements neither determine what every troubadour meant nor describe the performative function of his lyric. But they do serve to restore
in partial form historically grounded interpretive codes with which all individual interpretation
plays.

by the book that contains it. When not in such a state, it is a song—that is, an artifact embedded in a living culture apparently governed to a large extent by the characteristics of Ong's "secondary orality." In fact, the significance of the conjunction in time, space, and social class of the spread of literacy and the appearance of troubadour lyric has barely been raised with regard to the question of origins. The striking fact that the lyric arises so suddenly, "as if from nothing," has always seemed to demand an extrinsic explanation of some sort. That conclusion needs to be reevaluated, since the suddenness is not limited to troubadour poetry and may reflect rather the relatively rapid change in the means of and attitude toward preserving documents of all kinds, public as well as private. The equally sudden appearance of "personal" letters or "personal" poetry in Latin in this period supports the conclusion that the whole phenomenon of documentation, particularly of "personal" texts, underwent a relatively rapid change throughout the elite culture. From this perspective, we need to account less for the sudden rise than for the sudden preservation of the lyric—a very different question indeed.

A second tacit bias is introduced into the question of origins by the relative weight accorded to the compositional elements of lyric. Dante's well-known definition of troubadour poetry as *fictio rethorica musicaque poita* provides a useful illustration of the implications of this problem, especially since he himself proposes a strong revisionist reading (based on the classical poets) of the tradition in the text where this definition appears, the *De vulgari eloquentia* (ca. 1305).[2] Each of the components included in his succinct definition—fiction, ornamentation, form—has its own theory and history (including a theory of origins). All three of these theories/histories are valid: they represent different analytic structures applied to the same complex phenomenon.

The treatment of troubadour lyric primarily as *fictio* usually concentrates on the theories of love, particularly that of *fin'amor*. Even within this limited scope, problems of definition quickly arise. If, as many researchers have concluded, there was even in the twelfth century little agreement about the exact description of *fin'amor* despite general agreement about its desirability, then one's explicit or implicit preference for one poet or another will affect greatly one's notion of origins. Guillem de Peiteus, Marcabru, Jaufre Rudel, Bernard de Ventadorn, and Peire Vidal all display different conceptions of the same term (see Topsfield), obliging us in some measure to find separate "origins" for each. Other aspects of content besides love may

---

2. "Reviewing therefore what has been said, we recall that we have called 'poets' many of those people who make verses in the vernacular: which we presume beyond doubt to state on a rational basis because they are surely poets, if we consider poetry correctly, which is nothing else but an imaginative piece crafted with artful language and form" (*De vulgari eloquentia* 2.4).

show origins that shift with differing conceptions. They include the image of the lady, the voice of the lover, and the explicit aesthetic program.

When, however, one considers the lyric primarily as *poesis*, a very different picture emerges. The arts of composing and ornamenting texts, pleasing patrons, and persuading audiences have their own history and theory, in both the Latin and the vernacular cultures. The origins of these poetic practices can look very different from those of the "message" of the *fictio*. The search for poetic origins must be restricted to literary texts, while those of the *fictio* can range across the entire documentary record; at the same time, the former easily includes multigeneric evidence from debate songs, satires, etc., genres that the latter routinely ignores in its preoccupation with courtly love.

Similarly, the view of troubadour lyric as a primarily formal phenomenon—a sonic artifact—concerned with rhyme, meter, and music has yet another history and theory. Here the search for origins must be restricted to the various Latin and vernacular lyric traditions, a limitation at best unnecessary and at worst detrimental for the other views. But privileging the formal element has the virtue of maximizing the coherence of troubadour lyric as well as stressing its continuity with the Occitanian lyric traditions that surrounded it in time and space. From this perspective, it is important that we evaluate the extent to which what is usually called "context" should be included as an inseparable portion of the "text." Consider the following eyewitness description of a performance of Guillem de Peiteus reported in 1135 by Orderic Vitalis:

> Pictauensis uero dux . . . miserias captiuitatis suae . . . coram regibus et magnatis atque Christianis coetibus multotiens retulit rythmicis uersibus cum facetis modulationibus. (10.21; Chibnall ed., 5.342–43)

> Then the Poitevin Duke . . . related many times the miseries of his captivity before kings, magnates and Christian assemblies using rhythmic verses with witty measures.

His description is striking for its breadth of interest, as it records many simultaneous aspects of troubadour performance. In addition to specifying the song's content, form, and music, Orderic mentions its orality (*retulit*), its repetition (*multotiens*), and its community (*coram regibus*, etc.). As scholars of world song such as Charles Seeger have thoroughly demonstrated, living song includes each of these elements as an inseparable segment of the object, since an illiterate and notationless group of listeners does not readily distinguish between a song and its performance. The more troubadour lyric is considered as an event in time, as a true phenomenon, the more context must merge with text to become its co-text. In this manner, the uses of lyric performance for specific audiences become central rather than peripheral to the question of origins. Asking about the origin of troubadour lyric's particular status within its historical communities, for instance, will force us to examine its introduction as an integral but fragmentary portion of a much larger response by the Occitanian aristocratic court to the forces of change exerted upon it. The relationship between the production and patronage of artifacts, on the one hand, and the self-image of the noble court, on the other, would become a crucial area of inquiry.

Having attempted to describe major biases introduced by our conception of the object, I would like to look quickly at notions of source. It is one thing for an individual reader to note a parallel of some sort between two texts; this is a frequent and pleasurable accident of reading that is structured to a great extent by the knowledge, interests, memory, and abilities of the perceiving mind. It is quite another thing to propose a causal relation between the two within academic discourse. Such a second step transcends the individual experience of reading and requires answers to a variety of questions. What is the relative chronology of the two items? Did the second actually have access to the first? Did the second borrow from the first, or from its sources or derivatives? Where else can a parallel be found? What significance lies behind the fact that the second would turn to that particular source? Can one establish conclusively which way, in fact, the borrowing proceeded? Without answers to such often-unasked questions, the value of any perceived parallelisms remains indeterminate because of its unexamined subjectivity.

Answers do not come easily. For one thing, the uneven rate of literacy in the Latin and vernacular cultures means that requiring "proof"—i.e., relying on written sources—introduces a strong tacit bias toward the Latin and the ecclesiastic (Dronke 1966, 55). There is also a latent tendency to think that the direction of borrowing is almost exclusively from the Latin to the vernacular throughout the High Middle Ages, in spite of considerable evidence that court thinking as well as courtly literature continually exerted an influence, positive as well as negative, on all types of medieval Latin literature.

Moreover, sources vary across time. Even if we were to describe satisfactorily the entire set of sources for a given troubadour, that set would not remain the same for succeeding poets. Previous sources dry up or are ignored, new ones are found: Marcabru uses sacred sources untouched by Guillem de Peiteus, Peire Vidal borrows from new French narrative, Raimbaut de Vaqueiras introduces Ovid's *Heroides*, later troubadours adopt formal developments of dance songs. As the twelfth century progresses, the repertory created by other troubadours becomes itself an increasingly important source; eventually, in fact, it predominates over all other sources, helping to produce the characteristic poetics of the later periods.

Finally, we need to be more cautious in interpreting a given parallelism, determining case by case whether it represents a true source, an analogue, or an actual derivative. Let us take an example. Texts concerning *amor* in general and "true love" (*uerus amor*) in particular can be found among Latin poets and thinkers of the early period, yet their exact relationship to the troubadours remains to be ascertained. They may well have functioned as a source for the Old Occitan poets, but they may also derive some of their own salient features from recent developments within courtly discourse (or even literature) itself. Alternatively, the two might actually be analogues, representing two different reactions to the discussion of women, desire, and courtliness that had occupied at least some Occitanian courts throughout the eleventh century, as contemporary clerical condemnations indicate (Platelle).

I have given the questions themselves a great deal of attention in this chapter because I believe they have caused the gravest difficulties for this research. Unexamined assumptions about the object and the source have interfered so often with past work that its results have not proved persuasive. A thorough examination of these assumptions must accompany future research if it is to escape the current skepticism.

OVERVIEW

With the caveats established in the methodological section, we can now begin to review the results of a century of research. In this review, I shall concentrate on the amatory content of troubadour lyric, since other content will be discussed at sufficient length in the case study of Guillem de Peiteus below. We quickly notice the obvious stagnation that has characterized the field for some time. Many theories have been proposed, and many still appear viable. Not enough work has been done to accommodate them one to another, and few of them have been rejected with any finality. Much future effort is needed to adjudicate between rival theories, and it must be based on a preference for those theories that explain more, ignore less, and have greater probability.[3]

We can discern three broad types of textual sources that continue to attract scholarly attention: courtly texts from the Arabic culture in Spain, Latin literature (both ancient and medieval), and various forms of the cult

---

3. In the following resume, I shall ignore proposed origins which have not found substantial support and which, to my mind, only serve to confuse the picture even more: in particular, Cathar religious doctrine and practice, folk poetry and ritual, and Neoplatonism. In omitting them for the purposes of this summary, I do not mean to imply that they might not have relevance to the poetry of some troubadours at some time or other, only that they cannot be shown to have provided the main impulse of many of the troubadours most of the time. Theories of synchronic orientation (i.e., psychological), which are extraordinarily important for an understanding of troubadour lyric, have been omitted categorically from this chapter. The interested reader will find them summarized in Boase.

of the Virgin Mary. In addition, two other sources have been proposed that lie not in the world of texts at all, but rather in powerful social forces exerted on the traditional martial aristocracy by the lower aristocracy and by noble women.

The court culture of eleventh-century Arabic Spain was by all accounts brilliant, sophisticated, and particularly interested in artistic creation. Furthermore, secular as well as mystical love was a frequent topic of both lyric and didactic works; theories of profane love had been well worked out before 1100. Motifs (such as the need for secrecy), styles (such as difficult composition), and concepts (such as the *raqib* or "guard") similar or identical to those of troubadour poetry appear in the amorous verse of Muslim Spain. Reading such parallels as proof of influence, many scholars have asserted that the troubadours derived their main impulses from Arabic sources (Boase 62–75; Menocal).

It is certainly possible that the Muslim culture exerted a general influence on such areas as chivalry and courtliness (Nelli), and perhaps even on the social role of versemaking. This general and passive influence would have been the routine result of the interactions between the cultures brought about by the various activities of the Christian courts of northern Spain, which became increasingly powerful and wealthy as the eleventh century progressed. But specific and willful influences are less easily accepted. For one thing, of course, they would have to have been assimilated by Occitanian courts already by the time the first known troubadour began writing in the early years of the twelfth century. The late eleventh century was a period when contacts between the two cultures were few and—as the result of two very successful and lucrative invasions under Poitevin leadership (1064, 1086)—hardly conducive to imitation. Also, even the most lettered among the troubadours surely did not understand Arabic, and nothing is known to have been already translated. Perhaps the most damaging fact is that the generating metaphor of *fin'amor*, the service to a lady by a poet-lover who becomes gradually refined, is lacking from Muslim society and thought (Boase 74). In fact, strong indigenous sources can easily be found for this particular feature.

The Latin theory as a source for Occitan verse has not enjoyed the same favor in recent scholarship as it did formerly, perhaps as much because of the decline in the study of Latin in modern secondary education (especially in the United States) as anything else. Intended originally to describe the direct influence of classical authors such as Plato and Ovid (Scheludko), the theory has been modified over the last half century to focus on medieval Latin school poets and their students, the ubiquitous *clerici*, who themselves were confronted with the ideas and style of their classical predecessors. The notion of courtliness itself, for instance, has been traced to the Christian and Ciceronian mixture that provided the ideals for ecclesiastics at the imperial court in Germany during the tenth and eleventh centuries (Jaeger). Furthermore, a humanistic literary movement in central western France during the second half of the eleventh century, the "Loire school," produced influential poets such as Marbod of Rennes and Hildebert of Lavardin, whose epistolary poetry has been claimed as a major source of troubadour art (Brinkmann). Finally, it has been argued recently that the poetry of a minor figure of the Loire school, Baudri of Bourgueil, reveals the outlines of a regional "Ovidian subculture" extending well beyond the confines of the school, which could have provided the immediate background for the appearance of troubadour lyric (Bond 1986).

It is impossible to deny that some classical authors, particularly Ovid, exerted a significant influence on the troubadours. Guillem de Peiteus, Marcabru and others quote Ovid, sometimes by name, borrowing ideas and images, as do so many other writers of this *aetas ovidiana* centered at Orléans (Cahoon). In addition, the intermediary role of the medieval Latin poets at all levels not only makes intuitive sense, but also relies on demonstrable links, since clerics from bishop to notary constantly attended or were employed by the secular courts. Their poetic (and amorous) activity probably provided an important impulse and source for troubadour poetry. But the specific features of *fin'amor* can no more be derived from Ovidian practice than can those of form (including music). Ovid's lover is not a vassal, love service is absent, and there is no question of gradual refinement. Moreover, although explicit amorous verse was written by clerics, the poetic letters to ladies function less as love poems than as praise poems, and generally exclude sensuality.

The cult of the Virgin Mary, which was expanding at the time of the emergence of troubadour lyric, has received repeated attention from researchers (Boase 84–86). Certainly numerous possibilities existed for inspiration from this quarter, although most of the literary documents postdate the earliest lyric. As Reto Bezzola has demonstrated, however, the success of the reformer Robert of Arbrissel (d. 1117) placed him in a position to exert great influence over the Occitanian aristocracy in its conception of the lady and of male service to her. Indirect evidence shows the importance of the Virgin Mary to his thought, and his biographer quotes him on the centrality of *matronae* (noble, married women; i.e., *dompnas*) to his program of secular reform (see Dalarun). Moreover, Robert enjoyed close contact with and strong support from the Poitevin and Angevin houses, and is attested numerous times with Guillem de Peiteus or his wife, Philippa-Mathilda.

Since, as Bezzola pointed out (vol. 2, pt. 2, 293), Guillem seems to have composed a satire on Robert's principal foundation (1101) at Fontevrault, there can be little doubt that he and his male aristocratic contemporaries were well acquainted with Robert's ideas and practices. Yet no matter how well known, these cannot constitute the origin of the concept of *fin'amor* in general, although individual troubadours (such as Jaufre Rudel) may have derived much from the discourse associated with Robert's movement. The earliest troubadour poetry (see below) already satirizes a form of love— unworthy of a noble—that submissively awaits the mercy of a distant and haughty lady. Furthermore, the pedagogic program of *fin'amor* is distinctly ethical, not religious; perhaps we must assume some secularized version of the preacher's thoughts. Finally, we must be careful about accepting a simplistic interpretation of the similarities, for it cannot be ruled out that Robert himself could easily have adapted courtly practices, or at least their expectations, in order to draw ladies to religious goals.

An alternative direction of research looks to sociological factors for the origins of courtly love. It does not necessarily contradict the textual theses outlined above, but prefers to locate primary motivation in social rather than textual processes. One branch of the investigation concentrates on the courtly lover and his desire, while a second explores the role of the lady. Both examine the question from the standpoint of the consuming group rather than that of the producing individual, asking less about the sources of *fin'amor* than about its motives, less about material than about efficient cause.

The extent of the penetration of feudal thought into the conception and expression of courtly love has been apparent to all modern investigators: the poet-lover portrays himself as a vassal (*om*), the lady is treated as a feudal lord and often addressed in masculine form (*midons/sidons*), and contracts (*conven*), reward (*guizardon*), and other aspects of loyal and humble service are constantly under discussion. In a profound sense, courtly love is quintes-sentially feudal (Riquer 77–96), for it imitates the primary hierarchical principles increasingly employed to control as well as to justify hegemonic desire in the second feudal age.

A general acknowledgment of the feudal core of courtly love cannot account for its emergence in a particular time and space, however, and much recent work has attempted to identify more specific factors. It has been argued, for instance, that the ratio of males to females was particularly high at that time in Occitania; courtly love emerges, then, as an expression of the collective frustrated desire of young men to marry the few available females (Moller). Upward mobility among the lower aristocracy has also been proposed (Koehler): lacking titles of nobility yet possessing its wealth and power, the *miles* sought to define superiority in terms of personal rather than social excellence. The use of demonstrable facts particular to Aquitaine render this interpretation attractive; moreover, many of the earliest trou-badours (especially those of what I have called the "Poitevin school") composed satires against those claiming noble status without matching "deeds." Yet Guillem de Peiteus, Eble of Ventadorn, and Jaufre Rudel—

three of the most influential of the early troubadours—all belonged to the upper aristocracy. Furthermore, such an account omits questions of class and ideology, without which no social theory will be likely to succeed. This suggests that the currently favored sociological model lacks sufficient subtlety to explain the social phenomenon of courtly love lyric.

A different form of the sociological theory considers the roles of ladies and their courts, arguing that it is rather their "matronage" that finally causes and supports courtly love lyric (among other cultural artifacts). There is ample historical evidence from the second half of the twelfth century for such a position, but less work has been devoted to the earlier period (although Brinkmann did make it a serious part of his study of the Loire school). Poets associated with that group were the first to send Latin encomiastic verse to educated ladies of the secular court, such as Adela of Blois and her sister-in-law, Mathilda of England (Bezzola, Georgi), already in the 1090s; they had been sending them to educated noble nuns, of course, for some time, and nun poets (such as the "famous poet" Muriel of Wilton, dead by 1113) from the period are known (Dronke 1984). Clearly, at least leading Anglo-Norman ladies had become interested in supporting their own praise in poetry by the end of the eleventh century, an act accompanied by and accompanying the general rethinking of the status of women (or, at least, of ladies) that surely played an important role in the rise of courtly love lyric (Van Houts). Here again one must be very careful about the direction of influence, since it is very possible that those medieval Latin poets were adapting a discursive practice already well known at secular courts.

Finally, feminist scholars have begun to view the entire question in a different light. In a careful study that has not received as much attention as it deserves, Liebertz-Grün reoriented Koehler's general theories about the collective male desire for social station to emphasize the lady's active role. That work has been supported by scholars as different as Burns and Kay, both of whom have argued that "courtly love" requires rethinking in terms of gender ideology. The latter's proposal that the *domna* served as a kind of third and supplemental gender raises important theoretical and historical considerations for the questions of origins.

CASE STUDY: GUILLEM DE PEITEUS

There are obvious reasons for examining the origins of the extant songs of Guillem de Peiteus (William VII, count of Poitiers, ninth duke of Aquitaine), the first troubadour whose works are extant. The songs are attractive for their early date, of course, but also for other traits such as their explicit social investment and their generic and stylistic breadth. An acceptable model for these songs could provide a solid basis for answering the question for the entire corpus.

The lyric relics of this count of Poitiers (as he is always named in the lyric manuscripts) have slowly yielded up results for the question of origins. As new evidence comes to light, researchers (starting with Kolb) increasingly agree that the central notion of what we call "courtly love" was already in place by the time Guillem began composing around 1105. All but one of the songs treat of *amor;* in other words, the hegemony of "love" as lyric subject matter was established before he started writing. As a number of scholars (Lefèvre and Dronke, among others) have argued, moreover, the earliest poems already satirize an unrewarded and foolish form of masculine desire. Its object is repeatedly characterized as a beautiful but hostile lady wrongly rejecting a loyal knight's love; the lover is shown as lovesick, fated or crazed, and emasculated; and his love is distanced, without sexual pleasure, and concealed. Unless one wants to maintain that Guillem de Peiteus first invented then ridiculed this kind of love, we are led to conclude that he was familiar with an established and conventional concept of "courtly love." This recognition alters radically the question of origins for the first troubadour, since it shifts the locus of the investigation from an onymous poet whose texts are extant to anonymous poets whose texts do not exist. We will come back to the implications of this shift.

Opposing this type of "true" or "good" love (*fin'amor, bon'amor*) one finds Guillem promoting what has been termed "chivalric love" (Nelli) as worthy for a true knight. Here woman is treated as a pretext for and vehicle of male prowess and social standing. As Guillem argues repeatedly, a good woman is as essential a piece of "good equipment" as a good horse, both select markers of virile excellence for this group. Such a concept of a sexual love based on domination requires no literary source, for it is ubiquitous in time and space in forms of discourse and other sign systems that reflect the interests of a male elite glorifying its own potency.

There is a substantial amount of evidence that the first troubadour found both these forms of love already in existence when he began to write. They emerge from the attitudes embedded in the competing conceptions of courtly culture in western central France in the latter half of the eleventh century. "Chivalric love" expresses in its essence the attitude toward desire of the members of a martial culture that was founded on the warrior class and its acquisition of fame (*pretz*) and that placed a premium on prowess and loyalty. But although it may be safely surmised that sexual desire always played a significant role in the life of a *bellator*, it had not figured prominently in his idealizing discourse, as one quickly establishes from a reading of European heroico-feudal texts. Seen in this wider perspective, "chivalric love" represents a break with traditional concepts of nobility, without a significant change in its membership. Guillem's alterations were hardly isolated. One sees similar change in image in the literary figures of Olivier in the *Pèlerinage de Charlemagne* (ca.1120) and especially of Gauvain in Arthurian story, whose name became an aristocratic favorite in Poitou about this time (Gallais).

"Love from afar" (*amor de lonh*, to use Jaufre Rudel's famous term) was most likely a much more recent phenomenon. It is no longer possible to deny the links between such a conception of love and the emergence of a very different court culture, whose outlines have only been worked out in recent scholarship (Platelle). Condemnations by eleventh-century clerics reveal the emergence of a new aristocratic "courtliness" (*curialitas, cortezia*) based on a sophisticated aesthetic applied to language, dress, and social behavior. Mentions of "obscene talk" and "lovers' urbanities" imply that both the cult of noble women and stylized forms of amatory discourse were centrally connected to this new style. One cannot maintain, however, that Guillem's role was merely passive, for neither in conception nor in expression can his texts be considered routine. The theme of metaphysical *joi* (song 9), for instance, is lacking in the image of "love from afar" one sees in the early satires. Such an important aspect may be his own contribution, although the evidence is so scanty that it is difficult to judge.

The form of his lyric has led to a number of competing theories of origins. Liturgical origins have been concluded from formal parallels found in manuscripts associated with the abbey of St.Martial in Limoges, a renowned center of musical development for whose holdings Guillem served as feudal overlord (Spanke 1934). Support comes from the fact that the words for "song" (*vers*) and for "compose" (*trobar*) are most easily derived from Aquitanian liturgical vocabulary (Chailley). Another thesis locates the formal source in the *muwashshah* and the *zajal,* rhymed syllabic songs favored in Mozarabic Spain from the eleventh century onward (Menéndez Pidal, Nykl, Pollmann). Occasional Romance citations in the final couplet (the *harcha*) appear to reinforce this thesis; in addition, Guillem and his entourage can be demonstrated to have had strong connections to the courts beyond the Pyrenees.

Despite the current popularity of these two positions, it is a third—actually the earliest—that seems to me the strongest, since even in an era before Ockham the simplest of competing successful proposals must be considered the most likely. Detailed study of the lyric forms associated with the round dance (Verrier) links Guillem's forms strongly with an indigenous tradition known to have existed at least since the ninth century (Gougaud); it has been shown that his forms could have evolved easily from those of extant Romance songs from the early eleventh century (Le Gentil 1963); and his rhymes and meters indicate the prior use of refrains (Spanke 1936). If the form of his songs is closely and easily related to native refrain songs associated with the round dance and its amorous text—and dance itself often represents the ritualized expression of desire—there is no need for us to continue to entertain the notion of monastic or foreign sources. Since historical, formal, and documentary evidence attests to a long and stable tradition of amatory refrain songs in the vernacular, I follow others in concluding that Guillem founded his formal art upon an oral lyric practice that he had both means and motivation to exploit. This conviction does not deny, of course, substantial interaction with the art of liturgical and scholastic verse in the formal developments to come (Le Gentil 1954; Chailley).

Finally, a word about style. Difficult as the notion of style may be for theorists of the twentieth century, it is a reasonably clear construct for critics of troubadour poetry because of the constant cultural "pressure" exerted by the Latin rhetorical tradition inherited from antiquity and taught in the schools as the mark of true poetry (see Chapter 18 in this volume). The style found in Guillem de Peiteus's songs (as in those of later troubadours; see Paterson) is as diverse as the genre, as one might expect. On the one side, there are obvious instances of rhetorical *flores*, which betray clerical origins. In song 7, the most rhetorical of all, one finds *adnominatio* (lines 5–6), *ratiocinatio* (7–9), and *sententia* (9–12). All these figures were taught in the contemporary lower schools of the region, as demonstrated by Marbod of Rennes's popular summary *De ornamentis verborum* (written while he was head of the school at Angers between ca.1067 and 1096), and Guillem (or his clerics) could not have avoided them in the basic schooling that, as Marbod notes (in Jaeger 224), was customarily given to the young noble males in central France at this time.

On the other side, many techniques of Guillem's style originate in vernacular political and poetic practice. The erotic metaphors associated with the boasting songs (1–3, 5, 6), for instance, derive from characteristic postures within the martial aristocracy. Much of the language and imagery derives from the legal conceptions and practice that constituted the court's daily life (Press). The style of vernacular lyric dominates song 10, for instance, whose natural imagery and terms of complaint link it with pan-European and pre–courtly love song (Panzer). Song 11, a unique form of the *planh* or lament in which Guillem bemoans his "exile" and the accompanying personal and dynastic loss, belongs in style as in form and content to the discourse surrounding the most unstable moment in aristocratic political life: the death of a lord when the entire *linhage* lies in jeopardy. It is simple and unadorned, and shows little influence of school poetry.

If one tries to summarize the research on the origins of the poetry of the count of Poitiers while bearing in mind the methodological and conceptual cautions spelled out in the first sections of this chapter, one can place certain limits upon the range of possibilities. To begin with, one must accept the fact that the diversity of his poetry and the number of easily available sources is so great that no single body of literary, intellectual, or religious writing could claim paternity. We must conclude that the first troubadour constructed his lyric within the complex cultural nexus woven about his court and its interests.

At the base lay an indigenous lyric tradition in the vernacular, confirmed by much indirect evidence, which provided a formal repertory (based perhaps on refrain songs) with which Guillem could work. At the same time, it is highly likely that the incentive for Guillem's formal interests derives one way or another from the poetic and musical renaissance in Latin culture. We need not choose between the discrete origins implied by these statements. In fact, the complexities of "making a song" (*faire un vers*) suggest that we have identified here the two primary drives of all troubadour composition: a lyric drive derived from an oral, secular, vernacular, and public cult of song within the court, and a poetic drive derived from a written, ecclesiastic, Latin, and private cult of poem within the school. The interference and interaction of these two drives (and the groups they represent, the *joglar* and the *clericus*) strongly influenced the troubadours' compositions on a deep level—another indication that both are necessary to solve the problem of origins.

The content of Guillem's songs reflects the heterogeneous nature of court life and culture in early-twelfth-century Occitania. He speaks in many poems (as well as in historical sources) as an outrageously proud member of the male feudal elite, repeatedly asserting a conservative stance toward his class, viewed metonymically through the relationship between a real knight and a woman. Although in many ways this culture is very old, the centrality of love (as opposed to prowess) in the discussion of nobility marks a significant departure from the traditional model. A characteristic feature of the Occitanian court throughout the eleventh century tied by contemporary observers to the feminization (i.e., decadence) of the aristocracy, this new focus reflects a change in the perception of nature and of woman motivated, to some extent, by the presence of noble, powerful, and lettered women in court who had strong agendas concerning their own status.

In other poems (whether directly of indirectly), we see a very different "person," one to whom we cannot deny the title *fin'aman*. It is most unlikely that the figure is Guillem de Peiteus's invention; its origins must lie in the period before (and probably not long before) he began composing songs. Its particular features suggest that we should look for its source in the same combination of feudal and monastic thought (such as that found in the movement of Robert of Arbrissel) directed for the first time toward the Lady. This "courtly love" (or better: "true desire") must somehow relate to the radical reworking of the image of the aristocratic woman that one finds in various forms of the central French culture of the last years of the eleventh century. Although Guillem ridicules both participants of this love in most of his songs, he also portrays both its male lover (song 7) and its lady (song 9) in first-person terms so powerful that one shies away from making facile statements about his final attitudes.

Guillem's style does not provide great help in the search for origins. Some of his rhetoric derives from various forms of court discourse, some belongs to traditional genres of vernacular lyric, some he borrows indisputably from the Latin tradition practiced in the schools. In style as in content, his texts defy any attempt to identify a unique origin. This negative conclusion may only reflect a negative formulation, however, for the mixture of Latin and vernacular style in the troubadours' songs corresponds well to the cultural mixture represented by the young clerics and monks— *monges o clerga*, as Guillem calls them in a telling context (5.9)—in court service of various kinds. These lettered young men (such as the Renaud Quartald whose presence at his court was so disputed by his abbot, Geoffrey of Vendôme) often attempted "to render the conversation of the courts in the words of some poet," as Guibert of Nogent confessed (1.17) in his autobiography written in 1115, referring to his adolescent behavior at the courts of "France" in the late 1070s. If we want to find the origin of the very mixture that denies a single origin, then the hybrid culture associated with such figures (Keller) provides the most likely target.

Finally, it seems to me that one must widen the field of view in order to answer satisfactorily the question of the origins of troubadour lyric. It needs to be placed in the context of the cultural and especially literary changes occurring in central France at the end of the eleventh century. A sophisticated theory of play and an exaggerated consciousness of form, for instance, mark off troubadour lyric from other vernacular traditions as much as do the discussions of some kind of true love (Kendrick). Furthermore, the "self" that the troubadours present, an artist as much as a lover, was an amalgam new to medieval culture and obviously related to the artist-individual who dominates twelfth-century French culture (Stevens). Such features need to be studied against the broader background of the developments in the clerical culture at the schools and courts of central France, where they appear to have constituted the focus of the grammatical humanism that characterizes the earliest phase of the twelfth-century renaissance, from which the beginnings of troubadour poetry can hardly be separated.

CONCLUSION

In this chapter I have tried to clarify the question of the origins of troubadour lyric by complicating it. I have argued that we need to examine our conceptions both of the object whose origins we seek and of the origins whose product we are. The review of theories attempted to demonstrate that more work needs to be done in accommodating the theories one to another, and less in selecting one that simply pleases some prejudice. Finally, I have tried to interrogate the songs of Guillem de Peiteus, the first known troubadour. The results reinforce the utility of a theory that not only tolerates but actively seeks multiple sources for the creation and consumption of such an artifact within the complex conceptual space designated by the word *cort* in twelfth-century Occitania.

WORKS CITED

Axhausen, Käte. *Die Theorien über den Ursprung der provenzalischen Lyrik.* Düsseldorf: Nolte, 1937; repr. Geneva: Slatkine, 1974.

Bezzola, Reto. *Les Origines et la formation de la littérature courtoise en Occident (500–1200).* 3 vols. Paris: Champion, 1944–63.

Bloch, R. Howard. *Medieval French Literature and Law.* Berkeley and Los Angeles: University of California Press, 1977.

Boase, Roger. *The Origin and Meaning of Courtly Love.* Manchester: Manchester University Press, 1977.

Bond, Gerald A. *The Poetry of William VII, Count of Poitiers, IX Duke of Aquitaine.* New York: Garland, 1982.

———. "*Iocus amoris*: The Poetry of Baudri of Bourgueil and the Formation of the Ovidian Subculture." *Traditio* 42 (1986): 143–93.

Brinkmann, Hennig. *Entstehungsgeschichte des Minnesangs.* Halle: Niemeyer, 1926.

Burns, E. J. "The Man Behind the Lady in Troubadour Lyric." *Romance Notes* 25 (1985): 254–70.

Cahoon, Leslie. "The Anxieties of Influence: Ovid's Reception by the Early Troubadours." *Mediaevalia* 13 (1989, for 1987): 119–55.

Chailley, Jacques. "Les Premiers Troubadours et les versus de l'école d'Aquitaine." *Romania* 76 (1955): 212–39.

Dalarun, Jacques. "Robert d'Arbrissel et les femmes." *Annales* 39 (1984): 1140–60.

Dante Alighieri. *De vulgari eloquentia.* Vulgares Eloquentes, 3. Ed. Pier Vincenzo Mengaldo. Padua: Antenore, 1968.

Dronke, Peter. Review of *Les Origines et la formation de la littérature courtoise en Occident (500–1200),* by Reto Bezzola. *Medium Aevum* 35 (1966): 51–58.

———. *Women Writers of the Middle Ages.* Cambridge: Cambridge University Press, 1984.

Favati, Guido. "L'innovazione di Guglielmo IX d'Aquitania e un canto di Marbodo di Rennes." In *Présence des troubadours,* 65–76. Annales de l'Institut d'Etudes Occitanes, ser. 4, 2. Toulouse: Privat, 1970.

Gallais, Pierre. "Bleheri, la cour de Poitiers et la diffusion des récits arthuriens sur le continent." In *Actes du VIIème congrès national de la Société française de littérature comparée,* 47–79. Paris: Didier, 1967.

Georgi, Annette. *Das lateinische und deutsche Preisgedicht des Mittelalters.* Philosophische Studien und Quellen, 48. Berlin: Schmidt, 1969.

Gougaud, Lucien. "La Danse dans les églises." *Revue d'histoire ecclésiastique* 15 (1914): 5–22.

Jaeger, C. Stephen. *The Origins of Courtliness: Civilizing Trends and the Formation of Courtly Ideals, 939–1210.* Philadelphia: University of Pennsylvania Press, 1985.

Jauss, Hans Robert. "The Alterity and Modernity of Medieval Literature." *New Literary History* 10 (1979): 181–229.

Kay, Sarah. *Subjectivity in Troubadour Poetry.* Cambridge: Cambridge University Press, 1990.

Keller, Hans-Erich. "Le Climat prétroubadouresque en Aquitaine." In *Mittelalterstudien Erich Köhler zum Gedenken,* ed. Henning Krauss and Dietmar Rieger, 120–32. Heidelberg: Winter, 1984.

Kendrick, Laura. *The Game of Love: Troubadour Wordplay.* Berkeley: University of California Press, 1988.

Koehler, Erich. "Observations historiques et sociologiques sur la poésie des troubadours." *Cahiers de Civilisation Médiévale* 7 (1964): 27–51.

Kolb, Herbert. *Der Begriff der Minne und das Entstehen der höfischen Lyrik.* Hermea, 4. Tübingen: Niemeyer, 1958.

Lefèvre, Yves. "Réflexions sur une chanson de Guillaume IX." *Actes du IXème congrès d'études régionales de la Fédération historique du Sud-Ouest.* Bordeaux: n.p., 1956.

Le Gentil, Pierre. *Le Virelai et le villancico: le problème des origines arabes.* Paris: Les Belles Lettres, 1954.

———. "La Strophe zadjalesque, les khardjas et le problème des origines du lyrisme roman." *Romania* 84 (1963): 1–27, 209–50.

Liebertz-Grün, Ursula. *Zur Soziologie des "Amour courtois": Umrisse der Forschung.* Heidelberg: Winter, 1977.

Menéndez Pidal, Ramón. "Poesía árabe y poesía europea." In *Poesía árabe y poesía europea,* 9–67. Buenos Aires: n.p., 1941.

Menocal, María Rosa. *The Arabic Role in Medieval Literary History: A Forgotten Heritage.* Philadelphia: University of Pennsylvania Press, 1987.

Moller, Herbert. "The Social Causation of the Courtly Love Complex." *Comparative Studies of Society and History* 1 (1958–59): 137–63.

Nykl, Alois. *Hispano-Arabic Poetry and Its Relations with the Old Provençal Troubadours.* Baltimore: [Furst], 1946.

Ong, Walter. *Orality and Literacy: The Technologizing of the Word.* New York: Methuen, 1982.

Orderic Vitalis. *The Ecclesiastical History.* Ed. and trans. Marjorie Chibnall. 6 vols. Oxford: Clarendon Press, 1969–80.

Panzer, Friedrich. "Der älteste Troubadour und der erste Minnesinger." *Dichtung und Volkstum* 40 (1940): 133–45.

Paterson, Linda. *Troubadours and Eloquence.* Oxford: Clarendon Press, 1975.

Platelle, Henri. "Le Problème du scandale: les nouvelles modes masculines aux XIème et XIIème siècles." *Revue belge de philologie et d'histoire* 53 (1975): 1071–96.

Pollmann, Leo. "Dichtung und Liebe bei Wilhelm von Aquitanien." *Zeitschrift für romanische Philologie* 78 (1962): 326–57.

Press, Alan R. "L'Unité de la composition dans les chansons de Guillaume IX." In *Actes et mémoires du VIème congrès international de langue d'oc et d'études francoprovençales,* 2:417–34. Montpellier: Centre d'Estudis Occitans, 1971.

Riquer, Martín de. *Los trovadores: historia literaria y textos.* 3 vols. Barcelona: Planeta, 1975.

Scheludko, Dimitri. "Ovid und die Troubadours." *Zeitschrift für romanische Philologie* 60 (1940): 191–234.

Seeger, Charles. *Studies in Musicology, 1935–1977.* Berkeley and Los Angeles: University of California Press, 1977.

Spanke, Hans. "Zur Formenkunst des ältesten Troubadours." *Studi medievali,* n.s., 7 (1934): 72–84.

————. *Beziehungen zwischen romanischer und mittellateinischer Lyrik.* Abhandlungen der Gesellschaft zu Göttingen, 3. Folge 18. Berlin: Weidmann, 1936.

Stevens, Martin. "The Performing Self in Twelfth-Century Culture." *Viator* 9 (1978): 193–212.

Stock, Brian. *The Implications of Literacy.* Princeton: Princeton University Press, 1983.

Topsfield, Leslie. *Troubadours and Love.* Cambridge: Cambridge University Press, 1975.

Van Houts, Elisabeth. "Latin Poetry and the Anglo-Norman Court, 1066–1135: The *Carmen de Hastingae Proelio.*" *Journal of Medieval History* 15 (1989): 39–62.

Verrier, Paul. "Le Rondeau et formes analogues." *Neuphilologische Mitteilungen* 34 (1933): 102–25.

Wechssler, Eduard. *Kulturproblem des Minnesangs. Studien zur Vorgeschichte der Renaissance.* Vol. 1: *Minnesang und Christentum.* Halle: Niemeyer, 1909.

Zumthor, Paul. *Speaking of the Middle Ages.* Trans. Sarah White. Lincoln: University of Nebraska Press, 1986.

————. *La Lettre et la voix: de la "littérature" médiévale.* Paris: Seuil, 1987.

TEN

Northern France

Deborah H. Nelson

While it is impossible to establish when an unrecorded oral tradition in lyric poetry originated in either the langue d'oc or the langue d'oïl, mid-thirteenth-century manuscripts preserve the first recorded troubadour songs, from about 1120, and the earliest recorded trouvère work, a song from the Second Crusade, 1146–47 (Holmes 198). Two songs by Chrétien de Troyes are considered the earliest by an identified author in the langue d'oïl, written perhaps as early as 1160 (Dragonetti 662). Scholars generally accept that the genres, forms, and content of the lyric poetry of twelfth- and thirteenth-century France existed first in the south and then spread to the north. Although the physical movements of poets between these two regions are untraceable, circumstantial evidence points to the marriage in 1137 of Aliénor d'Aquitaine to Louis VII, king of France, as a major factor in the spread of troubadour poetry to the north. Aliénor's entourage would have supplied both poets and an audience for the secular and sophisticated verse hitherto unknown to or scorned by the austere royal court. Although Aliénor soon moved to England as the wife of Henry II, she passed on to her two daughters by Louis the literary tastes and bent for patronage that she had inherited from her grandfather Guillem de Peiteus, the first troubadour. Accordingly, under Marie and Aelis the courts of Champagne and Blois became cultural centers where literary activities of all sorts were fostered. In these and other northern courts, poets were supported financially, and their songs served as entertainment.

The trouvères, like the troubadours, came from all levels of the social scale: they were nobles, both powerful and unimportant, clergy, clerks, bourgeois, and even former jongleurs. Some of the better known trouvères, who lived between 1150 and 1300, included Chrétien de Troyes, Huon d'Oisi, Conon de Béthune, Gace Brule, Blondel de Nesle, le Châtelain de

Couci, Thibaut de Champagne, Colin Muset, Gautier d'Epinal, Renaut de Beaujeu, Gautier de Dargies, Richart de Semilli, Guiot de Provins, and Rutebeuf. All of them composed poetry with conventional techniques and subject matter for the pleasure of the aristocracy and were dependent on that group for an audience and generally also for financial sustenance. Both trouvères and troubadours lived at local courts or traveled from one to another.

The trouvères of thirteenth-century Arras were a notable exception to this general rule. In this town the citizens, enjoying newfound prosperity gained from commercial enterprises and wishing to imitate the lifestyle of the nobles, began to compose music and lyrics in the courtly tradition and also to serve as patrons to other poets. The names of two hundred poets from this commercial and literary center of twenty thousand inhabitants have survived, and their compositions make up more than half the lyric poetry written in Old French (Holmes 311). Although these poets also came from varied backgrounds, they organized themselves into literary guilds and seem to have composed their songs largely for each other and for a bourgeois, rather than a courtly, audience. Despite this social and poetic freedom, their songs display the same form and content as the poetry composed at courts for patrons in both the north and south.

While it cannot be assumed that the extant songs typify all those produced in the twelfth and thirteenth centuries, it is useful to note that we possess more than 2,500 songs (only about 250 of which still have melodies) composed by 460 troubadours; in contrast, about 200 trouvères have left about 2,000 songs, 1,500 or so of them with melodies (van der Werf 15). Critics often claim that the poetry of northern France in the twelfth and thirteenth centuries is merely a faint and less effective echo of its southern origins, a view that careful examination of the songs of both traditions does not contradict However, close scrutiny does reveal significant trends in the popularity of particular genres in the north and in the south, and in the form and content of the songs, that give clues to the extent and kind of influence exerted by the troubadours on the trouvères.

Lyric songs did exist in the north before the influx of Occitan influence. Some extant examples of the *chanson de toile* (weaving song), for example, are certainly very early, as evidenced by the frequency of Germanic names and the assonanced, ten-syllable lines associated with the epic (Frappier 29). The early existence of another genre is demonstrated in the *Chanson de Roland* (Brault, line 1014) by a reference to a satiric song. Most of the remaining lyric genres, including the *aube, sirventois, tenson, jeu parti, pastourelle*, crusade song, and love song, however, which serve as framework for the trouvère songs, most likely did originate in the south. Without exception, the earliest example of each of these genres is in Occitan, even though in some cases a larger number may have been preserved in the langue d'oïl. For example, northern French poets excelled at writing the *pastourelle* and the crusade song, although the earliest and possibly the best of both types that have been preserved were composed by Marcabru, ca. 1140 (Dejeanne, nos. 30, 35). Yet whereas only 25 *pastourelles* survive in Occitan (Jeanroy 338–39), 130 to 150 still exist in Old French (Frappier 57). As for crusade songs, we possess about the same number in each language: 35 in Occitan and 29 in Old French (Bec 152). It is important to note that the numbers mentioned here are open to dispute, since certain songs do not fit exactly into a strict definition of a particular genre. The popularity of the different genres may be roughly estimated by using these figures.

The *jeu parti* and the *tenson*, considered courtly counterparts of the Latin debate poem, differ slightly from each other in format. In the *jeu parti*, the first voice proposes to a colleague a love dilemma with two solutions and gives him the choice of the one he wishes to defend, whereupon the original poet takes the opposite position. Often, the *jeu parti* concludes with an appeal to a judge to declare the winner. The *tenson*, by contrast, is simply a debate between two poets who defend opposite opinions on a subject. Although the earliest extant examples of the *jeu parti* date from about 1200 in Occitan, with a total of 102 surviving (Jeanroy 263), this genre may well have originated in the langue d'oïl, in which 182 remain extant, more than three-fourths of them composed by poets from Arras (Långfors v, xxvi). As for the *tenson*, it proved to be more popular in the south, with 65 surviving (Jeanroy 371), compared to only 30 in Old French (Jeanroy 518). Similarly, there are 9 *albas* (dawn songs) preserved in Occitan, but only 5 *aubes* in Old French (Woledge 346).

Although these narrative and dramatic genres were used much more by the trouvères than the troubadours, both groups of poets wrote many more love songs (*cansos* or *chansons d'amour*) than any other kind of song. When considered superficially, the love songs in the langue d'oc and the langue d'oïl appear very similar. Although individual poets may show a preference for some themes over others, the troubadour and trouvère courtly love songs, taken as a group, are drawn from the same store. They all sing the praises or lament the disdain of the same distant, beautiful, married lady, whose attributes are described repeatedly in virtually the same language. The distance between the lady and the poet remains undeniable, whether owing to geography, class, or, most important of all, her attitude toward him. The songs focus on the poet's obsession with his own feelings and the intensity of his suffering much more than on his love for the lady. In the poets' eyes, it is through suffering that a lover is ennobled by love and thereby becomes worthy of an undefined "favor" from the lady. Therefore, a lover seeks to suffer, with death being the only release from his desperate situation. The poets sing of their timidity in their lady's presence and their fear of gossips' revealing their feelings or slandering their reputation in the lady's hearing. (For more on "courtly" love, see Chapter 3.)

Both the troubadours and the trouvères often cite the arrival of spring as their inspiration for songs about love. Although repetitious in terms of detail, the introductory strophes of both south and north remain surprisingly original and convincing in emotion through individual variations in form and emphasis. Ever seeking to embroider on a familiar theme, poets as early as Marcabru may, for example, reverse the nature introduction by describing a winter scene, stating that they sing of love despite the season.

Although the love songs in the langue d'oc and the langue d'oïl contain the same topoi (see Chapter 19), the difference in tone and intensity strike the modern reader immediately. The southern poetry is decidedly more sensual than its northern counterpart, occasionally to the point of obscenity; it is often apparent that the "favor" pleaded for by an Occitan poet was a sexual encounter, while the trouvère's longing remains vague. The northern poets cannot be considered prudish, however, since they did not hesitate to write quite erotic poetry in other genres. Perhaps the trouvères sought to make the *chansons d'amour* more tolerable to Christian morality (Zink 147). Be that as it may, neither the trouvères nor the troubadours seem to have perceived any conflict between their religious faith and the profane, adulterous love that they sought so passionately, if not to consummate, at least to enjoy; indeed, many from both groups called on God for help in amorous pursuits. Nevertheless, the religious language so common in many of the troubadour songs is rare in trouvère poetry.

Both the troubadours and the trouvères were conscious artists and regularly sang of their desire to perfect the words as well as the music. They demonstrated their great concern for their artistic reputation not only in the articulation of the theme but also in their preoccupation with form. Occitan poetry especially was marked by the poets' delight in innovation, refinement of expression, and the treatment of conventional motifs in ever more complex language and form (Zink 135). (For more on versification, see Chapter 4.) The troubadours tried to invent an original rhyme-scheme for every new song, since the tradition discouraged repetition or borrowing. The trouvères, for their part, imitated but did not duplicate the intricacy of the troubadour song; instead they contented themselves with less numerous and relatively simple rhymes that confined them to a rather limited vocabulary (Dragonetti 415). Their syntax and handling of the conventional motifs likewise remained low-key and repetitive in comparison to the snowballing of complex and esoteric expression that culminated in the *trobar clus* of the later troubadours, a style virtually unknown in the trouvère songs. If some troubadours wrote for only a small circle of the initiated, the trouvères, it seems, desired to remain intellectually accessible to almost any courtly audience.

The trouvères now considered most talented are those who produced songs with complex interwoven rhymes and themes in the troubadour style. The poetry of a few of them can in fact be concretely linked to that of specific troubadours (Dragonetti 457). For example, Conon de Béthune, who belonged to the first generation of trouvères (1180–1200), echoed the words of a song by Guiraut de Bornelh in "Chancon legiere a entendre" (Wallensköld, song 1) in which he declared his intent to compose a song easily understood by everyone to serve as the messenger of his love (Frappier 126). In "Belle doce Dame chiere" (Wallensköld, song 7), Conon used the same complex rhyme-scheme as Bertran de Born in "Chazutz sui de mal en pena" (Frappier 134) and composed two other songs for which he adapted the structure from the same troubadour (Frappier 139). Even though he imitated the songs of at least one troubadour, Conon did not use the same structure twice in his relatively few extant songs (ten). He also showed some originality by embroidering the traditional themes with a few new images. No historical evidence remains to demonstrate personal contact between Conon and any Occitan poet, but the form and content of his songs prove beyond any doubt his familiarity with the troubadour tradition.

Another first-generation trouvère, Gace Brule, also provides a solid link between the south and the north. Gace's most recent editor, Rosenberg, assigns him eighty-two songs, all of which exhibit characteristics usually associated with trouvère verse. For example, in dwelling on his suffering and melancholy feelings he falls into abstraction and a vagueness of expression, using few concrete images to give life and individuality to his artistic creation. Even so, he drew extensively from Bernart de Ventadorn for his overall perception of love, while echoes from the songs of Jaufre Rudel, Gaucelm Faidit, and Raimbaut d'Aurenga sound in the motif of nostalgia for a distant land and the use of birds (Rosenberg and Danon xxv). Underneath a certain monotony of *fond*, Gace used a wide variety of poetic techniques while carefully avoiding the repetition of any structure, characteristics that link him securely to the troubadour tradition. He experimented with the many possible relationships between strophes (*coblas singulars, unissonans, doblas, retrogradadas*) as well as with other poetic variables (rhyme schemes, interplay of masculine and feminine forms, etc.) (Rosenberg and Danon xxii). Gace Brule clearly imitated his Occitan counterparts, and he in turn was imitated and widely praised by his contemporaries and successors, and even by Dante. The troubadour Gaucelm Faidit, for one, was apparently so inspired by one of Gace's songs that he drew from both the text and melody for one of his own creations (Rosenberg and Danon xxv).

Another prolific trouvère, Thibaut de Champagne (1201–53), the grandson of Marie de Champagne, probably had extensive contact with the troubadour Rigaut de Berbezilh, who lived at the court of Champagne (Frappier 193). Like Rigaut, he used many bestiarial similes and metaphors, including among his images the phoenix, unicorn, swan, white deer, and pelican. In addition, the more than fifty songs positively attributed to Thibaut reveal an unusual level of education for a trouvère in their numerous literary allusions to mythology and the written and oral French tradition. His songs are individualized by his references to Narcissus, Piramus and Thisbe, Jason and the golden fleece, Roland and Olivier, Tristan, and Merlin, among others.

Both troubadours and trouvères composed for audiences that did not value originality; they were therefore encouraged to base their artistic creations on elements introduced and standardized by other artists. The *chanson d'amour* of the twelfth and thirteenth centuries was an exercise in composition that demanded that conventional themes be worked and reworked to satisfy a sophisticated secular audience of nobles, fellow poets, and bourgeois (especially in Arras). The songs are striking more for their conformity in form and content to a fixed tradition than for their expression of intimate and personal feelings. This conventionality and uniformity, which would greatly displease a modern audience, led to the enthusiastic reception of twelfth- and thirteenth-century poets (Dragonetti 545). The poets in both traditions express consistently the inseparability of love and singing. This link between desire and song has given rise to the suggestion (equally true for the troubadours) that "the frustrated quest for love" may be "in the end a fiction which both provides the matter for art to work on and masks the true object of the trouvère's passion: his song" (Rosenberg and Danon xxi). While belonging to the same lyric tradition and sharing the same images and form, the songs produced by these two groups of musician-poets are strikingly different in tone, intensity, and complexity of expression. Troubadour poetry is typified by an intricate interweaving of images, both religious and secular, while the trouvères remain content with a straightforward and much less complex lyrical expression. The trouvère songs contain much that is beautiful but lack the intellectual excitement inspired by their southern counterparts.

WORKS CITED

Bec, Pierre. *La Lyrique française au moyen âge (XIIe–XIIIe s.).* 2 vols. Paris: Picard, 1977–78.

Bédier, Joseph, and Pierre Aubry. *Les Chansons de croisades avec leurs mélodies.* New York: Franklin, [1909] 1971.

Brault, Gerard J. *The Song of Roland: An Analytical Edition.* University Park: Penn-sylvania State University Press, 1978.

Dragonetti, Roger. *La Technique poétique des trouvères dans la chanson courtoise.* Bruges: De Tempel, 1960.

Frappier, Jean. *La Poésie lyrique en France aux XIIe et XIIIe siècles.* Paris: Centre de Documentation Universitaire, 1962.

Holmes, Urban T. *A History of Old French Literature from the Origins to 1300.* New York: Crofts, 1948.

Jackson, W. T. H. *The Literature of the Middle Ages.* New York: Columbia University Press, 1960.

Jeanroy, Alfred. *Les Origines de la poésie lyrique en France au moyen âge.* Paris: Champion, 1969.

Långfors, Arthur. *Recueil général des jeux-partis français.* Paris: Champion, 1926.

Picot, Guillaume. *Poesie lyrique au moyen âge.* 2 vols. Paris: Larousse, 1963.

Rosenberg, Samuel N., and Samuel Danon. *The Lyrics and Melodies of Gace Brule.* New York: Garland, 1985.

Rosenberg, Samuel N., and Hans Tischler. *Chanter m'estuet: Songs of the Trouvères.* Bloomington: Indiana University Press, 1981.

van der Werf, Hendrik. *The Chansons of the Troubadours and Trouvères: A Study of the Melodies and Their Relation to the Poems.* Utrecht: Oosthoek, 1972.

Wallensköld, Axel. *Les Chansons de Conon de Béthune.* Paris: Champion, 1968.

Woledge, B. "Old Provençal and Old French." In *Eos: An Enquiry into the Theme of Lovers' Meetings and Partings at Dawn in Poetry,* ed. Arthur T. Hatto, 344–89. London: Mouton, 1965.

Zink, Michel. "Troubadours et trouvères." In *Précis de littérature française du moyen âge,* ed. Daniel Poirion, 128–55. Paris: PUF, 1983.

ELEVEN

The Minnesingers

Stephanie Cain Van D'Elden

Scholarship pertaining to the relationship between troubadour lyric and minnesang has had political and nationalistic overtones from the very beginning. The deeper the political differences were between France and Germany, the more German scholars sought to distance minnesang from troubadour lyric. The Germans strove to point out the "purity," "depth," and "richer spirit" of the "German" vis-à-vis the supposed "artificiality," "superficiality," and "moral wantonness" of the "French." Even in modern times the historian Karl Bosl (337) claimed that love service and love song were unchristian, erotic, and immoral in their Occitan homeland, but in Germany the sensual-aesthetic element was overcome by a spiritualization of love for the lady that placed the grace of the soul over that of the spirit.

Guillem de Peiteus (1071–1127) is the first troubadour whom we know by name; the first minnesinger whose name we know is der von Kürenberg, who was active in Austria or southern Germany in the middle of the twelfth century. We have eleven songs from Guillem and know many details of his life; we have only a dozen strophes from Kürenberg and know almost nothing about his life. And yet from their songs we can detect the distinct personalities of two poetic geniuses. Behind these two first names preserved through historical accident lie many years of anonymous Romance and Germanic songs. According to Peter Dronke,

> By looking at the surviving songs of these two poets we can glimpse behind them traditions of love-lyric of enormous vivacity and scope: they are relying on a wide, sophisticated range of expectations in an audience for such lyrics, they take for granted that this audience will be familiar with the mercurial nuances of a subtle poetic language, they count on the recognition of love as a complicated thing both poetically and humanly. It is scarcely possible to surmise how much of the poetic art of Guillaume and Kürenberc was their own

exclusive creation; what is certain is that neither was creating *ex nihilo*. (Dronke 118)

If we agree with Dronke that the love lyric, even the concept of courtly love, existed before Guillem and Kürenberg, what, then, are the relationships between troubadour lyric and minnesang? Did, as has been often stated, the troubadours influence the minnesingers, and if so, how?

Traditionally minnesang is divided into several stages of development, relative to the amount of French influence and level of sophistication evident.[1] In the first so-called indigenous stage, little Romance influence is perceived; it includes anonymous or little-known poets active along the Danube River in Austria and southern Germany, such as Kürenberg, Dietmar von Aist, Burggraf von Regensburg, Burggraf von Rietenburg, and Meinloh von Sevelingen.[2] Even at this early stage, however, contact with troubadour poetry cannot be discounted: in 1147 King Louis VII of France and Eleanor of Aquitaine gathered an army near Metz and traveled over the Rhine and down the Danube to Regensburg on the way to the Second Crusade. It is probable that both Jaufre Rudel and Cercamon were among the participants.

The next stage is usually characterized as fully developed courtly minnesang, demonstrating dependence on Romance models until "Walther von der Vogelweide shows a new way forward out of the *impasse* to which the

1. Schweilke presents the most recent scholarship in a well-organized, convenient form, 78–100. He divides minnesang into six phases: (1) early phase, 1150/60–1170; (2) first high phase, ca. 1170–1190/1200; (3) second high phase, 1190–1210/20; (4) climax, 1190–1230; (5) first late phase, ca. 1210–1240; (6) second late phase, 1210–1300.

2. The German *Minnelieder* (love songs) are preserved in collective manuscripts from a relatively late date. The most important are:

A The small Heidelberg MS, Universitätsbibliothek, Heidelberg, Cod. pal. germ. 357
   (end of 13th cent.)

B The Weingarten MS, Landesbibliothek, Stuttgart, HB XIII, poet. germ. 1 (beginning
   of 14th cent.), 25 illustrations

C The large Heidelberg MS (Codex Manesse), Universitätsbibliothek, Heidelberg,
   Cod. pal. germ. 848 (beginning of 14th cent.), 137 illustrations

J Jena Song MS, Universitätsbibliothek, Jena (14th cent.)

Editions of these manuscripts from which the identifying numbers for the songs come are:

MF *Des Minnesangs Frühling*, ed. Karl Lachmann and Moriz Haupt (Leipzig, 1857);
   30th ed. by Carl von Kraus (Leipzig, 1950); 37th rev. ed. by Hugo Moser and Helmut Tervooren (Stuttgart, 1982). Contains poets from the beginning down to Hartmann von Aue. Traditionally, and in all more recent editions, poems are quoted by
   the page and line number of the first edition.

L/K *Die Gedichte Walthers von der Vogelweide*, ed. Karl Lachmann (Berlin, 1827); 11th ed.
   by Carl von Kraus (Berlin, 1950).

MSH *Minnesänger. Deutsche Liederdichter des 12., 13. u. 14 Jahrhunderts*, Friedrich Heinrich von der Hagen, ed. 4 vols. (Leipzig/Berlin, 1838–56).

KLD *Deutsche Liederdichter des 13. Jahrhunderts*, vol. 1, text ed. Carl von Kraus (Tübingen, 1952); vol. 2, commentary by Hugo Kuhn (1958).

developed convention inevitably leads" (Walshe 106). The minnesingers geographically closest to France—Heinrich von Veldeke in Limburg, Friedrich von Hausen near Worms, Reinmar von Hagenau in Alsace, and Rudolf von Fenis in western Switzerland—are considered to demonstrate the most direct Romance influence. Other poets of "classical" minnesang include Wolfram von Eschenbach, Hartmann von Aue, Heinrich von Morungen, and Albrecht von Johansdorf. The kingdom of Arles (Provence and Burgundy) belonged to the Holy Roman Empire in the twelfth century, and the emperor frequently held court at Worms, Mainz, and Maastricht near French territory. Poets such as Heinrich von Veldeke and Friedrich von Hausen had opportunities to meet troubadour and trouvère poets on occasions such as the great festival at Mainz in 1184, attended also by Guiot de Provins and possibly Conon de Béthune. And of course, a number of German minnesingers, such as Friedrich von Hausen, who died in Asia Minor in 1190, took part in the Crusades, especially the Third Crusade (1189–92).

The essence of classical minnesang is achieved in the lyric of Reinmar von Hagenau (also known as Reinmar der Alte), who was active at the court in Vienna until his death ca. 1210. Reinmar frequently discusses the intellectual problems arising out of the convention of courtly love. He defines the conflict between the wish of the lover for the final "reward" and his wish that his beloved remain a paragon of purity (MF 165,10–166,6).[3] However, he never seems to be capable of resolving this dilemma.

Walther von der Vogelweide (d. ca. 1230), a pupil and rival of Reinmar at the court of Vienna, was a professional poet and, like many of the troubadours, was forced to spend time "on the road" searching for patrons. Walther, a true genius, excelled in the "classical" minnesang, then changed the course of development of the genre.

> He created a new type of poetic diction, in which the formal concepts of courtly love were expressed in a language that was stripped of its traditional formality. By this means he achieved a unique degree of immediacy by making possible an identification of poetic images with items of common experience. The figures of his poems are no longer the formal abstractions "lady" and "knight," but assume individual, human shape as girls and lovers. Moreover, the figures as well as their actions are part of the poetic environment, which is itself active. A linden tree and a meadow no longer merely symbolize spring or nature, as for instance in the poetry of Dietmar of Aist. They become active participants in the evocation of the experience; for instance, the grass and flowers, crushed and matted, testify to the meeting of lovers beneath the linden tree. (Bäuml 1969, 127)

Lyric poetry after Walther shows a vast increase in quantity but not necessarily in quality. The fashion of the courtly love lyric spread, and some

3. For full references of works cited in this essay, see note 2.

poets attempted to emulate the exaggerated rhyme-patterns of the trou-
badours and trouvères. The best poets include Neidhart von Reuental,
Burkhart von Hohenfels, Gottfried von Neifen, Ulrich von Winterstetten,
Konrad von Würzburg, Ulrich von Lichtenstein, and Prince Witzlaw von
Rügen. With Heinrich von Meissen (Frauenlob) at the end of the thirteenth
century, minnesang finally makes the transition to the meistergesang.

Most of the songs of the minnesingers are strophic in construction. The
word *liet* in Middle High German originally meant "strophe" in a lyrical
context; when a song consisted of more than one strophe, the plural *diu liet*
was used. Each strophe of a song was sung to the same melody. The extant
manuscripts have many identically constructed strophes placed next to each
other, making it difficult for scholars to determine which strophes constituted what we would today classify as a single song. The earliest lyrics appear
to be independent of Romance influence in their form. The type of strophe
used by Kürenberg, for example, is representative of the early stage: the
strophe is built up of long lines with a caesura, and marked by some
characteristic final cadence. Scansion is fairly free, and rhymes are often
mere assonances.

Romance influence is most obvious in the form and structure of the
classic minnesang. Here the strophe is usually tripartite, divided, according
to later German terminology, into an *Aufgesang* consisting of two identical
groups of lines called *Stollen* (*pedes*) and a third differing section, the *Abgesang* (*cauda*). The metrical structure is paralleled in the musical accompaniment, the *Stollen* having a repetition of the same melody, the *Abgesang* a
new one. The classical strophe varies and elaborates this pattern with subtle
rhythms and intricate rhyme-patterns. (For the troubadour strophic patterns, see Chapters 4 and 5.)

Two important genres (Schweilke 114–53) not found in troubadour lyric
appear in the very earliest minnesang: the *Wechsel* 'exchange', which has
early Germanic roots, and the *Frauenstrophe* 'woman's strophe'. Kürenberg
makes dramatic effective use of the *Wechsel*, or lyrical dialogue, alternating
speeches of identical length. Frequently the speeches do not make contact;
the man and woman talk past each other, remaining "shut each in their own
world of assumptions and inflexible wishes; it is a brilliant use of the
traditional form to convey an image of talking at cross purposes" (Dronke
113). Occitan genres that use dialogue have the speakers (rarely a man and
a woman) answer each other directly, almost always in alternating strophes.
Frauenstrophen, which present the woman's point of view, often take the form
of a *Frauenklage* 'woman's lament' in which the woman complains of separation, of desertion, or of envious rivals and ill-wishers. In a *Frauenklage* by
Albrecht von Johansdorf the woman laments the departure of her lover on
a Crusade (MF 94,15–95,15). Reinmar portrays the woman's conflicting
feelings in a monologue disguised as a *Botenlied* (an address to a messenger)

(MF 178,1–179,2). It is curious that the *Frauenstrophe* is absent from troubadour lyric in spite of the presence of women poets or trobairitz, who do not appear in the German sphere. In troubadour poetry when the woman appears as speaker, it is often in a "genre objectif," as in the *pastourelle* or *tenso*. The northern French *chansons de femme* are much closer to the German genre of *Frauenstrophe*. (See Chapter 8.)

While the early minnesingers Kürenberg, Dietmar von Aist, and also Meinloh von Sevelingen are considered part of the so-called indigenous tradition, their songs contain what also traditionally have been identified as "new" Romance features: in Kürenberg, the submissive role of the man, the mention of *merkære* 'slanderers' and *lügenære* 'liars'; in Dietmar, the man's submissiveness, the torments and sleeplessness of love, and the improving effect of love; in Meinloh, the ideas of the lady's supreme perfection and her sovereign power and use of the terms *dienest* 'service' and *dienen* 'to serve'. Kürenberg, in a *Wechsel*, parodies the figure of the lover who so idealizes his lady that he stands beside her bed and does not dare wake her up, much less think of enjoying her favors (MF 8,9–15). This *Wechsel* and an early-eleventh-century *Wechsel*, half Latin and half German, in which the lover twice implores "coro miner minne" (put my love to the test), seem to suggest the same concept of love service as was specified in Occitan (Dronke 131).

Throughout the twelfth century in Germany, such themes find expression not only in the lyrical poetry that shows Occitan influence, but also in songs that in their starkness of form and language are free of such influence and probably prior to it. Thus the southern influence, when it emerges, is most marked on the formal side; it is also perceptible in details of expression, but at a relatively superficial level. As István Frank shows, the incidence of trouvère influence is higher than that of the troubadours—thus Friedrich von Hausen indicates direct knowledge of six trouvère poems, but of only one troubadour poem, "En chanten m'aven a membrar" (P-C 155,8) by Folquet de Marseilla (ed., 27).

The early German minnesingers employed the Romance genre of *tageliet* (dawn song, *alba*), which reached its epitome in the songs of Wolfram von Eschenbach. While the earliest anonymous dawn song takes place in a natural setting without the figure of the watchman, it is nevertheless formally polished and already influenced by the idea of the woman's power to command (MF 39,18–29). Another fairly common convention is the address to the messenger (*Botenlied*). The whole poem may be addressed to or spoken by the messenger or the address to the messenger may form a link between the speeches in the *Wechsel*. This differs from the *tornada* or envoi, in which the messenger is merely the bearer of the message.

While dialogue proper is common in the narrative genres such as the dawn song and the village scenes of Neidhart von Reuenthal and his imitators, the argumentative dialogue, modeled on the Old Occitan *tenso* or debate, occurs for the first time in Albrecht von Johansdorf (MF 93,12–35). Ulrich von Lichtenstein employs the same form (KLD 58,XXXIII), as does Walther von der Vogelweide, who puts it to a somewhat different use (L/K 100,24), namely in a dialogue with *Frau Welt* 'Dame World' over the ultimate disposition of Walther's soul.

With a few notable exceptions, such as Guillem de Peiteus and Raimbaut d'Aurenga, the troubadours were professional poets, intellectual literati; they were not of the nobility but were dependent on their patrons for compensation (Kasten). Their songs tended to be panegyric in nature. They relied upon the rewards of the lady, monetary rewards being perhaps more important than amatory ones. They dedicated their songs to a lady who, in some cases, was a true ruler, one who may have ruled an area without the aid of her husband, father, or guardian, since in southern France, in contrast to Germany, it was possible for women to inherit and to take on the responsibilities of ruler. Thus the *midons* was both real and metaphorical. The German minnesingers, by contrast, were of the same class as the nobility; until the time of Walther von der Vogelweide they tended to be *ministeriales* who, unlike the troubadours, were not entirely dependent on the support of a noble patron.

Thus the panegyric element, so important in troubadour poetry, where it was politically advantageous for the singer of a lower social class to flatter his lady, is missing in minnesang. Moreover, the fact that the troubadours used *senhals*, secret names to hide the true name of the lady and of patrons, seems to point to a real-life situation rather than to the stylized fiction of the minnesingers. While the troubadours praised the beauty of their ladies, the minnesingers concentrated on praising the virtues of theirs. The troubadours, unlike the minnesingers, were not especially concerned with the *êre* 'honor and reputation' of the lady; nor did they engage in earnest debate over the conflict between God's love and woman's love. Anna Lüderitz (9) explains these differences by a stronger "contempt for women" on the part of Germans and by differences in social class between the minnesingers and troubadours.

The depiction of nature and the seasons is a common introductory topos, occurring in both the Romance and the German lyric. Typically the songs begin with a *Natureingang* 'nature introduction' that reflects the mood of the singer, summer being identical with joy, winter with sadness. Apart from the two chief protagonists, the hostile outer world is frequently mentioned, in the form of either envious rivals or society in general—particular figures include *lügenære* 'liars', *merkære* 'slanderers', and *huote* 'guards', influenced by Old Occitan *gardador* and *lauzenjador* and Old French *losengeor*. These figures serve important functions in minnesang: "as elements of the game of love, i.e. as opponents to the lovers; as clichés expected in the genre; as figures to be deceived and made foolish; as legitimizers and confirmers of the love affair. In each case [they] represent an outside order in conflict with the private order of the lovers" (Van D'Elden 1986a, 86). However, the *gilos* 'jealous husband' does not appear in minnesang.

Since almost no melodies of German songs survive from the early and classic period of minnesang, the concept of contrafacture is especially intriguing for Middle High German scholars. The term *contrafactum* has been used primarily in musicology, where it denotes the setting of new words to a borrowed melody. However, *contrafactum* may also involve a text translation or, more accurately, a text adaptation. Ulrich von Lichtenstein recounts in his *Frauendienst* that his lady sent him a tune unknown in Germany and requested that he compose a new song to it (Bechstein ed., 128). It has consequently been assumed that whenever a German poem is modeled in substance and form on a Romance lyric, the melody was also borrowed, though there is no direct evidence to support this view. Friedrich Gennrich emphasizes the notion that the German poets most certainly learned the Occitan songs with text and melody inextricably connected. Gennrich attempted "to remedy the paucity of musical material, by adducing *contrafacta* of existing tunes, usually of Romance origin, to fit particular poems, but these hypotheses carry little conviction" (Sayce 1976, xx). Yet a study of songs by Friedrich von Hausen and Rudolf von Fenis, identified as *contrafacta* of a song by Folquet de Marseilla (all three poets flourished from about 1180 to 1195 and possibly participated in the Third Crusade), indicates that the German songs really do not share much in form or in content with the Romance song (Van D'Elden 1986b). While the rhythmic forms are related, the rhyme-schemes differ. The content also does not represent translations, or even adaptations. Thus even in these songs, in which scholars see the most similarity, there is a great deal of difference.

A remarkably homogeneous "international courtly society" existed in the twelfth century. It should not surprise us that the literature it produced shows many affinities, for substantially the same cultural impetus (*Kulturgut*) existed in both France and Germany. The differences and similarities of troubadour lyric and minnesang are subtle and fascinating. As Theodor Frings pointed out, rather than focusing on regional and linguistic distinctions, we should look at the intrinsic merit of the individual troubadours and minnesingers, some of whom were more talented and had more vision than others.

WORKS CITED

Bäuml, Franz H. *Medieval Civilization in Germany, 800–1273*. London: Thames & Hudson, 1969.

———, ed. *From Symbol to Mimesis: The Generation of Walther von der Vogelweide*. Göppinger Arbeiten zur Germanistik, 368. Göppingen: Kümmerle, 1984.

Bechstein, Reinhold, ed. *Ulrich's von Liechtenstein. Frauendienst.* 2 vols. Leipzig: F. A. Brockhaus, 1880.

Bosl, Karl. *Die Grundlagen der modernen Gesellschaft im Mittelalter. Eine deutsche Gesellschaftsgeschichte des Mittelalters.* Monographien zur Geschichte des Mittelalters 4. Vol. 2. Stuttgart: A. Hiersemann, 1972.

Bumke, Joachim. *Ministerialität und Ritterdichtung. Umrisse der Forschung.* Munich: C. H. Beck, 1976.

Dronke, Peter. *The Medieval Lyric.* London: Hutchinson University Library, 1968.

Frank, István. *Trouvères et Minnesänger. Recueil de textes.* Saarbrücken: West-Ost-Verlag, 1952.

Frings, Theodor. "Erforschung des Minnesangs." *Forschung und Fortschritt* 26 (1950): 9–16, 39–43; also published in *Beiträge zur Geschichte der deutschen Sprache und Literatur* (Halle) 87 (1965): 1–39. [Text of a speech entitled "Minnesinger und Troubadours" delivered June 24, 1948.]

Gennrich, Friedrich. "Der deutsche Minnesang in seinem Verhältnis zur Troubadour-und Trouvère-Kunst." *Zeitschrift für deutsche Bildung* 2 (1926): 536–632.

Hatto, Arthur T., ed. *Eos: An Enquiry into the Theme of Lovers' Meetings and Partings at Dawn in Poetry.* London: Mouton, 1965.

Heffner, R.-M. S., and W. P. Lehmann. *A Word-Index to the Poems of Walther von der Vogelweide.* Madison: University of Wisconsin Press, 1950.

Heffner, R.-M. S., and Kathe Petersen. *A Word-Index to "Des Minnesangs Frühling."* Madison: University of Wisconsin Press, 1942.

Heinen, Hubert. *Mutabilität im Minnesang. Mehrfach überlieferte Lieder des 12. und frühen 13. Jahrhunderts.* Göppinger Arbeiten zur Germanistik, 515. Göppingen: Kümmerle, 1989.

Kaplowitt, Stephen J. *The Ennobling Power of Love in the Medieval German Lyric.* University of North Carolina Studies in Germanic Languages and Literatures, 106. Chapel Hill: University of North Carolina Press, 1986.

Kasten, Ingrid. *Frauendienst bei Trobadors und Minnesängern im 12. Jahrhundert.* Germanisch-Romanische Monatsschrift, 5. Heidelberg: Karl Winter, 1986.

Linker, Robert White. *Music of the Minnesinger and Early Meistersinger.* Chapel Hill: University of North Carolina Press, 1962.

Lüderitz, Anna. *Die Liebestheorie der Provençalen bei den Minnesingern der Stauferzeit.* Berlin/Leipzig, 1904; repr. Nendeln, 1976.

Räkel, Hans-Herbert S. *Der deutsche Minnesang. Eine Einführung mit Texten und Materialien.* Munich: C. H. Beck, 1986.

Ranawake, Silvia. *Höfische Strophenkunst. Vergleichende Untersuchungen zur Formentypologie von Minnesang und Trouvèrelied an der Wende zum Spätmittelalter.* Munich: C. H. Beck, 1976.

Salem, Laila. *Die Frau in den Liedern des "Hohen Minnesangs." Forschungskritik und Textanalyse.* Frankfurt a.M./Bern: Lang, 1980.

Saville, Jonathan. *The Medieval Erotic Alba: Structure as Meaning.* New York: Columbia University Press, 1972.

Sayce, Olive. *Poets of the Minnesang.* Oxford: Clarendon Press, 1976.

———. *The Medieval German Lyric 1150–1300. The Development of its Themes and Forms in their European Context.* Oxford: Clarendon Press, 1982.

Schnell, Rüdiger. *Causa Amoris. Liebeskonzeption und Liebesdarstellung in der mittelalterlichen Literatur.* Bern: Franke, 1985.

Scholz, Manfred Günter. *Bibliographie zu Walther von der Vogelweide.* Berlin: E. Schmidt, 1969.

Schweilke, Günther. *Minnesang.* Stuttgart: J. B. Metzler, 1989.

Taylor, Ronald J. "The Musical Knowledge of the MHG Poet." *Modern Language Review* 49 (1954): 331–38.

———. *The Art of the Minnesinger: Songs of the Thirteenth Century Transcribed and Edited with Textual and Musical Commentaries.* 2 vols. Cardiff: University of Wales Press, 1968.

Tervooren, Helmut. *Bibliographie zum Minnesang und zu den Dichtern aus "Des Minnesangs Frühling."* Berlin: E. Schmidt, 1969.

Thomas, Wesley, and Barbara Garrey Seagrave. *The Songs of the Minnesinger Prince Wizlaw of Rügen.* University of North Carolina Studies in the Germanic Languages and Literatures, 59. Chapel Hill: University of North Carolina Press, 1968.

Tubach, Frederic. *Struktur im Widerspruch.* Tübingen: Niemeyer, 1977.

Van D'Elden, Stephanie Cain. "Dark Figures of Minnesang: The *Merkære* and the *Huote.*" In *The Dark Figure in Medieval German and Germanic Literature,* ed. Edward R. Haymes and Stephanie Cain Van D'Elden, 66–88. Göppinger Arbeiten zur Germanistik, 448. Göppingen: Kümmerle, 1986a.

———. "Diversity Despite Similarity: Two Middle High German *Contrafacta* of an Occitan Song." In *Studia Occitanica in Memoriam Paul Remy,* ed. Hans-Erich Keller et al., 1:323–37. Kalamazoo: Western Michigan University Press, 1986b.

Walshe, Maurice O. *Medieval German Literature.* Cambridge, Mass.: Harvard University Press, 1962.

Werbow, Stanley N., ed. *Formal Aspects of Medieval German Poetry.* Austin: University of Texas Press, 1969.

TWELVE

The Iberian Peninsula

Joseph T. Snow

This chapter provides an overview of the presence, impact, and influence of the Occitan school of lyric in the Iberian peninsula. The subject is rich and complex and, as yet, still in need of critical attention and study. The early and suggestive works of Manuel Milá y Fontanals (1861), Carolina Michaelis de Vasconcellos (1904), and Ramón Menéndez Pidal (1924) have shed much light on the presence of trans-Pyrenean troubadours on Iberian soil, helping us to appreciate their roles at various of the royal courts, but especially those of Aragon and Castile.

Perhaps the first thing to note is that there was a strong and flourishing tradition of indigenous lyric in the Peninsula, dating back to the brief snatches of mozarabic song, preserved for us, at least in part, by Jewish and Muslim poets as final stanzas of poems written in either classical Arabic or Hebrew: these snippets of song are called *jarchas* and are thematically related to the Galician-Portuguese *cantigas d'amigo* 'lovers' songs', as well as to the Spanish *villancicos* 'folk songs', in which male poets speak through a female persona and tell of the pain of the lover's absence—in one form or another—and the longing for a happy reunion.[1]

It was the twelfth and thirteenth centuries that witnessed the troubadours' travels to and comments on Iberia and its kings and courts, many of which had—owing to the presence there of multiethnic and multinational

1. "Mozarabic" was the Latin dialect of Andalusia, analogous to Galician, Castilian, Leonese, Aragonese, etc., as Romance tongues in the eleventh and twelfth centuries. Little is known of its written forms. It was eventually—and completely—overshadowed by Castilian. Occasional words are preserved in the *jarchas*. A description of the *cantiga d'amigo* would be a song, often marked by the young girl's sadness at the absence of her lover (swain?). The *villancicos* are mostly two- to five-line strophes, lyric bursts more than extended poems, thematically akin to the *amigo* songs and to the mozarabic *jarchas*.

scholars and entertainers—a distinct international and multilingual character. The troubadours, from Marcabru to Guiraut Riquier and after, performed in Occitan. Through the entire period of the rise and fall of Occitan art forms, it may be said that the indigenous lyric of the Peninsula came under their spell, but in varying degrees. For example, they touched less the more popular *cantiga d'amigo* than they did the more formalized *cantiga d'amor*, the latter being more in line with the love *canso*. Another area of probable influence was on the native *cantigas d'escarnho e maldizer* 'songs of scorn and mockery' with their jocose satirical barbs: here the *sirventes* and the contentiousness of some of the *partimens* undoubtedly left their imprint. To date, however, there has been little study of the phenomenon of language in contact or of the impact of one lyric style on another, and a clear consensus on which directions such influences took is still to be achieved. The jury is still out on such thorny questions as the literary influences linking Arabic Spain and Occitania (for early and late assessments, see Nykl and Menocal, as well as Chapter 3 in this volume), or whether the Marian lyrics of Guiraut Riquier influenced—or were influenced by—those of Alfonso X, in whose court that troubadour spent nearly a decade.

From the outset, we may say that the impact of the Occitan troubadours must be limited to, principally, the courts of Aragon, Navarre, Castile, and Leon and, to a lesser degree, the courts of Portugal (d'Heur), from the early twelfth century to roughly 1300. The whole of the Peninsula would not qualify. In the eastern portion, Catalonia and the Levant had long enjoyed cultural, linguistic, commercial, and dynastic ties with southern France. The lyric poets of this part of the Peninsula were active participants in the poetic styles associated with Occitania and the Midi and composed in the same literary language as their trans-Pyrenean confrères. The use of Occitan in the region extended long past 1300, and its impact was still strong in such fifteenth-century poets as Ausias March. Thus, we would count poets from this area among those "Occitan" troubadours whose style and manner came into contact with the principal lyric language utilized by poets in the rest of the Peninsula: Galician-Portuguese (Riquer 21–196).

This hybrid lyric language was used by the cultured court poets in the rest of the Christianized Peninsula, where Castilian, the language that was gaining in linguistic as well as political hegemony throughout the thirteenth century in particular, was regularly employed for jongleuresque narrative, epic poetry, versified saints' lives, and poetic accounts of the exploits of classical heroes. It is Galician-Portuguese that is one of the six tongues used in the famed *descort* 'poem of discord' of Raimbaut de Vaqueiras (P-C 392,4). Galician-Portuguese is similarly employed (or imitated) in a composition (P-C 101,17) by Bonifaci Calvo, an Italian troubadour at the court of Alfonso X (r. 1252–84). (For more on Bonifaci Calvo, see Chapter 14.)

After 1300, when a significant portion of the Peninsula had been "pacified" or reconquered under the banner of Castile, Castilian clearly found its own lyric voice, and, little by little, the poets of the north and central regions abandoned the use of Galician-Portuguese and began exploring other lyric genres as well. Evolution in the language of Portugal created a poetic idiom more vibrant than the conventional and "tired"—by now even somewhat artificial—Galician-Portuguese. Thus it is that Galician-Portuguese, employed extensively in the western two-thirds of the Peninsula for lyrics in the period 1150–1300, attained the unique position of acting as a bridge for troubadour conceits, lexical terms, and, to a lesser extent, strophic forms and rhyme-schemes for the newly confident and dynamic lyric of both "Spain" (the Castilian-dominated areas) and Portugal.

This ascendancy is particularly attributable to the prestige and popularity of the troubadours and their art in several Iberian courts (Alvar 1977, 1978). Early monarchs who had contacts with the Occitan troubadours (or who were mentioned by them) include Alfonso VII (Castile and Leon), Sancho III (Castile), García V and Sancho VI (Navarre), Fernando II and Alfonso IX (Leon), and Alfonso VIII (Castile). The list of such troubadours for the period 1188–1228, a bare forty years, is impressive: Marcabru, Cercamon, Alegret, Peire d'Alvernhe, Bertran de Born, Guillem de Berguedan, Peire Vidal, Guiraut de Bornelh, Guillem Magret, Elías Cairel, Uc de Saint Circ, Raimon Vidal de Besalú, Gavaudan, Folquet de Marseilla, Aimeric de Peguilhan, Raimbaut de Vaqueiras, lo Monge de Montaudan, Guiraut de Calansó, Guillem Ademar, Guillem de Cabestanh, Uc de Lescura, and others (Alvar 1977). The monarch who inspired the most trust and extended the heartiest welcome to these artists was Castile's Alfonso VIII: eighteen troubadours sing his praises, and most of these enjoyed stays at his court.

The above-mentioned monarchs and troubadours, it may be said, flourished during the Golden Age of the troubadour tradition. It is for this same period that we would like more evidence of contact of the Galician-Portuguese poets with their Occitan counterparts in these courts. These invaluable meetings, when studied fully and assessed judiciously, will provide answers as to the specific impact—thematic and stylistic—on the principal lyric of the Peninsula's north-central regions. Compared with the Golden Age, fortunately, the thirteenth century has provided us with a greater abundance of texts, and we are thus better able to assess the relationships of these remarkable lyric styles. For the periods following the Albigensian Crusades, launched in 1209 and pursued for some two decades, many troubadours found it expedient to visit foreign lands. The Iberian courts, and Castile's in particular, were hospitable to a large number of troubadours, where the principal entertainment was provided by poets of Galician-

Portuguese. The favor found there earlier under Alfonso VIII had not waned, and the reigns of Fernando III, the Saint, and Alfonso X, the Learned (combined 1217–84), reflect a continuing respect for the skill and artistry of these professional singers.

Even though Fernando III devoted most of his energies to the Reconquest in the south of Spain, many troubadours were associated with his court, including Aimeric de Belenoi, Elias de Barjols, Sordel, Guillem Ademar, Ademar lo Negre, Uc de Saint Circ, Savaric de Mauleon, Peire Bremon Ricas Novas, and Arnaut Plagés (Alvar 1977, 165–79). One composition attributed to Fernando III, written in Galician-Portuguese, even has the hallmarks of troubadour art (nine-line stanza, rhyme-scheme, vocabulary). But whether or not it is in fact Fernando's, this poem certainly anticipates the troubadouresque *cantigas* of Alfonso X, Fernando's son. Alfonso speaks, in one of his secular poems, of the failure of a court poet to meet the high ideal of the Occitan poets. This admiration for the Occitan manner is borne out in the remainder of Alfonso's verse production. In fact, it may be thought that he pays the highest accolade to that art and style in his compilation of 420 songs to Mary, his *Cantigas de Santa Maria*, in which he introduces a second protagonist (probably himself) in the guise of a troubadour serving a Liege Lady (the Virgin) in hopes of winning the sought-after reward, Salvation. This embedded narrative (as well as many of the illustrations that illuminate one of the *Cantigas* manuscripts) not only adopts the external disguise of the troubadour figures with whom Alfonso must have associated as prince in his father's court, but also imitates—indeed, revitalizes—the forms and conceits of the then decadent poetic manner of the troubadours (Snow 1979, 1988).

The cast of troubadour characters would include most of those who frequented his father's court as well as some of the luminaries of this last great age of the practitioners of the Occitan style: Bonifaci Calvo, Guillem de Montanhagol, Cerverí de Girona, Folquet de Lunel, and Guiraut Riquier. Among others who *may* have visited (but certainly took an active part in recognizing Alfonso's generosity) are n'At de Mons, Bertolome Zorzi, Raimon de Tors, Bernart de Rovenac, and one who engages Alfonso in a *tenso*, Arnaut Catalan. There is, furthermore, one other interesting exchange that indicates the influence of Occitan art in Alfonso's court: it is the *supplicatio* directed to him by Guiraut Riquier in 1274, beseeching a clarification of the status of the various kinds of performers. Evidently there was a blurring of categories, and the genuine artists (like Guiraut Riquier?) were not credited with their full due. At any rate, Alfonso was willing to issue a clarification, sensitive as he was to the gradations of artists and their skills—both as patron and as composer of poems and music. He allowed Guiraut Riquier to promulgate (and author in Occitan) the royal decision of a year later (Bertolucci Pizzorusso).

If in Castile, in the wake of Alfonso, there is a sharp decrease in enthusiasm for and defense of the poetic manner of the troubadours of Occitania and their followers in Italy and Catalonia, it may be supposed that Alfonso was the last monarch with enough prestige as a poet to keep the dying flame alight. This seems to fit the facts, at least for Castile. But Alfonso's advocacy probably had other important consequences as well. It has been suggested that his well-ordered *Cantigas* were models of song cycles meant for preservation, and that Alfonso himself, an avid collector, may have personally assumed some oversight of the preservation of Galician-Portuguese poetic texts. In any case, the existing almost 1,600 texts (sadly, only 13 with their music) from Alfonso's century constitute the richest repository for future scholars tracing the path of the troubadours in the Peninsula. It is particularly rich in satiric and mocking verse genres, as well as in Galician-Portuguese *cantigas d'amor*, where the broad thematic variety of the Occitan models is sharply reduced to competing poetic portrayals of the effects of love's pain: Occitan *joi* is, seemingly, forgotten.

The second consequence of Alfonso's advocacy also concerns transmission: in this case, the advocacy was passed on to his grandson and the future king of Portugal, Diniz (1261–1325), who, like his talented grandfather, presided over a poetic court of some renown. It is not suspected that there was any direct contact between that king and late troubadours, but the models were in place from his early years, when he spent time at Alfonso's court, and in the poetry of the Galician-Portuguese troubadours still active in the four decades following Alfonso's death in 1284. Diniz likely oversaw the compilation of the *Cancioneiro da Ajuda*, a substantial collection of *cantigas d'amor*. Diniz's legacy was the propagation of the troubadour manner well into the Iberian fourteenth century (Snow 1984).

In the eastern sector of the Peninsula, where traditional ties to France had remained strong and the native poets adopted Occitan for lyric song (and this continued to hold true in the face of the generalized use of Catalan for prose works), the rich thematic array, including the crusading political spirit, was to remain intact. In the lands of the west, where the Galician-Portuguese lyric was cultivated and had a history of being "popular" (that is, it was enjoyed by the masses outside court circles as well as at court), the troubadours and their song had less of an impact. Owing to its nature as a personal art for a fairly small public, and in part to the "foreignness" of its extensive lexicon and its search for rhyming genius and strophic variety, Occitan song was appreciated most for its overlapping themes (especially the pain that love causes) and for the genres less courtly in overtone—the *alba*, the *pastorela*, the *estampie*, and particularly the satirical verse. Galician-Portuguese enjoyed, far more than did Occitan, a love affair with refrains (see Chapter 4 in this volume) and used them liberally. Where it did not was in the *cantigas d'amor*, the genre that more surely reflects the influence of the love *canso*. But even here, the established predilection for just a few themes (absence, hurt, sorrow) in the Galician-Portuguese songs limited the influence and reduced the potential impact of the variety attained by the Occitan singers. In such circumstances of languages in contact, one would expect the lexicon and the peculiar conceits of certain genres to have more of an impact on the analogous expression in the second language: the prestige and widespread renown of the art of the troubadours and its followers ensured that such influence flowed *toward* the Peninsula troubadours rather than *from* them. Still, even in these areas, there is much to be done to advance the state of our current knowledge: we think we know *what* was happening, but have not yet done enough close reading to understand better the *how*, or the *extent*, of it, although good models now exist (Ferrari).

The time is ripe. Over the past twenty-five years, many superb philologists—in the main from Italy—have set about editing individual *cancioneiros* of the Galician-Portuguese poets. Reliable editions of many of the Occitan troubadours with an interest in Spain are also available. The poetic strain we associate with the *fin'amor* of Occitania was very much present in twelfth- and thirteenth-century Iberia, and its shadow extended far into the fourteenth and fifteenth centuries in the lyric of Castilian, Catalan, and Portuguese poets, as much in love song as in satire. The foundation has been laid. New explorations will undoubtedly help us to gain an ever clearer understanding of the high esteem that was felt for the troubadour's art in the Spanish courts, as expressed in these two fragments:

> E car la manieyra es bela,
> En la valen cort de Castela
> Denan lo bon rey castelan
> C'a ferm pretz e fi e certan
> Sobre totz los autres que son
> En tot lo remanen del mon,
> Vuelh sia mos comtes retratz.
>
>   (Anonymous, Meyer 415)

And since the manner of it is good, I would like my story to be told in the rich court of Castile, before the good king of Castile, who has a solid reputation, a pure and certain one, greater than all others in all the rest of the world.

The second fragment is even more explicit:

> Si ia·m deu mos chans valer
> Ni far nulh be mos trobars
> Ni mos sabers pro tener,
> Er s'endressa mos afars,
> Qu'al paire d'entendemen
> E de saber e d'onor
> E de pretz e de lauzor,

On mos bos espers enten,
M'en vau, al bon rey n'Anfos.

(Guiraut Riquier 14:1–9)

If my song is ever to be appreciated, or my composing to do any good, or my knowledge stand me in good stead, now my affairs are looking up, for I am leaving to go to the father of understanding and knowledge and honor and fame and praise, to whom my best hope is directed, namely good king Alfonso.

WORKS CITED

Alfonso X. *Cantigas de Santa Maria.* Ed. Walter Mettman. 4 vols. Coimbra: University of Coimbra, 1959–72. Also 4 vols. in 2. Vigo: Ed. Xerais de Galícia, 1981.

Alvar, Carlos. *La poesía trovadoresca en España y Portugal.* Barcelona: Planeta, 1977.

———. *Textos trovadorescos sobre España y Portugal.* Barcelona: Planeta, 1978.

Anglés, Higini. *La música de las "Cantigas de Santa Maria" del rey Alfonso el Sabio.* Vol. 3. Barcelona: Diputación Provincial—Biblioteca Central, 1958.

Bertolucci Pizzorusso, Valeria. "La supplica de Guiraut Riquier e la risposta di Alfonso X di Castiglia." *Studi Mediolatini e Volgari* 14 (1966): 9–135.

Boase, Roger. *The Origin and Meaning of Courtly Love.* Manchester: Manchester University Press, 1977.

d'Heur, Jean-Marie. *Troubadours d'oc et troubadours galiciens-portugais.* Paris: Fundação Calouste Gulbenkian, 1973.

Ferrari, Anna. "Linguaggi lirici in contatto: trobadors e trobadores." *Boletim de filologia* 29 (1984): 35–58.

Menéndez Pidal, Ramón. *Poesía juglaresca y juglares.* Madrid, 1924. Reissued in an expanded version as *Poesía juglaresca y orígenes de las literaturas románicas.* Madrid: Inst. de Estudios Políticos, 1957.

Menocal, María Rosa de. *The Arabic Role in Medieval Literary History: A Forgotten Heritage.* Philadelphia: University of Pennsylvania Press, 1987.

Meyer, Paul. "Mélanges de littérature provençale." *Romania* 1 (1872): 401–19.

Michaelis de Vasconcellos, Carolina, ed. *Cancioneiro da Ajuda.* 2 vols. Halle: Niemeyer, 1904.

Milá y Fontanals, Manuel. *De los trovadores en España.* Barcelona, 1861; repr. Barcelona: CSIC, 1966.

Mölk, Ulrich, ed. *Guiraut Riquier: las cansos.* Studia Romanica 2. Heidelberg: Winter, 1962.

Nunes, J. J. *Cantigas d'amigo dos trovadores galego-portugueses.* 3 vols. Coimbra: University of Coimbra, 1928; repr. New York: Kraus, 1971.

———. *Cantigas d'amor dos trovadores galego-portugueses.* Coimbra: University of Coimbra, 1932; repr. New York: Kraus, 1971.

Nykl, Alardyce R. *Hispano-Arabic Poetry and Its Relations with the Provençal Troubadours.* Baltimore: Johns Hopkins University Press, [1946] 1970.

Riquer, Martín de. *Los trovadores: historia literaria y textos.* 3 vols. Barcelona: Planeta, 1975; 2d ed. Barcelona: Ariel—Colección Letras e Ideas, 1983.

Rodrigues Lapa, Manuel de. *Cantigas d'escarnho e de mal dizer.* Vigo: Galaxia,
   1970.
Snow, Joseph T. "The Central Rôle of the Troubadour Persona of Alfonso X in
   the *Cantigas de Santa Maria.*" *Bulletin of Hispanic Studies* 56 (1979): 305–16.
————. "Diniz, King of Portugal." In *Dictionary of the Middle Ages,* ed. Joseph R.
   Strayer, 4:148–91. New York: Scribner, 1984.
————. "Lo que nos dice la Cantiga 300 de Alfonso X." In *Studia Hispanica Medievalia,* ed. L. T. Valdivieso and J. H. Valdivieso, 99–110. Buenos Aires: Universidad Católica, 1988.

THIRTEEN

Italy

Ronald Martinez

THE SICILIAN SCHOOL

Despite important troubadours (including Peire Vidal, Raimbaut de Vaqueiras, Aimeric de Peguilhan, Gaucelm Faidit, and Uc de Saint-Circ) who
frequented the courts of northern Italy in the early years of the thirteenth
century,[1] troubadour imitation in Italian poetry begins with the formation
of a "Sicilian school" of poets, closely associated with the curia of Frederick II, between about 1230 and 1250.[2] High functionaries of Frederick,
like the imperial *podestà* of Treviso, Jacopo della Morra (a sponsor of Uc
Faidit's *Donatz proensals*, composed in Italy), were the probable midwives to
the birth of the Sicilian school.[3] By adopting wholesale the language and
situations of *fin'amor* (using figures like the *druz, lauzengier,* and *dompna;*
imitating the *canso* and its genres and adopting the *tenso;* and incorporating
into a new Italian poetic koiné nearly the full array of troubadour terminology),[4] this elite group established the mainstream of Italian lyric for
centuries to come.

1. For accounts of the troubadours at the Italian courts and their legacy, see Bertoni [1915]
1967; de Bartholomaeis 1930; Jeanroy 1934, 229–65; Viscardi [1948] 1971; and especially
Folena 1976 and Roncaglia 1981a.

2. For this school and Provençal influence on it, see Gaspary 1882, still useful, and Torraca
1902; a recent summary is Jensen 1986, xxxix–lii.

3. If not Frederick himself, to whom four extant lyrics are attributed (texts in Panvini 1972,
Jensen 1986). The best recent survey is Roncaglia 1981a.

4. There are analyses of this assimilation in Gaspary 1882, Torraca 1902, Bezzola 1924
(linguistic influence), and Jensen 1986, who lists troubadour terms and their Sicilian equivalents.

The Sicilians also imported from the troubadours similes and topics from natural science and from the bestiary tradition as well as a taste, conspicuous especially in Jacopo Mostacci, for elaborate stanzaic forms and verbal linkage (e.g., capcaudation and *replicatio*).[5] There are crucial differences, however: the *sirventes* is unknown, and the *senhal* and the separate *tornada* are unattested, no doubt reflecting the hermetic culture of Frederick's curia, which was dissociated from both political debate and social or erotic referentiality. The Sicilians, too, composed no melodies, and their poems were not sung, a fact that may have fostered a cult of stanzaic complexity.[6] The Sicilians evidently had before them the chansonniers compiled in northern Italy in the early thirteenth century.[7] In the most striking instance, Giacomo da Lentini's canzonetta "Madonna dir vi voglio," the Sicilian poet imitates two extant stanzas of Folquet de Marselh with flexible, mature mastery (Roncaglia 1975, 24–36).

GUITTONE D'AREZZO

Already by 1250 the Sicilian achievement had influenced Tuscan poets.[8] Guittone d'Arezzo, the most important Tuscan master of the midcentury, excelled in the political and moral canzone, a genre unknown to the *scuola siciliana*. Though derived from the *sirventes*, Guittone's achievement depends also on the prose treatise and the homily, and his language owes as much to Latin epistolography and Tuscan dialects as to Provençal models. Guittone's adherence to the *trobar clus*, for which he was celebrated, is most marked in his early love poetry. His sonnet "Tuttor ch'eo dirï gioi, gioiva cosa," which devotes thirty-three syllables to forms of *gioia*, represents *joi*

5. Natural scientific borrowings are conspicuous in Guido delle Colonnne; Rigaut de Barbezilh's animal similes in "Autressi com'l'olifanz" were especially influential. Contini 1960 and Panvini 1972 afford specimens of all these features; the English translations of Jensen 1986 are useful. E. H. Wilkins 1914–15 weighs the relative formal influences of troubadour, trouvère, and minnesinger poetry on the Sicilian school.

6. This thesis is in Roncaglia 1975, 34. Jensen 1986, lxii–lxviii, provides a useful survey of Sicilian poetics.

7. Roncaglia 1981a, 142–43, speculates that it was through the pro-imperial (after 1232) Ezzelino da Romano that a troubadour chansonnier made its way to Frederick's court. Italy was a center of study of the troubadours; in addition to Uc Faidit's *Donatz proensals* (see above) at least a substantial core of troubadour *vidas* was composed in Italy by Uc de Saint-Circ; Roncaglia 1981a, 122, also attributes to him the assembly of the oldest dated troubadour anthology, the Estense chansonnier (MS D, 1254). In a forthcoming study on the origins of humanism, Ronald Witt argues for the influence of troubadour lyricism on the classicizing Latin epistles of the Paduan prehumanist Lovati.

8. The imprisonment of Frederick's son Heinz (Re Enzo) in Bologna after 1249 is traditionally cited as the vehicle of transmission to the north; for the plausibility of this, see Contini 1960, 1:156.

through sheer excess.[9] The canzonetta "Tuttor s'eo veglio o dormo" contains an abundance of equivocal, rich, masculine, and broken rhymes, and concludes with a justification of the difficult style: "scuro saccio che par lo / mio detto . . . " (I know my poem seems obscure)—a "signature" that recalls those of Raimbaut d'Aurenga and Arnaut Daniel.[10]

GUINIZZELLI AND CAVALCANTI

While Chiaro Davanzati wrote in the *trobar leu* style, numerous Tuscan poets near the midcentury (Bondie Deitaiuti, Monte Andrea, Meo Abbracciavacca, Panuccio del Bagno) worked in the *trobar clus* style: Monte and Panuccio, for example, contain apparent imitations of Arnaut Daniel.[11] But the reaction to Guittone's labored and miscellaneous style is led by his own disciple Guido Guinizzelli of Bologna. Both Guinizzelli and the younger Guido Cavalcanti fully assimilated the poetic tradition derived from the troubadours through the Sicilians. The topoi of what was to become— thanks to Dante's invention of duecento literary history in the *Purgatorio*—a Guinizzelli-established *stil nuovo* have also been (if controversially) traced to troubadours like Guilhem de Montagnanol (de Lollis [1922] 1968, pro; Roncaglia 1967, contra). And Guinizzelli's precise and melodious use of the language of the schools, as in his epochal canzone "Al cor gentil rempaira sempre amore"—though spanking new and very much his own—marks the advent of a new kind of difficult poetry that joins up with the tradition of troubadour *conceptismo* going back to Raimbaut d'Aurenga and Marcabru.[12]

Much the same goes for the other forerunner of *stil nuovo* lyric, Guido Cavalcanti. Cavalcanti avoids the canzone (only two examples survive), choosing to ennoble lesser forms like the *ballata*, Provençal in origin but by then well established in Italy. Nevertheless, the Cavalcantian lyric persona, suffering from a relentless, destructive eros, is arguably the product of a self-consciously fashioned narrative *vida*—a project that may parallel or anticipate that of Dante's autobiographical *prosimetrum*, the *Vita nuova*. Cavalcanti's doctrinal canzone on the nature of love, "Donna mi prega" (Contini 1960, 2:522–29), with 54 of 154 syllables per stanza bound to the

---

9. Gaspary 1882, 135, quotes a Provençal example of *replicatio* on *gaug*.

10. For de Lollis ([1922] 1968, 13), Guittone's master in the obscure style was not Arnaut Daniel, but Peire Vidal. On Peire Vidal's influence in Italian poetry, see Paden 1976, 43.

11. On Monte Andrea, see Contini 1960, 1:447–48; for the *clus* tradition in Italy before Dante, see Toja 1976. Panuccio's phrase " . . . sembro lui *albore secco*" (de Lollis [1922] 1968, 13) may account for phrases in Guinizzelli like *secca la scoglia* (cf. Arnaut Daniel's *seca verga* and *l'escorz en la verga* in his sestina).

12. The tradition in Italy is summarized by Toja 1976.

frequent *rims tornatz* of its scheme (with much assonantal linking of rhymes between stanzas), is designed to outclass the *trobar clus* of Guittone. Cavalcanti's willfully obscure poem fairly claims a place in the hermetic tradition created by the troubadours.

DANTE

The *De vulgari eloquentia*

In his treatise *De vulgari eloquentia*, in addition to a discussion of Provençal as a literary language, Dante names eight troubadours: Peire d'Alvernha, Guiraut de Bornelh, Bertran de Born, Arnaut Daniel, Folquet de Marselh, Aimeric de Peguilhan, Aimeric de Belenoi, and Sordello. There is an example for each excepting Peire and Sordello; Guiraut and Arnaut rate four references apiece.[13] Bertran de Born, Guiraut de Bornelh, and Arnaut Daniel are chief among predecessors who treated the noblest subjects: arms, love, and rectitude; they are the troubadours who appear or find mention in the *Commedia*. Because Dante makes Guiraut de Bornelh the poet of rectitude, he ranks higher than Arnaut owing to the excellence of his subject matter; but Dante's reference to Arnaut in the *Commedia* as "miglior fabbro" has suggested to many that Dante's judgment in the treatise is merely categorical.[14] Special devotion to Arnaut Daniel as a master is suggested even in the treatise by the acknowledgment, unique for a troubadour, of him as a model ("eum secuti sumus").[15]

---

13. Mengaldo 1973 is a good summary of Dante's troubadour study; the notes to relevant passages of Mengaldo's edition (Dante Alighieri 1979) are indispensable. Santangelo's (1921) claim of Dante's scant early knowledge of the troubadours has been revised by Perugi 1978, 103–16, who builds on Contini's edition of the *Rime* ([1946] 1965). That Dante knew of Peire d'Alvernha except as a name (he was the first of the *maistres de trobar* and was typically listed first in early collections) is disputed, but the parallel between the first line of Dante's sestina ("Al poco giorno e al gran cerchio d'ombra") and that of Peire's "Dejosta'ls breus jorns e'ls loncs sers" is striking (the verse appears in the *vida*). Other verses of early troubadours often suggested as cited by Dante are Cadenet's "Qui non ereita lo sen e'l saber, / tenh que neys eretar degra l'aver" (see *Convivio* IV.xi.10); the incipit from Bernart de Ventadorn's "Can vei la lauzeta mover," possibly recalled in *Paradiso* XX.73–75 ("Quale allodetta si spazia . . . "); and vv. 17–18 of Guilhelm de Peitiu's "Ab la dolchor del temps novel," often quoted a propos of *Inferno* II.127–30. The fame of these latter two poems, however, suggests that Dante may have known excerpts or imitations, like Bondie Dietaiuti's imitation of Bernart de Ventadorn's famous incipit (Gaspary 1882, 47).

14. The implications of these several rankings have been studied recently by Barolini 1984, 85–123.

15. Toja 1976, 735–36, argues that for Dante the notion of *trobar clus* includes the *excelsa constructio* or syntactically complex and figurative style that is the explicit criterion of poetic excellence in the *De vulgari eloquentia*.

Early Lyrics and the *Vita nuova*

Like Guinizzelli, Dante inherited a poetic language already rich in the provençalisms and commonplaces of *fin'amor* and its poetic expression.[16] Dante's early exercises in *rimas caras* have led Perugi (1978, 69–74) to hypothesize that Dante knew Arnaut by the period of the *Vita nuova* (1294). An early moral canzone like "Poscia ch'amor," lamenting the decline of *leggiadria*, already reflects the manner of Guiraut de Bornelh, also called on in "Doglia mi reca."[17] At the other extreme, one of Dante's last canzoni, "Amor da che convien," which is related in theme to the *rime petrose*, was equipped by Dante himself with a *razo* in the form of an epistle.

Dante's first important consolidation of troubadour influence is the *Vita nuova*. Dante precedes his collection of lyrics with prose sections that are (as Rajna claimed) authentic *razos*. The work incorporates much of the apparatus of *fin'amor*. Love personified, screen ladies (drawn perhaps from the *vida* of Folquet de Marselh),[18] fear of the lady's *noia* (*enueg*), and need for consequent *escondig* and flight from the raillery (*gabbo*, Prov. *gap*) of other ladies.[19] Dante adopts the *senhal* in the naming of Beatrice, and adapts the *pastorela*, the *planh* ("Piangete, amanti . . . "), and the poem referred to in the text as a *sirventes*.[20] The poet as painter of and gazer at his lady's image, a topos widespread in Folquet and in the Sicilians, Dante turns into a narrative episode (chap. 33).[21] Use of the eaten heart motif early in the book stirs memories of the *vida* of Guilhem de Cabestanh. Even the book's quest for an adequate style to praise the lady, the *stile de la loda*, is a commonplace of troubadour verse (Jensen xlv).

The *Rime Petrose*

Dante's study and imitation, outside the *Commedia*, of Arnaut Daniel and the *trobar clus* culminates in the *rime petrose* (so called since the nineteenth

16. For Dante's early *plazer* "Guido i'vorrei," see Dante Alighieri [1946] 1965, 34 (Contini suggests Pistoleta's "Ar agues eu cen marcs" as a model). Thompson-Hill 1915, Paden 1976, and Suitner 1980 trace the history of the Italian versions of *plazer* and *enueg*.

17. See de Lollis [1901] 1971; Boyde 1971; and Barolini 1984, 108–10.

18. For the question of Folquet de Marselh's "screen ladies," which has provoked much debate, consult Zingarelli 1899, 45–46; and Suitner 1980, 162.

19. The *gap* tradition in the *Vita nuova* is studied by Picone 1979a, 99–128. The much-debated question of the *escondig* in relation to Bertran de Born is taken up again by Suitner 1980 (see below, note 29). Ferrers Howells [1921] 1968, 202, notes the use of the *enueg* and *escondig* in the *Vita nuova*.

20. Dante's lost poem listed Beatrice and other ladies, and might have been something like the *Carros* of Raimbaut de Vacqueyras, written at the court of Montferrat.

21. For this topic, see Zingarelli 1899, 24–25.

century), a series of four poems directed at a stony lady (*petra*) who frustrates the poet's desire. The sequence takes a commonplace of troubadour poetry—the attempt to persuade a recalcitrant, even hard-hearted *dompna*—and elaborates a poetics of microcosmic form that would decisively influence Dante's poetics in the *Commedia*.[22]

The parallel between the seasonal beginnings of Arnaut's "Can chai la fueilla" and Dante's "Io son venuto" (usually the first of the series) has often been recognized.[23] Although the sestina "Al poco giorno" echoes Arnaut's sestina "Lo ferm voler" in some respects, Dante's imitation is largely formal and conceptual.[24] "Amor tu vedi ben," Dante's "double" sestina, also echoes "Lo ferm voler," although the poem's complex form owes more, as Jeanroy (1913) observes, to the *canso redonda*.[25] The implicit self-definition of "Amor tu vedi ben" as a crystal fashioned by the poet's ardent desire (see vv. 64–66) draws on the troubadour conceit of crystalline ice as a lens: icy cold, but with the power to focus light and generate heat.[26] Central to the fourth of the *petrose*, "Così nel mio parlar voglio esser aspro," is the poet's role as craftsman, a role that Arnaut Daniel often takes in his *cansos* (see Perugi 1978, 77). Accordingly, of the *petrose*, "Così nel mio parlar" draws most extensively on Arnaut Daniel's mastery of *rimas caras*, of a difficult *ornatus*, in effect illustrating the link between Dante's theoretical discussion of rough or "shaggy" (*yrsuta*) and smooth or "combed" (*pexa*) words in the *De vulgari eloquentia* (II.vii) and Arnaut Daniel's shoptalk regarding his craft ("capuig e doli," X.2). The *petrose* confirm Dante's estimation of Arnaut Daniel as a master comparable in importance to Virgil.

The Troubadours of the *Commedia*

Over the last century, scholars have demonstrated to what extent Dante's presentation of four troubadours as characters in the *Commedia* entails reference to, indeed incorporation of, their texts. Still to emerge is the systematic nature of Dante's placement of troubadours in his poem.[27] The appearance of Sordello, scourge of princes, in the *Purgatorio*, follows on that

22. For parallels between Arnaut and the *petrose*, see Perugi 1978, 74–84; and König 1983, 247–50. A recent full study of the group is Durling and Martinez 1990, with bibliography.

23. See, inter alia, Renucci 1958, 67–70; and Goldin 1973, 345–51.

24. For some implications of sestina form, see Dragonetti 1982, 231–33; and Kropfinger 1988, 163–68.

25. For description of the form of "Amor tu vedi ben" and its meaning, see Durling and Martinez 1990, 138–64.

26. As in Peire Vidal XIII.25 and XXXV.21: " . . . car de la freida neu / Nais lo cristals, don hom trai foc arden: / E per esfortz venson li ben sufren." The topic and its use by the Sicilians is noted in Gaspary 1882, 97–98.

27. Dante's distribution of troubadours in the three realms of the *Commedia*, remarked by Hoepffner 1922, 196–97, has been recently discussed by Bergin 1965, 40; and Barolini 1984, 156–57.

of the "political" Bertran de Born, deep in hell (Barolini 153–73), while Sordello's *vida*, rich in erotic incident, commends him as a transition first to Arnaut Daniel, purged with the lustful in the fire, and finally to the once-ardent Folquet de Marselh, who companions, in Dante's heaven of Venus, a woman once Sordello's mistress, Cunizza da Romano. Dante thus appears to restate the paradigm of subject matter of the *De vulgari eloquentia*, passing from the militarism of Bertran de Born to the ardor of Arnaut Daniel and Folquet of Marselh, who, by virtue of his crusading episcopacy and his attack on the decretalists, can stand for *probitas armorum* and *directio voluntatis* as well.[28]

Dante's condemnation of Bertran de Born to the pit of the sowers of discord (*Inferno* XXVIII) derives from the text of the *vida* that records Bertran de Born's persistence in dividing Henry from the *jove rei engles*.[29] Dante's selections from Bertran de Born's poems reflect an estimation of Bertran de Born as a proponent of dispersion and schism, and provide the basis for a meditation, in the early cantos of the *Purgatorio*, on the stake of poets and poetry in the quest for civic peace and personal regeneration.[30] The common theme of poetry as an agent for, and reflection of, integration links Bertran de Born, albeit negatively, to Sordello in the *Purgatorio* (Barolini 168–72).

Scholars agree that Dante knew Sordello's *planh* for Blacatz and echoed it in the text of the *Purgatorio* where the troubadour is present (VI–VIII). Each poet discusses eight rulers, although the ranks are distributed differently. One ruler is shared: Henry III of England, newly ascended to the throne of his father, John Lackland, in 1236, and dead in Purgatory in 1300 (the fictional date of Dante's journey).[31] Dante draws on the *planh* for notions of negligent kingship (*nualhos, nescies* become Dante's *neghittosi*)

28. Zingarelli 1899, 55–62, showed that the reference to Joshua's victory at Jericho reflects Dante's knowledge of documents describing Folquet's role in the Albigensian Crusade (achieved, like Joshua's victory in Exodus 17:10–13, by lifting the arms, by prayer—the act of a bishop). For new documentation on Folquet de Marselh as bishop and his role in *Paradiso* IX, see Picone 1981.

29. Santangelo's insistence that Dante did not know the *vidas* of Bertran de Born has not convinced many scholars; for the majority view, see Scherillo 1897b, 90; and Barolini 1984, 165–69. For a recent assessment of the textual problems, see Suitner 1980, 598–604. Bertran de Born was well known in Italy and his poems influential; see Paden 1976; and Suitner 1980, 581–93.

30. The parallels between *Inferno* XXVIII and Bertran de Born's poems have been often tabulated and discussed: see Rua 1888; Boyers 1926; Bergin 1965, 15–17; Picone 1979b; Suitner 1980, 594–98; and Barolini 1984, 167. W. D. Paden, Bertran de Born's most recent editor, denies him the authorship of "Si tuit li dol . . . ," but that Dante thought it a composition of Bertran de Born seems well established.

31. Important readings of Dante's use of Sordello are in d'Ancona 1962; de Lollis 1896, 90–116; d'Ovidio 1901; Roncaglia 1956; Bergin 1965; Perugi 1983; and Barolini 1984, 153–56.

and for the spectacle of failed noble houses (echoing Sordello's reproach to the *deseretaz*). The centerpiece of Dante's passage is the sight of Charles of Anjou singing the *Salve regina* with his old rival, Peter of Aragon. This musical and spiritual *acort* ("cantano d'accordo"), itself embodied in complex but ordered verse, contrasts with the pursuit of discord Dante attributed to Bertran de Born.[32]

Arnaut Daniel's eight lines of Provençal (*Purgatorio* XXVI.140–47) come in a canto of poets (Arnaut is introduced by Guinizzelli) and establish his centrality in the sequence of troubadours.[33] The lines include allusion to the 'signature' of X.42 ("Ieu sui Arnaut . . . "). That Dante's incipit for Arnaut Daniel, *Tan m'abellis . . .* , is one of Folquet de Marselh's ("Tant m'abelhis l'amoros pessamens," a poem Dante cites in the *De vulgari eloquentia*) but also one of Sordello's, points to the key placement of Arnaut Daniel in Dante's overall scheme for his troubadours. Scholars like Sapegno and Bergin have seen Arnaut Daniel's lines of *trobar leu* in the *Purgatorio* as an imposed palinode of the poet's difficult style, but this does not prevent Dante from recuperating Arnaut Daniel's characteristic *trobar clus* in the language of canto XXVI itself (Martinez 1991).

With Folquet de Marselh's self-comparison to Dido in the *Paradiso* (IX.97) Dante consummates the series of links drawn between two schools of poetry, Latin and Provençal.[34] Looking back from Folquet de Marselh's perch in the heaven of Venus, we note that the exordium to *Inferno* XXVIII, imitating Bertran de Born, also draws on the *Aeneid* (VI.625–27) and that Sordello assumes the role taken by Anchises, Aeneas's father, in Virgil's underworld (Boni 1976, 332). Indeed, the embrace of Virgil and Sordello in the *Purgatorio*—the only successfully completed embrace between two poets in the whole *Commedia*—might be thought an emblem of the union of the two traditions, Latin and Provençal, which Dante held both alike in dignity.[35]

PETRARCH AND THE *RERUM VULGARIUM FRAGMENTA*

The only explicit indication of Petrarch's critical response to the troubadours is found in the *Triumphus cupidinis* IV.40–57, where Petrarch lists

32. For the relation of Sordello's poetry to Dante's invective against Florence in *Purgatorio* VI, see Perugi 1983.

33. On Arnaut Daniel, Contini 1970c and Perugi 1978, 116–44, are fundamental. See also Simonelli 1973; Folena 1977, 501–8; and Gruber 1983. Perugi and Folena include reconstructed *Urtexten* of the eight lines of Provençal that Dante gives his Arnaut.

34. For Folquet de Marselh's use of Latin poets, see Zingarelli 1899, 36–40; Stroński 1910, 78–81; Viscardi 1970; and for Folquet de Marselh's use of Ovid, Rossi 1989. For the interplay of Latin and vernacular canons, see Martinez 1995.

35. In Zingarelli's wake, Toja 1966; Suitner 1980, 619–43; Barolini 1984, 114–23, 184–87; Picone 1981; and Rossi 1989 provide good recent discussions of Folquet de Marselh in the *Commedia*. Space limitations prevent discussion here of the important Provençal culture of the Florentine Francesco da Barberino (1264–1348); see Thomas 1883.

fifteen troubadours in Love's train, with Arnaut in first place.[36] The list testifies to a wide knowledge of troubadour poetry and its reception in Italy.[37] Nicola Scarano long ago demonstrated, in exhaustive detail, Petrarch's integration of the poetic apparatus of the troubadours into the *Rerum vulgarium fragmenta* (or *Canzoniere*). Along with the forms of the canzone, the *ballata*, and the sestina, Petrarch rendered the psychology and language of *fin'amor* obligatory for Italian lyric poets of love until the present century.

Like the Sicilian poets, Petrarch drew on troubadours (Peire Vidal, Rigaut de Barbezilh, Aimeric de Peguilhan) for images and topoi derived from natural science, while Petrarch's preference for antithesis and paradox (e.g., poem 134) has often reminded readers of the riddle, or *devinalh* (like Guiraut de Bornelh's "Un sonet fatz malvatz e bo"). But prejudice about Petrarch's "originality" long impeded accurate study of Petrarch's exact debts to the troubadours.[38] Though Zingarelli (1930) was bound to acknowledge the copy of a scrap of paper on which Petrarch recorded that his composition of "Aspro core" (poem 265) was inspired by a verse of Arnaut Daniel (XIV.8: "car amans preians s'affranca cor uffecs"), the critic's allegorizing reading of the sonnet downgrades the import of Arnaut Daniel's text. Recently, however, Perugi (1985, 292–320) has shown that Arnaut's verses directly generate much of poem 265. Perugi goes on to suggest that Petrarch's study of Arnaut matched Dante's both in intensity and in fruitfulness.[39]

Of the troubadours, Arnaut is overwhelmingly the most important textual presence in Petrarch's collection, represented by the incorporation of Arnaut Daniel's famous signature ("Ieu sui Arnaut / qu'amas l'aura / que chatz la lebre ab lo bou / e nadi contra suberna") into several poems.[40] Of course, Petrarch's principal technical imitation of Arnaut consists of his nine sestinas, distributed through the whole *Canzoniere*. Much of what constitutes Arnaut Daniel's poetics for the Italian tradition is found in these sestinas: poems 30 and 66 are elaborations of the winter scenery dear to Arnaut Daniel and Raimbaut d'Aurenga; Arnaut Daniel's incipit *l'aur amara*

36. A useful recent edition and commentary can be found in Petrarca 1988, 176–79.

37. For example, Petrarch's list concludes with Uc de Saint-Circ and Gaucelm Faidit, whose editorial and biographical activity, conducted in Italy, largely determined the corpus as Petrarch might have known it.

38. Numerous parallels, rejected or downplayed by Zingarelli 1930, have been noted between passages in Petrarch and Aimeric de Belenoi, Peirol, Guilhelm Figueira, Peire Cardenal, and others.

39. Earlier studies of Arnaut's influence on Petrarch are included in the editions of Canello and Lavaud.

40. Noted by Diez 1829, 348; and before that by Tassoni in 1609 (Perugi 1985, 292; see also Perugi's lengthy note, 311). Petrarch's allusions to Arnaut Daniel's signature are densest in poems 212 and 239 (a sestina), and form the centerpiece of sonnet 212, "Beato in sogno."

and the *aura* of his signature also recur—as *L'auro* (gold) in 30, as *l'aura soave* in 80, and in the *aura amorosa* of 142 and the *dolce l'aura* of 239. These latter reflect the systematic development of Petrarch's *laura/ lauro* pun from Provençal models, a history traced by Gianfranco Contini (1970a).[41] Petrarch's favorites among Arnaut Daniel's incipits, XIII.1 ("Er vei vermeills, vertz, blaus, blancs, gruocs") and XIV.1 ("Amors e jois e liocs e temps"), appear together in sestina 142 (Perugi 1985, 308–9), while the incipit of Arnaut Daniel's sestina "Lo ferm voler" is quoted both in 22 and in 80. Indeed, all of Petrarch's sestinas, with the exception of the last (poem 332), are demonstrably influenced by the language of "Lo ferm voler."

With Petrarch's death (1374) close study of the troubadours largely ceased in Italy until Provençal studies, spurred by il Chariteo, Pietro Bembo, and Castelvetro, resumed in the cinquecento.[42] But by then the troubadours had lost to the Latin classics their primacy as models of the lyric. The rest is but Romance philology.

WORKS CITED

Abrams, Richard. "Illicit Pleasures: Dante Among the Sensualists (*Purgatorio* XXVI)." *MLN* 100 (1985): 1–41.

Asor Rosa, Alberto et al., eds. *Letteratura italiana: storia e critica.* Vol. 1: *Il letterato e le istituzioni.* Turin: Einaudi, 1981.

———. *Letteratura italiana: storia e geografia.* Vol. 1: *L'età medievale.* Turin: Einaudi, 1987.

Avalle, D'Arco Silvio. *La letteratura medievale in lingua d'oc nella sua tradizione manoscritta.* Turin: Einaudi, 1961.

Barolini, Teodolinda. *Dante's Poets: Textuality and Truth in the "Comedy."* Princeton: Princeton University Press, 1984.

Bergin, Thomas G. "Dante's Provençal Gallery." *Speculum* 40 (1965): 15–30.

Bertacchi, Giovanni. *Le rime di Dante da Maiano.* Bergamo: Istituto Italiano d'Arti Grafiche, 1896.

Bertoni, Giulio. *I trovatori d'Italia.* Rome: Società Multigrafica Editrice SOMU, [1915] 1967.

Bezzola, Reto R. *Abbozzo di una storia de gallicismi italiani nei primi secoli (750– 1300): saggio storico-linguistico.* Zurich: Seldwyla, 1924.

Blomme, Raoul. "Les Troubadours dans la Divine comédie: un problème d'onomastique poétique." In *Studia Occitanica: In Memoriam Paul Remy,* ed. Hans-Erich Keller, Jean-Marie d'Heur, Guy Mermier, and Marc Vuijlsteke, 1:21–30. Kalamazoo: Western Michigan University, Medieval Institute Publications, 1986.

---

41. Perugi 1978, 91–95, supplements Contini's study by tracing the history of Arnaut's *l'aura* in the text of Dante.

42. Described by Debenedetti 1911 and 1930.

Bologna, Corrado. "L'importazione della poesia occitanica in Italia: Il Nord-Ovest" and "La cultura occitanica in Lombardia e nel Veneto." Secs. 6 and 8 of "La letteratura dell'Italia settentrionale nel Duecento." In *Letteratura italiana: storia e geografia*, vol. 1: *L'età medievale*, ed. Alberto Asor Rosa et al., 123–29, 135–41. Turin: Einaudi, 1987.

Boni, Marco. "Sordello." *Enciclopedia dantesca* 5 (1976): 328–33.

Bowra, Sir Maurice A. "Dante and Arnaut Daniel." *Speculum* 27 (1952): 439–74.

Boyde, Patrick. "Style and Structure in 'Doglia mi reca.'" In *Dante's Style in His Lyric Poetry*, 317–31. Cambridge: Cambridge University Press, 1971.

Boyers, Hayden. "Cleavage in Bertran de Born and Dante." *Modern Philology* 24 (1926): 1–3.

Braccini, Mauro. "Paralipomeni al 'Personaggio-poeta' (*Purgatorio* XXVI.140–47)." In *Testi e interpretazioni: studi del Seminario di filologia romanza dell'Università di Firenze*, 169–256. Milan-Naples: Ricciardi, 1978.

Chambers, Frank M. "Imitation of Form in the Old Provençal Lyric." *Romance Philology* 6 (1952–53): 104–20.

Chaytor, Henry J. *The Troubadours of Dante*. Oxford: Clarendon Press, 1902.

Clausen, Anna Maria. *Le origini della poesia lirica in Provenza e in Italia*. Etudes Romanes de l'Université de Copenhague, Revue Romane numéro spécial 7. Copenhagen: Akademisk Forlag, 1976.

Contini, Gianfranco. "Préhistoire de l'aura de Pétrarque" (1957). In *Varianti e altra linguistica*, 193–99. Turin: Einaudi, 1970a.

———. "Alcuni appunti su *Purgatorio* XXVII" (1959). In *Varianti e altra linguistica*, 459–76. Turin: Einaudi, 1970b.

———. "Premessa a un'edizione di Arnaut Daniel" (1960). In *Varianti e altra linguistica*, 311–17. Turin: Einaudi, 1970c.

———, ed. *Poeti del duecento*. 2 vols. Milan-Naples: Ricciardi, 1960.

Crescini, Vincenzo. "Le razos provenzali e le prose della 'Vita nuova.' *Giornale storico della letteratura italiana* 32 (1898).

———. "Il canto XXVIII dell'*Inferno*." In *Letture scelte sulla "Divina Commedia,"* ed. G. Getto, 383–98. Florence: Sansoni, 1970.

———, ed. *Provenza e Italia*. Florence: Bemporad, 1930.

d'Ancona, Alessandro. "Il canto VII del *Purgatorio*." In *Letture dantesche*. Florence: Le Monnier, 1962.

Dante Alighieri. *Le rime*. Ed. Gianfranco Contini. 2d ed. Turin: Einaudi, [1946] 1965.

———. *De vulgari eloquentia*. Ed. Pier Vincenzo Mengaldo. In *Opere minori*, 2:3–237. Milan: Ricciardi, 1979.

de Bartholomaeis, Vincenzo. "La poesia trovadorica in Italia." In *Provenza e Italia*, ed. Vincenzo Crescini, 3–77. Florence: Bemporad, 1930.

———. *Poesie provenzali storiche relative all'Italia*. 2 vols. Rome: Tipografia del Senato, 1931.

Debenedetti, Santorre. *Gli studi provenzali in Italia nel Cinquecento*. Turin: Loescher, 1911.

———. "Tre secoli di studi provenzali in Italia (XVI–XVIII)." In *Provenza e Italia*, ed. Vincenzo Crescini, 145–81. Florence: Bemporad, 1930.

de Lollis, Cesare. *Vita e poesie di Sordello di Goito.* Halle: Max Niemeyer, 1896.
———. "Sul canzoniere de Chiaro Davanzati." *Giornale storico de letteratura italiana.* Suppl. 1 (1898): 82–1177.
———. "Arnaldo e Guittone" (1922). In Scrittori d'Italia, ed. G. Contini and C. Santoli, 3–20. Milan-Naples: Ricciardi, 1968.
———. "Quel de Lemosì" (1901). In *Scrittori de Francia,* ed. G. Contini and C. Santoli, 29–56. Milan-Naples: Ricciardi, 1971.
Diez, Friedrich Christian. *Lebens und Werke der Troubadours. Ein Beitrag zur nähern Kenntniss des Mittelalters.* Zwikkau: Gebrüder Schumann, 1829.
di Pino, G. *Il canto IX del Paradiso.* Lectura Dantis Romana. Turin: Società Editrice Internazionale, 1964.
d'Ovidio, Francesco. "Sordello." In *Studij sulla Divina Commedia,* 1–13. Milan-Palermo: Sandron, 1901.
Dragonetti, Roger. "The Double Play of Arnaut Daniel's Sestina and Dante's Divina Commedia." In *Literature and Psychoanalysis,* ed. Soshana Felman, 227–52. Baltimore: Johns Hopkins University Press, 1982.
Durling, Robert M., and Ronald L. Martinez. *Time and the Crystal: Studies in Dante's "Rime Petrose."* Berkeley and Los Angeles: University of California Press, 1990.
Edwards, Robert, ed. and trans. *The Poetry of Guido Guinizelli.* New York: Garland, 1987.
Egidi, Francesco. *Le rime di Guittone d'Arezzo.* Bari: Laterza, 1940.
Enciclopedia dantesca. 6 vols. Ed. Umberto Bosco et al. Rome: Istituto della Enciclopedia Italiana, 1970–78.
Ferrers Howells, E. "Dante and the Troubadours." In *Dante: Essays in Commemoration, 1321–1921.* Freeport, N.Y.: Books for Libraries Press, [1921] 1968.
Folena, Gianfranco. *Vulgares eloquentes: vite e poesie dei trovatori di Dante.* Padua: Liviana, 1961.
———. "Dante et les troubadours." In *Revue de langue et littérature d'oc* 12–13 (1962–63): 21–34.
———. "Tradizione e cultura trobadorica nelle corti e nelle città venete." In *AA.VV.: storia della cultura veneta,* vol. 1: *Dalle origini al trecento,* 453–562. Vicenza: Neri Pozza, 1976.
———. "Il canto XXVI del *Purgatorio.*" *Giornale storico della letteratura italiana* 154 (1977): 481–508.
Gaspary, Adolfo. *La scuola poetica siciliana del secolo XIII.* Trans. S. Friedmann. Leghorn: Vigo, 1882.
Goldin, Frederick. *German and Italian Lyrics of the Middle Ages.* Garden City, N.Y.: Anchor Books, 1973.
Gruber, Jörn. *Die Dialektik des Trobar. Untersuchungen zur Struktur und Entwicklung des occitanischen und französischen Minnesangs des 12. Jahrhunderts.* Beihefte zur Zeitschrift für romanische Philologie, 194. Tübingen: Niemeyer, 1983.
Hauvette, Henri. *La France et la Provence dans l'oeuvre de Dante.* Paris: Boivin, 1929.

Hoepffner, Ernest. "Dante et les troubadours." *Etudes italiennes* 4 (1922): 193–210.

Jeanroy, Alfred. "La 'Sestina doppia' de Dante et les origines de la sextine." *Romania* 42 (1913): 481–89.

———. *La Poésie lyrique des troubadours.* Vol. 1. Toulouse: Privat, 1934.

Jensen, Frede, ed. and trans. *The Poetry of the Sicilian School.* New York: Garland, 1986.

Ker, Walter P. "Dante, Guido Guinicelli, and Arnaut Daniel." *Modern Language Review* 4 (1909): 145–52.

Kolsen, Adolf. "Dante und der Trobador Arnaut Daniel." *Deutsches Dante-Jahrbuch* 8 (1924): 47–59.

König, Bernhard. "'La novità che per tua forma luce': Formville und Formkunst in Dantes Kanzonendichtung." In *Italia Mia: Studien zur Sprache und Literatur Italiens. Festschrift für Hans Ludwig Scheel,* ed. W. Hirdt and R. Klesczewski. Tübingen, 1983.

Kropfinger, Klaus. "Dante e l'arte dei trovatori." In *La musica nel tempo di Dante,* ed. Luigi Pestalozza, 130–74. Milan: Unicopoli, 1988.

Martinez, Ronald L. "Dante Embarks Arnaut." *NEMLA Italian Studies* 15 (1991): 5–28.

———. "Dante and the Two Canons." Forthcoming in *Comparative Literature Studies* (special issue) 32 (1995).

Mazzoni, G. "L'escondig del Petrarca." In *Convegno petrarchesco, tenuto in Arezzo il 25 e 26 novembre 1928,* 53–59. Arezzo: Presso la R. Accademia Petrarca, 1930.

Melli, Elio. "Dante e Arnaut Daniel." *Filologia romanza* 6 (1959): 423–48.

Meneghelli, Maria Luisa. *Il pubblico dei trovatori: ricezione e riuso dei testi lirici cortesi fino al XIVo secolo.* Modena: Panini, 1984.

Mengaldo, Pier Vincenzo. "Oc (oco)." *Enciclopedia dantesca* 4 (1973): 111–17.

Paden, William D. "Bertran de Born in Italy." In *Italian Literature, Roots and Branches: Essays in Honor of T. G. Bergin,* ed. Giosuè Rimanelli and Kenneth J. Atchity, 39–66. New Haven: Yale University Press, 1976.

Panvini, Bruno. *Le rime della scuola siciliana.* 2 vols. Florence: Leo S. Olschki, 1972.

Parducci, Amos. "Dante e i trovatori." In *Provenza e Italia,* ed. Vincenzo Crescini, 79–95. Florence: Bemporad, 1930.

Pasquazi, Silvio. "Il canto IX del *Paradiso* (Dall'amore passionale all'amore-milizia)." In *D'Egitto in Ierusalemme: studi danteschi,* 157–80. Biblioteca di Cultura, 311. Rome: Bulzoni, 1985.

Pastine, Luigi. "Dante e i trovatori." *Giornale dantesco* 26 (1923): 15–26, 128–41.

Pellizzari, Antonio. *La vita e le opere di Guittone d'Arezzo.* Pisa: Nistri, 1906.

Perugi, Maurizio. "Dante e Arnaut Daniel." *Studi danteschi* 51 (1978): 59–152.

———. "Il Sordello di Dante e la tradizione mediolatina dell'invettiva." *Studi danteschi* 55 (1983): 23–155.

———. *Trovatori a Valchiusa: un frammento della cultura provenzale del Petrarca.* Studi sul Petrarca, 18. Padua: Antenore, 1985.

Petrarca, Francesco. *Triumphi*. Ed. Marco Ariani and Roberto Fedi. Milan: Mursia, 1988.

Picone, Michelangelo. *"Vita nuova" e tradizione romanza*. Padua: Liviana Editrice, 1979a.

———. "I trovatori di Dante: Bertran de Born." *Studi e problemi di critica testuale* 19 (1979b): 71–94.

———. "Giraut de Bornelh nella prospettiva di Dante." *Vox Romanica* 39 (1980): 22–43.

———. "*Paradiso* IX: Dante, Folchetto e la diaspora trobadorica." *Medioevo Romanzo* 8 (1981): 47–89.

Pirot, F. "Dante et les troubadours." *Marche romane* 15 (1965): 213–19.

Rajna, Pio. *Lo schema della "Vita nuova."* Verona: Donato Tedeschi e Figlio, 1890.

———. "Per le 'divisioni' della 'Vita nuova.'" *Strenna dantesca* 1 (1902).

Renucci, Paul. *Dante*. Paris: Les Belles Lettres, 1958.

Rimanelli, Giosuè, and Kenneth J. Atchity, eds. *Italian Literature, Roots and Branches: Essays in Honor of T. G. Bergin*. New Haven: Yale University Press, 1976.

Roncaglia, Aurelio. *Il canto XXVI del Purgatorio*. Nuova Lectura Dantis. Rome: Signorelli, 1951.

———. "Il canto VI del *Purgatorio*". *Rassegna della letteratura italiana* 60 (1956): 409–26.

———. "Precedenti e significato dello 'stil novo' dantesco." In *Dante e Bologna nei tempi di Dante*. Bologna: Commissione per i Testi di Lingua, 1967.

———. "De quibusdam provincialibus translatis in lingua nostra." In *Letteratura e critica: studi in onore di Natalino Sapegno*, ed. Walter Binni et al., 2:1–36. Rome: Bulzoni, 1975.

———. "L'ingentilimento cortese" and "Federico II." Secs. 7 and 8 of "Le corti medievali." In *Letteratura italiana: storia e critica*, vol. 1: *Il letterato e le istituzioni*, ed. Alberto Asor Rosa et al., 105–47. Turin: Einaudi, 1981a.

———. "L'invenzione della sestina." *Metrica* 2 (1981b): 1–41.

———. "Per il 750° anniversario della scuola poetica Siciliana (1983)." *Atti dell' Accademia Nazionale dei Lincei: rendiconti della Classe di Scienze morali, storiche e filologiche* 28 (1984): 7–12, 331–39.

Rossi, Albert L. "E pos d'amor plus no·m cal: Ovidian Exemplarity and Folco's Rhetoric of Love in *Paradiso* IX." *Tenso* 5 (1989): 49–102.

Rua, G. "Gli accenni danteschi a Bertran de Born." *Giornale storico della letteratura italiana* 11 (1888): 376–77.

Santangelo, Salvatore. *Dante e i trovatori provenzali*. Catania: Giannotta, 1921.

Scarano, Nicola. "Fonti provenzali e romanze della lirica petrarchesca." *Studj di filologia romanza* 8 (1900): 250–360.

Scherillo, Michele. "Bertram dal Bornio e il re Giovane." *Nuova antologia* 154 (1897a): 452–78.

———. "Dante e Bertram dal Bornio." *Nuova antologia* 155 (1897b): 82–97.

———. "Dante et Folquet de Marseille." *Nouvelle Revue d'Italie* 18 (1921): 59–75.

Shapiro, Marianne. "The Fictionalization of Bertran de Born." *Dante Studies* 92 (1974): 107–16.

———. *Hieroglyph of Time: The Petrarchan Sestina.* Minneapolis: University of Minnesota Press, 1980.

Simonelli, Maria Picchio. "La sestina dantesca fra Arnaut Daniel e il Petrarca." *Dante Studies* 91 (1973): 131–44.

Smith, Nathaniel B. "Arnaut Daniel in the *Purgatorio*: Dante's Ambivalence Toward Provençal." *Dante Studies* 98 (1980): 99–109.

Spitzer, Leo. "Bemerkungen zu Dantes *Vita Nuova.*" *Publications de la Faculté des Lettres de l'Université d'Istanbul* 2, no. 1 (1937): 162–208.

Staüble, Antonio. "Le rime della 'rettitudine' nella coscienza poetica di Dante." *Studi e problemi di critica testuale* 8 (1974): 82–97.

Stroński, Stanisław. *Le Troubadour Folquet de Marseille.* Edition critique. Cracow, 1910; repr. Geneva: Slatkine, 1968.

Suitner, Franco. "Due trovatori nella Commedia (Bertran de Born e Folchetto di Marsiglia)." In *Atti della Accademia Nazionale dei Lincei: memorie, Classe di Scienze morali, storiche, e filologiche,* ser. 8, 24, no. 5 (1980): 579–643.

Thomas, Antoine. *Francesco da Barberino et la littérature provençale en Italie au moyen âge.* Paris: Thorin, 1883.

Thompson-Hill, R. "The *Enueg* and *Plazer* in Mediaeval French and Italian." *PMLA* 30 (1915): 42–63.

Toja, G. *Arnaut Daniel: canzoni.* Florence: Sansoni, 1960.

———. "Il canto di Folchetto di Marsiglia." *Convivium* 34 (1966): 234–56.

———. "Il canto XXVI del *Purgatorio.*" *Nuove letture dantesche* 5 (1972): 69–102.

———. "Trobar clus." *Enciclopedia dantesca* 5 (1976): 732–36.

Torraca, Francesco. *Studi su la lirica italiana del duecento.* Bologna: Zanichelli, 1902.

———. *Studi di storia letteraria.* Florence, 1923.

———. *Il canto XXVI del Purgatorio.* Florence: Sansoni, n.d. [1900?].

Ugolini, Francesco Alessandro. *La poesia provenzale e l'Italia.* Modena Società Tipografica Modenese, 1939.

Vallone, Aldo. *Studi sulla "Divina Commedia."* Biblioteca dell'*Archivum Romanicum,* ser. 1: Storia letteratura paleografia, 42. Florence: Leo S. Olschki, 1955.

———. "Il canto IX [*Paradiso*]." In *Nuove letture dantesche* 6. Florence: Le Monnier, 1973.

Varvaro, Alberto. "Un progetto innovatore: la lirica in volgare." Sec. 3.3 of "Il regno normanno-svevo." In *Letteratura italiana: storia e geografia,* vol. 1: *L'età medievale,* ed. Alberto Asor Rosa et al., 90–96. Turin: Einaudi, 1987.

Viscardi, Antonio. "Folchetto (Folco) di Marsiglia." In *Enciclopedia dantesca* 2 (1970): 954–56.

———. "La poesia trobadorica e l'Italia" (1948). In *Ricerche e interpretazioni mediolatine e romanze,* 345–81. Milan-Varese: Istituto Editoriale Cisalpino, 1971.

Vossler, Karl. *Medieval Culture,* 2:33–67. Trans. W. C. Lawton. New York: Harcourt Brace, 1929.

Wilhelm, James J. "Arnaut Daniel's Legacy to Dante and to Pound." In *Italian Literature, Roots and Branches: Essays in Honor of T. G. Bergin,* ed. Giosuè

Rimanelli and Kenneth J. Atchity, 67–84. New Haven: Yale University Press, 1976.

———, ed. and trans. *The Poetry of Arnaut Daniel.* New York: Garland, 1981.

———, ed. and trans. *The Poetry of Sordello.* New York: Garland, 1987.

Wilkins, Ernest H. "The Derivation of the Canzone." *Modern Philology* 12 (1914–15): 526–58.

Zingarelli, Nicola. *La personalità storica di Folchetto di Marsiglia nella "Commedia" di Dante.* Bologna: Zanichelli, 1899.

———. "Petrarca e i trovatori." In *Provenza e Italia,* ed. Vincenzo Crescini, 97–139. Florence: Bemporad, 1930.

FOURTEEN

Italian Troubadours

Hans-Erich Keller

Literary relations between Occitania and Italy were so close during the Middle Ages that, when scholarly research is able to observe them, they appear well established. In the second half of the twelfth century in Italy, only troubadour poetry was considered learned—and therefore respected—in its genre, giving rise to an indigenous courtly poetry with the concepts, motives, and formulas of the Occitan style, including the cult of form. That Occitan poetry should flourish, for instance, in the important university center of Bologna, where a great number of Occitans studied, is not surprising. The jurist Rambertino Buvalelli, writing between 1201 and 1221, is an excellent testimonial to this trend: ten of his poems, written in the purest Occitan, are preserved (Bertoni 1908).

Yet it was not at the universities that troubadour poetry could really flourish, since *studentes mali pagatores*. Whereas west of the Var River troubadours could be found in all social ranks, those who crossed the river or the Tenda Pass into Italy were mostly of humble origin and made a living from their pens, depending entirely on the patronage of courts, where music and poetry were cultivated in particular by ladies. The Upper Italy visited by the troubadours was then divided among the families of the Obertenghi, the Aleramici, and the Arduinici. The most famous branch of the Obertenghi was that of the Malaspinas, who controlled the mountainous Apennine region of Liguria and Emilia and held a splendid court in their castle of Oramala, already frequented by the first troubadours to appear in Italy. The marquises of Monferrat are the best-known descendants of the Aleramici; they held a territory stretching through southern Piedmont, with their court at Casale. Members of the Arduinici family held such important places as Turin, Ivrea, Asti, Alba, Mondovì, and the western part of the Ligurian coast.

In the latter part of the twelfth century these courts began to attract wandering minstrels (among whom quite a few also practiced the art of the troubadour), especially from Provence, where appreciation for the art of the troubadour—and hence patronage—was rapidly dwindling (Linskill 7). The earliest troubadour to arrive in Italy—as far as we know—was a knight of the Vienne region, Peire Bremon lo Tort, who must have spent some time at the court of Casale, since in 1176 or 1177 he addressed his poem "En abril, quant vey verdejar" (poem 1) to William Longsword, the eldest son of Marquis William III of Monferrat, then in Palestine.

The visits and sojourns of troubadours and jongleurs at this court became increasingly frequent and were already quite numerous when Boniface, the third son of William, began to rule in 1192. So much was he praised by the poets that the troubadour Peire Vidal, who in 1194–95 also spent time at that court, wrote that the jongleurs had already said so much good of the marquis that nothing was left for him to add (Avalle, No. 11).

The greatest glorification of the *Marques*, as Boniface was called by the troubadours and chroniclers alike, came from the troubadour Raimbaut de Vaqueiras. We know that

> Raimbaut, arriving at Montferrat during the eighth decade of the [twelfth] century, was to be united in a bond of sympathy which in due course ripened into one of the most intimate and affectionate associations ever recorded between a poet and his patron, and one which was only severed by Boniface's tragic death in 1207. (Linskill 8)

Raimbaut fought valiantly alongside the marquis on several occasions and was instrumental in saving his patron's life during Boniface's Sicilian campaign of 1194 for Emperor Henry VI, a fact that earned him knighthood. But before that he, too, was forced to wander across the plains of Lombardy, hungry and on foot, in search of hospitality, as recalled in his famous *tenso* with Marquis Albert of Malaspina (d. ca. 1210), a troubadour himself (poem 4).

It is during this period of wanderings that Raimbaut also stayed at the Malaspina court and composed the first of his *tensos*, in which certain stanzas are in a language other than medieval Occitan. Here he has a fictitious exchange of words with a Genoese lady who speaks her dialect and finally sends him to Lord Obizzino (Albert of Malaspina's older brother, Marquis Obizzo II Malaspina), who might provide him with a packhorse, since he is a minstrel (Linskill 101). After Raimbaut became attached to the court of Monferrat, however, his situation improved greatly, for that court reached its apogee under Boniface. This can be gleaned from a famous passage of Raimbaut's *Epic Letter*, 3.84–106 (Linskill 308):

> The poet has given us a colourful picture of the gaiety and brilliance of life at Montferrat, where all the courtly virtues were practised and all the courtly

customs honoured: fine raiment and armour, jousts, diversions and song formed a fitting background for the chivalry and hospitality which appeared to the poet to be the outstanding characteristics of Boniface's court. Boniface himself the poet has immortalised as the embodiment of the medieval knightly ideal; and compensating for the brevity of the references to him in contemporary chronicles, he portrays in vivid language and in lyrical accents the valour, the magnanimity, the justice tempered with mercy, the compassion for the weak and distressed, the respect for womanhood and the unusual self-restraint of the man who, by universal consent, was soon to be called on to lead the Fourth Crusade. (Linskill 18)

The years 1197–1202 were the happiest of Raimbaut's life, and in the congenial atmosphere at Casale his poetic talent and inventive genius reached full development. In the literary production of these years the so-called *Carros* must be singled out, for the brilliance and charm of this lively composition make it one of the jewels of Occitan literature. One critic offers the following observations:

Probably the last of the lyrical poems composed by Raimbaut prior to his departure on the Fourth Crusade, the *Carros* is devoted entirely to the glorification of Beatrice, daughter of his patron the Marquis. Intended also to entertain the refined society of the court of Monferrat, whose culture and tastes it accurately reflects, it describes an imaginary war for the prize of merit, beauty and youth between the patroness and a band of more than twenty ladies of the Italian nobility, all celebrated for their beauty and many of them mentioned by name. (Linskill 212)

In this happy period Raimbaut also composed his famous multilingual *descort* that contains one stanza in Occitan, another in Italian, a third in French, a fourth in a kind of Gascon, a fifth in a type of Galician-Portuguese, and a sixth in a combination of the five languages, each having two lines (poem 16). (See Chapter 12 in this volume.) Raimbaut's primary purpose here was no doubt to display his linguistic and artistic virtuosity. His bold innovation indeed impressed his contemporaries greatly, and he was even imitated by Dante in a *descort* in Occitan, Latin, and Italian.

Unfortunately, this glamor did not continue under Boniface's son William IV (1207–25), as the troubadour Aimeric de Peguilhan (ca. 1175–ca. 1225/1230) would discover: after a short stay, during which he urged the marquis to take the cross (Shepard and Chambers 86), he went on to the then brilliant court of Azzo VI (1196–1212) of Este, another descendant of the famous Obertenghi family, whose marquisate included Ferrara and Verona.

Scholars have noted that

Azzo's virtues were those dear to the troubadours: generosity first of all, and then courtesy, kindness, and the ability to recognize and reward merit. [However,] perhaps because he died shortly after Aimeric came to Este, Azzo appears in Aimeric's poems only as a dear memory, rather than as a living friend. (Shepard and Chambers 12)

Still, the Este family gained quite a reputation in the thirteenth century as a patron of Occitan poetry. Aimeric was among the first to profit from this hospitality, even though Azzo did not become for him what Boniface of Monferrat was for Raimbaut de Vaqueiras. That place was reserved for William, marquis of Malaspina and Massa (1194–1220), the nephew of Albert of Malaspina, who had joined in a *tenso* with Raimbaut de Vaqueiras. William's interest in Occitan poetry was therefore nothing new in the family. Aimeric expresses his opinion of William and defines their relationship succinctly:

> Lo pros Guillems Malespina soste
> Don e dompnei e cortesia e me.
>
> (41:41–42)

> The worthy William Malaspina upholds generosity and lady-service and courtesy and me. (trans. Shepard and Chambers 199)

Most famous is Aimeric's *planh* for William, in which he praises his patron for the qualities dear to the troubadours and compares him to Alexander, Gawain, Yvain, and even Tristan. After these conventional eulogies, Aimeric adds this stanza, which seems sincere:

> Belhs senher cars, valens, ieu que farai?
> Ni cum puesc sai vius ses vos remaner,
> Que·m saubes tan dir e far mon plazer
> Qu'autre plazers contra·l vostre·m desplai?
> Que tals per vos m'onrav' e m'aculhia
> Que m'er estrans cum si vist no m'avia;
> Ni ja nulh temps cambi no·n trobarai,
> Ni esmenda del dan qu'ai per vos pres,
> Nez ieu non cre qu'om far la m'en pogues.
>
> (10:37–45)

> Fair, dear and worthy Lord, what shall I do now? How can I remain alive here without you? You treated me so well in words and deeds that all other favors I scorn, in comparison with yours. Certain men, on your account, were wont to honor and welcome me, who now will be like strangers who have never seen me. I shall never, at any time, find one to take your place or who will make amends for your loss. I do not believe that anyone can do that for me. (trans. Shepard and Chambers 83)

Shepard and Chambers (18) sum up thus: "There can be little doubt that William Malaspina befriended Aimeric more than any other great lord whom he met in Italy, and that Aimeric repaid his beneficence with a very genuine affection."

Peire Raimon de Tolosa's career very much resembles that of Aimeric. He was at the courts of Alfonso II (1162–96) of Aragon, Raimon VI (1194–1222) of Toulouse, and Guilhem VIII (1177–1202) of Montpellier before turning to Italy, where his songs can be dated between 1218 and 1221. At the end of his poetic activity, he seems to have returned to the south of France and married at Pamiers in the county of Foix, where he died. Peire Raimon was first active in the court of Este, where he praises Azzo VI's daughter Beatrice in his song "Tostemps aug dir q'us ioys n'adutz," especially in the envoi, which is devoted entirely to her:

Prez e valor, beltat, ioi et ioven,
Ses faillimen,
Et toz bos aibs, totas belas faisos
Ha Na Beatrix d'Est, q'anc non cre qe fos
Don'ab tan bes ses tota malestansa.

(16:55–59)

Lady Beatrice of Este has merit and valor, beauty, joy and youth, is without any fault, and has all the good qualities and fine manners; so that I think there never was a lady with such immaculate qualities.

In the same period, Peire Raimon was also in contact with the other great patron of the troubadours in Italy, William of Malaspina. The poem "Pus vey parer la flor el glay" (poem 11) is addressed to him, and he is mentioned in the poem "Era pus l'invernz franh los broth" (poem 3), while the song "Si cum seluy qu'a servit son senhor" (poem 14) is addressed to his successor (in 1221), Conrad of Oramala. At much the same time Peire Raimon also wrote a poem dedicated to the Italian troubadour Rambertino Buvalelli ("De fin'amor son tuit mei pessamen," poem 5), a poem that contains one of the finest descriptions of *fin'amor* ever written.

Another Occitan troubadour who enjoyed the hospitality of the Malaspina court at Oramala was Uc de Saint-Circ, a poor vavasour from a village near Rocamadour who, after many peregrinations—also in Catalonia, Aragon, and Castile—arrived in Upper Italy ca. 1220, where he married and passed into the service of Alberico da Romano at Treviso; he died probably in 1253. His best-known poem is a *sirventes* of encouragement addressed to the defenders of the city of Faenza besieged in 1239–40 by Frederick II, in which he also exhorts the French king and the pope to conquer Apulia, Frederick's kingdom: "Quar selh qu'en Dieu non cre non deu terra tener" (For a person who does not believe in God should not hold land; 23:40). (On Uc de Saint-Circ, see also Chapter 7 in this volume.)

Aimeric also exchanged *coblas* with Sordel, the most famous of the Italian troubadours. Although Sordel was then (i.e., prior to 1229) still quite young, having been born ca. 1200 at Goito near Mantua, he was already quite well known, as evidenced by the fact that Aimeric also addresses a poem to him in which he appeals to Sordel to exculpate him of his lady's accusation that he is too old to love. Nevertheless, Sordel was still far from his fame, and soon afterward he had to flee Italy rather ignominiously; during this exile he crossed not only the Alps into Provence but also the Pyrenees, staying in Spain and perhaps even Portugal. Disappointed in the court of the king of Aragon, he returned to France and finally established residence in Aix at the court of Raimond Berenger V, count of Provence. Here he met the troubadour Blacatz, lord of Aups (ca. 1190–1237), with whom he became friends and to whose memory he dedicated what is considered one of the most famous works of medieval Occitan literature, a *planh* in which he employed the old myth of the eaten heart in a virulent attack on the politicians of his time (26:17–24). It is this *planh* that ingratiated Sordel with Dante, who chooses him as the guide of Virgil and himself in cantos VI–VIII of the *Purgatorio* and in particular has him pronounce a violent diatribe against Italy and its politicians, who lack any foresight and real love for their country.

In 1246 Charles of Anjou, the younger brother of Saint Louis, succeeded his father-in-law as count of Provence. Sordel finally reentered Italy in Charles's army in 1265, after more than thirty years of absence; but already a year later he was inexplicably a prisoner in Novara, perhaps because of difficulties encountered on the march to Naples. Pope Clement IV intervened personally to obtain his freedom, and in 1269 Charles of Anjou even endowed him with the seigniory of several castles in the Abruzzi. From a poor versifier in Occitan, the Italian Sordel thus became a valiant knight and a familiar of King Charles of Naples. In addition to the *planh* he left approximately ten *tensos*, about thirty *cansos*, and a moral poem that scholars have entitled "Ensenhamen d'onor." The *tenso* is Sordel's best poetry after the *planh*; vibrant and impetuous, these poems bear witness to a proud mind and original poetic talent (see Lafont and Anatole 138–41).

Perhaps an even better, certainly more lyrical troubadour than Sordel was Lanfranc Cigala, jurisconsult and councillor of the Genoese republic. He appears in documents in 1235, 1239, 1240, 1253, and 1257; in 1241 he served as ambassador of Genoa to Raymond Berenger V of Provence and died before September 24, 1258. Lanfranc's poetic output consists of eight early love poems (written in the 1230s), four *cansos* in honor of the Virgin, two crusade songs, and eighteen poems on varied topics. Among the latter is a violent *sirventes* against Marquis Boniface II of Monferrat, the nephew of Raimbaut de Vaqueiras's Boniface, because of his eternal navigating between the emperor and the pope: when in 1245 Boniface again adheres to the party of Frederick II, the poet (whose Genoa was allied with the pope) accuses him of heresy, perjury, accepting bribes, and worse. Here is, for instance, the beginning of stanza 4:

> Tant es avols e de menut coratge
> Q'anc iorn no·l plac prez de cavalaria,
> Per q'a perdut pro de son heritatge,
> Q'anc non reqeis per ardiment un dia.
> (21:25–28)

He is so vile and of such mean character that the *pretz* of knighthood never pleased him, so that he lost a great part of his inheritance, which not one day had he the courage to reclaim.

With these words troubadour poetry severed its relations with the house of Montferrat!

In the same period (1244–45), Lanfranc composed a crusade song in which he admonishes the kings of France and England, the Germans and the Spaniards, the count of Provence, and, in a first envoi, even the pope to take up the cross; in the second envoi he turns to Frederick II:

> Emperaire, del secors vos soveingna
> Car Dieus lo·us quier, per cui chascuns reis reingna,
> E fatz perdon de sai e lai secors,
> Car ben pot morz sobre·ls emperadors.
> (20:65–68)

Emperor, remember to lend your help, because God, thanks to whom every king reigns, asks it of you, and make peace here and succor there, since death spares emperors not.

His call would be answered a few years later by Saint Louis. Both his celebration of the lady's smile—that sweet smile that brings "joi e alegria e vol amoros" (joy and cheerfulness and amorous will)—which had made of Lanfranc Cigala the best troubadour ever to sing of smiling feminine lips, and his cult of the ideal woman, which had made him a precursor of the *dolce stil nuovo*, were now gone and had made room for a just bitterness. Soon after these years he abandoned amorous and political poetry for its religious counterpart: he now only sang and invoked Mary, the Lady of ladies, who represented for him feminine idealization in its supreme degree.

Compared to Sordel and Lanfranc Cigala, the other Italian troubadours do not have the same stature, although among the twenty-five other poets listed by Giulio Bertoni ([1915] 1967) there are two worthy to be mentioned here. The first is the Venetian Bertolome Zorzi, whose biography is known only from his two *vidas* (Boutière and Schutz 576–80), which, however, seem to be fairly accurate. According to these texts, Bertolome Zorzi was a merchant and, as such, undertook a journey to Constantinople in 1266. But the Genoese, in one of their frequent wars with Venice, seized the boat in the waters of Kithira Island (the ancient Cythera), and Bertolome—together with 108 prisoners, among them persons of high rank—was brought to Genoa, where he remained in prison until peace was concluded in 1273. During this time he continued to compose: in all, eighteen poems are preserved. In one *sirventes* with the Genoese troubadour Bonifaci Calvo, he answers the latter's accusation that the Venetians were cowards, using the same metrical schema and rhymes as those employed by Lanfranc Cigala. In another *sirventes*, in which he also mentions Saint Louis's death in Tunisia (August 25, 1270), he demands the liberation of the imprisoned Venetians. His most famous poem, though, is a moving *planh* for Conradin, the last of the Hohenstaufen dynasty, who had wanted to reconquer the kingdom of Naples from Charles d'Anjou but was defeated by the latter in 1268 in the battle of Tagliacozzo in the Abruzzi and summarily executed. As a sample of Bertolome's artistry, here is the envoi:

Als avinenz   recort   quel planhs faigz es
Ab gai sonet, coindet e d'agradage,
Qu'estiers m'albir   qu'om chantar no·l pogues,
Ni neis auzir,   tan mou de gran dampnage.
                    (18:60–63)

I remind the nobles that the *planh* is made with gay, gracious, and pleasing sounds, because I think that otherwise it could not be sung or even heard, so much is it inspired by destroying grief.

Among the other remaining works his two moving poems addressed to the Virgin (poems 1 and 5), probably written late in life, are particularly worthy of mention. The date of his death can only be surmised: ca. 1290.

The other noteworthy Italian poet is Zorzi's abovementioned adversary in the *sirventes* against the Venetians, Bonifaci Calvo, at that time already an older man who, after an eventful life as a troubadour, had retired to his hometown of Genoa (where he was not too happy, as we learn from the same *sirventes*, since he bitterly deplored the political dissension in that city). Bonifaci had spent most of his life at the courts of princes, especially that of Alfonso X the Wise of Castile (D'Heur 223–53), where he composed political *sirventes* in the style of Bertran de Born's "Be·m plai lo gais temps de pascor" (poem 30), inciting Alfonso to wars against the neighboring Navarre and even against the English King Henry III's possessions in Gascony. The three poems dealing with these matters can therefore be dated 1253 and 1254. The third one, which begins "Un nou sirventes ses tardar" (poem 7), is particularly interesting because, like Raimbaut de Vaqueiras's poem (which may have served here as model), it is composed in different languages: the first six lines of the first stanza are in Occitan, whereas the seventh is in Catalan (or perhaps Galician-Portuguese); in the second stanza, the first six lines continue in Catalan, while the seventh line, along with the first six lines of the third stanza, is in Old French; the seventh line of the third stanza returns to Occitan, in which the fourth stanza and the *tornada* are also written. The poem is composed according to the strophic schema *aababbc*, with *c* corresponding to the *a* of the next stanza, a schema known as *coblas capcaudadas*. Bonifaci also cultivated the genre of moral poems reminiscent, for instance, of Peire Cardenal, in which he—as usual—deplores the decay of *pretz* and *cortezia*. Fortunately, King Alfonso still personifies value and virtue: thanks to him, wise persons can continue to aspire to a better future. The traditional troubadour motifs can be found also in Bonifaci's love poems and in his two *cantigas de amor* in Portuguese (D'Heur 251–53). Perhaps his best poem in this genre is the *planh* on the death of a lady whom he calls *bella douz' amia* The expression is found in the envoi:

> Ai, flors de valor e de cortezia
> E de beutat! Ai, bella, douz'amia!
> Si·l mortz complic son voler qan vos pres,
> Ieu en remaing tan doloros, que res
> Alegrar ni conortar no·m poiria.
>
> (16:46–50)

Alas, flower of merit and courtesy and beauty! Alas, beautiful sweet friend! If death accomplished its will when it took you, I remain so sorrowful because of it that nothing could make me happy or comfort me.

Even this poem, however, cannot hide the fact that Bonifaci Calvo's poems, though the work of quite a skillful versifier, are not the fruit of the soul of a real poet. (For a fuller treatment of this poem, see Chapter 19 in this volume.) Occitan poetry in Italy comes to an end soon afterward. One of the last poems in that language, if not the very last, is a *tenso* between the Occitan troubadour Guillem Raimon (or Raimon Guillem) and the Ferrarese notary and *magister grammaticae* Ferrarino (attested in 1310 and possibly deceased at a very old age after 1330; see Boutière and Schutz 581–82). This poem in the *trobar clus* style sings the praise of a marquis of Este, probably Azzo VIII (1293–1308) (in Bertoni [1915] 1967, 461–62). After that, the Italian poetry of the *dolce stil nuovo*—itself an indirect fruit of Occitan poetry, since the Tuscan poets greatly admired the poetry of the so-called Sicilian school, which was in turn an emulation of troubadour poetry (Kleinhenz 10–16; see also Chapter 13 in this volume)—entirely supplanted the Occitan poetic tradition in Upper Italy. And very soon Italian poetry would find its own supreme expression in Petrarch.

Although Occitan poetry was now dead, though, interest in it did not disappear for a long time. More than half of the collections of lyric poems, the so-called chansonniers, composed between the thirteenth and fifteenth centuries are of Italian origin, which proves that Italians continued reading the Old Occitan songs. This continued interest is also evidenced by the composition of grammars of the Occitan language for Italians, to begin with Uc Faidit's well-known *Donatz proensals* of ca. 1240–45 (Marshall). The traces left by Occitan civilization and the ideal of *fin'amor* in Italy are indeed long-lasting.

WORKS CITED

The quotations in this chapter are from the critical editions cited in the List of Troubadour Editions in the Appendix, and in particular from the following editions: Bertran de Born (Paden et al.); Bonifaci Calvo (Branciforti); Lanfranc Cigala (Branciforti); Peire Vidal (Avalle); Sordel (Boni). All translations are my own except as indicated.

Appel, Carl, ed. *Provenzalische Chrestomathie.* 3d ed. Leipzig: O. Reisland, 1907.
Bertoni, Giulio, ed. *Rambertino Buvalelli trovatore bolognese e le sue rime provenzali.* Gesellschaft für romanische Literatur, 17. Halle: Niemeyer, 1908.
———. *I trovatori d'Italia (Biografia, testi, traduzioni, note).* Modena: Umberto Orlandini, 1915; repr. Rome: Somu, 1967.
Boutière, Jean, and Alexander H. Schutz, eds. *Biographies des troubadours: textes provençaux des XIIIe et XIVe siècles.* Paris: Nizet, 1964.
de Bartholomaeis, Vincenzo, ed. *Poesie provenzali storiche relative all'Italia.* 2 vols. Rome: Tipografia del Senato, 1931.
D'Heur, Jean-Marie. *Troubadours d'oc et troubadours galiciens-portugais: recherches sur quelques échanges dans la littérature de l'Europe au moyen âge.* Cultura medieval e moderna, 1. Paris: Centro Cultural Português, 1973.
Folena, Gianfranco. "Tradizione e cultura trobadorica nelle corti e nelle città venete." In *Storia della cultura veneta,* vol. 1: *Dalle origini al trecento,* 453–562. Vicenza: Neri Pozza, 1976.
Jeanroy, Alfred. "La Poésie provençale en Italie." In *La Poésie lyrique des troubadours,* 1:229–65. Toulouse: Privat; Paris: Didier, 1934.
Kleinhenz, Christopher. *The Early Italian Sonnet: The First Century (1220–1320).* Collezione di studi e testi, n.s., 2. Lecce, It.: Milella, 1986.
Lafont, Robert, and Christian Anatole. *Nouvelle Histoire de la littérature occitane.* Paris: PUF, 1970.
Linskill, Joseph, ed. *The Poems of the Troubadour Raimbaut de Vaqueiras.* The Hague: Mouton, 1964.
Marshall, J. H., ed. *The "Donatz Proensals" of Uc Faidit.* London: Oxford University Press, 1969.
Melli, Elio, ed. *Rambertino Buvalelli: le poesie. Edizione critica con introduzione, traduzione, note e glossario.* Bologna: Patròn, 1978.
Schultz-Gora, Oscar. "Die Lebensverhältnisse der italienischen Troubadours." *Zeitschrift für romanische Philologie* 7 (1883): 176–235.
Shepard, William P., and Frank M. Chambers. *The Poems of Aimeric de Peguilhan.* Evanston, Ill.: Northwestern University Press, 1950; repr. New York: AMS, 1983.
Ugolini, Francesco Alessandro. *La poesia provenzale et l'Italia.* Modena: Società Tipografica Modenese, 1939.

General and Technical Considerations

FIFTEEN

Manuscripts

William D. Paden

The oldest surviving physical traces of the Occitan language date from about A.D. 1000. Around that time scattered terms or phrases in the vernacular began to appear in legal documents, or charters, which were otherwise composed in Latin (Brunel 1922). Around the same time, too, a manuscript now at Rome in the Biblioteca Apostolica Vaticana (Regina 1462) was compiled at the Benedictine abbey of Fleury, later St-Benoît-sur-Loire. This manuscript contains a Latin *alba*, or dawn poem, with a puzzling refrain that has been interpreted by many scholars as archaic Occitan—although others see it as a different language altogether, either Romansh or popular Latin or even a fictional idiom intended to suggest the mumbled response of sleepers to the watchman's call.[1] We know that as early as 1059 oaths of fidelity to the lord of Montpellier, preserved today in a later copy, were written entirely in Occitan; original charters written essentially in Occitan survive from 1102 onward, and we have over five hundred of them from the twelfth century.[2] Although such an abundance clearly represents an established practice, the vernacular charters must have remained a minority in comparison to those that continued to be written in Latin.

The earliest surviving literary manuscripts were compiled in the late eleventh or the twelfth century. The first literary monuments, the *Boeci* and the *Chanson de Sainte Foy*, were perhaps composed around 1000 and 1050 respectively, but the manuscripts that transmit them to us are not the originals. The *Boeci* manuscript, now at Orléans (Bibliothèque Municipale 444), was perhaps written in the late eleventh century at the Benedictine

---

1. The date ca. A.D. 1000 and the last interpretation were proposed by Zumthor 1984. See also the two studies by Lazzerini. Avalle (33) dates the text in the tenth century.

2. Brunel 1921–22. See Brunel 1926, where the act appears as no. 7.

abbey of Saint-Martial in Limoges, and passed from there to the sister abbey of Fleury. The *Sainte Foy* manuscript was written at Fleury around the end of the eleventh century or the beginning of the twelfth, but it is now split into two pieces, one which contains the poem in the library of the University of Leiden (Vossianus latinus in-8°, 60) and the other at Orléans (Bibliothèque Municipale 347). We have Occitan versions of three originally French texts: two are known as the *Passion de Clermont-Ferrand* and the *Vie de Saint Léger*, both in an eleventh-century manuscript from the Limousin now at Clermont-Ferrand (Bibliothèque Municipale et Universitaire 240); the third, called the *Sponsus*, is in a late-eleventh-century manuscript from Saint-Martial now in the Bibliothèque Nationale (fonds latin 1139). The latter manuscript also contains three short religious lyrics in Occitan.[3] Also in the Bibliothèque Nationale are a collection of Occitan sermons written at St-Martial in the twelfth century (fonds latin 3548, B) and another twelfth-century manuscript from the Limousin region containing a vernacular life of Christ (fonds latin 11312).

These eight codices, including that of the bilingual *alba*, are the only literary manuscripts we have that were written in Occitan before the thirteenth century. As Avalle (19–41) has persuasively argued, all eight are associated directly or indirectly with the abbeys of Saint-Martial and Fleury. It is no accident that these Benedictine manuscripts contain texts on exclusively religious subjects (if we include the philosophical *Boeci*), nor is it accidental that religious texts join the charters as the two types of discourse that were the earliest to be preserved in the vernacular. The situation is different in French, where we have sixty-odd literary manuscripts from the twelfth century including secular texts such as chansons de geste and romances (Woledge and Short). The lack of secular literary texts in Occitan manuscripts of the twelfth century is a meaningful absence that needs to be explained.

In his *Bibliographie des manuscrits littéraires en ancien provençal*, Clovis Brunel cataloged a total of 376 codices containing Old Occitan literary texts, including the eight early ones already mentioned. Ninety-five of them contain lyric poetry of the troubadours.[4] Most of these chansonniers were compiled in the thirteenth and fourteenth centuries, a few in the fifteenth or sixteenth, and one as late as the nineteenth century.[5] The earliest one that may be dated exactly, perhaps, is manuscript *D* in Modena, which contains a statement that it was compiled in 1254—but the statement itself

---

3. Now edited in Switten et al. 18–34, with a recorded musical performance on cassette.

4. For explanation of sigla used for the chansonniers, see appendix to this chapter.

5. The manuscript compiled by Gioacchino Plà (Rome, Biblioteca Apostolica Vaticana, Barberiniani latini 3965 = Pillet-Carstens MS *e*), dated in the eighteenth century by Pillet-Carstens, is assigned to the period 1810–17 by Zufferey (157).

may be a copy rather than an original. The various sections of manuscript *D* were written by five scribes, three of whom were contemporary, active perhaps as early as 1254 (if the date is original) or perhaps as late as the end of the century (if it is a copy), while the other two scribes added passages in the mid–fourteenth century (*Il canzoniere provenzale estense* 1:19–28). The colophon of manuscript *V*, in Venice, indicates that it was compiled in 1268.[6] Manuscripts *D* and *V* are the only two chansonniers that bear specific dates prior to the fourteenth century.

It is a remarkable fact that few of these lyric manuscripts—precisely one-fifth of them, or nineteen, according to Avalle (44)—were compiled in the Occitan region. Among the others, fourteen originated in northern France, ten in Catalonia, and fifty-two (more than half the total number) in Italy. If we set aside the fragmentary chansonniers and focus on the major ones, we find this impression of Italian dominance strengthened. Riquer lists forty-one major manuscripts, of which twenty-seven are of Italian origin.[7] He finds ten major chansonniers from the thirteenth century, of which seven were compiled in Italy, one in Catalonia, one in Languedoc (west of the Rhône) and one in Provence (east of the Rhône). In the fourteenth century Languedoc is more strongly represented, with six out of twenty major chansonniers, but the predominance of the Italian tradition remains unquestionable with twelve. The significance of the Italian tradition is a problem to which we shall return later.

The sigla by which the chansonniers are commonly represented were first assigned in 1872 by Karl Bartsch in his *Grundriss*. Bartsch established the sound principle of referring to manuscripts on parchment with capital letters and to those on paper in lower case; less happily, he attempted to assign sigla in a rough order of merit rather than in some arbitrary way, a technique that has inevitably prejudiced subsequent investigations.[8] In

---

6. The colophon of *V* reads as follows (folio 148 recto):

Anno domini MCCLXVIII, II kalendas junii.
Signum R. de Capelades qui hoc scripsit.
Testes huic rei sunt cindipendium et pennam.

The name of the scribe refers to Capellades, a village near Barcelona. In the third line he takes his pen and another instrument of his trade as witnesses that he has completed his task. Regarding *cindipendium*, which has not been explained, Jean Dufour calls attention to the expression *scindere pennam*, "fendre le bec de la plume en deux parties inégales" (Stiennon 327); thus *(s)cindipendium* may be translated "fendoir à plume" (penknife). For more on *scindere pennam*, see Wattenbach 230 and his reference to the *Regulae de modo scindendi pennarum*, published from a fifteenth-century manuscript by Bech. For earlier discussion of the colophon in *V*, see *Colophons*, item 16221; and Crescini 39–40. I am grateful for this explanation of *cindipendium* to Jean Dufour and to Geneviève Brunel-Lobrichon, who communicated it to me.

7. *Los trovadores* 1:12–14. Similar figures in Zufferey (316).

8. "It was, to my mind, a great misfortune in Provençal studies that the attribution of the letters of the alphabet by Bartsch was not arbitrary: on the contrary, they corresponded in his

1916 Jeanroy added a number of new sigla for manuscripts recently discovered, while modifying Bartsch's use of Greek letters for those of lesser importance. In 1933 Pillet and Carstens were more faithful to Bartsch's original sigla in their *Bibliographie der Troubadours*, which remains the fundamental bibliographical reference on the subject. A small number of reasonable modifications to Pillet-Carstens were proposed by Zufferey in 1987.

Underlying these shifts in notation have been gains and losses in the number of known chansonniers. Since the end of the fifteenth century at least four have disappeared from view.[9] On the other hand, the discovery in Modena of manuscript a^1, composed in 1589, found in 1899, added a number of new attributions and entire new texts to the corpus.[10] New fragments also turn up from time to time.[11] During the 1980s, two fragments dating from around 1300 came to light in Torino and in Castagnolo Minore, north of Bologna; the former adds to our knowledge one new troubadour, three new songs, and two new stanzas of known songs (Gasca-Queirazza); the latter is interesting as an anthology of selected stanzas from previously known texts (Allegri). In 1989 a new manuscript turned up in Madrid; dating from the eighteenth century, it nevertheless contains one otherwise unknown *sirventes* (Careri 1989).

The great chansonniers, written in court hand on parchment, are elaborate artifacts that anticipate in many ways the work of modern editors. The richest is manuscript *C*, in the Bibliothèque Nationale, containing 1206 poems; in some ways the most impressive, especially for its lucid orthography, is manuscript *A*, with 626 poems, in the Vatican Library. Most of the anthologies are organized according to genre, beginning with the *canso*, which corresponds to the Italian *canzone*, the most prestigious lyric form in the peninsula at the time when the manuscripts were produced; others are organized according to author. An attribution is usually indicated at the

---

intention to a sort of order of merit, so that the MSS labelled *A*, *B* and *C* had, as it were, received a First, whereas *V* had barely earned a Pass degree, and *W*, *X* and *Y* were clear Fails. It is bad enough, no doubt, to label students in this way: worse still for manuscripts, which have a longer life-span—and which, like students, will commonly appear to conform to the grading placed upon them. Certainly all Provençal scholars are, in varying degrees, unconsciously affected by these letters" (Marshall 9).

9. See Pirot, who reviews and updates the conclusions of Chabaneau; further references in Avalle 127–28. One lost manuscript overlooked by Chabaneau and Pirot is (or was) a folio collection of poems of the *trobairitz*, reported in the library of the king of Spain in 1836 but since lost from view; see Paden 1989, 237.

10. On Bertoni's discovery, see his study of 1899 and *Il canzoniere provenzale estense* 1:12.

11. Fragmentary chansonniers that have been rediscovered or recognized since the publication of Bartsch's *Grundriss* include those denoted by Zufferey as *A'*, *K'*, *K''*, *m*, *p*, *r*, *s*, *x*, *y*, and *z*; see Zufferey 359–60.

head of the poem; when a given song is preserved in several manuscripts, it often happens that the attributions conflict. Some manuscripts have a table of contents or an index (in manuscript *C* the index provides a number of attributions that conflict with those given in the body). Four manuscripts (*G, R, W, X*) provide transcriptions of the melodies of some of the songs, 256 in all, or about 10 percent of the 2,500-odd extant texts. Nine troubadour manuscripts are ornamented with miniature paintings (Anglade; Huot; Meneghetti 1984, 323–63; Rieger). Eleven of the great chansonniers contain prose *vidas* and *razos* interspersed among the lyrics, sometimes written in red ink (as is suggested by the term *rubric*) in contrast to the black ink of the poems. A single fragmentary manuscript contains capital letters in gold leaf (*A'*, Zufferey 66); manuscript *A* has gold leaf backgrounds for capitals.

The luxury of the great chansonniers is reflected in the ranks of some of their early owners. A doge of Venice owned manuscript *A* during the fifteenth century, and a later doge held manuscript *K* during the sixteenth (Zufferey 65, 69). The dukes of Mantua held manuscript *N* from the fourteenth century to the sixteenth (Jeanroy 10); it has now come to rest in the library of J. Pierpont Morgan, New York. The Medici acquired manuscripts *P* and *U*, still today in the Biblioteca Medicea Laurenziana, Florence, where they may be inspected complete with the sturdy chains that once secured them against theft. The prime minister to Ferdinand II, king of Sicily, owned manuscript *M* in the late fifteenth century (Lamur-Baudreu). The counts of Foix and the viscounts of Béarn owned manuscript *C* until the sixteenth century (Jeanroy 3); in the seventeenth century the count of Sault owned manuscript *T* (Brunetti 1991). Manuscripts *K* and *M* in the Bibliothèque Nationale were confiscated from the Vatican by Napoleon as booty from his Italian wars (Zufferey 69; Jeanroy 10). The shift in balance of troubadour manuscripts from Italy, where over half of them were produced, to Paris, where half of them are found today, reflects their intrinsic worth and the power of an emperor.

Despite the passage of six centuries, more or less, which has produced occasional fading or chipping of ink, the typical court hand of the thirteenth and fourteenth centuries is clear and easily read—more easily than the cursive hand of a Renaissance paper text such as manuscript *a'* in Modena, compiled in 1589. Recent work tends to revise the low esteem implicit in Bartsch's sigla for manuscripts written in cursive. Manuscript *T*, parchment, now dated at the end of the thirteenth century, is therefore among the oldest chansonniers we have; its cursive hand corresponds to its origin as a private product for private use in an urban, bourgeois—perhaps mercantile—milieu (Brunetti 1990). Manuscript *H*, about as old as *T*, was also intended for the personal use of an amateur. It is a palimpsest: the parchment was originally employed about 1250 to record a Latin text in a scholastic hand, then erased and reused several decades later; after entering the Occitan texts in a court hand, the same scribe made additions in cursive, including glosses of various kinds and punctuation. The result records the scribe's reading and understanding of the texts in detail.[12] Manuscript N^2, paper, sixteenth century, also employs a cursive hand for purposes of personal consultation (Bologna).

TRANSMISSION

The transmission of troubadour poetry from the poets to the extant manuscripts is a subject that has exercised the ingenuity of many scholars and that has produced radically different hypotheses. The discussion has been oriented around the views of two towering figures in related fields, the classicist Karl Lachmann and the Old French scholar Joseph Bédier.

Lachmann formalized the tradition of textual criticism in Greek and Latin that had evolved since the Humanist Renaissance (see Timpanaro). In editions of the New Testament published from 1831 to 1850, he rejected the traditional text derived from Erasmus and based his version directly on manuscript sources. Categorizing New Testament manuscripts into two families, oriental and occidental, Lachmann reasoned that he must eliminate any reading attested in only one part of one family, and accept any reading common to both families. In 1850 Lachmann published his edition of Lucretius's *De rerum natura* ("On the Nature of Things"), a text well suited to his editorial method because there are relatively few medieval manuscripts of the work, and the genealogical relations among them can be reconstructed with relative ease. Assuming an absolutely mechanical transmission throughout the medieval period, Lachmann devised criteria for mechanical selection among variants in reconstituting the original text. Around the same time, other scholars developed techniques for investigating the genealogical relations among manuscripts and for reconstructing the history of the text, techniques based on the detection of common errors that were assumed to indicate affiliation between manuscripts—unless they were produced by contamination, in which one manuscript is not simply copied from a single source but incorporates readings from differing versions of the text. The affiliations among all versions of a text came to be symbolized in a stemma, or tree-diagram, which indicates their descent from the archetype. Though Lachmann himself never drew up a stemma, and showed slight interest in the history of the text as such, in his Lucretius he daringly reconstructed the exterior form of the long-lost archetype, specifying the number of lines on each page and the total number of pages in the book.

12. Careri 1988. I have not seen Careri 1991.

The Lachmannian method was challenged by Joseph Bédier in relation to the manuscript tradition of the the Old French *Lai de l'ombre*. Specifically, Bédier reacted against a version of Lachmann's technique proposed by Henri Quentin, who worked out his method in an edition of Genesis published in 1926 and described it the same year in his *Essais de critique textuelle*. Against Quentin's refinement of a mechanical process for determining the original, Bédier argued that the variants of the *Lai de l'ombre* were susceptible of analysis not in a single stemma, but in as many as eleven different stemmata, and that it was impossible to choose from among so many the one that would describe the true history of the text. Furthermore, Bédier observed that the stemmata proposed by the editors of over a hundred works in Old French were almost all bifid; that is, they were ultimately divided into two families rather than three or more. Casting doubt upon the near universality of such a pattern, Bédier argued that its very high frequency reflects editors' desire, conscious or unconscious, to regain the decisive role in determination of the text (which they enjoy whenever two traditions conflict) rather than to yield that power to a mechanical process (as they must whenever two out of three traditions agree). In the light of such considerations Bédier preferred to edit the *Lai de l'ombre* from one manuscript, the best manuscript insofar as he could determine, remaining faithful to that text whenever possible and marshaling variants in the apparatus.

Among Occitan scholars the viewpoint of Lachmann has been advocated by Gustav Gröber and more recently (as revised and called Neolachmannian) by D'Arco Silvio Avalle; that of Bédier has been represented by István Frank. Meanwhile, J. H. Marshall has claimed that the specific circumstances of the Occitan domain make both these programs inappropriate. Against the background of such cacophony in theoretical discussion, editors of troubadour texts have continued to produce editions based on widely varying assumptions, sometimes explicit and sometimes not. In general it has been the Italian scholars who have sustained the Lachmannian approach, while the French have tended to follow Bédier. German, English, and American scholars, while far from unanimous, may perhaps be characterized as more generally Bédiériste than Lachmannian. My own convictions are skeptical of the (Neo-)Lachmannian system, which is to say that they are essentially Bédiériste.

The grounds for my convictions are four. First, the Lachmannian system is built upon an axiom of mechanical transmission which presupposes that transmission was written, since any episode of oral transmission would introduce a flourishing of variants beyond any possibility of control (Avalle 45); but the axiom goes beyond any warrant of evidence. As Marshall points out, "we have extant sources which transmit this poetry to us precisely from the moment when the poetry itself was ceasing to be a living thing in its native land" (5). The manuscripts themselves, and of course the miniature paintings that depict the troubadours, cannot provide reliable information on the transmission that produced them, but only a retrospective and therefore unreliable view.[13] To bridge the gap between the composition of all but the latest poetry and its transcription on surviving parchment, we have in fact no direct evidence at all. When Marshall writes that "in so far as we can reconstruct the textual history of individual poets or songs, that history seems to be one of written texts, without interference (or with no demonstrable interference) from memorial transmission" (13–14), my reaction is to emphasize that the history *seems* so to Marshall only because he has applied an assumption congenial to him without finding it refuted by any evidence. This is not to say that he has found evidence to support his assumption. In the absence of direct evidence for either written or oral transmission in the early period, we are obliged to revert to whatever indirect traces we may feel able to detect, and to our general view of medieval culture—or simply to our predisposition in favor of one hypothesis or the other.

Memorial transmission, or oral transmission, seems a plausible alternative to written transmission in a culture where the literacy rate has been estimated at perhaps 1 or 2 percent of the population, and that small percentage composed principally of clergy and women of the nobility (Cipolla 55). In this view, which is my own, the reason we have no twelfth-century troubadour manuscripts is that lyric poetry was transmitted orally, and no manuscripts, or few, were compiled. Riquer (1:18) believes that we have indirect evidence of memorial transmission in the permutation of stanzas that may be observed among the manuscripts of many songs, since a strictly written transmission might change the order of textual passages by the column or the page, but not, presumably, by a unit of performance such as the stanza.[14] I have argued elsewhere (1984) that we have another form

13. A drawing in manuscript *N*, fol. 63r, shows Folquet de Marselha declaiming or perhaps composing at a writing desk with pen in hand and a roll of parchment before him. The drawing is a visualization of a passage in a poem transcribed on the same folio, in which the troubadour laments alone because his lady refuses to hear him. It provides clear evidence that the compilers of the manuscript conceived the troubadour's text inscribed on a roll, but is less persuasive that such was indeed the case. The manuscript was compiled in northern Italy at the end of the thirteenth century; the single testimony of this late Italian document must be suspected of anachronism. For the drawing, see Avalle, fig. 2A opp. p. 48; and Meneghetti 329–30n and 357, fig. 2; on rolls, see also note 16 below.

14. Permutation of stanzas has now been studied in detail by Van Vleck, who finds a correlation between stability of stanza order and two factors of stylistic complexity (stanza length and stanzaic linkage), but no evidence of a chronological trend toward greater stability (76–89). Her demonstration of the twelfth-century troubadours' ambivalence toward a concept of the fixed text corresponds, in my opinion, to their position early in the evolution of the low language into competition with the high language.

of indirect evidence in the troubadours' frequent instructions to a *joglar* to perform the song. Analysis of the incidence of such instructions reveals a steady decline over the twelfth and thirteenth centuries. If, as seems likely, the *joglars* were mostly illiterate, this steady decline in mentions made of them would correspond to a decline in memorial transmission and a corresponding increase in transmission through writing.

Tavera has analyzed in detail the textual relation between two manuscripts compiled in Languedoc, *C* and *R* (both now in the Bibliothèque Nationale), which are so alike that Avalle has called them "quasi gemelli" (114); but Tavera found that they also differ strikingly in numerous variant readings. Tavera accounts for this paradoxical relationship between *C* and *R* by positing an oral tradition on native ground: "S'ils voisinent si bien si souvent, au point qu'on ait pu s'y méprendre, c'est que les jongleurs du Languedoc avaient excellente mémoire; cependant le *support* n'était pas, comme un parchemin, stable et constant, mais sujet aux défaillances, aux caprices" (248). In Italy, by contrast, since it was a foreign country, the Occitan tradition was necessarily transmitted from one written text to another. To musicologists such as Friedrich Gennrich or Hendrik van der Werf, a shift from the apparently unwritten early transmission of melodies to written transmission in the extant manuscripts seems entirely plausible.

Such a shift of vernacular poetry from an oral medium into writing would make sense, too, in terms of the overarching development in the status of the vernacular, which may be taken to characterize the medieval period not only in the Midi but in Western Europe as a whole (see Paden 1983). Between antiquity and the Renaissance, the Middle Ages witnessed the transition from a sociolinguistic structure in which Latin, the prestige language, was the only language written, through the development of the Romance languages in predominantly oral discourse, to their gradual entry into writing and eventual displacement of Latin in an author such as Montaigne. This transition underlies the whole troubadour phenomenon, which is far more dynamic than has sometimes been thought. It underlies, for example, the change in attitude toward the Church—the institutionalization of Latin discourse—from Guillem de Peiteus to Matfre Ermengaud, whose Occitan discourse attempts to embrace ecclesiastical ethics. In this view, the Neolachmannian hypothesis in application to the Occitan domain seems to sweep away some of the most interesting phenomena that may be observed there, in the name of nothing more than a radical underestimation of the power of spoken language.

My second argument concerns the Lachmannian notion of error, which relates to several assumptions. Lachmann assumed that the scribe intended to produce a faithful copy, which may well have been true in relation to prestigious or authoritative texts such as Genesis in Hebrew, the New Testament in Greek, or Lucretius in Latin, but surely was not true in the same way of a vernacular text that the scribe found himself, exceptionally, copying. The status of the vernacular as low language in relation to Latin, the high language, must have invited more active participation by the scribe in the text. To the mechanical or closed recension that was a basic assumption for Lachmann, the Neolachmannians oppose what is called "open recension," in which the scribe enjoys greater liberty (Pasquali 126). Such open recension is implied by the whole impression of polish and sophistication that the Occitan chansonniers give. It is generally agreed that the texts were prepared by means of studious comparison of various versions, which were then conflated, perhaps by the director of the scriptorium who oversaw the efforts of individual scribes.[15] The ideal manuscript for Lachmannian analysis is a passive replica of its original; the chansonniers, with their elaborate evidence of philological effort of many kinds on the part of their producers, complicate the notion of error beyond any possibility of unraveling it.

In such a process of active, participatory reproduction, variants become possible on more than strictly written grounds. Indeed, the scribe becomes capable of introducing variants through his competence in active use of the poetic language, which is a specialized form of his competence in speech. The assumption that a given so-called error (better, perhaps, to speak of an innovative reading) can have been produced only once, and not on two independent occasions, begins to seem uncertain. Not only is the scribe capable of introducing innovative variant readings of a word, a phrase, or a line, but many editors believe that the isolated stanzas of certain songs that turn up in single manuscripts are also the work of the scribes of those manuscripts (see Pickens 1977); indeed, at least one entire song, an *alba* in manuscript *C*, has been attributed to a scribe (Poe). The very notion of error loses its certainty when we realize that more than one reading often makes sense in troubadour texts. If we lack confidence in our ability to identify errors, no stemma based on analysis of common errors will seem reliable.

Third, I cannot share the confidence with which a scholar such as Avalle feels able to reconstruct the past, either past textual detail or the overall process that led from the troubadours' composition to the manuscripts we have. Avalle follows Gröber in hypothesizing that the songs were originally written on individual pages or *Liederblätter*, and that these pages were eventually collected, by the author himself or by others, into songbooks or *Liederbücher*; another form of collection was the *Gelegenheitssammlung*, comprising songs composed or performed by several troubadours for some particular occasion. By conflation of *Liederbücher* and *Gelegenheitssammlungen* arose the chansonniers, or so the theory runs, which were compiled from various sources and so may be called *editiones variorum*, or editions that combine the insights and contributions of various editors. The remarkable

15. Avalle 58; Frank 1955, 472–73; Marshall 18–19; Riquer 1:12.

thing about Avalle's exposition of this elaborate process is that, as he scrupulously observes, we have no surviving *Liederblätter* (83–84), *Liederbücher* (83), *Gelegenheitssammlungen* (89), or overt *editiones variorum* (59) of troubadour songs. Gennrich argued that Gröber's case for *Liederblätter* applies equally well to medieval songs in Occitan, French, German, Catalan, and Galician: that in all these languages taken together we have at least ten thousand medieval songs, but we have no *Liederblatt* for any of them, not even the trace of one.[16] Gennrich concluded that the *Liederblätter* existed in small numbers if at all; that medieval songs—like the compositions of Bach, Mozart, or Beethoven—became widely known through performance, not through publication; and that medieval minstrels transmitted their knowledge of both music and text through oral performance.

For me Gröber's scaffolding of hypotheses places a greater strain upon credulity than does the alternative of accepting the evidence as it stands: an absence of written transmission followed by its presence. I feel the same way about the Lachmannian process of deducing original readings from analysis of variants and supposed errors. I am skeptical about our capacity to recover the past either in such fine textual detail or in such elaborate codicological process, because I do not believe that the past (or the future) necessarily functions in terms of any investigative principles we can bring to our analysis.

This is not to say that I deny the obvious affinities between certain troubadour manuscripts such as *A* and *B* or *I* and *K*, which may be regarded as two sets of twins (though not identical twins), each set derived from a common ancestor. Such affinities define what Avalle calls the *piani bassi*, or low levels in the stemma of the chansonniers. It is evident that there must have been manuscript sources of such twins which are no longer extant. Zufferey has reexamined the linguistic evidence for such sources and has arrived at plausible hypotheses of several manuscript traditions: one linking Auvergne and the Veneto, between which a movement of Occitan copyists and manuscripts produced chansonniers such as *D, A, I,* and *K;* another tradition linking Languedoc and Lombardy, which produced manuscripts *C* and *R;* and a third tradition in Provence. Zufferey has moved onto what Avalle called the *piani medi*, or middle levels of the textual history, and has done so with care and circumspection.[17]

---

16. It is true that we have a certain number of parchment rolls containing texts in other languages; such rolls seem to correspond to Gröber's hypothetical *Liederblätter*. They were inexpensive and ephemeral, and may have typically served as "the initial receptacle for new poems," as Rouse has argued (120). The Occitan word *role* was used for legal and fiscal documents, and in the epic *Roman de Fierabras* for the supposed ecclesiastical source, but not, to my knowledge, for the physical support of troubadour lyric. See also Avalle 83–84, and the study by Bäuml and Rouse of fragmentary rolls containing Middle High German lyric.

17. For reservations about Zufferey's geographical interpretations, however, see Leonardi.

Not so Avalle himself, who advanced boldly to the *piani alti*, the high levels, at which he proposed a single archetype for much of the Occitan lyric tradition, albeit subject to three traditions.[18] Not even Lachmann supposed that the tradition of every author returns to a unique archetype, but the great number of cases in which this seemed to be the case gradually produced the conviction among classicists that there must have been one archetype of every work (Timpanaro 227). However, even this strong claim falls short of Avalle's assertion of monogenesis of much of the troubadour corpus. Perhaps Avalle was led to make such a claim by the apparent danger that an admission of polygenesis might seem to imply a prior tradition of oral transmission—which would invalidate the claim of uninterrupted written transmission from the poet to us. If, as seems to be the case, the Lachmannian perspective implies, invites, or even requires a unique archetype, its systematic application to the Occitan lyric must be found untenable.

In the fiction of Arthur Conan Doyle, Sherlock Holmes had an older brother, Mycroft Holmes, whom he acknowledged as more gifted in deduction than himself. There is a scene in "The Greek Interpreter" in which the two brothers sit at a window of Mycroft's club observing traffic in the street while he performs prodigious feats of observation and deduction touching on the habits, careers, and private lives of passersby (Doyle 1:594). This entertaining fiction astonishes or flatters the reader with an image of human capacity to deduce hidden, detailed information from appearances. In contrast one may consider the *Warren Report*, which investigated the circumstances surrounding the assassination of John F. Kennedy. The commission found it impossible to determine either the precise number of shots that were fired or the assassin's motives (*Report* 22, 110–11). In reality, appearances are often more complicated than we wish them to be. As Aristotle remarks in the *Poetics*, it is the poet's task to describe "a kind of thing that might happen, i.e. what is possible as being probable or necessary," whereas the historian describes "the thing that has happened" (43). For me there is no doubt that a troubadour text established on Lachmannian principles, like an adventure of Sherlock Holmes, can be only a more or less plausible fiction.

Finally, one may speculate on the reason why Italian scholars tend to find the Lachmannian hypothesis persuasive, while French and other scholars tend not to (Meneghetti 1991, 168). I suspect that this is so because the assumptions necessary or helpful to the hypothesis—uninterrupted written tradition, closed recension, the long but well-known record of the past— find strong analogues in Italian culture, with its sense of secular continuity

---

18. Avalle 123–25; cf. Meneghetti 1991, 169.

since Aeneas and religious continuity since Saint Peter. In Italy written discourse has always flowed without interruption, and so it is natural for an Italian to suppose the same of a closely related culture such as that of the troubadours. This is not true to the same degree in French culture—Caesar may have marked the beginning of history in French schoolbooks, but he was certainly no Frenchman—much less in German, English, or American culture. In linguistic development, too, Italian has remained the most conservative of the major Romance languages, while French has been the most innovative. The strong continuity of literate culture in Italy made it natural to produce over half the troubadour manuscripts there, once the troubadours were accepted as part of the Italian literary heritage.[19] The Italian itinerary of the Occitan tradition also explains why so few songs have melodies, since in Italy the art of poetry had become separated from musical composition as early as Dante.[20] In contrast, the manuscripts of trouvère lyric in northern France, where poetry and music were associated throughout the fourteenth century by Guillaume de Machaut and his followers, provide a much higher proportion of melodies (about 75 percent).

This mildly Whorfian perspective suggests that it is natural for the Italians to accept Lachmann just because they are Italian, and for the French to reject him just because they are French—and for an American such as myself to reject him as well. To escape the limitations of such relativism we can only appeal to what we know about Occitan, which evolved from the status of an initially marginal, even defiant low language toward an increasing amalgamation with the broader concerns of the culture. As the sociolinguistic status of Occitan rose, its presence in the written medium expanded; the Lachmannian hypothesis thus gradually came to appear justified in retrospect, as though it were a newly adopted set of ancestral traditions or a newly gained title of ancient nobility. This is to say that the extant manuscripts are extant, and that they are manuscripts; that in all likelihood other manuscripts preceded them; but that we have good, though necessarily indirect,

19. Cf. Roncaglia in *Il canzoniere provenzale estense* (1:11–12): "La lirica dei trovatori costituisce infatti un passaggio obbligato e privilegiato a prender coscienza delle radici da cui è nata tutta la poesia occidentale moderna, delle matrici che hanno stampato un'impronta indelebile sui modi in cui l'uomo europeo ha atteggiato la propria vita sentimentale. In particolare per l'Italia, che con l'irradiazione del petrarchismo ha restituito all'Europa gli sviluppi più maturi dell'impostazione trovatoresca, si tratta d'un nodo storico nel quale non può non sentirsi vitalmente implicato chiunque si riconosca partecipe della nostra civiltà."

20. Cf. Pound (1968, 91): "Both in Greece and in Provence the poetry attained its highest rhythmic and metrical brilliance at times when the arts of verse and music were most closely knit together, when each thing done by the poet had some definite musical urge or necessity bound up within it. . . . It may be noted that the *canzon* of Provence became the *canzone* of Italy, and that when Dante and his contemporaries began to compose philosophic treatises in verse the *son* or accompaniment went maying on its own account, and in music became the sonata; and, from the date of the divorce, poetry declined."

reasons to doubt any uninterrupted, written, mechanical transmission of troubadour texts that began at the beginning.

In recent years the classical dialogue between followers of Lachmann and those of Bédier has been inflected into two distinctive new forms, the first of which is well developed by the present time, while the second remains embryonic. The first is predicated on the term and concept *mouvance,* coined by Paul Zumthor (1972, 65–72, 79, 507). Following in the wake of Lachmann, Zumthor considered the variants in vernacular texts in their relation to a unified text, but moved beyond Lachmann with his conviction that the frequency of variants is so great as to overwhelm the very assumption that they might realistically be called variants, that is, that they could be understood as marginal departures from a text assumed to underlie them in an essential, precise, form. Rather the variants seem to crowd about the text from which they supposedly vary in such numbers that the general principle of their generation, *mouvance,* comes to be seen as the normal process of textual transmission. This notion distinguishes the highly mobile vernacular text from authoritative, fixed or closed texts such as the Hebrew Old Testament, the Greek New Testament, and the Latin fathers of the Church. The open vernacular text, in contrast, invites innovation as part of the process of transmission.

The notion of *mouvance* was applied to troubadour lyric by Rupert T. Pickens in his important edition of Jaufre Rudel (1978). As Pickens explained, he undertook the project on the basis of essentially Lachmannian preconceptions, but found that the examination of variants gradually undermined his working principles. He arrived at the conclusion that the manuscript transmission of the seven songs did not permit reconstruction of authoritative original versions, and that therefore as editor he must adopt another format for the presentation of his materials. His solution was to present each song in as many distinctive versions as he found in the manuscripts. He did not abdicate entirely the editorial responsibility to reconstitute originals from differing attestations, since one version might reflect several manuscripts varying somewhat, but not essentially, from one to the other. But he did refuse to blend major textual variations among versions into one hypothetical original. Instead, on the basis of the versions of a given song—as many as nine—he proposed a skeletal Lachmannian original, including whatever specific elements (words, phrases, stanzas) he could confidently attribute to the point of departure, but refusing to commit himself where subsequent variation was too great. Having worked back from versions to the (incomplete, partial) original in his editorial process, he presented the results to his reader in the opposite order: the skeletal original followed by the various versions in the order of their differentiation from that first, authorial, but imperfectly known beginning. Pickens found the principal of *mouvance* asserted by the troubadour himself, since Jaufre Rudel could be understood to have invited subsequent performers to modify his compositions so as to improve them with increasing usage (1977).

Pickens's editorial policies have been greeted with widespread interest but have not been imitated. They may be criticized in three ways. First on pragmatic grounds, since they present the reader with a massive amount of information on each song. The works of Jaufre Rudel, which had been edited by Jeanroy in 38 pages, grew, in Pickens's treatment, to 281. An edition of one of the more prolific troubadours on these same principles might prove to be unpublishable, unpurchasable, unprintable, or simply impossible—and any of these alternatives could deprive the reader of access to a major body of work.[21]

Second, we must question the implication underlying the pragmatic difficulty: while the reader may find *mouvance* a phenomenon well worth study, he or she may not wish to plunge into it for every, or indeed any, troubadour song. The reader may wish to read a single text, in which case the editor is called upon to provide a transition between the medieval mode of existence of lyric song and a modern mode; and it is not obvious that the editor should deny the reader's right to such a transition, any more than that the editor should condemn the benevolent reader to return to the manuscripts and edit them again. An edition is and will be an instrument of communication; it must educate the reader to the original, convey the reader to the poetry, but it must also convey the poetry to the reader. An edition intrinsically does both these things. Pickens favors the former project over the latter. His *Jaufre Rudel* is of inestimable value for understanding *mouvance*, but *mouvance* is not the only reason to read the troubadours.

Third, the reader who is skeptical of Lachmannian principles in general may extend his or her doubts to their modified implementation by Pickens. In particular, one may doubt Pickens's reconstruction of the series of versions in increasing departure from the imperfectly known, but still firmly posited, original. For the skeptic it will come as no surprise that Pickens could not reconstruct the original with authority, since the skeptic never expected him to be able to do so in the first place. The skeptic may put in question Pickens's ability to reconstruct that series of increasingly independent versions, for reasons similar to those alleged above in discussion of Lachmann. Pickens's versions will then come to seem not genetically

21. For Van Vleck, Pickens's edition "offers a very desirable model for future editions of troubadour poetry," although she acknowledges that "such an edition is not practicable in every case" (205). Speer expresses concern over "the danger of alienating readers" (44). Rosenstein, citing errors of transcription in Pickens's edition, takes the view that every edition is a rewriting, every editor is a scribe, and every scribe is inevitably involved in prolonging medieval *mouvance*.

ordered by increasing departure from the author's original, as Pickens intends them, but descriptively ordered as variations on a pattern. They will not seem so different, essentially, from a mere series of manuscript versions. But we already possessed a series of manuscript versions before the editor took up his task.

Such a turn from the supposed authorial text toward its real attestations in tangible manuscripts on parchment or paper, a turn reminiscent of Bédier, has been advocated in a new guise by proponents of the recent American movement called the "New Philology."[22] Stephen G. Nichols has called for study of what he calls "the manuscript matrix," the mode of existence of the manuscript work, which he regards as essentially different from the existence of a work in print culture (1990, 1–10). He faults earlier philologists for treating works from manuscript culture as though they had been born in print, as when Auerbach insisted on a reading of Marcabru that required an essential hyphen. In this perspective *mouvance* is an undoubted truth, but the range of manuscript readings corresponding to a given textual moment becomes less interesting than the individual manuscript reading in relation to the rest of the same manuscript. Thus New Philology implies an interest in the detailed study of individual codices, in codicology, but an interest not restricted to positivist analysis; rather, the New Philology seeks to understand the manuscript matrix in terms of recent developments in literary theory such as Lacanian psychoanalysis. Nichols proposes that there need be no conflict between study of the text in its various manuscript instances and study of the manuscript, with all the texts it contains, aimed at understanding the conditions and processes inherent in the manuscript matrix (1994).

The New Philology has yet to produce editions of texts or manuscripts, but we may already ponder some of the implications of its program, which was anticipated, perhaps, in the anthology of troubadour poems published by the poet, mathematician, and linguist Jacques Roubaud in 1971. Roubaud announced the intention of transposing the disposition of his selections in manuscript *C*; each stanza therefore begins with a capital letter and runs as prose, interspersed with periods marking the end of verse lines. As the basis for an appreciation of the entire troubadour phenomenon, such semidiplomatic transcription of a single manuscript puts the modern reader in the position of an earlier one, perhaps an owner of manuscript *C*, too pressed for time to do more than browse. More recently Bernadette A. Masters has argued, in relation to Marie de France, that manuscript versions

22. The New Philology first attracted attention in the special issue of *Speculum* for January 1990, edited by Nichols; Nichols declared it a movement in "The New Medievalism: Tradition and Discontinuity in Medieval Culture" (1991). For further commentary, see Paden 1993.

are "more authentic, more 'medieval,' than editions"; that the icono-
graphic or traditional plastic arts of the Romanesque period, like the liturgy,
diminished any individual's claim to authority over a particular aesthetic
object; that the authority we have imputed to the original author was
accordingly shared, in the Middle Ages, by the scribe; and that therefore
"nothing less than diplomatic editions, with suggestions as to punctuation,
will do" for the needs of the present-day audience (285). The Hispanic
scholar John Dagenais, in a study of the fourteenth-century *Libro de buen
amor* (1994), refers to specific passages in the form of diplomatic transcriptions from the manuscripts that contain them, accompanied by an English
translation.

Diplomatic transcriptions are nothing new in troubadour studies, but
the favor accorded them by these scholars in preference to an edited text
certainly is. One may ask if the modern reader, put in the position of a
medieval one, has the means to understand the text as well as the earlier
reader did; one may ask, too, if the modern reader does not have greater
powers of understanding the effects of intervening literary and critical
traditions than the medieval, powers which this operation attemps to suppress. An edition may compensate for the modern reader's weaknesses by
offering informative material of many kinds, and it may attempt to capitalize on the reader's strengths by inviting an in-depth understanding of
the medieval text that will necessarily draw upon literary and critical resources of our day. None of these services is appropriate to a diplomatic
edition.

And yet, it is true that the fullest possible understanding of the medieval
artifact would be achieved through a direct contact with the manuscript—
the original, unique object—or, failing that, a high-quality facsimile, or,
failing that, a diplomatic edition. Such an understanding would liberate us
from the limitations of history, would expand our present to englobe the
past. We must grope for the most effective means to accomplish that expansion, that liberation.

EDITING

What, then, is an editor to do?

No doubt editors will continue to approach their task with varying assumptions about the transmission of the text. Some statement of these
assumptions, with reference to the grounds for entertaining them, should
be part of any edition that acknowledges the diversity of opinions among
its prospective readers. The editor's choice of methodology, as should be
apparent, will involve complex factors. Quite apart from the larger problem
of transmission, however, any editor confronts more ordinary tasks. Drawing

on personal experience and the opinions I have set forth, I shall conclude with some practical advice on how to deal with these tasks.[23]

First choose material to edit, primarily on grounds of its interest to you, while also considering the shortcomings of editions published already. Do not choose to edit material that strikes you as indifferent; though you un-doubtedly will learn to see more in it than you do at the beginning, extended study may turn your project into drudgery and you into a drudge. Know the text you plan to edit: if it is a lyric text it has already been edited, whether well or badly, accessibly or inaccessibly, and it would be inexcusable to ignore the work of your predecessor as you set about to improve upon it.

Next reconnoiter the field of combat. Determine all the editions that have been published already by consulting Pillet-Carstens for materials up to 1933, Frank's *Répertoire* to 1957, Chambers's *Proper Names* to 1971, Tay-lor's bibliography to 1977, and the *Year's Work in Modern Language Studies* to the present. You will also, of course, note studies on your subject. Set about to procure these published materials. If they are all available in your university library, be thankful; if not, use what you have and investigate avenues for getting what you do not. Exercise courtly blandishments upon your interlibrary loan officer. At this point you may already foresee the need to travel to European libraries and the need to find support for travel expenses from a benevolent sponsor.

You will now be ready to close upon the manuscripts, which you will do by consulting Pillet-Carstens in conjunction with published editions. Exactly which poems will you edit? If the canon of texts by your troubadour includes cases of conflicting attributions in the manuscripts—and even if earlier editors have set such cases aside—you are responsible for determining a policy of inclusion or exclusion from your edition on reasonable grounds. Perhaps some uncertain cases can be decided without going through the process of editing, or perhaps they cannot. Once you have set the contents of your edition, either definitively or tentatively, you must list all the manu-scripts containing your poems, along with the folios where they appear. Note that Pillet-Carstens's indications of folios, though indispensable, are im-perfect. Pillet-Carstens provides the number of the folio where a song begins, but gives no indication of where it ends; nor does Pillet-Carstens distinguish between recto and verso. In certain cases such as manuscript *N*, the old foliation has been revised for greater accuracy, and you must make use of the most recent reckoning; for manuscript *Z* in Barcelona, Pillet-Carstens provides only item numbers, and so on. Glean the best information

---

23. An application of the views expressed here may be found in the edition of Bertran de Born by Tilde Sankovitch, Patricia Harris Stäblein, and me. An excellent vade mecum for editors of Old French texts which should be familiar to any editor of Occitan is Foulet and Speer.

you can. Once you know what manuscripts will be involved, you must review what has been written about them. The most recent bibliography is provided by Zufferey, and it is very thorough; you should also check Avalle's index, and refer to Brunel, Jeanroy, and of course Pillet-Carstens (x–xxxv).

You have three ways of getting at the manuscripts. The diplomatic editions that have been published of a number of those in Italy and elsewhere (but of none at the Bibliothèque Nationale) are precious instruments to assist your own consultation of the original. They are listed by Zufferey; in some cases they include facsimiles. Of particular interest is the luxurious facsimile of manuscript *D*. The second way is by microfilm or photograph, available from the Institut de Recherche et d'Histoire des Textes, Paris (with its unpronounceable acronym IRHT)[24] or from individual libraries. The third way is by direct consultation. Although it is not always possible to consult every scattered manuscript, such as those in Berlin or Copenhagen, in person—and although the IRHT is dedicated to the proposition that photography has made direct consultation unnecessary—it remains desirable to see and handle, ever so gently, the codices. Photography provides a very high quality reproduction, but it cannot be perfect, and on occasion the original will provide readings in faint or faded ink, down the gutter or elsewhere, readings that have escaped the eye of the camera.[25]

You should transcribe every version of the text.[26] Your initial transcription should be diplomatic, preserving the appearance of the manuscript in regard to line divisions, abbreviations, and the like; after that you should make an interpretive transcription, with lines defined according to the metrical structure of the piece, abbreviations expanded (in italics), modern use of *u* or *v* and *i* or *j*, modern capitalization, and indication of numbers for stanzas and lines. Only by the rather laborious process of double transcription will you get an unambiguous record both of what the manuscript says and of what it means.

24. Write to the Institut de Recherche et d'Histoire des Textes (Section romane), 40 avenue d'Iéna, 75016 Paris. When requesting facsimiles, you must be totally explicit, and as exact as humanly possible; it is not useful to get the wrong folio, which obliges you to write again. For background on the IRHT, see the publications of Edith Brayer, Jean Glénisson with E. R. Labande, and J. Vielliard.

25. An estimate of the actual frequency of consultation of manuscript *D*, located somewhat off the beaten path in Modena, is possible because the Biblioteca Nazionale Estense has maintained an "Elenco dei lettori che hanno studiato il manoscritto" since 1886. In the century from that year until 1987, 207 consultations are listed, including several by scholars who have seen the manuscript more than once. Between 1912 and 1947 only a single consultation is recorded, by "Francois Chambers" (better known as Frank M.), on August 8–10, 1938. Before and after this period, the manuscript has been consulted on the average about three times a year.

26. If a diplomatic edition of your manuscript has been published, you should collate the original against it.

At this point you will be prepared to begin your edition proper. Determine the base manuscript for each text. The principal criterion in selection of a base must of course be the quality of the text; other factors that may come into consideration are homogeneity or diversity of base manuscripts throughout the edition, accessibility of individual manuscripts, the choice of base made by an earlier editor, and so on. If a given song is extant in versions that are so different as to constitute distinct works, you must decide whether to edit them all, as Pickens did in his edition of Jaufre Rudel, or to select a given version for inclusion and relegate others to the variants.

The heart of the editorial process is the treatment of the chosen base text. As editor you are responsible for reconstituting the poet's voice—you will "have men's hearts up from the dust" (Pound 1926, 151)—and you must not shirk that responsibility. Hence you are obliged to correct the manuscript whenever it fails to represent the poet as you yourself believe he spoke. The consensus holds that the troubadours made their poems rhyme; that is, there will be some recognizable rhyme-scheme which usually runs throughout the song or else varies in a comprehensible pattern. Normally the rhyme-sounds employed are perfect rhymes, distinguishing open and close *e* and *o*, front and back *a*, and so on. You must verify that the number of syllables in every line conforms with the stanzaic pattern of the song. If your base manuscript diverges from the apparent metrical structure of the piece, you must correct the base, drawing on the variant readings of other manuscripts to do so; or, if you cannot or will not correct it, point out the difficulty and explain your decision.[27]

More fundamental than metrical structure, but more delicate, is the language itself. Old Occitan was far from standardized, and the troubadour koiné accepted alternative forms in many graphic, phonological, and morphological functions. Do not impose a standardized language upon your helpless poet.[28] You must accept variations produced by the logic of the language, but not aberrations due to a scribe's carelessness or ignorance. To hew this difficult line, you must know all you can about the language of the troubadours. Zufferey's *Recherches linguistiques* is a mine of information. Consult Appel's *Chrestomathie* for a table of variant morphological forms in literary texts; if your manuscript offers something even stranger, consider the orthography of the charters as tabulated by Brunel. You must of course be a constant reader of the earlier editions of your poet, editions of other

---

27. The metrical form of every troubadour lyric was tabulated by Frank in his *Répertoire*. An invaluable discussion of every aspect of troubadour form is Chambers's *Introduction to Old Provençal Versification*; see also his essay in this volume (Chapter 4).

28. Like several reviewers, I remain unpersuaded by Zufferey's proposal of a standardized orthography, a "système décanté" (319); compare the reactions of Gouiran (294), Grafström (190), and Lamur-Baudreu (1987, 126).

troubadours (especially those with extensive glossaries), grammars, and all the dictionaries. If some surprising feature of your base manuscript (which was no doubt regularized by an earlier editor) can be paralleled in other passages or even in one other passage, there may be reason to believe it was a genuine feature of the language; and of course it may have been genuine even if it is unique in the surviving records.

Despite the Protean diversity of Occitan, as an editor you do have firm guidelines for your work. One of these concerns declension of substantives, at least in twelfth-century poets. Since Brunel found that the system of declension in two cases functioned without flaw in the twelfth-century charters, there is a strong presumption that any errors in declension in your (thirteenth- or fourteenth-century) manuscript are due to the scribe— especially if he was influenced by the Italian language, in which declension had already disappeared. During the thirteenth century, however, declension in Occitan became increasingly simplified, and the editor must be willing to follow along. Some statement of your policy should appear either in notes to particular passages or in your general statement of editorial procedures.

The final guideline is crystal clear. The troubadours must have made sense, and if your text does not make sense you are duty bound to correct it because you have not heard the poet's voice.[29] If the poet refers to historical events you must make sense of his reference, always reserving the possibility that his opinion, even of factual matters, differed from that of contemporary chroniclers. To sum it up, you should be alert to the need to correct your manuscript in regard to meter, language, or meaning.

The finished text must be presented to the reader in the most instructive and pleasurable way. You must provide a full translation, since the fluidity of Occitan will mask your understanding of the text without one. Provide variant readings according to some rational policy: the most satisfactory is perhaps to give all substantive variants, and to give them in their intrinsic order of divergence from your text. Annotate the text with care, but also with tact; do not indulge in annotation that is less than necessary for your reader, or that threatens to obscure the poetry. In the back matter be generous: provide your reader with all the information you can, in the glossary, tables, bibliography, and so on, reckoning that the needs he or she will bring to your edition may be different from yours. Finally, the front matter represents an opportunity for you to capitalize on all you will have learned about the poetry. Do not hasten to wrap up your edition once the editorial

29. Those of New Philological inclination may point out that manuscripts often contain passages of uncertain meaning, that such intermittences in communication are perfectly authentic. So they are, I say, but it is the editor's chosen duty to do everything possible to overcome them.

decisions are complete. You may never again know a text as well as you will upon completing your edition. Seize the moment to record your understanding and to deepen it further by writing the truest critical account of the poetry you can.

An edition represents an encounter with the text, which is a reading; and just as critical readings continually grow with the evolution of culture, so do editions. The activity of editing must continue to figure in the cultivation of troubadour lyric, even though this activity, which has never ceased since the earliest manuscripts, reached a new phase of intellectual seriousness with the first critical edition of a troubadour as early as 1857, in Bartsch's *Peire Vidal*, and has now produced an edition of every known troubadour lyric text.[30] As surely as we must continue to read, we must continue to edit. For only by editing anew do we gain the experience of direct contact—or the nearest approach to direct contact that is possible today—with the source of the text that interests us. In an impressive number of recent and imminent publications, scholars have returned to the manuscript sources in order to reexamine troubadour lyric in textual, linguistic, critical, and artistic perspectives. You must maintain the momentum of these investigations to assure the continued vitality of troubadour studies.

APPENDIX: SIGLA OF TROUBADOUR MANUSCRIPTS

The following sigla correspond to those in Zufferey, *Recherches linguistiques* 4–6 (omitting fragments), with a few corrections, and with indications of different sigla in Pillet-Carstens.

A: Rome, Biblioteca Apostolica Vaticana, latini 5232.
B: Paris, Bibliothèque Nationale, fonds français 1592.
C: Paris, Bibliothèque Nationale, fonds français 856.
D: Modena, Biblioteca Nazionale Estense, Estero 45 (Alpha R.4.4).
E: Paris, Bibliothèque Nationale, fonds français 1749.
F: Rome, Biblioteca Apostolica Vaticana, Chigiani L.IV.106.
G: Milan, Biblioteca Ambrosiana, R 71 superiore.
H: Rome, Biblioteca Apostolica Vaticana, latini 3207.
I: Paris, Bibliothèque Nationale, fonds français 854.
J: Florence, Biblioteca Nazionale Centrale, Conventi soppressi F.IV.776.
K: Paris, Bibliothèque Nationale, fonds français 12473.
Kp (Pillet-Carstens): see *Y.*
L: Rome, Biblioteca Apostolica Vaticana, latini 3206.
M: Paris, Bibliothèque Nationale, fonds français 12474.
N: New York, Pierpont Morgan Library, 819.
N² (Pillet-Carstens): see *d.*
O: Rome, Biblioteca Apostolica Vaticana, latini 3208.

---

30. As was first claimed by Frank 1950, and then again by Bond. Their claims are belied by the continuing discovery of new fragments or manuscripts.

P: Florence, Biblioteca Medicea Laurenziana, Plut. 41.42.

Q: Florence, Biblioteca Riccardiana, 2909.

R: Paris, Bibliothèque Nationale, fonds français 22543.

S: Oxford, Bodleian Library, Douce 269.

Sg (Pillet-Carstens): see *Z.*

T: Paris, Bibliothèque Nationale, fonds français 15211.

U: Florence, Biblioteca Medicea Laurenziana, Plut. 41.43.

V: Venice, Biblioteca Nazionale Marciana, 278 (fr. App. cod. XI).

Y: Copenhagen, Kongelige Bibliotek, Thott 1087 (Pillet-Carstens *Kp*).

Z: Barcelona, Biblioteca de Cataluña, 146 (Pillet-Carstens *Sg*).

a: The lost manuscript compiled by Bernart Amoros, represented by the following copies:

> Pillet-Carstens *a:* Florence, Biblioteca Riccardiana, 2814;

> Pillet-Carstens *a¹:* Modena, Biblioteca Nazionale Estense, Càmpori Appendice 426, 427, 494 (formerly Gamma.N.8.4.11–13).

b: The lost manuscript compiled by Miquel de la Tor, represented by the following copies:

> Pillet-Carstens *b:* Rome, Biblioteca Apostolica Vaticana, Barberiniani 4087;

> Pillet-Carstens *e:* Rome, Biblioteca Apostolica Vaticana, Barberiniani 3965.

c: Florence, Biblioteca Medicea Laurenziana, Plut. XC inferiore 26.

d: Berlin, Staatsbibliothek, Phillipps 1910 (Pillet-Carstens N^2; Pillet-Carstens *d* is merely a copy from *K,* and may be disregarded [Zufferey 7–8]).

e: Rome, Biblioteca Apostolica Vaticana, latini 7182 (no siglum in Pillet-Carstens; for Pillet-Carstens *e,* see under *b*).

f: Paris, Bibliothèque Nationale, fonds français 12472.

WORKS CITED

Allegri, Laura. "Frammento di antico florilegio provenzale." *Studi Medievali,* 3d ser., 27 (1986): 319–51.

Anglade, Joseph. "Les Miniatures des chansonniers provençaux." *Romania* 50 (1924): 593–604.

Appel, Carl, ed. *Provenzalische Chrestomathie mit Abriss der Formenlehre und Glossar.* 6th ed. Leipzig: Reisland, 1930; repr. Hildesheim: Olms, 1971.

Aristotle. *On the Art of Poetry.* Trans. Ingram Bywater. Oxford: Clarendon Press, 1920.

Avalle, D'Arco Silvio. *La letteratura medievale in lingua d'oc nella sua tradizione manoscritta: problemi di critica testuale.* Torino: Einaudi, 1961.

Bartsch, Karl, ed. *Peire Vidal's Lieder.* Berlin: Dümmler, 1857.

———, ed. *Grundriss zur Geschichte der provenzalischen Literatur.* Elberfeld: Friderichs, 1872.

Bäuml, Franz H., and Richard H. Rouse. "Roll and Codex: A New Manuscript Fragment of Reinmar von Zweter." *Beiträge zur Geschichte der deutschen Sprache und Literatur* (Tübingen) 105 (1983): 193–231, 317–30.

Bech, Fedor, ed. "Regulae de modo scindendi pennarum." *Zeitschrift für deutsche Philologie* 8 (1877): 348.

Bédier, Joseph. "La Tradition manuscrite du *Lai de l'ombre:* Réflexions sur l'art d'éditer les anciens textes." *Romania* 54 (1928): 161–96, 321–56.

Bertoni, Giulio. "Il complemento del canzoniere provenzale di Bernart Amoros." *Giornale storico della letteratura italiana* 34 (1899): 118–39.

Bologna, Corrado. "Giulio Camillo, il canzoniere provenzale N^2 e un inedito commento al Petrarca." *Cultura Neolatina* 47 (1987): 71–97.

Bond, Gerald A. "The Last Unpublished Troubadour Songs." *Speculum* 60 (1985): 827–49.

Brayer, Edith. "Section d'ancien français et d'ancien provençal." *Bulletin d'information de l'Institut de recherche et d'histoire des textes* 1 (1952): 10–22; 2 (1953): 44–64.

———. "Une filmothèque de la poésie lyrique médiévale." In *Mélanges de linguistique et de littérature romanes à la mémoire d'István Frank*, 75–86. Saarbrücken: Universität des Saarlandes, 1957.

Brownlee, Marina S., Kevin Brownlee, and Stephen G. Nichols, eds. *The New Medievalism.* Baltimore: Johns Hopkins University Press, 1991.

Brunel, Clovis. "Le Plus Ancien Acte original en langue provençale." *Annales du Midi* 33–34 (1921–22): 249–61.

———. "Les Premiers Exemples de l'emploi du provençal dans les chartes." *Romania* 48 (1922): 335–64.

———. *Bibliographie des manuscrits littéraires en ancien provençal.* Paris: Droz, 1935.

———, ed. *Les Plus Anciennes Chartes en langue provençale: recueil des pièces originales antérieures au XIIIe siècle.* Paris: Picard, 1926. *Supplément*, 1952.

Brunetti, Giuseppina D. B. "Sul canzoniere provenzale T (Parigi, Bibl. Nat. F. fr. 15211)." *Cultura Neolatina* 50 (1990): 45–73.

———. "Per la storia del manoscritto provenzale T." *Cultura Neolatina* 51 (1991): 27–41.

Il canzoniere provenzale estense, riprodotto per il centenario della nascita di Giulio Bertoni. "Presentazione" by Aurelio Roncaglia, "Introduzione" by D'Arco Silvio Avalle and Emanuele Casamassima. 2 vols. Modena: STEM Mucchi, 1979–82.

Careri, Maria. "Sul canzoniere provenzale H (Vat. Lat. 1207)." In *Actes du 18e Congrès International de Linguistique et de Philologie Romanes*, ed. Dieter Kremer, 6:100–107. Tübingen: Niemeyer, 1988.

———. "I sirventesi di Guillem Durfort de Caors in un apografo sconosciuto del 'Libre di Miquel de la Tor.'" *Vox romanica* 48 (1989): 77–84.

———. *Il canzoniere provenzale H (Vat. Lat. 3207): struttura, contenuto e fonti.* Modena: Mucchi, 1991.

Chabaneau, Camille. "Sur quelques manuscrits provençaux perdus ou égarés." *Revue des langues romanes* 21 (1882): 209–17; 23 (1883): 5–22, 70–80, 115–29; 26 (1884): 209–18; 27 (1885): 43–46; 28 (1885): 72–80.

Chambers, Frank M. *Proper Names in the Lyrics of the Troubadours.* Chapel Hill: University of North Carolina Press, 1971.

———. *An Introduction to Old Provençal Versification.* Philadelphia: American Philosophical Society, 1985.

Cipolla, Carlo M. *Literacy and Development in the West.* Harmondsworth, Eng.: Penguin Books, 1969.

Colophons des manuscrits occidentaux des origines au XVIe siècle. Ed. Bénédictins du Bouveret. 6 vols. Fribourg: Editions Universitaires, 1965–82.

Crescini, V. "Del canzoniere provenzale *V* (Marc. App. XI)." *Atti della R. Accademia dei Lincei,* ser. 4: *Rendiconti* 6, no. 2 (1890): 39–49.

Dagenais, John. *The Ethics of Reading in Manuscript Culture: Glossing the "Libro de Buen Amor."* Princeton: Princeton University Press, 1994.

Doyle, Arthur Conan. *The Annotated Sherlock Holmes.* Ed. William S. Baring-Gould. 2 vols. New York: Potter, 1967.

Foulet, Alfred, and Mary Blakely Speer. *On Editing Old French Texts.* Lawrence: Regents Press of Kansas, 1979.

Frank, István. "Ce qui reste d'inédit de l'ancienne poésie lyrique provençale." *Boletín de la Real Academia de Buenas Letras de Barcelona* 23 (1950): 69–81.

———. *Répertoire métrique de la poésie des troubadours.* 2 vols. Paris: Champion, 1953–57.

———. "De l'art d'éditer les textes lyriques." In *Recueil de travaux offert à M. Clovis Brunel,* 1:463–75. Paris: Société de l'Ecole des Chartes, 1955. Translated as "The Art of Editing Lyric Texts." In *Medieval Manuscripts and Textual Criticism,* ed. Christopher Kleinhenz, 123–38. Chapel Hill: University of North Carolina Press, 1976.

Gasca-Queirazza, Giuliano. "Un nouveau fragment de chansonnier provençal." *Marche Romane* 33 (1983): 93–99.

Gennrich, Friedrich. "Die Repertoire-Theorie." *Zeitschrift für französische Sprache und Literatur* 66 (1956): 81–108.

Glénisson, Jean, with E. R. Labande. "Formation et destin de l'Institut de Recherche et d'Histoire des Textes." *Cahiers de Civilisation Médiévale* 15 (1972): 53–60.

Gouiran, G. Review of *Recherches linguistiques sur les chansonniers provençaux,* by François Zufferey. *Revue de linguistique romane* 52 (1988): 290–94.

Grafström, Åke. Review of *Recherches linguistiques sur les chansonniers provençaux,* by François Zufferey. *Zeitschrift für romanische Philologie* 106 (1990): 182–90.

Gröber, Gustav. "Die Liedersammlungen der Troubadours." *Romanische Studien* 2 (1875–77): 337–670.

Huot, Sylvia. "Visualization and Memory: The Illustration of Troubadour Lyric in a Thirteenth-Century Manuscript." *Gesta* 31 (1992): 3–14.

Jeanroy, Alfred. *Bibliographie sommaire des chansonniers provençaux.* Classiques Français du Moyen Age, 16. Paris: Champion, 1916.

———, ed. *Les Chansons de Jaufré Rudel.* Classiques Français du Moyen Age, 15. Paris: Champion, 1915; 2d ed., rev., 1924.

Lamur-Baudreu, Anne-Claude. Review of *Recherches linguistiques sur les chansonniers provençaux,* by François Zufferey. *Romania* 108 (1987): 121–26.

———. "Aux origines du chansonnier de troubadours *M* (Paris: Bibl. Nat., fr. 12474)." *Romania* 109 (1988): 183–98.

Lazzerini, Lucia. "Nuova interpretazione dell'alba bilingue." *Studi Medievali* 20 (1979): 138–84.

———. "Nuove osservazioni sull'alba bilingue." *Medioevo Romanzo* 10 (1985): 19–35.

Leonardi, Lino. "Problemi de stratigrafia occitanica: a proposito delle *Recherches* di François Zufferey." *Romania* 108 (1987): 354–86.

Marshall, J. H. *The Transmission of Troubadour Poetry: An Inaugural Lecture Delivered at Westfield College, 5th March, 1975.* N.p.: n.p., n.d.

Masters, Bernadette A. "The Distribution, Destruction, and Dislocation of Authority in Medieval Literature and Its Modern Derivatives." *Romanic Review* 82 (1991): 270–85.

Meneghetti, Maria Luisa. *Il pubblico dei trovatori: ricezione e riuso dei testi lirici cortesi fino al XIV secolo.* Modena: Mucchi, 1984.

———. "De l'art d'éditer Jaufré Rudel." *Cahiers de Civilisation Médiévale* 34 (1991): 167–75.

Nichols, Stephen G. "Introduction: Philology in a Manuscript Culture." In *The New Philology*, ed. Stephen G. Nichols, 1–10. Special issue of *Speculum* 65, no. 1 (1990).

———. "The New Medievalism: Tradition and Discontinuity in Medieval Culture." In *The New Medievalism*, ed. Marina S. Brownlee, Kevin Brownlee, and Stephen G. Nichols, 1–26. Baltimore: Johns Hopkins University Press, 1991.

———. "Philology and Its Discontents." In *The Future of the Middle Ages: Medieval Literature in the 1990s*, ed. William D. Paden, 113–41. Gainesville: University Press of Florida, 1994.

Paden, William D. "Europe from Latin to Vernacular in Epic, Lyric, Romance." In *Performance of Literature in Historical Perspectives*, ed. David W. Thompson, 67–105. Lanham, Md.: University Press of America, 1983.

———. "The Role of the Joglar in Troubadour Lyric Poetry." In *Chrétien de Troyes and the Troubadours: Essays in Memory of the Late Leslie Topsfield*, ed. Peter S. Noble and Linda M. Paterson, 90–111. Cambridge: St. Catharine's College, 1984.

———, ed. *The Voice of the Trobairitz: Perspectives on the Women Troubadours.* Philadelphia: University of Pennsylvania Press, 1989.

———. "Is There a Middle in This Road? Reflections on the New Philology." In *Towards a Synthesis? Essays on the New Philology*, ed. Keith Busby, 119–30. Amsterdam: Rodopi, 1993.

Paden, William D., Tilde Sankovitch, and Patricia H. Stäblein, eds. *The Poems of the Troubadour Bertran de Born.* Berkeley and Los Angeles: University of California Press, 1986.

Pasquali, Giorgio. *Storia della tradizione e critica del testo.* 2d ed. Firenze: Le Monnier, 1952.

Pickens, Rupert T. "Jaufre Rudel et la poétique de la mouvance." *Cahiers de Civilisation Médiévale* 20 (1977): 323–37.

———, ed. *The Songs of Jaufré Rudel.* Toronto: Pontifical Institute of Medieval Studies, 1978.

Pillet, Alfred, and Henry Carstens, eds. *Bibliographie der Troubadours.* Halle: Niemeyer, 1933.

Pirot, François. "Sur quelques chansonniers provençaux perdus ou égarés." In *Mélanges de philologie romane dédiés à la mémoire de Jean Boutière*, ed. Irénée Cluzel and François Pirot, 1:466–80. Liège: Soledi, 1971.

Poe, Elizabeth Wilson. "The Lighter Side of the *Alba: Ab la genser que sia.*" *Romanistisches Jahrbuch* 36 (1985): 87–103.

Pound, Ezra. *Personae*. New York: New Directions, 1926.

———. "The Tradition." In *Literary Essays of Ezra Pound*, ed. T. S. Eliot, 91–93. New York: New Directions, 1968.

Quentin, Henri. *Essais de critique textuelle (ecdotique)*. Paris: Picard, 1926.

Report of the President's Commission on the Assassination of President John F. Kennedy. Washington, D.C.: Government Printing Office, 1964.

Rieger, Angelica. " 'Ins e·l cor port, dona, vostra faisso': image et imaginaire de la femme à travers l'enluminure dans les chansonniers des troubadours." *Cahiers de Civilisation Médiévale* 28 (1985): 385–415.

Riquer, Martín de, ed. *Los trovadores: historia literaria y textos*. 3 vols. Barcelona: Planeta, 1975.

Rosenstein, Roy. "*Mouvance* and the Editor as Scribe: *Trascrittore Tradittore?*" *Romanic Review* 80 (1989): 157–71.

Roubaud, Jacques, ed. *Les Troubadours: anthologie bilingue*. Paris: Seghers, 1971.

Rouse, Richard H. "Roll and Codex: The Transmission of the Works of Reinmar von Zweter." *Münchener Beiträge zur Mediävistik und Renaissance-Forschung* 32 (1982): 107–23.

Speer, Mary B. "Textual Criticism Redivivus." *L'Esprit Créateur* 23, no. 1 (Spring 1983): 38–48.

Stiennon, Jacques, with Geneviève Hasenohr. *Paléographie du moyen âge*. Paris: Armand Colin, 1973.

Switten, Margaret, et al. *The Medieval Lyric, Anthology I: Monastic Song, Troubadour Song, German Song, Trouvère Song*. Rev. ed. South Hadley, Mass.: Mount Holyoke College, 1988.

Tavera, Antoine. "Le Chansonnier d'Urfé et les problèmes qu'il posc." *Cultura Neolatina* 38 (1978): 233–50.

Taylor, Robert A. *La Littérature occitane du moyen âge: Bibliographie sélective et critique*. Toronto: University of Toronto Press, 1977.

Timpanaro, Sebastiano, Jr. "La genesi del 'metodo di Lachmann.' " *Studi italiani di filologia classica* 31 (1959): 182–228; 32 (1960): 38–63. Revised and expanded under the same title. Firenze: Le Monnier, 1963.

van der Werf, Hendrik. *The Chansons of the Troubadours and Trouvères: A Study of the Melodies and Their Relation to the Poems*. Utrecht: Oosthoek, 1972.

Van Vleck, Amelia E. *Memory and Re-Creation in Troubadour Lyric*. Berkeley and Los Angeles: University of California Press, 1991.

Vielliard, J. "L'Institut de Recherche et d'Histoire des Textes de Paris." *Anuario de estudios medievales* (Barcelona) 2 (1965): 597–603.

Wattenbach, W. *Das Schriftwesen im Mittelalter*. 3d ed. Leipzig: Hirzel, 1896.

Woledge, Brian, and Ian Short. "Liste provisoire de manuscrits du XIIe siècle contenant des textes en langue française." *Romania* 102 (1981): 1–17.

Zufferey, François. *Recherches linguistiques sur les chansonniers provençaux*. Publications romanes et françaises, 176. Paris: Droz, 1987.

Zumthor, Paul. *Essai de poétique médiévale*. Paris: Seuil, 1972.

———. "Un trompe-l'oeil linguistique? Le refrain de l'aube bilingue de Fleury." *Romania* 105 (1984): 171–92.

SIXTEEN

Translation

Roy S. Rosenstein

The translation of poetry is so difficult and thankless a task that no one, unless he greatly loves and admires a poem, will think of attempting it.

(AUDEN 5)

Whether in general anthologies or critical editions, troubadour texts as published in our century are almost invariably accompanied by facing verse or following prose translations.[1] The troubadours have been presented in this dual-language format many times and in almost as many languages, far more often than the trouvères or the Minnesänger, for example.

Bilingual editions are standard practice for two major reasons. Like Old French or Middle High German, Old Occitan is no one's native language. Indeed, it is frequently maintained that this was a koiné, an artificial, literary language, even for all or most of the poets who composed in it and the scribes who copied its literature. Today a reading knowledge of the other principal medieval languages can be readily developed by anyone who has already mastered their modern descendants. By contrast, comparatively few people know contemporary Occitan well; fewer still have studied the language of earlier periods in its long history. An informal and conservative estimate suggests that today only some 200–300 scholars read Old Occitan with ease (Caluwé vii). Any translation thus provides greater visibility among a wider audience. Still, the language barrier is not the only reason troubadour lyrics are translated; some would maintain that it is not even the chief one.

The other reason is literary in nature. Even those learnèd, happy few who know Occitan find the poetry of the troubadours to be difficult of access. Several studies see ambiguity as central to troubadour lyric, or as a value generally in medieval literature (Paden, Ferrante, Duggan). Old Occitan

---

1. A rare exception is the collection published by the Centre d'Etudes Occitanes and providing texts exclusively in Occitan for students of that language (Lafont 1972). One of the comparative anthologies presumes easy reading knowledge of medieval Latin, Occitan, French, Castilian, Galician-Portuguese, and Italian (Brittain).

can be remarkably succinct and synthetic, as recently renewed attention to its proverbial expressions has reminded us (Goddard). In vocabulary Occitan may seem deceptively simple (e.g., *joi*: Cropp 334; cf. Dembowski), and in syntax it is often immediately obscure (see Skårup on Jaufre Rudel, the single most studied troubadour). Reference is frequently unclear, both grammatically and contextually. The so-called clear style of *trobar leu* may still require a translation; even seasoned French medievalists can and do make serious gaffes in Occitan.[2] Robert Lafont, the dean of Occitan poets and critics, has warned of this chiaroscuro effect: "La poésie dite claire n'est pas moins obscure souvent (telle chanson de Jaufre Rudel . . .) que celle qui se proclame verrouillée" (Poetry said to be limpid [a Jaufre Rudel song for example . . .] is often no less obscure than that which asserts its hermeticism; 1963, 163). Consequently, a troubadour translation is also a practical exercise in applied hermeneutics. Aristotle had already said as much about all translating (Richards 111).

For reasons of both access and interpretation, then, troubadour texts are most often presented in bilingual format. Whether in tandem with the originals or published independently, translations of the troubadours are most numerous in English and French, but they are also available in many other languages (e.g., Czech, Černý; Norwegian, Gundelach; Romanian, Boşca). Even Catalan and contemporary Occitan, the two modern languages closest to that of the troubadours, are well served by translations (Serra-Baldó, Moreno, Badia; Cordes 1975). In this short essay I will examine selected English, French, and modern Occitan translations.

The most influential nonacademic translators of Old Occitan into English have been two American poets, Ezra Pound (1885–1972) and Paul Blackburn (1926–71), both of whom studied Occitan with renowned troubadour specialists. Pound began at Hamilton College under W. P. Shepard (whose troubadour library is still preserved there) and continued at the University of Pennsylvania. Blackburn studied at the University of Toulouse under Jean Seguy and René Nelli, but he acknowledged that it was Pound's translations that had inspired him (Apter). Among French translators, it is largely the Occitan poets and troubadour scholars Nelli, André Berry, Robert Lafont, and Pierre Bec who have themselves popularized the troubadours through their studies in and translations into French. Most recently, a French mathematician, poet, and critic, Jacques Roubaud, has done much to make troubadour lyric accessible in French through two collective vol-

---

2. A much-respected scholar once wrote of Arnaut Daniel's "Jauzirai joi en vergier ou dins cambra" that "*Joi* est ici le pronom personnel" (Payen 43). Of course, the precise meaning of the key term *joi* 'joy' has been much debated; but Payen was likely alone in thinking that it could ever compete with *ieu* as a reflex of EGO in this common *figura etymologica* (of the PUGNARE PUGNAM type), or anywhere else. "Paiens ad tort," as the *Song of Roland* might have said.

umes of free translations, a bilingual anthology of his own, and a critical study.

The great diversity of poetic and academic translations invites more subtle categorization than the preliminary distinctions between literary and literal, free and close, or verse and prose might permit. We may further distinguish between word-for-word and literal translations, and between free and poetic ones; suggest a few possible distinctions between translation, adaptation, recreation, imitation, and transposition; and ultimately consider briefly their different purposes, varying audiences, and relative successes.

Despite the importance and variety of academic and popular translations of the troubadours, to date little attention has been given to the problems they raise, and comparative translation studies remain scarce (Tomlinson xvii). This lack is readily if only incompletely explained. With the exception of the literary versions mentioned above, translations—especially in a bilingual format—are often intended as intermediaries providing access to difficult texts written in an unfamiliar language. Where studies of troubadour translations do exist, they are usually either *ad hominem* critiques of a poet-translator as scholar or of a scholar-translator as poet (Schutz, Economou, Riggs) or *pro domo* apologias by these translators themselves (Cordes 1978; Bec; Hutchinson 1987, 1990).

For our purposes it should be helpful to compare several medieval and modern translations of the single best known troubadour lyric. Jaufre Rudel's "Lancan li jorn," his famous song of distant love, has been copied, cited, anthologized, and translated repeatedly since the thirteenth century (Gauchat; Raupach and Raupach 96). Similar comparative translation exercises have proven useful in examining representative passages from the *Song of Roland* and *The Odyssey* through the mirrors of their multiple English versions (Cook, Borges).

Given below is the first stanza of the original Occitan song from manuscript *B* as reproduced in the most comprehensive edition (Pickens 164; a typographical error at line 1 is corrected). This is the same base manuscript used in the fundamental critical edition and study of this song (Lejeune 416; her punctuation and word division differ slightly).

> Lan qand li jorn son lonc en mai,
> M'es bels douz chans d'auzels de loing,
> E qand me sui partitz de lai
> Remembra·m d'un'amor de loing.
> Vauc de talan enbroncs e clis
> Si que chans ni flors d'albespis
> No·m platz plus que l'inverns gelatz.
>
> (P-C 262,2)

On most levels, this stanza seems quite limpid in both language and meaning. Certainly none of the critical editions draws attention to a *crux desperationis* in its seven lines. Yet translations from the thirteenth to the twentieth century are distinctly at variance with one another, highlighting differences of interpretation and difficulties of translation. Like the poet, a translator must make choices at every step, so that each new translation is also a new reading. But while there is usually a single textual reading (*leçon*) in each medieval manuscript or modern text, multiple interpretive readings (*lectures*) are always possible in the translations. We will successively look at word-for-word gloss (Jean Renart), metaphrase or literal version (Rupert Pickens), close translation (Margaret Switten), free translation (Sally Purcell), verse translation (Barbara Smythe), paraphrase or literary version (Paul Blackburn), poetic imitation (Ezra Pound), and poetic re-creation (Léon Cordes).

An early French version of this stanza that was incorporated into Jean Renart's *Roman de la Rose ou de Guillaume de Dole* (1228) is given below (significantly normalized text from Lecoy 41; Gégou 321–22). Based on the only surviving manuscript of the romance (MS ε), it can be compared to the gallicized Occitan versions in the two French manuscripts (*W* and *X*) that are given by Pickens (Pickens 206, 210); more conservative transcriptions of all three manuscripts, with facsimiles of *W* and *X*, are also now available (Wolf and Rosenstein 165–67, 189, 193).

> Lors que li jor son lonc en mai,
> m'est biaus doz chant d'oisel de lonc.
> Et quant me sui partiz de la,
> menbre mi d'une amor de lonc.
> Vois de ça embruns et enclins
> si que chans ne flors d'aubespin
> ne mi val ne qu'ivers gelas.

Jean Renart, perhaps the most famous writer of medieval French romances after Chrestien de Troyes, here provides a decidedly French version ("Lors que") within a longer French text, not just an Occitan text with gallicisms as in the songbooks *W* and *X* ("Lan que" and "Lan qant"). His French deliberately relies on cognates, straying farther from the original only when an immediate calque is not possible. On the positive side, his French gloss preserves meter and some effective devices by rigidly seeking cognates. It maintains the stanza-initial alliteration of *Lan can* in "Lors que" and the echoing *mot-refrain loing* in "lonc," which in French further collapses the Occitan original's paronomastic *lonc* 'long' and *loing* 'far'. These are the fruits of chance good fortune in this word-by-word, line-by-line attempt at carbon copying in French an Occitan original.

However, when an obvious French calque is not available for *talan* 'desire', Renart is evidently at a loss and the word is omitted in the gloss. "Gelas" may seem to transcribe *gelatz*, but it is an unfamiliar occitanism, not an acceptable standard French lexeme. This *hapax legomenon* (attested nowhere else) was likely forged by the would-be translator. Because Old Occitan was probably not fully accessible even to this medieval Frenchman, he limped from word to word—until he ran into a wall, which he plastered up as best he could. In order to translate terms that he perhaps did not know and that had no obvious parallels in Old French, he imagined equivalents. Rupert Pickens is right to include in his edition the closer-to-Occitan transcriptions in manuscripts *W* and *X* despite their gallicisms and to exclude this would-be French translation that is not entirely French (cf. Zufferey 281n). Worse, like any other word-for-word trot, Jean Renart's version banalizes by cavalierly ignoring larger concerns, like word groups and suprasegmental units.

One further note is in order on this so-called French translation. "Val" in the last line is not even the one creative innovation in this unimaginative and imperfect rendering. Instead of the expected Old French "plaist" for *platz*, "val" simply reflects the variant *val* in the song's manuscript tradition. Most manuscripts give *val* where only a few give the *dificilior* and more natural Occitan *platz*. Jean Renart evidently knew a version from some manuscript other than *B* (*pace* Gégou 322). To avoid potential confusion in presenting a translation, whether the original accompanies it or not, a translator must always take special care to make clear what manuscript's text is translated.[3]

Even as concerns *val*, then, the word-for-word translation remains extremely conservative, when it does not break down because of complicated syntax or the unavailability of an immediate calque.

Old Occitan and Old French are of course closely related languages, yet only a very few poets have succeeded in composing well in both (see Brugnolo). Other Romance or non-Romance target languages will force more and more complicated interpretive decisions on the translator. One editor translates literally the base manuscript *B* as follows (Pickens 165). For convenient comparison, his word-for-word prose is here presented as if it were verse:

> When the days are long in May
> I like a sweet song of birds from afar,
> And when I have gone away from there

3. One bilingual anthology sometimes gives an Occitan text from one manuscript opposite a translation based on a slightly different version from a second manuscript, much to the justified frustration of readers who attempt to compare the English translation and the supposed Occitan original.

I am reminded of a love from afar;
I go bent and bowed with desire,
So that song nor hawthorn flower
Pleases me more than frozen winter.

Pickens is quite aware that as a *fidèle* transposition into a noncognate language this one is far from *belle*. Like the French *mot-à-mot*, it aims at word-for word equivalents. Any one-to-one correspondence, however, sometimes imposes an inelegant and only marginally standard contemporary English (line 6, for example, requires a "neither"). Consequently, the translation may be accurate but not particularly felicitous. And while it shares the defects of the French gloss above, its English cannot offer the number of easy cognates that bolstered the French attempt to replicate the original. To a person who cannot also read the Occitan, it would not begin to suggest why this or any such text could have so distinguished a reputation. Since the intention is to assist specialists who can and will read the original, this version is fine. But if the translation were for those who read only the English, there would be a serious problem.

The issue is addressed well by the editor-translator, who notes that his renderings are no literary masterpieces but rather literal keys to the originals, intended to elucidate all meanings and ambiguities without resolving them (Pickens 43). But as this example already anticipates, the same method, if not controlled or if pushed to a myopic extreme, could lead to an unreadable word-for-word gloss that would dangerously approximate gibberish. Any concerted effort to calque a source text can lead to an embarrassingly heavy-handed literal-mindedness, which in turn gives fewer and fewer clues about the original's global meaning. Kolsen's German translations of Guiraut de Bornelh sometimes suffer from just this malady. Happily, Ruth Sharman's new edition with idiomatic English renderings promises to supersede Kolsen's outdated texts and translations at long last.

Another working translation of the text of manuscript *B* is that by Margaret Switten. Designed for classroom use only, and until now unpublished, it is faithful but also direct, eschewing woodenness or artificiality. More than a pedagogical tool for study of the facing original, it succeeds independently in maintaining and communicating the song's atmosphere of enchantment. In text and translation, the repeated key phrase *de loing* 'from afar' expresses the inexpressible. In so doing this version illuminates the ambiguity of a central concept (distance on temporal, spatial, spiritual, and psychological planes), where a more opaque translation might only have added impenetrability to an already difficult original.

When the days are long in May,
I like the sweet song of birds from afar,
And when I have departed from there,

> I remember a love from afar:
> I go sad and bowed with desire
> So that songs or hawthorn flowers
> Please me no more than icy winter.

As always, a genuine translation represents a series of choices. Here the translator has wisely chosen to go beyond the literal and the obvious. The punctuation is interpretive, suggesting with a colon some of the logical links in a series of paratactic phrases. For *gelatz*, "icy" is an excellent choice over the literal "frosty" or the weaker "frozen." Though differing in number from the original's singular *chans ni flors*, the appropriate idiomatic plural "songs or hawthorn flowers" corresponds to standard contemporary English usage. For these reasons, even in translation the stanza makes a uniformly strong beginning to a lyric whose subsequent Occitan strophes vary widely in the manuscripts as a function of different word choice and different stanzaic orders.

Still, this translation is not the work of a poet, nor is it intended to be, in an academic context that focuses on the Occitan text. Faithfulness to the original imposes a certain neutrality or even flatness in the diction: "I go sad." Some of the poetic effects of the original, such as the frequent nasalized vowels, are inevitably missed. If, as Robert Frost maintained, poetry is what is lost in translation, then some of this lyric's magic has been sacrificed to accuracy, or at least closeness.

To the word-for-word gloss, the literal version, and the close rendering we might now contrast a few other varieties: the free translation, the verse translation, the free verse translation, and the transposition. Naturally enough, these latter types are intended less for comparison with the original and usually are published independently; they are more often the work of poets, not scholars. With or without a facing Occitan text, they are meant to be able to stand alone, as original poetry as much as or more than faithful translation. Indeed, according to this taxonomy of translations, the translations proper are situated between the opposite poles of word-for-word gloss and free transposition.

Sally Purcell provides a free translation of the same text. An Oxford author and scholar, she knows the language of the troubadours well enough to compose in it, an experiment rarely undertaken (see, e.g., Purcell 1970, Richardson, Buche; on Bartsch, see Riquer 1705). But rather than pursue an illusory linguistic faithfulness, she seeks fidelity instead in sentiment and mood. Purcell modernizes and interprets as she translates for a contemporary audience. The twelfth-century Blaye troubadour comes to life in the twentieth-century Oxford poet (Purcell 1969, 34):

> Now that the days are long in May
> I hear the gentle song of distant birds,

and when I leave the song behind
my thoughts turn to my distant love;
I walk with mind so overcast and sad
that birdsong or the whitethorn flower
please me no more than icy winter.

This translation perhaps began as a close rendering by an academic and a linguist. But in its finished form it has been rewritten by a poet, trimmed of all artificial language and unfamiliar sentiments. The text is indeed contemporary, for it is in its final state the work of a modern poet, not a medieval troubadour. "Now" as the first word forcefully underlines this contemporaneity of text and translation. It is a commonplace to say that each generation must retranslate its classics. Here the Occitan classic re-appears rejuvenated in entirely modern garb, no longer shabby in its out-worn and unfashionable (read: unidiomatic) dress. *Vauc* is not the literal "go" but the more exact "walk," and indeed the entire poem moves effortlessly, gracefully. Old Occitan *vauc* meant precisely "walk" in a time when means of locomotion were not as varied as in our own day.

The original poem shines through in its new and polished form. The repeated line-final *de loing* is less prominent in the two verses where it has now been integrated, and the translation follows broadly verse by verse rather than slavishly word by word. Though the rhyme-scheme has been sacrificed the freedom of this free translation still does not extend to complete liberation from its model's structures. Other successful translations in this vein have been undertaken by equally professional and expe-rienced translators (Trask 25, Wilhelm 130). But to this reader, at least, none rings quite as true as the version of Sally Purcell.

Whether labeled free or close by their authors, many early translations did attempt to follow as closely as possible the versification of the original lyric. When the verse is not free, the translation necessarily will be. The strictures of metrics and rhyme—whether those of the source that are preserved or those of the target language that are introduced—often lead to semantic drift or even outright filler (the *chevilles* of French poetry), most often in line-final position (Smythe 18).

Whenas the days are long in May
I love the song of birds afar,
And when no more I hear their lay
Then I recall my love afar.
Sorrow so sore my heart doth blight,
Nor nightingale nor may-flower white
Can please me more than winter drear.

From its opening "Whenas," perhaps intended to suggest to a modern age the distant quaintness of Herrick's time, this 1929 version "doth" stubbornly cling to outdated and artificial vocabulary, syntax, and rhyme. There is no room for "now" in so artificial and "drear" a construct. The rhyme configuration obsequiously follows the medieval original, even to including the unfamiliar (in English) *rim estramp* (or *rim dissolut*) of the last verse, which rhymes only with the last verse of the other stanzas. The singsong internal rhyme of "no more"/"so sore" is deliberately intended to parallel the *lanqan/qan/talan* echo and the *chans* repetition, probably unnoticed by most readers and perhaps unintended by the poet. "May" provokes archaic "lay," just as a lost etymological "white" in *albespi* summons up a Blakean "blight," though nothing resembling either appears in the Occitan. A further danger is that the unwary reader might mistakenly think that Occitan *lai* 'there' corresponds to Old French *lai* and thence the English "lay" of this translation.[4]

Undue attention to details of metrics and rhyme has "blighted" Jaufre's lyricism, substituting forced structures and even more artificial diction. Worse, tone and interpretation are determined not by the original's poetic voice but by its rhyme-pattern. While it is crucial to remember that each troubadour strove to innovate in meter and rhyme, all Jaufre's efforts on other levels are here subordinated or neglected by the translator. The 1970s saw many volleys of reproaches fired off in tests of translation when such belletristic, scholarly-genteel versions deservedly came under attack from several sides (Economou). Similar complaints might be leveled at the "dour" "flower" that is Muriel Kittel's version of the same song (Flores 176). Even Helen Waddell's sensitive rendering is a victim of the pitfalls of rhymed translation (221–22).

Archaizing translations are no longer in vogue, and deservedly so. The medieval text may sometimes seem to be a dead artifact, but its translation at least must be a living song. The poet's purpose is to disinter and reinterpret, not remold an old poem in another dead tongue. The French mercifully learned their lesson long ago when Marcel Schwob (1867–1905) failed in his attempt to translate *Hamlet* into late Renaissance French. Only the rare poet succeeds in translating Shakespeare even into contemporary French, as Yves Bonnefoy has taught us (Bonnefoy 350, Heylen). Similarly, to entomb (like a *fausse morte!*) Jaufre's undying inspiration in a second dead language is also a double disservice to medieval poet and modern reader alike.

---

4. This danger in paraphrases is well known. Thus Pasero unwisely includes a gratuitous Italian "simboli" in his translation of Guillem de Peiteus's *sembeli* (Bond 360). Even an accurate translation can be confusing enough. Years ago one of my students in France saw in Villon's phrase *Jehanne la bonne Lorraine* a vision of Joan of Arc as domestic servant (i.e., *la bonne lorraine*)—confirmed, or so the student thought, by Galway Kinnell's "The Maid of Orleans."

At the opposite extreme of the archaizing translation, Paul Blackburn's poem is more than idiomatic. It is contemporary and colloquial: with him, we might say of it, "it's good," "all that song." Forsaking the dynamics of twelfth-century lyricism, he draws our attention instead to his own poetic stance (Blackburn 68).

> When the days are long in May
> it's good,
> soft birdsong from afar,
> and when the melody leaves me
> I remember my love afar.
> I've been bent and thoughtful with desire until
> hawthorn flowers & all that song
> mean no more to me than snow in winter.

The configuration of this free verse on the page highlights modern typography and layout, not medieval metrics and rhyme as the Smythe version attempted to do. As if in response to that stiff and artificial translation, Blackburn's poetry cuts to the quick by relying on the most direct and blunt language. Rather than translate words and rhymes, he has transposed expressions and sentiments. The eight lines paraphrase the feelings of the seven-line original, never submissively attempting to reconstruct its linguistic and other formal scaffolding. Though it will not reach all modern readers, some of whom will not be touched by his "soft birdsong from afar," Blackburn's text is accessible beyond dispute. Were easy readability the sole criterion, his work would receive high marks. But what has become of Jaufre Rudel's moving *canso* in Blackburn's free verse?

As often happens in translation, the missing dimension is inspiration and originality. Poetic translation should make the poet and his song live again through the strong voice of a new poet in a new song. This poem, for all its readability and clarity, is transparently a translation. It fails to transcend the original; instead, it is merely a contemporary rewriting. Perhaps because Blackburn has muted his own voice, he has stilled that of the troubadour. To this reader's taste, neither poet speaks through this translation. High fidelity to an earlier poet's words and sentiments, even in the language of one's own time, can bring death to the poetry.

Finally, let us consider two poets who do not simply recast Jaufre's lyric in a modern tongue. Rather, they also create a new poem that can develop beyond the source it echoes. The results are more than translations, for they are in different degrees independent works by modern poets. Yet they are also witnesses to the continued vitality of Jaufre's lyrics, which spoke to the translator as he now speaks to us.

"Lancan li jorn" also furnishes a model for Ezra Pound's "Canzon: The Spear," which borrows its form as well as its theme from Jaufre's famous lyric. But the poetry is Pound's. In 1910 in "Proensa," a chapter of his first published prose work, *Spirit of Romance*, Pound presented troubadour lyrics and translated competently the first stanza of "Lancan li jorn" along with other texts.[5] More pertinently for us, in his *Provença* poetry collection of the same year he goes one step further in articulating Jaufre's preoccupations (Pound 134). In this imitation, the theme of absence remains the poet's guiding light: the Lady represents an ideal that cannot be attained (McDougal 85–87). Here the troubadour's lyricism has been rediscovered, assimilated, and above all reinterpreted by his translator and fellow poet. The first of its eight stanzas bears close comparison specifically to Jaufre's lyric—not broadly to the sestina form, as one critic has intimated (Jackson 206).

> 'Tis the clear light of love I praise
> That steadfast gloweth o'er deep waters,
> A clarity that gleams always.
> Though man's soul pass through troubled waters,
> Strange ways to him are openèd.
> To shore the beaten ship is sped
> If only love of light give aid.

Whatever its failings, including a lingering aftertaste of the now dated, genteel, belletristic tradition, the strength of Pound's lyric stems from his affection for Jaufre's song, itself "a clarity that gleams always." Pound's adaptation acknowledges its thematic debt by borrowing his source's rhyme-scheme. Even the *rim estramp* of the last verse and the repeated rhyme-word of lines 2 and 4 are intact. But that *mot tornat* is not the same word as in Jaufre: here the distance is transmuted and actualized as "waters" separating the lovers, probably reflecting the legendary *vida* in which Jaufre crosses the seas to reach his distant love. As this shift in key word demonstrates, theme and form have been assimilated and renewed by Pound. To cite his own programmatic formula, the poet has "made it new." The new lyric is not a translation: it is another poet's response in homage to Jaufre, an imitation by a modern poet and a transposition into his own terms (with some probable interference from Baudelaire's image of "Les Phares").

This necessarily schematic survey of modes and techniques in translating the troubadours began with an unnatural, unsuccessful gloss by the thirteenth-century French writer Jean Renart. It seems fitting to conclude with

---

5. Charlotte Ward has now unearthed a previously unpublished, experimental version by Pound midway between the banausic translation in "Proensa" and the free imitation of the "Canzon" (Ward 4).

an unpretentious but effective translation by a modern Occitan poet (Cordes 1975, 44):

> Quand los jorns s'alongan en Mai
> m'es bèl doç cant d'aucèl de luènh,
> e quand ieu soi partit delai
> me remembra un amor de luènh.
> E me'n vau sornarut, cap clin,
> sens que cant ni flor d'albespin
> m'agrade mai qu'ivèrn gelat.

Léon Cordes is not Pierre Menard, who in Borges's story "Pierre Menard, Author of the *Quixote*" translated *Don Quixote* into Cervantes's Spanish: a "translation" in the sense that the original Spanish can only be understood differently in today's world (cf. Steiner 71). Robert Lafont has undertaken a somewhat similar task when he modernizes Jaufre's orthography in the *Trobar* anthology intended for today's students at the Centre d'Etudes Occitanes in Montpellier. But Cordes has neither recomposed his original, like Menard, nor retranscribed it, as Lafont did his. Instead he has translated it into his own idiolect of modern Occitan. More than the imaginary Pierre Menard and more than the historical Jean Renart, Cordes as a modern Occitan poet recognizes that a word-for-word gloss, even where possible, is not always desirable.

Cordes also provides an embarrassingly awkward, banalizing French translation that does justice neither to Jaufre's original nor to his own Occitan adaptation: "Quand les jours s'allongent en Mai me souvenant de mon amour lointain je ressens [*sic*] l'hiver parmi les fleurs." Like his medieval fellow translator, Cordes could not be expected to be equally at home in Occitan and French. But unlike Jean Renart, he pursues in his own language an inspiration that is rich and appropriate: "sornarut" is a common enough word in modern Occitan, but it has no single parallel in French, where it corresponds to both "sombre" and "sournois, taciturne"; "cap clin" innovates with respect to the standard modern Occitan "cap bas" but is at the same time faithful to the original *clis* (Fourvières s.v. *sournaru*, *cap*).

Cordes has accomplished more here than adapting Old Occitan into modern Occitan: like Sally Purcell, he has instilled a translation with the breath of a living poet in his or her own idiolect. As has so often been repeated, perhaps none but a poet should undertake to translate poetry. It is just that vibrancy which makes Cordes's poem faithful in a deeper sense, true both to the art of translation and to the energy of life. Translations of the same poem through centuries of historical and linguistic change allow us to measure both the extent of our evolution and the unity of our poetic nature, a unity that still defies the disparity of different cultures, different times.

WORKS CITED

Apter, Ronnie. "Paul Blackburn's Homage to Ezra Pound." *Translation Review* 19 (1986): 23–26.

Auden, W. H. Preface to *Jean sans terre*, by Yvan Goll. New York: Thomas Yoseloff, 1958.

Badia, Lola, ed. and trans. *Poesia trobadoresca: antologia*. Barcelona: Edicions 62, 1982.

Bec, Pierre. "La Sextine d'Arnaut Daniel: essai de traduction poétique." *Perspectives Médiévales* 8 (1982): 93–103.

Blackburn, Paul, trans. *Proensa: An Anthology of Troubadour Poetry*. Berkeley and Los Angeles: University of California Press, 1978; repr. New York: Paragon, 1986.

Bond, Gerald A. Review of *Guglielmo IX d'Aquitania*, by Nicolò Pasero. *Romance Philology* 30 (1976): 343–61.

Bonnefoy, Yves. "Comment traduire Shakespeare?" *Etudes Anglaises* 17 (1964): 341–51.

Borges, Jorge Luis. "Some Versions of Homer." Trans. and ed. Suzanne Jill Levine. *PMLA* 107 (1992): 1134–38.

Boşca, Teodor, trans. *Poezia trubadurilor provensali[,] italieni, portughezi, a truverilor*. Cluj-Napoca, Rom.: Dacia, 1980.

Brittain, F[rederick], ed. *The Medieval Latin and Romance Lyric to A.D. 1300*. Cambridge: Cambridge University Press, 1951.

Brugnolo, Furio. *Plurilinguismo e lirica medievale da Raimbaut de Vaqueiras a Dante*. Rome: Bulzoni, 1983.

Buche, Raymond. "Une oeuvre inédite d'un troubadour inconnu, Raimonet de la Faia(?)." *Lemouzi* 53 (1972): 299–303.

Caluwé, Jacques de. Preface to *Répertoire des traductions des oeuvres lyriques des troubadours*, by Marcelle D'Herde-Heiliger. Béziers: Centre International de Documentation Occitane, 1985.

Černý, Václav. *Vzdálený slavíků zpěv, výbor z poesie trobadorů*. Prague: Státní, 1963.

Cook, Robert Francis. "Translators and Traducers: Some English Versions of the *Song of Roland*, Stanzas 83–85." *Olifant* 7 (1980): 327–42.

Cordes, Léon. "Quelques notes sur une translation de troubadours." In *Mélanges Charles Camproux*, 1:71–74. Montpellier: Centre d'Etudes Occitanes, 1978.

———, ed. and trans. *Troubadours aujourd'hui*. Raphèle-les-Arles: CPM, 1975.

Cropp, Glynnis M. *Le Vocabulaire courtois des troubadours de l'époque classique*. Geneva: Droz, 1975.

Dembowski, Peter F. "Lexicology and Stylistics: Vocabulary of Provençal Courtly Lyrics—Introductory Remarks." *Proceedings of the Berkeley Linguistics Society* 8 (1982): 18–27.

Duggan, Joseph J. "Ambiguity in Twelfth-Century French and Provençal Literature: A Problem or a Value?" In *Jean Misrahi Memorial Volume*, ed. Hans R.

Runte et al., 136–49. Columbia, S.C.: French Literature Publications Co., 1977.

Economou, George. "Test of Translation X: Guillem Comte de Peitau's 'Ab la dolchor.'" In *A Caterpillar Anthology*, ed. Clayton Eshleman, 346–57. Garden City, N.Y.: Doubleday, 1971.

Ferrante, Joan. "'Ab joi mou lo vers e·l comens.'" In *The Interpretation of Medieval Lyric Poetry*, ed. W. T. H. Jackson, 112–41. New York: Columbia University Press, 1980.

Flores, Angel, ed. *Medieval Age*. New York: Dell, 1963.

Fourvières, Xavier de. *Lou Pichot Tresor*. Avignon: Aubanel, 1975.

Gauchat, Louis. "Les Poésies provençales conservées par des chansonniers français." *Romania* 22 (1893): 364–404.

Gégou, Fabienne. "Jean Renart et la lyrique occitane." In *Mélanges Pierre le Gentil*, 319–23. Paris: SEDES, 1973.

Goddard, R. N. B. "Marcabru, *Li proverbe au vilain*, and the Tradition of Rustic Proverbs." *Neuphilologische Mitteilungen* 88 (1987): 55–67.

Gundelach, Kristen, trans. *Luth og skalmeie. Fransk poesi fra middelalderen i norsk gjendigtning*. Kristiana: Aschehoug, 1920.

Heylen, Romy. "*La Tragédie d'Hamlet*: Bonnefoy's (In)verse Translation Theory." *French Review* 66, no. 2 (1992): 275–85.

Hutchinson, Patrick. "Les Chemins du traduire: entre anglais et français, les médiations des *Trobars* d'Arnaud Daniel et de Raimbaut d'Aurenga." *Sud* 17, nos. 69–70 (1987): 198–209.

———. "La traduction des trobadors: vers une approche pré- (ou hypo-)sémantique." In *L'Identité occitane: réflexions théoriques et expériences*, ed. François Pic, 125–35. Montpellier: Association Internationale des Etudes Occitanes, 1990.

Jackson, Thomas H. *The Early Poetry of Ezra Pound*. Cambridge, Mass.: Harvard University Press, 1968.

Kolsen, Adolf, ed. and trans. *Sämtliche Lieder des Trobadors Guiraut de Bornelh*. 2 vols. Halle: Niemeyer, 1910–35.

Lafont, Robert. "Pour lire les troubadours." *Cahiers du Sud* 50 (1963): 163–94. Reprinted in *Poésie méditerranée*, 91–122. Marseilles: Rivages, 1982.

———, ed. *Trobar, XIIe–XIIIe siècles*. Montpellier: Centre de Documentation Occitane, 1972.

Lecoy, Félix, ed. *Jean Renart: le Roman de la Rose ou de Guillaume de Dole*. Paris: Champion, 1962.

Lejeune, Rita, ed. and trans. "La Chanson de l''amour de loin' de Jaufre Rudel." In *Studi in onore di Angelo Monteverdi*, 1:403–42. Modena: Mucchi, 1959.

McDougal, Stuart Y. *Ezra Pound and the Troubadour Tradition*. Princeton: Princeton University Press, 1972.

Moreno, Toni, ed. and trans. *Cançons de trobadors*. Barcelona: Edicions del Mall, 1981.

Paden, William D. "*Utrum Copularentur*: Of *Cors*." *L'Esprit Créateur* 19 (1979): 70–83.

Payen, [Jean-Charles]. *Les Origines de la courtoisie dans la littérature française médiévale*. Paris: CDU, [1968].

Pickens, Rupert, ed. and trans. *The Songs of Jaufre Rudel*. Toronto: Pontifical Institute of Mediaeval Studies, 1978.

Pound, Ezra. *Collected Early Poems*. New York: New Directions, 1976.

Purcell, Sally. "Poëmas en ancian occitan." *Obradors* 3 (1970): 5–8.

———, trans. *Provençal Poems*. London: Carcanet, 1969.

Raupach, Manfred, and Margaret Raupach. *Französierte Trobadorlyrik*. Tübingen: Niemeyer, 1979.

Richards, Earl Jeffrey. "Finding the 'Authentic' Text: Editing and Translating Medieval and Modern Works as Comparable Interpretive Exercises." *L'Esprit Créateur* 27, no.1 (1987): 111–21.

Richardson, Beverly Danuser. *Plazer ed enueg*. Gurnee, Ill.: Vanishing Press, 1972.

Riggs, Donald Albert. "On Translating: Twentieth-Century Translations of the Troubadours." *DAI* (University of North Carolina) 43, no. 5 (1982): 1536A.

Riquer, Martín de, ed. and trans. *Los trovadores: historia literaria y textos*. Barcelona: Planeta, 1975.

Roubaud, Jacques. *La Fleur inverse: essai sur l'art formel des troubadours*. Paris: Ramsay, 1986.

———, ed. and trans. *Les Troubadours: anthologie bilingue*. Paris: Seghers, 1971.

———, ed. *Troubadours*. Thematic issue of *Action Poétique* 64 (1975).

———, ed. *Les Trobairitz*. Thematic issue *Action Poétique* 75 (1978).

Schutz, Alexander H. "Pound as Provençalist." *Romance Notes* 3 (1962): 58–63.

Serra-Baldó, Alfons, ed. and trans. *Els trobadors*. Barcelona: Barcino, 1934.

Skårup, Povl. "Quelques strophes de Jaufré Rudel dont la syntaxe a été mal interprétée." *Revue Romane* 19 (1984): 71–84.

Smythe, Barbara, trans. *Trobador Poets*. London: Chatto, 1929; repr., Folcroft, N.Y.: Norwood, 1975.

Steiner, George. *After Babel*. Oxford: Oxford University Press, 1975.

Switten, Margaret. *Study Materials on the Troubadours*. South Hadley, Mass.: Mount Holyoke College, 1981.

Tomlinson, Charles, ed. *The Oxford Book of Verse in English Translation*. Oxford: Oxford University Press, 1980.

Trask, Willard R., trans. *Medieval Lyrics of Europe*. New York: New American Library, 1969.

Waddell, Helen. *The Wandering Scholars*. Garden City, N.Y.: Doubleday, 1961.

Ward, Charlotte, ed. *Ezra Pound: Forked Branches, Translations of Medieval Poems*. Iowa City: Windhover Press, 1985.

Wilhelm, James J., trans. *Medieval Song: An Anthology of Hymns and Lyrics*. New York: Dutton, 1971.

Zufferey, François. *Recherches linguistiques sur les chansonniers provençaux*. Geneva: Droz, 1987.

SEVENTEEN

Language

Frede Jensen

Until recently, scholars made use of the term *Provençal* to describe the language in which the troubadours wrote their poetry, but this designation has now largely been replaced by *Occitan*, considered a more appropriate label. The ambiguity inherent in the traditional term stems from the fact that *Provençal*, in dialectological parlance, refers to a very specific region, located on the eastern side of the Rhone river and having Marseille and Aix-en-Provence as its major centers, while the word *Occitan* is applied to the much broader area where southern-type dialects, different from French proper, were spoken. The exact geographical limits of Occitan are difficult to circumscribe. Roughly speaking, the Occitan linguistic domain lies between the Atlantic, the Pyrenees, and the Alps; its northern boundary, which is far more difficult to draw, passes somewhat south of the Loire River at a distance that varies from one region to the next.

While the Ile-de-France dialect was able to establish itself fairly early as the main literary language of the north, the south lacked an important literary-cultural center capable of exerting firm control over the region, and as a result a generally recognized label for the language was slow to develop. The term *Provençal* was little used in the Middle Ages. Raimon Feraut, author of a life of Saint Honorat, makes use of it, and it appears in the title of a mid-thirteenth-century grammatical treatise, known as the *Donatz proensals*, but this work was probably put together in Italy, where the word *provenzale* was traditionally used.

In the medieval period the language of the south was referred to simply as *romans* or *lenga romana*. This term is encountered in the *Leys d'Amors*, a fourteenth-century grammatical and poetic treatise composed in Toulouse, and it is still maintained by Raynouard in his *Lexique roman*—although post-Raynouard scholarship has wasted little time in discarding this designation as inappropriate, since it may be applied not only to Occitan, but to Romance languages in general.

The thirteenth-century Catalonian-born poet and grammarian Raimon Vidal de Besalù, author of the *Razos de trobar*, chose the term *limousin* as the designation for the poetic language, presumably because of the prominence of several poets from that region, chief among them Bernart de Ventadorn. Yet to Raimon Vidal de Besalù, as well as to the author of the *Leys d'Amors*, this label, far from being restricted to the Limousin area proper, also applies to regions such as Provence, Auvergne and Quercy, to which Raimon Vidal adds a vague "and all the neighboring areas." What is truly remarkable in Raimon Vidal's description is the fact that he appears keenly aware of the difficulty of isolating the exact dialectal base. He is aware, in other words, of the koiné or supradialectal aspect of the artistic language in which the troubadours expressed their thoughts on *fin'amor*. *Limousin* thus is no more than a convenient label, representing not the cradle of the poetic language of the troubadours, but the much broader area where the medieval courtly-love poets lived and worked: le Midi. Launched by a Catalonian, the term *limousin* further came to designate the language in which the thirteenth- and fourteenth-century Catalan imitators of the troubadour love lyrics expressed themselves. In Spain, the terms *poesía lemosina* and *lengua lemosina* were used in reference to the troubadour medium as well as to literary Catalan.

In his *De vulgari eloquentia*, Dante uses a labeling based on the form of the affirmative particle: the troubadour medium is the *langue d'oc*, French the *langue d'oïl*, and Italian the *langue de si*. Basing these important linguistic divisions on as trivial a fact as the affirmative particle did, of course, cause a certain amount of confusion. The *langue de si* label applies as much to Spanish as it does to Italian, yet Dante actually uses the term *oc* about Spanish. A brief mention in the *Vita nuova* of the langue d'oc as being the language of the troubadours cleared up this misunderstanding, but a new source of confusion arose with the use of the word to designate the geographical province of Languedoc, created in the late thirteenth century when the county of Toulouse was ceded to the king of France.

The exact dialectal base of the troubadour medium cannot be defined with precision. The refinement process that a spoken dialect must undergo in order to attain the level of a medium capable of literary expression is in no small measure responsible for having obscured the geographical provenance of the troubadour koiné. In their efforts to throw light on this perplexing mystery, dialectologists have focused their attention on a series of important phonological fluctuations present in the lyrical corpus: the retention or elimination of the so-called unstable -*n* (*barōne* > *baron* vs. *baró*), retention or palatalization of initial *c* [*k*] before *a* (*cantāre* > *cantar* vs. *chantar*), the change of the *ct* cluster to *i̯t* or [*tš*] (*factu* > *fait* vs. *fach, fag*),

TABLE 1.   Tonic Vowels, Occitan and Old French

VL	Occitan	Old French, Free	Old French, Blocked
i (CL ī)	i	i	i
ẹ (CL ĭ, ē, oe)	ẹ	ei > oi > [wa] *or* wẹ > ẹ	ẹ
ę (CL ĕ, ae)	ę	ie	ę
u (CL ū)	[y]	[y]	[y]
ọ (CL ŭ, ō)	ọ	ou > eu > [œ]	ou
ǫ (CL ŏ)	ǫ	uo > ue > [œ]	ǫ *or* ọ
a (CL ā, ă)	a	e	a

and a few less important developments. These features all come together in a central region, corresponding approximately to the ancient Languedoc province. As a result of these probings, central dialects have replaced *limousin* as the most probable source of the poetic medium of the troubadours, but certain difficulties remain. These findings presuppose that we have before us the primitive version of the poems as they were written down or dictated by the troubadours themselves. The vicissitudes of the transmission process are overlooked, yet it seems quite plausible that scribes may have weeded out archaisms or deviant dialectal features or interfered in other ways with the original version. That the above-mentioned dialectological findings are confirmed by the *ALF* (Gilliéron and Edmond's *Atlas linguistique de France*) raises yet another question: to what extent can we be certain that the trajectory of modern-day isoglosses accurately reflects the linguistic conditions of another era?

The following discussion of the historical development of Occitan traces the phonology and the morphology of the language of the troubadours back to its origin in Vulgar Latin, while there is no need to view syntax in a diachronic perspective. A comparison of the Occitan evolution with that of Old French is given for many features.

PHONOLOGY

Vowels

The Classical Latin vocalic system comprising five long and five short vowels had been reduced to a quality-based system of seven vowels in Vulgar Latin: *i, u*, a close *e* (*ẹ*), an open *e* (*ę*), a close *o* (*ọ*), an open *o* (*ǫ*), and *a*. Of the Latin diphthongs, *oe* had merged with close *e* and *ae* with open *e*, leaving *au* as the only surviving diphthong in Vulgar Latin. Table 1 serves as an illustration of the development of the tonic vowels in Occitan and Old French, as they evolve from the Vulgar Latin base; for French, but not for Occitan, the nature of the syllable, whether free or blocked, is important.

The Vulgar Latin vocalic system is much better preserved in Occitan than in French. In the tonic syllable, six of the seven vowels are kept unchanged: *rīpa* > *riba*; *vĭce* > *vetz*; *nĕpos* > *neps*; *mŭndu* > *mon*; *cŏrpus* > *cors*; *lātus* > *latz*, but Occitan shares with French the fronting or palatalization of *u* to [y]: *mūru* > *mur*. One of the most important distinguishing features between Occitan and French vocalism is the retention of stressed free *a* in the south as opposed to the change of *a* to *e* in the north: *mare* > Oc. *mar* vs. Fr. *mer*; *tale* > Oc. *tal* vs. Fr. *tel*. The Vulgar Latin diphthong *au* is retained unchanged in Occitan, while French monophthongizes it to *o*: *auro* > Oc. *aur*, Fr. *or*; *audit* > Oc. *au*, OFr. *ot*; *pauper* > Oc. *paubre*, OFr. *povre*.

A very prominent feature is the total lack in the south of the spontaneous diphthongization that affects the close and open *e* and *o* in French in a stressed, free syllable: *habēre* > Oc. *aver*, Fr. *avoir*; *fĭde* > Oc. *fe*, Fr. *foi*; *pĕde* > Oc. *pe*, Fr. *pied*; *flōre* > Oc. *flor*, Fr. *fleur*; *gŭla* > Oc. *gola*, Fr. *gueule*; *mŏla* > Oc. *mola*, Fr. *meule*. In the blocked position, where French does not diphthongize, Occitan respects the Vulgar Latin vowel quality far better than French, which opens *e* to *e*, while tending to close a primitive *o* to *u*: *mĭttĕre* > Oc. *metre*, Fr. *mettre*; *vĭrĭde* > Oc. *vert*, Fr. *vert*; *bŭcca* > Oc. *boca*, Fr. *bouche*; *sŭrdu* > Oc. *sort*, Fr. *sourd*; *cŏhŏrte* > VL *corte* > Oc. *cort*, Fr. *cour*.

The conditioned diphthongization of short *e* and short *o* is a feature that occurs in both Gallo-Romance languages, although the conditioning factors and the outcome and implementation of the diphthongization process display no rigorous parallelism. In Occitan, the conditioned diphthongization may be triggered by a variety of factors: the presence of a palatal, of a final long *i*, of the semivowel *u* (whether original or following from the vocalization of final *v* or *b*), and, less commonly, of a velar *c*, while blocked short *e* and short *o* are subject to diphthongization in French only when followed by a palatal. Whereas the conditioned diphthongization is compulsory in the north, it is only optional in the south: *lĕctu* > *leit*, *lieit*; *vĕtulu* > VL *veclu* > *velh*, *vielh*; VL *vendēdī* > *vendei*, *vendiei*; *lĕve* > *leu*, *lieu*; *mĕu* > *meu*, *mieu*. The diphthongized stage of the short *o* is either *uo* or *ue*: *ŏcto* > *oit*, *uoit*, *ueit*; *ŏcŭlu* > *olh*, *uolh*, *uelh*; *fŏlia* > *folha*, *fuolha*, *fuelha*; VL **ŏvu* > *ou*, *uou*, *ueu*; *fŏcu* > *foc*, *fuoc*, *fuec*. The free close *e* becomes *i* in French if preceded by a palatal: *mercēde* > *merci*; *cēra* > *cire*; this feature, known as Bartsch's Law, is unknown in the south: Oc. *merce*, *cera*.

Other features differentiate the vowel system of Occitan from that of French. The instability of final *n* offers proof that nasalization was not a prominent feature in the south, but prior to its falling or weakening the nasal had brought about a closure of the open-vowel quality, changing *e* to *e* and *o* to *o*: *bĕne* > *ben*, *be*; *rĕm* > *ren*, *re*; *bŏnu* > *bon*, *bo*. Similarly the stable

TABLE 2.   Pretonic Vowels in Occitan

VL	Occitan
i	i
ẹ	ẹ
ę	ę
u	[y]
ọ	ọ
ǫ	ǫ
a	a
au	au

n exerts a closing influence on the preceding vowel without otherwise affecting its quality: *vĕntu* > *vẹn*; *pŏnte* > *pǫn*. Closure of *e* to *i* in hiatus before *a* occurs in *vĭa* > *via* and **sĭam* > *sia* (vs. Fr. *voie*, OFr. *soie*), while *o* is subject to a fluctuating hiatus treatment: *sŭa* > *soa* and *sua*. Umlaut or apophony occurs under the influence of final long *i* in both languages; *e* is closed to *i*, *o* to *u*: *ecce-ĭllī* > *cil*; *prĕhĕnsī* > VL *prēsī* > *pris*; *fŭī* > VL *fǫi* > *fui*; VL *tōttī* > *tuit, tug.* The simplification of diphthongs is a common trend: *magis* > *mais* > *mas*; **frĭgĭdu* > *freit* > *fret.* The diphthong *iu*, on the other hand, is quite frequently enlarged to *ieu*: *vīvo* > *viu* > *vieu*; *rīvu* > *riu* > *rieu.*

The pretonic vowels change little from Vulgar Latin to Occitan (Table 2). The diphthong *au* is retained: *audīre* > *auzir*, and *ū* palatalizes to [y]: *hūmōre* > *umor*, just as in the tonic syllable. *A* and *i* are not subject to change: *amōre* > *amor*; *hĭbĕrnu* > *ivern*, while a general trend toward a close pronunciation in the pretonic position reduces the remaining four vowels to two, a close *e* and a close *o*: *lĭcēre* > *lẹzer*; *lĕvāre* > *lẹvar*; *aetāte* > *ẹdat*; *cōrtēnse* > *cǫrtes*; *mŏrtāle* > *mǫrtal.* There are sporadic occurrences of a further closure of pretonic *o* to *u*: **mŏrīre* > *morir* and *murir*; **sŭfferīre* > *sofrir* and *sufrir*; **cōperīre* > *cobrir* and *cubrir*, while the change of pretonic *e* to *i* seems dependent upon a preceding palatal: *zelōsu* > *gilos*; *gelare* > *gelar* and *gilar*; *gĕnŭcūlu* > *genolh* and *ginolh.*

Some vowel changes do not occur in a fixed pattern. Cases of vowel dissimilation are quite common, whether they date back to Vulgar Latin or come about later: *vīcīnu* > *vezin, vezí*; *dīvīnu* > *devin, deví*; *sŏrōre* > *seror*; *hŏnōre* > *onor, enor.* Loss of the pretonic vowel has taken place in *directu* > *dreit* and *quiritāre* > *cridar*, and the same development may occur through aphaeresis in the absolute initial position: *ecclesia* > *gleiza*; *epĭscopu* > *bisbe.*

The treatment of unstressed vowels offers other features that differentiate Occitan from French. Final vowels are dropped, with the exception of *a*, which survives intact, as opposed to its weakening to *e muet* in French: *flōre*

> *flor*; *mūru* > *mur*; *amat* > *ama*, Fr. *aime*. A supporting vowel, which may be either *e* or *i*, in French only *e*, is added following certain consonant clusters, mostly an occlusive plus liquid combination, but also elsewhere: *patre* > *paire*; *bĭbĕre* > *beure*; *dŭbĭto* > *dopte, dopti*. Specifically Occitan is the insertion of the supporting vowel between the two consonants in a palatal and *r* sequence: *sĕnior* > *sénher*; *maior* > *máier*. The intertonic vowel, placed between the initial and the main stress, is treated like the final vowel: *collŏcāre* > *colgar*; *verĕcŭndia* > *vergonha*; *ornamentu* > *ornamen*; *quadri-fŭrcu* > *caireforc*.

The most striking feature in the treatment of weak vowels is the frequent retention of the post-tonic nonfinal vowel at the expense of the final. This is common with the unstressed *-ĕre* infinitive, but occurs also elsewhere: *vĭncĕre* > *vénser*; **nascĕre* > *naisser*; *plangĕre* > *plánher*; **cassanu* > *casse(r)*; *fraxĭnu* > *fraisse(r)*. The treatment of this vowel is not uniform, however, and elimination is a common occurrence just as in French: *anĭma* > *anma*; *dŏmĭna* > *domna*; *sŭbĭtu* > *sobde*. Some cases of retention are easily traced to analogical pressure: *fenimen* from *fenir*; *mezurar* from *mezura*. Although generally speaking Occitan like French tolerates only one syllable following the accent, true proparoxytones seem to have been preserved exceptionally in old documents: *dimenegue* < *die domĭnĭcu*; *canonegue* < *canonĭcu*; *monegue* < *monacu*; *canebe* < *cannabis* as archaic variants of *dimergue, canorgue, morgue*, and *carbe*. These words seem to count metrically as having only one post-tonic syllable, but one may cite a few additional words that seem to prove the existence of a proparoxytone stress at an early period: *pertega* < *pertĭca*; *femena* < *fēmĭna*; *lagrema* < *lacrĭma*.

Consonants

The consonantal system characteristic of French seems to extend a little farther south into the Occitan domain than, for example, the treatment of the vowel *a*. This is specifically true of the palatalization of initial *c* and *g* to [*tš*] and [*dž*] before *a*, encountered in the northern sections of the Occitan domain. Both palatalized and nonpalatalized forms are commonly used by the troubadours: *capu* > *cap* and *chap*; *caballu* > *caval* and *chaval*; *gallu* > *gal* and *jal*; **gaudīre* > *gauzir* and *jauzir*. Initial *c* before *e* and *i* is assibilated to [*ts*] with a subsequent reduction to *s*, which seems to have taken place earlier in Occitan than in French, judging from the frequency of the *s* spelling: *cĕrtu* > *cert* and *sert*. Initial *g* before *e* and *i* develops like initial *i̯* and *di̯* to [*dž*]: *gĕnte* > *gen*; *jŭvĕne* > *jove*; *jŏcu* > *joc*; *diŭrnu* > *jorn*. There is little else to say about consonants in initial position: [*kʷ*] is reduced to *k*, which, before *a*, may be spelled either *c* or *qu*: *quantu* > *can* and *quan*; *quattuor* > *catre* and *quatre*. The Germanic *w* moves via [*gʷ*] to *g*: **werra* > *guerra*. Both the Latin mute *h* and the Germanic aspirated *h* are lost: *hĕrba* > *erba*; **hapja* > *apcha*. Initial clusters containing *l* are kept unchanged just like in French: *plangĕre*

> *plánher*; *clave* > *clau*, and a prosthetic *e* develops before *s* plus consonant: *stāre* > *estar*.

Substantial changes take place in intervocalic position. The weakening process encountered here, known as lenition, leads to the voicing of *p* to *b*, of *t* to *d*, and of *s* to [z]: *sapēre* > *saber*; *vīta* > *vida*; *ausāre* > *auzar*, and infrequently of *f* to *v*: *dēfēnsu* > *deves*, while elsewhere *f* receives treatment as initial in compounds and is kept: *profĕctu* > *profieg*. Intervocalic *d* evolves to a voiced *s*: *vĭdēre* > *vezer*, a change that may be placed chronologically around the middle of the twelfth century. This fairly late development is accountable for a considerable amount of graphic vacillation: *adorāre* > *azorar* and *adorar*; *audīre* > *auzir* and *audir*. To this may be added cases of the complete elimination of *d* in the northern regions of the Occitan domain in accordance with conditions in French: *crūdēle* > *cruzel, crudel, cruel*; **tradīre* > *trazir, tradir, trair*. The *Boeci*, an eleventh-century text from the Limousin region, has *fiar* < *fĭdāre*; *veüt* < *vĭdūtu*; *traazo* < **tradatiōne*.

Some consonants show specific conditioned developments. This is the case with intervocalic *b* and *v*, which merge into *v*: *dēbēre* > *dever*; *lavare* > *lavar*, but which drop before and quite often also following a back vowel: *pavōre* > *paor*; *nŏvĕllu* > *novel, noel*; *provĭnciāle* > *provensal, proensal*. The development of intervocalic *c* and *g* is particularly complex, for not only is it tied very closely to the vocalic environment, but the graphical representation of the outcome is at times quite difficult to interpret. If the following vowel is *a*, intervocalic *c* may voice to *g*, or it may evolve to *i*, a spelling that may be interpreted either as yod or as [dž]: **prĕcāre* > *pregar, preiar, prejar*, while *g* alone represents the norm before a velar vowel: *acūtu* > *agut*. *Pauca*, from Latin *pauca*, shows no lenition, since *au* does not create a true intervocalic position. Intervocalic *g* yields much the same results as *c*: *nĕgāre* > *negar, neiar, nejar*, but it displays a certain tendency to drop before a velar vowel: *augŭstu* > VL *agosto* > *agost, aost*. The prepalatal *c* moves to a voiced *s* in intervocalic position: *vĭcīnu* > VL *vēcīnu* > *vezin, vezí*, while prepalatal *g* yields [dž] or yod, or else it may drop altogether: *sagĭtta* > *sageta, saieta, saeta*. Geminates are simplified: *bŭcca* > *boca*, but the resulting single consonant is not subject to any further change. Intervocalic *i* gives *i* or [dž]: *maiōre* > *maior, major*—with the proviso, however, that the interpretation of these graphs is uncertain.

While, basically, lenition affects single consonants lodged between two vowels, voicing may also occur in intervocalic clusters with *r* as the second element: *capra* > *cabra*. Primary *cr* voices to *gr*: CL *álacer* > VL *alécre* > *alegre*, while the secondary cluster becomes *ir*: CL *cŏquĕre* > VL *cŏcĕre* > *coire*. The development of the internal *gr* cluster shows a fair amount of fluctuation: *nĭgru* > *ner, negre*; *flagrāre* > *flairar*. Vocalization commonly affects certain consonants tied to *r* in internal groupings. The already-mentioned *coire* and *flairar* displaying a change of *c* and *g* to *i* are cases in point, but there are many others besides. A *u̯* results from *b* and *v*, while *t* and *d* move to *i̯* when followed by *r*: *bĭbĕre* > *beure*; *vīvĕre* > *viure*; *matre* > *maire*; *tropātor* > *trobaire*; *crēdĕre* > *creire*. The internal *pl* cluster undergoes voicing in *dŭplu* > *doble*, while *bl* is retained intact, aside from an occasional vocalization in the secondary cluster: *fabula* > *fabla, faula*.

Specific combinations have led to the creation of a palatal *l* and a palatal *n* in both Gallo-Romance languages. If *l* is preceded by *c* or *g*, or followed by *i̯*, the outcome is a palatal *l̦*, represented graphically in a number of ways, of which it will suffice to mention the characteristic *lh* spelling: *apĭcula* > *abelha*; *vĭgĭlāre* > *velhar*; *mēliōre* > *melhor*, while a palatal *n*, similarly of varied graphical representation, but often spelled *nh*, evolves from the combination of *n* and a palatal: *sĕniōre* > *senhor*; *plangĕre* > *plánher*. A syllabic division usually prevents a merger of *n* and *c* from taking place: *vĭncĕre* > *vénser*, but the *nct* group may yield a palatal *n*: *planctu* > *planh*, along with other outcomes: *planch, plaint*.

As in Old French, the presence of a yod after a consonant modifies its development. The *di̯* and *gi̯* clusters evolve to [*dž*], or else they are reduced to *i̯*: *ĭnvĭdia* > *enveja* or *enveia*; *corrĭgia* > *correja* or *correia*, while *ti̯* is resolved as a voiced *s*: *prĕtiāre* > *prezar*; *ratiōne* > *razon, razó*. A number of outcomes are noted for *pi̯*: *sapiātis* > *sapchatz, sachatz, sapiatz*, while *bi̯* and *vi̯* suffer vocalization of the labial: **grĕviāre* > *greujar* (which could reveal influence of *greu* < **grĕve*); *rabia* > *rauja*. *Si̯* evolves to [*i̯z*], *i̯* or [*dž*]: *mansiōne* > *maizó, maió*, while *ssi̯* and *sci̯* yield voiceless results: **bassiāre* > *baissar, baichar*; *fascia* > *faissa*. *Ci̯* evolves to a voiceless affricate [*ts*], and there is no yod-release; the affricate [*ts*] is reduced to *s* very early: *faciat* > *fassa*, but survives in final position: *brachiu* > *bratz*; *vīvaciu* > *viatz*. Anticipation of yod is the norm for the *ri̯* cluster: *variu* > *vair*; *matĕria* > *madeira*. The development of *mi̯* is varied: *commeātu* > *comnhat, comiat*.

Other palatal clusters are *cs* and *ct*. Of these, *cs*, spelled *x*, is resolved as yod and a voiceless *s*: *laxāre* > *laissar*, while the evolution of *ct* is less homogeneous, the outcome being either *i̯t* or [*tš*]: *factu* > *fait, fag*; *lacte* > *lait, lag, lach*. The secondary *t'c* and *d'c* clusters both give [*dž*]: *viatĭcu* > *viatge*; *mĕdĭcu* > *metge*.

The labial-dental combinations *pt, bt,* and *vt* are subject to considerable fluctuation in their evolution, running the gamut from retention, simplification, voicing, and unvoicing to vocalization: **accaptāre* > *acaptar, acatar*; *adaptāre* > *azautar*; *dēbĭtu* > *depte, deute*; *cīvĭtāte* > *ciptat, ciutat, ciudat*. *Ps* is either kept, or it may develop in a manner that suggests a confusion with *cs*: *ŏpus* > *ops*; *capsa* > *caissa, caisha*.

The vocalization of *l* before a consonant is not carried nearly as far as in French, being restricted to the position before a dental or a palatal, and being optional only: *alteru* > *autre, altre*; *falsu* > *faus, fals*; *dŭlce* > *doutz, dolz*. Before other consonants, *l* is kept: *alba* > *alba*; *salvāre* > *salvar*. The insertion of glides is another feature that does not command the same frequency as in French, presumably because the weak vowels were retained longer in the south. Standard in *m'r* and *m'l* clusters: *camĕra > cambra*; *sĭmūlāre > semblar*, glide insertion is optional only with *n'r* and *l'r* and, on the whole, is not too commonly found: *honorāre > onrar* and *ondrar*; *tŏllĕre > tolre* and *toldre*.

Very few consonants occur in final position. Of these, *m* survives only in monosyllables in Vulgar Latin, and it is continued in Occitan as an unstable *n*: *rĕm > ren, re*. Final *s* is kept and continues to play an extremely important role in the declension and conjugation systems: *mūros > murs*; *cantas > cantas*. Final *t* is dropped, including from verbal endings: *amat > ama*; *dēbet > deu*; *cantant > cantan, canton*, while French keeps *t* when following a consonant: *doit, chantent*, but drops it fairly early after a vowel: *amat > aimet > aime*. The northern regions of the Occitan domain retain the *-ant* and *-ont* endings. Final *c* is mostly dropped: *nec > ne, ni*; it survives in *hŏc > oc* and may move to yod in *(il)lac > lai* or *la*; *ecce-hac > sai* or *sa*. The imperative *fac* is continued as *fai*. Romance or secondary final consonants may be retained, changed, or lost. Chief among the changes are desonorization: *Hūgo > Uc*; *nūdu > nut*, and vocalization: *nave > nau*; *dēbet > deu*. Final *n* becomes unstable: *pane > pan, pá*, and the same is true of *n* before a flexional *s*: *latrōnes > lairons, lairós*, while final *nt* and *nd* are reduced to a stable *n*: *mŏnte > mon*; *mŭndu > mon*. Final *rr* is mostly simplified, but it may be retained intact, in which case a supporting vowel is added: *carru > car* or *carre*. The prepalatal *c*, when becoming final, evolves to [*ts*] in Occitan, but unlike in French, there is no yod-release: *vōce > Oc. votz*, OFr. *voiz*.

MORPHOLOGY

Nouns

Occitan, like Old French, has a two-case declension system for each number, based on the Latin nominative and accusative. The feminine declension in *-a*, derived from the Latin first declension, has only one form for each number: sing. *filha < fīlia* and pl. *filhas < fīlias*. Other words have joined this group, chiefly reflexes of Latin neuter plurals: *fŏlia > folha* and pl. *folhas*.

The two-case declension system, based on the presence or the absence of a flexional *s* in direct continuation of conditions in Latin, is above all characteristic of masculine nouns derived from the Latin second declension in *-us* and inflected as shown in Table 3. Parisyllabic third-declension masculine nouns join this flexion through the creation of a separate nom. pl. form, whether in Vulgar Latin or in early Gallo-Romance. This is achieved by adapting the uniform *-es* ending of the Classical Latin plural (*canes-canes*, *patres-patres*, etc.) to the *mūri-mūros* system (Table 4).

TABLE 3.   Standard Masculine Declension

	VL	Occitan	Old French
nom. sing.	mūrus	murs	murs
acc. sing.	mūru(m)	mur	mur
nom. pl.	mūrī	mur	mur
acc. pl.	mūros	murs	murs

TABLE 4.   Third-Declension Masculine Nouns,
Adapted to the Standard Flexion

	CL	VL	Occitan	Old French
nom. sing.	canis	canis	cans, cás	chiens
acc. sing.	canem	cane	can, cá	chien
nom. pl.	canes	*cani	can, cá	chien
acc. pl.	canes	canes	cans, cás	chiens

Many fourth-declension nouns swell the ranks of the standard flexion because of their *-us* ending: *frūctus > frugz*; *portus > portz*. A flexional *s* may be added optionally to the nom. sing. of nouns lacking it in Latin: *pater > paire(s)*. These changes converge in a system in which a subject and oblique case are distinguished in both singular and plural of most masculine nouns but an invariable category is formed by nouns whose stem ends in *s* or *tz*: *cŏrpus > cors*; *tĕmpus > tems*; *brachiu > bratz*.

Other third-declension nouns are imparisyllabic, counting one syllable less in the nom. sing. than in the rest of the paradigm. Many of these had joined the regular parisyllabic flexion by aligning their nom. sing. with the remaining forms (Table 5). In a couple of cases it is only the theme that differs, not the stress: *cŏmes-cŏmĭte > coms-comte*; *hŏmo-hŏmĭne(m) > om-ome* (Table 6).

All other surviving imparisyllables display an additional difference in accentuation that, far more than the imparisyllabic feature itself, is responsible for setting the nom. sing. apart from the rest of the paradigm. It is mainly nouns designating persons that are able to maintain two very distinct forms for the nominative and the accusative singular. Among such nouns are those formed with the *-ātor, -atóre(m)* and the *-tor, -tóre(m)* suffixes: *trŏpātor-trŏpatóre > trobaire-trobador*; *ĭmperātor-imperatóre > emperaire-emperador*; *pastor-pastóre > pastre-pastor* (Table 7).

Another important group is made up of nouns built on the *-o, -óne* suffix: *lātro-latróne > laire-lairó* (Table 8). This Latin suffix was adopted by many nouns of Germanic origin: *baro-baróne > bar-baró*, including a few proper

TABLE 5. Realigned Masculine Imparisyllables

	CL	VL	Occitan
nom. sing.	mons	*montis	montz
acc. sing.	montem	monte	mon
nom. pl.	montes	*monti	mon
acc. pl.	montes	montes	montz

TABLE 6. Flexion of om

	CL	VL	Occitan
nom. sing.	hŏmo	hŏmo	om(s)
acc. sing.	hŏmĭnem	hŏmĭne	ome
nom. pl.	homĭnes	*hŏmīnī	ome
acc. pl.	homĭnes	homines	omes

TABLE 7. Flexion of trobaire

	CL	VL	Occitan
nom. sing.	trŏpātor	trŏpātor	trobaire
acc. sing.	trŏpatōrem	trŏpatōre	trobador
nom. pl.	trŏpatōres	*tropatōri	trobador
acc. pl.	trŏpatōres	tropatōres	trobadors

TABLE 8. Flexion of laire

	CL	VL	Occitan
nom. sing.	lātro	lātro	laire
acc. sing.	latrōnem	latrōne	lairó
nom. pl.	latrōnes	*latrōni	lairó
acc. pl.	latrōnes	latrones	lairós

nouns of persons: *Carles-Carló*; *Uc-Ugó*. Some geographical names are inflected similarly: *Bret-Bretó*; *Gasc-Gascó*.

The plural of third-declension masculine nouns, whether parisyllabic or imparisyllabic, follows the pattern of the second, establishing a formal differentiation between the two case-forms: *fraire-fraires*; *trobador-trobadors*; *baró-barós*.

TABLE 9.   Flexion of *naus*

	VL	Occitan
nom. sing.	navis	naus
acc. sing.	nave(m)	nau
nom. pl.	naves	naus
acc. pl.	naves	naus

TABLE 10.   Flexion of *sor*

	VL	Occitan
nom. sing.	sŏror	sor
acc. sing.	sŏrōre	seror
nom. pl.	sŏrōres	serors
acc. pl.	sŏrōres	serors

While first-declension feminine nouns like *filha* are not susceptible to any case variation, most third-declension feminines have an *s* in the nom. sing.: *navis* > *naus*, as opposed to the oblique *nave(m)* > *nau*. Nouns ending in *e*, such as *maire* < *mater*, form an exception to this case differentiation. The plural of all feminine nouns counts only one form (Table 9).

Only two feminine nouns are imparisyllabic: *sŏror-sŏrōre(m)* > *sor-seror* and *mŭlier-mŭliere(m)* > *mólher-molhér* (Table 10). All other feminine imparisyllables had become parisyllabic in Vulgar Latin: *cīvĭtas-cīvĭtātem* > VL **cīvĭtātis-cīvĭtāte* > Oc. *ciutatz-ciutat*; *dŏlor-dŏlōrem* > VL **dŏlōris-dŏlōre* > *dolors-dolor*.

In the late thirteenth century the two-case system begins to fall into disuse, and Raimon Vidal de Besalù censures various troubadours for violations of declension rules. Because of its numerical strength, it is the accusative that tends to replace the nominative, but the reasons for the case breakdown are very complex.

Adjectives

Adjectives do not have an inherent gender, but agree in gender, number, and case with the noun they modify. Their flexional system parallels that of nouns, but the adjective has kept a neuter form, which differs from the masculine nom. sing. through its lack of a flexional *s*. There are two major categories of adjectives in Occitan: one that displays a formal distinction in gender, and another that does not: masc. *bós-bó* and fem. *bona* vs. masc. and fem. *fortz-fort*. Their flexion is illustrated in Tables 11 and 12.

TABLE 11.   Flexion of *bons*

	masculine		feminine		neuter	
	VL	Occitan	VL	Occitan	VL	Occitan
nom. sing.	bŏnus	bons, bós	bona	bona	bonu(m)	bon, bó
acc. sing.	bŏnu	bon, bó	"	"		
nom. pl.	bŏnī	bon, bó	bonas	bonas		
acc. pl.	bŏnos	bons, bós	"	"		

TABLE 12.   Flexion of *fortz*

	masculine		feminine		neuter	
	VL	Occitan	VL	Occitan	VL	Occitan
nom. sing.	fortis	fortz	fortis	fortz	forte	fort
acc. sing.	forte	fort	forte	fort		
nom. pl.	*forti	fort	fortes	fortz		
acc. pl.	fortes	fortz	fortes	fortz		

Bós-bona are inflected like *murs* and *filha*, respectively, *fortz* like *cans* for the masculine, like *naus* for the feminine. These noun flexions may be consulted for all pertinent details. It is to be noted that the gender identity of the *fortz* category is not complete: the feminine counts only one plural form. The imparisyllabic flexion, which is so strongly represented in the realm of nouns, is limited to a few synthetic comparatives, continued from Latin: *mĕlior-mĕliōre* > *mélher-melhór*; *pĕior-pĕiōre* > *péier-peiór*; *maior-maiōre* > *máier-maiór*; *mĭnor-mĭnōre* > *ménre-menór*. *Fel-felon, feló* is originally a noun. All present participles had lost their imparisyllabic feature through the refashioning of analogical nominative singulars: CL *cántans-cantántem* > VL **cantántis-cantánte* > *cantantz-cantan*. Many invariable adjectives tended to move into the gender-distinguishing category: *granda*, but most occurrences of this development are late medieval: *tala, difficila*.

Occitan forms the comparative degree of adjectives analytically by means of adding *plus* to the positive: *plus cortes*, while the use of *melhs* and *mais* in this role is limited to participles that have kept their verbal force: *la melz amada* 'the most loved' (Sordel); *qu'es forser e mais tirans* 'for it is stronger and more powerful' (A. de Peguilhan). Occitan has also inherited from Latin a few synthetic comparatives, the most common ones of these being listed above. The relative superlative is formed by adding a determiner, usually the definite article or a possessive adjective, to the comparative degree: *lo plus cortes.* The use of a determiner is less stringent in the medieval period, and it is not uncommon to find *plus* itself used unmodified with the value of a superlative: *cill qe el mon plus mi platz* 'the lady in this world who pleases me the most' (G. Faidit). The absolute superlative is expressed by means of reinforcing adverbs: *mout honratz, be clara,* or through prefixation: *perluzens, sobrebella.*

Numerals

Lat. *ūnus,* which has also yielded the indefinite article, evolves with a full flexion: masc. *u(n)s, u(n), u(n), u(n)s* and fem. *una, unas.* For the masculine form of the number "two" a separate nominative *dūi* was created in Vulgar Latin; it is continued either as *dui,* with an *ī*-caused metaphony of *o,* or as *doi,* which may owe its *o* to the accusative *dos* from *dŭos.* Noteworthy is the regular use of a feminine *doas < dŭas,* while OFr. *doues* is dialectal and little used. The feminine, as to be expected, has no separate nominative form: *aquist son dui e vos est doas* 'they are two [i.e., squires], and you are two [i.e., ladies]' (*Flamenca*). The numeral two is often reinforced by means of *ambo* 'both': *amdui, amdoas, ambedoi,* etc. Continuations of *ambo* may also serve independently, though with less frequency: *n'ams los flancs* 'in both sides' (A. Daniel); *ab ambas mans* 'with both hands' (*Sainte Foi*). Analogically from *dui, doi,* Occitan draws a nom. *trei,* while the etymological *tres* is kept as an accusative and used throughout in the feminine, which, as usual, shows no case distinction. A plural *vintz* is encountered in *quatre-vins* (*Croisade Albigeoise*) and in other rare instances of the vigesimal counting system: *seis-vintz. Cen* takes an *-s* in the "plural hundreds": *trezens, dozentas. Mil* is a singular, *milia* a plural; they are both invariable, while the suffixated *milher* consistently serves as a noun: *per mil marcs* 'for a thousand marks' (B. de Born); *per cinc milia solz* 'for five thousand sous' (*Chartes*); *apres lui van ben tres miller de cavalliers* 'after him follow well over three thousand knights' (*Flamenca*), this last example with *miller* as a nominative plural. Compound numerals regularly link the units with *e: setenta e doas lengas so* 'there are seventy-two languages' (*Sermons*).

Prim from Lat. *prīmu* has been replaced by *premier,* leaving only rare vestiges: *non er segons ni tertz ans prims* 'it will not be the second nor the third, but the first' (A. Daniel). A few Latin ordinals have survived: *segon, tertz, cart, quint,* and a rare *sest,* while the remainder are formed on the *-e(n)* suffix: *seize(n), seten.* In enumerations, *l'altre* is more commonly used than *segon.*

Articles

Characteristic of the definite article is the lack of any case distinction in the masc. sing., where both cases have *lo,* aside from rare occurrences of a nom. *le* in certain narrative texts. The plural has a nom. *li* and an acc. *los,* while

TABLE 13.   Flexion of the Definite Article

	masculine		feminine	
	Occitan	Old French	Occitan	Old French
nom. sing.	lo < ĭllu(m), var. le < ĭlle	li < *ĭllī	la < ĭlla, var. li < *ĭllī	la
acc. sing.	lo < ĭllu(m)	le	la < ĭlla(m)	la
nom. pl.	li < ĭllī	li	las < ĭllas	les
acc. pl.	los < ĭllos	les	las < ĭllas	les

the feminine forms are sing. *la* and pl. *las*, with an alternate nom. sing. form *li*, which may have been drawn from the relative *qui* (Table 13). Contractions of the masculine article with some of the most common prepositions is standard: *al, del, el,* etc.; in the plural, these contractions are less violent than in French: Oc. *als, dels, els* vs. OFr. *as, des, es.* The forms of the indefinite article are listed above under "Numerals"; there is no partitive article.

Pronouns

Personal Pronouns

Subject pronouns are tonic. *Tu, nos,* and *vos* are regular reflexes of Latin, while CL *ĕgo,* reduced to VL *eo,* evolves to *eu* or *ieu* with optional diphthongization. The third person has *el, ela, il, elas,* with variants displaying a palatal *l: elh, elha,* etc. The fem. sing. variant form *il, ilh* is obtained in the same manner as the feminine article *li* (Table 14).

First- and second-person oblique forms lack any distinction between tonic and weak and between accusative and dative. The alternation of *me* and *mi, te* and *ti,* and *se* and *si* may stem from the influence of the dative *mi < mĭhī,* or else the forms in *i* may have originated from antevocalic use. *Nos* and *vos* pose no problems. The third-person oblique forms of the tonic series are masc. sing. *el < ĭllu* and *lui < (il)luī* and fem. sing. *ela < ĭlla* and *l(i)ei, l(i)eis < ĭllaei,* with some influence of *eius* accounting for the variant ending in *s.* The plural has masc. *els < ĭllos* and fem. *elas < ĭllas;* a major difference from French is the use of *lor* as a tonic oblique form, masculine as well as feminine (Table 15). The weak pronouns maintain a formal difference between the accusative: *lo, la, los, las,* and the dative: sing. *li* and pl. *lor.* The dative forms are identical for both genders (Table 16). Weak pronouns often lean enclitically on a preceding word for support: *lo·t < lo te; que·s < que* and *se* or *si.* The neuter *o < hŏc* is an accusative. The pronominal adverbs are *ne* or *en(t) < ĭnde* and *i < ĭbī.*

TABLE 14.   Flexion of the Subject Pronouns

	singular	plural
1st pers.	ĕgo > VL eo > eu, ieu	nōs > nos
2d pers.	tū > tu	vōs > vos
3d pers. masc.	ĭlla > el, elh; rare var. il, ilh	ĭllī > il, ilh
3d pers. fem.	ĭlla > ela, elha; var. il, ilh	ĭllas > elas, elhas
3d pers. neut.	ĭllu(m) > lo	—

TABLE 15.   Flexion of the Tonic Oblique Personal Pronouns

	singular	plural
1st pers.	mē > me, mi	nōs > nos
2d pers.	tē > te, ti rare var. tu from the nom.	vōs > vos
3d pers. masc.	ĭllu > el, elh; ĭllui > lui	ĭllos > els, elhs; ĭllōrum > lor, lur
3d pers. fem.	ĭlla > ela, elha; ĭllaei > l(i)ei, l(i)eis	ĭllas > elas, elhas; ĭllōrum > lor, lur
reflexive	sē > se, si	

TABLE 16.   Flexion of the Weak Personal Pronouns
(*Limited to the Third Person*)

	accusative	dative	reflexive
masc. sing.	ĭllu(m) > lo	ĭllī > li	sē > se, si
masc. pl.	ĭllos > los	ĭllōrum > lor, lur	"
fem. sing.	ĭlla(m) > la	ĭllī > li	"
fem. pl.	ĭllas > las	ĭllōrum > lor, lur	"
neut.	ĭllu(m) > o, lo; hŏc > o	—	—

Possessive Pronouns

The possessives consist of a strong or pronominal and a weak or adjectival category, though with no clear distinction between the two in the realm of possessives designating a plurality of owners. A conspicuous feature is the modeling of the masculine *tŭus* and *sŭus* on *mĕus*, giving a hypothetical **tĕus* and **sĕus* base, hence *m(i)eus*, *t(i)eus*, and *s(i)eus*, with optional diphthongization. These forms are inflected as follows: nom. sing. *m(i)eus*, acc. sing. *m(i)eu*, nom. pl. *m(i)ei*, acc. pl. *m(i)eus*, and a neuter *lo m(i)eu*. The postulated base for the feminine is **mēa* (cf. OFr. *meie*, *moie*), which changes its *e* to *i*

TABLE 17.   Flexion of the Tonic Possessives

	masculine	feminine
nom. sing.	mĕus, *tĕus, *sĕus > m(i)eus, t(i)eus, s(i)eus	*mēa > mia *and var.* m(i)eua; tŭa > toa, tua *and var.* t(i)eua; sŭa > soa, sua *and var.* s(i)eua
acc. sing.	mĕu(m), *tĕu(m), *sĕu(m) > m(i)eu, t(i)eu, s(i)eu	″
nom. pl.	mĕī, *tĕī, *sĕī > m(i)ei, t(i)ei, s(i)ei	mēas > mias *and var.* m(i)euas; tŭas > toas, tuas *and var.* t(i)euas; sŭas > soas, suas, *and var.* s(i)euas
acc. pl.	mĕos, *tĕos, *sĕos > m(i)eus, t(i)eus, s(i)eus	″

TABLE 18.   Flexion of the Possessive Adjectives

	masculine	feminine
nom. sing.	mĕus > VL *mos > mos; tŭus > VL *tos > tos; sŭus > VL *sos > sos	m(e)a > ma; t(ŭ)a > ta; s(ŭ)a > sa
acc. sing.	mĕum > VL *mom > mon, mó; tŭum > VL *tom > ton, tó; sŭum > VL *som > son, só	″
nom. pl.	mĕī, *tĕī, *sĕī > m(i)ei, t(i)ei, s(i)ei	m(e)as > mas; t(ŭ)as > tas; s(ŭ)as > sas
acc. pl.	mĕos > VL *mos > mos; t(ü)os > VL *tos > tos; s(ŭ)os > VL *sos > sos	″

in hiatus: *mia,* while a similar change of the hiatus *o* to *u* in *tŭa, sŭa* is optional only: *toa, tua* and *soa, sua.* Common also are feminine forms drawn ana-logically from the masculine: *m(i)eua, t(i)eua, s(i)eua.* The plural forms are *mias, m(i)euas,* etc. (Table 17). The possessive adjectives are *mos, tos, sos* in the masc. nom. sing. and acc. pl., derived from the reduced Vulgar Latin forms **mos, *tos, *sos,* while the masc. acc. sing. has *mo(n), to(n), so(n)* with an unstable *n.* The masc. nom. pl. is not kept distinct from the correspond-ing tonic forms. The feminine adjectival forms are *ma, ta, sa* in the singular, *mas, tas, sas* in the plural (Table 18). The possessives of plurality are *nostre, vostre,* and an invariable *lor, lur. Nostre* and *vostre* may optionally add a flexional *s* to the masculine nom. sing. form: *nostre(s), nostre, nostre, nostres* and *vostre(s), vostre, vostre, vostres,* while the feminine has *nostra, nostras* and *vostra, vostras* (Table 19).

TABLE 19.   Flexion of the Possessives of Plurality

	masculine		feminine	
	1st/2d pers.	3d pers.	1st/2d pers.	3d pers.
nom. sing.	noster > nostre(s); voster > vostre(s)	lor, lur < īllōrum	nostra > nostra; vostra > vostra	lor, lur < īllōrum
acc. sing.	nostru(m) > nostre; vostru(m) > vostre	″	″	″
nom. pl.	nostrī > nostre; vostrī > vostre	″	nostras > nostras; vostras > vostras	″
acc. pl.	nostros > nostres; vostros > vostres	″	″	″

Demonstrative Pronouns

The demonstratives are mostly derived from Lat. *īlle* and *ĭste*, reinforced by *ecce*: *ecce-īlle* > *cel* and *ecce-ĭste* > *cest*, with identical forms for the accusative, while the Old French nominatives *cil* and *cist* go back to a hypothetical *ĕcce-īllī* and *ĕcce-ĭstī* base, with an *i*-caused metaphony of *e* to *i*. The plural has *cil* and *cist* in the nominative and *cels*, *ceus* and *cestz* in the accusative. The feminine forms are *cela*, *cesta* in the singular and *celas*, *cestas* in the plural (Tables 20 and 21). Contrasting with the binary division in Old French: *cil* vs. *cist*, Occitan demonstratives carry a third dimension: masc. *aquel*, *aquest*, fem. *aquela*, *aquesta*, denoting what is far removed both from the person speaking and the person spoken to, and obtained through a reinforcement with *atque*, while an *atque* and *ecce* combination yields the forms *aicel* and *aicest*. The relatively infrequent feminine variants *cilh* for *cela*, *cist* for *cesta*, and *aquist* for *aquesta* are obtained in the same manner as the feminine article *li*, while alternate forms of the *cel* group, displaying a palatal *l*, have a parallel in third-person personal pronoun morphology. All these forms may serve either as adjectives or as pronouns.

Other demonstratives are masc. *celui* and fem. *cel(i)ei(s)*, paralleling the personal pronouns *lui* and *l(i)eis*, and found mostly in pronominal function. The uncompounded *ĭste* is continued as *est*, while *īlle* has yielded the definite article. Of the Latin demonstrative *hic*, only the neuter *hŏc* is kept; it is continued as *o* and enters into the formation of a variety of reinforced forms: *aco*, *aisso*, *so*, *zo*. The pronoun denoting identity is masc. *eis*, *eus*, *eps*, fem. *eissa*, *epsa*, drawn from Lat. *ĭpse* and often reinforced by *met-*: *mezeis*, *meteis*, *medeis* < *met-ĭpse*, while the French-type *mezesme*, *medesme* < *met-ĭpsĭmu* is rare.

TABLE 20. Flexion of *cest*

	masculine			feminine		
	VL	Occitan	OF	VL	Occitan	OF
nom. sing.	ecce-ĭste	cest	cist (< *ecce-ĭstī)	ecce-ĭsta	cesta, *var.* cist	ceste
acc. sing.	ecce-ĭstu	cest	cest	"	"	"
nom. pl.	ecce-ĭstī	cist	cist	ecce-ĭstas	cestas	cez, *rare and dial.* cestes
acc. pl.	ecce-ĭstos	cestz	cez	"	"	"

TABLE 21. Flexion of *cel*

	masculine			feminine		
	VL	Occitan	OF	VL	Occitan	OF
nom. sing.	ecce-ĭlle	cel	cil (< *ecce-ĭllī)	ecce-ĭlla	cela, *var.* cil	cele
acc. sing.	ecce-ĭllu	cel	cel	"	"	"
nom. pl.	ecce-ĭllī	cil	cil	ecce-ĭllas	celas	celes
acc. pl.	ecce-ĭllos	cels, ceus	cels, ceus	"	"	"

Relative and Interrogative Pronouns

The relative and interrogative pronouns are practically identical. Most distinctions of gender and number had disappeared already in Vulgar Latin, and a strong trend is noted in Occitan toward an even greater simplification: the indiscriminate use of *que* regardless of syntactical function. The nominative has *qui* or *que*, the oblique case *cui* or *que*, the neuter *que*. In addition, Occitan also has *cals* and *lo cals*, inflected like the third-declension adjective group, a relative adverb *que*, and an adverbial-pronominal *don* and *on*. The interrogative *quinhs-quinha* is of obscure origin. The indefinite or generalizing relatives are formed by adding an indefinite *que*, while the initial element may be interrogative rather than relative: *qui que* 'whoever'; *que que* 'whatever'; etc.

Indefinite Pronouns

This pronoun category constitutes a heterogeneous group, presenting relatively few specific morphological problems. The pronoun *om*, which serves

TABLE 22.   Flexion of *totz*

	masculine	feminine
nom. sing.	totz	tota
acc. sing.	tot	"
nom. pl.	tuit, tug, tuch	totas
acc. pl.	totz	"

as subject only, is derived from the nom. sing. of the Latin noun *hŏmo* 'man'. Its use parallels that of the French *on*. *Pluzor* is derived from a **plūriōri* base, with analogical influence of *plus*. *Autrui*, drawn from *autre*, is modeled on *cui*, *lui*, and Occitan shows instances of an erroneous plural formation *autruis*, unknown to French. *Cascu*, like OFr. *chascun*, may be either pro-nominal or adjectival, but an adjectival *casque* is created fairly early in Occitan. Lat. *quĭsque* is continued as *quec-quega*, which may serve either as a pronoun or as an adjective. *Manh*, *maint* is usually explained as stemming from a combination of *magnu* and *tantu*, but some scholars suggest Germanic or Celtic sources. *Totz* is inflected as shown in Table 22.

Of pronouns with indefinite-negative value, we may note *negu-neguna* < *nec-ūnu* and a dissimilated *degu-deguna*. *Nul* is flanked by the palatalized variants *nulh*, *lhun*, and *lunh*. *Neisun* or *nesun* can be traced to a **nec-ĭpse-ūnu* base. *Ren*, *re* is used not only about things, but also about persons, meaning either 'nothing' or 'nobody', and it may serve as a strong negation, in which case it may add an adverbial *s*: *re* or *res*. Occitan has several neuter indefinite pronouns, among them *al* < **alid* < CL *aliud* and *alre*, representing a combination of *al* and *re*.

Indeclinabilia

The *indeclinabilia*, which is to say adverbs, prepositions, and conjunctions, present little of interest to a morphological study. Many adverbs are formed by adding *-men* to the feminine form of the adjective, with *-men* stemming from the Latin feminine noun *mente*: *ricamen*, *doussamen*. French uses *-ment* in the same manner, but only Occitan shows sporadic examples of the primitive separability of the two constituent elements. The only other fea-ture worthy of note is that of the so-called adverbial *s*. Its origin is tradi-tionally traced to the frequency in Latin of adverbs ending in *-s*: *mĕlius*, *pĕius*, etc. An adverbial *s* may appear in the *-men* formation: *doussamentz*, and it spreads to other word categories. Affected are prepositions: *ses* (cf. Fr. *sans*) < *sĭne* + *s*, conjunctions: *sempre(s) que* < *sĕmper* + *s*, and indefinite pronouns: *al(s)*, *alre(s)*, *alque(s)*.

Verbs

It is in verb morphology that Occitan manifests its greatest individuality. It has preserved the pluperfect indicative of Latin, which has left only scant traces in the most archaic French; it abandons almost completely the weak *-avi* perfect, uses the *-dĕdī* perfect very widely, even with verbs of the *-ar* conjugation, and its future formation is subject to separability.

The Infinitive

The infinitive endings of Latin are *-āre, -ēre, -ĕre,* and *-īre,* and these develop as follows: *-are* is continued as *-ar*: *cantāre > cantar, -ēre* as *-er*: *jacēre > jazer,* and *-īre* as *-ir*: *servīre > servir,* while the unstressed *-ĕre* ending mostly gives *-re*: *perdĕre > perdre.* At times, however, it is the final vowel that is dropped in this category, not the post-tonic nonfinal *e,* and this phonological feature is responsible for leaving Occitan with instances of an unstressed *-er* ending: *vĭncĕre > vénser; plangĕre > plánher; essĕre > ésser.* There are numerous cross-overs from one infinitive category to another: *sapĕre >* VL *sapēre > saber,* and this may lead to the existence of alternate forms, mostly in the *e* conjugations: *ardre* and *arder; querre* and *querer; creire* and *creer,* but also *segre* and *seguir.* The *-ar* and *-ir* conjugations absorb all new formations: *agradar, abelir.*

Endings

There are several conspicuous features in the area of verbal endings. The supporting vowel, which in French is consistently *-e,* can be either *-e* or *-i* in Occitan: *ŏpero > obre, obri,* and this feature occurs even with verbs where no support is phonologically needed: *adōro > azor, azori: *trŏpo > trop, trobi.* Characteristic of 1st pers. pl. endings throughout is the loss of final *s* of Latin: *cantam, vendem, partem.* In the 2d pers. sing., *cantas* gives *cantas*; it is perhaps through an analogy from here that the other conjugations show a variant syllabic ending: *partz* and *partes; ventz* and *vendes.* In the 2d pers. pl., *-atz* is regular, while the other conjugations have *-etz,* in spite of the close quality of *e* in the Latin *-ētis, -ĭtis* endings. The opening of the vowel is usually accounted for through an analogy with *etz < ĕstis.* In the 3d pers. pl., the instability of *n* affects even *nt,* yielding the variants *parton* and *parto, vendon* and *vendo.* In the *-ar* group, however, final *n* is never allowed to drop, presumably to prevent confusion with the singular, but *cantan* is found alternating with *canton* and *canto,* obtained analogically from the other conjugations. In the 1st and 2d pers. pl., the *-em* and *-etz* endings of *e* verbs have spread to the *-ir* group, where they have completely ousted *-īmus* and *-ītis,* and these same forms are unaffected by the inchoative flexion: *florem, floretz* vs. *florisc, floriscon* (Table 23).

TABLE 23.   The Present Indicative

-ar	-re	-ir	-ir
cant, can	ven	part, parti, parte	floris, florisc
cantas	vens, vendes	partz, partes	floris, florisses
canta	ven	part	floris
cantam	vendem	partem	florem
cantatz	vendetz	partetz	floretz
cantan (-on, -en)	vendon (-o, -en)	parton (-o, -en)	florisson (-o, -en)

Changes in the Stem

Changes may occur in the stem owing to phonological factors. The stem-vowel may diphthongize if the required conditions are present, but it remains intact if the ending carries the stress: *vuelh, vuolh* vs. *volem, voletz*; *muer* vs. *morem, moretz*. Consonants are treated differently, depending on whether they become final or remain intervocalic: *trop* vs. *trobam*. In final position *nt* and *nd* may be reduced to a stable *n*, but they remain unchanged internally: *can* < *canto* vs. *cantam*; *ven* < *vendo* vs. *vendem*. If *v* becomes final, it vocalizes and may cause diphthongization: *mueu, muou* < *mŏvet* vs. *movem*. A variant *cant* of *can* < *canto* owes its unreduced consonant cluster to the rest of the paradigm.

The Imperfect Indicative

The imperfect indicative of *-are* verbs follows regularly from Lat. *-abam*. In the other groups, the Latin intervocalic *b* was lost, presumably through dissimilation in such common verbs as *habebam, debebam*, and the resulting *-ea* then evolved to *-ia* because of the hiatus position of *e* before *a*. In all imperfects, regardless of category, *-am* and *-atz* are stressed. The imperfect of the inchoative conjugation is similar to the noninchoative, with *floria* following the pattern of *partia* (Table 24). The imperfect of *esser* is *era*, from Lat. *eram* (Table 25).

The Future

As in most other Romance languages, the future is formed by means of the infinitive, to which the present tense of *aver* is added, though with elimination of the *av-* portion of *avem, avetz*. Unlike in French, separable futures and conditionals are not uncommon in Occitan: *dir-vos-ai per que* 'I shall tell you why'. The *a* vowel of the infinitive is regularly kept: **cantare aio > cantarai*, while *e* and *i* drop in this weak, intertonic position: **vendere aio > vendrai*;

TABLE 24.   The Imperfect Indicative

-ar	*-re*	*-ir*
cantava	vendia	partia
cantavas	vendias	partias
cantava	vendia	partia
cantavam	vendiam	partiam
cantavatz	vendiatz	partiatz
cantavan	vendian	partian
(-on, -o, -en)	(-on, -o, -en)	(-on, -o, -en)

TABLE 25.
Imperfect of *esser*

era
eras
era
eram
eratz
eran (-on, -o, -en)

*partire aio > partrai, although *i* is retained in the common variant flexion *partirai*, probably under analogical pressure from the infinitive or with some influence of *cantarai* (Table 26).

Conditional I

The conditional (conditional I) is formed in the same manner from the infinitive and the imperfect of *aver*, but with elimination of the initial *av-* portion of *avia*: *cantaria, vendria, partria,* or *partiria* (Table 27).

Conditional II

A notable characteristic of Occitan is the existence of a second conditional (conditional II), which formally represents a direct continuation of the Latin pluperfect indicative, with the exception, however, that verbs of the *-ar* group adopt the vowel *e* characteristic of the perfect: *ama(ve)ram > amara > amera*. These forms usually carry the value of conditionals or past conditionals: *amera* 'I would love' or 'I would have loved'; *fora* 'I would be' or 'I would have been'. The conditional II forms of *esser* and *aver* are *fora* and *agra*, respectively (Table 28).

TABLE 26.   Future

-ar	-re	-ir
cantarai	vendrai	partrai
cantaras	vendras	partras
cantara	vendra	partra
cantarem	vendrem	partrem
cantaretz	vendretz	partretz
cantaran (-au)	vendran	partran

TABLE 27.   Conditional I

-ar	-re	-ir
cantaria	vendria	partria
cantarias	vendrias	partrias
cantaria	vendria	partria
cantariam	vendriam	partriam
cantariatz	vendriatz	partriatz
cantarian	vendrian	partrian

TABLE 28.   Conditional II

-ar	-re	-ir	esser	aver
amera	vendera	partira	fora	agra
ameras	venderas	partiras	foras	agras
amera	vendera	partira	fora	agra
ameram	venderam	partiram	foram	agram
ameratz	venderatz	partiratz	foratz	agratz
ameran	venderan (-on, -o)	partiran	foran	agran

The Present Subjunctive

The present subjunctive continues the Latin forms, with the exception that *-iam* is reduced to *-am* (Table 29).

The Imperfect Subjunctive

Noteworthy for the imperfect subjunctive are the existence of a syllabic ending in the 2d pers. sing. and the alignment of *a* verbs with the perfect,

TABLE 29.   Present Subjunctive

-ar	-re	-ir
cant	venda	parta
cantz	vendas	partas
cant	venda	parta
cantem	vendam	partam
cantetz	vendatz	partatz
canten (-on)	vendan (-on, -o, -en)	partan

TABLE 30.   Imperfect Subjunctive

-ar	-re	-ir
cantes	vendes	partis
cantesses	vendesses	partisses
cantes	vendes	partis
cantessem	vendessem	partissem
cantessetz	vendessetz	partissetz
cantessen (-on)	vendessen (-on)	partissen (-on)

from which the vowel *e* is adopted. *Canta(vi)ssem* should have evolved to *cantas*, but this form is replaced by *cantes* (Table 30).

The Imperative

The imperative forms are *canta, cantatz* and *part, partetz.* It is the subjunctive that is used in exhortations: *cantem,* while French makes use of the indicative: *chantons.*

The Weak Perfect

Weak perfects are uniformly stressed on the ending. Of the weak Latin perfects in *-ii (-ivi), -evi* and *-avi,* only the *-ii* type survives: *partii (partivi)* > *partí,* while *-evi* is lost. Noteworthy is the almost complete disappearance of the *-avi* perfect, retained only in the 3d pers. sing.: *cantāvit* > **cantāt* > *cantat* (cf. Fr. *chanta*) and very seldom used. Many verbs of the two *e* groups adopted a new perfect based on Lat. *dĕdī,* perfect of *dare: vend(i)ei, perd(i)ei.* Significantly, it is this formation that has replaced the *-avi* type: *cant(i)ei, am(i)ei,* with optional diphthongization of *ĕ* caused by the final long *i.* This ranks easily as one of the most striking features of Occitan verb morphology.

TABLE 31.   Weak Perfect

-ar	*-ir*
cant(i)ei	parti
cant(i)est	partist
cantet	parti, partit
cantem	partim
cantetz	partitz
canteren (-on, -o)	partiron (-o, -en)

French has only very few vestiges of the *dĕdī* perfect formation; they are limited to the 3d pers. sing. and pl.: *perdiet, perdieron,* and none of these verbs belongs to the *-avi* group (Table 31).

The Strong Perfect

The strong perfects comprise both strong and weak forms, the strong ones being those that are stressed on the stem, while the weak ones are stressed on the ending. The distribution of these forms is not the same as in Latin; in Occitan, as well as in French, the 1st pers. sing. and the 3d pers. sing. and pl. are strong, while the other forms are weak. The 1st pers. pl. is strong in Latin, but *tráxĭmus* has undergone the influence of *traxístis,* becoming *traxímus,* and in the 3d pers. pl. the stressed *-ērunt* ending yields to the unstressed *-ĕrunt.* Strong perfects are commonly found with verbs of the *e* conjugations and a few others, but not with any verbs of the *-ar* group.

Latin had strong perfects in *-i: vīdī, fēcī,* in *-si* or *-xi: mīsī, dīxī,* and in *-ui: sapui.* Of these, the first group is limited to *fui, vi* and *fi, fezi* in Occitan, while the sigmatic type expanded its domain in Vulgar Latin: *fregi* is replaced by *franxi, quaesīvi* by *quaesi,* etc. Most *-ui* perfects are continued in a development that treats *u* like the initial Germanic *w-: tenuĭstī > *tenwist > tenguist; tĕnuit > *tengu(et) > tenc,* this latter form having undergone desonorization in final position after the regular loss of the *-et* ending. An exception to this development is constituted by all *-ui* perfects whose final stem consonant is *p,* where metathesis or anticipation of *u̯* represents the norm, with *pu̯* evolving to *u̯p* as in *sapuit > saup; recĭpuit > receup.* Forms such as *tenc, volc, poc* are responsible for the existence of alternations in the 3d pers. sing. perfect ending: *vi* and *vic.* Other characteristic features are metaphony in the 1st and 2d pers. sing., caused by the final long *i* of Latin: *tĕnuī > tinc,* not **tenc; tenuĭstī > tenguist,* not **tenguest,* and the alternation in the 3d pers. pl. between strong and weak forms: *tengron* and *tengueron; aguen* and *agueron; preiron* and *prezeron* (Table 32).

TABLE 32. Strong Perfect

vezer	prendre	tener	saber
vi	pris	tinc	saup
vist	prezist	tenguist	saubist
vi, vic	pres	tenc	saup
vim	prezem	tenguem	saubem
vitz	prezetz	tenguetz	saubetz
viron	preiron	tengron	saupron

The Present Participle

The present participles fall into two categories: those of the *-ar* group end in *-an*, all others in *-en*, as in *cantan, venden, parten*, this in contrast to French, where *-ant* is generalized throughout.

The Past Participle

The weak past participles end in *-at, -it,* or *-ut*: *cantát < cantātu, partit < partītu, agut <* VL **habūtu*. We may take note of the analogical extension of the *-ūtu* ending: *vendut, tenut, agut, vengut, dolgut, begut*, etc. The close relationship between *-ūtu* participles and *-ui* perfects is evident in the many forms in *g*; as an example, CL *ventum* is replaced in Vulgar Latin by *venūtu* and hence *venut* and Fr. *venu*, but far more common in Occitan is *vengut*, influenced by *venguist, venc*. Most of the strong, i.e., stem-stressed, past participles are derived from Latin formations in *-sum* and *-tum*: *mes < mĭssu*; *pres <* VL *preso < CL prĕhĕnsu*; *fait, fag < factu*; *rot < rŭptu*.

The Future Participle

A specific feature of Occitan is the existence of a future participle in *-dor <* Lat. *-tōriu* or *-tŭriu*: *endevenidor* 'that is to happen'. For transitive verbs the value of this participial formation is passive: *fazedor* 'that is to be done'; *punidor* 'that is to be punished'.

SYNTAX

Nouns

Case

Relationships that today are made by means of prepositions or through word order are often expressed in the old language by the surviving case system.

The principal uses of the nominative case are those of subject or predicate of *esser* or other copulative verbs, such as *devenir, remaner,* or *tornar: li pastor tornan lop raubador* 'the shepherds turn into ravenous wolves' (N'At de Mons); *lanquand li jorn son lonc en mai* 'when the days are long in May' (J. Rudel). Verbs for "to be called" are constructed with the nominative: *er' amics clamatz* 'he was called a friend' (G. de Bornelh); *a nom n'Ugos* 'his name is lord Hugo' (B. de Born). The nominative has by and large taken over the domain of the Latin vocative, though with some competition from the accusative: *messatgiers, vai e cor* 'messenger, run hastily' (B. de Ventadorn) vs. *messatgier, vai* 'go, messenger' (ibid.), and it is the norm in comparisons: *per so n'estaran vergonhos com lo lops* 'therefore they will be ashamed like the wolf' (B. de Born).

The accusative serves chiefly as direct object: *dos cavalhs ai* 'I have two horses' (Guillem de Peiteus), as prepositional complement: *guerra ses fuoc* 'a war without fire' (B. de Born), and in apposition with another accusative: *que Nostre Seinor portet effant* 'who carried our Lord when he was a child' (*Sermons*).

Double Accusatives

Not infrequently, a noun or an adjective is used in an attributive role with another accusative: *et avia moler na Elizabet* 'and he had for a wife lady Elizabeth' (*Sermons*); *clama sos vezins coartz* 'he calls his neighbors cowards' (P. d'Alvernhe); *qe·l vil fai car e.l nesci gen parlan* 'for it makes the wretched man friendly and the stupid man eloquent' (A. de Peguilhan); *si tolc marit un gentil baron* 'she married a noble baron' (*Vida*). However, prepositional constructions offer strong competition to this syntax: *no·l volg Boecis a senor* 'Boeci did not want him as a lord' (*Boeci*); *e fesetz de l'aiga vin* 'and you turned water into wine' (P. d'Alvernhe).

The Accusative in Genitive Function

With nouns designating individuals, the possessive relationship may be expressed through the juxtaposition of two nouns without the use of a preposition. The noun indicating the possessor is always in the accusative case, and it usually follows immediately upon the noun it determines: *pel cap sanh Gregori* 'by Saint Gregory's head' (Guillem de Peiteus); *per amor Deu* 'for the love of God' (ibid.); *Marcabrus, fills Marcabruna* 'Marcabru, son of Marcabruna' (Marcabru); *qu'ieu non ai ges tot lo sen Salamo* 'for I do not in any way have all Solomon's wisdom' (A. de Peguilhan). The same syntax is seen in Old French: *vos estes niece mon pere* 'you are my father's niece' (*Erec*). The reversed order of the two nouns is not uncommon with *dieu: per la Dieu voluntat* 'by the will of God' (*Sainte Enimie*). As in French, the juxtaposition genitive is also encountered with the pronouns *autrui* and *cui*; they both precede: *en l'autrui ueil* 'in your neighbor's eye' (G. Faidit); *lui cui sui amia* 'him whose friend I am' (B. de Dia). Occitan alone may make *autrui* "agree," as it were, with a following plural noun: *fan los autrus enfans als maritz tener e noyrir* 'they make the husbands raise and bring up other people's children' (Marcabru). Rivaling genitive constructions with *de* or *a* and an accusative are used with plural possessors and whenever the possessor is not referred to as a distinct individual, but as a member of a class: *reis dels Engles* 'king of the English' (B. de Born); *filla semblaz d'emperador* 'you seem to be the daughter of an emperor' (*Sainte Foi*). The same rules apply to Old French: *l'ost as Franchois* 'the army of the French' (Robert de Clari); *malvais fix a putain* 'you evil son of a bitch' (*Aucassin et Nicolete*). The preposition *de* is obligatory when the possessor is an animal or a thing: *las voltas dels auzeus* 'the warblings of the birds' (G. de Bornelh); *ab la dolchor del temps novel* 'with the sweetness of the new season' (Guillem de Peiteus).

The Accusative as an Unmarked Dative

Closely related to the juxtaposition genitive is the use of the accusative in the role of an absolute or unmarked dative. Used only about human beings or about God, the prepositionless dative may either precede or follow the verb: *Mon Conort dei grat saber* 'I must be thankful to Mon Conort' (B. de Ventadorn); *lo somnhe comtei mo senhor* 'I told the dream to my lord' (G. de Bornelh). The dative may also be expressed by means of *a* followed by a noun in the accusative case: *gran honor aves faita a mun seinor* 'you have greatly honored my lord' (*Jaufré*).

The Adverbial Accusative

The accusative serves in indications of point in time, duration, measure, and manner: *l'altrer, lo primer jorn d'aost, vinc en Proensa* 'recently, on the first day of August, I came to Provence' (G. de Bornelh); *cant ac un gran briu anat* 'when he had traveled quite a while' (*Jaufré*); *cascus se lonja .i. mezurat arpen* 'everybody withdraws by exactly one *arpent*' (*Daurel et Beton*); *vai t'en dreich viatge lai on ill es* 'go straight to where she is' (Peirol). An accusative may serve to express accompanying circumstance in absolute locutions: *puis venc . . . ves Fellon, escut abrassat* 'then he moved toward Fellon, holding his shield in his arms' (*Jaufré*).

Number

Collectives

Some collective singulars are originally neuter plurals, which are able to preserve a value of plurality, as is the case with *folha*, which often denotes 'all the leaves of a tree, foliage': *ans que·l cim reston . . . despoillat de fuoilla* 'before the treetops remain stripped of their foliage' (A. Daniel). Other instances of this feature may be seen in the following passages: *esquinta sa vestimenta* 'he ruined his clothes' (*Sainte Enimie*); *bastir la mura* 'to build the city walls' (ibid.); *sa pluma li trembla* 'its plumage is trembling' (D. de Pradas). *Brassa* is used globally for 'both arms': *mort te veg e tenc en ma brassa* 'dead I see you and hold you in my arms' (*Marienklage*).

Agreement of Collectives

Though formally singular, collectives denote a plurality of beings or things and are therefore subject to a vacillating agreement pattern: *e fes castiar sa mainada que non fasson bruida* 'and she urged her servants not to make any noise' (*Jaufré*); *bella foil gentz, si fosson san* 'the people would have been beautiful, if they had been healthy' (*Sainte Foi*).

Abstracts

Abstracts often appear in plural form in what may originally have been some kind of augmentative process serving to mark either intensity or repeated occurrence as in Lat. *calores* 'intense heat' and *amicitiae* 'proofs or manifestations of friendship'. Occitan examples are: *ac ne grans alegriers* 'he rejoiced over it' (*Daurel et Beton*); *can vei vostras beltatz* 'when I see your beauty' or 'your beautiful features' (G. de Bornelh). The plural is particularly common in prepositional locutions: *en grans pessamens* 'in great anguish' (Perdigon); *quar ylh es ses totas merces* 'for she is completely without mercy' (A. de Maruelh).

Adjectives

Substantival Use of Adjectives

Adjectives often serve as nouns, designating a person or a group of persons endowed with a certain quality or characteristic: *ieu vuoill mais esser paubres honratz c'avols manens* 'I will rather be a poor man living honorably than a vile person of great wealth' (A. de Peguilhan); *e·l vielh laissan als joves lor maisos* 'and the old leave their houses to the young' (B. de Born), or denoting an abstract concept: *sabra·n lo ver* 'she will learn the truth about it' (Cercamon).

Agreement of the Adjective

Adjectives agree in gender, case, and number with the noun they modify: *vuel un novel chant comenzar* 'I want to begin a new song' (Cercamon); *ab tan doussa pena* 'with such sweet suffering' (Peirol); *e·l pans fo blancs e.l vins fo bos* 'and the bread was white and the wine was good' (Guillem de Peiteus);

et ag loncz guinhos 'and it had long whiskers' (ibid.); *en las ricas cortz* 'in the powerful courts' (P. Vidal). Agreement is usually made with the closer of two coordinated nouns: *vengutz es lo temps e la sazos* 'the time and the moment have arrived' (A. de Peguilhan); *maint mur, mainta tor desfacha veirem* 'we shall see many a wall and many a tower destroyed' (B. de Born).

The Neuter Adjective

The neuter adjective refers to such neuter antecedents as *so* and *tot* or to the content of a clause: *so que vas totz es comunal* 'what is common to everybody' (G. de Bornelh); *mas anc non fo crezut qu'ella li fezes amor de la persona* 'but it was never believed that she had made love to him' (*Vidas*). As in French, *es vers* and *es dreitz* contain correctly inflected masc. nom. sing. nouns and not adjectives: *conosc que vers es* 'I know that it is the truth' (E. de Barjols); *et es ben dreytz e razos* 'and it is truly just and right' (ibid.). The neuter form of several adjectives, among them *aut, clar, bas, gen, greu, fort*, etc., is often used adverbially: *e·l rossinhols autet e clar leva sa votz* 'and the nightingale raises its voice loudly and clearly' (B. de Ventadorn); *am fort* 'I love sincerely' (Ussel); *parla bas* 'he speaks softly' (R. d'Aurenga). It is an uninflected masculine accusative rather than a neuter adjective that appears in such impersonal locutions as *faire bo(n), faire bel*: *en totas res fai bo menar mesura* 'it is good to show moderation in all things' (G. de Cabestanh); *porc . . . fai melhor escoutar que vos* 'it is better to listen to a pig than to you' (B. de Born).

Numerals

An approximate number may be expressed by means of *tal*: *nos fom tal trenta guerrier* 'we were some thirty warriors' (B. de Born), while proportional relations are expressed by means of a substantival *tan*: *eras ay de mal dos tans* 'now I suffer twice as much pain' (G. Riquier), or through the use of the preposition *per*, followed by *un* and another cardinal: *e qan vos vi, amei vos per un cen, e chascun jorn creis l'amors per un dos* 'and when I saw you, I loved you a hundredfold, and every day my love grows twofold' (A. de Peguilhan). This construction is extremely rare in the north, where it never achieved the formulaic status it holds in the south.

Articles

The definite and the indefinite articles are used much less in the medieval language than in later periods, and there is no partitive article: *liura uous e fromatge* 'he distributes eggs and cheese' (B. de Born). Locutions such as *aver paor, prendre comjat, aver esperansa* may be relics of a primitive syntax, which tended to leave the direct object unmodified. Furthermore, it may be said of abstracts in general that they carry no article. The personification of abstract qualities is a highly favored stylistic device in Romance medieval literature. Such personifications are treated like proper nouns, remaining unmodified: *Pres es mortz e Jois sos compain* 'Merit is dead and Joy its companion' (*Flamenca*). Nouns used generically, whether in the singular or in the plural, to designate a species or a class are unmodified: *salamandra viu de pur foc* 'the salamander lives of fire alone' (*Bestiaire*); *volon mais raubar que lop non fan* 'they want to take more than wolves do' (P. Cardenal). The definite article is rarely used with the demonstrative force of its Latin source: *per so·n cazec lo dia* 'therefore he fell that day' (R. de Vaqueiras). Nouns taken in a general, indefinite sense are unmodified: *e d'ome qu'es aissi conques, pot domn' aver almorna gran* 'and for a man who is thus conquered, a lady may have great pity' (i.e., 'any man' and 'any lady') (B. de Ventadorn). Omission of the article often follows from a negative or conditional sentence structure: *si gaugz entiers no m'en socor* 'if a perfect joy does not assist me' (P. Vidal).

The Plural Indefinite Article

The plural indefinite article is most commonly used about objects that occur in pairs, or that are somehow viewed as consisting of two identical halves: *la valensa d'us gans* 'the value of a pair of gloves' (*Croisade Albigeoise*); *ac . . . us bels estivals biais* 'he wore a pair of sharp-pointed boots' (*Flamenca*); *ab unas forfes ben tallanz* 'with a sharp pair of scissors' (ibid.). Occitan does not seem to use this syntax with parts of the body, as opposed to Old French, which has such forms as *unes levres* 'lips' and *unes joes* 'cheeks'. The plural indefinite article may also serve to stress the notion of a unit made up of a set of individual elements: *demandet us escaxs d'evori* 'he asked for a chess-board of ivory' (*Chanson d'Antioche*).

Emphatic Use of Un

The indefinite article *un* may assume the strong meaning of 'one and the same, identical, one single', which brings it close to the qualifying adjective in syntactic behavior: *d'un paire son tut l'enfan?* 'are all the children of the same father?' (Perdigon); *tro qu'Espanha fos tota d'una fe* 'until Spain would be all of one single faith' (P. Vidal); *e son andui d'un pretz e d'un parage* 'and they are both of equal merit and of equal rank' (R. de Vaqueiras). Old French has the same usage: *sol une nuit sont en un leu* 'they spend only one night in the same place' (Béroul).

Pronouns

Personal Pronouns

Subject Pronouns.   Since verbal endings afford a clear indication of person, subject pronouns are usually left unexpressed: *ar' auzires qu'ai respondut* 'now you shall hear what I answered' (Guillem de Peiteus), and the same holds true of the impersonal construction: *quan mi soven de la cambra* 'when I remember the room' (A. Daniel). However, subject pronouns may appear for a variety of syntactical and rhythmical reasons, serving above all to mark emphasis or contrast: *e ilh an lui per dessenat* 'and *they* believe that *he* has gone mad' (P. Cardenal); *nos fom austor et ylh foro aigro* 'we were hawks, and they were herons' (R. de Vaqueiras). They are also used in coordinations: *en breu serem ja velh et ilh et eu* 'soon we shall be old both she and I' (P. Vidal).

Tonic Oblique Pronouns.   The tonic pronoun serves above all as a prepositional complement: *pus me mirei en te* 'since I looked at myself in you' (B. de Ventadorn). In a characteristic structure of Medieval Gallo-Romance, the pronoun that stands between a preposition and an infinitive assumes tonic form, being considered a prepositional complement rather than the object of the infinitive: *e faitz issir vostras jenz per el aculhir* 'and have your people come out to receive him' (*Jaufré*); *de liey servir sui volontos* 'I am eager to serve her' (G. de Cabestanh); *c'anc de lui amar no m'estrais* 'for I never gave up loving him' (B. de Dia). Similarly for Old French: *de moi desarmer fu adroite* 'she was very skilled at unarming me' (*Yvain*). The same structure is encountered with infinitives that would require an indirect object: *a lui ajudar e servir* 'to help and serve him' (*Flamenca*), and in Old French: *por els doner a boivre* 'to give them (wine) to drink' (*Saint Eustace*). The tonic pronoun may occasionally follow the infinitive: *ges no·m recre d'amar leis* 'I never give up loving her' (G. Faidit), or the pronoun may be omitted altogether: *c'om no pot cor destrenher ses aucire* 'for one cannot torment a heart without killing it' (B. de Ventadorn), but Occitan never inserts a weak pronoun between preposition and infinitive, and cases of this construction are extremely rare in Old French: *por la mener a chief* 'in order to bring it to an end' (*Queste del Saint Graal*). Cases such as *pres suy del penr' e del grazir* 'I am ready for the taking and for the acceptance' (Guillem de Peiteus) do not contain pronouns, but substantival infinitives preceded by the definite article. Tonic pronouns are used with the gerund: *vau leis seguen* 'I am following her' (B. de Ventadorn), and they may be contrasted with one another or with a noun for emphasis: *non blasmetz mi mas vos eissa et Amor* 'do not blame me, but yourself and Love' (A. de Peguilhan).

Weak Pronoun Combinations.   If the context calls for both a direct and an indirect object pronoun, Occitan keeps the full form of the accusative, adding the dative enclitically in weakened form: *eu non lo·lh aus dire* 'I do not dare tell it to her' (P. Vidal), with *lo·lh* from *lo li*, whereas Old French drops the accusative altogether in a development known as *écrasement*: *les armes quiert et l'an li baille* 'he asks for his weapons, and they give them to him' (*Erec*). Hitherto undocumented for the south, this feature

appears in: *e ques lil cors demantenen. Ses contradir autreiet li* 'and he immediately asked him for the body. Without objecting, he granted it to him'
(*Marienklage*). Striking is the ease with which Occitan is able to combine
two non-third-person pronouns, one an accusative and the other a dative:
qu'ie·us mi don ses bauzia 'for I surrender myself to you without deceit' (B.
Carbonel); *eu qe·us mi complaing* 'I who complain to you' (R. de Vaqueiras);
paratges sai que·us mi defen 'I know that rank forbids me (to love) you'
(Ussel). Such combinations are impossible in Old French. Ethical-dative
syntax even allows for the grouping together of two datives: *diguas li·m* 'tell
her for me' (Cercamon); *so lor mi digatz* 'tell them that for me' (Peirol).
Two datives are very rarely combined outside of this specific case: *cant li·m
plac senher lo bran* 'when it pleased her to gird upon me the sword' (R. de
Vaqueiras).

Pronoun and Verb.   Since weak pronouns cannot open a sentence, they
are placed after the verb: *trobei la sotz un fau* 'I found her under a beech-tree'
(Marcabru); *meravilh me com posc durar* 'I wonder how I can go on' (B. de
Ventadorn), but they resume their accustomed place before the verb if other
elements are present at the head of the sentence: *enquer me menbra d'un mati*
'I still remember one morning' (Guillem de Peiteus); *a manjar mi deron capos*
'they gave me capons to eat' (ibid.). Similarly with the imperative: *paia mi*
'pay me' (G. Ademar) vs. *ab joi t'en vai* 'sally forth with joy' (G. de Bornelh).
Weak pronouns are normally placed before the entire auxiliary plus infinitive group rather than before the infinitive: *pos no·l sai far* 'since I do not
know how to do it' (G. de Bornelh); *mas eu non lo·lh aus dire* 'but I do not
dare tell it to her' (P. Vidal), even in cases where the infinitive is separated
from the auxiliary by a preposition: *car lo menasava a pendre* 'for he threatened to hang him' (*Jaufré*).

The Ethical Dative.   It will suffice to briefly mention the frequent use of
me as an ethical dative, translating as 'for me' or 'on my behalf': *vay me ad
Aspremon* 'go to Aspremon for me' (*Dauel et Beton*). The most striking feature
of the ethical dative is the ease with which it allows for joining two datives
together: *e potz li·m ben dire qu'en breu la verai* 'and you can truly tell her for
me that I shall see her shortly' (Peirol).

The Dative Constructed with an Adverb.   It is not uncommon for verbs
indicating a sudden or surprising and often hostile movement to be constructed with an adverb and a dative rather than with a prepositional phrase:
lieis, ce·m fug denan 'the lady who flees before me' (Ricas Novas); *ez ab aitan
lor saill denan lo senescal* 'and at that moment the seneschal appears before
them' (*Jaufré*), and similarly with verbs marking a state: *quant eu li sui denan*
'when I am in front of her' (P. Vidal). The corresponding prepositional

phrases are, of course, also in common use: *tu venras denan leis viatz* 'you will quickly appear before her' (G. de Bornelh).

Reflexive Pronouns

The use of a reflexive in lieu of a personal pronoun is common in Gallo-Romance: *e dui apostol devon ben un cavallier aver ab se* 'and two cardinals truly ought to have one knight with them' (*Flamenca*), while the reverse trend in Occitan is restricted to the plural, where *lor* may replace the reflexive *se, si*: *ben an mort mi e lor mei huel galiador* 'my treacherous eyes have killed me and themselves' (F. de Marseilla). *Se* is occasionally encountered as a prepositional complement even where no reflexive function is present: *e s'acordet ab se* 'and he reached an agreement with him' (B. de Born); *s'ilh non a de me merce, pot saber que murai de se* 'if she shows no pity on me, she may learn that I shall die because of her' (G. Faidit). Reflexives are usually left unexpressed with nonfinite verb forms: *que·l jorns es aprosmatz* 'for the day has drawn near' (F. de Marseilla), from *aprosmar se*.

Possessive Pronouns

The tonic possessives serve unmodified as predicates of *esser* and other copulative verbs: *l'anta er soa el dans mieus* 'the shame will be its and the harm mine' (*Flamenca*); *sieus son e sieus serai jase* 'I am hers, and I shall be hers forever' (Peirol). They may also appear directly before the noun, competing with the adjective, seemingly with no added emphasis: *era tan grans li sieua honestatz* 'her honesty was so great' (*Sancta Doucelina*). *Lor* is originally invariable in conformity with its Latin source: *tol lor chastels* 'he takes their castles' (B. de Born), but a plural form *lors* is created fairly early in the south: *lurs sermos* 'their words' (Perdigon); *totas lurs molhers* 'all their women' (*Daurel et Beton*), and there are even instances of a nom. sing. *lors*, pointing to the establishment of a *lors, lor, lor, lors* flexion: *tot so qe lurs seinhers lur di* 'everything their lord tells them' (B. de Bondeilhs); *ans m'es lurs brutz honors* 'on the contrary, their talk is to me an honor' (A. de Peguilhan). Possession is marked pleonastically far more often in the south than in the north: *per vos mi creys ma grans dolors* 'because of you my great sadness grows' (Marcabru); *mas camjatz l'es sos coratges* 'but changed is her heart' (R. de Vaqueiras).

The possessive may express a subjective as well as an objective genitive: *la nostr' amor vai enaissi* 'the love we feel fares like this' (Guillem de Peiteus) vs. *lo sant paes on venc per nostr' amor morir* 'the holy land where he came to die because of his love for us' (P. Vidal); *sos amars m'es prezius* 'loving her is precious to me' (G. Riquier); *am mais la sua vista* 'I prefer seeing her' (G. de Biars). Similarly, *mos conoissens* 'my friends' or 'my acquaintances' are 'those who know me' (B. de Born). It may also be the equivalent of a dative:

cre far son pro e·l mieu dan 'I believe that I am doing what is good for her and bad for me' (Uc de Saint-Circ), or it may serve as the equivalent of various prepositional constructions: *qui no vol prendre son plait o sa mercei* 'if one does not want to accept a pact or a reconciliation with her' (Guillem de Peiteus); *contra la soa batailla non qier ja repaus aver* 'I do not wish to have any respite in my struggle against it [i.e., love]' (Peirol).

Demonstrative Pronouns

Celui and *cel(i)ei(s)* mostly serve as oblique forms, and they usually function solely as pronouns, their primary function being that of antecedents of a relative clause: *cel que cellui combat que no·is deffen* 'he who fights against a person who does not defend himself' (A. de Peguilhan); *quar eu d'amar no·m posc tener celeis don ja pro non aurai* 'for I cannot refrain from loving the lady from whom I shall never have any favor' (B. de Ventadorn). An adjectival *celui* is extremely rare, and I can cite only one such instance: *en cellui temps* 'at that time' (Raimon Vidal de Besalù, *Judici d'Amor*), while a similar syntax is not uncommon in Old French: *cestui Jason* 'this Jason' (*Roman de Troie*); *de celui lac* 'from that lake' (*Queste del Saint Graal*); *par celi Dieu en cui je croi* 'by the God in whom I believe' (*Guillaume d'Angleterre*).

Eis 'same, self, own' expresses insistence or identity: *quelh eys Dieus . . . la fetz de sa eyssa beutat* 'for God himself made her from his own beauty' (G. de Cabestanh). It often serves to reinforce a personal or a reflexive pronoun: *ill eis sent de l'espaven* 'he himself feels scared' (P. d'Alvernhe); *car se eis destrui* 'for he destroys himself' (G. de Bornelh). It may be used adverbially with the meaning of 'even': *eiss saintz Caprasis* 'even Saint Caprasis' (*Sainte Foi*).

Relative Pronouns

The neuter relative pronoun is *que*, which usually refers to the neuter antecedent *so*: *e·m fetz encobir so que no·m pot avenir* 'and she made me desire what cannot fall to my lot' (G. de Bornelh), but it may also stand alone: *Alixandres fo niens contra qu'eu seria* 'Alexander was nothing compared to what I would be' (P. Vidal). It is a neuter *que* that is contained in sentences like *fesetz que fols* 'you acted foolishly', lit. 'you did what a fool (would have done)' (R. de Vaqueiras): *que malvatz fai* 'he acts in an evil manner' (B. de Born); *amors . . . fai que corteza* 'love acts in a courtly manner' (Peirol).

The use of *que* following a preposition is a common occurrence, although Schultz-Gora (§124) declares this syntax nonexisting. It may refer not only to things and abstracts: *la tenda . . . en que jasia Brunesens* 'the tent in which Brunesen was sleeping' (*Jaufré*); *las penas en que·m fai estar* 'the sufferings in which she makes me live' (G. Godi), but also to animals and persons: *vostr' aucel, cel ab que cassest el pradel* 'your bird, the one with which you were hunting in the meadow' (*Jaufré*); *una santa pieusela, per que·l mons es salvatz* 'a holy virgin by whom the world is saved' (P. Cardenal).

Lo cal is mostly found in texts of a juridical or ecclesiastical nature; essentially pronominal, it mostly serves as a prepositional complement: *un balcet lonc lo cal eu . . . mis una peira* 'an escarpment alongside which I placed a stone' (*Chartes*); *en Bernart Aton de qual tu es preinz* 'lord Bernart Aton with whose child you are pregnant' (ibid.). The adjectival *lo cal* is restricted to a technical style: *delz pasturals de las Olmeiras, los quals pasturals afermava per seus l'abas del Loc Deu* 'of the pastures of las Olmeiras, which pastures the abbot of Loc Deu was claiming as his' (ibid.).

The relative *cui* is mostly used in reference to persons, serving, just as in Old French, as a dative: *lo reis cui el laisset la terr'* 'the king to whom he left his land' (Cercamon); *cui que plass' o cui que pes* 'whomever it may please, or whomever it may displease' (ibid.), and is at times preceded by *a* in this function: *Fin'Amors a cui me sui datz* 'True Love to which I have given myself' (J. de Puycibot). It may also serve as a genitive, expressing a relationship which is not essentially different from that of the dative: *cella cui soi amis* 'the lady whose friend I am' or 'the lady to whom I am a friend' (A. Daniel). *Cui* may express possession: *·l marques cui es Salonics* 'the marquis to whom Saloniki belongs' (P. Vidal), and is found alternating in this acceptation with *de cui*: *al rei Peire, de cui es Vics* 'to King Peire to whom Vic belongs' (ibid.). *Cui* may further serve as an emphatic direct object: *vos, cuy yeu am et azor* 'you whom I love and adore' (Ricas Novas), and as a prepositional complement, mostly in reference to persons: *tal seingnor ai, en cui a tant de be* 'I have a lord in whom there is so much good' (R. de Berbezilh), but also quite commonly to abstracts: *us novels jois en cui ai m'esperansa* 'a new joy in which I have placed my hope' (F. de Marseilla), while nonpersonal use of *cui* following a preposition is undocumented for Old French.

The relative adverb *don* usually marks point of departure or origin: *la terra don son* 'the land I am from' (*Jaufré*), but may also mean 'where', specifically when designating a person's birthplace: *torna t'en en Persa, don es natz e noiritz* 'go back to Persia where you were born and raised' (*Croisade Albigeoise*). Noted is also its use as a relative with instrumental value: *m'espasa, don tant baron ai mort* 'my sword, with which I have killed so many a baron' (*Jaufré*).

Local adverbs meaning "where" are commonly used in relative function. Old French has *ou*, from Lat. *ŭbī*, while the south uses *on* from *ŭnde*: *a Cardoil, on a vit Taulat* 'at Cardoil where he saw Taulat' (*Jaufré*). *On* often has an adverb of place as its antecedent: *de lai on s'abriva·l Nils tro sai on sols es colgans* 'from where the Nile flows to here where the sun sets' (G. de Bornelh). With the meaning of 'in whom', it refers to a person in this passage: *scellui on tut peccador troban fi* 'the one in whom all sinners find peace' (Guillem de Peiteus). Found only in Occitan is the use of *on* and a comparative adverb in expressions of a proportional relationship: *on plus es autz, gieta mais de calor* 'the higher it [i.e., the sun] is in the sky, the more heat it irradiates' (P. de C. d'Aorlac); *on plus la prec, plus m'es dura* 'the more I plead with her, the more cruel she is to me' (B. de Ventadorn). *O* from *ŭbī* is extremely rare and archaic in the south.

The relative adverb *que* is often favored over a more precise and often cumbersome linking: *una ma filha que sos maritz mor es* 'a daughter of mine whose husband is dead' (*Daurel et Beton*), with *que sos maritz* for *cui maritz.*

Qui is used without an antecedent in broad, generalizing statements: *qui ama de cor non vol garir* 'he who loves from the heart does not want to be cured' (A. de Peguilhan). This *qui* is often thought of as having hypothetical value: *fora be grans tortz qui m'en tolgues lo desirier* 'it would have been a great wrong if someone would have taken away from me the desire [to do so]' (Peirol). It may establish a dative relationship: *del vers vos dig que mais en vau qui ben l'enten* 'I am telling you that the poem is worth more to the person who understands it well' (Guillem de Peiteus); *greu partir si fa d'amor qui la trob' a son talen* 'it is difficult to separate oneself from love for the person who finds it to his liking' (ibid.).

Interrogative Pronouns

It is *cal* rather than *lo cal* that serves to express an alternative: *ges non sai ab qual mi tengua de N'Agnes o de N'Arsen* 'I do not know at all which one to choose, whether lady Agnes or lady Arsen' (Guillem de Peiteus); *triatz de doas cal val mays* 'choose which one of the two ladies is better' (F. de Marseilla), although *lo cal* does take this usage: *no sai re loqual d'ams ai pejor* 'I do not know at all which one of the two I consider worse' (A. de Peguilhan). An adjectival *lo cal* is rare: *pois apenrés la qual vía deu tener bar* 'then you will learn which course a baron must follow' (P. Cardenal).

Indefinite Pronouns

The Latin noun *hŏmo* 'man' is continued as an indefinite pronoun *om* in the south, paralleling the development of Fr. *on*: *per un albre c'om hi tailla* 'for one tree they cut there' (Guillem de Peiteus); *ardre·ls degr' om* 'one ought to burn them' (Cercamon). The use of third-person plural verbs in the present indicative in this acceptation is restricted to *dizen* 'they say, people say' (P. d'Alvernhe).

Autre is sometimes used pleonastically in Medieval Gallo-Romance: *fora mielhs . . . que visques el que maint autre enoios* 'it would have been better if he [i.e., the Young King] had lived than many annoying people' (B. de Born)— and not '*many other annoying people*', since the king is not part of this larger group. Here is a similar example from Old French: *en bois estes com autre serve* 'you [i.e., Yseut] live in the woods like a bondwoman' (Béroul). The *l'us-l'autre* structure does not normally allow for any gender distinction, as in this passage, which refers to a man and a woman: *non poiria l'uns ses l'autre joi aver* 'one could find no joy without the other' (Sordel).

A singular *tan* serves with countables to emphasize individual occurrence rather than the mass aspect: *tanta veuza, tant orfe cosselhar e tant mesqui vos ai vist ajudar* 'I have seen you help so many a widow, so many an orphan and so many a weak person' (R. de Vaqueiras); *m'espasa, don tant baron ai mort* 'my sword, with which I have killed so many a baron' (*Jaufré*). The same syntax may be seen with *molt*: *estat ai molta setmana abrossitz en gran languor* 'for many a week I have been sad [?] and languishing' (D. de Pradas), and this represents the most characteristic usage of *maint*: *mainta malanansa i hai suffert, e maint turmen* 'many a misfortune have I suffered there and many a torment' (G. Faidit); *aqui auzim vas manhtas partz sonar manh corn, manh gralle, manhta senha cridar* 'there we heard on many sides the sounding of many a horn, of many a clarion, and the shouting of many a war cry' (R. de Vaqueiras).

Serving as adverbs of quantity in a construction with *de, tan, molt,* and *maint* may show grammatical agreement with the prepositional complement: *car m'a fait tanta d'onor* 'for she has bestowed so much honor on me' (P. Vidal); *en mantas de maneiras* 'in many ways' (*Croisade Albigeoise*); *en motas de maneiras* 'in many ways' (*Sancta Doucelina*).

Verbs

Faire faire qch. à qn.

The *faire faire qch. à qn.* construction, 'to have or make somebody do something', is commonly found: *fan los autrus enfans als maritz tener* 'they make the husbands raise other people's children' (Marcabru); *e fa a la gaixa sonar los cavalers* 'and have the watchman call the knights' (*Jaufré*), and the same syntax is often observed with the verbs of perception *vezer* and *auzir*: *eu l'audi leger a clerczons* 'I heard clerics recite it' (*Sainte Foi*); *so que auch dir a vos* 'what I am hearing you say' (Perdigon); *ieu vi als fals los fis amonestar, e als lairos los leials prezicar* 'I see the disloyal admonish the sincere and thieves preach to the loyal' (P. Cardenal).

Pronominal Verbs

The use of a reflexive pronoun with verbs indicating movement, mode of being or rest is widespread in Medieval Gallo-Romance; it is a popular feature, which has its roots in Vulgar Latin. Verbs used pronominally, such as *morir se* for *morir*, do not normally present any difference in meaning, the pronoun being essentially expletive in nature, serving at the most to stress such vague notions as participation or interest in the stated action: *on que·m an* 'wherever I go' (B. de Tot-lo-mon); *si·m sui estatz lonc tems iratz* 'if I have been sad a long time' (G. de Bornelh); *ab leis me remanh* 'I remain with her' (ibid.); *el castel s'en es intratz* 'he entered the castle' (*Jaufré*).

The Reflexive Passive

The reflexive passive, which is documented only very sporadically in Old French: *car amors ne se puet celer* 'for love cannot be hidden' (Béroul), is present in the work of one of the earliest troubadours: *ni res tant greu no·s covertis* 'and nothing is obtained with as great a difficulty' (Cercamon); *sobre tota·s deu prezar* 'more than anybody else she must be esteemed' (ibid.), and it gains in frequency later on: *c'autre viure no·s deu vid' apellar* 'for a different way of living should not be called life' (Sordel).

Impersonal Verbs

As a rule, the impersonal construction does not carry a formally expressed subject, but it is not uncommon for it to be accompanied by various complements, notably by a dative pronoun: *a chantar m'er* 'I shall have to sing' (B. de Dia); *puois de me no·us chal* 'since you do not care about me' (B. de Born), or by *de* introducing the true or logical subject: *assatz m'es bel del temps essuig* 'the dry season pleases me very much' (Marcabru); *be sapchatz que·m peza del dan* 'you well know that the harm grieves me' (G. de Bornelh); *puois als baros enoia e lor pesa d'aquesta patz* 'since this peace annoys the barons and grieves them' (B. de Born). A substantival complement is often added, originally an accusative of measure, but soon taken to be the true subject, hence the preference for the nominative case: *estrains consiriers m'en ve* 'a terrible worry besets me' (Peirol); *a pauc pietatz no m'en pren* 'I almost feel pity for him' (P. d'Alverne), while the accusative is relatively rare: *no mi cal guiren* 'I do not need any witness' (Perdigon); *de lai don plus m'es bon e bel no·m ve mesager ni sagel* 'from where it pleases me the most, there comes to me neither messenger nor sealed letter' (Guillem de Peiteus).

Auxiliaries

Transitive and some intransitive verbs are constructed with *aver*. In the formation of its compound tenses, *anar* shows some hesitation between *esser* and *aver*: *pois l'inverns d'ogan es anatz* 'since this year's winter has departed' (Marcabru) vs. *cant ac anat un petit* 'when he had walked a little' (*Jaufré*). In most instances where *aver* is used, an adverbial indication of measure is present. *Aver* itself may be constructed with *esser*, but only when used intransitively as the equivalent of *estar*: *a Lombers etz ahutz* 'you have been to Lombers' (R. de Miraval); *suy pessius avutz* 'I have been absorbed in thought'

(G. Riquier); *sirvens sui avutz . . . , e sui estatz arbalestiers* 'I have been a servant, and I have been a crossbowman' (R. d'Avinhon). Compound tenses of reflexive verbs are usually formed with *esser*: *Jaufre s'es vestitz e causatz* 'Jaufré put on his clothes and shoes' (*Jaufré*), while the use of *aver* as auxiliary seems confined to cases where the reflexive pronoun serves as a dative: *lo reis joves s'a pretz donat* 'the young king has gained fame' (B. de Born), or where it is purely expletive: *no sai de que m'ai fach chanso* 'I do not know what I have written my song about' (G. de Bornelh).

Another common auxiliary is *anar*, which, combined with a gerund, serves to mark ongoing action: *so qu'ieu vau deziran* 'what I am wishing for' (Cercamon); *ja non anetz domnejan ses deners* 'do not ever court the ladies without money' (Marcabru); *trobat avem que anam queren* 'we have found what we are looking for' (Guillem de Peiteus). The auxiliary *soler*, which expresses habitual action, is often used in the present, where a past tense would have seemed a more logical choice: *ieu non sui cel que suoill* 'I am not the person I used to be' (G. Ademar); *qu'il solon anar prezicant, mas eras van peiras lansan* 'for they used to go about preaching, but now they are throwing stones' (P. Cardenal). This does not exclude the use of past tenses, however: *cil c'amar solia* 'the lady I used to love' (Peirol).

The Substantival Infinitive

The infinitive is easily substantivized. When used thus, it most often carries a determiner, although this is not an indispensable ingredient in the substantivization process: *chantars no pot gaire valer* 'singing can hardly be worthwhile' (B. de Ventadorn). The substantival infinitive follows the flexion of *murs-mur* and may assume the various functions of a noun, such as subject, predicate, direct object, and prepositional complement: *lor parlars sembla lairars de cans* 'their speech resembles the barking of dogs' (P. Vidal); *per tostemps lais mon chantar* 'I shall forever abandon my singing' (R. de Berbezilh); *al coronar fui del bon rei d'Estampa* 'I attended the crowning of the good king of Etampes' (A. Daniel). As a verb form, the substantival infinitive may carry a direct object: *al sagramen passar* 'when taking the oath' (P. d'Alvernhe); *prec midons al vers finir* 'I beg my lady, as I finish the poem' (G. Ademar). Since this occurs only with the prepositional infinitive, its seems likely that we are dealing with replacements of the gerund.

The Negated Infinitive

A negated infinitive achieves modal value when serving to express a prohibition: *ai Amors, no·m aucire* 'oh, Love, do not kill me' (Peirol); *ja no·t fizar en Velay* 'never trust Velay' (P. Cardenal). Preceded by *a* and the definite article, the infinitive may express an exhortation: *drutz, al levar* 'lover, rise', while Old French uses the preposition *de* in this structure: *or del monter* 'now let us get on our horses' (*Mort Artu*).

The Passive Infinitive

Since the Occitan infinitive does not per se express voice, it is often used with passive meaning: *quant hom ses querre fai be* 'when a man does good without being asked' (Peirol); *amors per decelar dechai* 'love declines by being divulged' (G. Faidit); *car paor a gran de nafrar sun caval* 'for he is very much afraid that his horse will be wounded' (*Jaufré*). Though far more widespread in the south, this syntax is also encountered in the north: *trop estoit haus hons pour pendre* 'he was too high-ranking a man to be hanged' (Robert de Clari). Passive infinitives are mostly found in prepositional locutions, but occur also elsewhere: *adoncs veirem aur et argen despendre* 'then we shall see gold and silver be spent' (B. de Born). A passive infinitive is often found after the locution *faire a* 'to deserve to be': *aitals amors fai a prezar* 'such a love deserves to be praised' (Marcabru); *no fai ad amar rics hom* 'a rich man does not deserve to be loved' (B. de Born). This syntax is common in the north: *molt font lor cop a redoter* 'their blows truly deserve to be feared' (*Yvain*).

Accusativus cum infinitivo

The *accusativus cum infinitivo* construction is found mainly with *faire, laissar*, and verbs of perception and command: *e·m fai amar cal que·lh plass* 'and it makes me love whoever pleases it' (B. de Ventadorn); *ara no vei luzir solelh* 'now I do not see the sun shining' (ibid.); *ni ja apres sopar no l'auziretz re dir* 'and never after supper will you hear her say anything' (G. de Bornelh); *e manded la ant se venir* 'and he ordered her to appear before him' (*Sainte Foi*). In late texts, the *accusativus cum infinitivo* construction is encountered as a learned Latinism: *lhi magi . . . conuogro Crist esser nat* 'the wise men realized that Christ had been born' (*Pseudo-Turpin*).

The Present Participle

The present participle normally serves in a purely adjectival role: *tant es nobla e plazens dona* 'she is such a noble and pleasant lady' (G. Riquier); *ela cavalga .i. palafre corren* 'she is riding on a swift horse' (*Daurel et Beton*), and it shares with adjectives the ability to be used substantivally: *l'estela que guía los passans* 'the star that guides the travelers' (P. Cardenal), but it may also appear in a periphrastic verbal locution with *esser*: *ja Dieus no·l sia perdonans* 'may God never forgive him' (Marcabru); *tan com la vida m'er durans* 'as long as my life lasts' (B. de Ventadorn); *s'oms es lo mon seguens* 'if man follows the world' (P. d'Alvernhe). The verbal character of this locution notwithstanding, the participle is inflected here, too, which sets it apart from the *anar* plus gerund syntax. The present participle may give rise to a verbal adjective used with passive meaning; this is particularly common with *prezan* and *blasman* 'worthy of praise/blame': *un sirventes prezan vuoill far* 'I want to write a *sirventes* worthy of praise' (R. de Vaqueiras); *per re non es om tan prezans com per amor* 'nothing makes man worthier of praise than love' (B. de Ventadorn). This syntax is very rare in the north.

The Gerund

The gerund, which has verbal force, is found alternating with the infinitive following verbs of perception: *ylh m'auzi chantan* 'she heard me sing' (Ussel), and particularly after the causative *faire*: *fai son seinhor sufren* 'he makes his lord suffer' (Marcabru); *so que m'ai faich perden* 'what she made me lose' (G. Faidit) vs. *sola lieis, c'Amors m'a faich chausir* 'only the lady whom Love made me choose' (ibid.). Used in adverbial function, the gerund marks simultaneity, means, manner: *en chantan vos apel* 'while singing I call you' (G. de Bornelh); *sai perden gazanhar* 'I know how to win by losing' (P. Vidal); *nostra mort aucis moren* 'he killed our death by dying' (D. de Pradas). The gerund usually refers to the subject of the main verb, but it may also be linked to the direct or the indirect object, mostly in contexts where a misunderstanding is not likely to occur: *trobei en ma via un pastor . . . cantan* 'I found along my way a shepherd singing' (Cadenet); *on troba las domnas ploran* 'where he finds the ladies in tears' (*Jaufré*); *en chantan m'aven a membrar so qu'ieu cug chantan oblidar* 'while I am singing, it happens to me that I remember what by singing I intend to forget' (F. de Marseilla). It occasionally refers to an unexpressed indefinite *om*: *donan, metén, plazers fazén es valors acampada* 'by giving, spending and acting in a pleasant manner, worth is accumulated' (P. Cardenal). Though carrying verbal force, gerunds are occasionally inflected, probably by analogy with present-participle syntax: *be·m dey en chantans esbaudir* 'I truly ought to rejoice while singing' (E. de Barjols). Like the infinitive, the gerund may be used substantively: *a l'issen d'us ortz* 'at the gate of a garden' (G. de Bornelh); *al mieu viven* 'in my lifetime' (A. de Peguilhan).

Combined with *anar*, the gerund forms a verbal locution expressing continuing action and paralleling the *esser* plus present participle periphrasis: *aissi·s vai lo pretz menuzan* 'thus merit is diminishing' (Marcabru); *trastota dia vai la mort reclaman* 'all day he keeps pleading with death' (*Boeci*); *anavan vacas sercan* 'they were looking for cows' (*Sainte Enimie*). *Estar* is occasionally used instead of *anar* in this construction: *pus qu'estrus . . . , que estay esguardan sos huous* 'more than an ostrich that is keeping watch over its eggs' (R. de Miraval).

The gerund of *vezer* and *auzir* is used in an absolute construction rendering the notion of somebody witnessing a happening; it carries an accusative subject, as is normal for absolute constructions: *vezen lieys que·m ten pres* 'in front of her [lit. 'she seeing'] who holds me imprisoned' (Sordel); *vezentz totz los decipols venc una nivols* 'in front of all the disciples there appeared a cloud' (*Sermons*).

In some instances, the present participle/gerund approaches the past participle in value: *trians* and *triatz*, from the verb *triar*, both mean 'distinguished, excellent'; *celan* and *celat*, from *celar*, both mean 'discreet, reserved'; *aprenen* and *apres*, from *aprenre*, both render the notion of 'informed'. Two gerunds are often joined together paratactically, expressing either related or contrasting notions: *mas ara dic rizen gaban* 'but now I say while laughing and joking' (R. de Miraval); *la bella . . . on m'esta·l sens dormen veillan* 'the fair lady in whom my heart and my mind are, whether I am asleep or awake' (A. Daniel).

The Past Participle

It is above all the past participle that may lay claim to being the adjectival form of the verb. Its major grammatical function is that of serving in the formation of compound tenses, and it may appear in a late and Latinizing absolute construction: *e en aprop, aisso augit, Karle fo alegres* 'and afterwards, having heard that, Charles was happy' (*Pseudo-Turpin*). The past participle may be used with active meaning, so, for example, *apres* 'who has learned' and hence 'who is informed, experienced': *dona franca e corteza e de repondre ben apreza* 'a noble and courteous lady and who has learned well how to answer' (Lo Monge de Montaudon), and *jurat* 'who has sworn' and *plevit* 'who has pledged': *c'ambedui me son jurat e plevit per sagramen* 'for both are sworn to me and bound by oath' (Guillem de Peiteus).

TENSES AND MOODS

The Past Tenses

The use of tenses and moods can only be sketchily outlined here. The preterite is commonly used in descriptions: *cavaliers fon vostre paire* 'your father was a knight' (Marcabru), and it may even appear where repetition is implied: *cascun mati, quan si levet, l'emage de Guillem miret* 'every morning when she got up, she looked at the picture of Guilhem' (*Flamenca*). It may acquire the value of an inchoative past, *saup* coming to mean 'I learned', *aic* 'I received', etc.: *Augiers, can lo vi venir, conuc lo* 'when Augier saw him coming, he recognized him' (*Jaufré*); *quant saup ben per ver que n'Archimbautz era garitz* 'when she learned for a fact that lord Archimbaut had recovered' (*Flamenca*). The pluperfect and the past anterior are used indiscriminately, with a preference in narrative texts for the latter of these tenses following a temporal conjunction: *e can fo el castel intratz, troba sa domna Brunissen* 'and when he had entered the castle, he found his lady Brunesen' (*Jaufré*).

The Future and the Two Conditionals

The future may compete with the imperative in the formulation of orders or instructions. As a tense, conditional I marks the future in the past, while as a mood it may render such notions as politeness and modesty: *ben volria saber que vai queren* 'I would like to know what he is looking for' (Albertet). Conditional II, which is derived from the Latin pluperfect indicative, appears with its etymological value only in a couple of archaic texts: *preget los ministres . . . que no l'i messeso(s) de tal mesura quo N.S. i fora mes* 'he asked the servants not to put him [on the cross] in the same manner as our Lord had been placed there' (*Sermons*). The troubadours make use of this form with values that relate it closely to conditional I: *cantera* 'I would sing' or 'I would have sung'. The true domain of conditional II is thus the hypothetical systems where, emphasizing the *irrealis* aspect of a hypothesis, it appears in the main clause, while the conditional clause is in the imperfect subjunctive: *s'ieu saubes la gent enquantar, miei enemic foran enfan* 'if I knew how to put a spell on people, my enemies would be children' (B. de Ventadorn); *s'ieu pogues contrafar Fenis, . . . ieu m'arsera* 'if I could imitate the phoenix, I would burn myself' (R. de Berbezilh). It may, like conditional I, express a notion of politeness: *al sieu marit volgr' ieu un pauc atanher* 'I would like to be related in some way to her husband' (Albertet).

The Subjunctive

The independent subjunctive expresses a wish: *los pros sal Dieus* 'may God save the worthy' (Marcabru). It may serve to formulate an order in the third person: *en amor s'entenda qui pretz vol aver* 'let him turn his thoughts to love who wants to attain merit' (Peirol), and it may express a prohibition, serving in the role of a negative imperative: *no m'oblidetz mia* 'do not forget me' (G. Faidit); *no temas ni ven ni gelada* 'fear neither wind nor frost' (B. de Born). The imperfect subjunctive may be used in the independent clause to render a notion of politeness where an imperative would have been felt as too direct: *puois no·m voletz colgar, donassetz m'un baisar* 'since you do not want to sleep with me, you might give me a kiss' (B. de Born). In the noun clause, the relative and interrogative clause and in the adverbial clause, the subjunctive is used whenever doubt or wish is implied.

Negation Auxiliaries

Adverbs, prepositions, and conjunctions give rise to few observations of a syntactical order. Negative auxiliaries such as *mia* and *ges* may be constructed with *de* or with the pronominal adverb *ne*, even when applied to something that is not divisible by nature. In such contexts, these words may be rendered by 'not any trace of' or 'not at all': *de me non an mia* 'they will not see any trace of me' (Peirol); *qu'er'ai leis, era no·n ai ges* 'for now I possess her, and now I do not own a trace of her' or 'I do not own her at all' (B. de Ventadorn).

The Restrictive Si-Non

Among the locutions serving to express the restrictive notion of 'only, except' is the separable *si-non*. The excepted or restricted element is placed between *si* and *non*: *que d'als no pens si de lieys no* 'for I think of no other woman except of her' (G. Faidit); *non s'i bainet si rix hom no* 'only a rich man took a bath there' (*Flamenca*).

Negation Reinforcements

A negation may be reinforced by a number of popular expressions, used mainly with the verbs *prezar* and *valer*. Not true auxiliaries of negation, these nouns are clearly perceived as direct objects, and they are usually combined with *un*, serving with numerical value: *no·m pretz un jau* 'I do not care one rooster' (Guillem de Peiteus); *anc no·m costet un alh* 'it never cost me one bulb of garlic' (B. de Born); *no lur valra una pluma de pau* 'that would not be worth one peacock feather to them' (P. Vidal).

The Expletive Negation

The expletive negation is used most consistently in comparisons of inequality: *l'am mais . . . que Jacobs no fetz Rachel* 'I love her more than Jacob did Rachel' (P. Vidal); *mens a de sen non a l'enfans que teta* 'he has less reason than the child who still suckles' (P. Cardenal). It appears in noun clauses governed by verbs of prohibition and prevention: *per so no·is recre c'ades non chant* 'therefore it does not refrain from singing' (A. de Peguilhan); *non puosc mudar qu'eo no m'effrei* 'I cannot help feeling disturbed' (Guillem de Peiteus), or by verbs of fearing: *tal paor ai c'ades no·us pes* 'I am so afraid that it will grieve you immediately' (A. de Maruelh); *soven ai gran doptansa que no·s mi fass' oblidar non-calers* 'I often have great fear that indifference may make you forget me' (F. de Marseilla), and it is found after certain conjunctions.

The Pronominal Adverbs

Representing a construction with *de, ne* may regularly denote persons as well as things or abstracts: *si lonhar m'en volia* 'if I wanted to depart from her' (B. de Palol), and it is often used pleonastically: *mas peccat n'aia de l'aman* 'but may she have pity on the lover' (P. Vidal). It may serve as a partitive, providing a reference to something already mentioned: *l'autra n·a dos* 'the other has two of them [i.e., cloaks]' (P. Cardenal). *I* represents *a* and a complement: *tant hi vey de be . . . qu'ie·us am per bona fe* 'I see so much good in you that I love you sincerely' (B. de Palol). Like *ne*, it is often used pleonastically: *al valen rey . . . te y ta via* 'go to the noble king' (G. de Montanhagol). An adverb of place often serves as a reference to a person; this is standard in the poetry with *aillor* 'elsewhere', since *amar aillor* is a common expression for 'to be in love with another woman': *s'ieu anc jorn amei aillor* 'if I ever was in love with another woman' (Uc de Saint-Circ).

Prepositional Complements in the Nominative Case

The prepositional complement is in the accusative case, but there are infrequent occurrences of the nominative, notably following *tener se per* 'to consider oneself to be', since this locution is the semantic equivalent of a predicate denoting existence: *era·m tenh per enganatz* 'now I consider myself deceived' (P. Vidal), but also with a few additional expressions: *be·s deu guardar qui a drutz si depeis* 'he must watch out who described himself as a lover' (B. de Born). The complement of *fors* is often aligned with the subject, marking a restriction: *res fors Deus no·m pot pro tener de peiurar* 'nobody except God can protect me against decline' (G. de Bornelh).

The Coordinating Ne, Ni

As a coordinating conjunction, *ne, ni* serves mostly in negative, interrogative or conditional contexts, with generalizing relatives and in comparisons: *era no·us ai ni vos non avetz mi* 'now I do not have you, nor do you have me' (F. de Marseilla); *si·l donna es valentz ni pros* 'if the lady is worthy and noble' (Perdigon); *on qu'ieu an ni·m vir* 'wherever I may go, and wherever I may turn' (E. de Barjols); *anz me son tuich plus que fraire ni oncle* 'but they are all more to me than brothers or uncles' (A. Daniel), but it is even found in sentences that contain no underlying negative connotations: *quar tan vos am ni·us dezir* 'for I love and desire you so much' (P. Vidal); *cel q'es e mun verger intratz, qe als ausels espaventatz nils a faitz giqir de cantar* 'he who has entered my garden, and who has scared the birds and made them stop singing' (*Jaufré*). The same usage is found in Old French: *dehors ont veü ceminer dames, chevaliers ne puceles* 'outside they saw ladies, knights and maidens walking' (*Bel Inconnu*).

The Comparison of Two Clauses

Where two clauses are compared, the resulting combination "(more) than that" is expressed by means of one *que* only: *doncs m'es mielhs que mueir' en bon esper qu'aia vida que ja pro no·m tengues* 'therefore it is better for me to die in good hope than to lead a life that would bring me no profit' (Perdigon); *mais voil morir . . . qe prenda 'st vostre nuiriment* 'I would rather die than accept the pledge you propose' (*Sainte Foi*). Old French also uses one *que* only: *melz sostendreiet les empedemenz qu'elle perdesse sa virginitet* 'she would rather undergo torture than lose her virginity' (*Sainte Eulalie*).

Proportional Comparisons

Several constructions are available for the expression of proportional comparisons, among them *on plus . . . (e) plus*: *on plus la prec, plus m'es dura* 'the more I plead with her, the more cruel she is to me' (B. de Ventadorn). *Mais* may replace *plus* in this structure: *on mais n'i a e la flam' es plus grans* 'the more (wood) there is, the bigger the flame' (G. Faidit), and a late variant of *on mais* is *al mai*: *quar al may hom met al forn de lenha al may sertanamen de calor hi a* 'for the more wood you put into the furnace, the more heat there certainly is' (Jutgamen general). Commonly used is *com plus . . . (e) plus*: *cum plus m'en cuich partir, plus mi referm* 'the more I think of leaving you, the more I stay put' (A. de Peguilhan); *cum maier es, plus art lo focs* 'the bigger the fire is, the more it burns' (G. Ademar). *Com* may be introduced by *aissi* in this locution: *c'aissi cum plus la vuoill, e pieitz m'en pren* 'for the more I want her, the worse I fare' (G. Faidit); *aissi con son major an peior sen* 'the bigger they are, the worse their mind is' (P. Cardenal). Another locution expressing a proportional comparison is *tant plus . . . cant plus*, including slight variations in the arrangement of these elements: *tant cant val mais tant n'es plus encolpatz* 'the more value he has, the guiltier he is' (F. de Marseilla).

Inverted Word Order

In the area of word order, the most striking feature in the medieval language is inversion or the change from a subject-verb to a verb-subject sequence. Inversion is the norm whenever the clause opens with other sentence elements, such as a direct object: *lo vers a faich Peirols* 'Peirol wrote the *vers*' (Peirol); a prepositional locution: *per tot lo cor m'intra l'amors* 'love penetrates all through my heart' (ibid.); an adverb or other circumstantial complements: *car tan l'am eu* 'for so much do I love her' (B. de Ventadorn); *ab tan se resida Jaufres* 'then Jaufré woke up' (*Jaufré*); *tot l'an mi ten Amors* 'all year Love holds me' (Perdigon). Conjunctions, on the other hand, do not normally cause inversion by themselves: *tem que la dolors me ponja* 'I fear that the pain may sting me' (Guillem de Peiteus); *can l'altre s'en van, eu venh* 'when the others leave, I arrive' (G. de Bornelh). As a rule, it is only when other sentence elements stand before the verb that the inversion mechanism is triggered in the subordinate clause: *chantars no pot gaire valer, si d'ins dal cor no mou lo chans* 'singing can have no merit if the song does not come from the bottom of the heart' (B. de Ventadorn); *e·il fai creire qu'aillors es sos camis* 'and he makes him believe that his path lies elsewhere' (Perdigon); *qu'eu sai que perdutz es l'argenz* 'for I know that the money is lost' (Peirol). Stylistic considerations may account for the use of inversion where the conjunction alone precedes the verb: *mas quan chai la plueg* 'but when the rain falls' (ibid.). Inversion is the rule in the incidental clause and in the direct question: *femna, dis el, as ton enfant?* 'woman, he said, do you have your child [with you]?' (*Jaufré*); *de que sun li degra?* 'what are the steps made of?' (*Boeci*). Inversion is common in the independent optative clause and in exclamations: *e vailla mi ma fina voluntatz!* 'and may my sincere desire avail me!' (Peirol); *mor se·l vostr' amaire!* 'your lover is dying!' (B. de Ventadorn). The relative clause shows some fluctuation in word order: *belha domna, en cui renha senz e beutatz* 'fair lady in whom reason and beauty dwell' (Peirol) vs. *la comtess' en cui jois e pretz reigna* 'the countess in whom joy and merit dwell' (ibid.).

Word Order and the Two-Case System

The two-case system allows for a certain latitude in word order: *jes las donsellas non oblida Guillems* 'Guillaume does not at all forget the ladies' (*Flamenca*); *dison . . . quel comte de la Marca a Guillems de Nevers ferit* 'they say that Guillaume de Nevers has hit the count of la Marca' (ibid.). Meaning may offer an important guiding principle where morphological distinctions are unhelpful: *anz vol guerra mais que qualha esparviers* 'on the contrary, he wants war more than a sparrow-hawk wants a quail' (B. de Born), and not '*more than a quail [wants] sparrow-hawks'.

The Proleptic De

The so-called proleptic *de* 'concerning, as to, as regards' offers a convenient device for emphasizing the subject of a dependent clause by moving it forward to the governing clause. The use of *de* usually precludes any misinterpretation of the role of such anticipated nouns: *veiran de mon bran com talha* 'concerning my sword, they will see how it cuts' or 'they will see how my sword cuts' (B. de Born). Other examples of this feature are: *ben vuelh que sapchon li pluzor d'est vers si's de bona color* 'I want people to know whether this poem is finely colored' (Guillem de Peiteus); *eu sai de paraulas com van* 'I know how words go' (ibid.); *non saps d'Amor cum trais Samson?* 'don't you know how Love betrayed Samson?' (Marcabru); *paor ai del trachor que l'ausiza* 'I am afraid the traitor will kill him' (*Daurel et Beton*); *d'aquestz sap Marcabrus qui son* 'Marcabru knows who these people are' (Marcabru). If an object is emphasized in this manner, it is usually represented at its habitual place by the corresponding weak pronoun: *ara sai ieu de pretz quals l'a plus gran* 'now I know who has the greatest merit' (B. de Born). Anticipation may also be made without the use of *de*: *calacom cre c'aura verguina* 'I believe that somebody will be ashamed' (*Jaufré*); *totz lo mons cre que m'azire* 'I believe that everybody hates me' (E. de Barjols).

Occitan has its own individual characteristics that distinguish it from French, making the scientific study of its phonology, morphology, and syntax both challenging and indispensable. A precise understanding of the earliest European lyrics, the troubadour poetry of the south of France, can be achieved only if the literary koiné of these remote ancestors of modern poetry continues to be explored with the logical rigor of modern philology.

WORKS CITED

Anglade, J. *Grammaire de l'ancien provençal ou ancienne langue d'oc.* Paris: Klincksieck, 1921.

Appel, C. *Provenzalische Lautlehre.* Leipzig: Reisland, 1918.

Bec, Pierre. *La Langue occitane.* Paris: Presses Universitaires de France, 1967.

———. *Manuel pratique de philologie romane.* 2 vols. Paris: Picard, 1970–71.

Bourciez, Edouard. *Eléments de linguistique romane.* 5th ed. Paris: Klincksieck, 1967.

Crescini, V. *Manuale per l'avviamento agli studi provenzali.* Milano: Ulrico Hoepli, 1926.

Grafström, Å. *Etude sur la graphie des plus anciennes chartes languedociennes avec un essai d'interprétation phonétique.* Uppsala: Almqvist, 1958.

———. *Etude sur la morphologie des plus anciennes chartes languedociennes.* Stockholm: Almqvist, 1968.

Grandgent, C. H. *An Outline of the Phonology and Morphology of Old Provençal.* Boston: D. C. Heath, 1905.

Hamlin, F. R., P. T. Ricketts, and J. Hathaway. *Introduction à l'étude de l'ancien provençal.* Geneva: Droz, 1967.

Henrichsen, A.-J. *Les Phrases hypothétiques en ancien occitan.* Bergen: University of Bergen Årbok, 1955.

Jensen, F. *Old Provençal Noun and Adjective Declension.* Odense: Odense University Press, 1976.

———. *Provençal Philology and the Poetry of Guillaume of Poitiers.* Odense: Odense University Press, 1983.

———. *The Syntax of Medieval Occitan.* Tübingen: Niemeyer, 1986.

———. *Old French and Comparative Gallo-Romance Syntax.* Tübingen: Niemeyer, 1990.

Lausberg, H. *Romanische Sprachwissenschaft.* 3 vols. Berlin: W. de Gruyter, 1956–62.

Levy, Emil. *Petit Dictionnaire provençal-français.* Heidelberg: C. Winter, 1966.

———. *Provenzalisches Supplement-Wörterbuch.* 8 vols. Leipzig: Reisland, 1894–1924; 2d ed. Hildesheim-New York, 1973.

Linder, K. P. *Studien zur provenzalischen Verbalsyntax.* Tübingen: Niemeyer, 1970.

Loos, T. "Die Nominalflexion im Provenzalischen." Diss., Marburg, 1884.

Nyman, W. *Etude sur les adjectifs, les participes et les nombres ordinaux substantivés en vieux provençal.* Vol. 13. Göteborg: University of Göteborg Årsskrift, 1907.

Pellegrini, G. B. *Appunti di grammatica storica del provenzale.* 3d ed. Pisa: Libreria Goliardica, 1965.

Pfister, M. "Beiträge zur altprovenzalischen Grammatik." *Vox Romanica* 17 (1958–59): 281–362.

Raynouard, J.-F. *Lexique roman.* 2d ed. 6 vols. Heidelberg: C. Winter, 1927–29.

Reimann, P. "Die Declination der Substantiva und Adjectiva in der Langue d'Oc bis zum Jahre 1300." Diss., Danzig, 1882.

Richter, Elise. "Beiträge zur provenzalischen Grammatik." *Zeitschrift für romanische Philologie* 41 (1921): 81–95.

Roncaglia, A. *La lingua dei trovatori.* Roma: Ateneo, 1965.

Schultz-Gora, O. *Altprovenzalisches Elementarbuch.* Heidelberg: C. Winter, 1906.

———. "Vermischte Beiträge zum Altprovenzalischen." *Zeitschrift für romanische Philologie* 53 (1933): 87–112; 58 (1938): 63–80.

Stimming, A. *Bertran de Born, sein Leben und seine Werke.* Halle: Niemeyer, 1879.

EIGHTEEN

Rhetoric

Nathaniel B. Smith

The troubadours aimed, above all, to be convincing. Convincing audiences and patrons that the poetic voice spoke truthfully marked the troubadours' route to material rewards and prestige. Prestige, indeed, proved as durable as their texts, which yielded up ostensibly factual data from which the medieval biographers imaginatively founded the continuing cult surrounding these Occitan singers and poets. Poets of the twelfth and thirteenth centuries (like more recent ones) strove to sound more sincere than their rivals, as does Bernart de Ventadorn in this song:

> Non es meravelha s'eu chan
> Melhs de nul autre chantador,
> Que plus me tra·l cors vas amor
> E melhs sui faihz a so coman.
>
> (1:1–4)

> It is no wonder if I sing better than any other singer, for my heart draws me more toward love and I am better made to its command.

Thanks in part to such self-advertising by Bernart, his medieval biographer and many modern scholars have depicted him as the ideal troubadour, uniquely worthy of being the protégé of that courtliest of ladies, Eleanor of Aquitaine, just as the politically virulent Bertran de Born became, in his own *vida* and in Dante's *Inferno*, a famed "sower of discord." Most troubadours contentedly played along with this game of words, the fiction that their fictions are not fictitious. Some, though, in moments of candor, confess a more self-interested motive, like Elias Cairel in his *tenso* with Isabella:

> E s'ieu en dizia lauzor
> En mon chantar, no·l dis per drudaria,

Mas per honor e pro qu'ieu n'atendia,
Si com joglars fai de domna prezan.

(7:12–15)

and if I praised you in my singing, I didn't say it from love, but for the honor
and profit that I expected, as a jongleur does with a worthy lady.

What on the whole caused the poetry of the troubadours—even the
forthright or self-deprecating ones—to supersede the details of their actual
lives is their artful use of language or, in a word, rhetoric: that is, the
traditional Western repertory of means for organizing and expressing
thoughts persuasively to others, whether orally or in writing. Rhetorical
techniques are at their most evident when they are indubitably intentional,
as in the intense alliteration of Arnaut Daniel's line "Sols sui qui sai lo
sobrafan qe·m sortz" (I alone know the great suffering that rises in me;
15:1); or in Rigaut de Berbezilh's use of comparison in the opening lines
of a poem that, already in the Middle Ages, was regarded as his trademark:
"Atressi con l'orifanz / que quant chai no·s pot levar . . ." (Just like the
elephant who, when he falls, cannot raise himself; 2:1–2).

The stylistic difference between such lines and normal speech patterns
forms the substance of rhetoric. Certainly some poets push rhetoric to the
point where expression, nominally the medium, becomes the message; but
on the whole, the troubadours exercise due restraint, finding that this
bundle of inherited techniques is most useful when least obtrusive. Rhetoric, a conscious and unconscious element in Western letters for the past
three millennia, lives on today not only in formal discourse but also in
traditional sayings, popular poetry, and Top Forty songs. There is rhetoric
even if the writer or speaker and audience remain unaware of its use: it is
so internalized in our linguistic heritage that we all use it, just as Monsieur
Jourdain in Molière's *Le Bourgeois Gentilhomme* used prose.

Still, consciousness of rhetoric has not died. A fairly recent work by
Willard R. Espy, *The Garden of Eloquence*, is devoted to the almost countless
rhetorical devices described in the sixteenth century by the Reverend Henry
Peacham, who wrote: "By the great might of figures (which is no other thing
than wisdom speaking eloquently), the orator may lead his hearers which
way he lists, and draw them to what affection he will" (11).

The English term *rhetoric* comes down to us, through French and Latin,
from the Greek *rhetorike*, based on a root designating speech, from Indo-
European *wer-*, the ultimate source of our *word* and *verb*, among many
others. The Bible and Homer established a repertory of rhetorical devices
that over time came to be expanded, analyzed, and codified. The first known
genuine textbook of rhetorical analysis was Aristotle's *Rhetoric*, which distinguishes that art from dialectic (logic), poetry, and grammar. But this

Aristotelian treatise, virtually unknown in the Middle Ages, was replaced by the Latin tradition associated with Cicero.

In various works including *De inventione* (known respectfully to the Middle Ages as the "first" or "old Rhetoric"), Cicero gave prime attention to legal oratory and to the proper selection and ordering of convincing arguments. At about the same time, an anonymous author wrote the *Rhetorica ad Herennium*, known in the Middle Ages as the "second" or "new Rhetoric" and believed to be by Cicero himself. The *Herennium* distinguished three levels of expression—*gravis* (grand, high), *mediocris* (moderate, middle), and *adtenuata* (subdued, plain)—as well as the two sorts of *exornationes* (adornments) that we now call "figures of speech" (or of diction) and "figures of thought" (or of idea or sense). *Herennium* inventoried forty-five figures of speech (including ten later labeled "tropes," that is, "turnings" of the ordinary meanings of words) and nineteen figures of thought. This repertory was rearranged and modified by the mid-fourth-century grammarian Aelius Donatus in his *Ars minor* and *Ars maior*, the latter of which includes as its book 3 a treatment of rhetoric known as *Barbarismus*. By his terminology, his conflation of the grammatical and rhetorical traditions, and his idea that what is regarded as a "vice" of expression in ordinary speech or prose can, in poetry, become an intentional schema and thus a "virtue," Donatus exercised incalculable influence over medieval rhetoric.

Espy, in lamenting the decline of formal rhetoric, states that "Rhetoric and eloquence make us nervous because we sense in them a terrible power" (15). Indeed, even before the collapse of the empire that codified rhetoric, the "pagan" eloquence of Virgil and his peers made early Christian thinkers exceedingly nervous. A strong fourth-century movement against all use of pagan literature, philosophy, and rhetoric regarded classical letters as a siren luring people away from the spirit and toward the flesh. But others, more moderate, felt that non-Christian learning should be taken over, cautiously and with the necessary modifications, for Christian purposes. The leader of this school of thought, St. Augustine, introduced an influential comparison: just as the Israelites took from Egypt what was useful to them— "vases and ornaments of gold and silver and clothing"—while leaving behind "idols and grave burdens," so pagan learning contains not only things to be avoided but "also liberal disciplines more suited to the uses of truth" (*On Christian Doctrine* 75=2:40). Thus, he says, we should use images, figures, and literature itself *in bono* and not *in malo*: for good and not for evil.

In fact, much of book 4 of *On Christian Doctrine* derives from Cicero, including the concept that "wisdom without eloquence is of small benefit to states; but eloquence without wisdom is often extremely injurious and profits no one" (121=4:7, based on the first sentence of *De inventione*). With

St. Augustine's blessing, the cultivation of rhetoric continued vigorously through and beyond the Middle Ages. Under the influence of Donatus and Priscian (early 6th cent.) among others, "grammar"—taken in the literal sense of writing about writing—came to usurp much of the domain of rhetoric. These two liberal arts, together with dialectic, made up the three areas known together to medieval schools as the *trivium.*

Continued knowledge of the classical rhetorical tradition produced many medieval commentaries and reworkings. These Latin treatises, from the later twelfth century on, are devoted in varying proportions to what today we would call grammar, rhetoric, and literary studies. The first of these works, Matthew of Vendôme's *Ars versificatoria,* written in the troubadours' Golden Age a bit before 1175, is typical in identifying the figures of word, tropes, and figures of thought largely derived from *Herennium.* Also important are Geoffrey of Vinsauf's *Poetria nova* and *Documentum de modo et arte dictandi et versificandi,* both probably composed just before the symbolic year 1213, which marks the Battle of Muret and the subsequent decline of the culture that nourished the troubadours. (In speaking of rhetoric and rhetoricians, I include authors who, like Geoffrey, regard rhetoric primarily as an annex to grammar.)

As suggested by Matthew's title, many of these treatises aimed specifically to counsel aspiring versifiers and to train their audiences in appreciating verse. Medieval rhetorical doctrine was preceptive, that is, it recommended techniques thought to be effective in carrying out the goals of the writer of poetry and prose and also, in a different series of manuals, those of the preacher and the composer of formal letters. Since these precepts were based on oral and written examples, they depend not on the whims of individual codifiers but on a series of sources reaching back to the earliest works in the Western tradition. Ultimately, the tradition is based in an epistemology of absolutes which holds that human reason can distinguish what is good and proper from what is bad and undesirable.

As J. J. Murphy says, "The ubiquity of the figures and tropes . . . should be kept in mind during any study of medieval uses of language" (191). Although it is not clear what knowledge the troubadours may have had of specific treatises, there is no doubt that, whether through formal education, independent study, word of mouth, or imitation, the precepts of classical and medieval rhetoric were readily available to them, as to all even semi-sophisticated western European poets of the Middle Ages.

Throughout the Middle Ages, rhetoric was regarded as a basic curricular element—required in high school, we would say. This, perhaps, is the reason that "the study of formal rhetoric did not flourish at the universities even as much as it had done in the best schools of the early Middle Ages" (Paetow 70). The troubadours were not university graduates, but they certainly were literate; many were well schooled and, like their medieval biographers, conscious of the stylistic individuality of the leading contemporary and earlier troubadours.

Evidence supporting the foregoing points includes the activities of four individuals (see Smith 1976b, chap. 1). Peire d'Alvernhe (fl. 1158–80) and the Monk of Montaudon (fl. 1180–1215) wrote satires making fun of other troubadours for personal and stylistic reasons; Uc de Saint-Circ (fl. 1211–53), a troubadour and author of troubadour biographies, wrote among other satires one imitating a certain Guilhem Fabre's use of alliteration, root repetition, and other rhetorical techniques (see Smith 1976a); and the Italian Ferrari de Ferrara (late 13th–early 14th cent.) was, according to his biographer (Boutière and Schutz 581–583), not only an accomplished troubadour but also an authority on the Occitan language and the compiler of a troubadour anthology.

As these individuals show, active poetry writing and what we would call literary history and scholarship were intertwined. Scholarship was a flourishing Occitan enterprise. The grammatical-rhetorical tradition is reflected in a number of treatises written in medieval Occitan, beginning with *Las razos de trobar*, the first known grammatical treatise in a Romance language, written in prose by the Catalan troubadour Raimon Vidal de Besalù, probably between 1190 and 1213. A long line of Occitan authors leads on to works written in Catalonia, where poetic "floral games" were revived in 1393 on the model established earlier in Toulouse.

The most impressive author in the Occitano-Catalan tradition—although he lived after the definitive decline of the troubadours—was Guilhem Molinier, who in 1328–37 wrote *Las leys d'amors* (The laws of love), a prose codification of phonetics, grammar, rhyme, genres, rhetoric, and related themes. A shorter version omitting rhetoric was officially promulgated in 1356 as the guide to the poetic contests of the Consistori del Gay Saber in Toulouse, and Molinier also wrote a simplified rhymed version entitled *Las flors del Gay Saber*. This indefatigable compiler drew primarily on Donatus's *Ars maior* and on Isidore of Seville's early-seventh-century *Origines* (also known as *Etymologia*). Yet Molinier, confident in the excellence of the vernacular tradition, also proposes "to make laws of love [that is, of poetry] according to the good troubadours of old" and to follow "long and accustomed usage" (Guilhem Molinier 1:2). To illustrate various genres and rhetorical points, he uses mostly examples of his own creation but also some quotations from N'Ath de Mons, a now little-studied troubadour of the second half of the thirteenth century, as well as one each from Peire Vidal, Raimbaut de Vaqueiras, and Rigaut de Berbezilh.

Part 3—for us the most important—of the full prose version of the *Leys* is loosely structured as an allegory that shows how "vices" of language can become "virtues" of poetry. Three kings—Barbarismus, Solecismus, and

Allebolus, representing vices of word, grammar, and meaning—make war on Queens Dictio (Word), Oratio (Speech), and Sentensa (Idea). Through Lady Rhetoric's intervention, the kings marry the three queens' sisters, Metaplasmus, Schema, and Tropus. The resulting daughters and grand-daughters, along with the presents bestowed by Lady Rhetoric, are the "figures" and "flowers" by which rhetoric adorns poetry. (Since his alle-gory cannot cover everything he has to say, Molinier is also obliged to add in, at the end, a large number of "nonprincipal figures" and "other flowers of rhetoric.")

Molinier's treatment is particularly useful for several reasons: it is quite complete, it draws on a tradition known directly or indirectly to the trou-badours, it is written in Occitan and gives copious examples in that lan-guage, and it respects the necessity of adapting Latin rhetoric to vernacular usage. However clumsy, Molinier's allegory has the benefit of dramatizing an important point: a linguistic feature that is undesirable when used carelessly or without design can become a desirable stylistic feature when used intentionally and with regularity ("scienmen per dreg compas," as he often says). Molinier, though not alone among rhetoricians in dwelling on this point, does make it with particular force.

Rhetoric was traditionally divided into five parts:

1. *inventio*, the "finding" of suitable material
2. *dispositio*, the orderly arranging of the materials
3. *elocutio*, including means of "adornment" divided into
    a. *ornatus difficilis* ("difficult adornment") or similar terms, com-prising the tropes
    b. *ornatus facilis* ("easy adornment," also known as *ornata facilitas*, colors of rhetoric, etc.), divided into figures of word (flowers of diction) and figures of thought
4. *memoria*, memorization
5. *actio* or *pronuntiatio*, oral delivery

A distinction relevant to both *dispositio* and *elocutio* is that between (a) *amplificatio*, emphasizing and developing the material, and (b) *abbreviatio*, shortening the material (not a high priority in most medieval literature).

These often imprecise and arbitrary categories, applicable primarily to the art of the orator, are not terribly helpful to us as modern readers of Romance poetry. Furthermore, the various medieval authorities treat rhet-oric idiosyncratically and often give different classifications or definitions of the same terms. Among other works, Faral's is still useful for its Latin texts and its analysis; several works by Lausberg have done much schematizing based on sources through the sixth century; and Murphy's volume is also valuable. Nevertheless, Ernst Robert Curtius's statement that "the study of figures has never been satisfactorily systematized" (45) still holds true today.

This being the case, I will present various techniques of rhetoric—whether traditionally labeled figures, flowers, colors, or tropes—in groupings intended to appear logical to the late-twentieth-century mind. Without at all aiming at completeness, I have selected those techniques that seem most important for appreciating lyric poetry in general and in particular the troubadours' art. I leave aside techniques that pertain more to non-lyric forms of discourse or to versification (for which see Chapters 4 and 6 in this volume). Where equivalent or overlapping terms exist, I generally prefer a Latin term, except that I favor Greek for figures of transfer of sense. Though I adopt medieval terminology and concepts where possible, I also add some modern distinctions and terms, particularly when English terms are well established and unambiguous. In any case, I indicate alternate terms in parentheses. Since colors and figures are not clearly distinguished from each other, I will use the term *figures* to include both.

FIGURES OF REPETITION

The first group of rhetorical techniques that we shall examine involves the repetition of words or their component roots or sounds (for the term *figures of repetition*, see Smith 1976b, 64–67). Repetition was no doubt particularly helpful for the medieval audience, which had to catch and connect the meanings of words as they were sung or recited. But more than merely repeating for the sake of clarity, the troubadours, like other medieval poets, use this large family of techniques to enhance and structure their literary message.

Given the many ways of repeating elements of words, it is not surprising that traditional rhetorical terminology exhibits much confusion. The term *annominatio* (*paronomasia*), for example, is variously applied to the repetition of initial letters, of final letters, of syllables, and of most of a word. Moreover, most authorities do not distinguish whether the affected words are etymologically related to each other or not; thus the *Leys'* examples of *annominatio* (3:170) include *corta/cortz/cortezia* 'short/court/courtesy', where the second term is of a different word family from the others.

Alliteration (*alliteratio*, a late-fifteenth-century term for what was earlier known as *paranomeon* or *homoeoprophoron*) is the use of the same sound at the beginning of two or more words in proximity. This is one of the troubadours' favorite techniques, whether in syntactically parallel structures, as in the three *v*'s of Bernart de Ventadorn's "Lo tems vai e ven e vire" (Time goes and comes and turns; 44:1), or in the looser syntactical relationship between the two words beginning with *m* in his "en un miralh que mout me plai" (in a mirror that pleases me much; 31:20). The troubadours occasionally use thorough-going alliteration as a tour de force, as in the verse of Arnaut Daniel cited above ("Sols sui qui sai lo sobrafan qe·m sortz") or in Guillem de Montanhagol's "A Lunel lutz una luna luzens . . ." (In Lunel shines a shining moon; 2:1).

Although alliteration is often considered to include repetition of vowels, that subtype is today generally labeled assonance, as in Guillem de Peiteus's expressions "la pessa e·l coutel" (the slice of bread and knife; 10:30), with two tonic open *e*'s; and "joi e deport" (joy and amusement; 11:39), with two tonic open *o*'s. Here the assonating terms are in parallel constructions, but other relations are possible, as in the same poet's line "E per la carn renovellar" (And to renew the flesh; 9:35). Nontonic vowel repetition also has its importance, as here in the definite article *la* reinforcing the two following tonic *a*'s.

The terms *similiter desinens* (*homoeoteleuton*) and *similiter cadens* (*homoeoptoton*) both designate phonetic identity of the final part of nearby words. In principle, the affected words are final in their clause or line of verse, but such is not always the case in fact. According to some rhetoricians, *similiter desinens* involves verbs and *similiter cadens* nouns and adjectives, but others tell us that *similiter cadens* includes the tonic vowel while *similiter desinens* need not. At any rate, in the Romance languages the two devices generally merge as rhyme—that is, phonetic identity of the tonic vowel and all following phonemes. When final in the verse, rhyme forms the basic structural principle of troubadour poetry; when internal in the line (and not recurring at regular intervals) it comprises what Guilhem Molinier calls *rim fayshuc* 'annoying rhyme'. But whatever that authority may have later thought, the troubadours constantly use irregular internal rhyme. Expressions like *aman baizan* 'loving and kissing' and *amors/dolors* 'love/sadness' involve repetition of the gerundive ending *-an* and the substantival suffix *-or(s)*, but we can just as easily find morphemically unrelated rhyming words, as in Jaufre Rudel's expression "belhs uelhs" (beautiful eyes; 6:14, as spelled in manuscripts *C* and *e*^*b*; *bels huelhs* in manuscript *R*).

Annominatio (*paronomasia*) usually designates an even higher degree of phonetic similarity. The troubadours skillfully use such near-homophony to make a relation of sound into a relation of meaning, as in the frequent opposition of *cor(s)* 'heart' and *cors* 'body', or in Guillem de Peiteus's line "Si·m vol midons s'amor donar" (If my lady wishes to give me her love; 9:37), where juxtaposition of two etymologically unrelated words identifies the lady as one who gives.

When, however, the affected words belong to the same family, we can speak of "organic" *annominatio*. Guilhem Molinier's study of lexical compounds includes *dreyta compositio* 'proper compounding' (2:100–102), which modifies the meaning of a root by prefixation, thus *cortes/descortes* 'courtly/uncourtly' or, in Bernart de Ventadorn, "C'astrucs sojorn' e jai / e malastrucs s'afana" (For the fortunate one lingers and stays and the unfortunate one tires himself out; 26:49–50). Molinier also discerns *motz biaysshatz* 'diverted words' (2: 214), which change a word by suffixation, thus *falha/falhensa* 'fault/failing' or *plazen/plazensa* 'pleasing/pleasure'. The device now called "etymological figure" (*derivatio, figura per pleonasmum, figura etymologica, paregmenon*) associates two cognate words such as *flor/florar* 'flower/to flower' or Bernart de Ventadorn's *chan/chantador* in the lines cited at the beginning of this chapter. Finally, *variatio* (*declinatio, derivatio, polyptoton,* etc.) involves various forms of a single word differentiated by declension or conjugation: *flor/flors* 'flower' (in different cases), *am/amarai* 'I love/I will love', *bel/belazor* 'beautiful/more beautiful'. A related device, which we might label "nonetymological morphological figure," involves morphologically associated forms derived from different roots, as in *bo/melhor* 'good/better'.

Often, the troubadours combine two or more such devices, as when Bernart says, with compounding and *variatio,* "C'aissi com las solh chaptener, / enaissi las deschaptenrai" (For just as I am used to defend them, so I will attack them; 31:27–28). Indeed, the various types of *annominatio* can become the structural principle of whole sections of poems built around word families like those of *amar, chantar, jauzir, planher, poder,* etc. For example, the poem of Guillem de Montanhagol cited above as an example of alliteration continues for a whole stanza to heap up words signifying light.

Such phonetic similarities readily lead to punning (*traductio, antanaclasis*), as in the frequent juxtaposition *marit/marrit* 'husband/sad' (e.g., Elias d'Uisel 14:48) or, with two perfect homophones, *cozina/cozina* 'kitchen/cousin' (*Leys* 3:108). A special twist of punning, *interpretatio per etymologiam,* develops a meaning from a proper name such as Valflor 'Flower Valley' or Bonifaci 'May-He-Do-Well'.

When a word is repeated without any sort of variation at all, we enter the domain of *conduplicatio* (*repetitio*). As Guilhem Molinier, ever concerned with justifying the use of rhetorical devices, says: "You should know that the repetition that one makes of words . . . is to show better the great feeling of the person who says the words and to move and excite the hearts of the audience" (3:170). At the beginning of successive verses (or, by extension, nearby ones), word repetition is called anaphora (*repetitio, epanaphora*). Anaphora can involve a small word like *e* 'and', *ni* '(n)or', or *anc* 'ever', or it can flourish in complex and variable series, as when Bertran de Born writes of youth and age:

> Jov'es dona que sap honrar paratge,
> Et es joves per bos fagz—quan los fa.
> Joves se te quan a adreg coratge . . .
>
> (24:17–19)

Young is a woman who knows how to honor nobility, and she is young by good deeds—when she does them. Young she remains when she has an honest heart . . .

Another special type of *conduplicatio* is *conversio* (*epistrophe, epiphora*), which occurs at the ends of successive clauses, as in the *Leys'* example: "Savis es, bels es, discretz es" (Is wise, is handsome, is discrete; 3:166).

Extended to their logical limit, the various types of repetition yield various sorts of stanza; thus, *anadiplosis* (for an example, see the first paragraph of this chapter), when applied at the stanzaic level, produces *coblas capfinidas.* Indeed, a whole poetic genre, the *plazer*, is dominated by anaphoric expressions meaning "it pleases me. . . ." And when such figures of repetition are placed at the ends of verses, we have derivative (or grammatical) rhyme, equivocal rhyme, and a host of other types (for which see Chapter 4 in this volume).

FIGURES OF SYNTAX

We turn now to a group of techniques that, because they involve the functions of words in the sentence and the relations between words, might well be labeled "figures of syntax." Like figures of repetition, figures of syntax operate on the level of linguistic units; but figures of syntax usually have an even more indirect relation to meaning. Sometimes, figures of syntax give an impression of emphasizing certain ideas, though they often contribute little more than a sense of structure or stylistic ingenuity.

First we have a group of procedures that describes ways of enumerating ideas. *Asyndeton* (*dissolutio, dialyton, dissolutum*) juxtaposes two parallel terms or expressions with no conjunction, as in "cors ferms fortz" (solid strong body; Arnaut Daniel 9:45). Conversely, *polysyndeton* (*conjunctum*) links parallel elements by means of conjunctions: "Manjar ni beure ni dormir" (Eating or drinking or sleeping; Bertran de Born 30:42).

Zeugma (including various types known as *conjunctio, adjunctio*, etc.) is the coordination of two or more subjects governing a single verb, as in Guillem de Peiteus's lines "Totz joys li deu humiliar / et tota ricors obezir, / Midons . . ." (All joy should bow down to her, and all nobility obey My Lady; 9:19–21), where *deu* is understood as the verb of which *tota ricors* is subject. Like *asyndeton, zeugma* can be regarded as a form of ellipsis—that is, omission of words felt as normally necessary—as in Folquet de Marseilla: "Vers Dieus, e·l vostre nom e de sancta Maria" (True God, in your name and [that] of Saint Mary; 28:1).

The order of words, which in Provençal is grammatically freer than in English, enables a great variability. (For normal word order, see Jensen 385–397; and Smith and Bergin 235–238.) A change of word order for emphasis or another special effect is *transgressio* (*hyperbaton*), as in "Fetz Marcabrus los motz e·l so" (Marcabru made the words and the music; 35:2).

One of the many subtypes of *transgressio* is *hysterologia* (hysterology, *hysteron proteron*), which puts, as it were, the cart before the horse, in that the term that should logically be second is first, thus: "Lai on fo mortz e vius / nostre Seigner" (Where our Lord died and lived; Peire Vidal 2:43–44). (This particular example may, however, be designed to call attention to the resurrection, in which death did precede life; for a clearer example of hysterology, see Bernart de Ventadorn's "Lo tems vai e ven e vire," cited above). Another subtype of *transgressio* is *parenthesis*, in which a thought is momentarily interrupted and then returned to, as when the imperative "—Escoutatz!—" '—Listen!—' is inserted in the middle of each stanza of Marcabru's poem 18. *Chiasmus* (a postmedieval term; one chief type is traditionally labeled *antimetabole*, *commutatio*, or *permutatio*) involves, in its purest form, pairs of words that recur with or without changed endings in the order *abba*, but by extension it applies to words of similar meaning or to the same parts of speech. For example, Peire Cardenal's line "Que·l [ricz] laire penda·l lairo mesqui" (That the rich thief hangs the petty thief; 56:24) shows the chiastic structure adjective + noun in the subject case . . . + the same noun in the object case + a second adjective.

These examples show the richness of syntax as a linguistic feature and the variety of its contributions to the poetic voice.

FIGURES OF DESCRIPTION AND ARGUMENTATION

A large group of rhetorical techniques helps the speaker or writer to describe, demonstrate, present, and argue. To us, these may often seem no more than natural ways of expressing oneself, but in the Middle Ages they were carefully calculated and well-defined procedures.

Definitio (*horismos*) briefly identifies the essential properties of a person or thing, as in Guiraut de Bornelh's male-centered definition of his lady: "Ilh es cela per cui eu chan e plor" (She is the one because of whom I sing and weep; 1:10).

Descriptio is the describing of any thing in some detail and vividness. The troubadours, for instance, enjoy depicting natural scenes, as in Bernart de Ventadorn's "Can l'erba fresch' e·lh folha par / e la flors boton' el verjan" (When the fresh grass and leaf appear and the flower buds on the branch; 20:1–2). Often, as here, the *exordium* (the initial segment of the poem, thus the first phase of *dispositio*) contains such nature descriptions, for which German gives us the handy term *Natureingang*. Frequent too are descriptions of individuals, notably the lady or the subject of a *planh*.

Physical description is called *effictio*, thus in Arnaut Daniel: ". . . sa crin saura / e·l cors gai, grailet e nou" (her blond hair and her lively, slender, young body; 10:19–20). And character description is *notatio*, as in Guiraut de Bornelh: "Dolz' e bona, umils, de gran paratge, / en fachs gentils, ab solatz avinen" (Sweet and good, humble, of great nobility, noble in deeds, of pleasant company; 1:16–17). A more developed technique is *demonstratio*, which describes an event together with what comes before and after, its circumstances, and its consequences; this figure can be seen in many of the troubadours' depictions of crossed love or in narrative genres like the *pastorela*.

Distributio (*merismus*) is the attribution of various functions or roles to a series of individuals. In a negative variant, Bertran de Born writes:

> Regisme son, mas rei no jes;
> E contatz, mas non comt ni bar;
> Las marchas son, ma no·il marqes,
>
> (42:17–19)

There are kingdoms, but no kings at all, and counties, but no counts or barons; there are marquisates, but no marquises.

Another way of adding further dimensions to one's discourse is *exemplum*, the citing of authorities or well-known examples, as in Marcabru's: "Non saps d'Amor cum trais Samson?" (Don't you know how love betrayed Sampson? 6:14). Peire Cardenal among others enjoys *sententia*, the use of maxims and proverbs: "Anz es ben ditz un reprochiers pe·l mon: / Sel qu'una ves escorja autra non ton" (A proverb is well said in the world: The one who once flays, the next time does not shave; 75:47–48)—or, more or less, as the French say, "qui vole un oeuf, vole un boeuf."

An obvious way of emphasizing ideas is by repeating them in other terms through *congeries* (*synathroismos*), literally 'accumulation'. One type is *interpretatio* (*synonymia*, synonymic iteration): *planc e plor* 'I lament and weep'. Often we find more or less synonymous terms designating personal qualities: the lady is noble, well-born, kind; the late king is rich, generous, powerful; and so on. Another type of *congeries* associates complementary terms that represent a single category or a totality: *aur e argen* 'gold and silver', designating wealth in general; *Cristiana ni Juzeva* 'Christian or Jewish woman', standing for all women; *tot quant es ni er ni fo* 'all that is or was or will be'. Or, more complexly, Guillem de Peiteus says in three different ways that his lady's nobility has no equal: "Pus hom gensor non pot trobar / ni huelhs vezer ni boca dir" (Since a nobler one cannot be found nor seen by eyes nor described by mouth; 9:31–32).

Next, a series of devices relate the speaker to others. Apostrophe (*apostrophatio*) addresses a person (including oneself) or a personified thing. Thus, the first word of each strophe of a *tenso* addresses the poetic adversary ("Amics Bernartz de Ventadorn . . . , Peire . . . ," etc.; Bernart de Ventadorn 28:1, 8, etc.). Guiraut de Bornelh offers a more developed example: "Reis glorios, verais lums e clartatz, / Deus poderos, Senher, si a vos platz" (Glorious king, true light and clarity, Mighty God, Lord, if you please; 54:1–2).

An often-associated figure is *exclamatio*, which expresses a strong emotional outcry, as in Gaucelm Faidit's *alba*: "Ai las! quan pauca nueytz fai!" (Alas! how little night is left! 68:23). *Licentia* (*parrhesia*) is asking to be excused for speaking frankly, as when Peire Cardenal ends a diatribe against false clerics by saying: "E si mal o ai dig, que·m sia perdonatz" (And if I've spoken wrongly, may I be pardoned for it; 34:36).

In *sermocinatio*, the speaker puts appropriate-sounding words in another's mouth, including imagined dialogues such as that between the Monk of Montaudon and God (poem 13) and between Lanfranc Cigala, his heart, and his wisdom (poem 10).

The various figures that involve questions include *interrogatio* (rhetorical question, *erotesis*), where the speaker asks a question whose answer is not given but is implied: "No deu om los oblitz / ni·ls velhs fachs remembrar?" (Should one not recall the forgotten ones and the deeds of old? 65:63–64). (The poet's answer, obviously, would be: Yes, one should.) A variant is the *ubi sunt* topos, as in the same poem: "On son gandit joglar / que vitz gen acolhitz?" (Where have the jongleurs vanished to, whom one used to see so well received? 65:41–42). When the speaker asks a question and then proceeds to answer it, we have *ratiocinatio*, as where Peire Cardenal writes:

Saps qu'endeven la ricor
De sels que l'an malamen?
Venra un fort raubador . . .

    (74:17–19)

Do you know what will become of the wealth of those who acquire it by evil?
A mighty robber will come . . .

Whole strophes built on this principle combined with *sermocinatio* have the persona dialoguing interrogatively with himself or an imagined interlocutor.

When rather than implicitly or actually answering the question the author calls on the interlocutor or audience to reply or judge, we have *permissio* (*concessio, epitrope, synchoresis*), as in Bernart de Ventadorn: "Era·m cosselhatz, senhor, / vos c'avetz saber e sen" (Now give me advice, sirs, you who have knowledge and wisdom; 25:1–2). (In a different technique also known as *permissio*, the speaker submits to another party, as in Guillem de Peiteus 8:7–8, discussed below.)

Where the speaker expresses real doubt about a point or a choice of words, we have *dubitatio*. This principle leads Raimbaut d'Aurenga to create a new genre, the *No sai que s'es*, by saying he does not know what genre he is using:

Escotatz, mas no say que s'es
Senhor, so que vuelh comensar.

Vers, estribot, ni sirventes
Non es, ni nom no·l sai trobar;
(24:1-4)

Listen, but I don't know what this is, sirs, that I want to begin. It's not a *vers*,
estribot, or *sirventes*, and I don't know how to find it a name.

Another group of techniques is built around the principle of opposition, for
which the general term is *contentio* (*antithesis*). *Contentio* is usually considered
a figure of word in simple pairs, like *joi e dolor* 'joy and sadness', but a figure
of thought when more developed, as in Peire Cardenal: "Clergue si fan
pastor / e son aucizedor" (Clerics pretend to be shepherds and they are
killers; 29:1-2). Examples like this one, in which a person is not what he or
she seems, are very common in the *canso*: the beloved seems merciful but
is really cruel, etc. Or he or she has both qualities at once, being merciful
to all but cruel only to the lover, as in the Countess of Dia's complaint: "Mi
faitz orguoill en digz et en parvenssa / e si etz francs vas totas autras gens"
(You're overbearing toward me in words and in appearance, yet you act
nobly toward all other people; 2:13-14).

A distinct type of *contentio* contrasts individuals, as in Bertran de Born's
"Di·n en Richart qu'il es leos, / e·l reis Felips agnels me par" (Tell Sir
Richard that he's a lion, and King Philip appears a lamb to me; 42:50-51).
According to the *Leys* (3:186), this is a type of *antitheta* or *syndiasmos*, of
which another mode contrasts before and after states, as in Marcabru:
"Amors soli' esser drecha, / mas er' es torta e brecha" (Love used to be
straight, but now it's twisted and nicked; 18:25-26). Sometimes, the two
contrasting states are seen in a process of evolution, as in Cercamon:
"Malvestatz puej' e Jois dissen" (Evil rises and Joy declines; 1:5). If one
alternative were to destroy the other, then, in the *Leys*' terminology (3:184),
we would have *antitheton*.

Often, the poet delights in contrasting ideas that seem mutually contradictory, as in Guillem de Peiteus's "nonsense poem" (*devinalh*, 13) beginning "Farai un vers de dreit nïen" (I'll make a verse about nothing at all;
4:1), which is full of mutually contradictory ideas like "Anc non la vi ez am
la fort" (I never saw her and I love her lots; 4:31). This principle can
produce whole series of images of the type "In the heat you feel great cold,"
as described in the *Leys* (3:188) under the label *reversari*.

Another group of techniques helps emphasize the main ideas of a discourse. *Commoratio* (*epimone*) reiterates a point by using, among other figures, synonymy and word repetition, already discussed. *Expolitio* (*exargasia*)
polishes an idea through many techniques gathered in one place, but the
term is also used broadly of amplifying techniques. *Frequentatio* (*synathroismos*) gathers together scattered points in one place for greater impact; it can
also indicate a heaping together of synonyms, as in *congeries*. Given the

variability of definitions, it is not easy to distinguish these figures, which occur in the *canso* around the central image of noble but incompletely requited love, as well as in some other genres like the *planh* in its reiteration of the virtues of the departed and the grief of those left behind. We can see all these figures and more where Bertran de Born dwells on universal sadness at Young King Henry's death:

Rema pretz e jovens doloros
E·l mon oscurs e teintz e tenebros,
Sems de tot joi, ples de tristor e d'ira
(Hill-Bergin 75:6–8)

Merit and youth remain sad and the world obscure and dark and shadowy, deprived of all joy, full of grief and dolor.

FIGURES OF TRANSFER OF SENSE

Finally, the group comprising most of the ten traditional tropes and some other techniques will here be labeled "figures of transfer of sense," since in some way they all challenge the reader's creativity by moving the discourse to a new level or locus that transcends the literal meaning of the words. As Geoffrey of Vinsauf says of tropes, the object of our discourse "shrouds itself in mist, as it were, but in a luminous mist" (*Poetria nova* 54, line 1050). Within this group of figures, allegory, metaphor, metonymy, personification, simile, symbol, and synecdoche are the only "common types distinguished now" (*Princeton Encyclopedia* 365).

Geoffrey tells us: "Since a word . . . passes swiftly through the ears, a step onward is taken when an expression made up of a long and leisurely sequence of sounds is substituted for the word. In order to amplify the poem, avoid calling things by their names . . ." (24, lines 226–240). In short, he is recommending periphrasis (*circumlocutio, circumitio, circuitio*). In a broad sense, this figure includes many others like hyperbole, litotes, irony, and antonomasia, which say things in less than direct fashion. In its more specific sense, periphrasis is also very common in the troubadours.

Not surprisingly, periphrasis often designates the lady by using terms like *lai* 'there [where she is]', as in Guiraut de Bornelh's "Soven sospir e soplei et azor / vas lai on vi resplandir sa beltat" (Often I sigh and bow and worship toward where I see her beauty shine; 1:12–13). Other particularly noteworthy examples of periphrasis are Bertran de Born's designation of paradise as "Lai on anc dol non ac ni aura ira" (Where grief there never was nor will be sadness; Hill-Bergin 75:40) and Arnaut Daniel's reference to his mother as "la seror de mon oncle" (the sister of my uncle; 18:19).

A variant of periphrasis, euphemism, is used of an unpleasant or taboo topic, as in Marcabru: "Anz . . . / c'ajam la boca ni·ls huoills claus" (Before . . . our mouth and eyes are closed; 35:24–25). Such periphrases offer a chance to amplify the essential characteristics of a person, thing, or situation.

Next, personification (*conformatio, prosopopeia*) challenges the audience to accept the attribution of human characteristics to a thing, an animal, or a concept. This device helps bring to life abstract qualities like *Joy* (Joy) and *Pretz* (Merit), as when Marcabru writes: "Mas Escarsedatz e No·fes / part Joven de son compaigno" (Niggardliness and Faithlessness separate Youth from his companion; 35:19–20). More dramatically, the female persona in Raimbaut de Vaqueiras's *cantiga d'amigo* exhorts the waves to bring news of her absent friend (24:1–3), and Guillem Figueira devotes a whole *sirventes* to denouncing Rome, represented as having a full range of human vices such as a gullet full of ire (2:141).

In departing from literalness, the author often leaves the truth of the matter to be determined by the audience. *Hyperbole* (*superlatio*) or exaggeration is a favorite device of the troubadours beginning with Guillem de Peiteus: "Quar senes lieys non puesc viure, / . . . / Que plus ez blanca qu'evori" (Without her I cannot live . . . she is whiter than ivory; 8:11, 13). The contrary figure is *diminutio* (*meiosis*), or understatement, as when the warlike Bertran de Born concludes a threat with surprising meekness:

> Fals enveios fementit lausengier,
> Pois ab midonz m'avetz mes destorbier
> Be lausera qe·m laissasetz estar.
>   (6:49–51)

> False, jealous, perjured flatterers, since you have caused trouble between me and my lady, I would be grateful if you left me alone.

(In modern terminology this device is usually called litotes, which properly is reserved for the type "not small," meaning "large.")

Irony (*eironeia*, literally 'dissimulation') can be seen as comprising a whole group of interrelated figures like *diminutio, hyperbole*, various types of ambiguity including punning, and false innocence (as in the deceptive nonsense utterance "Babariol," etc., in Guillem de Peiteus 5). One of the more specific meanings of irony is sarcastic speech, saying the contrary of what one means, as in Peire Cardenal's diatribe against the order of nuns known as Beguines: "Tals miracles fan, aiso sai per ver: / de saintz paires saint podon esser l'er" (Such ones [Beguines] perform miracles, this I know as true: of saintly fathers saints can be the heirs [and children]; 28:55–56).

Another challenge to our creativity as readers, *antonomasia* (*pronominatio*) involves a substitution of or for a proper name. In one type, a general term designates an individual member of that class, thus Verge for the Virgin Mary, Apostol for the Apostle Peter, and Sepulcre for the Sepulcher of

Christ. In another type, a characterization designates an individual, as in the list of attributes representing God cited earlier, the expression "cill del temple Salamo" (those of Solomon's temple) for the Knights Templar (Marcabru 35:56), or *senhals* like Rigaut de Berbezilh's hyperbolic "Miels de Domna" (Better than Lady; 2:50).

In a comparison (*similitudo, collatio, comparatio*), the grammar tips us off that one thing is being characterized or amplified by reference to another thing. Often the mark of comparison is a word meaning "like" or "as," for example in Marcabru: "Amors vai com la belluja . . ." (Love acts like the spark; 18:13). Or the overt mark of comparison can be a verb designating resemblance or appearance, as in Peire Vidal: "E lor parlars sembla lairar de cas" (And their speech resembles the barking of dogs; 21:12). Or a form meaning "more than" or "less than" can be used, as by Peire Cardenal: "Mens a de sen non a l'enfans que teta" (Has less sense than does the babe that suckles; 56:31). Comparisons often become digressions, and *exempla* can be phrased as comparisons.

A metaphor (*translatio*) is a shortened comparison, a juxtaposition of two things without any grammatical evidence of the link; thus in Raimbaut de Vaqueiras: "Nos fom austor et ylh foro aigro" (We were hawks and they were herons; Epic Letter 2:54). Feudal metaphors are frequent, from Guillem de Peiteus on: "Qu'ans mi rent a lieys e·m liure / qu'en sa carta·m pot escriure" (For rather, I surrender to her and give myself up, and she can write me in her charter; 8:7–8). Similarly, the joy of love "flowers" (Guillem de Peiteus 9:9–10), the lady is "a beautiful lily" (Guiraut de Bornelh 1:6), and so on.

A similar transfer of sense, metonymy (*denominatio*), uses one thing in place of another to which it stands in some relation of logical contiguity, such as invention for inventor, instrument for user, cause for effect, container for content, abstract for concrete, material for the object it forms, property for thing, possession or quality for possessor, and, in many cases, the reverse of these relations. It is not easy to distinguish the types of metonymy, and various authorities define them differently, but here are three examples: (1) possessor for quality, in Peire Vidal: "Non auzim pueis l'Emperador / creisser de pretz ni de bontat" (Since then, we have not heard the Emperor grow in renown or kindness; 6:28–29) (it is not the Emperor but his qualities that are not growing); (2) quality for possessor and abstract for concrete, in the same troubadour: "Bell' es sobre tota beutat" (She is beautiful above all beauty; 6:53); and (3), in Marcabru, container for content: "Sai plora Guiana e Peitaus" (Here, Guyenne and Poitou weep; 35:68) (i.e., the inhabitants of these provinces lament). Metonymy is a broad enough category that it can include other figures like personification (quality for possessor) and, in many cases, periphrasis.

Synecdoche (*intellectio*), the use of a part for the whole or vice versa, is not always easy to distinguish from metonymy. A frequent sort of synecdoche is the use of *cors* 'body' to represent the entire person (including soul and personality); on the other hand, according to the *Leys* (3:226), if we speak of burying a person we use the whole for the part, since in fact only the body, and not the soul, is buried.

Last of all, allegory (*permutatio, inversio*) can be seen as an extended metaphor that replaces one idea by another. In the Middle Ages, allegory (which is not always easily distinguished from several other figures of transfer of sense) could be as brief as a single line, but in the more developed sense it implies a whole figurative level corresponding to the literal level of a narrative. For example, Raimbaut de Vaqueiras's *Carros* 'War-Chariot' (poem 18) ostensibly recounts a military campaign, but on another level details the competing qualities of a number of noble ladies; or, Peire Cardenal's "fable" (poem 80) makes a little story out of St. Paul's idea that the wisdom of God is opposed to human folly. Courtly love itself has been treated (by C. S. Lewis) as one vast allegory; it is very fitting that the intertwining of rhetoric and the troubadours' favorite subject matter should be recognized in this way.

A CONCLUDING WORD OR TWO

Rhetoric comprises a largely fixed inventory. Almost all the troubadours' techniques of expression are already embodied in Guillem de Peiteus, who himself invented little or nothing; this is not surprising, given that the troubadours drew both on the classical-medieval tradition and on the works of their Provençal predecessors. What can be called a "troubadour style" is heavily marked by rhetoric and by a strong interaction of form and content.

Yet this does not mean that rhetorical usage remains unchanged. Within one generation, there are notable differences in emphasis: one troubadour may prefer comparisons, another word repetition, and so on. As time goes on, some devices, such as alliteration or comparison, seem to gain in popularity, while others decline. In the postclassical period, after about 1210, it seems that rhetoric often became a pretext for writing poetry, even a game for its own sake. In the mid–fourteenth century, with the codification of the *Leys d'amors*, rhetoric took on a new life adapted to a vastly altered poetic content, and still today it exists in new avatars, even though the troubadours' poetry died out six centuries ago.

This persistence of rhetoric testifies to the continuity of the values that inform Western society. In one analysis, at least, medieval rhetoric expressed the ethos and interests of a ruling class. The troubadours dispensed to their patrons not only self-satisfaction, public praise, and fame, but also something more subtle. Western society has largely been characterized by a striving to amass power and material resources; yet on the whole the greatest prestige has been conferred by a sort of distillation of the material into artistic and linguistic refinement. Thus medieval lords, themselves usually unlettered, promoted and by their largesse controlled those who by background and talent could master language and song. In return, the troubadours, like the artists and musicians in Marcel Proust's *A la recherche du temps perdu,* received some access to the higher reaches of a hierarchical socio-economic system.

These outspoken individuals who staked their livelihoods on pleasing the noble class through a conventional rhetoric were by that fact prevented from expressing new political or social values. They might attack individual lords and ladies, but not the existence and preeminence of the noble class. In other words, the rhetorical system and the concomitant assumption that texts should be seen as aesthetic products (as opposed to, say, commentaries on relations between socio-economic, ethnic, or gender groups) can be seen as conservative forces that upheld class-oriented, male-dominated, formalistic, ostensibly orderly and rational, ultimately self-serving structures. As St. Augustine and his contemporaries were aware, the genius of the rhetorical system is to organize, persuade, and embellish, but not necessarily to promote the true and overthrow the false. Rhetoric, like all sign systems, can be turned in any direction; it exists at the service of whatever force in society—whether in the fourth, twelfth, or twentieth century—has the resources to appropriate it.

Ultimately, rhetoric can be seen as a means by which author, reader, and critic alike assert their control over the text. The persistence of the Western rhetorical tradition gives the twentieth-century American scholar the illusion of "correctly" interpreting the work of a western European medieval poet who in turn, consciously or unconsciously, used—also presumably "correctly," or in line with the teachings of normative manuals—forms of expression legitimized by the classical Greeks and Romans but going back even farther in time. No one, however, can lock a text into a given system of interpreting sounds, words, symbols, and other exterior manifestations of the human mind. In studying the troubadours, we must be aware that we approach them with a set of assumptions conditioned by our own culture, which, though related to theirs, prevents us from thinking and reacting as they did. We cannot read or listen as the troubadours' audience did, any more than we can write or sing as the troubadours did. The problem is the same as with their grammar and pronunciation: we can try to go back in time, using all the evidence we can muster, but we cannot hope to become twelfth-century Occitan people.

Certainly, then, the passage of time has not entirely illuminated rhetorical practice and its social function, nor will it. Nevertheless, we can learn from asking and attempting to answer many pertinent questions. The following issues seem preeminent among the many that need further consideration:

1. How can we best understand and appreciate the attitudes of the troubadours and their audiences toward rhetoric and style?

2. How conscious of literary style were the troubadours and their audiences? Did they use and appreciate rhetorical devices out of habit and intuition? Did they analyze them in the manner of medieval rhetoricians and modern scholars? Or did they do both in varying degree?

3. Is there a rhetorical "norm" against which individual and collective practices can be measured?

4. What about the "originality" of certain troubadours: Is it a breaking away from tradition in the manner of the Romantic poets? Or is it merely a use of conventions so skilled that the conventions are concealed from view?

5. What about the claim to "sincerity": is it just one more convention?

6. Is the rhetoric of the trobairitz similar to or different from that of the male troubadours?

7. Are there real rhetorical differences between *trobar clus* and *trobar leu*, the "difficult" and "easy" styles? Or do both styles, as well as the intermediate *trobar ric*, basically use the same old rhetorical devices in similar proportions?

8. How can we describe and measure the role of rhetoric in the postclassical decline as compared to its role in the flowering of the troubadours?

WORKS CITED

The quotations in this chapter are from the critical editions cited in the List of Troubadour Editions in the Appendix, and in particular from the following editions: Arnaut Daniel (Toja); Bertran de Born (Paden, Sankovitch, and Stäblein); Cercamon (Wolf and Rosenstein); Jaufre Rudel (Wolf and Rosenstein); Guillem de Montanhagol (Ricketts); Guillem de Peiteus (Bond); Guiraut de Bornelh (Kolsen); Monge de Montaudon (Routledge); Peire Vidal (Avalle); Rigaut de Berbezilh (Várvaro). Unless otherwise indicated, quotations in the present chapter are taken from Bergin et al. All translations are my own.

Augustine, Saint. *On Christian Doctrine.* Trans. D. W. Robertson Jr. Indianapolis: Bobbs-Merrill, 1958.

Bergin, Thomas G., et al., eds. *Anthology of the Provençal Troubadours.* 2d ed. 2 vols. New Haven: Yale University Press, 1973.

Bogin, Meg, ed. *The Women Troubadours.* New York: Paddington Press, 1976.

Boutière, Jean, and Alexander H. Schutz, eds. *Biographies des troubadours: textes provençaux des XIIIe et XIVe siècles.* Paris: Nizet, 1964.

Curtius, Ernst Robert. *European Literature and the Latin Middle Ages.* Trans. Willard R. Trask. New York: Harper & Row, 1963.

Espy, Willard R. *The Garden of Eloquence: A Rhetorical Bestiary.* New York: Harper & Row, 1983.

Faral, Edmond. *Les Arts poétiques du XIIe et du XIIIe siècle.* Paris: Champion, 1924.

Geoffrey of Vinsauf. *Poetria nova.* Trans. with an introduction by Margaret F. Nims. Toronto: Pontifical Institute of Mediaeval Studies, 1967.

————. *Documentum de modo et arte dictandi et versificandi.* Trans. with an introduction by Roger P. Parr. Milwaukee: Marquette University Press, 1968.

Guilhem Molinier. *Las flors del Gay Saber, estiers dichas Las leys d'amors.* Ed. and trans. Adolphe-Félix Gatien-Arnoult et al. 3 vols. 1841–43; repr. Geneva: Slatkine, 1977.

Jensen, Frede. *The Syntax of Medieval Occitan.* Tübingen: Max Niemeyer, 1986.

Lausberg, Heinrich. *Elemente der literarischen Rhetorik.* 3d ed. Munich: Max Hueber, 1967.

Lewis, C. S. *The Allegory of Love.* London: Oxford University Press, 1936.

Marshall, John H., ed. *The "Donatz Proensals" of Uc Faidit.* London: Oxford University Press, 1969.

————, ed. *The "Razos de trobar" of Ramon Vidal and Associated Texts.* London: Oxford University Press, 1972.

Matthew of Vendôme. *The Art of Versification.* Trans. with an introduction by Aubrey E. Galyon. Ames: Iowa State University Press, 1980.

Murphy, James. J. *Rhetoric in the Middle Ages: A History of Rhetorical Theory from Saint Augustine to the Renaissance.* Berkeley and Los Angeles: University of California Press, 1974.

Paetow, Louis J. *The Arts Course at Medieval Universities, with Special Reference to Grammar and Rhetoric.* Champaign-Urbana: University of Illinois Press, 1910.

Princeton Encyclopedia of Poetry and Poetics. Ed. Alex Preminger et al. Princeton: Princeton University Press, 1965.

Smith, Nathaniel B. "Guilhem Fabre, Uc de Saint-Circ, and the Old Provençal Rime Dictionary." *Romance Philology* 29 (1976a): 501–7.

————. *Figures of Repetition in the Old Provençal Lyric: A Study in the Style of the Troubadours.* University of North Carolina Studies in the Romance Languages and Literatures, 176. Chapel Hill: Department of Romance Languages, University of North Carolina, 1976b.

Smith, Nathaniel B., and Thomas G. Bergin. *An Old Provençal Primer.* New York: Garland, 1984.

NINETEEN

Topoi

Elisabeth Schulze-Busacker

Whenever medieval, and in particular Occitan, literature is examined closely, it soon becomes evident that it is difficult for us to appreciate an art that does not stem from the personal expression or individual characteristics of a feeling, experience, or action; in brief, an art in which there is no authentic relationship to the life of the artist.

While leafing through a chansonnier, romance, or chanson de geste from the twelfth or thirteenth century, it is easy to feel a sense of lassitude: such useless repetition, especially of so many well-known motifs and so many overused themes. In fact, the principal intent of medieval literature is not to exteriorize a fact or sentiment that (individually or collectively) really existed; rather, "the [medieval] epic raises the history of the social group to the heights of the universal; the lyric song transposes an individual experience out of its time" by positing it as a typical human experience (Zumthor 1963, 13).

How, then, does one learn to recognize and appreciate the originality of a different "poetics" so far removed from that to which we have become accustomed since the Romantic movement? In order to grasp what, for the medieval audience, can be translated into aesthetic pleasure and a conscious perception of art, it is necessary to analyze the texts (and their music, in those cases where it has survived), not simply read them. One needs to follow the movement, relationship, and combination of *all* the elements in the text, paying as much attention to the perceptible value of the theme as

Translated from the French by Dorothy Flaherty, University of Minnesota, and Brenda Hosington, Université de Montréal. Quotations originally in languages other than English have been translated, and the original is not provided here, although the documentation refers the reader to the foreign-language source. Unless otherwise indicated, the translators have rendered into English the modern French translations provided by the author.

to the expressive quality of the formal play on the level of style and the spellbinding power of the formula, the word itself and its sound.

Only by grasping the authentic tone of the work can one appreciate and evaluate this product of a very learned art. To open the way to such a perception of medieval works of literature, it is first of all necessary to understand the contours of a rhetoric, or of a very specific poetic technique, in which the artist's freedom consists in choosing from among the possibilities of a deliberately limited network of references. In fact, the lyric text, just like the medieval narrative, is built on the "commonplace": the language of convention, the cliché, and the topos. The artist's subtlety is thus measured by his capacity to create a new work in a traditional thematic and stylistic framework. Although we agree therefore with Robert Guiette ([1949] 1972, 61) that medieval art is characterized by a traditional background against which the perception of the formal elements—of playing with form—can be distinguished, we must review the different ways in which this form is achieved.[1]

The present study seeks to tackle the issue in two stages: first, we will give a brief sketch of the research on the notion of topos; then, we will attempt to demonstrate the various applications of this notion in Occitan literature, with the help of an example.

The tradition living on in medieval art goes back to Antiquity, touches on folklore, and includes the Celtic heritage, without our being in a position to identify the origin of each element in this system of signals by which the author transmits his poetic message. It is a question of a "universe of reference both imaginary and verbal" (Zumthor 1972, 82), which has been the object of research using different approaches, either in the manner of Ernst Robert Curtius, Eugene Vinaver, Robert Guiette, and Paul Zumthor, who aim for a global interpretation of the medieval poetic, or in the more restricted mode that traces various themes, motifs, or stylistic or lexical elements in a specific network of references.

The first, most wide-ranging and influential attempt to deal with the subject was that of Curtius, presented, after numerous preparatory publications, in his 1948 book *Europäische Literatur und lateinisches Mittelalter*. Looking at stereotyped and recurrent textual elements in Western literature, Curtius establishes a line of continuity between the topos of Greco-Latin rhetoric, on the one hand, and the "clichés" one encounters in literary works, on the other. This equation constitutes, in his opinion, not only proof of a cultural continuity between classical Antiquity, the Latin Middle Ages, and vernacular literature, but also the best common denominator to measure the aesthetic value of literature in general, and medieval

---

1. See Gruber 1–7, 242–57, criticizing this type of research. See also Emrich 251: "An investigation that does not limit its scope by too narrow a concept of topic and topos must lead to the conclusion that we are dealing with support devices."

literature in particular. Curtius's literary theory is thus based on rhetoric because the *topic*, as he uses the term, is close to its meaning in classical rhetoric, which designates by topos the treasury "of subjects and forms that constitute the common fund of tradition and culture. A personal use of themes represents only one choice offered among the possibilities in a collective topic" (Butters 264n.7, quoting Genette).[2]

On the basis of this definition, Curtius himself analyzed the "topic of discourse" (for example, affected modesty, the *exordium*, the *Natureingang*, the world upside down); figures of style like metaphors relating to people, parts of the body, and navigation; certain topoi such as that of inexpressibility (the author declares himself "incapable of treating the subject") or of "outdoing" (the author praises a character or a thing as surpassing all that can be compared); and certain typical descriptions, such as those of heroes and sovereigns, beauty, or an ideal landscape, in poetry and the epic.

Inspired by Curtius, whose subject was above all the Latin tradition and its multiple Western repercussions, not just the Middle Ages, Guiette, Vinaver, and Zumthor continued in the same theoretical vein but concentrated expressly on medieval literature, especially French and Occitan. Guiette, seeking to pin down the particularity of French medieval poetry, finds it in formal invention:

> The courtly chanson is a genre that deliberately excludes the originality of musical thought and the originality or sincerity of poetic thought. . . . The courtly chanson, for the langue d'oïl poets, is an artistic and rhetorical creation. From all the given elements, they set out to make or construct an "objet," a new reality. What they are making is not an admission, but a song. The action that solicits their attention is that of "composition": the placement of known elements, the elaboration of a definitive verbal grouping, of a text to be sung, of a sung text. (Guiette [1949] 1972, 28–30)

Vinaver, who is especially interested in the specificity of medieval epic and romance composition, states that

> the work is presented like an organism that unites two seemingly contradictory principles: that of *cohesion* and that of *multiplicity*. It is, on the one hand, impossible to take away anything without disrupting the whole; on the other hand, one can never gather together this whole at a central point, each of the interlacing themes having its own central point. (Vinaver 44–45)

Once again, it becomes clear that we are dealing with cleverly constructed works, controlled by an arrangement of episodes, themes, and recurring motifs.

---

2. "The justification for the historical topic by Curtius I see confirmed on the one hand in the multiplicity of the aspects offered by topic and topoi in Antiquity, and on the other in the effect of rhetoric upon texts, but above all in the conversion of a system (or tool) serving literary production into its opposite: a tool for the comprehension of texts" (Emrich 251).

Zumthor extends the field of investigation, aiming to prepare a doctrine that would be valid for all medieval literature. To do this, he adopts the various methods previously used for the interpretation of medieval poetry and presents, in detail, the different "models of writing" that characterize the era: the *grant chant courtois* and its repercussions, the *récit* with its multiple manifestations, and the dialogic genres, including the theater. He proposes an analytic grid applicable to all the texts which distinguishes five strata of meaning (phonic, morpho-syntactic, lexical, minimal figurative units, thematic) connected to three levels of analysis: first, the form of the message made up of sounds and syntagmatic bonds; second, the composition of the work by lexical units and figures of style; third, the message as communication through themes and motifs (Zumthor 1972, 148–49).

Levels 2 and 3 are concerned with what Curtius had included under the term topos. Level 2 deals with lexical units and figures of style, paying attention to key words (or families of words), fixed locutions, metaphors, and grammatical figures (Zumthor 1972, 152)—in other words, what used to be called "formulaic style." The third level, that of the *motifs*, seeks to identify recurring traditional elements, for example the motif of the troubadour's love service toward women, or that of birdsong, which belongs to the theme of Spring (Zumthor 1972, 152). It is only in order to designate some structured group of motifs, for example the request for love or the epic battle, that the author refers to the term *theme.*

Curtius had considered such a grouping (=theme) as one of the possible forms for a general topos; thus the *locus amoenus* "forms the principal motif of all nature description" (Curtius 1963, 195). It is levels 2 and 3—the "topic of discourse" according to Zumthor's analytic grid, or the topos in its various realizations according to Curtius—that will be the subject of this chapter, which is based on an already long series of works published since the appearance of Curtius's fundamental work (1948) and on subsequent reflections by Guiette (1949, 1960/1972), Vinaver (1970, based on four articles published between 1959 and 1968), and Zumthor (1963, 1972). The studies that put the theoretical analysis to the test by applying it to medieval French and Occitan texts are in fact close to one or other of these theoretical writings.

La Technique poétique des trouvères dans la chanson courtoise ([1960] 1979) by Dragonetti shares the viewpoint found in Curtius and Guiette; Zumthor himself said in his first publication about medieval poetry, *Langue et techniques poétiques à l'époque romane* (1963), that he was a follower of de Bruyne, Vinaver, and Guiette, before he presented, in 1972, his own system for the interpretation of medieval French literature.

Also to be considered are books and articles in the same line of thought but less general, being more concerned with particular aspects of medieval stylistics such as metaphors, comparisons, and images (Ziltener 1972, with two appendices 1972, 1983), figures of repetition (Smith), and portraits (Colby, Leube-Fey); or studies of semantic fields (for example, "pretz e valor," "joi e solatz," "aiza/aizimen," "obediens," "mezura," "cortezia") and conceptual fields such as joy and sadness (Camproux, Bec, Lavis), repentance (Payen), the heart (Ertzdorff) and courtly love (among others Akehurst; Frappier 1959, 1969, 1971; Lazar; and Schnell 1985, 1989).

All these works dealing with themes, motifs, and recurring stylistic and lexical elements underline the fact that medieval poetry is based on a system of rhetorical codification, which I will now describe using a lyric piece as an example. For purposes of demonstration, I chose a piece from a genre with a universal theme, at once close to the classical tradition and specifically Occitan: the *planh* or lament for the dead.

It is true that "the works of classical rhetoric—whether they were writings from Antiquity or their medieval descendants—offered writers lists of *figurae* suitable for translating emotion and of topoi likely to provoke compassion in the listener as well as frameworks for panegyric poetry and eulogistic description . . ." (Thiry 26). Nevertheless, medieval authors did not rely wholly on the tradition of Antiquity, but turned just as often to Occitan examples from before their time.

In the case of Bonifaci Calvo, a Genoese troubadour from the mid–thirteenth century (for more on whom, see Chapters 13 and 14 in this volume), this Occitan tradition was already a century old, and it continued as late as 1343. In all, forty-four *planh* have been preserved, which express an individual or collective funeral lament for a great personage, a protector, a friend or relative, or a lady. Whether the *planh* concern the death of a prince or of a woman, the essential themes are the same: general sorrow, praise for the deceased, and prayer for his or her soul (Aston 1969, 1971; Cohen; Rieger; Schulze-Busacker 1979, 1981, 1986; and Thiry). The amount of emphasis placed on each of these elements can, however, be quite remarkably varied, so much so in fact that it is even possible to distinguish three types of *planh*: (1) the moralizing *planh*, in which the expression of grief is only a point of departure for moral and social criticism of the epoch; (2) the true lament, where the expression of grief forms the central idea through the notion of sorrow and of its manifestation by the song, the *planh*; and (3) the courtly *planh*, which combines the expression of grief with the related idea of loss of joy or courtly gaiety. Bonifaci Calvo chose this last type for his lament on the death of a woman. This *planh* probably dates from the years 1250–60 and may have been written at the court of Alphonse X, the Learned of Castile, where Bonifaci spent a considerable amount of time.

> I. S'ieu ai perdut, no se·n podon iauzir
>   Mei enemic, ni hom que be no·m vueilla,
>   Car ma perda es razos qu'a els dueilla
>   Tan coralmenz, que·s deurian aucir,

E totz lo monz aucire si deuria,   5
Car morta es midonz, per cui valia
Pretz e valors; e s'eu, chaitius, saupes
Chauzir tal mort, que piegz far mi pogues
Que ma vida, senz tardar m'auciria.

II.   E car non posc peiurar ab murir,   10
Mi lais viure tant trist, que flors ni fueilla
Ni nuls deportz non a poder que·m tueilla
Ren del dolor, que·m fai metr'en azir
Tot zo que mais abellir mi solia,
Car despiegz mi capdell'e ira·m guia   15
E·m met en luec, on no viuria res,
Mas ieu, qu'ai tant de mal suffrir apres,
Qu'eu viu d'aisso, don totz autr'om morria.

III. E viu tan grieu, qu'eu no·m posc ges soffrir,
Que plors non semen e dols non recueilla   20
Per la mort de la bella, que·m despueilla
De tot conort; pero eu non dezir
Aver poder, ni voler, nueg ni dia,
De mi loingnar del maltrag que·m languia,
Pois c'a Dieu plac que mortz cella·m tolgues   25
Dont venia totz mos gaugz e mos bes
E tot cant ieu d'avinen far sabia.

IV.   Tant er'adreich'en tot ben far e dir,
Qu'eu non prec Dieu qu'en paradis l'acueilla,
Quar, per paor q'aia ni aver sueilla   30
Qu'el l'aia mes en soan, non sospir
Ni plaing, car, al mieu senblan, non seria
Lo paradis gent complitz de coindia
Senz leis; per qu'eu non tem ni dupti ges
Que Dieus non l'ai'ab se lai on el es,   35
Ni·m plaing mas, car sui loing de sa paria.

V.   Fols mi par cel que cor met ni consir
El ioi del mon, e plus fols qui s'orgueilla
Per tal ioi, car autr'uichaizos non mueilla
Mon vis de plors, ni als no·m fai languir,   40
Mas la menbranza del ioi, qu'eu avia
Del bel capteing e de la cortezia
Qu'eu trobav'e mi donz; e s'eu agues
Saubut que tant mal prendre me·n degues,
Non prezera·l ioi, ni ar me·n dolria.   45

VI.   Ai, flors de valor e de cortesia
E de beutat! Ai, bella, douz'amia!
Si·l mortz complic son voler qan vos pres,

Ieu en remaing tan doloros, que res
Alegrar ni conortar no·m poiria.   50

(poem 16)

I. Although I have had a loss, my enemies cannot rejoice, nor can anyone who dislikes me because it is just that my loss should sadden them to such a point that they should kill themselves and everyone should kill himself, for my lady is dead, thanks to whom Pretz (=breeding) and Valor (=innate qualities) were prized; and if I, unfortunate person that I am, knew how to find a manner of death that would be more painful to me than life, I would kill myself without hesitation.

II. And since my plight cannot be worsened through death, I allow myself to live, so sadly that neither flowers nor leaves, nor a single diversion has the power to take away a little of the pain that makes me abhor all that once pleased me, for sadness governs me and sorrow guides me and places me in a position where no one but I could live, I who have learned to suffer so much unhappiness that I live on what would make any other person die.

III. And I live so painfully that I can hardly keep myself from sowing tears and reaping sorrow because of the beautiful woman whose death deprives me of all consolation; and yet I do not desire either the power or the will, night or day, to abandon the suffering that afflicts me, since it pleased God that death took away the one from whom came all my joy and happiness and all the good that I could do.

IV. She was so perfect in actions and speech that I do not even pray God to take her into Paradise because I neither sigh nor complain as I could from fear, and as I used to, that He had scorned her, for in my opinion, Paradise would not be completely perfect without her; thus, I do not fear or doubt that God has placed her at His side, where He is, and I no longer lament because I am deprived of her company.

V. Foolish is he, it seems to me, who places his heart and thoughts in worldly joy, and more foolish is he who is proud of such a joy, for not a single other reason can moisten my face with tears, no other reason makes me languish, other than the memory of the joy I so deeply felt for the noble behavior and the *courtoisie* that I found in my lady; and if I had known that there was to be so much unhappiness for me as a result, I would never have esteemed joy nor be suffering now on its account.

VI. Oh, flower of excellence and *courtoisie* and beauty! Oh beautiful and sweet friend! How death imposed its will when it took you away; as for me, I remain here so unhappy that nothing could console me or make me joyful.

Let us try to follow the topical discourse at its various levels. According to the tradition of classical rhetoric, the *planctus* or funeral lament belongs to panegyric oratory that is, in its turn, a subcategory of epideictic or eulogistic discourse (Curtius 1963, 154–59).

The Occitan *planh* retains the three constituent elements of such a lament (grief, eulogy, and consolation) while giving a new twist to the classical and medieval Latin theme.[3] The lament forms the central element (strophes I, lines 1–4; II; III, lines 1–6; V; VI, lines 4–5); eulogy becomes a supplemental element in the form of a description of the effects of death on the suffering individual and group (strophes I, lines 6–7; III, lines 3–4, 9; IV, lines 5–7; V, lines 6–7; VI, lines 1–2); and consolation loses its Christian tone and is transformed into a sort of courtly *credo* (strophe IV, lines 1–5, 7–9).

Various motifs are evoked in order to fill in and give structure to this thematic framework. Motifs from a long-standing tradition are mingled with more recent topical elements.

The first stanza is the most conventional. It is the exordium of a lament as characteristic of medieval Latin and vernacular funeral laments, using three motifs:

the invitation to *compassio* (lines 1–4),
the announcement of death (line 6),
the desire to die of despair in light of the deceased's death.

Stanzas 2 and 3 combine three motifs in a similar manner, one that is typical of the courtly *planh*:

grief as the absence of "joi," of courtly gaiety (strophes II, lines 2–7;
    III, lines 1–4, 8–9),
acceptance of sorrow by the mourner on the basis of this same
    courtly idea (strophes II, lines 7–9; III, lines 4–9),
submission to divine will (strophe III, line 7).

The structure of the fourth stanza is drawn from the three elements fundamental to the funeral lament. The author introduces *praise for the deceased* (lines 1, 5–7, 9) while at the same time denying the usefulness of prayer (lines 2–5, 7–9), which normally accompanies *consolation* in the *planh*, and abandoning *grief* faced with the certainty that the perfection of the deceased guarantees her a place in Paradise (lines 3–5, 7–9).

The fifth stanza develops this same idea even further. The certainty that the perfect lady is in Paradise (lines 5–7) causes rejection of terrestrial "joi" (of the "world"; lines 1–3, 8–9) and gives preference to memory (lines 3–7) and to the resulting state of the no longer suffering soul (lines 7–9). Apparently, then, courtly love, which is at the basis of this *hyperbolic praise* of the deceased, leads toward sublimated love and to the *absence of grief*, the pinnacle of *consolation*. The *dolce stil nuovo* will elaborate this same idea, for example in the role that Beatrice plays for Dante.[4]

---

3. This corresponds to the Christian concept expressed in an exemplary manner by St. Augustine; cf. Moos 3:1, under C28 and C146–50.

4. See also Boethius: "Sed hoc est quod recolentem uehementius coquit; nam in omni aduersitate fortunae infelicissimum est genus infortunii fuisse felicem" (But this is what burns

The sixth stanza is the envoi (or, following the tradition of classical rhetoric, the *conclusio*). It brings together once more the three motifs that form the thematic nucleus of the piece:

praise for the deceased as the pinnacle of *courtoisie* (lines 1–2),
evocation of Death the abductor (line 3), whose central position in
    the stanza is not accidental,
grief as the absence of "joi" (lines 4–5).

Let us once again look at the most important of the motifs already mentioned in order to specify, at the stylistic level, the details of the topical discourse. I shall not take into consideration the classical legacy of the following:

polysyndeton (Lausberg par. 267), for example in lines 1–2, 4–5, 46–
    47;
anaphora (Lausberg pars. 265–66), for example in lines 37–38;
parallelism in the syntactic construction (Lausberg par. 337), for ex-
    ample in lines 6–7, 21–22, and 15;
contrasting pairs (Lausberg par. 389) such as *perdre/jauzir* (line 1),
    mort/vida (lines 8–9), *murir/viure* (lines 10–11, 18), *deportz/dolor*
    (lines 12–13), *azir/abellir* (lines 13–14), *semenar/recolhir* (line 20),
    mal prendre/prezar (lines 44–45);
iteratio of synonyms (Lausberg par. 244), for example in lines 15 (*cap-
    delhar-guiar*), 31–32 (*sospir-planher*), 34 (*non tem ni dupti ges*), 37 (*cor
    met ni consir*).

Rather I am concerned with the syntactic and lexical aspects of the three motifs that form the thematic nucleus of Bonifaci Calvo's *planh*. Concerning the *eulogy for the deceased*, certain key words that use the themes of the *canso d'amor* will be discussed. The evocation of death will be examined with reference to the formula "morta es" (line 6). The motif of *grief* will demonstrate the particularity of the *planh courtois* at the stylistic level and the play of contrasts between the conceptual fields of *joy* and *pain*.

In the Occitan *planh*, the *eulogy for the deceased* is not based on the recipes of classical or postclassical rhetoric of the *descriptio*, which insists on physical

---

the rememberer most violently; for in any misfortune, the most unhappy kind of misfortune is to have been happy) (Anicii Manlii Severini Boethii *Philosophiae Consolatio*, ed. L. Bieler, Corpus Christianorum, ser. Latina 94 [Turnhout: Brepols, 1957], p. 23); and Dante: "E quello a me: "Nessun maggior dolore / que ricordarsi del tempo felice / ne la miseria; e ciò sa'l tuo dottore" (And he said to me: there is no greater sorrow than remembering happy times when in misery; and this your doctor knows) (Dante Alighieri, *La commedia secondo l'antica vulgata*, ed. G. Petrocchi [Milan: Mondadori, 1966], 2:92.5, 121–23).

beauty much more than on moral and social qualities;[5] instead it follows the Occitan code of courtly love. Bonifaci Calvo chooses three names for the lady: *midons* (lines 6, 43), *bella* (line 21), and *bella, douz'amia* (line 47). Each term evokes another aspect of the perfection of the deceased in the courtly sense. The term *midons*, designating both the superiority of the lady and the distance that separates her from her lover, appeals to *cortesia, pretz,* and *valor* and thus to moral and social qualities that characterize the lady and govern her relationship with the lover.[6] *Cortesia* represents "the climate favorable to [courtly] love," demanding of the lady "on the one hand, excellence of character [*valor*], and on the other, refinement of behavior and a respect for propriety [*pretz*]" (Cropp 100–101).[7] (For *cortesia*, see also Chapter 3 in this volume.)

The sum of these two components makes the lady worthy of adoration: "bella" designates the lady who is loved (Cropp 150–53). She is loved for her pleasant and gracious way of conducting herself in the world (*coindia, adreich'en tot ben far e dir*) and preferred for her correct moral behavior (*bel capteing, tot ben far,* Cropp 161–64), because, after all, she is the pinnacle of all the qualities, "flors de valor e de cortesia e de beutat."

But courtly love is not only adoration of the lady; there is also "the affection the lover feels, as well as the charm, kindness, and sympathy the lady has for him" (Cropp 153, cf. 37–41). Like so many other troubadours, Bonifaci designates this by the apostrophe "bella, douz'amia" (line 47). Courtly love, which is thus situated between adoration and affection, procures "[lo] ioi," courtly gaiety as social diversion (*deport,* line 12; Cropp 324–27); gladness, which is expressed in song (*alegrar,* line 50; Cropp 322–24; *tot cant ieu d'avinen far sabia,* line 27); but also "mos gaugz e mos bes" (line 26), that is to say, the experience of love (Cropp 334–35, 359–62); and the "ioi del mon" (line 38), which could and should be followed

5. This "register" exists but belongs to the *descriptio*, to the canon of physical and moral qualities one uses in the description of a person; cf. Colby (chap. 1) and Leube-Fey, but see also the *planh* of Aimeric de Peguilhan on the death of Beatritz (poem 22), the only *planh* that makes use of so many of these elements: for example, "sos belhs cors gen noiritz" (her fair, well-nurtured body; line 9); "sos parlars fis ez aperceubutz" (her speech witty and intelligent; line 19); "sos esguars dous, um pauc en rizen" (her glances sweet, smiling a little; line 21); and "de totz bos ayps avia mais ab se / que'autra del mon" (she had more good qualities than any other lady in the world; lines 23–24) (translation Shepard/Chambers).

6. Cf. Cropp 29–37 and the works cited there.

7. ". . . The two terms complete each other. If the word *pretz* designates the merit, esteem, approbation that courtly society awards to its happy members, then it assumes that these individuals also possess a certain level of knowledge and *savoir vivre*. On the other hand, the word *valor* designates rather the quality of the human personality; it is, of course, concerned with inborn quality, but since the courtly 'ideal' demands perfection, it is also a question of acquired quality" (Cropp 437–38).

by the "menbranza del ioi" (line 41) that as the sublimation of terrestrial love extinguishes suffering and grief.

For the grieving poet this consoled state of mind is only hypothetical, for he is still feeling the loss of his lady: "car morta es midonz" (line 6). Such an announcement of death seems to be the simplest and most universal, because it is necessary to the *planh*. It does indeed correspond to the rule of the *Artes dictaminis* on the *propositio* (cf. Moos T79–87, C146–50), the announcement of the subject, but it finds in the poetry of the troubadours a variety of expression that constitutes a specifically Occitan topical element. The causal sentence chosen by Bonifaci was not placed at the beginning of the sixth line by accident. It is placed there in accordance with a stylistic constraint specific to the genre of the Occitan *planh* as it existed in the thirteenth century. In the first Occitan *planh*, for example those of Cercamon (1137), Guiraut de Bornelh (two texts from 1173 and 1199), and Bertran de Born (three texts from 1183 and 1186), the simple statement "es mortz" occupies various places in the first stanza. Starting from the famous *planh* of Gaucelm Faidit on the subject of the death of Richard Lion-Heart in 1199, however, "es mortz" becomes a fixed formula occupying a very specific place: the end of the first period, which coincides with the beginning or the end of the seventh or eighth line of the first stanza. Consider the example of Gaucelm Faidit: "Lo rics valens Richartz, reis dels Engles / es mortz! . . ." (The noble and valiant Richard, king of the English, is dead! 50:6–7); and a lament from 1209 by Guilhem Augier Novella: "Lo pro vescomte, que morts es . . ." (The good viscount, who is dead; 2:7). Aimeric de Peguilhan makes this a characteristic trait in the four *planh* preserved from his work dating from 1212 and 1220 (poems 10, 22, 30, 48).

The poets of the thirteenth century use the formula frequently, always in a marked place within a subordinate clause that can be either relative (the type closest to Gaucelm Faidit or Aimeric de Peguilhan) or causal (most frequent type, also chosen by Bonifaci Calvo). A late text furnishes proof that both types of subordinate clause (relative and causal) were consciously used; the author, Paulet de Marseille, clearly combines them when he says: "Qu'es mortz, don ai ira et malsabensa" (For he is dead, and thus I am in despair and despondence; 6:6).

Although Bonifaci Calvo chooses for his announcement of death the procedure preferred by Occitan rhetoric of his time, he does not do so for another form of codification of topical discourse: the personification of death (cf. Moos T207–10). When he says, "A Dieu plac que mortz cella·m tolgues dont venia . . ." (It pleased God that death took away the one from whom came; lines 25–26) and "Si·l mortz complic son voler qan vos pres" (Thus death accomplished its will when it took you away; line 48), Bonifaci is clearly choosing a middle path between, on the one hand, the attribution of an active role to God, which characterizes the religiously oriented *planh* using stylistic formulae such as "Dieus le volc" (it was God's will; Guilhem de Hautpoul in Meyer 41–43; cf. Rigaut de Berbezilh, app. 1, p. 286; and Peire Bremon Ricas Novas, Zingarelli 41), and, on the other hand, the personification of death of the type "Mortz m'a tout mo fizel companho" (Death has taken my faithful companion from me; Bertran Carbonel 15:3). Missing in Bonifaci's *planh*, however, is the *insultatio amarae mortis* for which Moos gives medieval Latin examples (T207–10) and which can also be found in troubadour poetry and the epic, for example in *Ronsasvals* and *Jaufre*.[8]

Concerning the third motif, the expression of grief and its stylistic realizations, Bonifaci, like other troubadours who chose the *planh courtois* type, develops his lament along three principal lines:

grief as distaste for life,
grief as absence of joy,
(hypothetical) consolation.

Behind these three elements there is obviously a medieval-Latin legacy such as that described by Moos, the classical and postclassical *taedium vitae*, the *maeror et gaudium* of the Christian Latin lament, and the *iucunda recordatio* of the deceased from the classical and medieval traditions. Their stylistic realization in troubadour poetry is, however, from the first *planh* of 1137 on, governed more by the conceptual networks of *dolor-dan-planh* and their opposite *joi-solatz-chan*, which correspond to the opposition between suffering and joy—sorrow (of loneliness) and gaiety (of the court)—lament and (courtly) song. For each of these concepts, Bonifaci chose a hyperbolic form of expression.

The idea of distaste for life (=*taedium vitae*) becomes death sought out of despair, not only for the grieving person, but also for his enemies, and in fact for everyone: "totz lo monz aucire si deuria" (line 5). Bonifaci thus takes up, and strengthens, an idea already expressed by other troubadours. Gavaudan, the first to have formulated it in 1200, was speaking only of his own death:

Mielhs fora qu'ieu muris premiers
Que ses joy visques ab dolor
(3:9–10)

8. *Ronsasvals*, ed. Roques, lines 1544–47, 1529; *Jaufre*, ed. Brunel, lines 8450–8695. See also the lyric poems: Gaucelm Faidit (poem 50), Gavaudan (poem 3), Joan Esteve (poems 10,11), Pons de Chapteuil (poem 24), Raimon Menudet (P-C 405,1 [ed. Mahn, *Gedichte* 153]), Raimon Gaucelm de Beziers (P-C 401,7 [ed. Azaïs 9]), and anonymous poems (P-C 461,2 [Stengel VII] and 234 [Bertoni 480]).

It would have been better had I died first instead of living without consolation in sorrow.

Others like Peire Bremon Ricas Novas (1237) and Pons de Chapteuil (first third of 13th cent.) followed the same path:

> Per que volgra morir e foram gen
> Que m'ausies, quar trop viu esperdus;
> E viures m'es marrimenz et esglais,
>
> (Pons de Chapteuil 24:3–5)

Therefore I would like to die, and killing myself would be pleasant for I am so desperate that living is pain and affliction.

But Bonifaci goes still further in desiring the hardest death, rather than the life of a "chaitius" (unfortunate person; lines 7–9).

No other troubadour chose such an extreme expression. Stylistically, however, it allows the author to pass to the second concept, grief as the absence of joy (of living). Balancing between the opposites *viure* and *murir*, the author introduces a certain number of the key words of the *canso d'amor*. First of all, let us consider the two elements belonging to the "Spring stanza": *flors ni feuilla* and *deport* (lines 11–12). This is a briefer form of another topos of classical tradition, the description of nature. It was introduced into troubadour poetry above all in the form of the *Natureingang* or Spring theme, which normally serves as an introduction or conclusion to a *canso*, a *sirventes*, and sometimes even other lyric genres (Schulze-Busacker 1974, 1978). In the *planh*, there is only one other example that is a little more developed, the *planh* of Cerveri de Girona, which begins:

> Joys ne solaz, pascors, abrils ne mays,
> Xans ne jardis, ortz ne vergers ne pratz,
> Cortz ne domneys ne hom pros ne presetz,
> Ans, tems ne mes ne jorns no·m playra mays,
> Que·ls ans e·l tems e·l jorns e·ls mes azir
> Per est mal mes, que no pogues venir
> Juyn, c'a desjuyns de joy totz los valenz,
> E juns ab dol adolitz e dolenz.
>
> Vers ne xanços, plasenz motz, sos ne lays,
> Cortz ne juglar, re no say que·us façatz
> Car mort es cel per que·l plus valiatz,
>
> (39:1–11)

Joy and distraction, Spring, April, and May, song and garden, orchard, meadow, and field, life at the court in the service of love and man of distinction and nobility, year, season, month, and day will please me no more. The enjoyment of year, season, and month is out of place. June cannot come back, for it has separated all valorous men from joy and bound them to pain and grief.

Verse and song, pleasant words, sound and melody, courtly life and distractions—I do not know what it means to you now, for dead is he who brought you most honor.

If Cerveri de Girona, a Catalan troubadour of the second half of the thirteenth century, consciously evokes at least three of the six elements of the Spring stanza (the season, lines 1, 4–8; vegetation, line 2; animals, line 2), leaving aside allusions to atmospheric conditions and aquatic phenomena, Bonifaci reduces it even more. His "flors ni fueilla," in terms of binary grouping, is quite frequent in a Spring stanza, since thirty-two troubadours use it (Schulze-Busacker 1974, 1119–24), but it is one of the simplest evocations of vegetation (Schulze-Busacker 1974, 1148–82), very different from another stanza with the same information such as Marcabru's:

> Lanquan fuelhon li boscatge
> E par la flors en la prada
> M'es belhs dous chanz per l'ombratge,
> Que fan desus la ramada
> L'auzelet per la verdura;
>
> (28:1–5)

When the groves are in leaf and the flower blossoms in the meadow, I love to hear the birds sweetly singing in the shade, in the midst of the greenery.

The term *deport* is even vaguer and laden with diverse connotations, for it suggests references to the songs of birds in the manner of the early troubadours such as Guiraut de Bornelh:

> E·lh gen deport d'auzelhs els plais
> Mostro·m a far
> Un cortes vers
>
> (35:5–7)

And the warbling of the birds in the bushes shows me how to write a courtly verse

or to the general joy elicited by Spring's revival such as that of Jaufre Rudel:

> E·l riu son clar e·l prat son gen,
> Pel novel deport que·y renha,
> Mi ven al cor grans joys jazer.
>
> (5:5–7)

And the streams are clear and the meadows fair, because of the new pleasure which prevails. (trans. Wolf and Rosenstein 143)

It nevertheless also evokes the diversions of the courtly life, "the amusement by which the court seeks out joy . . ." (Cropp 324–27, esp. 325).[9]

The verb *alegrar* (line 50) in the envoi can furthermore suggest the same type of connotations, when lines like the following by Daude de Pradas are recalled:

> Al temps d'estiu, qan s'*alegron* l'ausel
> (Schutz ed., app. II, p. 91, line 1)

In summer when birds are rejoicing

and these by Arnaut de Marueil:

> E pus tota res terrena
> S'*alegra* quan fuelha nais
> (17:9–10)

While every creature rejoices at the rebirth of the greenery

and these by the same poet:

> Belhs m'es lo dous temps amoros,
> Lanquan lo mons reverdezis,
> Per qu'ieu *m'alegr'*e m'esbaudis
> Ab joy de las novellas flors
> (16:1–4)

I love the sweet and gentle season when the world is green once more, for I am cheerful and happy in the joy of the fresh blossoms

or finally these by Raimbaut d'Aurenga:

> Domn'am que me fai *alegrar*
> Qu'ieu am plus c'om non sap pensar
> Tant ben cum ieu am . . .
> (35:15–17)

The lady who gives me joy, for I love her more then anyone could imagine.

Alegrar evokes, therefore, for those readers sensitive to topical discourse whom Bonifaci addresses, the joy of both Spring and love and the love song that results from that joy.[10]

---

9. Lerch (223) saw the notion of "self-consolation" in the semantic evolution of this very term.

10. Cf. the lines by Guilhem de Saint-Didier: "Per vostra mort metrai a nonchaler / joi e solatz e alegrar e chan" (because of your death, joy and distractions, and pleasure and song mean nothing more to me; 10:4–5).

Even more laden with connotations of this type is the semantic and stylistic network of *joi* and *dolor* which underlies the entire piece:

	Dolor	*Joi*
strophe I	-perdre	-iauzir (line 1)
strophe II	-trist	-deport (lines 11–12)
	-dolor, azir	-abellir (lines 13–14)
	-despieg, ira, suffrir (lines 15, 17)	
strophe III	-soffrir, plors, dols	-conort (lines 19–20, 22)
	-maltrag, languir	-gaug, ben, far avinen (lines 24, 26–27)
strophe IV	-paradis	-non sospir ni plaing (lines 29, 31–33)
		-non tem ni dupti ges (line 34)
		-ni·m plaing mas (line 36)
strophe V		-ioi del mon (line 38)
		-s'orgueillar (line 39)
		-non mueilla mon vis de plors (lines 39–40)
		-no·m fai languir (line 40)
		-menbranza del ioi (line 41)
	-non prezera·l ioi	-ni ar me·n dolria (line 45)
strophe VI	-doloros	-alegrar, conortar (line 50)

This simple juxtaposition of elements not only retraces the poetic message of the piece and its thematic bipartition for which the evocation of Paradise is the turning point (strophe IV), but it also draws attention to the topic of courtly love examined in detail by Lavis and Cropp, among others. "The expression of joy in the work of the troubadours, and particularly in the love song, cannot be separated from its antithetical corollary: pain, always present in counterpoint, even whenever the poet is singing about joy" (Lavis 191). This statement is equally valid, as we have seen, for the courtly *planh*. Let us point out briefly the significance of the terms in the context of Bonifaci's poem.

Joi, "a key word in the poetic imagery of the troubadours" (Lazar 103), is accompanied in the *planh,* as in the *canso d'amor,* by morphologically related terms (*iauzir, gaug*) to translate the general idea of joy, or the joy of love (Lavis 155–91; Cropp 334–36). *Abellir* expresses "the effect that is produced on the poet by the sight or thought of the lady" and "is identified in fact . . . with the feeling of love" (Lavis 39). The conceptual chain "totz mos gaugz e mos bes e tot cant ieu d'avinen far sabia" (lines 26–27), preceded by "tot conort" (line 22), evokes the lessening of the lover's suffering (*conort;* Lavis 147n.182; Cropp 331n.48) by "the good that is derived from courtly love, the moral good as well as the good bestowed by favors, the sense of well-being and the sensual pleasure of love" (Cropp 334–40, 362; Lavis 155–79, 319).

"Avinen far" maintains the ambiguity between the perfect behavior of the lover in regard to his lady and the idea of poetic creation evoked by love, in which it is comparable, for example, to a piece by Folquet de Marseilla, based entirely on this ambiguity (poem 7).

Concerning the gamut of terms designating pain, Bonifaci proceeds by degree of intensity. If *trist* still encompasses all of life, *dolor* is already more specific in its immediate context (lines 13–14), referring to the suffering of love (cf. Lavis 191–94). *Despieg* and *ira* evoke the two poles of pain, absence of pleasure (the loss of *joi*) and depression or painful thoughts (cf. Lavis 195–96), and this provokes both the outward signs of pain—*plors e dols* (cf. Lavis 193; Bec 560–61)—and the expression of gentle pain (cf. Lavis 203; Cropp 284–85) as a desired state of mind.

While using the terms of the topical description of courtly love, Bonifaci nevertheless arrives at a third and new concept, that of the *menbranza del ioi* (line 41). This motif is conventional insofar as it uses first the lexicon of manifest pain (*sospir, planher, plors, languir*) and then the image of a Paradise in need of the beloved lady. In this, it is comparable to other *planh* on the death of a lady, for example those by Gavaudan and Pons de Chapteuil.[11] The concept is new, however, in that it extols not only distant love (*loing de sa paria*, line 36), as other troubadours had done, but also immaterial love, *la menbranza del ioi* (cf. note 5). For Bonifaci, this may still constitute the last stage in his style of hyperbolic eulogy, in his praise of his lady and of love; the poets of the *dolce stil nuovo* will find a new topos.

WORKS CITED

The quotations in this chapter are from the critical editions cited in the List of Troubadour Editions in the Appendix, and in particular from the following editions: Arnaut de Marueil (Johnston); Bertran Carbonel (Contini); Bonifaci Calvo (Branciforti); Gavaudan (Guida); Guiraut de Bornelh (Kolsen); Jaufre Rudel (Wolf and Rosenstein); Joan Esteve (Vatteroni); Paulet de Marseilla (Riquer); and Rigaut de Berbezilh (Anglade). All translations are my own except as indicated.

---

11. Gavaudan 3:49–52: "Dompna, grans joys, grans alegriers, / vos met'el renc del cel aussor / ab los angils que fan lauzor, / aissi cum Sanhs Johans retrays" (Lady, the great joy and elation which emanate from you place you in the highest rank in heaven, among the angels who sing songs of praise, as Saint John says). And Pons de Chapteuil 24:28–36: "Aras podem saber que l'angel sus / son de sa mort alegre e jauzen, / qu'auzit ai dir, e trobam o ligen: / Cui lauza pobles, lauza Dominus. / Per que sai be qu'ill es el ric palais, / en flors de lis, en rozas et en glais, / la lauzon l'angel ab joi et ab chan. / Cella deu be, qui anc no fo mentire / en paradis sobre totas assire" (Now we are assured that the angels on high are joyful and glad she is dead. I have heard it said and it is written in the books: He who is beloved of men, is beloved of God. This is how I know for sure that she is in a heavenly mansion, amidst lillies, roses, and gladioli, and the angels sing her praises with joy and melody. She who never betrayed herself must surely be seated above all others in paradise).

Akehurst, F. R. P. "The Paragram *Amor* in the Troubadours." *Romanic Review* 69 (1978): 15–21.

Aston, S. C. "The Provençal *Planh* II: The Lament for a Lady." In *Mélanges offerts à Rita Lejeune*, 1:57–65. Gembloux: Duculot, 1969.

———. "The Provençal *Planh* I: The Lament for a Prince." In *Mélanges de philologie romane dédiés à la mémoire de Jean Boutière*, 1:23–30. Liège: SOLEDI, 1971.

Azaïs, Gabriel. *Les Troubadours de Béziers*. Béziers, 1869; repr. Geneva: Slatkine, 1973.

Baeumer, Max. *Toposforschung*. Wege der Forschung 395. Darmstadt: Wissenschaftliche Buchgesellschaft, 1973.

Bec, Pierre. "La Douleur et son univers poétique chez Bernard de Ventadour: essai d'analyse systématique." *Cahiers de Civilisation Médiévale* 11 (1968): 545–71; 12 (1969): 25–33.

Bertoni, Giulio. *I trovatori d'Italia: biografie, testi, traduzioni, note*. Modena: Mucchi, 1915.

Bruyne, Edgar de. *Etudes d'esthétique médiévale*. 3 vols. Bruges: Publications de l'Université de Gand, 1946; repr. Geneva: Slatkine, 1975.

Butters, Gerhard. "La Théorie des topiques comme modèle de production de texte. Quelques hypothèses sur E. R. Curtius et le *Grant et vray art de pleine rhétorique* by Pierre Le Fèvre." In *Du mot au texte: actes du IIIe Colloque International sur le Moyen Français, Düsseldorf, 1980*, ed. Peter Wunderli, 263–75. Tübingen: Niemeyer, 1982.

Camproux, Charles. *Joy d'amor (jeu et joie d'amour)*. Montpellier: Causse & Castelnau, 1965.

Cohen, Caroline. "Les Eléments constitutifs de quelques planctus des Xe et XIe siècles." *Cahiers de Civilisation Médiévale* 1 (1958): 83–86.

Colby, Alice M. *The Portrait in Twelfth Century French Literature: An Example of the Stylistic Originality of Chrétien de Troyes*. Geneva: Droz, 1965.

Cropp, Glynnis M.. *Le Vocabulaire courtois des troubadours de l'époque classique*. Geneva: Droz, 1975.

Curtius, Ernst Robert. *Europäische Literatur und lateinisches Mittelalter*. Bern: Francke, 1948. English translation: *European Literature and the Latin Middle Ages*. New York: Pantheon Books, 1953; repr. New York: Harper Torchbooks, 1963. French translation: *La Littérature européenne et le moyen âge latin*. 2 vols. Paris: PUF, 1956.

Dragonetti, Roger. *La Technique poétique des trouvères dans la chanson courtoise: contribution à l'étude de la rhétorique médiévale*. 1960; repr. Geneva: Slatkine, 1979.

Emrich, Berthold. "Topik und Topoi." In *Toposforschung* 1973:210–51.

Ertzdorff, Xenia von. "Die Dame im Herzen und das Herz bei der Dame. Zur Verwendung des Begriffs Herz in der höfischen Lyrik." *Zeitschrift für deutsche Philologie* 84 (1965): 6–46.

Frappier, Jean. *Amour courtois et Table ronde*. Publications romanes et françaises 126. Geneva: Droz, 1973. Articles no. 1: "Vues sur les conceptions courtoises dans les littératures d'oc et d'oïl au XIIe siècle" (1959), 1–31; no. 2: "Amour courtois" (1971), 33–41; no. 3: "Le Concept de l'amour dans les romans arthuriens" (1969), 43–56.

Gruber, Jörn. *Die Dialektik des Trobar. Untersuchungen zur Struktur und Entwicklung des occitanischen und französischen Minnesangs des 12. Jahrhunderts.* Beihefte zur Zeitschrift für romanische Philologie, 194. Tübingen: Niemeyer, 1983.

Guiette, Robert. "D'une poésie formelle en France au moyen âge." *Revue des sciences humaines* (Lille) 54 (1949): 61–68. A revised version appeared in *Romanica Gandensia* 8. Ghent: Université de Gand, 1960; repr. Paris: Nizet, 1972.

Hill, Raymond T., and Thomas G. Bergin, eds. *Anthology of the Provençal Troubadours.* 2d ed., 2 vols. New Haven: Yale University Press, 1973.

Lausberg, Heinrich. *Handbuch der literarischen Rhetorik.* 2 vols. Munich: Max Hueber, 1975.

Lavis, Georges. *L'Expression de l'affectivité dans la poésie lyrique française du moyen âge (XIIe–XIIIe siècles): étude sémantique et stylistique du réseau lexical joie-dolor.* Bibliothèque de la Faculté de Philosophie et Lettres de l'Université de Liège 200. Paris: Les Belles Lettres, 1972.

Lazar, Moshe. *Amour courtois et fin'amors dans la littérature du XIIe siècle.* Paris: Klincksieck, 1964.

Lerch, Eugen. "Trobadorsprache und religiöse Sprache." *Cultura Neolatina* 3 (1943): 214–30.

Leube-Fey, Christiane. *Bild und Funktion der dompna in der Lyrik der Trobadors.* Studia Romanica 21. Heidelberg: Winter, 1971.

Meyer, Paul. *Les Derniers Troubadours de la Provence.* Paris 1871; repr. Geneva: Slatkine; Marseilles: Lafitte, 1973.

Moos, Peter von. *Consolatio. Studien zur mittellateinischen Trostliteratur über den Tod und zum Problem der christlichen Trauer.* 4 vols. Münstersche Mittelalter-Schriften 3. Munich: Fink, 1971–72.

Payen, Jean-Charles. *Le Motif du repentir dans la littérature française médiévale (des origines à 1230).* Geneva: Droz, 1967.

Pillet, Alfred, and Henry Carstens. *Bibliographie der Troubadours.* Halle, 1933; repr. New York: Burt Franklin, 1968.

Pollmann, Leo. "*Joi e solatz* (Zur Geschichte einer Begriffskontamination)." *Zeitschrift für romanische Philologie* 80 (1964): 256–68.

Rieger, Dietmar. *Gattungen und Gattungsbezeichnungen der Trobadorlyrik.* Beihefte zur Zeitschrift für romanische Philologie, 148. Tübingen: Niemeyer, 1976.

Riquer, Martín de, ed. *Los Trovadores: historia literaria y textos.* 3 vols. Barcelona: Editorial Planeta, 1975.

Rohr, Rupprecht. "Zur Skala der ritterlichen Tugenden." *Zeitschrift für romanische Philologie* 8 (1962): 292–325.

Roncaglia, Aurelio. "Obediens." In *Mélanges de linguistique romane et de philologie médiévale offerts à M. Delbouille,* 2:567–614. Gembloux: Duculot, 1964.

Schnell, Rüdiger. *Causa amoris. Liebeskonzeption und Liebesdarstellung in der mittelalterlichen Literatur.* Bibliotheca Germanica. Bern/Munich: Francke, 1985.

———. "L'Amour courtois en tant que discours courtois sur l'amour (I–II)." *Romania* 110 (1989): 72–126, 331–63.

Schulze-Busacker, Elisabeth. "Le Vocabulaire de la nature dans la poésie des troubadours—étude descriptive." Thesis, 3e cycle, Paris-Sorbonne, 1974.

———. "En marge d'un lieu commun de la poésie des troubadours." *Romania* 99 (1978): 230–38.

———. "La Complainte des morts dans la littérature occitane." In *Le Sentiment de la mort au moyen âge*, 228–48. Montréal: L'Aurore, 1979.

———. "Etude typologique de la complainte des morts dans le roman arthurien en vers du 12e au 14e siècle." In *An Arthurian Tapestry: Essays in Memory of Lewis Thorpe*, 54–68. Glasgow: University of Glasgow, 1981.

———. "La Conception poétique de quelques troubadours tardifs." In *Studia Occitania: In Memoriam Paul Remy*, ed. Hans-Erich Keller, Jean-Marie d'Heur, Guy Mermier, and Marc Vuijlsteke, 1:265–77. Kalamazoo: Western Michigan University, Medieval Institute Publications, 1986.

———. "La Datation de *Ronsasvals* (I–II)." *Romania* 110 (1989): 127–66, 396–425.

Schutz, Alexander H. "The Provençal Expression *Pretz e valor.*" *Speculum* 19 (1944): 488–93.

Smith, Nathaniel B. *Figures of Repetition in the Old Provençal Lyric: A Study in the Style of the Troubadours.* University of North Carolina Studies in the Romance Languages and Literatures 76. Chapel Hill: University of North Carolina Press, 1976.

Stengel, Edmund. *Die beiden ältesten provenzalischen Grammatiken: "Lo donatz proensals" und "Las rasos de trobar."* Marburg: Elwert, 1878.

Thiry, Claude. *La Plainte funèbre.* Typologie des sources du moyen âge occidental 30. Turnhout: Brepols, 1978; rev. ed. 1985.

Vinaver, Eugène. *A la recherche d'une poétique médiévale.* Paris: Nizet, 1970.

Ziltener, Werner. *Studien zur bildungsgeschichtlichen Eigenart der höfischen Dichtung.* Romanica Helvetica 83. Bern: Francke, 1972.

———. *Repertorium der Gleichnisse und bildhaften Vergleiche der okzitanischen und der französischen Versliteratur des Mittelalters.* Fasc. 1: Literaturverzeichnisse; Natur I. Teil (Unbelebte Natur); fasc. 2: Natur II. Teil (Belebte Natur). Bern: Francke, 1972–83.

Zingarelli, Nicola. *Intorno a due trovatori in Italia.* Florence: Sansoni, 1899.

Zumthor, Paul. "Etude typologique des planctus contenus dans la *Chanson de Roland.*" In *La Technique littéraire des chansons de geste.* Bibliothèque de la Faculté de Philosophie et Lettres de l'Université de Liège, 150. Paris: Les Belles Lettres, 1959a.

———. "Recherches sur les topiques dans la poésie lyrique des XIIe et XIIe siècles." *Cahiers de Civilisation Médiévale* 2 (1959b): 409–27.

———. *Langue et techniques poétiques à l'époque romane (XIe–XIIIe siècles).* Paris: Klincksieck, 1963a.

———. "Les *Planctus* épiques." *Romania* 84 (1963b): 61–69.

———. *Essai de poétique médiévale.* Paris: Seuil, 1972.

TWENTY

Imagery and Vocabulary

Eliza Miruna Ghil

Students of the troubadours' language concur nowadays on several basic characteristics of its vocabulary, such as the following: (1) the lexical corpus of Old Occitan poetry is very limited in size (Zumthor 182; Pfister 317; Cropp 1975, 11), much as is, for instance, that of seventeenth-century classical French poetry; (2) this corpus becomes highly specialized and rich in nuances when it attempts to articulate the concept of *fin'amor* and the realm of affectivity surrounding it (Pfister 317; Cropp 1975, 282, 449, and passim); (3) its lexemes exhibit a misleading semantic transparency, and renditions of key terms with apparently identical modern ones often blur the original connotations (Lazar 17; Cropp 1975, 13; Akehurst 19); (4) a historical tendency to expansion (e.g., quantitative: through the creation of partial synonymns placed in binomial constructions or in series of accumulations; or qualitative: through the appearance of new connotations) compensates for the initial lexical scarcity (Cropp 1975, 451; Dembowski 775); (5) the terminology of courtliness and its corollary, *fin'amor*, was built mainly on borrowings from domains other than the strictly psychological language of behavior and feeling (Dembowski 775); and (6) the connotations of the borrowed terms become, in the lyric, considerably more complex than in their usage outside it, since the courtly corpus represents a tightly knit verbal universe endowed with an equilibrium similar to "the equilibrium of a well-structured phonological system" (Dembowski 776).

   I shall concentrate in the present chapter on the last two points, in an attempt to discern the main sources of the troubadours' vocabulary and imagery.

ADMINISTRATIVE LANGUAGE

The first major linguistic area worth mentioning in this respect is what I would call, broadly speaking, *administrative language*. It consists of words and phrases that designate in documents (and presumably often also in common parlance) the various types of social relations typical of life in medieval Occitan communities. In twelfth-century Occitania, although documents concerning noblemen were generally drafted in Latin, settlements with representatives of the bourgeois class were already, and in increasing numbers, being drafted in langue d'oc (Pfister 309–10). We may also presume that in legal matters the vernacular language must have been overwhelmingly present in oral court proceedings, even though these were subsequently recorded in writing in official Latin (Wüest 557). As for transactions with or among townsmen, charters, trade agreements, and wills involving artisans and merchants were generally formulated in the vernacular language that the partners could understand and master (Pfister 310).

Among the types of social relations articulated by officials in this administrative language, three, namely the *feudal*, *legal*, and *commercial*, will retain my attention here. Their essence is based on service, the law, and the use of money, and both traditional and more "modern" types of connections between humans come to the fore in medieval documentary sources thanks to this language.

Feudal Terminology

Troubadour poetry was born and evolved in a feudal society. It is therefore only normal that the institutions of feudalism (and the terminology naming them) are a constant presence in these poets' works, whether as a diffuse social background or as an explicit frame of reference for human relations, amorous or otherwise. Some of the central actants in the troubadours' semantic universe bear appellatives that are to be found in feudal terminology, such as *midons*, applied to the beloved lady, a term present in vernacular documents of the eleventh and twelfth centuries (Cropp 1975, 30) and already used by the first troubadour Guillem de Peiteus in his song "Mout jauzens me prenc en amar" (9:21, 37); or such as *drut* and *amic*, designations used for the courtly lover, but also functioning as appellatives for members of the feudal lord's entourage (Cropp 1975, 59, 70).

The *cort* itself, the setting par excellence of *fin'amor* (< late Lat. *cortis*, *curtis*), appears frequently in charters; as for the adjective *cortes* (< late Lat. *curtensis*), an essential attribute of the participants in the love game, an eleventh-century Latin chronicle already attests its semantic evolution from the descriptive connotation of "participant in court life" to the judgmental one of "one who respects the social and moral norms appropriate for court life" (Cropp 1975, 97).

Several series of attributes considered essential to the perfect lover's persona evoke an individual's status within the feudal hierarchy. One of these series connotes nobility or distinction and is actualized through terms like *franc* 'noble, generous, excellent' (< Frankish **frank* and late Lat. *Francus* 'name of the Frankish people'), *pro, pros* 'valiant, worthy' (< late Lat. *prodis* 'deserving'), and *ric* 'noble, prestigious, rich' (< Frankish **rīki* 'powerful'). Other series articulate the subordinate position of the lover with respect to the beloved *domna* (thus evoking the vassal's ties of dependence on his lord), stressing either his humility (*aclin, obedien, umil*) or his truthfulness (*fizel, leial, verai*, etc.).

The beloved lady also exhibits certain attributes that echo the terminology of feudalism. She is herself often *franca, francha* 'noble, excellent' or *pros* 'noble'; but when called *umils*, the connotation seems to be 'gracious' rather than 'humble', as in these lines by Bernart de Ventadorn:

> Doussa res, conhd' et avara,
> Umils, franch' et orgolhoza.
> (12:45–46)

Sweet creature, charming and stingy, gracious, noble and haughty.

She is elsewhere *de bon linhatge, de bon paratge* 'of noble birth', which should not prevent her from accepting the humble lover's courtship, since true love, as Bernart puts it: "Paubres e rics fai amdos d'un paratge" (Whether poor or rich, she [love] makes them both of the same rank; 7:18).

When everything goes well between the humble lover and the gracious *domna*, the latter grants some *(h)onor* to the former. The expression *ben et onor* may connote a significant sensual reward, as in Gaucelm Faidit, where the poet-lover mentions fondly the memory "de l'onor e del be" (the honor and the good things; 33:35) he once enjoyed. *Onor* designates in feudal language the fief granted by the lord to his vassal, while the phrase *ben et onor* renders faithfully *honor et beneficium* 'office bestowed by the king and the benefits appertaining to it' from Latin documents (Bloch 274).

But when the love relationship breaks up, the formula *se recreire* occurs (< Lat. *recredere* 'to renege, back out of an agreement'), a feudal term that connotes acceptance of defeat, discouragement, renunciation. Bernart de Ventadorn, in the famous "lauzeta" song, gives up love in these terms: "Aissi·m part de leis e·m recre" (I thus separate from her and give up love service; 31:53).

The most striking reusage of feudal language for poetic purposes involves the constantly reiterated parallel between love service and feudal service. Commentators have noted, for instance, that two songs by Guillem de Peiteus, "Farai chansoneta nueva" (8) and "Mout jauzens me prenc en amar" (9), reproduce formulas from eleventh-century acts of homage (Lejeune passim; Ourliac 161–62), particularly from those that use Occitan phrases with ritual value in the Latin text. Thus, the poet-lover speaks in poem 8 about his unwillingness to be delivered of his pledge to *ma domna* ("son liam," line 6) and about his total surrender to her authority:

> Qu'ans mi rent a lieys e·m liure
> Qu'en sa carta·m pot escriure.
>
> (8:7–8)

> On the contrary, I surrender and give myself to her, so that she can write me down in her charter.

The last formula may allude to the obligation, incurred by vassals in Poitou, of surrendering their castle upon the presentation of a charter written by their lord, in order for the latter to hold garrison in it.

Ritual gestures of the ceremony of homage often provided troubadours with verbal material used to articulate the lover's subservient posture in the *fin'amor* relationship. We thus leave the domain of pure naming to reach the domain of imagemaking, as in this beautifully wrought sustained metaphor by Bernart de Ventadorn in which the lover-vassal, head bowed, hands clasped and on his knees, as in the ceremony of homage, implores the favor of his suzerain, i.e., the gift of her intimacy:

> Qu'eu sui sos om liges, on que m'esteya,
> Si que de sus del chap li ren mo gatge;
> Mas mas jonchas li venh a so plazer,
> E ja no·m volh mais d'a sos pes mover,
> Tro per merce·m meta lai o·s despolha.
>
> (7:38–42)

> Since I am her liege subject wherever I find myself, to the point that I pledge myself to her, head bowed in absolute submission; and hands clasped, I surrender myself to her pleasure, and I wish to remain at her feet until she, as a sign of mercy, admits me where she undresses [to her private chamber].

As some commentators remark, however, the reproduction of feudal ceremonies remains very approximate in courtly rites; the formulas thus reused should therefore be interpreted with utmost caution. (For a systematic treatment of the expressions *mans jonchas* and *a(de) genolhos*, see Cropp 1991.)

It is to servile homage rather than to feudal homage that some formulations allude (Ourliac 164), such as the following by Uc de Saint-Circ:

> E fis sers remaing
> A l'adreich gai cors plazen
> Cui ill son obedien.
>
> (1:16–18)

And I remain a true serf to the adroit, joyful and pleasant creature whom they [my eyes and my heart] obey,

or the line where the poet-lover describes himself in the service of Amor as "humils, francs, sers e leials" (humble, generous, serflike, and loyal; 6:22). Bernart de Ventadorn also refers to the lover persona as "sers e bric / . . . de joi" (serflike and crazy . . . with joy; 6:44–45) when the lady responds to his love .

The recourse to the servile homage rather than to the feudal homage may have served better, at times, the expressive demands of the hyperbolic laudatory tone so essential to the poetic diction in the *canso*. Such is the language of feudalism in troubadour songs: enduring over time (more than a century separates Guillem de Peiteus from Uc de Saint-Circ) and responsive to poetic needs rather than to referential exigencies.

Legal Terminology

The second social area that Occitan poets tapped for their own purposes is the law with its jargon, often related to the feudal language, but sometimes covering aspects other than class relations *stricto sensu*. A key term from this lexical field seems to have given shape to an important trait of Occitan mentality in the twelfth and the thirteenth centuries: that is, *covinen, covinensa* 'agreement, accord' (< Lat. *convenientia* 'accord'). Historians tell us that southern feudal relations were based more often on the personal pledge of loyalty (*plevina*) than on the granting of a fief. The vassal served his lord for love and honor, and the lord responded to this service with *largueza*. The *covinen* was thus sealed by a verbal promise that did not involve the formal oath, a rather exceptional procedure in Occitania until late into the thirteenth century (Ourliac 165).

We encounter this *covinens(a)* early in the troubadour vocabulary when Cercamon refers to *fin'amor* as to a trustworthy partner: "Qu'anc non passet covinens ni los frays" (Since she [Amor] never circumvented or broke an agreement; 8:11). We also encounter it, predictably enough, in accusations of broken promises, leveled by the poet-lover against his *dona*, as in this example from Peire Vidal:

De ma dona . . .
Me clamera, qu'a tan gran tort me mena
Que no m'atent plevi ni covinensa.
                    (41:2–4)

I would complain against my lady . . . , since she behaves toward me so unjustly and observes neither promises nor agreements.

The "partnership" *fin aman/domna* thus posited entails benefits and damages. The legalese borders, in some instances, on the commercial, as in the case of the term *gazardo, guizardo* 'reward' (< Frankish *widarlon 'what is given as a reward with security', later *widardonum, through a contamination with the Lat. *donum* 'gift'). In the same stanza of song 8, Cercamon extolls the gain potential of a lover's partnership with love, since

> Aquest'amor no pot hom tan servir
> Que mil aitans no·n doble·l gazardos.
> > (8:7–8)

This love cannot be served too long before the reward [for service] multiplies a thousand times.

The lover then awaits confidently this happy result of his love service, as Gaucelm Faidit tells us:

> E selh que ser Amor dreg ses biays . . .
> Consec hom ben guizardo qui l'aten.
> > (4:32, 34)

And the one who serves Love squarely without deceit . . . reaches certainly the reward that awaits him.

Once received, this benefit or reward greatly repays the lover for past efforts, as Bernart de Ventadorn shows:

> Tot can m'avia forfaih,
> Val ben aquest guizerdos.
> > (16:27–28)

Whatever damages she [Amor] has caused me, this reward compensates for it greatly.

What does, in fact, the *guizardo* imply? The same troubadour suggests elsewhere the shape it may take, in the following terms:

> Be for' oimais sazos,
> Bela domna e pros,
> Que·m fos datz a rescos
> En baizan guizardos.
> > (17:49–52)

It might be appropriate now, beautiful and noble lady, that a kiss be given me in secrecy, as a reward.

The lover expects the *guizardo* and fights for it, since his love service, often externalized through songmaking in praise of the *domna*, certainly warrants it. Guiraut de Bornelh puts it bluntly:

> Per que·m par nescietatz
> Qu'eu chan, si no m'en venia
> Gazardos o gratz.
> > (16:66–68)

It seems foolish to me to sing (in her praise) if no rewards or favors come my way.

If the reward does not materialize, the love partnership founded on *covinensa* becomes painful and unbalanced for the lover. Instead of the expected *gazardos* or *gratz*, we then encounter the *dan* (< Lat. *damnum* 'damage, wrong, prejudice, loss') or *damnatge* (< Lat. **damnaticum* 'damage') 'damage, loss'. This *damnatge* becomes all too often the *fin aman*'s lot, as Marcabru suggests:

> On plus n'ay meilhor coratge
> D'amor, mielhs m'es deslonhada,
> Per qu'ieu no·m planc mon dampnatge?
> > (28:15-17)

The more I have my heart set on love, the more she eludes me; why not complain then of my damage?;

or as Bernart de Ventadorn does in a particularly legalistic context:

> Que m'alonje ma dolor,
> S'eu aquest plaih li cossen,
> E s'aissi·l dic mon pessat,
> Vei mo damnatge doblat.
> > (25:11-14)

If I concede this litigious matter to her [that the lady has another lover], I prolong my pain; and if I tell her what I think, I see my damage doubled.

Besides Love herself or the *domna*, external enemies may also inflict damage upon the *fin aman*. Bernart de Ventadorn alludes to some of these:

> E lauzenger volon mo dan d'amor
> E diran l'en be leu adiramen.
> > (13:35-36)

And the flatterers want to damage me in my love, and could tell her things to incite her anger.

The partners' lot is obviously unequal in the *fin'amor* game, especially in the initial phase when the terms of the agreement are still uncertain. Bernart de Ventadorn tells us that:

> Pois ela no·n pert lo rire,
> E me·n ven e dols e dans,
> C'a tal joc m'a faih assire
> Don ai lo peyor dos tans . . .
> Tro que fai acordamen.
> > (44:8-11, 14)

While she does not lose her good spirits, I get the pain and the loss, since she had me seated at such a game in which I am twice the loser . . . until the [mutual] agreement is struck.

But Bernart's lover knows how to stand such ills:

> E can bes no m'ave,
> Sai be sofrir lo dan.
> (18:41–42)

And when no good comes my way, I know well how to suffer the damage,

and finds antidotes to pain and loss through the power of his own longing:

> Encontra·l damnatge
> E la pena qu'eu trai,
> Ai mo bon uzatge:
> C'ades consir de lai.
> (38:73–76)

To the loss and the pain that I endure, I oppose my good habit: I often contemplate in my mind the place where she dwells.

Fin'amor thus appears, in one of its facets, as an institution in need of (and benefiting from) some rules and regulations. This is what the frequent phrase *en dreit d'amor* 'according to the legislation [law] of love' seems to suggest, particularly in thirteenth-century *cansos* and in the *vidas* and *razos*. We thus read in the latter corpus of texts that Rigaut de Berbezilh's lady "no·l avia fait null plaser en dreit d'amor" (granted him no pleasure according to the law of love; Boutière and Schutz 153), and that Gaucelm Faidit "anc non ac plazer en dreg d'amor" (never received any pleasure according to the law of love; ibid. 170) from his *dona*, Maria de Ventadorn. Uc de Saint-Circ's *dompna Clara*, for her part, promises her suitor "de far plaser en dreit d'amor" (to give him pleasure according to the law of love; ibid. 244). This expression occurs several times in Aimeric de Peguilhan's *cansos* (e.g., 21:10, 28:70), in Uc de Saint-Circ (15:53–54), in Aimeric de Belenoi (4:40, 10:32, 17:40), and probably in many others. Here is such an example from Aimeric de Peguilhan:

> E si Merces merceyan no·m defen
> Endreg d'Amor pretz pauc merceyamen.
> (21:9–10)

And if merciful Mercy does not defend me, I estimate mercy very little [i.e., it is of little importance] within the law of love.

Quotations of this phrase could be multiplied *ad libitum,* and "en dreg d'amor" would probably deserve a separate exhaustive study.

The use of legal notions increases over time in the troubadours' vocabulary. One of the major poets of the thirteenth century, Peire Cardenal, uses them so abundantly that some scholars think he must have studied *legalis scientia* in the canonical school at Le Puy (Ourliac 169). Speaking about a dishonest oath in a matter of succession, for example, this troubadour mentions the culprit's *trebellian* mind (22:20), a technical term designating a fiduciary lawyer, a participant in the debts of a succession. The historical character to whom this *sirventes*, "Senh En Ebles, vostre vezi," seems to allude is Blanche de Castille, whose rough treatment of Raymond VII of Toulouse in the Meaux-Paris accords of 1229, concluded in the aftermath of the Albigensian Crusade, incurred the wrath of many troubadours. Peire Cardenal was otherwise no friend of lawyers (identified by the Occitan public at the time with the new order of the French/Roman intruders). He accuses them elsewhere of public abuses and threatens them with divine punishment:

Aus tu, que t'iest fatz legista
E tols l'autrui dreg a vista?
Al partir n'er t'arma trista
S'as fortjutjada la gen.
      (55:105–8)

Listen here, you who made yourself into a lawyer and take away the rights of another in full public view! At departure time [the Last Judgment] your soul will be mighty sad if you have judged the people wrongfully.

But whether sympathetic to lawyers or not, Occitan poets kept on subverting their professional language for their own poetic purposes. Another term borrowed from the language of successional law was destined to achieve great prominence in thirteenth-century epic and lyric poetry, namely *paratge*.

Used first in the courtly *canso* as a laudatory epithet for the beloved *domna*, who is at times *de gran paratge*, *d'aut paratge* 'of high rank', this term (< Lat. *paragium, paraticum* 'equality of condition, of nobility') originally designated the institution that regulated the successional rights of the firstborn and of his younger brothers in the inheritance of the paternal fief (Cropp 1975, 149). In courtly parlance, "om de paratge" came to mean a person distinguished in moral and social qualities, and therefore worthy of admiration.

A rather rare word in twelfth-century lyricism, *paratge* was to blossom into a key term of the troubadour ethico-poetic universe in thirteenth-century political lyricism (the *sirventes*), and particularly in the anonymous *Canso de la Crozada* (1228). This vast epic work centers its poetic axiology on a revised concept of *paratge* that now connotes legitimacy, continuity in one's native space, and moral nobility. From a technical form of successional law, this type of inheritance becomes in this work the vehicle for moral law and for southern courtly superiority in the face of foreign (northern) invasion.

Often coupled with *pretz*, in one of those binomial constructions so frequent in the troubadour style, *paratge* and the search (or fight) for it reign supreme in the pantheon of virtues erected by the anonymous Toulousan poet (Ghil 1984, 143; 1989, chap. 3). One of the most eloquent spokesmen in the elaboration of this pantheon is, in the epic, the poet-knight Gui de Cavaillon. An alter ego of the anonymous author within the text, Gui articulates at some point, for the benefit of the Toulousan heir, the future Raymond VII, the importance of this concept and of the young count's role in its preservation. Here are some of his arguments:

> Oimais es la sazo
> Que a grans obs Paratges que siatz mals e bos,
> Car lo coms de Montfort que destrui los baros
> E la gleiza de Roma e la prezicacios
> Fa estar tot Paratge aunit e vergonhos. . . .
> E si Pretz e Paratges no·s restaura per vos,
> Doncs es lo mortz Paratges e totz lo mons en vos.
>
> (*laisse* 154, lines 7–11, 14–15)

Now is the time that *Paratge* needs badly that you be both worthy and mean, since the count of Montfort, who ruins the barons, and the church of Rome and the predication [by preachers sent by the pontiff, especially Dominicans] push *Paratge* into dishonor and shame. . . . And if *Pretz* and *Paratge* are not restored by you, then *Paratge* is dead and the whole world with it, in you.

Paratge is here erected into a mythlike entity that embodies the integrity of southern society and its chance for survival.

The systematic reuse of the legal language for poetic purposes testifies to the Occitan poets' normative vocation. Troubadours celebrate courtliness in general, and *fin'amor* in particular, as normative behaviors, to be learned and emulated by all members of the elite society. They use the official language of documents to legitimize surreptitiously their system of values (Warning 93) and to make it into a kind of ruling law.

Commercial Terminology

The third type of social relations (and the terminology that names them) used by Occitan poets in some of their pronouncements belongs to the domain of *business and trade*. Let us analyze briefly, in this category, the above-quoted concept of *pretz* 'personal worth, social prestige, reputation' (< Lat. *pretium* 'price, computable worth').

Pretz designates in Old Occitan an eminently changing type of moral value that a person has to reestablish for him- or herself constantly, and that goes up and down all the time (*mont' e poya, enansa, dechai*). *Pretz* is an entity based on factual reality: the "quotation" of a person's worth in the "stock market" of moral values depends first on deeds, and only afterward on flattering words. Raimbaut d'Aurenga describes it, in a *tenso* with Peire Rogier, as follows:

> Q'en dich non es bos pretz saubutz,
> Mas el faich es puois conogutz,
> E pelz faitz veno il dich apres.
> > (Peire Rogier ed., 8a:19–21)

For good reputation is not revealed through words, but is made known through facts instead, and, based on deeds, the accounts come afterwards.

More externally oriented than moral values such as *proeza, mezura,* or even *valor,* one's *pretz* depends on the opinion of peers and is often an equivalent of reputation. Thus, a lover's *pretz* increases thanks to a lady's influence, as Bernart de Ventadorn declares:

> Be conosc que mos pretz melhura
> Per la vostra bon'aventura.
> > (13:14–15)

I know well that my merit increases thanks to the good fortune that emanates from you [in my direction],

or thanks to his suitability for love and his readiness to sing it publicly, as the same Bernart tells us elsewhere:

> Me creis l'aventura,
> Per que mos chans mont' e poya,
> E mos pretz melhura.
> > (4:6–8)

My good luck increases, because my song climbs and soars and my merit improves.

Pretz also appears often among the attributes of the beloved lady, beside physical beauty, pleasant manners, and intelligence:

> Pretz e beutat, valor e sen
> A plus qu'eu no vos sai dire.
> > (Bernart de Ventadorn 19:39–40)

She has merit and beauty, worth and good sense more than I could ever tell you.

But this *pretz* is an eminently unstable asset; inappropriate deeds may easily undermine it, as Marcabru suggests:

> C'aissi pot savis hom reignar,
> E bona dompna meillurar;
> Mas cella qu'en pres dos ni tres

E per un non si vol fiar,
Ben deu sos pretz asordeiar,
E sa valors a chascun mes.

(15:25–30)

It is thus that a wise man should behave [i.e., with *mesura* and *cortesia*] and a good lady should improve herself; but the one who takes two or three [lovers] and refuses to put her faith in just one depreciates her reputation, and also her worth every month.

Bound to diminish easily, a lady's *pretz* may fortunately also rise, as Bernart tells the addressee of his *canso* "Ab joi mou lo vers e·l comens" in these terms:

Bels Vezers, senes doptansa
Sai que vostre pretz enansa,
Que tantz sabetz de plazers far e dir.

(3:57–59)

Good Appearance, I know without a doubt that your reputation improves, since you know so well how to do and how to say pleasing things.

Based on actions and socially oriented, *pretz* is the outer manifestation of *valor* (personal worth) and, as such, the key entity in the courtly behavioral ethic. Without it, an individual does not gain a prominent place in his community, as Guillem de Montanhagol makes it clear in a *sirventes*:

E hom que pretz ni do met en soan,
Ges de bon loc no·l mou, al mieu semblan.

(1:8–9)

And a man who despises reputation and generosity is not of good moral stock, in my view.

Moreover, this *pretz* is, for some later troubadours and for the anonymous poet of the *Canso de la crozada*, validated by God himself, and by the Christian ethic as well: "Quar Dieus vol pretz e vol lauzor" (Since God wants a good reputation and wants praise [to be deserved]; ibid., line 10). God is thus the arbiter (dare we say "arbitrager?") in the stock market of courtliness, which is as unstable as any stock market: one makes gains in it only if one takes action—and risks.

Other terms from the language of business shine in poetic contexts in thirteenth-century *cansos*, where they often serve as a vehicle for intricate amorous metaphors. Here is such an example, from Aimeric de Peguilhan:

I. Pus ma belha mal' amia
M'a mes de cent sospirs captal,
A for de captalier lial
Los ai cregutz quascun dia

D'un mil, per q'ueimais seria,
Sol qu'a lieys plagues, cominal,
Que los partissem per egual,
Qu'aissi·s tanh de companhia.

II. Pero, si·n vol senhoria,
Ben es dregs, quar mais pot e val,
Et hie·l port tan d'amor coral
Que no·n puesc. Neus s'ieu podia,
Son voler non desvolria
Mas sol d'aitan, non de ren al,
D'amar son fin cors natural:
Ve·us tot quan li desdiria.

(43:1–16)

I. After my beautiful and wicked beloved has committed to me more than one hundred sighs as a fund, like a trustworthy partner I have since increased them every day by a thousand, so that from now on it should be common stock, if she agrees with it, in such a way that we might share them equally, for this is appropriate in a partnership.

II. However, if she wants authority over it [i.e., a senior partner's share], this is quite right, for she has more power and worth than I, since I love her with such sincere love that I have no power in the matter. Even if I could, I would not contradict her will, save only insofar, and in no other matter, as to love her noble and genuine person. You see, this is all in which I might go against her will.

The terminology of capital investment, profit sharing and business partnerships serves in this *canso* to articulate in a most striking fashion the escalation in the *fin aman*'s suffering and the partners' uneven status in the *fin'amor* relationship. Aimeric de Peguilhan reuses this investment metaphor elsewhere (in 29, stanza 1); Uc de Saint-Circ similarly uses a commercial metaphor to allude to the lover persona's precarious position with respect to Amor:

Mas Amors ditz q'anz mi penda
Qe ja li menta de re.
Mas dreitz es c'ab aital fe
Cum ill compra q'ieu li venda.

(6:15–18)

But Love says that I should hang myself rather than transgressing the word I gave her. But it is only right that, based on equal terms, I sell to her exactly as she buys from me.

The use of commercial terms by thirteenth-century troubadours deserves a special study, in my view. Poets such as Aimeric de Peguilhan, Uc de Saint-Circ, Aimeric de Belenoi, and Peire Cardenal are not simple lexical epigones of their predecessors. While preserving intact the traditional courtly vocabulary of their forerunners, they venture more systematically into stylistic areas less explored by Bernart de Ventadorn or by Guiraut de Bornelh in the twelfth century, often with felicitous results. (See also the medical terminology discussed below.)

RELIGIOUS LANGUAGE

The second major linguistic area used by troubadours as a source of vocabulary and imagery is *religious language.* We deal, in this case, with another institutionalized terminology of high prestige, adopted by Occitan poets in order to legitimize their conception of love and social behavior (Warning 81). A systematic analogy between the Christian notion of *service to God* (reinforced by the feudal connotations analyzed above) and the secular *love service* emerges early in the lyric tradition, beginning with the *cansos* of Guillem de Peiteus.

Several elements combine to articulate this analogy throughout the troubadour corpus, including: (1) the beloved lady's lofty qualities that transform her into an awe-inspiring *summum bonum*, worthy of being implored and adored; (2) her usual inaccessibility and/or physical absence; (3) the power of psychological and corporeal renewal that she holds and exercises at will; (4) the amorous martyrdom undergone by the *fin aman* in the attempt to reach her; and (5) the paradisiacal experience produced by her embrace.

The beloved lady is often addressed, in *cansos*, as *bona domna* (e.g., in Bernart de Ventadorn's "Non es meravelha s'eu chan" [1:49]) and referred to at times, in *tornadas*, by means of the telling *senhal* Mieils-de-ben 'Better than good' (e.g., in Bertran de Born's "Domna, puois de mi no·us cal" [7:47]). Her mere presence is awesome to the lover persona, as Bernart describes it in the *canso* just cited:

> Cant eu la vei, be m'es parven
> Als ohls, al vis, a la color,
> Car aissi tremble de paor
> Com fa la folha contra·l ven.
> $\qquad$ (1:41–44)

When I see her, it [the sincerity of my love] is clearly apparent, from my eyes, my facial expression, my color, since I tremble with fear like the leaf blown in the wind.

She overwhelms with desire the lover who breaks down in tears and lamentations:

> Las! tan l'aurai dezirada
> Qe per lei plaing, plor, e sospir,
> E vau cum res enaurada.
> $\qquad$ (Cercamon 4:12–14)

Alas! I will have desired her so that for her I lament, shed tears and sigh, and go about like a person out of his mind.

Planher, plorar, sospirar serve, in the Old Testament, to express man's anxiety while overwhelmed by carnal and spiritual desires (such as in the psalms; see Cropp 1975, 309). Guiraut de Bornelh's lover "planh e sospir" (laments and sighs) for his lady (21:24), and so repeatedly does Bernart de Ventadorn's lover, who "planh e sospir" (5:34), "planh e plor" (laments and weeps; 17:7), "clam" (weeps; 17:9), "planha" (complains; 38:61), etc.

A rich series of synonyms taken from various lexical areas names the love request that the *fin aman* addresses to this beautiful and awe-inspiring creature. Let us mention among these: *demandar, enquerre, pregar, mercejar, orar, soplegar.* The first two of this series are neutral in their connotations, while *pregar, mercejar,* and *orar* belong to the religious language, and *soplegar* to the feudal one (< Lat. *supplicare* 'to ply, humble oneself, render homage').

Pregar (< Lat. *precari* 'to pray, to implore') has in Old Occitan connotations both strictly religious and amorous. The analogy between the two speech acts—that is, praying to God and imploring the lady—is made explicit by Raimbaut d'Aurenga in these lines:

Mas Dieu, que no faill en re,
Pregua lo hom de son be,
E doncx ben dei ieu vos preguar.
(26:7–9)

But since one prays God, who is unfailing, for his own well-being, so must I pray you.

Gaucelm Faidit spells out the rationale for this imploring posture in "Tant aut me creis amors en ferm talan," where he states it redundantly in stanza 6, yet in a hopeful mood:

E s'ieu merce li clam, com fin aman,
La prec d'amor, e·ill leialmens servis,
Be·m degr'auzir, pos fis pretz es assis
El sieu gen cors, en cui ai m'alegransa,
Que, lai on es beutatz e pretz valens,
Non deu faillir merces ni chauzimens,
Ni guizardos de fin joy, ses duptansa.
(6:22–28)

And if I cry for mercy from her, as a perfect lover should, if I pray for her love and serve her loyally, she should indeed listen to me, because a high merit inhabits her beautiful person who is source of my joy; since a person in whom beauty and worthy merit dwell must lack neither mercy nor pity, nor the giving of rewards of refined joy, I believe.

We encounter above, in lines 22–23, the imploring vocabulary couched in religious terms ("merce li clam," "la prec d'amor") and associated with the notion of amorous service. This is what love service consists of, in fact: imploring love, through speech acts and poetic acts, while hoping that the worthy addressee will wish to take part in the communicative exchange.

The *pregar* is doubled, in this stanza, by the more potent *mercejar* (< Lat. *mercediare*) 'to cry mercy, to implore', rendered here through one of its several synonymous phrases: *merce clamar*. The phrase, as well as the verb, contains in itself the object of request, precisely the *merce* (line 27), a term that overlaps several linguistic areas, among which is the religious one.

The extreme potency of *mercejar* appears clearly in these lines from Bernart de Ventadorn:

Tant sui vas la bela doptans,
Per qu'e·m ren a leis merceyans:
Si·lh platz, que·m don o que·m venda!
(29:26–28)

I am so awe-stricken with respect to the beautiful one, that I surrender myself to her while crying mercy; if she pleases, may she give me as a gift or sell me!

Several linguistic areas discussed in the present chapter converge in these lines to produce an especially powerful cry for love: the awe-inspiring nature of the beloved ("doptans"); the lover's surrender to her, expressed in military/religious terms (*clamar merce* means also to beg for mercy by someone defeated in battle, while "e·m ren" may allude at once to a prisoner's surrender and to entrance into a monastic order [Gay-Crosier 47]); the metaphor of servile homage, used to articulate the lover's submission to the beloved.

The object of *mercejar*, the *merce* (< Lat. *merces, -edis*; VLat. acc. *mercem* 'wages, price of an article; reward'), seems to have kept both Latin connotations in Old Occitan. Its proximity to *guizardos* in the stanza from Gaucelm Faidit quoted above (6:28) and to *venda* in Bernart's line 28 above actualizes the commercial connotation. But its proximity to *prec d'amor* in Gaucelm's stanza (6:23) and to *doptans* in Bernart's line 26 points rather to the expression *merces Dei* from medieval Church Latin, where *merces* often occurs as a synonym for *misericordia* 'compassion, charity' (Gay-Crosier 47).

Other synonyms with religious connotations may replace *merce* in troubadour vocabulary, such as *almorna* (< Lat. *alemosina*; Church Lat. *eleemosyna* 'alms'), used by Bernart de Ventadorn:

E d'ome qu'es aissi conques,
Pot domn'aver almorna gran.
(1:47–48)

For a man who is so utterly conquered, a lady can certainly have great compassion.

The most technical element among the verbs of the love request is *orar*. Less frequently used than *pregar* or *mercejar*, *orar* was the officially accepted Church Latin term for praying (Gay-Crosier 57). Formulas such as *oremus* and *ora pro nobis* interspersed liturgical prayers and prayers to the Virgin. Jaufre Rudel remembers them and echoes them thus:

> D'un'amistat suy enveyos—
> Quar no sai joya plus valen—
> C'or e dezir.
>
> > (5:8–10)

I am eager for an amorous friendship, since I know of no other more precious jewel, for which I pray and long.

Besides inciting the lover to supplication, the *domna* is also worthy of adoration. *Adorar, azorar* (< Lat. *adorare* 'to worship, pray, entreat the gods or the ancestors') surfaces early in troubadour lyric, basically as an enhanced synonym of *amar*. Guillem de Peiteus is the first to use it, in "Farai chansoneta nueva," where he states that "autra non azori" (I adore no one else but her; 8:14). Bernart de Ventadorn follows suit:

> Domna, per vostr'amor
> Jonh las mas et ador!
>
> > (4:57–58)

Lady, for your love I clasp my hands [in prayer] and adore you!

Later on, Gaucelm Faidit's lover uses it thus:

> Liei desire,
> Si c'allior
> Mon desir no vire,
> Car lieis am e lieis ador
> E causisc per la miglior.
>
> > (20:13–17)

I desire her so that I turn my desire nowhere else, since it is she whom I love and adore, and choose as the best there is.

The beloved lady emerges, from all these contexts, as a *summum bonum* of intrinsic virtues that make her gracious response to the *fin aman*'s request (be it through *merce, almorna, guizardos,* or *gratz*) a highly desirable commodity. But this commodity is hard to come by because of the desired object's inaccessibility and/or remoteness. Many variants actualize, in the troubadour corpus, this semantic feature of the *fin'amor* relation. Let us invoke here only the variant that may well be the most famous, at least for modern readers, among the treatments of this feature: Jaufre Rudel's *amor de lonh*.

Though rather earthly and sensuous in its ultimate intent (Lazar 86), this *amor de lonh* often sounds religious in its wording, as in this stanza of Jaufre Rudel:

Be tenc lo Seignor per verai
Per q'ieu veirai l'amor de loing,
Mas per un ben qe m'en eschai
N'ai dos mals, car tant m'es de loing;
Ai! car me fos lai pelleris,
Si que mos fustz e mos tapis
Fos pels sieus bels oills remiratz!

(6:8–14)

I consider the Lord truthful, since thanks to Him I shall see this love from afar; but for one good thing that befalls me I get two evils, for she [this love] is so far away. Ai! I wish I were a pilgrim there, so that my staff and my prayer rug might be reflected in her beautiful eyes.

This contact with the beloved, though precarious and hard to attain, is eagerly sought after because of its beneficial effects on the *fin aman*'s person. The *domna* may restore the lover to well-being and renewed vitality, as in a kind of emotional resurrection. This is how Guillem de Peiteus describes this effect:

Pus hom gensor non pot trobar
Ni huelhs vezer ni boca dir,
A mos ops la·m vuelh retenir:
Per lo cor dedins refrescar
E per la carn renovellar,
Que no puesca envellezir.

(9:31–36)

Because a more beautiful one than her cannot be found—neither eyes can see nor mouth can describe such a one—I wish to retain her for myself, in order to refresh my heart and to reinvigorate my flesh, so that it won't ever get old.

The expression of the inability to describe beauty (line 32) parallels similar biblical phrases applied to the impact of the divinity, while terms such as *refrescar* and *renovellar* bring forth the salutary nature of the lady's being who performs miracles on the lover's persona with a Christ-like healing power.

Bernart de Ventadorn also acknowledges this salutary power over his lover persona:

Francha, doussa, fin' e leiaus,
En cui lo reis seria saus;
Bel' e conhd', ab cors covinen,
M'a faih ric ome de nien.

(2:39–42)

A noble lady, sweet, refined, and loyal, thanks to whom the king himself would find his salvation; beautiful and graceful, with an attractive body, she made me a man rich in happiness out of mere nothing.

Let us note here the use of the adjective *saus* 'saved' and the notion of overall transformation of the lover's being (line 42) under the lady's influence. The *domna*'s rejuvenating powers bring the *fin aman* back to life, while her continuous goodwill keeps him in a state of joy fit for a king. Bernart uses also a synonym of *saus*, namely *resperitz* 'resuscitated', in "Can lo boschatges es floritz" (42:24).

The quest for the contact with this beneficial being, the object of desire in the courtly *canso*, may take the lover to extremes of suffering. The readiness to die or to be killed (*aucir, morir*) for one's love is a recurrent feature in the semantic universe of *fin'amor*. One notion from Christian hagiography proved useful to Occitan poets in their attempt to articulate this feature, that of martyrdom: *martir* (< Church Lat. *martyrium* 'sacrificial death for one's belief') 'torment, agony' (Gay-Crosier 49).

Martyrdom does not necessarily imply death, but it certainly implies indescribable tortures. Thus the troubadours found the hyperbolic emotional tone fit to articulate their cry for love. Here is how Peire Vidal describes a *fin aman*'s love pains:

E per s'amor suefri tan greu martire,
Que la dolors m'a ja del tot conquis.
                    (19:27–28)

And for her love I suffered such intense pain that I am already completely overwhelmed with grief.

Bernart de Ventadorn also uses the notion of martyrdom in a general way, as for instance here:

La pena e la dolor
Que·n trac, e·l martire.
                    (4:75–76)

The pain and the grief that I suffer for her, and the martyrdom.

A more specific martyrdom—i.e., by fire—appears in another of Bernart's songs:

C'aitan doloirozamen
Viu com cel que mor en flama.
                    (12:63–64)

Since I live as painfully as the one who is dying in the flames.

The counterpart of this extreme suffering is, in the Christian ethic, the "consolation" received from God, and even, in the case of the martyr's

physical death, eternal salvation and the extreme bliss that the supreme
sacrifice entails. Such experiences are to be found also within the realm of
fin'amor, through the various degrees of communion with the beloved. The
concept of *joy*, so central to Occitan poetic lovemaking in the Middle Ages,
is at times actualized by terms with religious connotations. Two of these
terms are *solatz* and *benanansa*.

   Solatz (< Lat. *solacium* 'consolation, comfort') was often used in conjunction with *joy* in the Vulgate (Gay-Crosier 54). When the troubadours
adopted the two terms in their poetry, a partial semantic leveling seems to
have occurred, with the result that *joy* and *solatz* became quasi-synonymous.
In the love lyric, *solatz* implies a comforting of the suffering lover to be
achieved through either social or private contact with the beloved. Jaufre
Rudel dreams about such a comforting moment in these terms:

> Qu'en un petit de joy m'estau,
> Don nulhs deportz no·m pot jauzir
> Tan cum solatz d'amor valen.
>
> (1:6–8)

However, I have very little joy, since no amusement can cheer me up as much
as the comfort given by a noble love.

As for Bernart de Ventadorn, he evokes it fondly thus:

> De solatz m'es umana
> Can locs es ni s'eschai.
>   (26:45–46)

She is humane to me and gives me comfort, whenever the place and the
occasion allow.

Elsewhere, however, Bernart deplores the lack of *solatz* in a reversed context:

> Qu'eu vei que de nien m'apana
> Cilh que no·m vol esser umana,
> E car no·n posc aver joi ni solatz,
> Chan per conort cen vetz qui sui iratz.
>
> (36:29–32)

Since I see that she feeds me pure nothing, the one who does not want to be
humane toward me, and since I can have neither joy nor solace from her I sing
a hundred times that I am distressed, for consolation.

   A stronger joy than mere solace is rendered by the term *benanansa*
'happiness, complete success in love'. This term is based on the noun *ben*
'good', and represents probably the closest lexical approximation in Occitan of an amorous communion with the *summum bonum*. *Benanansa* implies
a complete union with the beloved, a state that is rare and precious, and that

ought to be protected at all cost from outside harm. Bernart de Ventadorn's poet-lover advises complete discretion about it, once *benanansa* is achieved:

> Car no·m par bos essenhamens,
> Ans es foli' et efansa
> Cui d'amor a benanansa
> Ni·n vol so cor ad autre descobrir.
> (3:20–23)

Since it does not seem to me a reasonable behavior, but it is rather childish and foolish for the one who enjoys happy love to go about disclosing the state of his heart to others.

Less vague in its implications than in the lyric, this happiness will become more explicit in the courtly narratives of the thirteenth century, for instance in *Le Roman de Flamenca*, where it connotes the ultimate bliss of the *fin amans'* intimacy. Here is an enlightening passage in this respect:

> Que non es hom pogues notar
> Ni bocca dir ni cors pensar
> La benanansa c'uesquex n'a;
> A negus homes meils non va.
> (lines 5977–80)

Since there is no one who could describe, nor mouth could tell, nor heart could conceive, the bliss that each of them receives; nobody in the world can do better than that.

The phrase about the impossibility of telling the magnitude of the lovers' bliss (line 5978), also used elsewhere in the troubadour style to describe the lady's beauty, is taken from Isaiah 64:4. Employed in the present context as a qualifier of amorous *benanansa*, this phrase applies to sensual intimacy the wording reserved by the scriptural style for mystical experiences. The subversion of the religious language for secular purposes seems here complete, since what appears to the Christian ethic as carnal sin is depicted for us in this passage as the ultimate bliss.

The reuse of theological words and phrases to articulate a secular religion of love represents probably the most daring stylistic undertaking performed by troubadour poetry within the context of medieval culture.

PROFESSIONAL LANGUAGE

I shall conclude with a few words about a third linguistic area that troubadours mined profitably: namely, *professional language*. I apply this term to the terminologies of various actual professions that surface intermittently in the troubadour style, including the military and the medical, but also including the field of entertainment—games and amusements such as chess, cards, dice, hunting, and banqueting.

Space does not permit a full treatment of this third area here. As far as military imagery is concerned, we already encountered it when I analyzed the expression *merce clamar* and in the quotations that included terms such as *conques* 'conquered' or *me ren a lieis* 'I surrender myself to her'. Instead I would like to focus briefly, in conclusion, on *medical imagery*. Though taken mostly from classical sources such as Ovid, this imagery often achieves in the troubadours' verses a certain freshness and power. This seems to be the case particularly for such terms as *languir, guerir/garir*, and *metge*.

Languir (< Lat. *languere* 'to be sick') 'to languish' describes a prolonged state of physical despondency, a result of the powerful emotions that often are the *fin aman*'s lot. Both intense joy and intense pain may be covered by this quasi-clinical term of physical discomfort. Guiraut de Bornelh uses it in a context of mixed emotions in a *canso* in which the poet-lover laments his confused emotional state:

> Mas com m'ave, Deus m'aiut,
> Qu'era, can cut chantar, plor?
> Seria ja per Amor
> Que m'a sobrat e vencut?
> E per amor no·m ve jais?
> Si fai! Donc per que m'irais
> Ni que·m fai languir?
> Que? non o sabria dir?
>
> (21:1–8)

But by God, how does it come about that now, when I mean to sing, I cry? Would that be because of Love, who overwhelmed and vanquished me? And doesn't Love bring me joy? Yes, indeed! Then why am I so sad, and what makes me languish so? What? Could I really not say?

Aimeric de Belenoi also eloquently expresses the same state of mind of the lover torn between the possibility of joy and the pain of being deprived of it:

> No·m laissa ni·m vol retener
> Amors, ni no li puesc fugir;
> Ans me fai enaissi languir,
> Cum selh que cuyda d'aut chazer
> Quant en somnhans ve en son cor
> Sa mort, si chai, et a son for
> No conoys que·lh valha raubirs;
> Aissi·m fai Amors e Sospirs
> Languir, quar nulhs joys no·m refranh
> L'afan del ric joy que·m sofranh.
>
> (5:1–10)

Love neither abandons me nor retains me [as her vassal], and neither can I
escape from her; but she makes me languish so, as the one who thinks that
he is falling from high up, when, while asleep, he sees in his heart his own
death if he falls; and according to his judgment, [once awake] he does not
know what good this dream did to him. Thus, Love and Sighing make me
languish, since no joy assuages the pain that I feel because of the exquisite joy
that is being denied me.

The reiterated usage of *languir* frames, in this stanza, an intricate dream
metaphor thanks to which the sinking feeling produced by an amorous joy
simultaneously desired and denied takes poetic shape. Intense joy may also
bring about this state of physical despondency, as Jaufre Rudel suggests in
connection with a *colps de joi* 'stroke of joy':

Et anc mais tan greu no·m feri,
Ni per nuill colp tan no langui.
(3:16–17)

And no other stroke ever hit me so hard, and for no other stroke did I so
languish.

Aimeric de Belenoi echoes this usage in "Nulhs hom no pot complir
adrechamen" when he evokes the lover's ecstasy while contemplating in his
mind the beloved lady:

Quant e mon cor remir so belh cors gen,
Lo dous pessars m'abelhis tant, e·m plai,
Qu'ab joy languisc.
(6:25–27)

When I contemplate in my heart her beautiful and graceful person, the sweet
thought delights me so, and pleases me, that I languish with joy.

The utter physicality of overwhelming amorous emotions: this is what *languir*
describes so well in many powerful contexts.

The antidote to *languir* is *guerir* (< Frankish *warjan* 'guarantee') 'to heal'.
Guillem de Peiteus is the first to use this term, evoking the lady's healing
powers within a context in which the medical connotation seems stronger
than the possible religious one: "Pus sap qu'ab lieys ai a guerir" (Since she
knows that only thanks to her I shall be healed; 9:48). The healing power
of the beloved emerges also in one of Jaufre Rudel's *cansos*, in a context of
praise to Love. The love longing, however painful, will easily be healed by
her kiss (1:52), better than by any other medical treatment, since

Bona es l'amors, e molt per vau,
E d'aquest mal mi pot guerir
Ses gart de metge sapien.
(1:54–56)

Good is this love, and highly worthy it is! And she [the lady] can heal me thus [with one kiss] of this illness, without the need of any wise physician.

The term *metge*, used here by Jaufre Rudel, also enjoyed some original usages in troubadour poetry. The most striking metaphorical treatment of this medical term occurs, to my knowledge, in Aimeric de Peguilhan's *sirventes* in praise of the emperor Frederick II. The object of praise is compared throughout the text to a doctor whose arrival restored the courtly world to good health and well-being. Here is how this efficient medical intervention is presented in stanza 2:

Pretz es estortz, qu'era guastz e malmes,
E Dons gueritz del mal qu'avia pres,
Q'un bon metge nos a Dieu sai trames
Daves Salern, savi e ben apres,
Que conoys totz los mals e totz los bes
E mezina quascun segon que s'es.

(26:9-14)

Merit, which was wasted and mistreated, is restored [to good health], and Generosity is cured of the illness that had seized it, since God sent us here, from Salerno, a good physician, wise and well taught, who knows all the illnesses and all the treatments for them and who doctors everyone as suits him best.

In this astute exercise in encomiastic style, the medical imagery is an attempt to articulate the beneficial influence on the world of this particular ruler's reign. The second *tornada* closes this verbal *tour de force* with a flourish, in a final address to medical science itself, here personified for the occasion:

Al bon metge maistre Frederic
Di, meggia, que de meggar no·s tric.

(26:48-49)

To the good physician, Master Frederic, say, O Medicine, to keep on doctoring.

This brief overview of vocabulary and imagery in medieval Occitan poetry leads to several conclusions: (1) although limited in size, the troubadours' vocabulary is endowed with considerable depth, which results from complex lexical interferences between different linguistic areas; (2) an attempt to reconstruct these interferences and their resonance in the context of their time reveals a much more colorful choice of words than we may be able to perceive through modern translations into Western languages (the apparently similar terms of which are weakened by seven centuries of repeated poetic usage); (3) key terms often come in pairs and series that reinforce the words' suggestive power; (4) though highly stable throughout the tradition, the troubadour vocabulary deserves more scholarly attention in the later period of its historical development, a period in which refreshing treatments of conventional images produce quite a few pleasant surprises; and (5) certain coined phrases are in great need of a more specific study, my favorite one in this respect being *en dreg d'amor.*

WORKS CITED

The quotations in this chapter are from the critical editions cited in the List of Troubadour Editions in the Appendix, and in particular from the following editions: Aimeric de Belenoi (Dumitrescu); Bernart de Ventadorn (Lazar); Bertran de Born (Paden et al.); Cercamon (Wolf and Rosenstein); Guiraut de Bornelh (Kolsen); Guillem de Peiteus (Bond); Peire Vidal (Avalle); Rigaut de Berbezilh (Várvaro); *La Chanson de la croisade albigeoise* (Martin-Chabot); *Le Roman de Flamenca* (Gschwind). All translations are my own.

Akehurst, F. R. P. "La Folie chez les troubadours." In *Mélanges de philologie romane offerts à Charles Camproux,* 1:19–28 Montpellier: Centre d'Estudis Occitans, 1978.

Bloch, Marc . *La Société féodale.* Paris: Albin Michel, 1968.

Cropp, Glynnis M. *Le Vocabulaire courtois des troubadours de l'époque classique.* Geneva: Droz, 1975.

———. "Les Expressions *mans jonchas* et *a (de) genolhos* dans la poésie des troubadours." In *Mélanges de langue et de littérature occitanes en hommage à Pierre Bec,* 103–12. Poitiers: Publications de l'Université de Poitiers, 1991.

Dembowski, Peter F. "Vocabulary of Old French Courtly Lyrics: Difficulties and Hidden Difficulties." *Critical Inquiry* 4 (1976): 763–79.

Gay-Crosier, Raymond. *Religious Elements in the Secular Lyrics of the Troubadours.* Chapel Hill: University of North Carolina Press, 1971.

Ghil, Eliza Miruna. "Ideological Models and Poetic Modes in *The Song of the Albigensian Crusade.*" *Romanic Review* 75 (1984): 131–46.

———. *L'Age de Parage: essai sur le poétique et le politique en Occitanie au XIIIe siècle.* University Studies in Medieval and Renaissance Literature 4. New York/Bern: Peter Lang, 1989.

Lazar, Moshe. *Amour courtois et fin'amors dans la littérature du XIIe siècle.* Paris: Klincksieck, 1964.

Lejeune, Rita. "Formules féodales et style amoureux chez Guillaume IX d'Aquitaine." In *VIIIo congresso di studi romanzi,* 227–48. Florence, 1956.

Ourliac, Paul. "Troubadours et juristes." *Cahiers de Civilisation Médiévale, Xe–XIIe siècles* 2 (1965): 159–77.

Pfister, Max. "Die Anfänge der altprovenzalischen Schriftsprache." *Zeitschrift für romanische Philologie* 3–4 (1970): 305–23.

Warning, Rainer. "Moi lyrique et société chez les troubadours." In *L'Archéologie du signe,* ed. Lucie Brind'Amour and Eugène Vance, 63–100. Papers in Medieval Studies 3. Toronto: Pontifical Institute of Medieval Studies, 1982.

Wüest, Jakob. "Remarques sur le langage juridique au moyen âge." In *Mélanges d'études romanes du moyen âge et de la renaissance offerts à Jean Rychner*, 557–66. Strasbourg: Centre de Philologie et de Littérature Romanes, 1978.

Zumthor, Paul. *Langue et techniques poétiques à l'époque romane (XIe–XIIIe siècles)*. Paris: Klincksieck, 1963.

TWENTY-ONE

Bibliography

Robert Taylor

Finding one's way to the riches of troubadour scholarship is not always an easy task. In spite of remarkable advances in the technology of information processing, and contrary to the wishful thinking of many scholars, the science of bibliography remains an inexact one. There are many helpful sources of several types, which will be outlined in this chapter, but when it comes down to a particular quest for up-to-date references to scholarship in a particular area, the quest will sooner or later take on aspects of a detective mystery (or a game of blindman's buff!) as clues to research are tracked down in the most unlikely places and appear now and then seemingly out of nowhere, by pure chance.

This disconcerting capriciousness is encountered in most humanistic fields of scholarship, but it is especially true in Old Occitan studies. Many scholars tend to approach the troubadour lyrics from their own area of specialization and from widely varying perspectives, rather than as a complete and self-sufficient field of study. Troubadour studies belong to everyone and yet, paradoxically, to no one.

The fascinating but vexed problem of the origins of Western poetry has been fought out largely through the troubadour corpus, and has not yet been entirely resolved. Those who would define the elusive but powerful notion of "courtly love" must deal with its manifestations in the troubadours, since it appears there earlier than anywhere else in Europe. Religious and social historians have tried to identify a link between the poetry of *fin'amor* and the Cathar heresy or between the troubadour love ethic and the particular configuration of the social classes in the twelfth century. Students of early Italian poetry have sought the beginnings of Italian lyrics and some of the inspiration of Dante and Petrarch in the troubadours, as students of German, Spanish, Portuguese, Catalan, and French literature have linked the early history of their disciplines to the influential vigor of troubadour verse (see Chapters 9–14 herein). Musicologists have given much attention to the melodies without, until recently, attempting to link them meaningfully to the corresponding texts (see Chapter 5). Arabicists have cataloged the many parallels in form, vocabulary, and motifs with earlier Arabic poetry. More recently, students of feminist literature have been drawn to examine the strangely ahistorical attitude of many troubadours toward the women of whom they sing, or the verses of the trobairitz, who are the earliest named women poets in Western vernacular (see Chapter 8). The "occitaniste" movement in southern France has claimed the troubadours as its cultural ancestors for reasons that may be as strongly motivated by politics as by aesthetics.

Naturally each of these groups will approach the troubadour poems from a different perspective. Some of them may be familiar with the work of one or more of the other groups, and a few may be familiar with the whole range of troubadour scholarship and be capable of relating their own interests to it, but all too often studies take place in a partial vacuum. Many articles, even books, continue to be written in curious isolation, as though the writers were unaware that anyone else might be undertaking research related to their own but from within a different discipline. Thus the troubadours belong to everyone, but to no one.

The point of this cautionary statement is a practical one, as far as bibliographical guidance is concerned: troubadour studies are to be found scattered in the most unlikely places, in periodicals of many kinds, or as chapters of books whose titles give no hint of their particular content. One of the more interesting articles about Guillem de Peiteus, an early study by Roger Dragonetti, for example, is a chapter in a book about psychology (*Sexualité humaine*). For some reason, that chapter is omitted, without comment, from the second edition of the book (1972). Similarly, a detailed factual presentation by Henry Farmer on Arabic sources for the European names of musical instruments and notions of rhythm is printed in the journal of the Oriental Society of Glasgow University. One of the best introductions to troubadour poetry is that of Claude Marks, but its title, *Pilgrims, Heretics, and Lovers: A Medieval Journey*, has caused the book to be classified as history, and does not indicate that it is concerned entirely with the Occitan area and contains a solid presentation of eight of the most interesting troubadours.

Dependable and up-to-date bibliographical references are not always easy to come by, let alone references to work in press or in progress. Help is to be found, however, in a number of sources outlined below in the following categories: (1) introductory guides for the beginner and non-specialist; (2) general bibliographies offering an overview; (3) specialized bibliographies on particular topics; (4) serial bibliographies listing new studies year by year; (5) helpful hints on discovering new articles and books before they find their way into the serial bibliographies; and (6) a brief mention of several influential works that have helped shape the evolution of troubadour studies.

INTRODUCTORY GUIDES

The volume that you are now perusing is intended to provide initial orientation to graduate students who are beginning their study of the troubadours and to scholars from neighboring disciplines who require succinct information about the troubadours for use as background or comparison in their own studies.

A good orientation in English is found in the book by Claude Marks mentioned above. Historical and literary documentation is dependable, and the poetry of eight major troubadours is discussed within its sociohistorical context.

A more literary introduction is provided by Leslie Topsfield, who analyzes the work of eleven troubadours to illustrate the major stages in the evolution of the poetry.

In French, the best short introduction is that of Henri Marrou, which is written from a historical perspective but which gives a lively overview and a most helpful summary of the importance of troubadour melodies.

The most complete and dependable work of orientation is in Spanish: Martín de Riquer, *Los trovadores*. A rich introduction to medieval Occitan poetry is followed by a presentation of 122 individual troubadours, giving a trustworthy outline of historical facts and examining the poets' place within the Occitan tradition.

All of these books contain references that will lead the reader into the whole spectrum of troubadour studies and may make one seek help in ordering further reading.

GENERAL BIBLIOGRAPHIES

The only comprehensive bibliography of the troubadours is that of Alfred Pillet and Henry Carstens dating from 1933. It remains an essential research tool in spite of its age and its several weaknesses (there is neither table of contents nor index; abbreviations are not explained; the presentation is excessively condensed). In the evolution of troubadour studies, it has played an incalculably valuable role in opening up the discipline to scholars around the world. Although several people have broached the possibility of preparing a revised version of the book, the task now seems too enormous to be feasible in our world of exploding information.

A selected bibliography was prepared in 1977 by myself. This kind of presentation aims to give practical help through critical annotation and by choosing only the most helpful or the most representative works. References are limited to recent work wherever possible, with the idea that retrospective bibliography is relatively easy to establish simply by working backward through footnotes from the modern works. Naturally such a work begins to diminish in usefulness as the years pass, because new studies continue to appear. Until a revised edition appears, the book will still provide a useful overview of the field, but references to particular topics will require updating through the serial bibliographies for each year following the effective cut-off date of its entries.

The older bibliographies by David Cabeen (1947, 1952) and Joseph Anglade (1921) may still be helpful for their evaluative remarks concerning studies not listed in Taylor, but they are dependable only up to 1949 and 1920, respectively. Both cover lyric as well as non-lyric writing, as does Taylor; Pillet/Carstens covers only the troubadour lyrics.

SPECIALIZED BIBLIOGRAPHIES

For language studies dealing with medieval and modern usage, the *Guide des études occitanes* by Pierre Berthaud and Jean Lesaffre will be helpful, but it and its supplements are incomplete in coverage and are now outdated. Some supplementary references up to 1986 are provided by François Zufferey (363–68); see also "The State of Occitan Linguistic Studies" by Kathryn Klingebiel.

For the manuscript collections of troubadour poetry, referred to commonly as chansonniers, bibliographical information is supplied by Clovis Brunel, supplemented by updated references in István Frank and in Zufferey (349–62). See also the article by Michael Routledge in *Tenso*.

For troubadour melodies and the continuing scholarly debate over their interpretation, Andrew Hughes has compiled a remarkable guide that contains references (144–78) to studies of the troubadours, trouvères, and Minnesinger.

For those who are interested in the evolving history of troubadour scholarship itself, Eleonora Vincenti has provided references to troubadour scholarship from the early sixteenth to the early nineteenth century.

SERIAL BIBLIOGRAPHIES

In order to keep up with troubadour studies in a systematic way, consultation of the periodic listings of articles and books in the field will be required.

The most specific of these is provided by *Tenso*, the journal of the Société Guillaume IX, which lists medieval and Renaissance Occitan bibliography annually in its spring number, covering the period of the previous calendar year.

The Year's Work in Modern Language Studies contains a section on Occitan scholarship every other year. A choice of works from the two-year period is presented with some critical commentary.

The International Courtly Literature Society publishes each year *Encomia*, a bibliographical bulletin covering the previous year's scholarship in the broad area of courtliness, which naturally includes all of the troubadour studies.

The Modern Language Association of America publishes annually the *MLA International Bibliography of Books and Articles on the Modern Languages and Literatures*, with troubadour references listed under "Provençal and Catalan." This is available on CD-ROM for sophisticated electronic searches based on title, author, subject, key word, etc.

The *Cahiers de civilisation médiévale* publish a separate fascicle annually, listing studies dealing with all cultural aspects of the tenth, eleventh, and twelfth centuries in Europe.

Several other serial bibliographies are published which might be useful (International Medieval Bibliography, Romanische Bibliographie, etc.), but these tend to be either incomplete in coverage or several years out of date.

HELPFUL HINTS

Since even the best of serial bibliographies are at least a year and a half out of date when they appear (often more), further updating will be required in order to be on the cutting edge of scholarship regarding a particular topic. There is no easy way to carry out this exciting but unpredictable quest, since articles involving the troubadours may appear almost anywhere, and books with important material in our field may carry no hint in their title that they contain scholarship dealing with the troubadours.

For articles, a systematic scanning of nine key journals will provide references to most of the current work on the troubadours. These journals are

Tenso: Bulletin of the Société Guillaume IX (articles, reviews, announcements, yearly bibliography)
Revue des langues romanes (articles, many brief reviews)
Cahiers de civilisation médiévale (many articles and reviews, yearly bibliography)
Annales du Midi (articles on historical subjects, many reviews)
Cultura neolatina (many articles)
Le Moyen Age (articles and reviews)
Romance Philology (articles on linguistic and philological subjects, many trenchant reviews)

Romania (many articles and reviews)
Zeitschrift für romanische Philologie (many articles and reviews).

Many others could be added to this short list. *Encomia*, for example, regularly scans over three hundred journals for its yearly bibliography of courtly literature. Many of these periodicals could be expected to publish articles in the area of troubadour studies from time to time.

The Arts and Humanities Citation Index may help to locate new books and articles that are relevant to a particular topic. If one begins with a key work in a given area (a standard edition of a given poet, an important book on a critical topic, etc.), the index will identify recent works that make reference to this key work and hence are likely to deal with the topic under investigation. Other sorts of indexes provide more traditional references according to subject, author, or geographic location.

In many libraries, facilities for electronic searches for defined bibliographical material are becoming available and should be exploited as funding and expertise allow.

For very recent publications and for work in progress, one must rely on such things as publishers' catalogs and leaflets (from Garland Press, Harvard University Press, University of Toronto Press, etc.) and especially on word of mouth. Attendance at one of the major conferences in the field will present opportunities to examine publishers' displays and to speak with active researchers and teachers in the area, who may be able to furnish information on particular topics.

The major conferences that offer focused sessions in troubadour studies are those of the Société Guillaume IX, the International Courtly Literature Society (ICLS), the Association Internationale d'Etudes Occitanes (AIEO), the Société de Linguistique Romane, the International Congress on Medieval Studies (Kalamazoo), the Medieval Academy of America, and the Modern Language Association of America (MLA) and its regional branches.

Often it is helpful to visit large research libraries in order to scan the shelves for recent books that may not have come to one's attention yet by other means. One should also scan Festschrift volumes and published "Acts" of conferences or colloquia dealing with any area in French or Romance literature or history, since these frequently contain articles touching on troubadour research. In fact, Festschriften have become in recent years one of the principal avenues of publication of articles in the area, grouping as many as forty specialized articles at a time (e.g., recent volumes in honor of Paul Remy and Pierre Bec).

LANDMARK STUDIES

A certain number of influential books have become a part of the discipline by setting a tone or direction to ongoing research. One must be aware of these books, nor only for their own merits, but in particular because their presence informs many individual studies, whether they are directly quoted or not.

These include, of course, the major reference tools: the bibliography of Pillet and Carstens, the dictionaries of Raynouard and Levy, the *Répertoire métrique* of István Frank have made the poetry accessible to scholars, although they may not have set any particular direction to their users' work.

Alfred Jeanroy's *La Poésie lyrique des troubadours* (1934) set the tone for a whole generation of troubadour scholarship. Jeanroy typified the interest of his period in historical background, identifications, and the philological study of the texts. This scrupulous examination of the texts as documents remained curiously detached from an understanding of their vitality and functioning as poetry. In a paradoxical way, Jeanroy devoted his life to studying the troubadours, but he seems not to have understood—or to have refused to understand—what the poetry was really about.

Moshe Lazar's study *Amour courtois et fin'amors* is the most influential of several works that opened up the poetry to fuller understanding by insisting on its direct sensuality—in opposition to those, like Jeanroy, who refused to see anything other than Platonic idealism in its underlying love ethic.

Paul Zumthor's *Essai de poétique médiévale* is the fullest expression of the renewed understanding of the poetry as poetry, in which the formal elements of the poems are given at least as much importance as the ideas expressed by the poet.

WORKS CITED

Anglade, Joseph. *Bibliographie élémentaire de l'ancien provençal.* Barcelona: Institut d'Estudis Catalans, 1921.

Arts and Humanities Citation Index. Philadelphia: Institute for Scientific Information, 1975–.

Bartsch, Karl. *Grundriss zur Geschichte der provenzalischen Literatur.* Elberfeld: Friderichs, 1872.

Berthaud, Pierre, and Jean Lesaffre. *Guide des études occitanes.* Paris: Les Belles Lettres, 1947; 2d ed. 1953. Supplemented by Jean Lesaffre and Jean-Marie Petit: *Bibliographie occitane, 1967–71* and *1972–73.* Montpellier: Centre d'Etudes Occitanes, Université Paul Valéry, 1973, 1974.

Brunel, Clovis. *Bibliographie des manuscrits littéraires en ancien provençal.* Paris: Droz, 1935.

Cabeen, David. *A Critical Bibliography of French Literature.* Vol. 1. Syracuse: Syracuse University Press, 1947; 2d ed. 1952.

Dragonetti, Roger. "Aux origines de l'amour courtois: la poétique amoureuse de Guillaume IX d'Aquitaine." In *Sexualité humaine,* 130–70. Paris: Aubier-Mont, 1966. Reprinted in *La Musique et les lettres: études de littérature médiévale,* 161–200. Publications Romanes et Françaises 171. Geneva: Droz, 1986.

Farmer, Henry G. "The Arabic Influence on European Music." *Glasgow University Oriental Society* 19 (1961–62): 1–15.

Frank, István. *Répertoire métrique de la poésie des troubadours.* 2 vols. Paris: Champion, 1953–57.

Hughes, Andrew. *Medieval Music: The Sixth Liberal Art.* Toronto: University of Toronto Press, 1974.

Jeanroy, Alfred. *La Poésie lyrique des troubadours.* 2 vols. Paris: Privat, 1934.

Klingebiel, Kathryn. "The State of Occitan Linguistic Studies: A Retrospective from the Bibliographer's Viewpoint, with a Look Forward." *Tenso: Bulletin of the Société Guillaume IX* 8 (Spring 1973): 107–15.

Lazar, Moshe. *Amour courtois et fin'amors dans la littérature du XIIe siècle.* Bibliothèque Française et Romane, ser. C: Etudes littéraires 8. Paris: Klincksieck, 1954.

Levy, Emil. *Provenzalisches Supplement-Wörterbuch.* 8 vols. Leipzig: Reisland, 1894–1918.

———. *Petit Dictionnaire provençal-français.* 4th ed. Heidelberg: Winter, 1966.

Marks, Claude. *Pilgrims, Heretics, and Lovers: A Medieval Journey.* New York: Macmillan, 1975.

Marrou, Henri. *Les Troubadours.* Paris: Seuil, 1961.

Pillet, Alfred, and Henry Carstens. *Bibliographie der Troubadours.* Halle: Niemeyer, 1933.

Raynouard, François. *Lexique roman, ou dictionnaire de la langue des troubadours.* 6 vols. Paris: Silvestre, 1836–44.

Riquer, Martín de. *Los trovadores: historia literaria y textos.* 3 vols. Barcelona: Planeta, 1975.

Routledge, Michael. "An Etat-Présent of Occitan Lyric: Editions Extant and Desiderata." *Tenso: Bulletin of the Société Guillaume IX* 8 (Spring 1993): 116–31.

Taylor, Robert. *La Littérature occitane du moyen âge: bibliographie sélective et critique.* Toronto: University of Toronto Press, 1977.

Topsfield, Leslie. *Troubadours and Love.* Cambridge: Cambridge University Press, 1975.

Vincenti, Eleonora. *Bibliografia antica dei trovatori.* Milan: Ricciardi, 1963.

Zufferey, François. *Recherches linguistiques sur les chansonniers provençaux.* Publications Romanes et Françaises 176. Paris: Droz, 1987.

Zumthor, Paul. *Essai de poétique médiévale.* Paris: Seuil, 1972.

Appendix:
Editions of the Troubadours
and Related Works

F. R. P. Akehurst and Robert Taylor

The numbers preceding the troubadour names are those assigned to the troubadours by Bartsch, and subsequently used by Pillet and Carstens (P-C) in their listings. They are traditionally, but not invariably, used to refer to troubadours and their poems. The troubadours listed here are all those to whom eight or more poems are attributed in Frank's *Répertoire*, along with a few others whose importance justifies their inclusion even though fewer poems are attributed to them (for example, Jaufre Rudel). After the poet's name (in capital letters), a full citation of the major edition(s) of his or work is given; when more than one edition exists, each one is numbered. All poets quoted or cited by the authors of the various chapters in this book are included. The list is arranged numerically, according to the P-C numbers; it is approximately alphabetical. The compilers wish to thank Professor Deborah Hovland of Buffalo State University College for assistance in compiling this list.

9. AIMERIC DE BELENOI. 1. Dumitrescu, Maria. *Poésies du troubadour Aimeric de Belenoi*. Société des Anciens Textes Français 80. Paris: Champion, 1935. Repr. New York: AMS, 1983. 2. Ruffino, Mario. *Il trovatore Aimeric de Belenoi*. Turin: L'Aquila, 1951.

10. AIMERIC DE PEGUILHAN. Shepard, William P., and Frank M. Chambers. *The Poems of Aimeric de Peguilhan*. Evanston, Ill.: Northwestern University Press, 1950. Repr. New York: AMS, 1983.

16. ALBERTET DE SESTARO. Boutière, Jean. "Les Poésies du troubadour Albertet." *Studi Medievali* 10 (1937): 1–129. Repr. New York: AMS, 1983.

27. ARNAUT CATALAN. Blasi, Ferruccio. *Le poesie del trovatore Arnaut Catalan*. Biblioteca dell'Archivum romanicum 24. Florence: Olschki, 1937.

29. ARNAUT DANIEL. 1. Toja, Gianluigi. *Arnaut Daniel: Canzoni*. Florence: Sansoni, 1960. 2. Perugi, Maurizio. *Le canzoni di Arnaut Daniel*. Milan and Naples: Ric-

ciardi, 1978. 3. Wilhelm, James J. *The Poetry of Arnaut Daniel.* Garland
Library of Medieval Literature 1. New York: Garland Press, 1981. 4. Eusebi,
Mario. *Arnaut Daniel: Il sirventese e le canzoni.* Milan: Scheiwiller,
1984.

30. ARNAUT DE MARUEILL. 1. Johnston, Ronald C. *Les Poésies lyriques du troubadour
Arnaut de Mareuil, publiées avec une introduction, une traduction, des notes et un
glossaire.* Paris: Droz, 1935. Repr. Geneva: Slatkine, 1973. 2. Bec, Pierre. *Les
Saluts d'amour du troubadour Arnaut de Mareuil: Textes publiés avec une introduction, une traduction et des notes.* Bibliothèque Méridionale, 1st ser., 31. Toulouse: Privat, 1961.

46. LA COMTESSA DE DIA. Kussler-Ratyé, Gabrielle. "Les Chansons de la comtesse
Béatrice de Die." *Archivum Romanicum* 1 (1917): 161–82.

47. BERENGUIER DE PALAZOL. 1. Partial edition: Jeanroy, Alfred, and Pierre
Aubry. "Huit chansons de Bérenger de Palazol." *Anuari de l'Institut d'Estudis
Catalans* 2 (1908): 520–40. 2. Newcombe, Terence H. "The Troubadour Be-
renger de Palazol: A Critical Edition of his Poems." *Nottingham Medieval Stud-
ies* 15 (1971): 54–95. 3. Spampinato, Margherita B. *Berenguer de Palol.*
Modena: Mucchi, 1978.

63. BERNART MARTI. 1. Hoepffner, Ernest. *Les Poésies de Bernart Marti.* Classiques
Français du Moyen Age 61. Paris: Champion, 1929. 2. Beggiato, Fabrizio. *Il
trovatore Bernart Marti.* Modena: Mucchi, 1984.

70. BERNART DE VENTADORN. 1. Appel, Carl. *Bernart von Ventadorn, seine Lieder,
mit Einleitung und Glossar.* Halle: Niemeyer, 1915. Repr. New York: AMS,
1983. 2. Nichols, Stephen G., John A. Galm, A. Bartlett Giamatti, Roger J.
Porter, Seth L. Wolitz, and Claudette M. Charbonneau. *The Songs of Bernart de
Ventadorn.* University of North Carolina Studies in the Romance Languages
and Literatures, 39. Chapel Hill: University of North Carolina Press, 1962; 2d
ed. 1965. 3. Lazar, Moshe. *Bernart de Ventadour, troubadour du XIIe siècle: Chansons d'amour.* Bibliothèque Française et Romane, ser. B: Editions critiques de
textes, 4. Paris: Klincksieck, 1966.

71. BERNART DE VENZAC. Picchio Simonelli, Maria. *Lirica moralistica nell'Occitania
del XII secolo: Bernart de Venzac.* Modena: Mucchi, 1974.

74. BERTOLOME ZORZI. Levy, Emil. *Der Troubador Bertolome Zorzi.* Halle: Niemeyer,
1883.

76. BERTRAN D'ALAMANON. Salverda de Grave, Jean-Jacques. *Le Troubadour Bertran
d'Alamanon.* Bibliothèque Méridionale 7. Toulouse: Privat, 1902.

80. BERTRAN DE BORN. 1. Stimming, Albert. *Bertran von Born. Sein Leben und seine
Werke.* Halle: Niemeyer, 1879. 2. Gouiran, Gérard. *L'Amour et la guerre: L'Oeuvre de Bertran de Born.* Aix-en-Provence: Publications de l'Université de Provence, 1985. 3. Paden, William D., Tilde Sankovitch, and Patricia H. Stäblein.
The Poems of the Troubadour Bertran de Born. Berkeley and Los Angeles: University of California Press, 1986.

82. BERTRAN CARBONEL. 1. Jeanroy, Alfred. "Les 'Coblas' de Bertran Carbonel."
Annales du Midi 25 (1913): 137–88. 2. Contini, Gianfranco. "Sept poésies
lyriques du troubadour Bertrand Carbonel de Marseille." *Annales du Midi* 49
(1937): 5–41, 113–52, 225–40.

96. BLACASSET. Klein, Otto. *Der Troubadour Blacassetz.* Städtische Realschule zu Wiesbaden, Jahresbericht über das Schuljahr 1886/87. Wiesbaden: Ritter, 1887.

97. BLACATZ. Soltau, Otto. "Die Werke des Trobadors Blacatz." *Zeitschrift für romanische Philologie* 23 (1899): 201–48; 24 (1900): 33–60.

101. BONIFACI CALVO. 1. Branciforti, Francesco. *Le rime de Bonifacio Calvo.* Catania: Università di Catania, 1955. 2. Horan, William D. *The Poems of Bonifacio Calvo.* The Hague: Mouton, 1966.

106. CADENET. 1. Appel, Carl. *Der Trobador Cadenet.* Halle: Niemeyer, 1920. Repr. Geneva: Slatkine, 1974. 2. Zemp, Josef. *Les Poésies du troubadour Cadenet.* Bern: Lang, 1978.

109. CASTELLOZA. Paden, William D., et al. "The Poems of the *Trobairitz* Na Castelloza." *Romance Philology* 35, no. 1 (August 1981): 158–82.

112. CERCAMON. 1. Jeanroy, Alfred. *Les Poésies de Cercamon.* Classiques Français du Moyen Age 27. Paris: Champion, 1922. 2. Tortoreto, Valeria. *Il trovatore Cercamon.* Unione Academica Nazionale Roma, Subsidia al Corpus des Troubadours, 7; Istituto di Filologia Romanza dell'Università di Roma, Studi, Testi e Manuali, 9. Modena: Mucchi, 1981. 3. Wolf, George, and Roy Rosenstein. *The Poetry of Cercamon and Jaufre Rudel.* Garland Library of Medieval Literature 5. New York: Garland Press, 1983.

For CERVERI DE GIRONA, *see* 434, 434a.

119. DAUPHIN D'AUVERGNE. Brackney, Emmert M. "A Critical Edition of the Poems of Dalfin d'Alvernhe." Thesis, University of Minnesota, 1937. Partial editions listed in Chambers, Frank M., *Proper Names in the Lyrics of the Troubadours,* 21. Chapel Hill: University of North Carolina Press, 1971.

124. DAUDE DE PRADAS. Schutz, Alexander H. *Poésies de Daude de Pradas.* Bibliothèque Méridionale 22. Toulouse-Paris: Privat, 1933.

132. ELIAS DE BARJOLS. Stronski, Stanislaw. *Le Troubadour Elias de Barjols.* Bibliothèque Méridionale 10. Toulouse: Privat, 1906.

133. ELIAS CAIREL. Jaeschke, Hilde. *Der Trobador Elias Cairel. Romanische Studien* 20 (1921).

136. ELIAS D'UISEL. Edition in Jean Audiau. *Les Poésies des quatre troubadours d'Ussel.* Paris: Delagrave, 1922.

154. FOLQUET DE LUNEL. Eichelkraut, Franz. *Der Troubadour Folquet de Lunel.* Berlin, 1872. Repr. Geneva: Slatkine, 1975.

155. FOLQUET DE MARSEILLA. Stroński, Stanisław. *Le Troubadour Folquet de Marseille.* Cracow: Spolka Widawnicza Polska, 1910. Repr. Geneva: Slatkine, 1968.

156. FALQUET DE ROMANS. 1. Zenker, Rudolf. *Die Gedichte des Folquet von Romans.* Halle: Niemeyer, 1896. 2. Arveiller, Raymond, and Gérard Gouiran. *L'Oeuvre poétique de Falquet de Romans, troubadour.* Aix-en-Provence: Publications de l'Université de Provence, 1987.

167. GAUCELM FAIDIT. Mouzat, Jean. *Les Poèmes de Gaucelm Faidit, troubadour du XIIe siècle.* Paris: Nizet, 1965. Repr. Geneva: Slatkine, 1989. [A new edition by Agostino Ziino is announced.]

173. GAUSBERT DE PUICIBOT. Shepard, William P. *Les Poésies de Jausbert de Puycibot.* Classiques Français du Moyen Age 46. Paris: Champion, 1924.

174. GAVAUDAN. 1. Jeanroy, Alfred. "Poésies du troubadour Gavaudan." *Romania* 34 (1905): 497–539. 2. Guido, Saverio. *Il trovatore Gavaudan*. Unione Academica Nazionale Roma, Subsidia al Corpus des Troubadours, 6; Istituto di Filologia Romanza dell'Università di Roma, Studi, Testi e Manuali, 8. Modena: Mucchi, 1979.

183. GUILLEM COMTE DE PEITEUS. 1. Jeanroy, Afred. *Les Chansons de Guillaume IX, duc d'Aquitaine (1071–1127)*. Classiques Français du Moyen Age 9. 1913; Paris: Champion, 1964. 2. Pasero, Nicolò. *Guglielmo IX d'Aquitania: Poesie*. Subsidia al Corpus dei Trovatori 1. Rome and Modena: Mucchi, 1973. 3. Bond, Gerald A. *The Poetry of William VII, Count of Poitiers, IX Duke of Aquitaine*. New York: Garland Press, 1982.

194. GUI D'UISEL. 1. Edition in Audiau, Jean. *Les Poésies des quatre troubadours d'Ussel*. Paris: Delagrave, 1922. 2. Billet, Léon. *Généalogie de de la famille "d'Ussel": Les Quatre Troubadours d'Ussel*. Tulle: Orfeuil, 1982.

202. GUILLEM ADEMAR. Almqvist, Kurt. *Poésies du troubadour Guilhem Adémar*. Uppsala: Almqvist & Wiksells, 1951. Repr. New York: AMS, 1983.

205. GUILHEM AUGIER NOVELLA. Calzolari, Monica. *Il trovatore Guillem Augier Novella*. Modena: Mucchi, 1986.

210. GUILLEM DE BERGUEDAN. Riquer, Martín de. *Guillem de Berguedà*. Vol. 1: *Estudio histórico literario y lingüístico*; vol. 2: *Edición crítica, traducción, notas y glosario*. Scriptorium Populeti 5. Barcelona: Abadía de Poblet, 1971.

213. GUILLEM DE CABESTANH. Långfors, Arthur. *Les Chansons de Guillem de Cabestanh*. Classiques Français du Moyen Age 42. Paris: Champion, 1924. [A new edition by Aimo Sakari is announced.]

217. GUILLEM FIGUEIRA. Levy, Emil. *Guilhem Figueira, ein provenzalischer Troubadour*. Berlin: Liebrecht, 1880.

223. GUILHEM MAGRET. Naudieth, Fritz. *Der Trobador Guillem Magret*. Halle: Karras, 1913. Also in *Beihefte zur Zeitschrift für romanische Philologie* 52:81–144. Halle: Niemeyer, 1914.

225. GUILLEM DE MONTANHAGOL. Ricketts, Peter T. *Les Poésies de Guillem de Montanhagol*. Toronto: Pontifical Institute of Mediæval Studies, 1964.

226. GUILHEM DE MUR. Partial edition in Pfaff ed. of Guiraut Riquier; *see* 248 below.

227. GUILHEM PEIRE DE CAZALS. Mouzat, Jean. *Guilhem Peire de Cazals, troubadour du XIIIe siècle*. Paris: Les Belles Lettres, 1954. Repr. in repr. of Gaucelm Faidit; *see* 167 above.

234. GUILLEM DE SAINT-DISDIER. Sakari, Aimo. *Poésies du troubadour Guilhem de Saint-Didier*. Mémoires de la Société Néophilologique de Helsinki 19. Helsinki: Société Néophilologique, 1956. Repr. New York: AMS, 1983.

236. GUILLEM DE LA TOR. Blasi, F. *Le poesie di Guilhem de la Tor*. Biblioteca dell'Archivum romanicum. 21. Florence: Olschki, 1934.

242. GUIRAUT DE BORNELH. 1. Kolsen, Adolf, trans. *Sämtliche Lieder des Trobadors Guiraut de Bornelh*. 2 vols. Halle: Niemeyer, 1910–35. 2. Sharman, Ruth. *The Cansos and Sirventes of the Troubadour Giraut de Borneil: A Critical Edition*. Cambridge: Cambridge University Press, 1989.

243. GUIRAUT DE CALANSO. Ernst, Willy. "Die Lieder des provenzalischen Trobadors Guiraut von Calanso." *Romanische Forschungen* 44 (1930): 255–406.

244. GUIRAUT D'ESPANHA. Hoby, Otto. "Die Lieder des Trobadors Guiraut d'Espanha." Thesis, Fribourg (Switz.), 1915.

246. GUILHEM DE L'OLIVIER (D'ARLES). Schultz-Gora, Oskar. *Provenzalische Studien*, 1:24–82 Strasbourg: Trübner, 1919.

248. GUIRAUT RIQUIER. 1. Pfaff, S. L. *Guiraut Riquier*. Vol. 4 of Mahn, Carl A., *Die Werke der Troubadours in provenzalischer Sprache*. Berlin: Dümmler; Paris: Klincksieck, 1853. 2. Mölk, Ulrich. *Guiraut Riquier: Las Cansos—Kritischer Text und Kommentar*. Studia Romanica 2. Heidelberg: Winter, 1962. 3. Linskill, Joseph. *Les Epitres de Guiraut Riquier, troubadour du XIIIe siècle: Edition critique avec traduction et notes*. London: AIEO, 1985.

262. JAUFRE RUDEL. 1. Jeanroy, Alfred. *Les Chansons de Jaufre Rudel*. Classiques Français de Moyen Age 15. Paris: 1915; 2d rev. ed. 1924. 2. Pickens, Rupert T. *The Songs of Jaufré Rudel*. Toronto: Pontifical Institute of Mediæval Studies, 1978. 3. Wolf, George, and Roy Rosenstein. *The Poetry of Cercamon and Jaufre Rudel*. New York: Garland Press, 1983. 4. Chiarini, Giorgio. *Il canzoniere di Jaufre Rudel*. Romanica Vulgaria 5. L'Aquila: Japadre, 1985.

266. JOAN ESTEVE. 1. Edition in Azaïs, Gabriel. *Les Troubadours de Béziers*, 59–119. Béziers: Malinas, 1869. 2. Vatteroni, Sergio. *Le poesie del trovatore Johan Esteve*. Biblioteca degli Studi Mediolatini e Volgari, n.s. 10. Pisa: Pacini, 1986.

281. RAMBERTINO BUVALELLI. 1. Bertoni, Giulio. *Rambertino Buvalelli trovatore bolognese e le sue rime provenzali*. Gesellschaft für romanische Literatur 17. Dresden: Gesellschaft für romanische Literatur, 1908. 2. Melli, Elio. *Rambertino Buvalelli: Le poesie*. Testi i Saggi di Letterature Moderne, Sezione di Letteratura Francese, Occitanica e Letterature Francofone, Testi, 2. Bologna: Pàtron, 1978.

282. LANFRANC CIGALA. Branciforti, Francesco. *Il canzoniere di Lanfranco Cigala*. Biblioteca dell'Archivum romanicum 37. Florence: Olschki, 1954.

290. LUQUET GATELUS. Boni, Marco. *Luchetto Gattilusio, liriche*. Biblioteca degli Studi Mediolatini e Volgari 2. Bologna, 1957.

293. MARCABRU. Dejeanne, J.-M.-L. *Poésies complètes du troubadour Marcabru*. Bibliothéque Méridionale 12. Toulouse: Privat, 1909. [An edition by Simon Gaunt, Ruth Harvey, John Marshall, and Linda Paterson is announced; an edition by Aurelio Roncaglia has long been awaited.]

305. LO MONGE DE MONTAUDON. 1. Philippson, Emil. *Der Mönch von Montaudon, ein provenzalischer Troubadour. Sein Leben und seine Gedichte*. Halle: Lippertsche Buchhandlung, 1873. 2. Klein, Otto. *Die Dichtungen des Mönchs von Montaudon neu herausgegeben*. Ausgaben und Abhandlungen aus dem Gebiete der romanischen Philologie, 7. Marburg: Elwert, 1885. 3. Routledge, Michael J. *Les Poésies du Moine de Montaudon*. Montpellier: Centre d'Etudes Occitanes, Université Paul Valéry, 1977.

319. PAULET DE MARSEILLE. 1. Levy, Emil. "Le Troubadour Paulet de Marseille" *Revue des langues romanes* 21 (1882): 261–89. 2. Riquer, Isabel de. "Las poesías del Trovador Paulet de Marselha." *Boletín de la Real Academia de Buenas Letras de Barcelona* 38 (1979–82): 133–205.

323. PEIRE D'ALVERNHE. 1. Zenker, Rudolf. *Die Lieder Peires von Auvergne*. Erlangen: Fr. Junge, 1900. Also in *Romanische Forschungen* 12 (1899): 653–924. 2. Del Monte, Alberto. *Peire d'Alvernha: Liriche*. Collezione di Filologia Romanza. Turin: Loescher-Chiantore, 1955.

330. PEIRE BREMON RICAS NOVAS. Boutière, Jean. *Les Poésies du troubadour Peire Bremon Ricas Novas.* Bibliothèque Méridionale 21. Toulouse: Privat, 1930.

331. PEIRE BREMON LO TORT. Boutière, Jean. "Peire Bremon lo Tort." *Romania* 54 (1928): 427–52.

335. PEIRE CARDENAL. Lavaud, René. *Poésies complètes du troubadour Peire Cardenal (1180–1278): Texte, traduction, commentaire, analyse des travaux antérieurs, lexique.* Bibliothèque Méridionale, 2d ser., 34. Toulouse: Privat, 1957.

349. PEIRE MILON. Partial edition by Carl Appel in *Revue des langues romanes* 39 (1896): 185–216.

355. PEIRE RAIMON DE TOULOUSE. Cavaliere, Alfredo. *Le poesie di Peire Raimon de Tolosa.* Biblioteca dell'Archivum romanicum 22. Florence: Olschki, 1935. Repr. New York: AMS, 1983.

356. PEIRE ROGIER. Nicholson, Derek E. T. *The Poems of the Troubadour Peire Rogier.* Manchester: Manchester University Press; New York: Barnes & Noble, 1976.

362. PEIRE DE VALEIRA. Jeanroy, Alfred. *Jongleurs et troubadours gascons des XIIe et XIIIe siècles.* Classiques Français du Moyen Age 39. Paris: Champion, 1957.

364. PEIRE VIDAL. 1. Bartsch, Karl. *Peire Vidal's Lieder.* Berlin: Dümmler, 1857. 2. Anglade, Joseph. *Les Poésies de Peire Vidal.* 2d ed. Classiques Français du Moyen Age 11. Paris: Champion, 1923. 3. Avalle, d'Arco Silvio. *Peire Vidal: Poesie.* 2 vols. Milan and Naples: Riccardo Ricciardi, 1960. Repr. in one vol. New York: AMS, 1983.

366. PEIROL. Aston, Stanley C. *Peirol, Troubadour of Auvergne.* Cambridge: Cambridge University Press, 1953. Repr. New York: AMS, 1983.

370. PERDIGON. Chaytor, H. J. *Les Chansons de Perdigon.* Classiques Français du Moyen Age 53. Paris: Champion, 1926.

372. PISTOLETA. Nestroy, E. *Der Trobador Pistoleta.* In Beihefte zur Zeitschrift für romanische Philologie 52, i–xvi, 1–77. Halle: Niemeyer, 1914. Repr. New York: AMS, 1983.

375. PONS DE CHAPTEUIL. Napolski, Max von. *Leben und Werke des Trobadors Ponz de Capduoill.* Halle: Niemeyer, 1879. Repr. New York: AMS, 1983.

377. PONS DE LA GARDA. Frank, István. "Pons de la Guardia, troubadour catalan du XIIe siècle." *Boletín de la Real Academia de Buenas Letras de Barcelona* 22 (1949): 229–327.

389. RAIMBAUT D'AURENGA. Pattison, Walter T. *The Life and Works of the Troubadour Raimbaut d'Orange.* Minneapolis: University of Minnesota Press, 1952, 1980. Repr. New York: AMS, 1983. [A new edition by Luigi Milone is announced.]

392. RAIMBAUT DE VAQUEIRAS. Linskill, Joseph. *The Poems of the Troubadour Raimbaut de Vaqueiras.* The Hague: Mouton, 1964. Repr. New York: AMS, 1983.

401. RAIMON GAUCELM DE BEZERS. Edition in Azaïs, Gabriel. *Les Troubadours de Béziers,* 3–41. Béziers: Malinas, 1869.

404. RAIMON JORDAN. Kjellman, Hilding. *Le Troubadour Raimon Jordan, vicomte de Saint-Antonin.* Uppsala: Almqvist & Wiksells, 1922. [A new edition by S. Asperti is announced.]

406. RAIMON DE MIRAVAL. 1. Topsfield, Leslie T. *Les Poésies du troubadour Raimon de Miraval.* Les Clasiques d'Oc 4. Paris: Nizet, 1971. 2. Partial edition: Switten, Margaret L. *The "Cansos" of Raimon de Miraval: A Study of Poems and Melo-*

dies. Medieval Academy Books, 93. Cambridge, Mass.: Medieval Academy of America, 1985. 3. Partial edition: Nelli, René. *Raimon de Miraval: Du jeu subtil à l'amour fou.* Lagrasse: Verdier, 1979.

421. RIGAUT DE BERBEZILH. 1. Vàrvaro, Alberto. *Rigaut de Berbezilh: Liriche.* Biblioteca de Filologia Romanza 4. Bari: Adriatica, 1960. Repr. New York: AMS, 1983. 2. Braccini, Mauro. *Rigaut de Barbezieux: Le canzoni.* Florence: Olschki, 1960.

427. ROSTANH BERENGUIER. Meyer, Paul. *Les Derniers Troubadours de la Provence.* Paris: Franck, 1871. Repr. Geneva: Slatkine, 1973.

434, 434a. CERVERI DE GIRONA. Riquer, Martín de. *Obras completas del trovador Cerverí de Girona.* Publicaciones sobre Filologia y Literatura. Barcelona: Instituto Español de Estudios Mediterráneos, 1947.

437. SORDEL. 1. Boni, Marco. *Sordello, le poesie.* Biblioteca degli "Studi Mediolatini i Volgari" 1. Bologna: Libreria Antiquaria Palmaverde, 1954. 2. Wilhelm, James J. *The Poetry of Sordello.* New York: Garland Press, 1987.

457. UC DE SAINT-CIRC. Jeanroy, Alfred, and Jean-Jacques Salverda de Grave. *Poésies de Uc de Saint-Circ.* Bibliothèque Méridionale, 1st ser., 15. Toulouse: Privat, 1913.

461. ANONYMOUS. No complete edition of the anonymous troubadour songs exists. The songs are edited in various publications; see Frank, *Répertoire,* 183–92.

ANTHOLOGIES

Appel, Carl. *Provenzalische Chrestomathie, mit Abriss der Formenlehre und Glossar.* 1895; 6th ed. Leipzig, 1930. Repr. Geneva: Slatkine, 1974.

Bartsch, Karl, and Edouard Koschwitz. *Chrestomathie provençale.* 6th ed. Marburg: Elwert, 1904. Repr. Hildesheim: Olms, 1971.

Bec, Pierre. *Anthologie de la prose occitane du moyen âge.* Avignon: Aubanel, 1970.

———. *Anthologie des troubadours.* 10/18, Série "Bibliothèque médiévale." Paris: Union Générale des Editions, 1979.

———. *Burlesque et obscénité chez les troubadours: Le Contre-texte du moyen âge.* Paris: Stock Plus, 1984.

Goldin, Frederick. *Lyrics of the Troubadours and Trouvères: An Anthology and a History.* Garden City, N.Y.: Anchor, 1973.

Hamlin, Frank R., Peter T. Ricketts, and John Hathaway. *Introduction à l'étude de l'ancien provençal: Textes d'étude.* Geneva: Droz, 1967; 2d rev. ed. 1987.

Hill, R. T., and Thomas G. Bergin, with the collaboration of Susan Olson, William D. Paden, and Nathaniel Smith. *Anthology of the Provençal Troubadours.* 2 vols. New Haven: Yale University Press, 1973.

Lavaud, R., and René Nelli. *Les Troubadours.* 2 vols. Bruges: Desclée de Brouwer, 1966.

Lommatzsch, Erhard. *Leben und Lieder der provenzalischen Troubadours.* 2 vols. Berlin: Akademie-Verlag, 1957–59; 2d ed. Munich: W. Fink, 1972.

Mahn, Carl A. F. *Die Werke der Troubadours in provenzalischer Sprache.* 4 vols. Berlin and Paris, 1846–53. Vol. 4, an edition of the works of Guiraut Riquier, was recently reprinted, ed. S. L. Pfaff. Geneva: Slatkine, 1975.

Nelli, René. *Ecrivains anticonformistes du moyen âge occitan.* 2 vols. Paris: Phébus, 1977.
Press, Alan R. *Anthology of Troubadour Lyric Poetry.* Austin: University of Texas Press, 1971.
Riquer, Martín de. *Los trovadores: Historia literaria y textos.* 3 vols. Barcelona: Planeta, 1975.

VIDAS

Boutière, Jean, and Alexander H. Schutz. *Biographies des troubadours: Textes provençaux des XIIIe et XIVe siècles.* Paris: Nizet, 1964.

TROBAIRITZ

Bogin, Meg. *The Women Troubadours.* New York: Paddington, 1976.
Bruckner, Matilda Tomaryn, Laurie Shepard, and Sarah White. *The Songs of the Women Troubadours.* Garland Library of Medieval Literature 97. New York: Garland, 1995.
Rieger, Angelica. *Trobairitz: Der Beitrag der Frau in der altokzitanischen höfischen Lyrik. Edition des Gesamtkorpus.* Beihefte zur Zeitschrift für romanische Philologie 233. Tübingen: Niemeyer, 1991.
Schultz-Gora, Oskar. *Die provenzalischen Dichterinnen.* Leipzig: Gustav Foch, 1888.

OTHER TEXTS

Bond, Gerald. "The Last Unpublished Troubadour Songs." *Speculum* 60 (1985): 827–49.
CHANSON DE LA CROISADE ALBIGEOISE. 1. Martin-Chabot, Eugène. *La Chanson de la croisade albigeoise.* 3 vols. Paris: Société d'Edition "Les Belles Lettres," 1957–61. 2. Gougaud, Henri. *La Chanson de la croisade: Texte du manuscrit original conservé à la Bibliothèque Nationale.* Paris: Berg, 1984.
FLAMENCA. Gschwind, Ulrich. *Le Roman de Flamenca, nouvelle occitane du 13e siècle.* 2 vols. Berne: Francke, 1976.
Frank, István. "Ce qui reste d'inédit de l'ancienne poésie lyrique provençale." *Boletín de la Real Academia de Buenas Letras de Barcelona* 23 (1950): 69–81.

DICTIONARIES

Cropp, Glynnis. *Le Vocabulaire courtois des troubadours de l'époque classique.* Geneva: Droz, 1975.
Levy, Emil. *Provenzalisches Supplement-Wörterbuch.* 8 vols. Leipzig: Reisland, 1894–1918.
———. *Petit Dictionnaire provençal-français.* 4th ed. Heidelberg: Winter, 1966.
Raynouard, François. *Lexique roman, ou dictionnaire de la langue des troubadours.* 6 vols. Paris: Silvestre, 1836–44.

CONTRIBUTORS

F. R. P. Akehurst is professor of French at the University of Minnesota and the translator of *The "Coutumes de Beauvaisis" of Philippe de Beaumanoir* (Philadelphia: University of Pennsylvania Press, 1992).

Gerald A. Bond is emeritus professor of French and German at the University of Rochester and the editor of *The Poetry of William VII, Count of Poitiers, IX Duke of Aquitaine*, Garland Library of Medieval Literature 4 (New York: Garland, 1982).

Matilda Tomaryn Bruckner is professor of French at Boston College and coeditor, with Laurie Shepard and Sarah White, of *The Songs of the Women Troubadours*, Garland Library of Medieval Literature 97 (New York: Garland, 1995).

Frank Chambers is professor emeritus of French at the University of Arizona, Tucson, and the author of *An Introduction to Old Provençal Versification*, Memoirs of the American Philosophical Society 167 (Philadelphia: American Philosophical Society, 1985).

Judith M. Davis is professor of French at Goshen College and coauthor, with F. Xavier Baron, of *Amour Courtois, the Medieval Ideal of Love: A Bibliography* (Louisville: University of Louisville, 1973).

Suzanne Fleischman is professor of French at the University of California, Berkeley, and the author of *Tense and Narrativity: From Medieval Performance to Modern Fiction* (Austin: University of Texas Press/London: Routledge, 1990).

Eliza Miruna Ghil is professor of French at the University of New Orleans and the author of *L'Age de Parage: Essai sur le poétique et le politique en Occitanie au XIIIe siècle*, University Studies in Medieval and Renaissance Literature 4 (New York/Bern: Peter Lang, 1989).

FREDE JENSEN is professor of French at the University of Colorado, Boulder, and the author of *The Syntax of Medieval Occitan* (Tübingen: Niemeyer, 1986).

HANS-ERICH KELLER is professor emeritus of Romance languages at the Ohio State University and the author of *Autour de Roland: Recherches sur la chanson de geste,* Nouvelle Bibliothèque du Moyen Age 14 (Paris: Champion, 1989).

MOSHE LAZAR is professor of comparative literature, University of Southern California, and the author of *Amour courtois et fin'amors dans la littérature du XIIe siècle* (Paris: Klincksieck, 1964).

RONALD MARTINEZ is associate professor of Italian at the University of Minnesota and coauthor, with Robert M. Durling, of *Time and the Crystal: Studies in Dante's "Rime Petrose"* (Berkeley: University of California Press, 1990).

DEBORAH H. NELSON is professor of French at Rice University and coauthor, with Hendrik van der Werf, of *The Lyrics and Melodies of Adam de la Halle,* Garland Library of Medieval Literature 24 (New York: Garland, 1985).

WILLIAM D. PADEN is professor of French at Northwestern University and coeditor, with Tilde Sankovitch and Patricia H. Stäblein, of *The Poems of the Troubadour Bertran de Born* (Berkeley: University of California Press, 1986).

ELIZABETH W. POE is professor of French at Tulane University and the author of *From Poetry to Prose in Old Provençal* (Birmingham, Alabama: Summa Publications, 1984).

ROY S. ROSENSTEIN is professor of comparative literature at the American University of Paris and coeditor, with George Wolf, of *The Poetry of Cercamon and Jaufre Rudel,* Garland Library of Medieval Literature 5 (New York: Garland, 1983).

ELISABETH SCHULZE-BUSACKER is professor of Romance philology at Université de Montréal and the author of *Proverbes et expressions proverbiales dans la littérature narrative du moyen-âge français* (Geneva: Slatkine, 1985).

NATHANIEL B. SMITH is executive assistant to the Vice President of the College at Franklin and Marshall College and the author of *Figures of Repetition in the Old Provençal Lyric: A Study in the Style of the Troubadours* (Chapel Hill: Department of Romance Languages, University of North Carolina, 1976).

JOSEPH T. SNOW is professor of Spanish at Michigan State University and the author of *The Poetry of Alfonso X, el Sabio: A Critical Bibliography* (London: Grant and Cutler, 1977).

ROBERT TAYLOR is professor of French at Victoria College, University of Toronto, and the author of *La Littérature occitane du moyen âge: bibliographie sélective et critique* (Toronto: University of Toronto Press, 1977).

STEPHANIE CAIN VAN D'ELDEN has taught at the University of Minnesota and is the author of *Moriz von Craûn,* Garland Library of Medieval Literature 69 (New York: Garland, 1990).

HENDRIK VAN DER WERF is emeritus professor of music at the Eastman School of Music, University of Rochester, and the author of *The Chansons of the Troubadours and Trouvères: A Study of the Melodies and Their Relation to the Poems* (Utrecht: Oosthoek, 1972).

AMELIA E. VAN VLECK is assistant professor of French at the University of Texas, Austin, and the author of *Memory and Re-Creation in Troubadour Lyric* (Berkeley: University of California Press, 1991).

PAUL ZUMTHOR was professor emeritus at Université de Montréal until his death in 1995. He is the author of *Essai de poétique médiévale* (Paris: Seuil, 1972).

INDEX

Troubadours are indexed under their first names (e.g. Peire Vidal is found under P, rather than V). The editors gratefully acknowledge the aid of University of Minnesota students John Durant, Sarah Grace Heller, Michelle Reichert, Jean Luc Roche, Timothy Tomasik, and Ellen Wormwood in compiling this index.

Compositor: Braun-Brumfield, Inc.
       Text: 10/12 Baskerville
    Display: Baskerville
    Printer: Braun-Brumfield, Inc.
     Binder: Braun-Brumfield, Inc.